GM X-CARS

Buick Skylark · Chevrolet Citation
Oldsmobile Omega · Pontiac Phoenix

1980-1985

SHOP MANUAL

By
RON WRIGHT

ALAN AHLSTRAND
Editor

JEFF ROBINSON
Publisher

CLYMER PUBLICATIONS

World's largest publisher of books devoted exclusively to automobiles and motorcycles

12860 MUSCATINE STREET • P.O. BOX 4520 • ARLETA, CALIFORNIA 91333-4520

FIRST EDITION
First Printing 1982

SECOND EDITION
Updated by Kalton C. Lahue to include 1981-1982 models
First Printing July, 1983

THIRD EDITION
Updated by Kalton C. Lahue to include 1983 models
First Printing April, 1984

FOURTH EDITION
Updated by Kalton C. Lahue to include 1984-1985 models
First Printing April, 1985
Second Printing July, 1986

Printed in U.S.A.

ISBN: 0-89287-348-5

Production Coordinator, Paul Purkhiser

COVER: Photographed by Michael Brown Photographic Productions, Los Angeles, California. Assisted by Dennis Miller and Ned Quick. Automobiles courtesy of Chevrolet and Pontiac Motor Divisions, General Motors Corporation.

CONTENTS

QUICK REFERENCE DATA

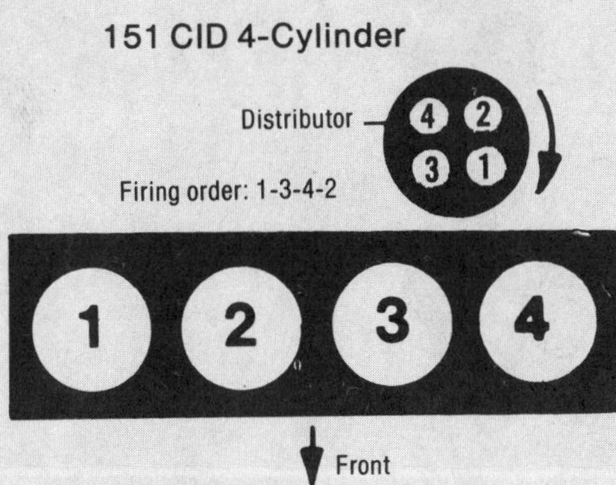

ENGINE TUNE-UP SPECIFICATIONS

Spark plug type	
151 cid	**R43TSX**
173 cid (1980)	**R44TS**
173 cid (1981-on)	**R43TS**
Spark plug gap	
151 cid	**0.060 in. (1.52 mm)**
173 cid	**0.045 in. (1.15 mm)**
Ignition timing	**See Vehicle Emission Control Label**
Idle speed	**See Vehicle Emission Control Label; not adjustable on 1981-on models with Idle Speed Control**

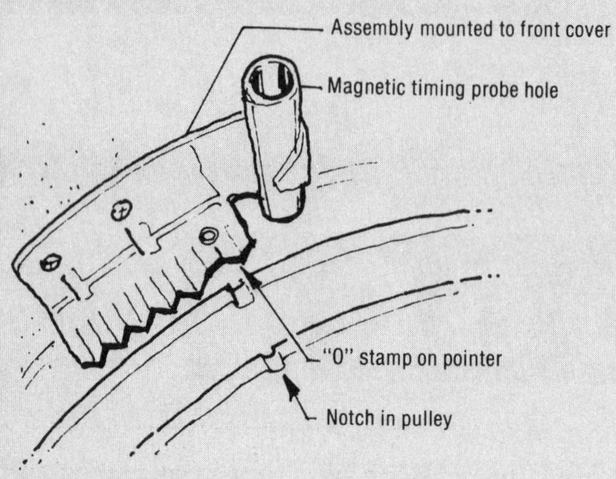

TIMING MARKS (TYPICAL)

WHEEL ALIGNMENT SPECIFICATIONS

1980-1981	
Camber (left and right side to be within 1/2°)	**±1/2 ±1/2°**
Toe-in	**+2.5 ±2.5 mm**
1982-on	
Camber (left and right side to be within 1/2°)	**0 ±1/2°**
Toe-in	
1982	**0 ±2.5 mm**
1983-on	**0 ±0.5 mm**

COOLING SYSTEM CAPACITY

Engine	Capacity
4-cylinder	
With air conditioning	9 3/4 quarts (9.3 liters)
Without air conditioning	9 1/2 quarts (9.0 liters)
V6	
With air conditioning	11 3/4 quarts (11.2 liters)
Without air conditioning	11 1/2 quarts (10.8 liters)

RECOMMENDED LUBRICANTS

Item	Lubricant
Engine oil	API service SE
Brake fluid	DOT 3
Engine coolant	Ethylene Glycol type
Manual transaxle	ATF (DEXRON-II)
Automatic transaxle	ATF (DEXRON-II)
Power steering system	GM power steering fluid or equivalent
Manual steering gear	GM lubricant #1052182 or equivalent
Chassis lubrication	Chassis grease (GM specification #6031-M) or equivalent
Lock cylinders	WD-40 spray or equivalent
Clutch linkage	
Pivot points	Engine oil
Push rod to clutch fork joint	Chassis grease (GM specification #6031-M or equivalent)
Manual transaxle shift linkage	Chassis grease

DRIVE BELT TENSION

Belt	Torque*
Alternator belt	
New	135 ft.-lb. (605 N•m)
Used	55 ft.-lb. (205 N•m)
Power steering belt	
New	135 ft.-lb. (605 N•m)
Used	55 ft.-lb. (205 N•m)
Air conditioning belt	
New	150 ft.-lb. (605 N•m)
Used	80 ft.-lb. (360 N•m)

*Do not adjust any used belt if initial reading is 50 ft.-lb. (205 N•m)

BULB SPECIFICATIONS

Bulb	SAE No.
Headlamp	6052
Front park and directional signal	1157NA
Front side marker	194
Rear side marker	194
Tail & stop light	1157
License plate	194
Backup	1156
Directional signal (rear)	1156
Luggage compartment	1003
Indicator lamps	194 (1)
Instrument panel	194
Radio dial	1893
Header map lamp	211-2
Underhood lamp	631
Courtesy	906
Dome	561 (2)
Reading lamp	1004

(1) Headlamp Hi Beam indicator lamp 161
(2) Dome with reading lamp 212

LUBRICANT AND FUEL CAPACITIES

Item	Capacity
Engine oil	
151 cid	3.0 qt. (2.8 lit.)
173 cid	4.0 qt. (3.8 lit.)
Manual transaxle	3.0 qt. (1.5 lit.)
Automatic transaxle	5.0 qt. (4.6 lit.)
Fuel	14.0 U.S. gal. (53 lit.)

RECOMMENDED GRADES OF OIL

Oil Grade	Temperature Range
5W-20*, 5W-30	20° F and below
10W, 5W-30, 10W-30, 10W-40	0° to 60° F
20W-20, 10W-30, 10W-40, 20W-40, 20W-50	20° F and above

*If the vehicle is being operated at sustained highway speeds, the next heavier grade of oil should be used.

—NOTES—

GM X-CARS

Buick Skylark · Chevrolet Citation
Oldsmobile Omega · Pontiac Phoenix

1980-1985

SHOP MANUAL

INTRODUCTION

This detailed, comprehensive manual covers 1980-1985 General Motors X-car (Buick Skylark, Chevrolet Citation/Citation II, Oldsmobile Omega and Pontiac Phoenix) models. The expert text gives complete information on maintenance, repair and overhaul. Hundreds of photos and drawings guide you through every step. The book includes all you need to know to keep your car running right.

Chapters One through Twelve contain general information on all models and specific service information on 1980 models. The Supplement at the end of the book contains specific service information on 1981 and later models.

Where repairs are practical for the owner/mechanic, complete procedures are given. Equally important, difficult jobs are pointed out. Such operations are usually more economically performed by a dealer or independant garage.

A shop manual is a referencc. You want to be able to find information fast. As in all Clymer books, this one is designed with this in mind. All chapters are thumb tabbed. Important items are indexed at the rear of the book. Finally, all the most frequently used specifications and capacities are summarized on the *Quick Reference* pages at the front of the book.

Keep the book handy. Carry it in your glove box. It will help you to better understand your car, lower your repair and maintenance costs, and generally improve your satisfaction with your vehicle.

CHAPTER ONE

GENERAL INFORMATION

The troubleshooting, tune-up, maintenance, and step-by-step repair procedures in this book are written for the owner and home mechanic. The text is accompanied by useful photos and diagrams to make the job as clear and correct as possible.

Troubleshooting, tune-up, maintenance, and repair are not difficult if you know what tools and equipment to use and what to do. Anyone not afraid to get their hands dirty, of average intelligence, and with some mechanical ability can perform most of the procedures in this book.

In some cases, a repair job may require tools or skills not reasonably expected of the home mechanic. These procedures are noted in each chapter and it is recommended that you take the job to your dealer, a competent mechanic, or machine shop.

MANUAL ORGANIZATION

This chapter provides general information and safety and service hints. Also included are lists of recommended shop and emergency tools as well as a brief description of troubleshooting and tune-up equipment.

Chapter Two provides methods and suggestions for quick and accurate diagnosis and repair of problems. Troubleshooting procedures discuss typical symptoms and logical methods to pinpoint the trouble.

Chapter Three explains all periodic lubrication and routine maintenance necessary to keep your vehicle running well. Chapter Three also includes recommended tune-up procedures, eliminating the need to constantly consult chapters on the various subassemblies.

Subsequent chapters cover specific systems such as the engine, transmission, and electrical systems. Each of these chapters provides disassembly, repair, and assembly procedures in a simple step-by-step format. If a repair requires special skills or tools, or is otherwise impractical for the home mechanic, it is so indicated. In these cases it is usually faster and less expensive to have the repairs made by a dealer or competent repair shop. Necessary specifications concerning a particular system are included at the end of the appropriate chapter.

When special tools are required to perform a procedure included in this manual, the tool is illustrated either in actual use or alone. It may be possible to rent or borrow these tools. The inventive mechanic may also be able to find a suitable substitute in his tool box, or to fabricate one.

The terms NOTE, CAUTION, and WARNING have specific meanings in this manual. A NOTE provides additional or explanatory information. A CAUTION is used to emphasize areas where equipment damage could result if proper precautions are not taken. A WARNING is used to stress those areas where personal injury or death could result from negligence, in addition to possible mechanical damage.

SERVICE HINTS

Observing the following practices will save time, effort, and frustration, as well as prevent possible injury.

Throughout this manual keep in mind two conventions. "Front" refers to the front of the vehicle. The front of any component, such as the transmission, is that end which faces toward the front of the vehicle. The "left" and "right" sides of the vehicle refer to the orientation of a person sitting in the vehicle facing forward. For example, the steering wheel is on the left side. These rules are simple, but even experienced mechanics occasionally become disoriented.

Most of the service procedures covered are straightforward and can be performed by anyone reasonably handy with tools. It is suggested, however, that you consider your own capabilities carefully before attempting any operation involving major disassembly of the engine.

Some operations, for example, require the use of a press. It would be wiser to have these performed by a shop equipped for such work, rather than to try to do the job yourself with makeshift equipment. Other procedures require precision measurements. Unless you have the skills and equipment required, it would be better to have a qualified repair shop make the measurements for you.

Repairs go much faster and easier if the parts that will be worked on are clean before you begin. There are special cleaners for washing the engine and related parts. Brush or spray on the cleaning solution, let it stand, then rinse it away with a garden hose. Clean all oily or greasy parts with cleaning solvent as you remove them.

WARNING

Never use gasoline as a cleaning agent. It presents an extreme fire hazard. Be sure to work in a well-ventilated area when using cleaning solvent. Keep a fire extinguisher, rated for gasoline fires, handy in any case.

Much of the labor charge for repairs made by dealers is for the removal and disassembly of other parts to reach the defective unit. It is frequently possible to perform the preliminary operations yourself and then take the defective unit in to the dealer for repair, at considerable savings.

Once you have decided to tackle the job yourself, make sure you locate the appropriate section in this manual, and read it entirely. Study the illustrations and text until you have a good idea of what is involved in completing the job satisfactorily. If special tools are required, make arrangements to get them before you start. Also, purchase any known defective parts prior to starting on the procedure. It is frustrating and time-consuming to get partially into a job and then be unable to complete it.

Simple wiring checks can be easily made at home, but knowledge of electronics is almost a necessity for performing tests with complicated electronic testing gear.

During disassembly of parts keep a few general cautions in mind. Force is rarely needed to get things apart. If parts are a tight fit, like a bearing in a case, there is usually a tool designed to separate them. Never use a screwdriver to pry apart parts with machined surfaces such as cylinder head and valve cover. You will mar the surfaces and end up with leaks.

Make diagrams wherever similar-appearing parts are found. You may think you can remember where everything came from — but mistakes are costly. There is also the possibility you may get sidetracked and not return to work for days or even weeks — in which interval, carefully laid out parts may have become disturbed.

Tag all similar internal parts for location, and mark all mating parts for position. Record number and thickness of any shims as they are removed. Small parts such as bolts can be identified by placing them in plastic sandwich bags that are sealed and labeled with masking tape.

Wiring should be tagged with masking tape and marked as each wire is removed. Again, do not rely on memory alone.

When working under the vehicle, do not trust a hydraulic or mechanical jack to hold the vehicle up by itself. Always use jackstands. See **Figure 1**.

Disconnect battery ground cable before working near electrical connections and before disconnecting wires. Never run the engine with the battery disconnected; the alternator could be seriously damaged.

Protect finished surfaces from physical damage or corrosion. Keep gasoline and brake fluid off painted surfaces.

Frozen or very tight bolts and screws can often be loosened by soaking with penetrating oil like Liquid Wrench or WD-40, then sharply striking the bolt head a few times with a hammer and punch (or screwdriver for screws). Avoid heat unless absolutely necessary, since it may melt, warp, or remove the temper from many parts.

Avoid flames or sparks when working near a charging battery or flammable liquids, such as brake fluid or gasoline.

No parts, except those assembled with a press fit, require unusual force during assembly. If a part is hard to remove or install, find out why before proceeding.

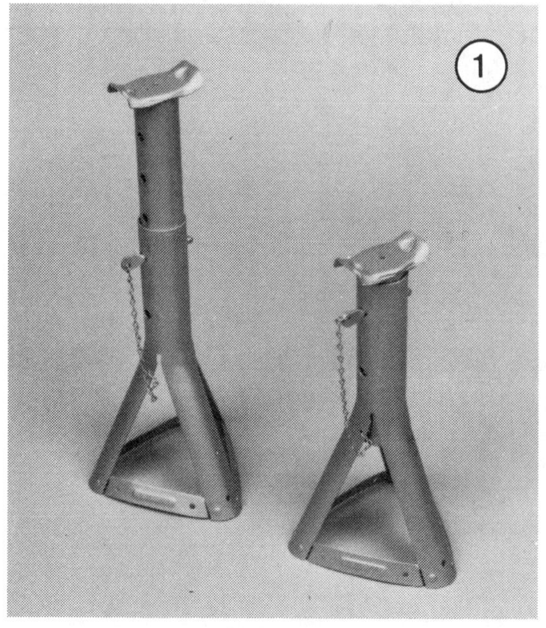

Cover all openings after removing parts to keep dirt, small tools, etc., from falling in.

When assembling two parts, start all fasteners, then tighten evenly.

The clutch plate, wiring connections, brake shoes, drums, pads, and discs should be kept clean and free of grease and oil.

When assembling parts, be sure all shims and washers are replaced exactly as they came out.

Whenever a rotating part butts against a stationary part, look for a shim or washer. Use new gaskets if there is any doubt about the condition of old ones. Generally, you should apply gasket cement to one mating surface only, so the parts may be easily disassembled in the future. A thin coat of oil on gaskets helps them seal effectively.

Heavy grease can be used to hold small parts in place if they tend to fall out during assembly. However, keep grease and oil away from electrical, clutch, and brake components.

High spots may be sanded off a piston with sandpaper, but emery cloth and oil do a much more professional job.

Carburetors are best cleaned by disassembling them and soaking the parts in a commercial carburetor cleaner. Never soak gaskets and rubber parts in these cleaners. Never use wire to clean out jets and air passages; they are easily damaged. Use compressed air to blow out the carburetor, but only if the float has been removed first.

Take your time and do the job right. Do not forget that a newly rebuilt engine must be broken in the same as a new one. Refer to your owner's manual for the proper break-in procedures.

SAFETY FIRST

Professional mechanics can work for years and never sustain a serious injury. If you observe a few rules of common sense and safety, you can enjoy many safe hours servicing your vehicle. You could hurt yourself or damage the vehicle if you ignore these rules.

1. Never use gasoline as a cleaning solvent.

2. Never smoke or use a torch in the vicinity of flammable liquids such as cleaning solvent in open containers.

3. Never smoke or use a torch in an area where batteries are being charged. Highly explosive hydrogen gas is formed during the charging process.

4. Use the proper sized wrenches to avoid damage to nuts and injury to yourself.

5. When loosening a tight or stuck nut, be guided by what would happen if the wrench should slip. Protect yourself accordingly.

6. Keep your work area clean and uncluttered.

7. Wear safety goggles during all operations involving drilling, grinding, or use of a cold chisel.

8. Never use worn tools.

9. Keep a fire extinguisher handy and be sure it is rated for gasoline (Class B) and electrical (Class C) fires.

EXPENDABLE SUPPLIES

Certain expendable supplies are necessary. These include grease, oil, gasket cement, wiping rags, cleaning solvent, and distilled water. Also, special locking compounds, silicone lubricants, and engine cleaners may be useful. Cleaning solvent is available at most service stations and distilled water for the battery is available at most supermarkets.

SHOP TOOLS

For proper servicing, you will need an assortment of ordinary hand tools (**Figure 2**).

As a minimum, these include:

a. Combination wrenches
b. Sockets
c. Plastic mallet
d. Small hammer
e. Snap ring pliers
f. Gas pliers
g. Phillips screwdrivers
h. Slot (common) screwdrivers
i. Feeler gauges
j. Spark plug gauge
k. Spark plug wrench

Special tools necessary are shown in the chapters covering the particular repair in which they are used.

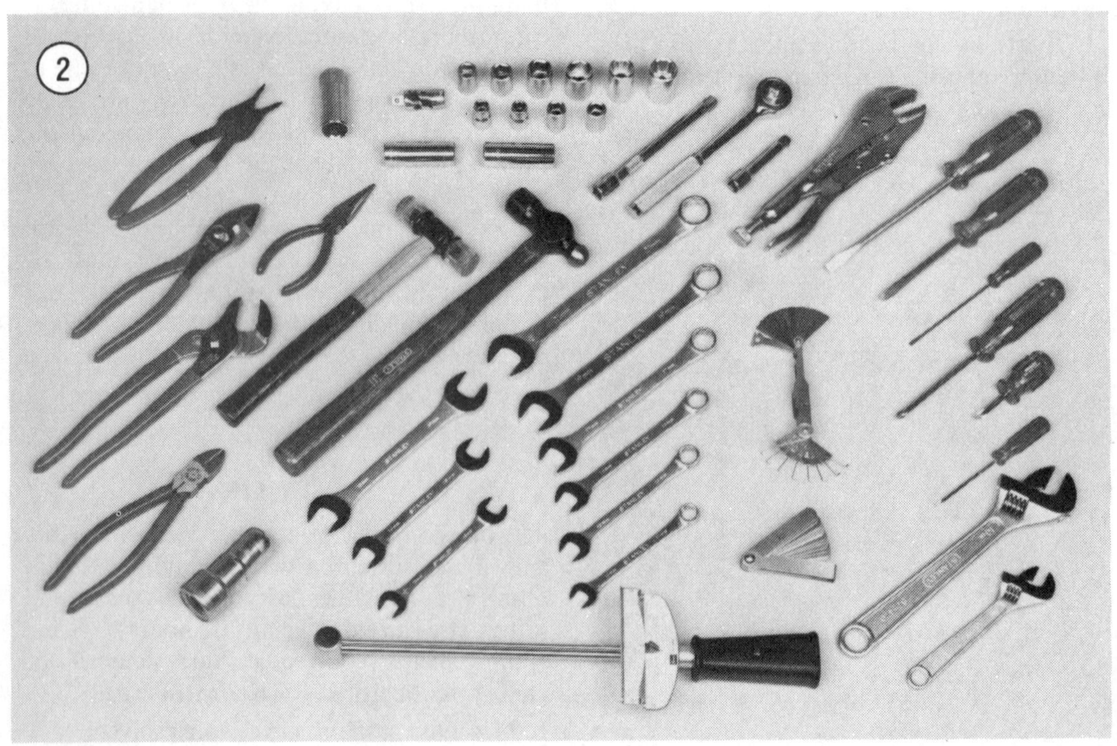

Engine tune-up and troubleshooting procedures require other special tools and equipment. These are described in detail in the following sections.

EMERGENCY TOOL KIT

A small emergency tool kit kept in the trunk is handy for road emergencies which otherwise could leave you stranded. The tools listed below and shown in **Figure 3** will let you handle most roadside repairs.

a. Combination wrenches
b. Crescent (adjustable) wrench
c. Screwdrivers — common and Phillips
d. Pliers — conventional (gas) and needle nose
e. Vise Grips
f. Hammer — plastic and metal
g. Small container of waterless hand cleaner
h. Rags for clean up
i. Silver waterproof sealing tape (duct tape)
j. Flashlight
k. Emergency road flares — at least four
l. Spare drive belts (water pump, alternator, etc.)

TROUBLESHOOTING AND TUNE-UP EQUIPMENT

Voltmeter, Ohmmeter, and Ammeter

For testing the ignition or electrical system, a good voltmeter is required. For automotive use, an instrument covering 0-20 volts is satisfac-

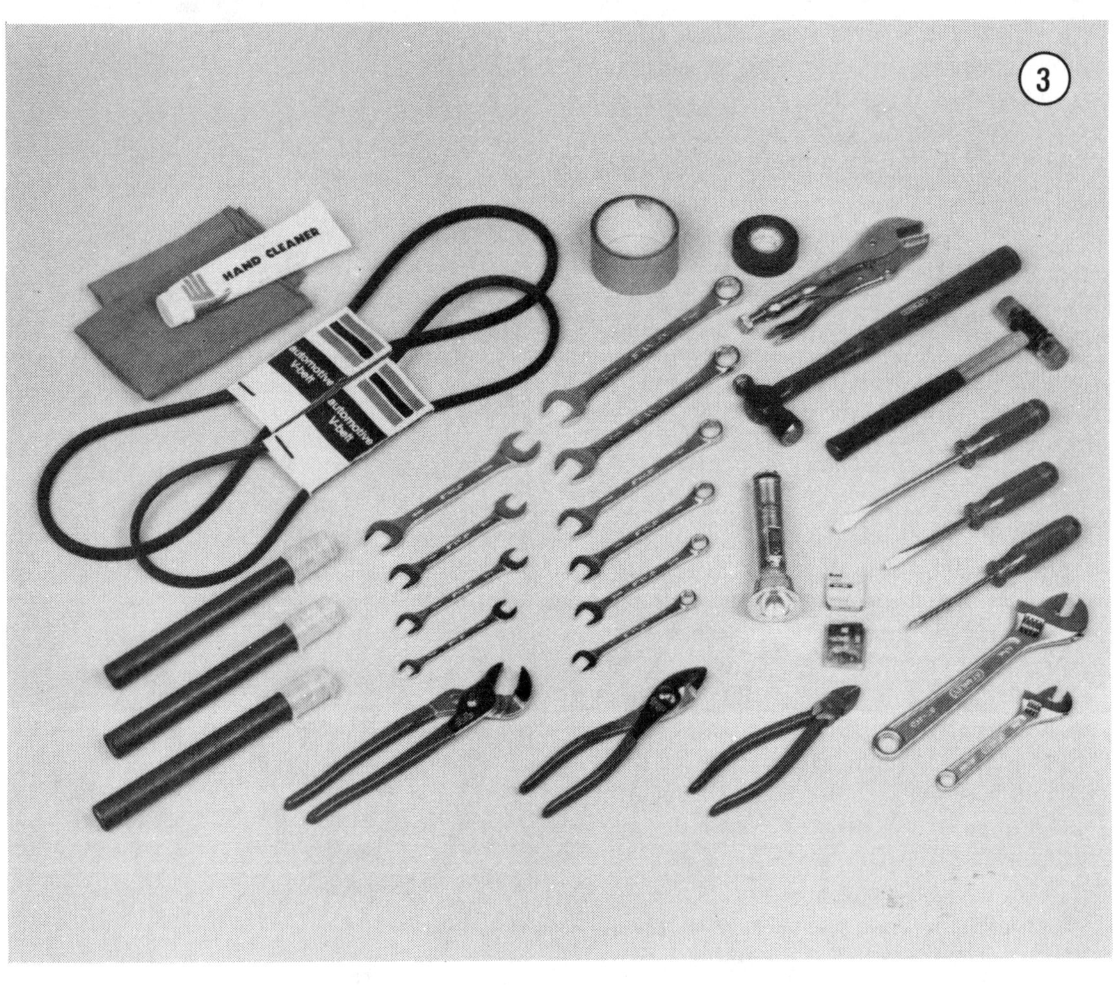

tory. One which also has a 0-2 volt scale is necessary for testing relays, points, or individual contacts where voltage drops are much smaller. Accuracy should be ± ½ volt.

An ohmmeter measures electrical resistance. This instrument is useful for checking continuity (open and short circuits), and testing fuses and lights.

The ammeter measures electrical current. Ammeters for automotive use should cover 0-50 amperes and 0-250 amperes. These are useful for checking battery charging and starting current.

Several inexpensive VOM's (volt-ohm-milliammeter) combine all three instruments into one which fits easily in any tool box. See **Figure 4**. However, the ammeter ranges are usually too small for automotive work.

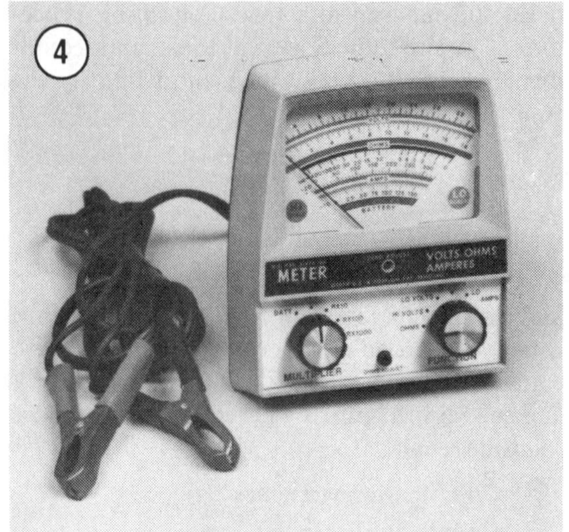

Hydrometer

The hydrometer gives a useful indication of battery condition and charge by measuring the specific gravity of the electrolyte in each cell. See **Figure 5**. Complete details on use and interpretation of readings are provided in the electrical chapter.

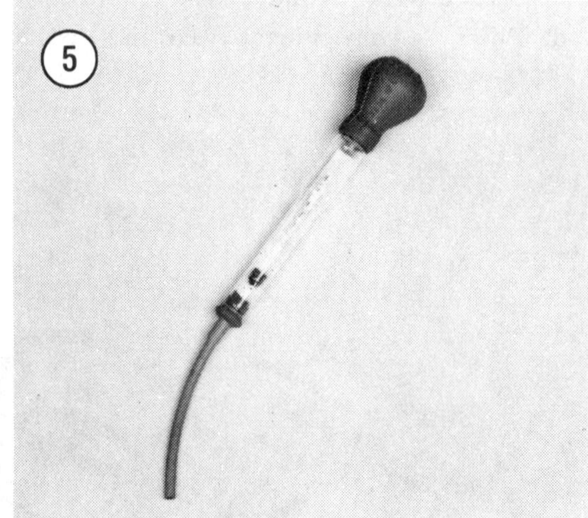

Compression Tester

The compression tester measures the compression pressure built up in each cylinder. The results, when properly interpreted, can indicate general cylinder and valve condition. See **Figure 6**.

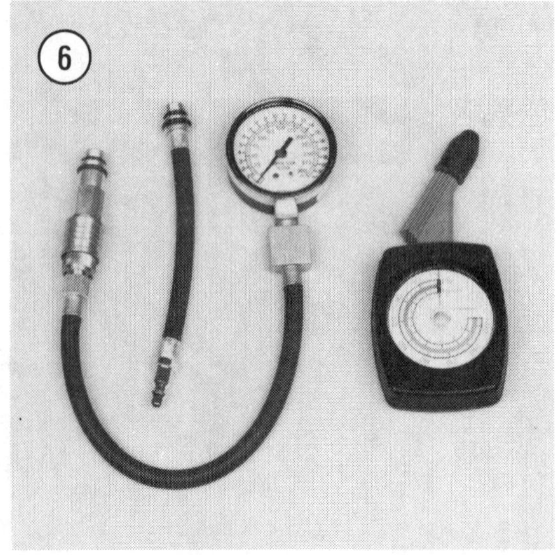

Vacuum Gauge

The vacuum gauge **(Figure 7)** is one of the easiest instruments to use, but one of the most difficult for the inexperienced mechanic to interpret. The results, when interpreted with other findings, can provide valuable clues to possible trouble.

To use the vacuum gauge, connect it to a vacuum hose that goes to the intake manifold. Attach it either directly to the hose or to a T-fitting installed into the hose.

> NOTE: *Subtract one inch from the reading for every 1,000 ft. elevation.*

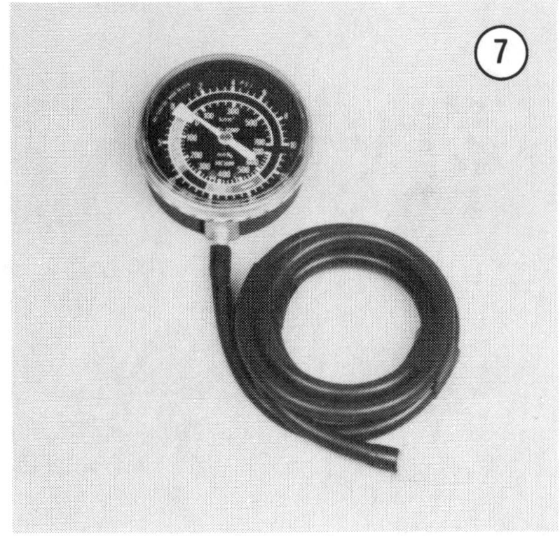

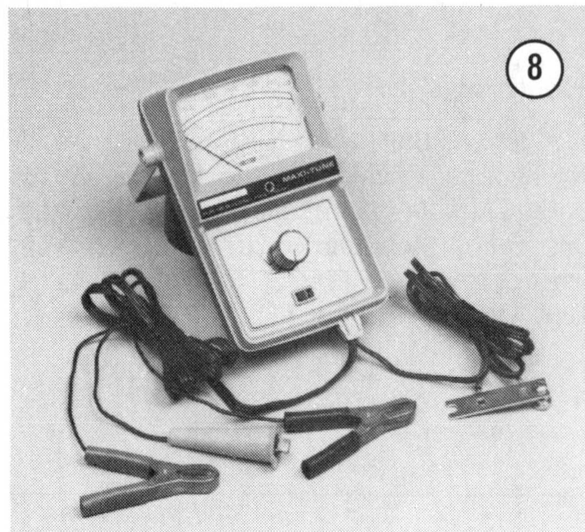

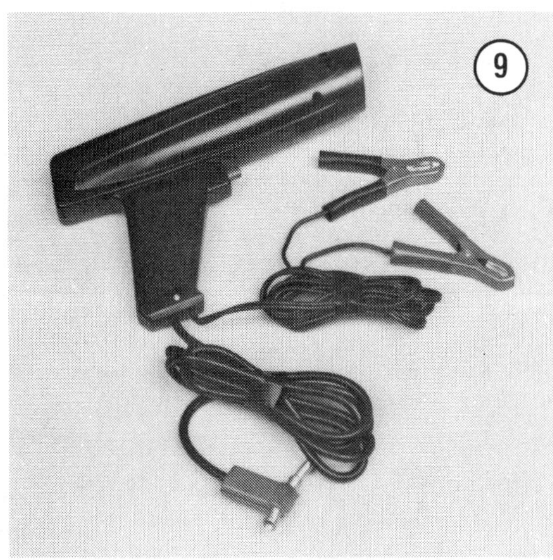

Fuel Pressure Gauge

This instrument is invaluable for evaluating fuel pump performance. Fuel system troubleshooting procedures in this manual use a fuel pressure gauge. Usually a vacuum gauge and fuel pressure gauge are combined.

Dwell Meter (Contact Breaker Point Ignition Only)

A dwell meter measures the distance in degrees of cam rotation that the breaker points remain closed while the engine is running. Since this angle is determined by breaker point gap, dwell angle is an accurate indication of breaker point gap.

Many tachometers intended for tuning and testing incorporate a dwell meter as well. See **Figure 8**. Follow the manufacturer's instructions to measure dwell.

Tachometer

A tachometer is necessary for tuning. See **Figure 8**. Ignition timing and carburetor adjustments must be performed at the specified idle speed. The best instrument for this purpose is one with a low range of 0-1,000 or 0-2,000 rpm for setting idle, and a high range of 0-4,000 or more for setting ignition timing at 3,000 rpm. Extended range (0-6,000 or 0-8,000 rpm) instruments lack accuracy at lower speeds. The instrument should be capable of detecting changes of 25 rpm on the low range.

Strobe Timing Light

This instrument is necessary for tuning, as it permits very accurate ignition timing. The light flashes at precisely the same instant that No. 1 cylinder fires, at which time the timing marks on the engine should align. Refer to Chapter Three for exact location of the timing marks for your engine.

Suitable lights range from inexpensive neon bulb types ($2-3) to powerful xenon strobe lights ($20-40). See **Figure 9**. Neon timing lights are difficult to see and must be used in dimly lit areas. Xenon strobe timing lights can be used outside in bright sunlight. Both types work on this vehicle; use according to the manufacturer's instructions.

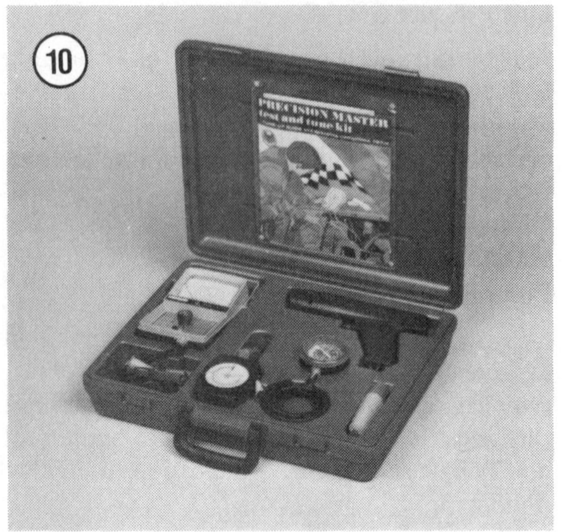

Tune-up Kits

Many manufacturer's offer kits that combine several useful instruments. Some come in a convenient carry case and are usally less expensive than purchasing one instrument at a time. **Figure 10** shows one of the kits that is available. The prices vary with the number of instruments included in the kit.

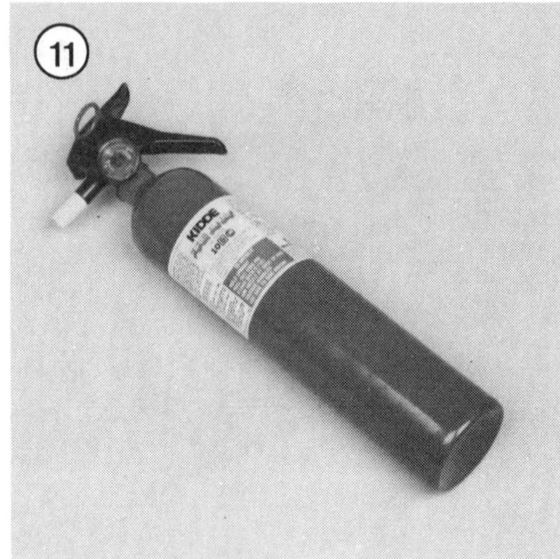

Fire Extinguisher

A fire extinguisher is a necessity when working on a vehicle. It should be rated for both *Class B* (flammable liquids—gasoline, oil, paint, etc.) and *Class C* (electrical—wiring, etc.) type fires. It should always be kept within reach. See **Figure 11**.

CHAPTER TWO

2

TROUBLESHOOTING

Troubleshooting can be a relatively simple matter if it is done logically. The first step in any troubleshooting procedure must be defining the symptoms as closely as possible. Subsequent steps involve testing and analyzing areas which could cause the symptoms. A haphazard approach may eventually find the trouble, but in terms of wasted time and unnecessary parts replacement, it can be very costly.

The troubleshooting procedures in this chapter analyze typical symptoms and show logical methods of isolation. These are not the only methods. There may be several approaches to a problem, but all methods must have one thing in common — a logical, systematic approach.

STARTING SYSTEM

The starting system consists of the starter motor and the starter solenoid. The ignition key controls the starter solenoid, which mechanically engages the starter with the engine flywheel, and supplies electrical current to turn the starter motor.

Starting system troubles are relatively easy to find. In most cases, the trouble is a loose or dirty electrical connection. **Figures 1 and 2** provide routines for finding the trouble.

CHARGING SYSTEM

The charging system consists of the alternator (or generator on older vehicles), voltage regulator, and battery. A drive belt driven by the engine crankshaft turns the alternator which produces electrical energy to charge the battery. As engine speed varies, the voltage from the alternator varies. A voltage regulator controls the charging current to the battery and maintains the voltage to the vehicle's electrical system at safe levels. A warning light or gauge on the instrument panel signals the driver when charging is not taking place. Refer to **Figure 3** for a typical charging system.

Complete troubleshooting of the charging system requires test equipment and skills which the average home mechanic does not possess. However, there are a few tests which can be done to pinpoint most troubles.

Charging system trouble may stem from a defective alternator (or generator), voltage regulator, battery, or drive belt. It may also be caused by something as simple as incorrect drive belt tension. The following are symptoms of typical problems you may encounter.

1. ***Battery dies frequently, even though the warning lamp indicates no discharge*** — This can be caused by a drive belt that is slightly too

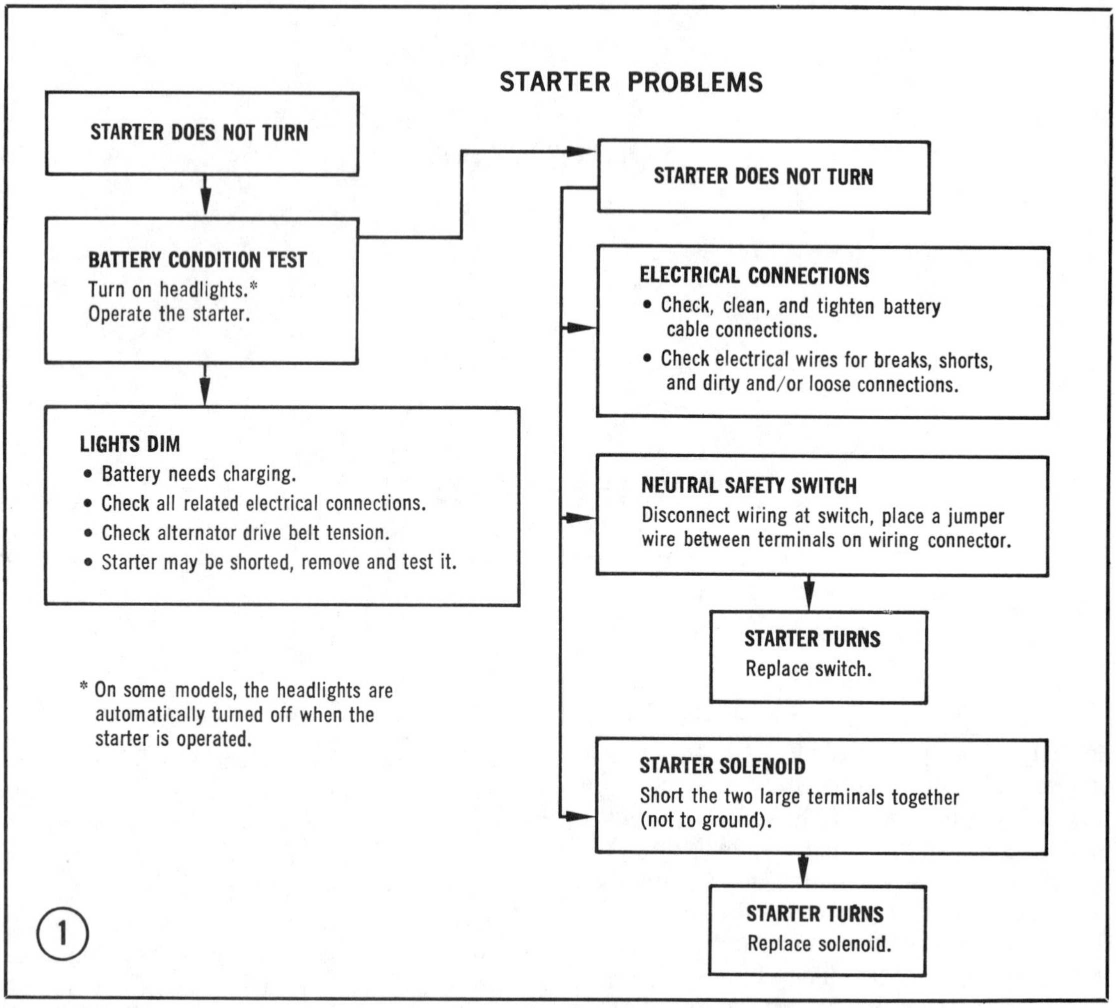

STARTER PROBLEMS
STARTER DOES NOT TURN
BATTERY CONDITION TEST
Turn on headlights.*
Operate the starter.
LIGHTS DIM
• Battery needs charging.
• Check all related electrical connections.
• Check alternator drive belt tension.
• Starter may be shorted, remove and test it.
* On some models, the headlights are automatically turned off when the starter is operated.
STARTER DOES NOT TURN
ELECTRICAL CONNECTIONS
• Check, clean, and tighten battery cable connections.
• Check electrical wires for breaks, shorts, and dirty and/or loose connections.
NEUTRAL SAFETY SWITCH
Disconnect wiring at switch, place a jumper wire between terminals on wiring connector.
STARTER TURNS
Replace switch.
STARTER SOLENOID
Short the two large terminals together (not to ground).
STARTER TURNS
Replace solenoid.
1

STARTER PROBLEMS
STARTER TURNS
DOES NOT ENGAGE WITH ENGINE
Check pinion or solenoid shifting fork and teeth on flywheel gear.
ENGAGES WITH ENGINE — WILL NOT RELEASE
Check for sticking solenoid or jammed pinion onto flywheel.
LOUD GRINDING NOISE
Check flywheel to pinion alignment. The overrunning clutch may be broken.
Remove the starter and examine the gear teeth; replace if necessary.
2

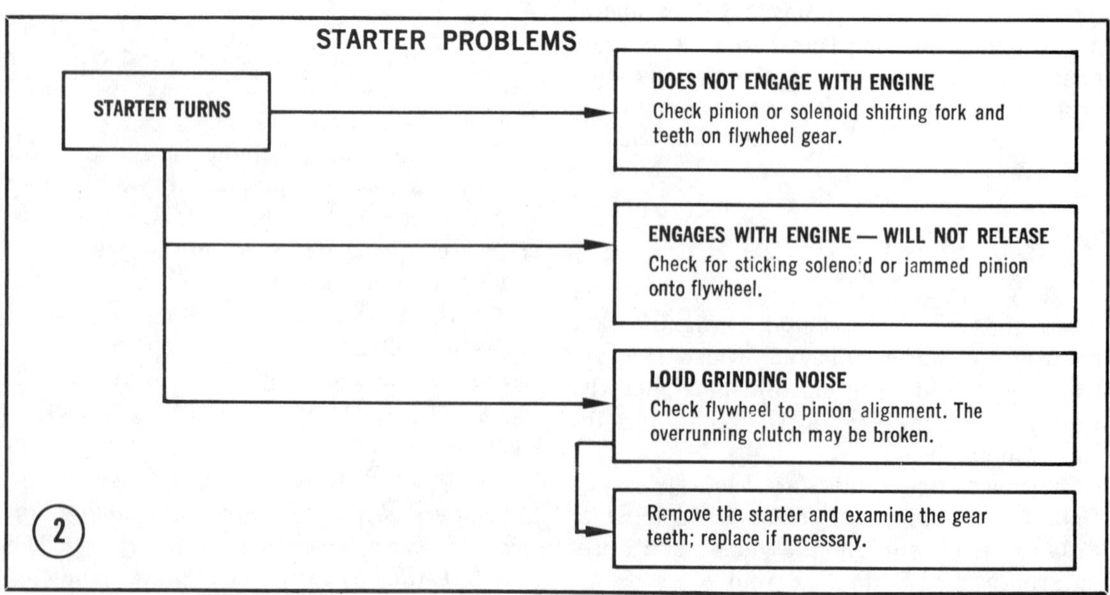

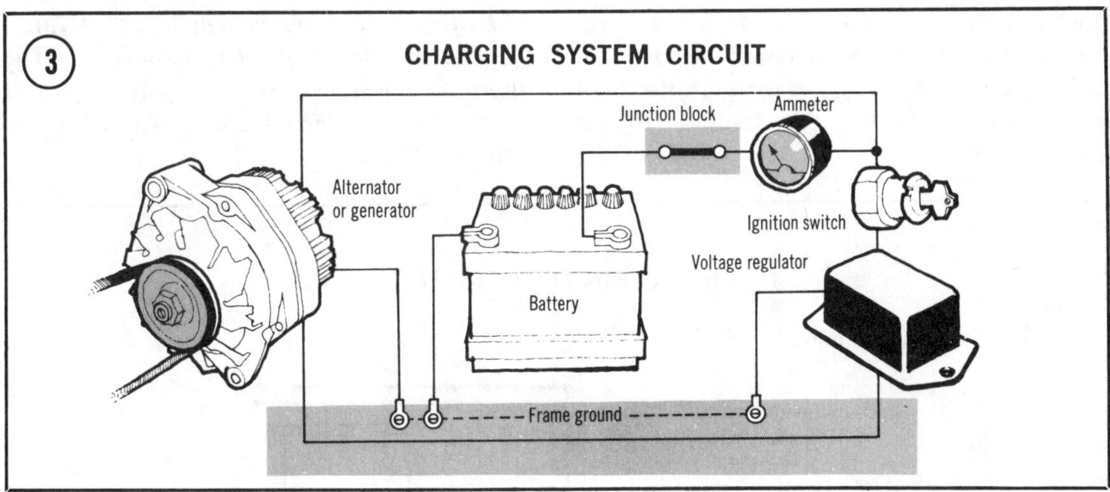

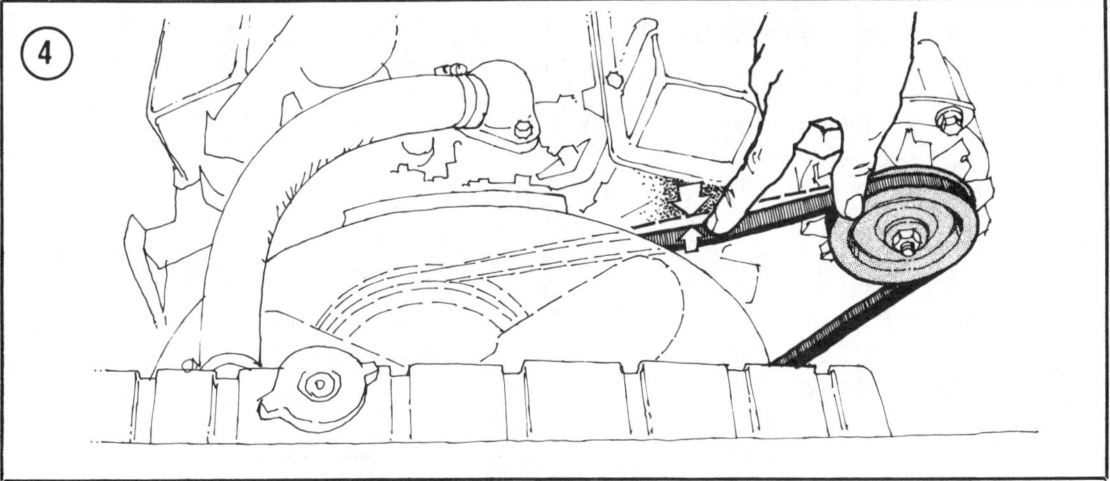

loose. Grasp the alternator (or generator) pulley and try to turn it. If the pulley can be turned without moving the belt, the drive belt is too loose. As a rule, keep the belt tight enough that it can be deflected about ½ in. under moderate thumb pressure between the pulleys (**Figure 4**). The battery may also be at fault; test the battery condition.

2. ***Charging system warning lamp does not come on when ignition switch is turned on*** — This may indicate a defective ignition switch, battery, voltage regulator, or lamp. First try to start the vehicle. If it doesn't start, check the ignition switch and battery. If the car starts, remove the warning lamp; test it for continuity with an ohmmeter or substitute a new lamp. If the lamp is good, locate the voltage regulator and make sure it is properly grounded (try tightening the mounting screws). Also the alternator (or generator) brushes may not be making contact. Test the alternator (or generator) and voltage regulator.

3. ***Alternator (or generator) warning lamp comes on and stays on*** — This usually indicates that no charging is taking place. First check drive belt tension (**Figure 4**). Then check battery condition, and check all wiring connections in the charging system. If this does not locate the trouble, check the alternator (or generator) and voltage regulator.

4. ***Charging system warning lamp flashes on and off intermittently*** — This usually indicates the charging system is working intermittently.

Check the drive belt tension **(Figure 4)**, and check all electrical connections in the charging system. Check the alternator (or generator). *On generators only*, check the condition of the commutator.

5. ***Battery requires frequent additions of water, or lamps require frequent replacement*** — The alternator (or generator) is probably overcharging the battery. The voltage regulator is probably at fault.

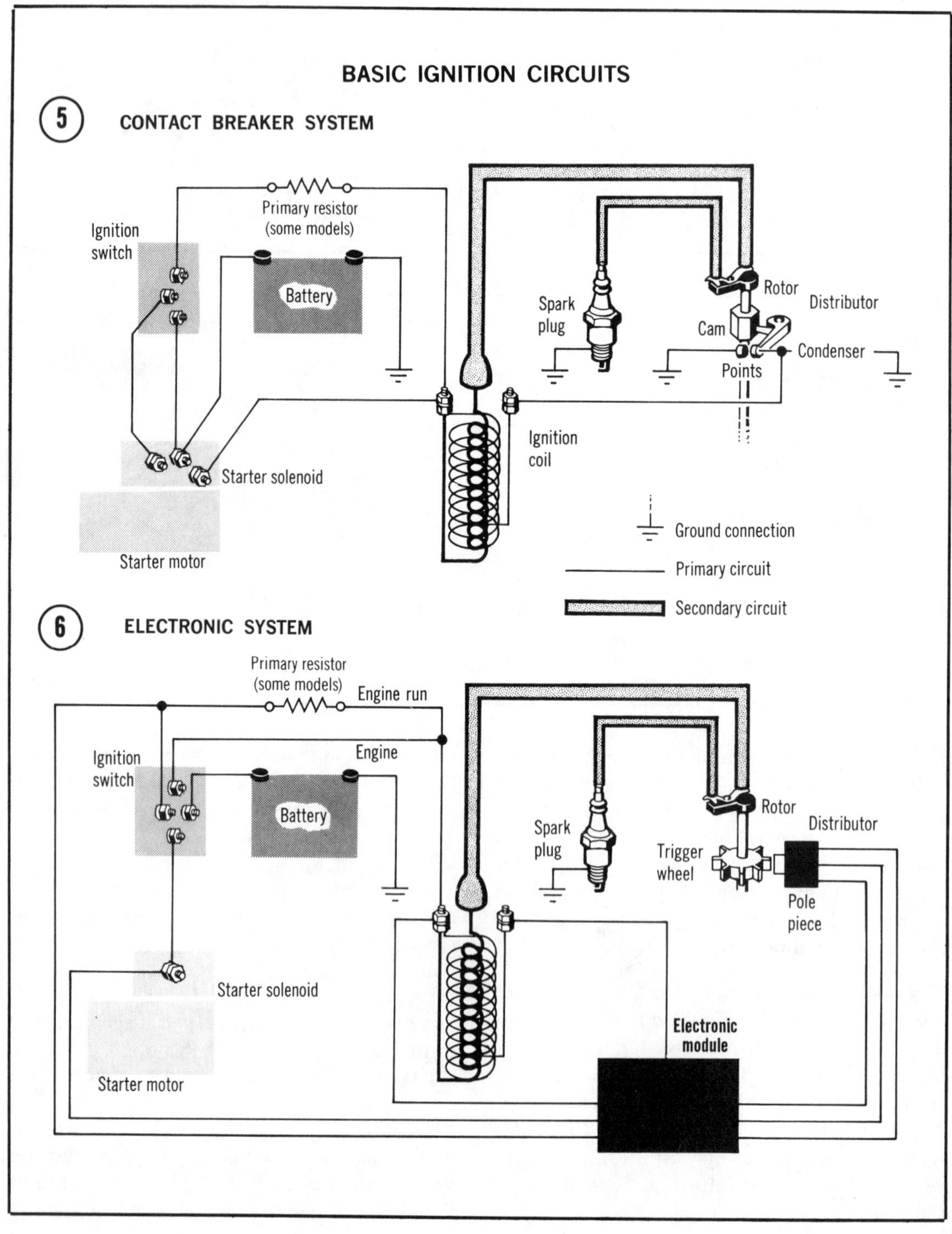

6. ***Excessive noise from the alternator (or generator)*** — Check for loose mounting brackets and bolts. The problem may also be worn bearings or the need of lubrication in some cases. If an alternator whines, a shorted diode may be indicated.

IGNITION SYSTEM

The ignition system may be either a conventional contact breaker type or an electronic ignition. See electrical chapter to determine which type you have. **Figures 5 and 6** show simplified diagrams of each type.

Most problems involving failure to start, poor performance, or rough running stem from trouble in the ignition system, particularly in contact breaker systems. Many novice troubleshooters get into trouble when they assume that these symptoms point to the fuel system instead of the ignition system.

Ignition system troubles may be roughly divided between those affecting only one cylinder and those affecting all cylinders. If the trouble affects only one cylinder, it can only be in the spark plug, spark plug wire, or portion of the distributor associated with that cylinder. If the trouble affects all cylinders (weak spark or no spark), then the trouble is in the ignition coil, rotor, distributor, or associated wiring.

The troubleshooting procedures outlined in **Figure 7** (breaker point ignition) or **Figure 8**

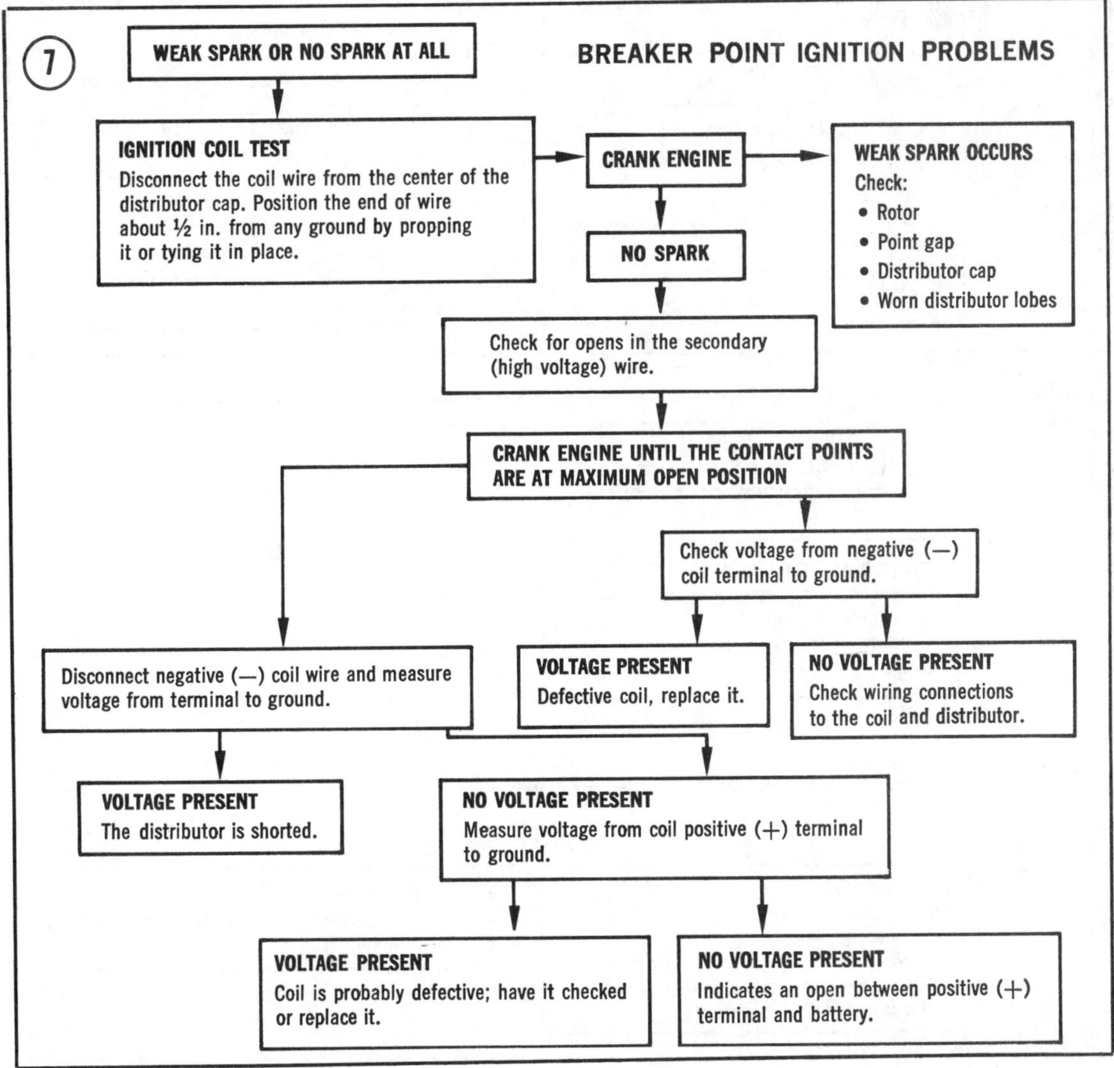

(electronic ignition) will help you isolate ignition problems fast. Of course, they assume that the battery is in good enough condition to crank the engine over at its normal rate.

ENGINE PERFORMANCE

A number of factors can make the engine difficult or impossible to start, or cause rough running, poor performance and so on. The majority of novice troubleshooters immediately suspect the carburetor or fuel injection system. In the majority of cases, though, the trouble exists in the ignition system.

The troubleshooting procedures outlined in **Figures 9 through 14** will help you solve the majority of engine starting troubles in a systematic manner.

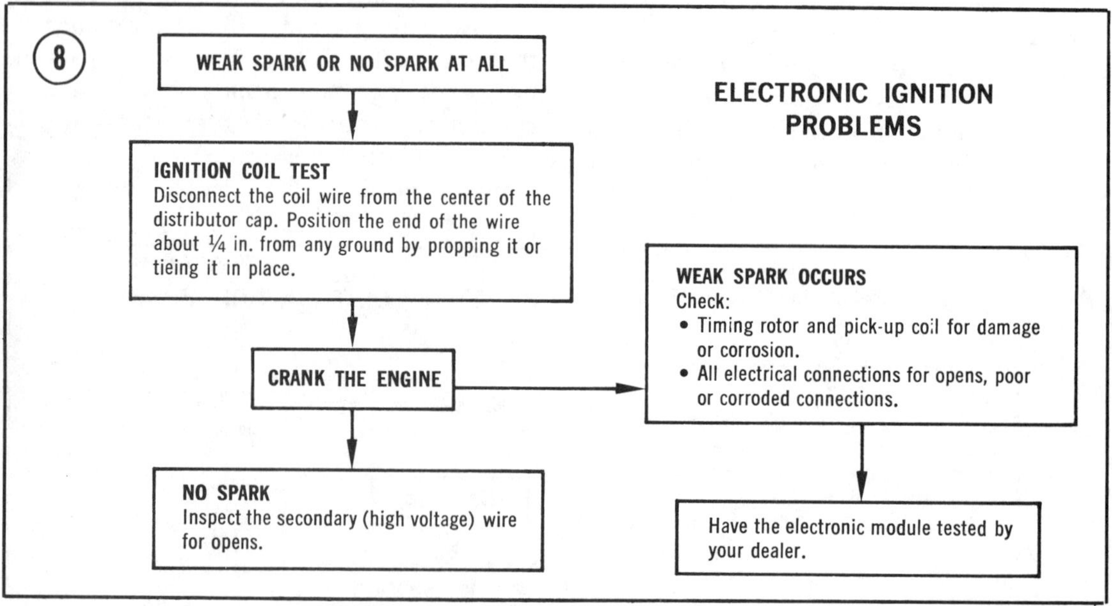

8
WEAK SPARK OR NO SPARK AT ALL
ELECTRONIC IGNITION PROBLEMS
IGNITION COIL TEST
Disconnect the coil wire from the center of the distributor cap. Position the end of the wire about ¼ in. from any ground by propping it or tieing it in place.
CRANK THE ENGINE
WEAK SPARK OCCURS
Check:
• Timing rotor and pick-up coil for damage or corrosion.
• All electrical connections for opens, poor or corroded connections.
NO SPARK
Inspect the secondary (high voltage) wire for opens.
Have the electronic module tested by your dealer.

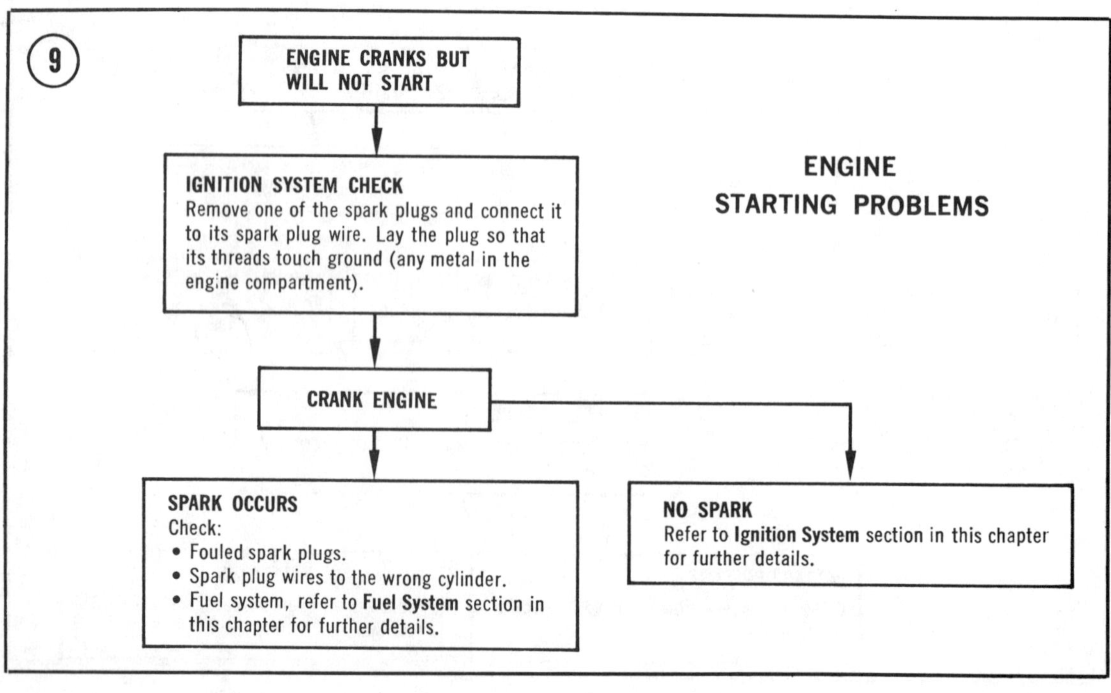

9
ENGINE CRANKS BUT WILL NOT START
ENGINE STARTING PROBLEMS
IGNITION SYSTEM CHECK
Remove one of the spark plugs and connect it to its spark plug wire. Lay the plug so that its threads touch ground (any metal in the engine compartment).
CRANK ENGINE
SPARK OCCURS
Check:
• Fouled spark plugs.
• Spark plug wires to the wrong cylinder.
• Fuel system, refer to Fuel System section in this chapter for further details.
NO SPARK
Refer to Ignition System section in this chapter for further details.

10
STEADY ENGINE MISS
ENGINE MISSES STEADILY
DISCONNECT ONE SPARK PLUG WIRE AT A TIME
START ENGINE AND LET IT IDLE
MISS REMAINS THE SAME
That cylinder is not operating correctly.
Check:
• Spark plug condition and gap.
• Spark plug wires for opens or cracks in the insulation.
• Distributor cap.
MISS INCREASES
That cylinder is operating correctly—continue to next cylinder.

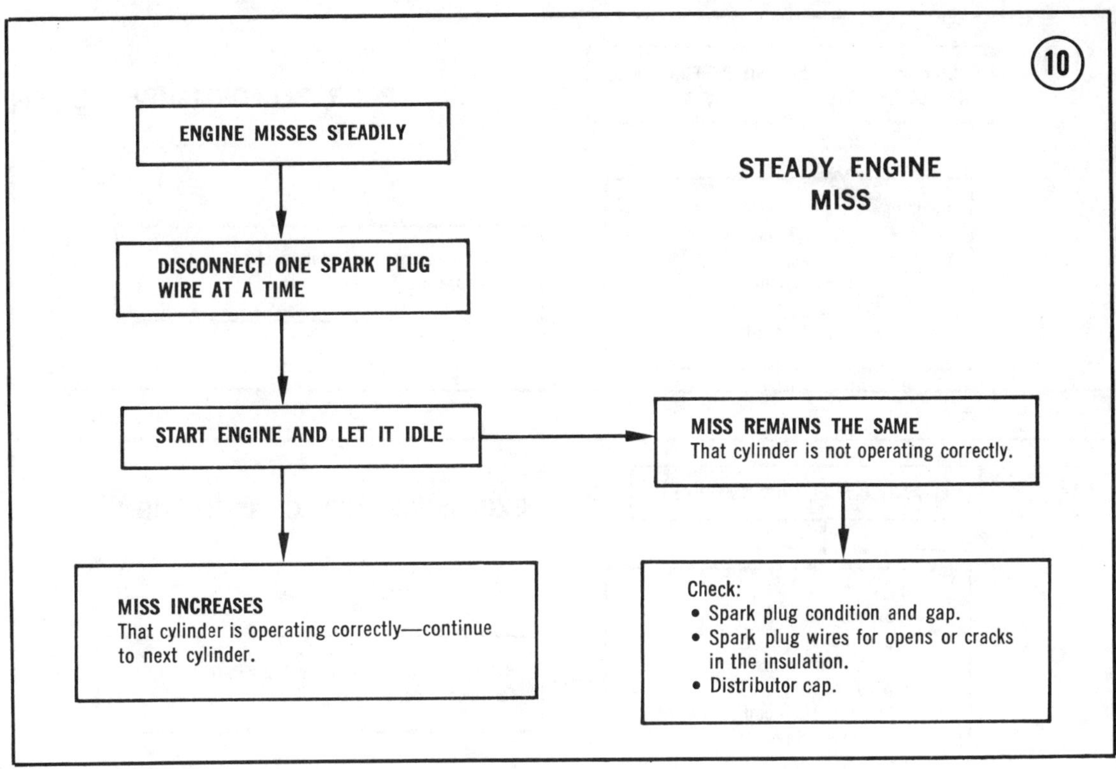

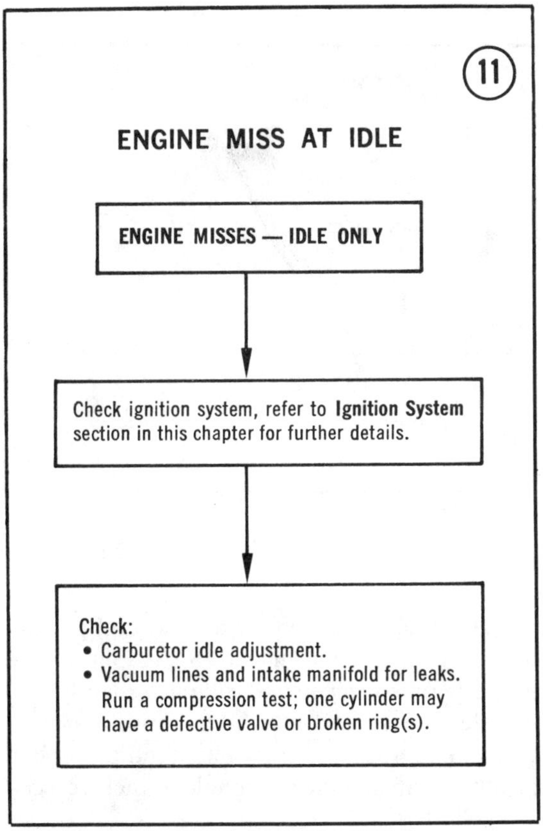

11
ENGINE MISS AT IDLE
ENGINE MISSES — IDLE ONLY
Check ignition system, refer to Ignition System section in this chapter for further details.
Check:
• Carburetor idle adjustment.
• Vacuum lines and intake manifold for leaks.
Run a compression test; one cylinder may have a defective valve or broken ring(s).

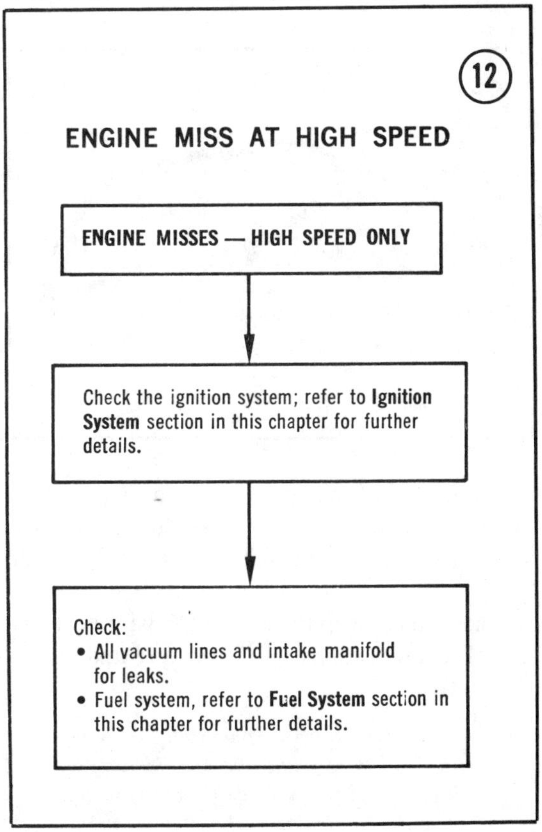

12
ENGINE MISS AT HIGH SPEED
ENGINE MISSES — HIGH SPEED ONLY
Check the ignition system; refer to Ignition System section in this chapter for further details.
Check:
• All vacuum lines and intake manifold for leaks.
• Fuel system, refer to Fuel System section in this chapter for further details.

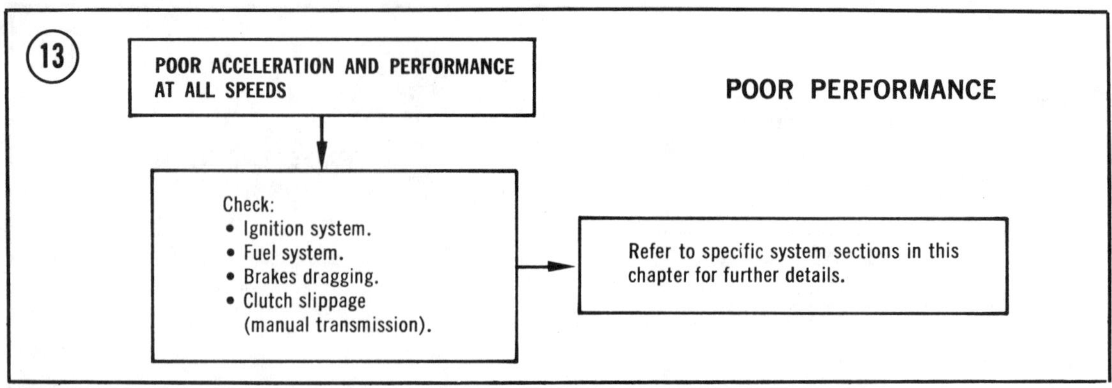

13
POOR ACCELERATION AND PERFORMANCE AT ALL SPEEDS
POOR PERFORMANCE
Check:
• Ignition system.
• Fuel system.
• Brakes dragging.
• Clutch slippage (manual transmission).
Refer to specific system sections in this chapter for further details.

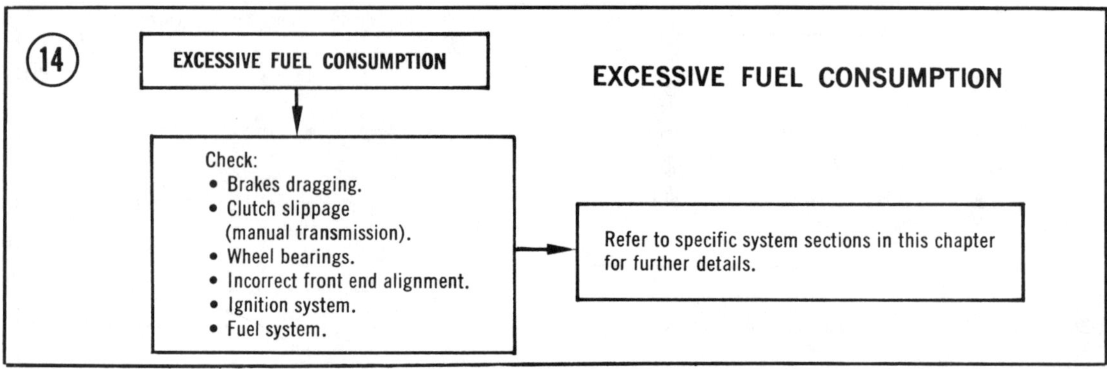

14
EXCESSIVE FUEL CONSUMPTION
EXCESSIVE FUEL CONSUMPTION
Check:
• Brakes dragging.
• Clutch slippage (manual transmission).
• Wheel bearings.
• Incorrect front end alignment.
• Ignition system.
• Fuel system.
Refer to specific system sections in this chapter for further details.

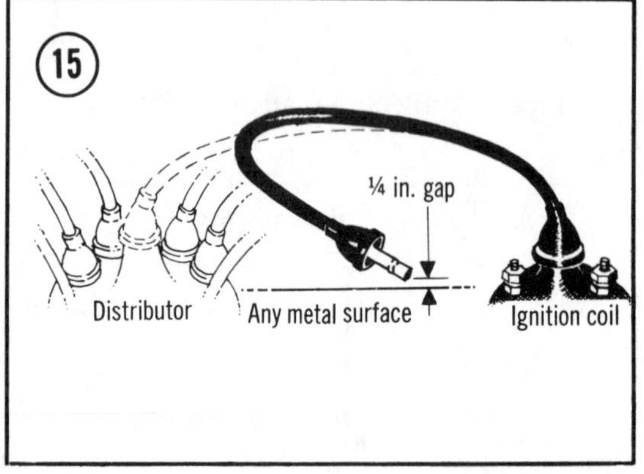

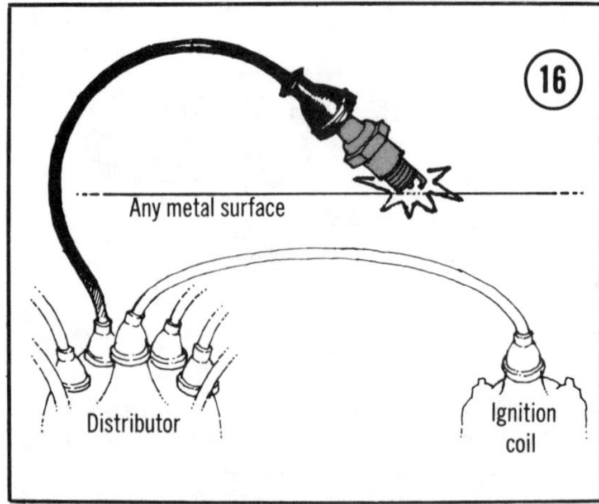

Some tests of the ignition system require running the engine with a spark plug or ignition coil wire disconnected. The safest way to do this is to disconnect the wire with the engine stopped, then prop the end of the wire next to a metal surface as shown in **Figures 15 and 16**.

WARNING

Never disconnect a spark plug or ignition coil wire while the engine is running. The high voltage in an ignition system, particularly the newer high-energy electronic ignition systems could cause serious injury or even death.

Spark plug condition is an important indication of engine performance. Spark plugs in a properly operating engine will have slightly pitted electrodes, and a light tan insulator tip. **Figure 17** shows a normal plug, and a number of others which indicate trouble in their respective cylinders.

• Appearance—Firing tip has deposits of light gray to light tan.
• Can be cleaned, regapped and reused.

• Appearance—Dull, dry black with fluffy carbon deposits on the insulator tip, electrode and exposed shell.
• Caused by—Fuel/air mixture too rich, plug heat range too cold, weak ignition system, dirty air cleaner, faulty automatic choke or excessive idling.
• Can be cleaned, regapped and reused.

• Appearance—Wet black deposits on insulator and exposed shell.
• Caused by—Excessive oil entering the combustion chamber through worn rings, pistons, valve guides or bearings.
• Replace with new plugs (use a hotter plug if engine is not repaired).

• Appearance — Yellow insulator deposits (may sometimes be dark gray, black or tan in color) on the insulator tip.
• Caused by—Highly leaded gasoline.
• Replace with new plugs.

• Appearance—Yellow glazed deposits indicating melted lead deposits due to hard acceleration.
• Caused by—Highly leaded gasoline.
• Replace with new plugs.

• Appearance—Glazed yellow deposits with a slight brownish tint on the insulator tip and ground electrode.
• Replace with new plugs.

• Appearance — Brown colored hardened ash deposits on the insulator tip and ground electrode.
• Caused by—Fuel and/or oil additives.
• Replace with new plugs.

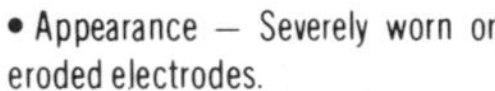

• Appearance — Severely worn or eroded electrodes.
• Caused by—Normal wear or unusual oil and/or fuel additives.
• Replace with new plugs.

• Appearance — Melted ground electrode.
• Caused by—Overadvanced ignition timing, inoperative ignition advance mechanism, too low of a fuel octane rating, lean fuel/air mixture or carbon deposits in combustion chamber.

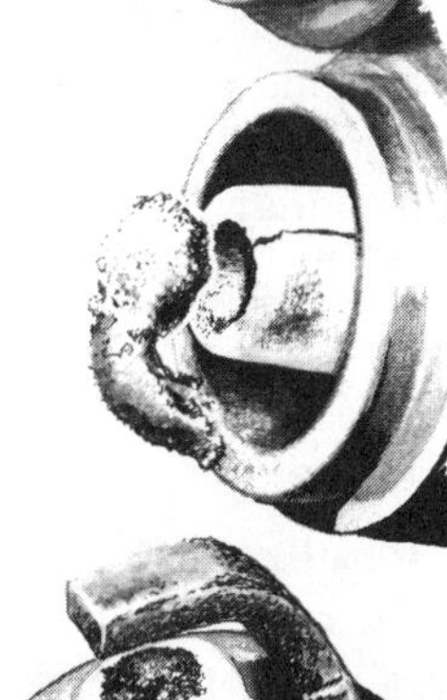

• Appearance—Melted center electrode.
• Caused by—Abnormal combustion due to overadvanced ignition timing or incorrect advance, too low of a fuel octane rating, lean fuel/air mixture, or carbon deposits in combustion chamber.
• Correct engine problem and replace with new plugs.

• Appearance—Melted center electrode and white blistered insulator tip.
• Caused by—Incorrect plug heat range selection.
• Replace with new plugs.

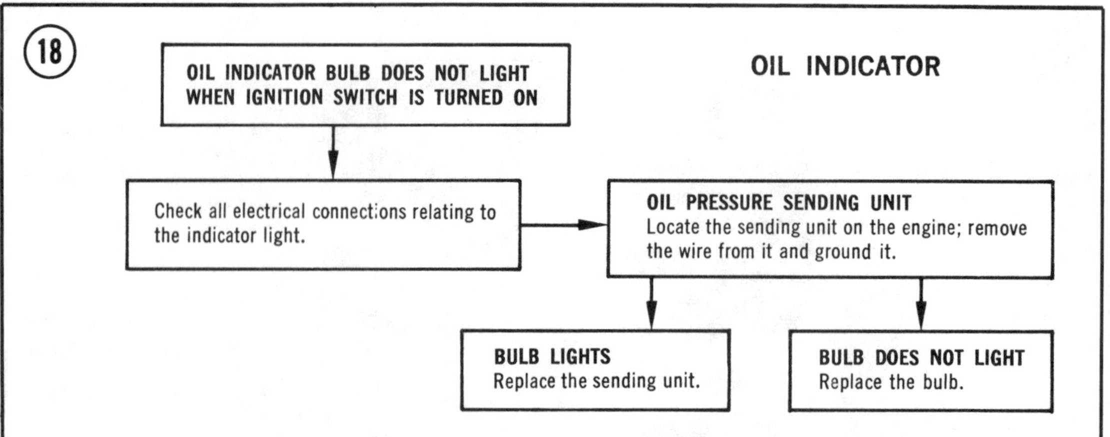

ENGINE OIL PRESSURE LIGHT

Proper oil pressure to the engine is vital. If oil pressure is insufficient, the engine can destroy itself in a comparatively short time.

The oil pressure warning circuit monitors oil pressure constantly. If pressure drops below a predetermined level, the light comes on.

Obviously, it is vital for the warning circuit to be working to signal low oil pressure. Each time you turn on the ignition, but before you start the car, the warning light should come on. If it doesn't, there is trouble in the warning circuit, not the oil pressure system. See **Figure 18** to troubleshoot the warning circuit.

Once the engine is running, the warning light should stay off. If the warning light comes on or acts erratically while the engine is running there is trouble with the engine oil pressure system. *Stop the engine immediately*. Refer to **Figure 19** for possible causes of the problem.

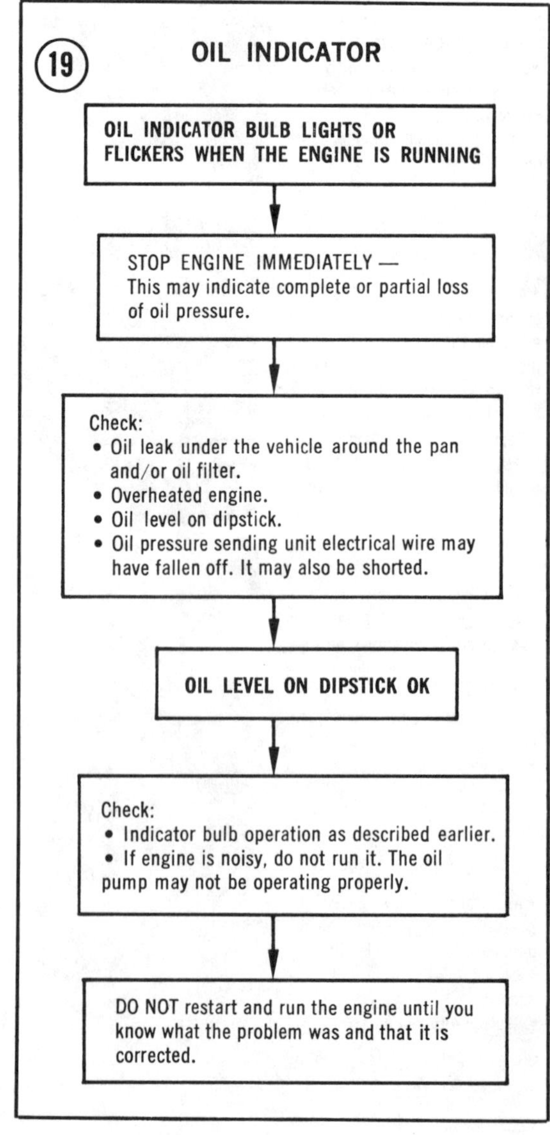

19
OIL INDICATOR
Locate the sending unit on the engine; remove the wire from it and ground it.
OIL INDICATOR BULB LIGHTS OR FLICKERS WHEN THE ENGINE IS RUNNING
STOP ENGINE IMMEDIATELY —
This may indicate complete or partial loss of oil pressure.
Check:
• Oil leak under the vehicle around the pan and/or oil filter.
• Overheated engine.
• Oil level on dipstick.
• Oil pressure sending unit electrical wire may have fallen off. It may also be shorted.
OIL LEVEL ON DIPSTICK OK
Check:
• Indicator bulb operation as described earlier.
• If engine is noisy, do not run it. The oil pump may not be operating properly.
DO NOT restart and run the engine until you know what the problem was and that it is corrected.

FUEL SYSTEM (CARBURETTED)

Fuel system problems must be isolated to the fuel pump (mechanical or electric), fuel lines, fuel filter, or carburetor. These procedures assume the ignition system is working properly and is correctly adjusted.

1. ***Engine will not start*** — First make sure that fuel is being delivered to the carburetor. Remove the air cleaner, look into the carburetor throat, and operate the accelerator

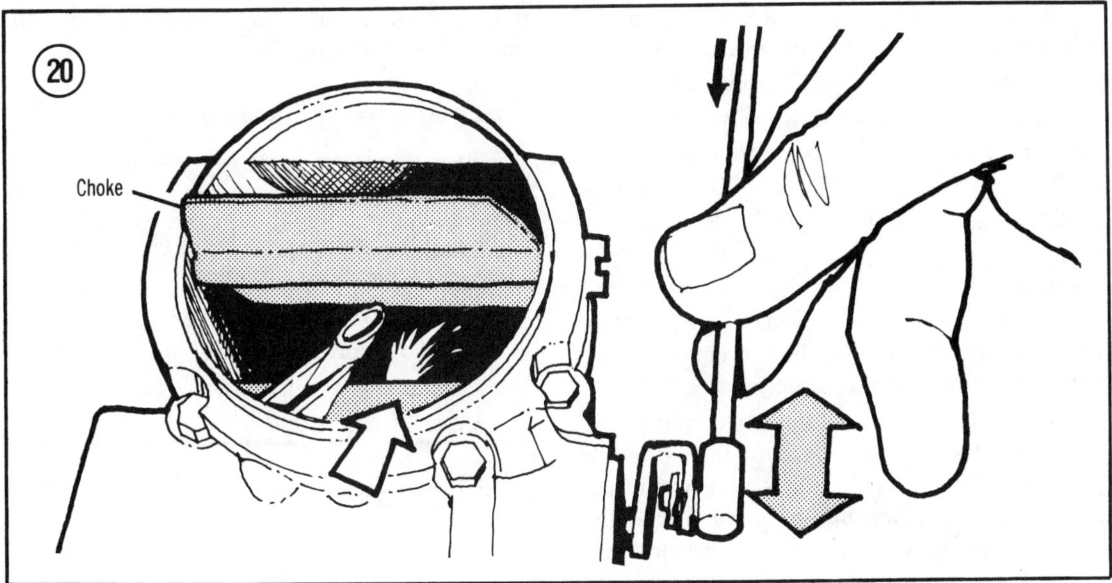

linkage several times. There should be a stream of fuel from the accelerator pump discharge tube each time the accelerator linkage is depressed (**Figure 20**). If not, check fuel pump delivery (described later), float valve, and float adjustment. If the engine will not start, check the automatic choke parts for sticking or damage. If necessary, rebuild or replace the carburetor.

2. ***Engine runs at fast idle*** — Check the choke setting. Check the idle speed, idle mixture, and decel valve (if equipped) adjustment.

3. ***Rough idle or engine miss with frequent stalling*** — Check idle mixture and idle speed adjustments.

4. ***Engine "diesels" (continues to run) when ignition is switched off*** — Check idle mixture (probably too rich), ignition timing, and idle speed (probably too fast). Check the throttle solenoid (if equipped) for proper operation. Check for overheated engine.

5. ***Stumbling when accelerating from idle*** — Check the idle speed and mixture adjustments. Check the accelerator pump.

6. ***Engine misses at high speed or lacks power*** — This indicates possible fuel starvation. Check fuel pump pressure and capacity as described in this chapter. Check float needle valves. Check for a clogged fuel filter or air cleaner.

7. ***Black exhaust smoke*** — This indicates a badly overrich mixture. Check idle mixture and idle speed adjustment. Check choke setting. Check for excessive fuel pump pressure, leaky floats, or worn needle valves.

8. ***Excessive fuel consumption*** — Check for overrich mixture. Make sure choke mechanism works properly. Check idle mixture and idle speed. Check for excessive fuel pump pressure, leaky floats, or worn float needle valves.

FUEL SYSTEM (FUEL INJECTED)

Troubleshooting a fuel injection system requires more thought, experience, and know-how than any other part of the vehicle. A logical approach and proper test equipment are essential in order to successfully find and fix these troubles.

It is best to leave fuel injection troubles to your dealer. In order to isolate a problem to the injection system make sure that the fuel pump is operating properly. Check its performance as described later in this section. Also make sure that fuel filter and air cleaner are not clogged.

FUEL PUMP TEST (MECHANICAL AND ELECTRIC)

1. Disconnect the fuel inlet line where it enters the carburetor or fuel injection system.

2. Fit a rubber hose over the fuel line so fuel can be directed into a graduated container with about one quart capacity. See **Figure 21**.

3. To avoid accidental starting of the engine, disconnect the secondary coil wire from the coil or disconnect and insulate the coil primary wire.

4. Crank the engine for about 30 seconds.

5. If the fuel pump supplies the specified amount (refer to the fuel chapter later in this book), the trouble may be in the carburetor or fuel injection system. The fuel injection system should be tested by your dealer.

6. If there is no fuel present or the pump cannot supply the specified amount, either the fuel pump is defective or there is an obstruction in the fuel line. Replace the fuel pump and/or inspect the fuel lines for air leaks or obstructions.

7. Also pressure test the fuel pump by installing a T-fitting in the fuel line between the fuel pump and the carburetor. Connect a fuel pressure gauge to the fitting with a short tube **(Figure 22)**.

8. Reconnect the coil wire, start the engine, and record the pressure. Refer to the fuel chapter later in this book for the correct pressure. If the pressure varies from that specified, the pump should be replaced.

9. Stop the engine. The pressure should drop off very slowly. If it drops off rapidly, the outlet valve in the pump is leaking and the pump should be replaced.

EMISSION CONTROL SYSTEMS

Major emission control systems used on nearly all U.S. models include the following:

a. Positive crankcase ventilation (PCV)
b. Thermostatic air cleaner
c. Air injection reaction (AIR)
d. Fuel evaporation control
e. Exhaust gas recirculation (EGR)

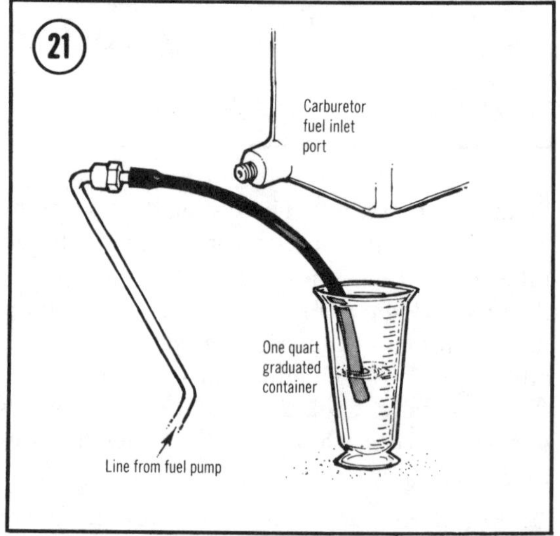

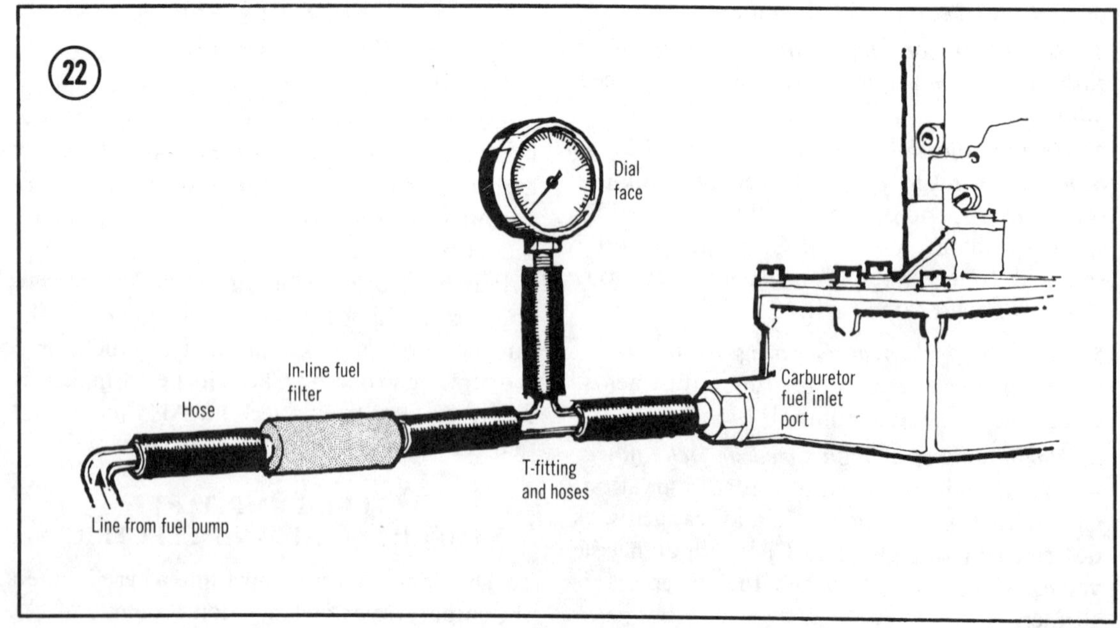

Emission control systems vary considerably from model to model. Individual models contain variations of the four systems described here. In addition, they may include other special systems. Use the index to find specific emission control components in other chapters.

Many of the systems and components are factory set and sealed. Without special expensive test equipment, it is impossible to adjust the systems to meet state and federal requirements.

Troubleshooting can also be difficult without special equipment. The procedures described below will help you find emission control parts which have failed, but repairs may have to be entrusted to a dealer or other properly equipped repair shop.

With the proper equipment, you can test the carbon monoxide and hydrocarbon levels. **Figure 23** provides some sources of trouble if the readings are not correct.

Positive Crankcase Ventilation

Fresh air drawn from the air cleaner housing scavenges emissions (e.g., piston blow-by) from the crankcase, then the intake manifold vacuum draws emissions into the intake manifold. They can then be reburned in the normal combustion process. **Figure 24** shows a typical system. **Figure 25** provides a testing procedure.

Thermostatic Air Cleaner

The thermostatically controlled air cleaner maintains incoming air to the engine at a predetermined level, usually about 100°F or higher. It mixes cold air with heated air from the exhaust manifold region. The air cleaner in-

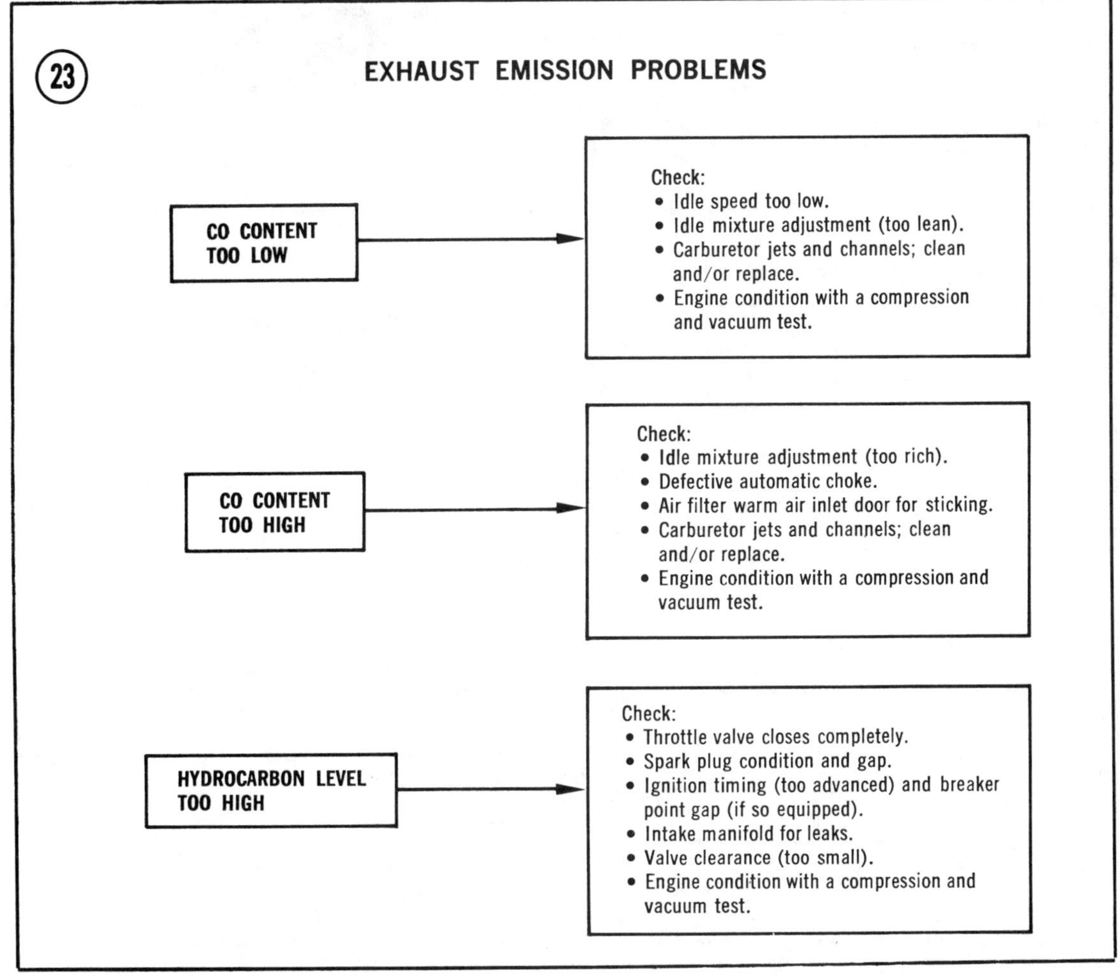
23
EXHAUST EMISSION PROBLEMS
CO CONTENT TOO LOW
Check:
• Idle speed too low.
• Idle mixture adjustment (too lean).
• Carburetor jets and channels; clean and/or replace.
• Engine condition with a compression and vacuum test.
CO CONTENT TOO HIGH
Check:
• Idle mixture adjustment (too rich).
• Defective automatic choke.
• Air filter warm air inlet door for sticking.
• Carburetor jets and channels; clean and/or replace.
• Engine condition with a compression and vacuum test.
HYDROCARBON LEVEL TOO HIGH
Check:
• Throttle valve closes completely.
• Spark plug condition and gap.
• Ignition timing (too advanced) and breaker point gap (if so equipped).
• Intake manifold for leaks.
• Valve clearance (too small).
• Engine condition with a compression and vacuum test.

cludes a temperature sensor, vacuum motor, and a hinged door. See **Figure 26**.

The system is comparatively easy to test. See **Figure 27** for the procedure.

Air Injection Reaction System

The air injection reaction system reduces air pollution by oxidizing hydrocarbons and carbon monoxide as they leave the combustion chamber. See **Figure 28**.

The air injection pump, driven by the engine, compresses filtered air and injects it at the exhaust port of each cylinder. The fresh air mixes with the unburned gases in the exhaust and promotes further burning. A check valve prevents exhaust gases from entering and damaging the air pump if the pump becomes inoperative, e.g., from a fan belt failure.

Figure 29 explains the testing procedure for this system.

Fuel Evaporation Control

Fuel vapor from the fuel tank passes through the liquid/vapor separator to the carbon canister. See **Figure 30**. The carbon absorbs and

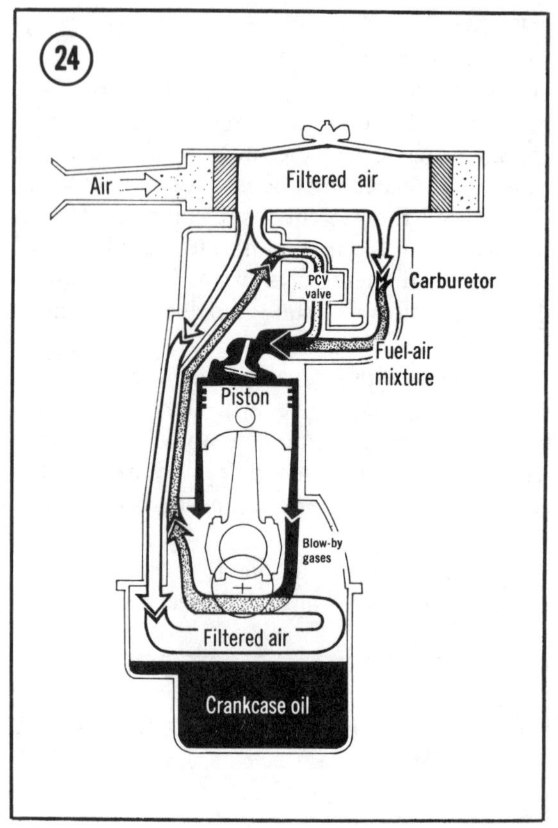

(24)

Air
Filtered air
PCV valve
Carburetor
Fuel-air mixture
Piston
Blow-by gases
Filtered air
Crankcase oil

(25)

PCV VALVE TEST
START ENGINE
Let it idle, remove oil fill cap and place a piece of paper over the opening. The paper should be sucked onto the opening by vacuum.
VACUUM PRESENT
Valve is operating correctly.
NO VACUUM PRESENT
Valve is stuck closed.
Remove PCV valve and shake it, it should rattle.
VALVE RATTLES
Check hose from valve for obstructions. Clean out or replace it.
VALVE DOES NOT RATTLE
Take it apart and clean or replace it.

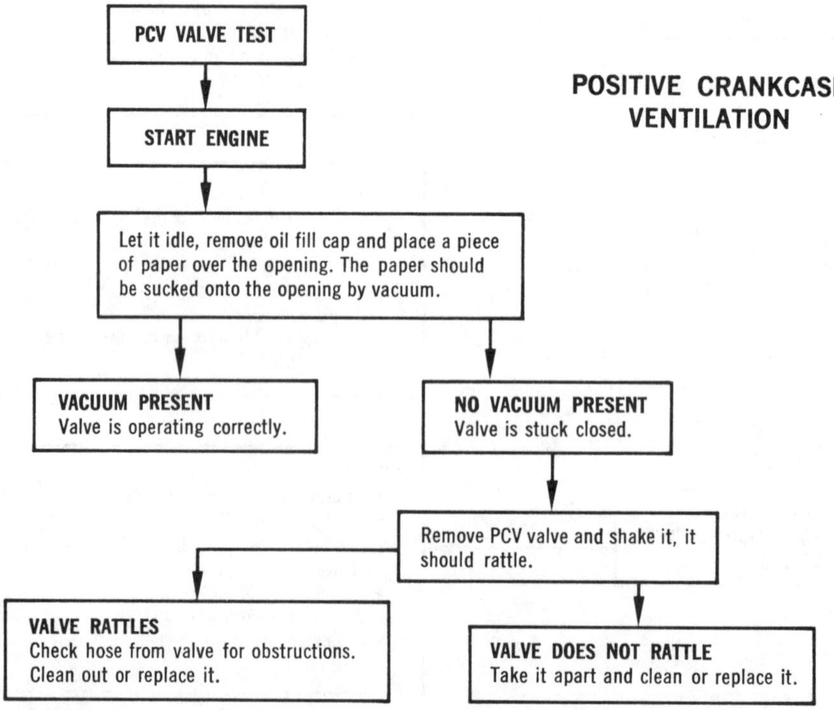

POSITIVE CRANKCASE VENTILATION

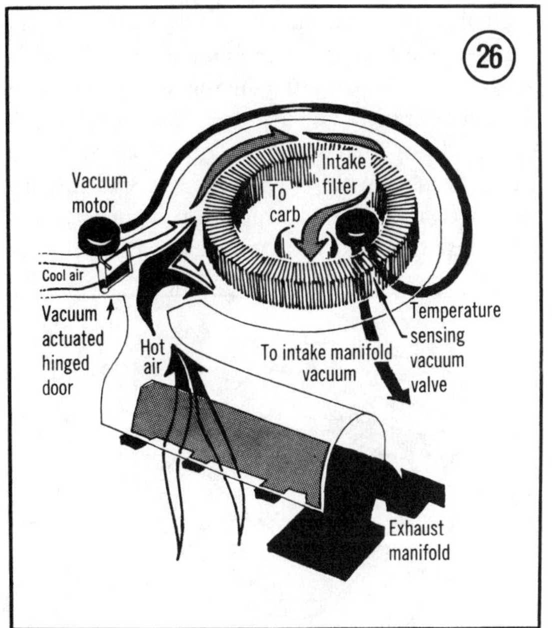
26
Vacuum motor
Intake filter
To carb
Cool air
Vacuum actuated hinged door
Hot air
To intake manifold vacuum
Temperature sensing vacuum valve
Exhaust manifold

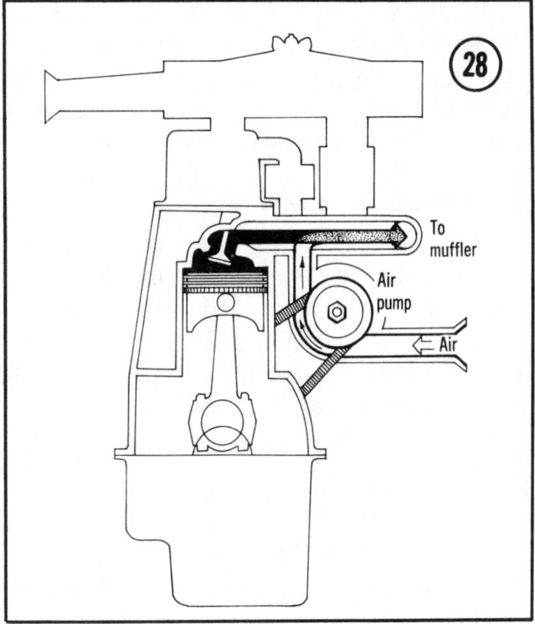
28
To muffler
Air pump
Air

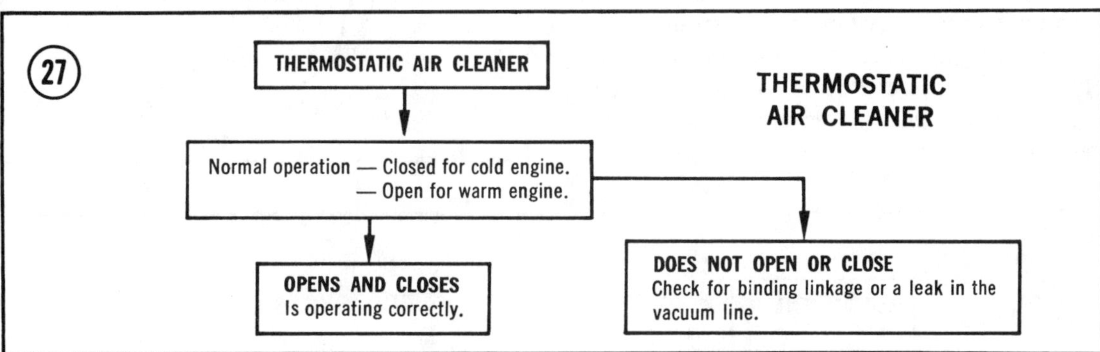
27
THERMOSTATIC AIR CLEANER
THERMOSTATIC AIR CLEANER
Normal operation — Closed for cold engine.
— Open for warm engine.
OPENS AND CLOSES
Is operating correctly.
DOES NOT OPEN OR CLOSE
Check for binding linkage or a leak in the vacuum line.

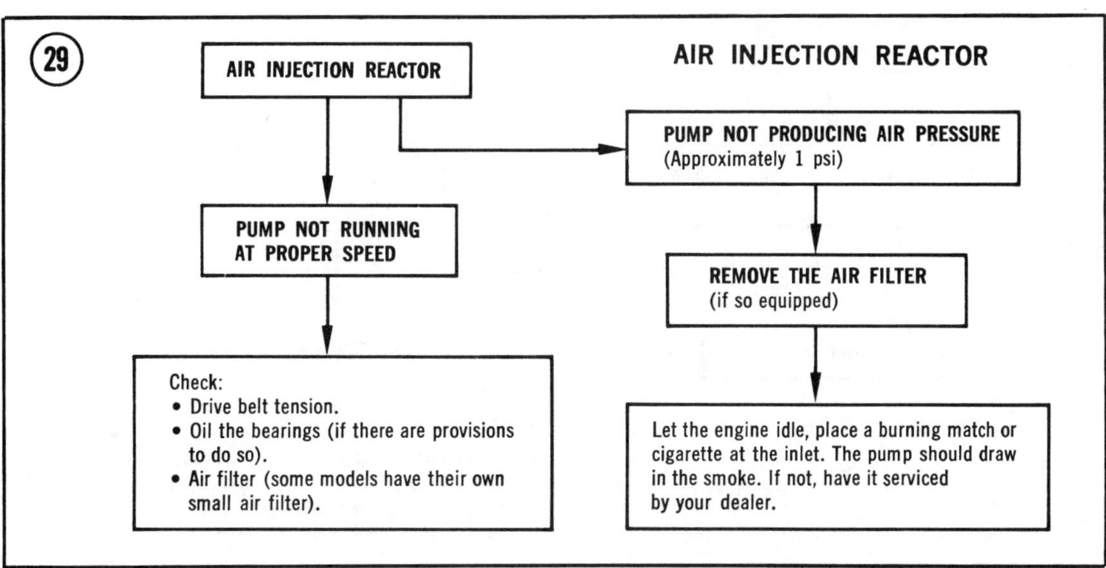
29
AIR INJECTION REACTOR
AIR INJECTION REACTOR
PUMP NOT RUNNING AT PROPER SPEED
Check:
• Drive belt tension.
• Oil the bearings (if there are provisions to do so).
• Air filter (some models have their own small air filter).
PUMP NOT PRODUCING AIR PRESSURE
(Approximately 1 psi)
REMOVE THE AIR FILTER
(if so equipped)
Let the engine idle, place a burning match or cigarette at the inlet. The pump should draw in the smoke. If not, have it serviced by your dealer.

stores the vapor when the engine is stopped. When the engine runs, manifold vacuum draws the vapor from the canister. Instead of being released into the atmosphere, the fuel vapor takes part in the normal combustion process.

Exhaust Gas Recirculation

The exhaust gas recirculation (EGR) system is used to reduce the emission of nitrogen oxides (NO_x). Relatively inert exhaust gases are introduced into the combustion process to slightly reduce peak temperatures. This reduction in temperature reduces the formation of NO_x.

Figure 31 provides a simple test of this system.

ENGINE NOISES

Often the first evidence of an internal engine trouble is a strange noise. That knocking, clicking, or tapping which you never heard before may be warning you of impending trouble.

While engine noises can indicate problems, they are sometimes difficult to interpret correctly; inexperienced mechanics can be seriously misled by them.

Professional mechanics often use a special stethoscope which looks similar to a doctor's stethoscope for isolating engine noises. You can do nearly as well with a "sounding stick" which can be an ordinary piece of doweling or a section of small hose. By placing one end in contact with the area to which you want to listen and the other end near your ear, you can hear

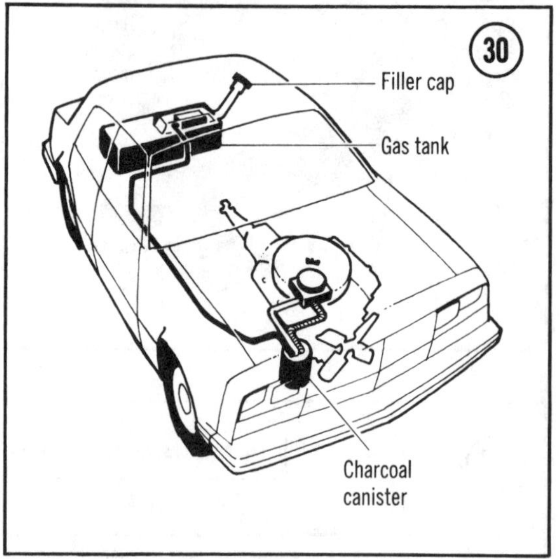
30
Filler cap
Gas tank
Charcoal
canister

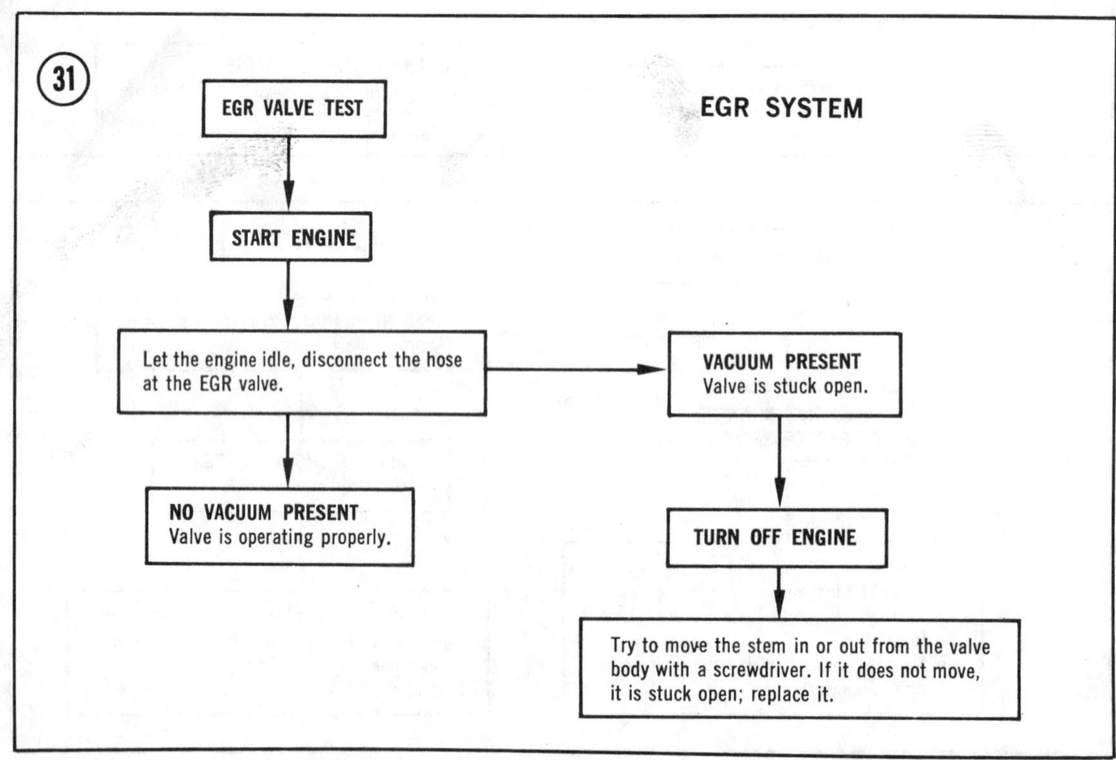
31
EGR VALVE TEST
EGR SYSTEM
START ENGINE
Let the engine idle, disconnect the hose at the EGR valve.
VACUUM PRESENT
Valve is stuck open.
NO VACUUM PRESENT
Valve is operating properly.
TURN OFF ENGINE
Try to move the stem in or out from the valve body with a screwdriver. If it does not move, it is stuck open; replace it.

sounds emanating from that area. The first time you do this, you may be horrified at the strange noises coming from even a normal engine. If you can, have an experienced friend or mechanic help you sort the noises out.

Clicking or Tapping Noises

Clicking or tapping noises usually come from the valve train, and indicate excessive valve clearance.

If your vehicle has adjustable valves, the procedure for adjusting the valve clearance is explained in Chapter Three. If your vehicle has hydraulic lifters, the clearance may not be adjustable. The noise may be coming from a collapsed lifter. These may be cleaned or replaced as described in the engine chapter.

A sticking valve may also sound like a valve with excessive clearance. In addition, excessive wear in valve train components can cause similar engine noises.

Knocking Noises

A heavy, dull knocking is usually caused by a worn main bearing. The noise is loudest when the engine is working hard, i.e., accelerating hard at low speed. You may be able to isolate the trouble to a single bearing by disconnecting the spark plugs one at a time. When you reach the spark plug nearest the bearing, the knock will be reduced or disappear.

Worn connecting rod bearings may also produce a knock, but the sound is usually more "metallic." As with a main bearing, the noise is worse when accelerating. It may even increase further just as you go from accelerating to coasting. Disconnecting spark plugs will help isolate this knock as well.

A double knock or clicking usually indicates a worn piston pin. Disconnecting spark plugs will isolate this to a particular piston, however, the noise will *increase* when you reach the affected piston.

A loose flywheel and excessive crankshaft end play also produce knocking noises. While similar to main bearing noises, these are usually intermittent, not constant, and they do not change when spark plugs are disconnected.

Some mechanics confuse piston pin noise with piston slap. The double knock will distinguish the piston pin noise. Piston slap is identified by the fact that it is always louder when the engine is cold.

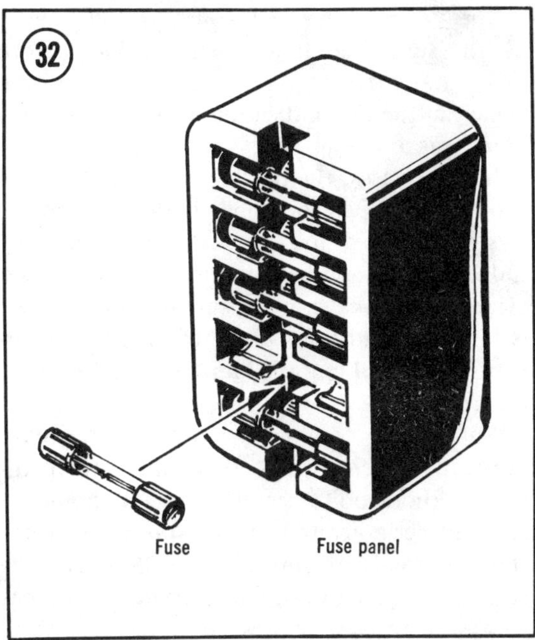

ELECTRICAL ACCESSORIES

Lights and Switches (Interior and Exterior)

1. ***Bulb does not light*** — Remove the bulb and check for a broken element. Also check the inside of the socket; make sure the contacts are clean and free of corrosion. If the bulb and socket are OK, check to see if a fuse has blown or a circuit breaker has tripped. The fuse panel **(Figure 32)** is usually located under the instrument panel. Replace the blown fuse or reset the circuit breaker. If the fuse blows or the breaker trips again, there is a short in that circuit. Check that circuit all the way to the battery. Look for worn wire insulation or burned wires.

If all the above are all right, check the switch controlling the bulb for continuity with an ohmmeter at the switch terminals. Check the switch contact terminals for loose or dirty electrical connections.

2. ***Headlights work but will not switch from either high or low beam*** — Check the beam selector switch for continuity with an ohmmeter

at the switch terminals. Check the switch contact terminals for loose or dirty electrical connections.

3. ***Brake light switch inoperative*** — On mechanically operated switches, usually mounted near the brake pedal arm, adjust the switch to achieve correct mechanical operation. Check the switch for continuity with an ohmmeter at the switch terminals. Check the switch contact terminals for loose or dirty electrical connections.

4. ***Back-up lights do not operate*** — Check light bulb as described earlier. Locate the switch, normally located near the shift lever. Adjust switch to achieve correct mechanical operation. Check the switch for continuity with an ohmmeter at the switch terminals. Bypass the switch with a jumper wire; if the lights work, replace the switch.

Directional Signals

1. ***Directional signals do not operate*** — If the indicator light on the instrument panel burns steadily instead of flashing, this usually indicates that one of the exterior lights is burned out. Check all lamps that normally flash. If all are all right, the flasher unit may be defective. Replace it with a good one.

2. ***Directional signal indicator light on instrument panel does not light up*** — Check the light bulbs as described earlier. Check all electrical connections and check the flasher unit.

3. ***Directional signals will not self-cancel*** — Check the self-cancelling mechanism located inside the steering column.

4. ***Directional signals flash slowly*** — Check the condition of the battery and the alternator (or generator) drive belt tension (**Figure 4**). Check the flasher unit and all related electrical connections.

Windshield Wipers

1. ***Wipers do not operate*** — Check for a blown fuse or circuit breaker that has tripped; replace or reset. Check all related terminals for loose or dirty electrical connections. Check continuity of the control switch with an ohmmeter at the switch terminals. Check the linkage and arms for loose, broken, or binding parts. Straighten out or replace where necessary.

2. ***Wiper motor hums but will not operate*** — The motor may be shorted out internally; check and/or replace the motor. Also check for broken or binding linkage and arms.

3. ***Wiper arms will not return to the stowed position when turned off*** — The motor has a special internal switch for this purpose. Have it inspected by your dealer. Do not attempt this yourself.

Interior Heater

1. ***Heater fan does not operate*** — Check for a blown fuse or circuit breaker that has tripped. Check the switch for continuity with an ohmmeter at the switch terminals. Check the switch contact terminals for loose or dirty electrical connections.

2. ***Heat output is insufficient*** — Check the heater hose/engine coolant control valve usually located in the engine compartment; make sure it is in the open position. Ensure that the heater door(s) and cable(s) are operating correctly and are in the open position. Inspect the heat ducts; make sure that they are not crimped or blocked.

COOLING SYSTEM

The temperature gauge or warning light usually signals cooling system troubles before there is any damage. As long as you stop the vehicle at the first indication of trouble, serious damage is unlikely.

In most cases, the trouble will be obvious as soon as you open the hood. If there is coolant or steam leaking, look for a defective radiator, radiator hose, or heater hose. If there is no evidence of leakage, make sure that the fan belt is in good condition. If the trouble is not obvious, refer to **Figures 33 and 34** to help isolate the trouble.

Automotive cooling systems operate under pressure to permit higher operating temperatures without boil-over. The system should be checked periodically to make sure it can withstand normal pressure. **Figure 35** shows the equipment which nearly any service station has for testing the system pressure.

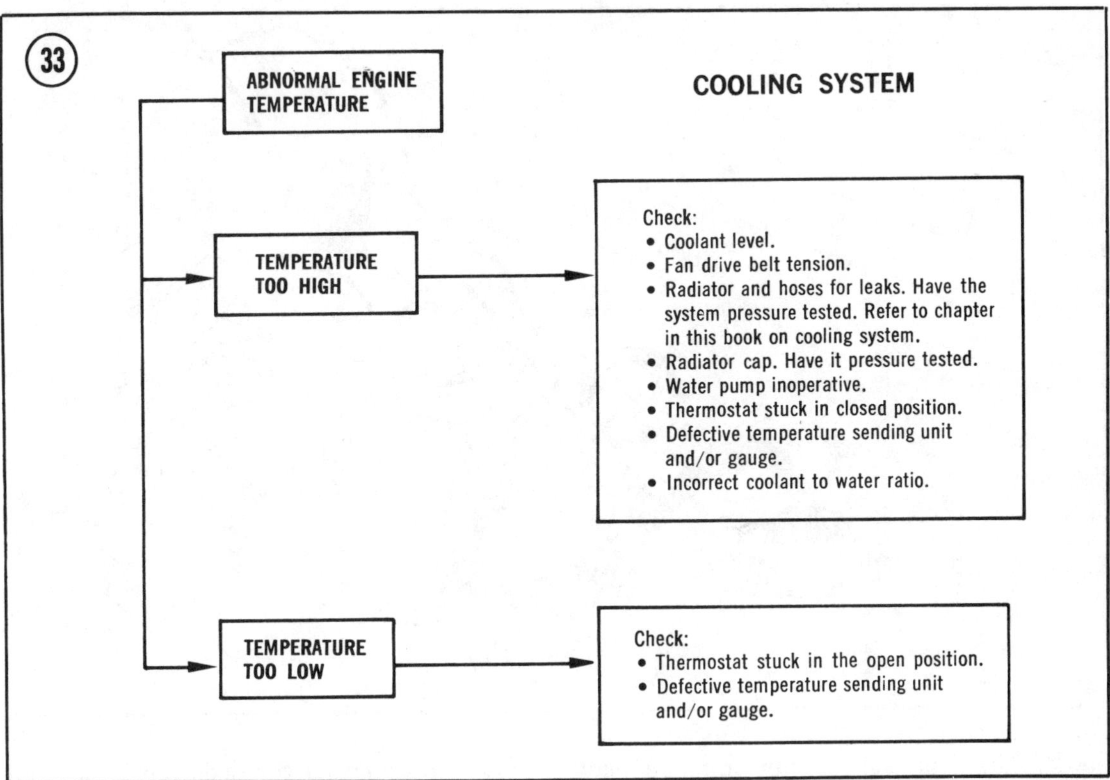

33
ABNORMAL ENGINE TEMPERATURE
COOLING SYSTEM
TEMPERATURE TOO HIGH
Check:
• Coolant level.
• Fan drive belt tension.
• Radiator and hoses for leaks. Have the system pressure tested. Refer to chapter in this book on cooling system.
• Radiator cap. Have it pressure tested.
• Water pump inoperative.
• Thermostat stuck in closed position.
• Defective temperature sending unit and/or gauge.
• Incorrect coolant to water ratio.
TEMPERATURE TOO LOW
Check:
• Thermostat stuck in the open position.
• Defective temperature sending unit and/or gauge.

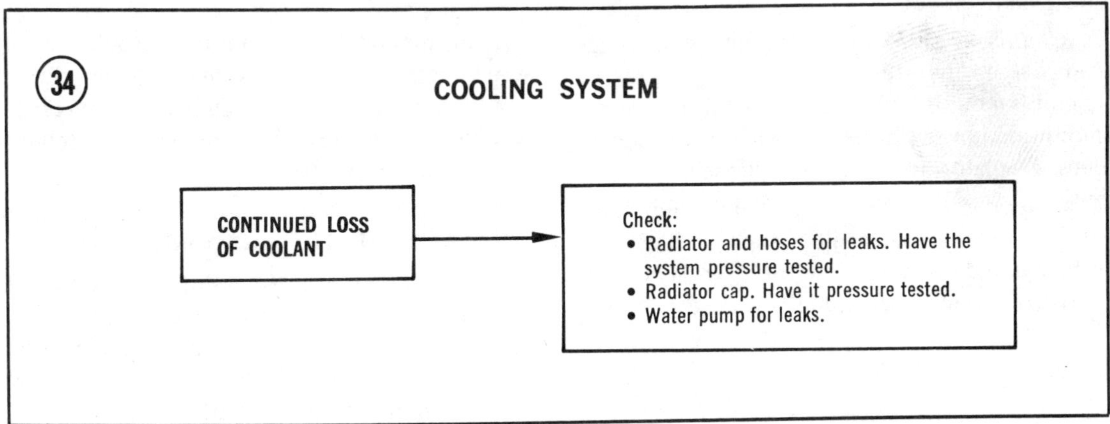

34
COOLING SYSTEM
CONTINUED LOSS OF COOLANT
Check:
• Radiator and hoses for leaks. Have the system pressure tested.
• Radiator cap. Have it pressure tested.
• Water pump for leaks.

CLUTCH

All clutch troubles except adjustments require transmission removal to identify and cure the problem.

1. ***Slippage*** — This is most noticeable when accelerating in a high gear at relatively low speed. To check slippage, park the vehicle on a level surface with the handbrake set. Shift to 2nd gear and release the clutch as if driving off. If the clutch is good, the engine will slow and stall. If the clutch slips, continued engine speed will give it away.

Slippage results from insufficient clutch pedal free play, oil or grease on the clutch disc, worn pressure plate, or weak springs.

2. ***Drag or failure to release*** — This trouble usually causes difficult shifting and gear clash, especially when downshifting. The cause may be excessive clutch pedal free play, warped or bent pressure plate or clutch disc, broken or

loose linings, or lack of lubrication in pilot bearing. Also check condition of transmission main shaft splines.

3. *Chatter or grabbing* — A number of things can cause this trouble. Check tightness of engine mounts and engine-to-transmission mounting bolts. Check for worn or misaligned pressure plate and misaligned release plate.

4. *Other noises* — Noise usually indicates a dry or defective release or pilot bearing. Check the bearings and replace if necessary. Also check all parts for misalignment and uneven wear.

MANUAL TRANSMISSION/TRANSAXLE

Transmission and transaxle troubles are evident when one or more of the following symptoms appear:

a. Difficulty changing gears
b. Gears clash when downshifting
c. Slipping out of gear
d. Excessive noise in NEUTRAL
e. Excessive noise in gear
f. Oil leaks

Transmission and transaxle repairs are not recommended unless the many special tools required are available.

Transmission and transaxle troubles are sometimes difficult to distinguish from clutch troubles. Eliminate the clutch as a source of trouble before installing a new or rebuilt transmission or transaxle.

AUTOMATIC TRANSMISSION

Most automatic transmission repairs require considerable specialized knowledge and tools. It is impractical for the home mechanic to invest in the tools, since they cost more than a properly rebuilt transmission.

Check fluid level and condition frequently to help prevent future problems. If the fluid is orange or black in color or smells like varnish, it is an indication of some type of damage or failure within the transmission. Have the transmission serviced by your dealer or competent automatic transmission service facility.

BRAKES

Good brakes are vital to the safe operation of the vehicle. Performing the maintenance speci-

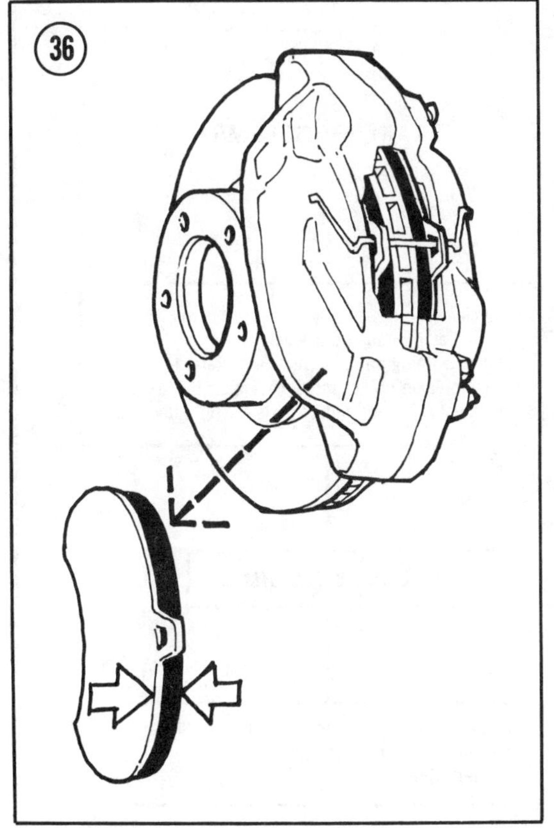

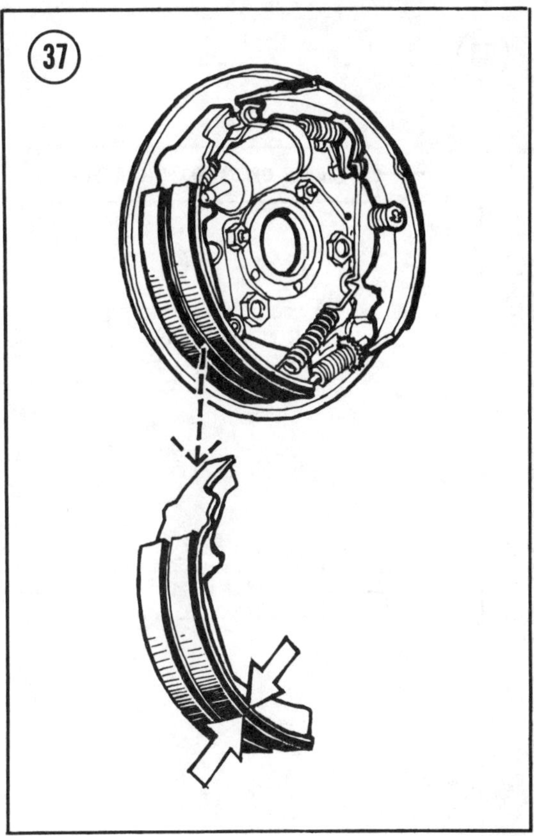

2

fied in Chapter Three will minimize problems with the brakes. Most importantly, check and maintain the level of fluid in the master cylinder, and check the thickness of the linings on the disc brake pads (**Figure 36**) or drum brake shoes (**Figure 37**).

If trouble develops, **Figures 38 through 40** will help you locate the problem. Refer to the brake chapter for actual repair procedures.

STEERING AND SUSPENSION

Trouble in the suspension or steering is evident when the following occur:

a. Steering is hard
b. Car pulls to one side
c. Car wanders or front wheels wobble
d. Steering has excessive play
e. Tire wear is abnormal

Unusual steering, pulling, or wandering is usually caused by bent or otherwise misaligned suspension parts. This is difficult to check without proper alignment equipment. Refer to the suspension chapter in this book for repairs that you can perform and those that must be left to a dealer or suspension specialist.

If your trouble seems to be excessive play, check wheel bearing adjustment first. This is the most frequent cause. Then check ball-joints (refer to Suspension chapter). Finally, check tie rod end ball-joints by shaking each tie rod. Also check steering gear, or rack-and-pinion assembly to see that it is securely bolted down.

TIRE WEAR ANALYSIS

Abnormal tire wear should be analyzed to determine its causes. The most common causes are the following:

a. Incorrect tire pressure
b. Improper driving
c. Overloading
d. Bad road surfaces
e. Incorrect wheel alignment

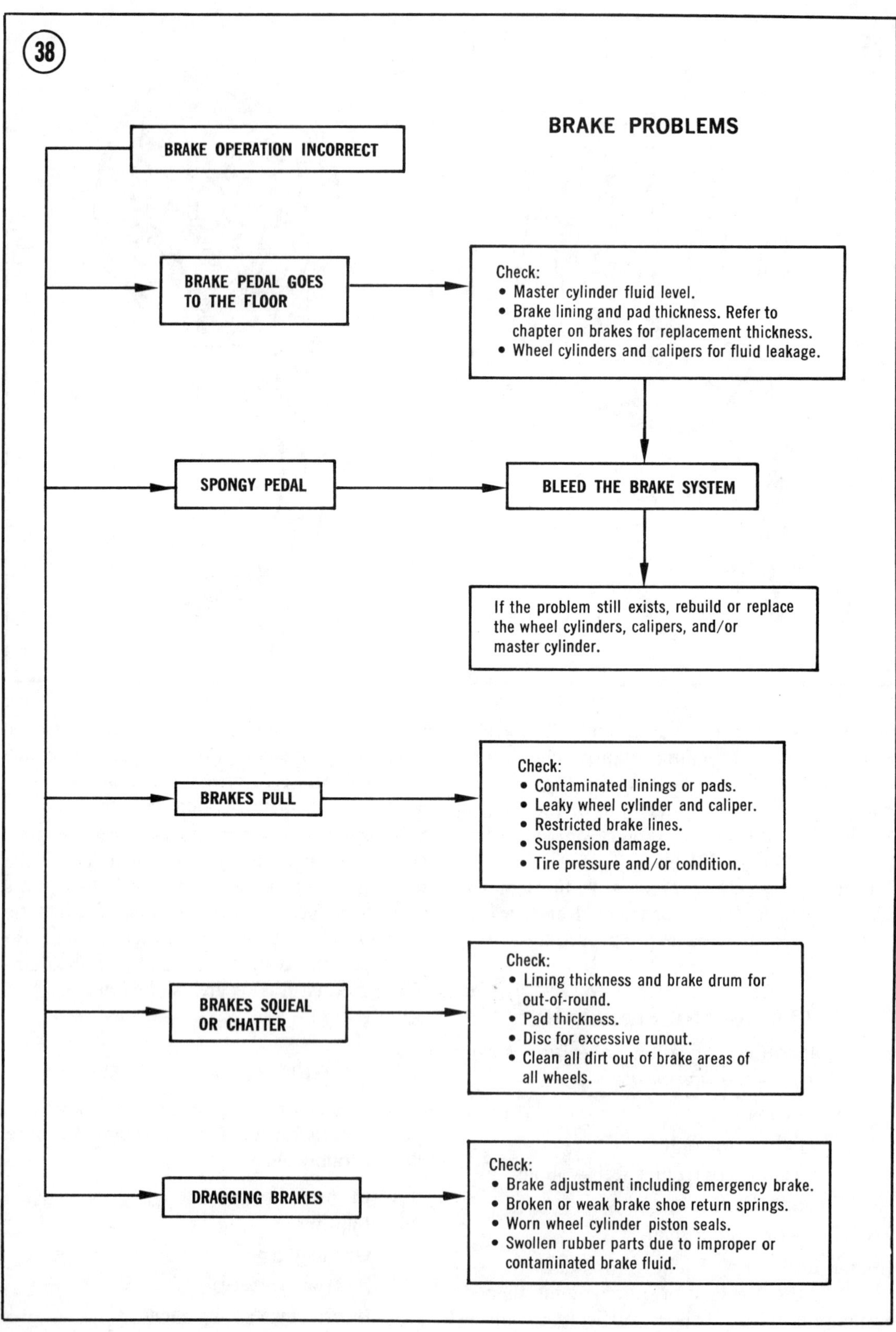
38
BRAKE PROBLEMS
BRAKE OPERATION INCORRECT
BRAKE PEDAL GOES TO THE FLOOR
Check:
• Master cylinder fluid level.
• Brake lining and pad thickness. Refer to chapter on brakes for replacement thickness.
• Wheel cylinders and calipers for fluid leakage.
SPONGY PEDAL
BLEED THE BRAKE SYSTEM
If the problem still exists, rebuild or replace the wheel cylinders, calipers, and/or master cylinder.
BRAKES PULL
Check:
• Contaminated linings or pads.
• Leaky wheel cylinder and caliper.
• Restricted brake lines.
• Suspension damage.
• Tire pressure and/or condition.
BRAKES SQUEAL OR CHATTER
Check:
• Lining thickness and brake drum for out-of-round.
• Pad thickness.
• Disc for excessive runout.
• Clean all dirt out of brake areas of all wheels.
DRAGGING BRAKES
Check:
• Brake adjustment including emergency brake.
• Broken or weak brake shoe return springs.
• Worn wheel cylinder piston seals.
• Swollen rubber parts due to improper or contaminated brake fluid.

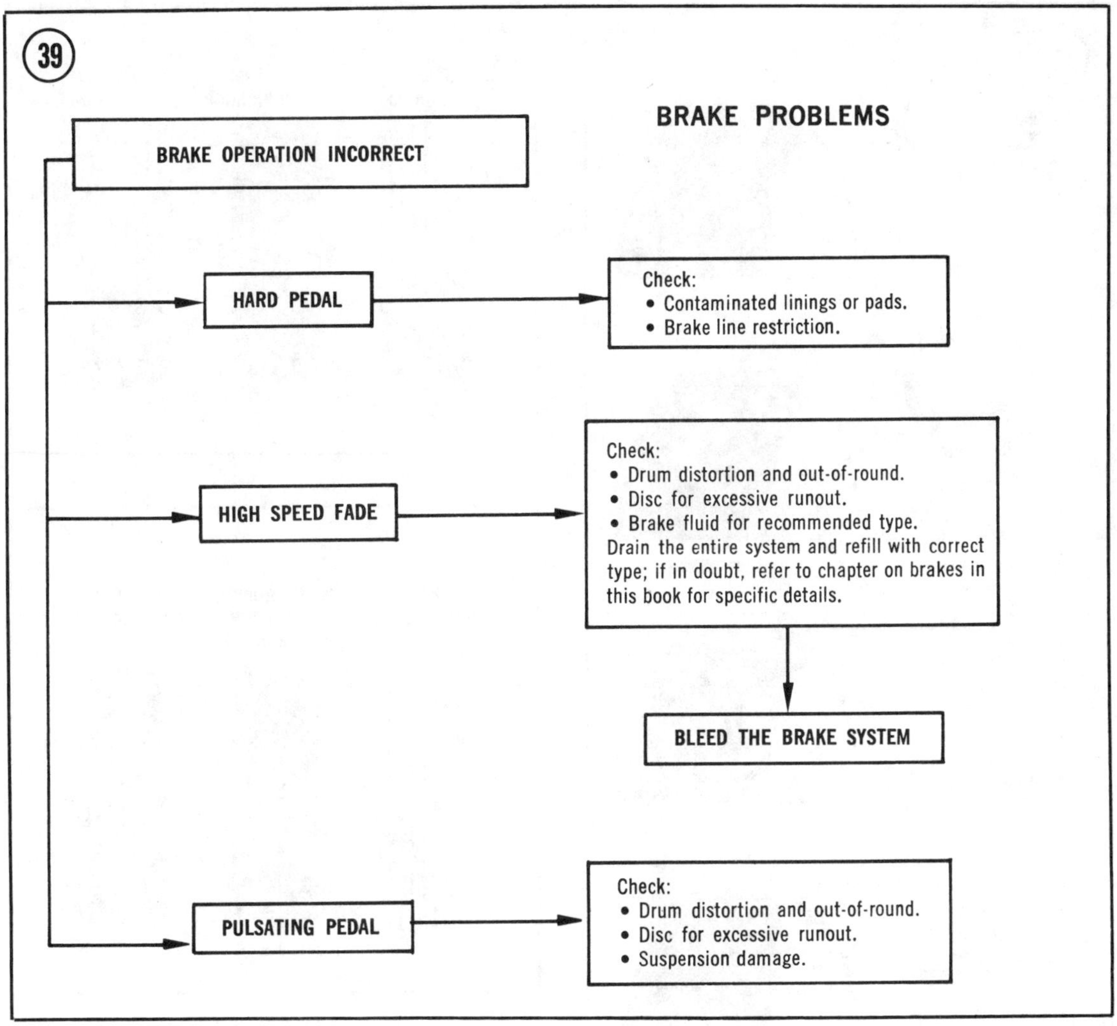

39

BRAKE PROBLEMS

BRAKE OPERATION INCORRECT

HARD PEDAL

Check:
- Contaminated linings or pads.
- Brake line restriction.

HIGH SPEED FADE

Check:
- Drum distortion and out-of-round.
- Disc for excessive runout.
- Brake fluid for recommended type.

Drain the entire system and refill with correct type; if in doubt, refer to chapter on brakes in this book for specific details.

BLEED THE BRAKE SYSTEM

PULSATING PEDAL

Check:
- Drum distortion and out-of-round.
- Disc for excessive runout.
- Suspension damage.

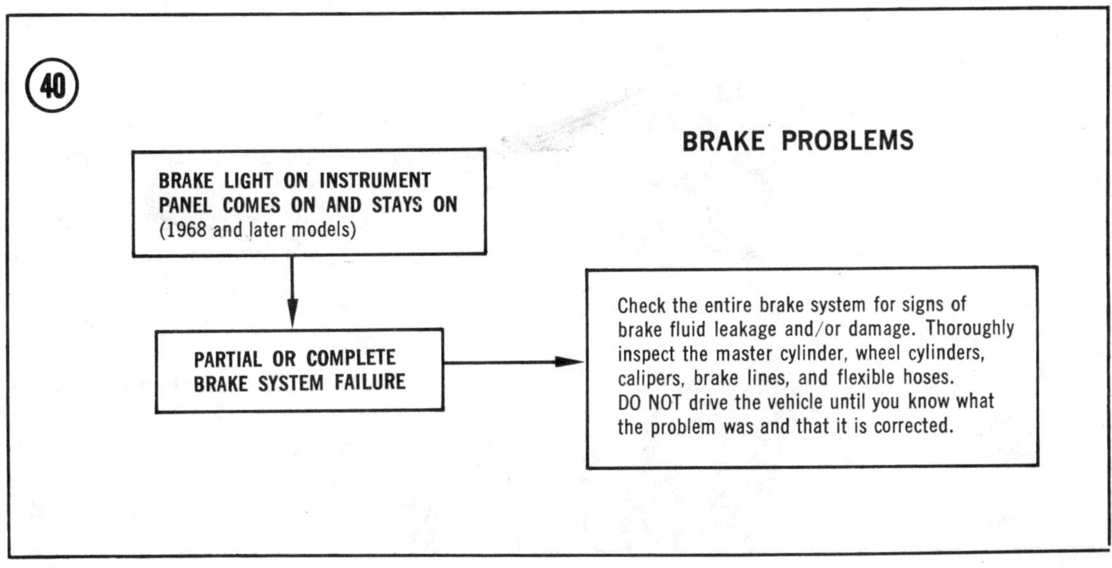

40
BRAKE PROBLEMS
BRAKE LIGHT ON INSTRUMENT PANEL COMES ON AND STAYS ON (1968 and later models)
PARTIAL OR COMPLETE BRAKE SYSTEM FAILURE
Check the entire brake system for signs of brake fluid leakage and/or damage. Thoroughly inspect the master cylinder, wheel cylinders, calipers, brake lines, and flexible hoses.
DO NOT drive the vehicle until you know what the problem was and that it is corrected.

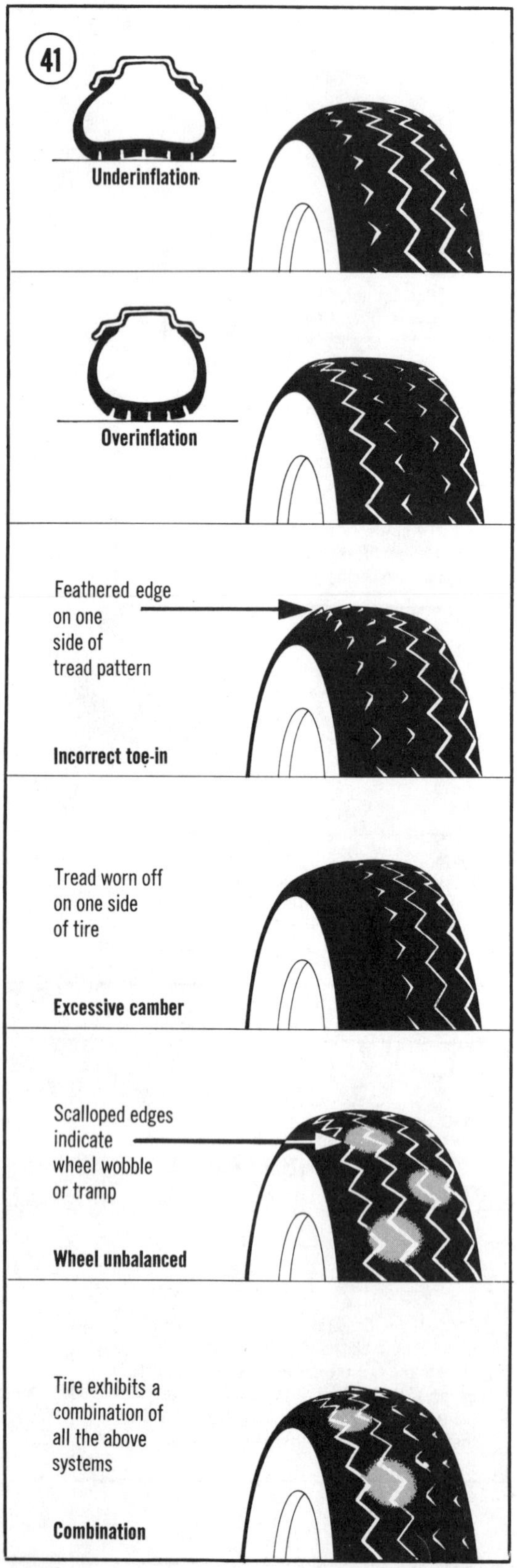

(41)

Underinflation

Overinflation

Feathered edge on one side of tread pattern

Incorrect toe-in

Tread worn off on one side of tire

Excessive camber

Scalloped edges indicate wheel wobble or tramp

Wheel unbalanced

Tire exhibits a combination of all the above systems

Combination

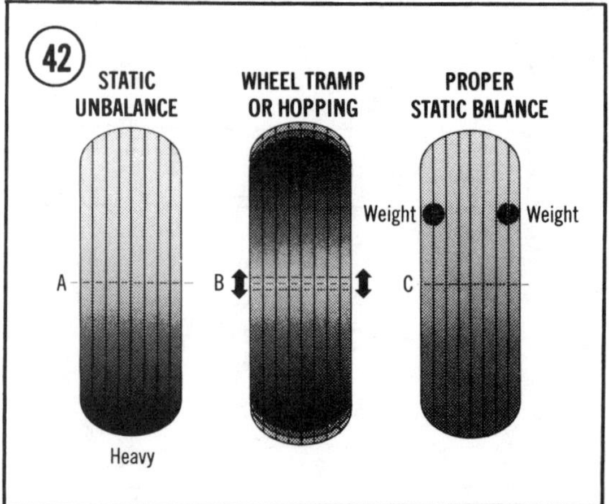

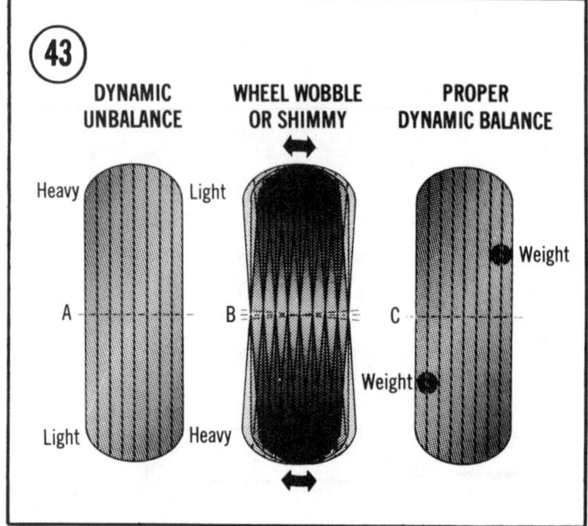

Figure 41 identifies wear patterns and indicates the most probable causes.

WHEEL BALANCING

All four wheels and tires must be in balance along two axes. To be in static balance **(Figure 42)**, weight must be evenly distributed around the axis of rotation. (A) shows a statically unbalanced wheel; (B) shows the result — wheel tramp or hopping; (C) shows proper static balance.

To be in dynamic balance **(Figure 43)**, the centerline of the weight must coincide with the centerline of the wheel. (A) shows a dynamically unbalanced wheel; (B) shows the result — wheel wobble or shimmy; (C) shows proper dynamic balance.

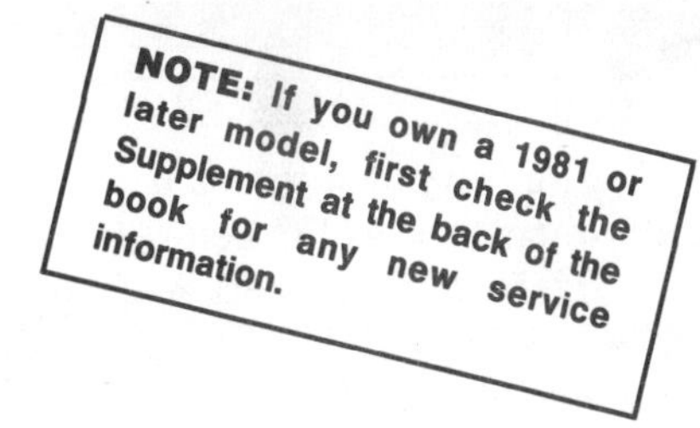
NOTE: If you own a 1981 or later model, first check the Supplement at the back of the book for any new service information.

CHAPTER THREE

3

LUBRICATION, MAINTENANCE, AND TUNE-UP

To ensure good performance, dependability and safety, regular preventive maintenance is necessary. This chapter outlines periodic lubrication and maintenance for a car driven by an average owner. A car driven more than average may require more frequent attention, but even without use, rust, dirt and corrosion may cause unnecessary damage. Whether performed by the owner or dealer, regular routine attention helps to avoid expensive repairs.

The recommended schedule in this chapter includes routine checks which are easily performed at each fuel stop and periodic maintenance to prevent future trouble. Also included is a systematic engine tune-up procedure which simplifies this important task. **Table 1** summarizes all periodic maintenance required in an easy-to-use format.

Tables 1-5 are at the end of the chapter.

1

2

ROUTINE CHECKS

The following simple checks should be performed at each fuel stop.

1. ***Check engine oil***—Shut off the engine and allow a few moments for the oil to return to the crankcase. Remove the dipstick, wipe it off and reinstall it, making sure it is seated in the tube. See **Figure 1** (4-cylinder) or **Figure 2**

(V6). Remove it again and inspect; add oil only when the level is below the ADD mark. See **Figure 3**. One quart will raise the level from ADD to FULL. See **Table 2** for recommended oil grades.

2. ***Check battery condition***—Observe the indicator on top of the battery. See **Figure 4**. If the indicator is dark with a green dot showing, the battery is fully charged. If the indicator is dark, but no green dot is showing, the battery needs charging. If the indicator is light or yellow, the battery should be replaced. See **Figure 5**.

3. ***Check drive belt condition and tension***—Correct tension depends on the distance between the pulleys. See **Figure 6**. The alternator drive belt should deflect about 1/4 in. (6 mm) under moderate thumb pressure. The air conditioner belt should deflect about 1/2 in. (13 mm). If necessary, adjust tension as described later in this chapter. See **Figure 7** (4-cylinder) or **Figure 8** (V6) for drive belt and pulley diagrams.

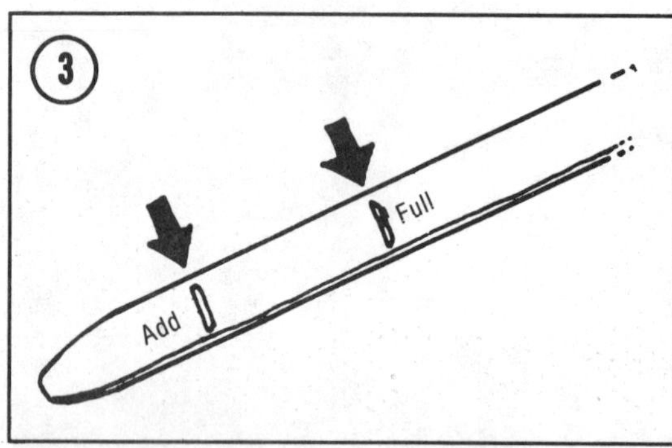

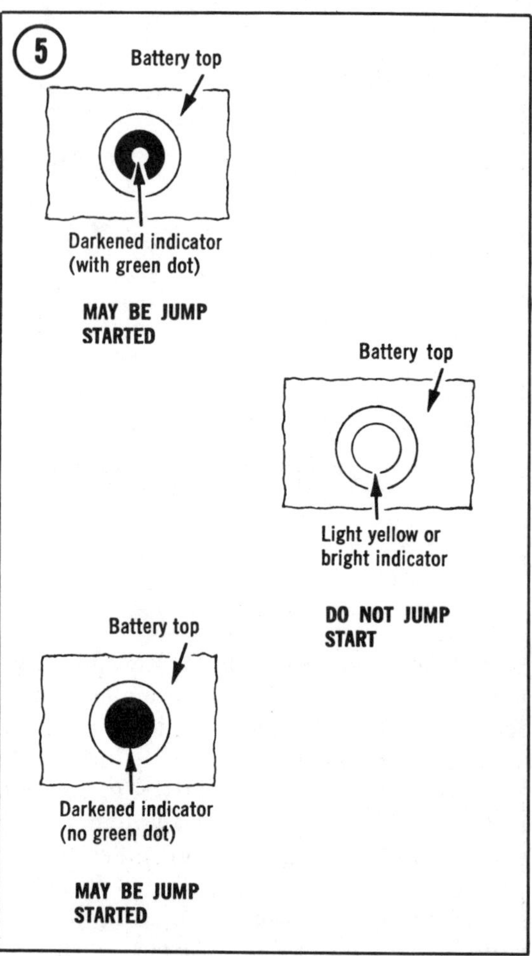

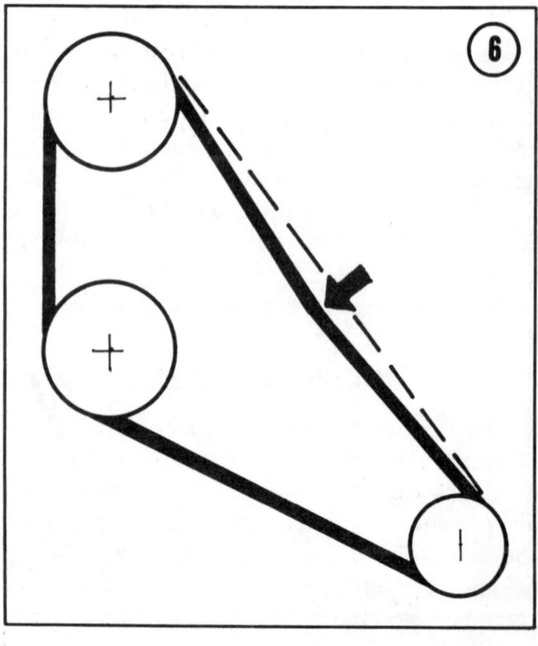

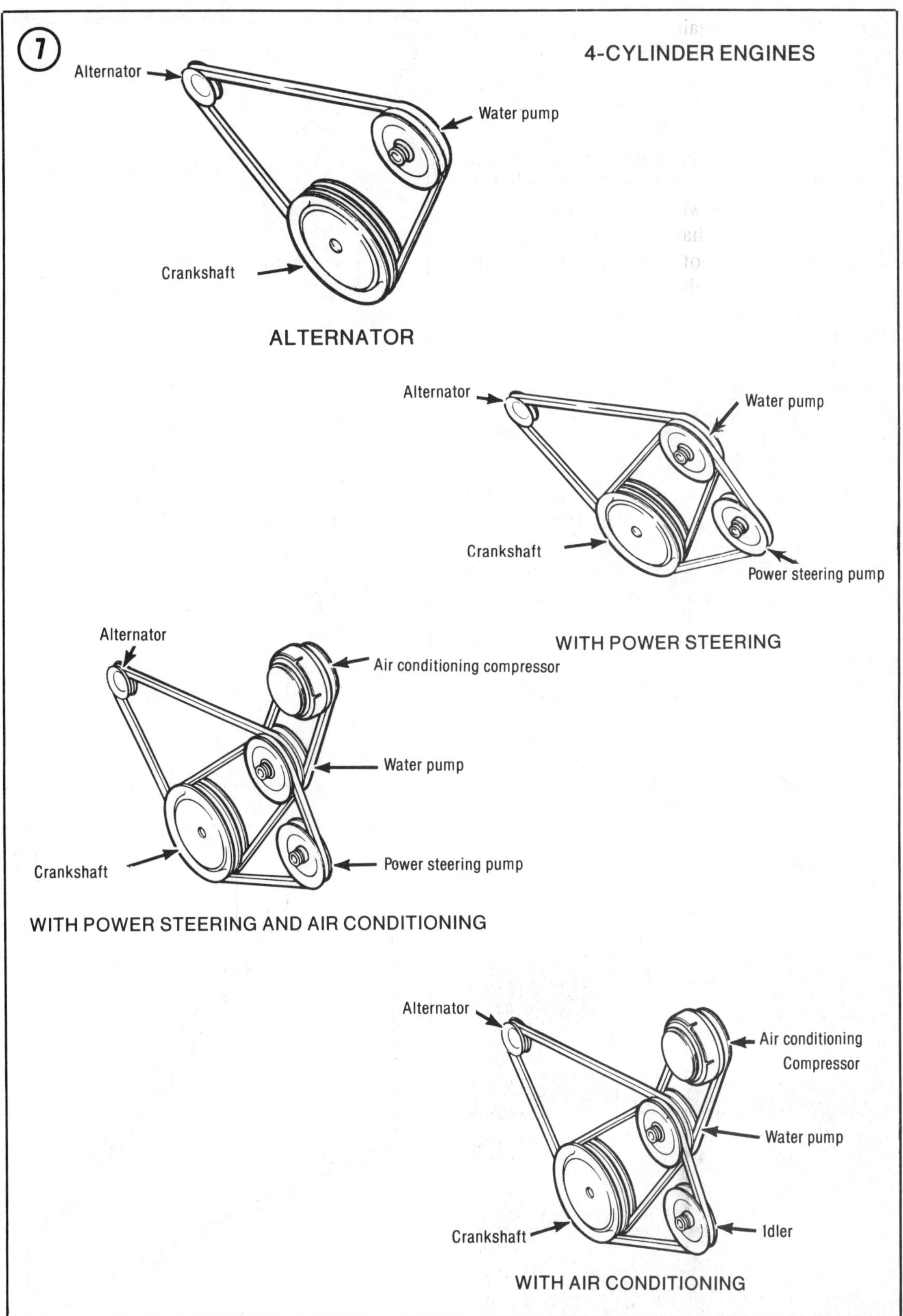
7
4-CYLINDER ENGINES
Alternator
Water pump
Crankshaft
ALTERNATOR
Alternator
Water pump
Crankshaft
Power steering pump
WITH POWER STEERING
Alternator
Air conditioning compressor
Water pump
Crankshaft
Power steering pump
WITH POWER STEERING AND AIR CONDITIONING
Alternator
Air conditioning
Compressor
Water pump
Crankshaft
Idler
WITH AIR CONDITIONING

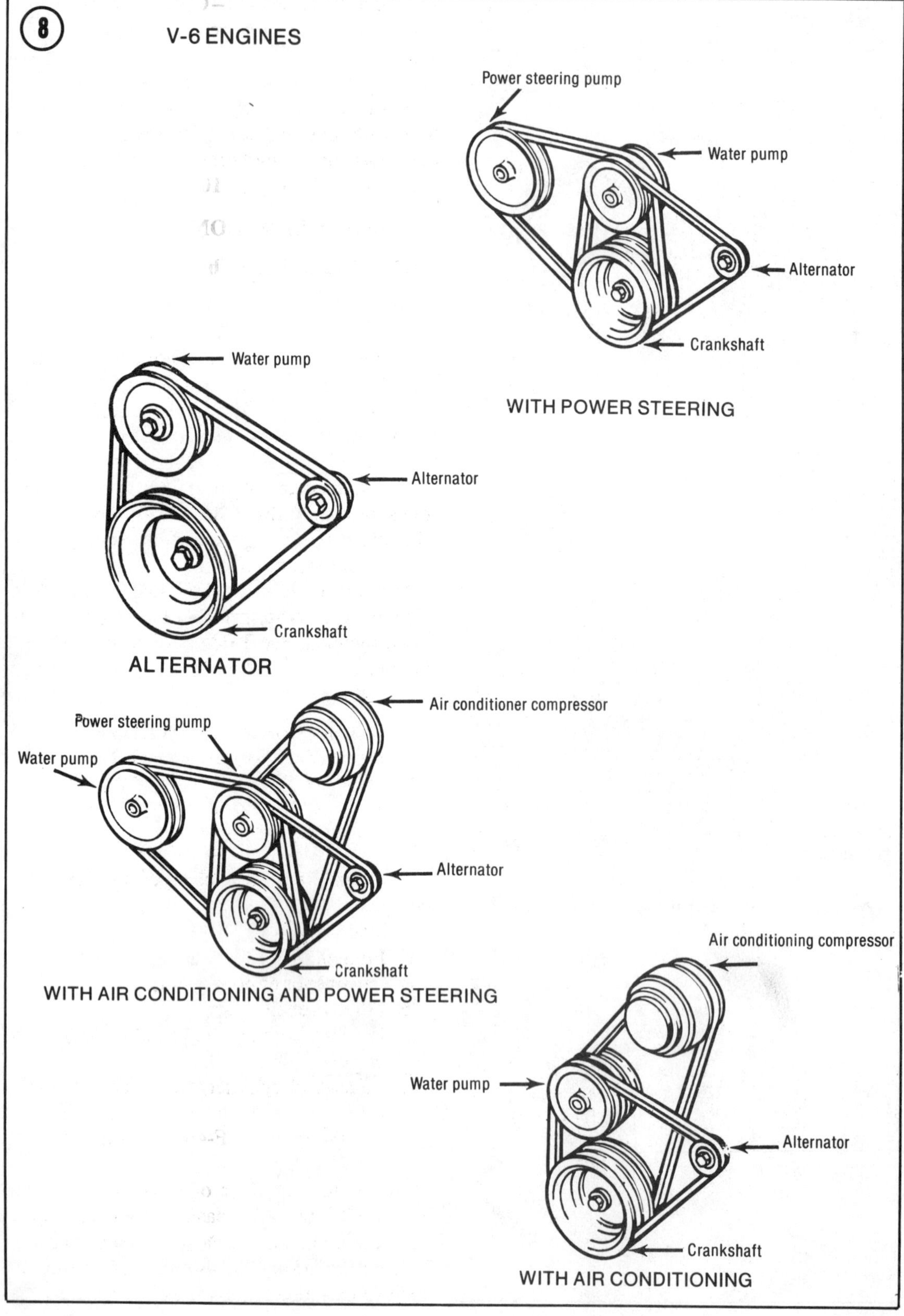
8
V-6 ENGINES
Power steering pump
Water pump
Alternator
Crankshaft
WITH POWER STEERING
Water pump
Alternator
Crankshaft
ALTERNATOR
Air conditioner compressor
Power steering pump
Water pump
Alternator
Crankshaft
WITH AIR CONDITIONING AND POWER STEERING
Air conditioning compressor
Water pump
Alternator
Crankshaft
WITH AIR CONDITIONING

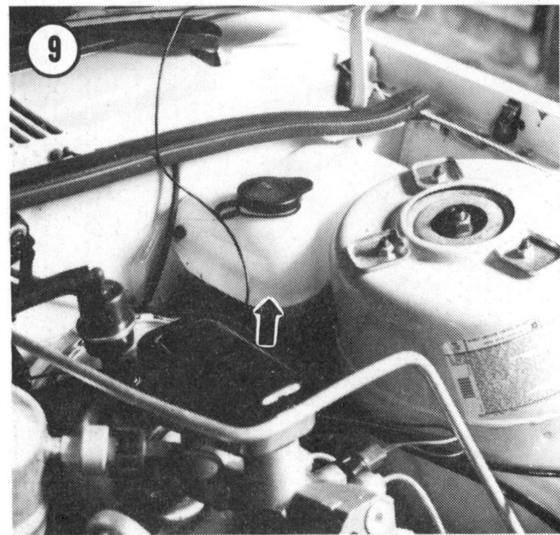

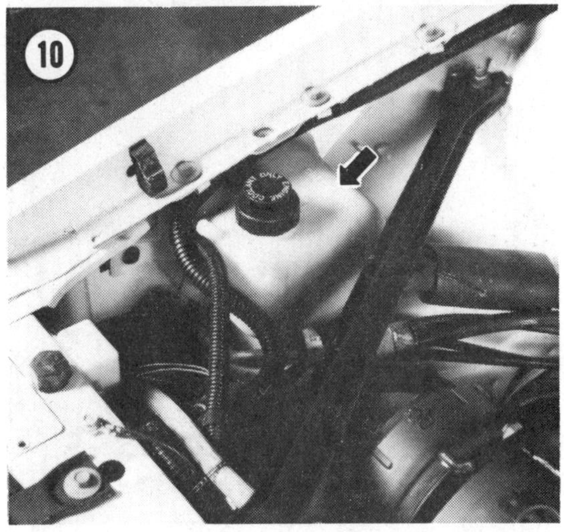

4. ***Check tire pressure***—Check when tires are cold. Maximum pressure is imprinted on each tire.

5. ***Check windshield washer container level***—It should be kept full. See **Figure 9**.

6. ***Check coolant level in reservoir***—Note markings indicating correct level for hot and cold engine. See **Figure 10**.

7,500 MILE/6 MONTH SERVICE

Engine Oil and Filter Change

The oil and filter change interval varies depending on the type of driving that you do. For normal driving, including some city traffic, change oil and filter every 7,500 miles or 6 months, whichever comes first. If driving is primarily stop-and-go traffic, includes trailer hauling or involves short trips in cold climates, change oil and filter every 3,000 miles or 3 months. Change oil and filter at least twice a year if the car is driven only a few hundred miles a month.

Any oil used must be rated "SE." See **Figure 11**. Non-detergent oils are not recommended. See **Table 2** for recommended oil grades.

CAUTION

General Motors specifically warns against the use of non-detergent oil, low quality oil or any oil not having the SE designation. The regular use of oil additives is specifically not recommended.

To drain the oil and change the filter, you will need:

a. Drain pan.
b. Funnel.
c. Can opener or pour spout.
d. Filter wrench.
e. 15 mm wrench (adjustable will also work).
f. 3 quarts (4-cylinder) or 4 quarts (V6) of oil.
g. Oil filter: AC PF-40 (4-cylinder); AC PF-51 (V6).

There are a number of ways of discarding the old oil safely. The easiest way is to pour it from the drain pan into a gallon bleach bottle. Tighten the cap and throw it in your household trash (if local regulations allow) or recycle it.

1. Warm engine to operating temperature, then shut it off.
2. Put drain pan under oil drain plug and remove plug with 15 mm wrench.
3. Let oil drain for at least 10 minutes.
4. Unscrew oil filter counterclockwise by hand or use a filter wrench. See **Figure 12**.

NOTE

Because of oil filter positioning on the 4-cylinder engine, filter removal requires removing the right front wheel ***(Figure 13)****. The oil filter on the V6 engine is located up front beside the starter* ***(Figure 14)****.*

5. Wipe the gasket surface of the engine block with a clean, lint-free cloth.
6. Coat the neoprene gasket on the new filter with clean oil. See **Figure 15**.
7. Screw the filter onto the engine *by hand* until the filter gasket just touches the base, i.e., until you feel the slightest resistance when turning the filter. Then tighten the filter *by hand* 2/3 turn more.

CAUTION

Do not overtighten and do not use a filter wrench or the filter will leak.

8. Install oil drain plug and tighten securely.
9. Remove the oil filler cap. See **Figure 16** (4-cylinder) or **Figure 17** (V6).
10. Add 3 quarts (4-cylinder) or 4 quarts (V6) of oil recommended in **Table 2**. Lubricant capacities are found in **Table 3**.
11. Start the engine and let it idle. The oil pressure light on the instrument panel will remain on for a short time (15-30 seconds), then it will go out.

CAUTION

Do not rev engine to make oil light go out. It takes time for the oil to reach all areas of the engine—excessive engine speed could damage dry parts.

12. While the engine is running, make sure that the drain plug and oil filter are not leaking.
13. Turn the engine off and check the oil level with the dipstick. See **Figure 3**. Add oil if necessary to bring oil up to the FULL mark, but *do not overfill.*

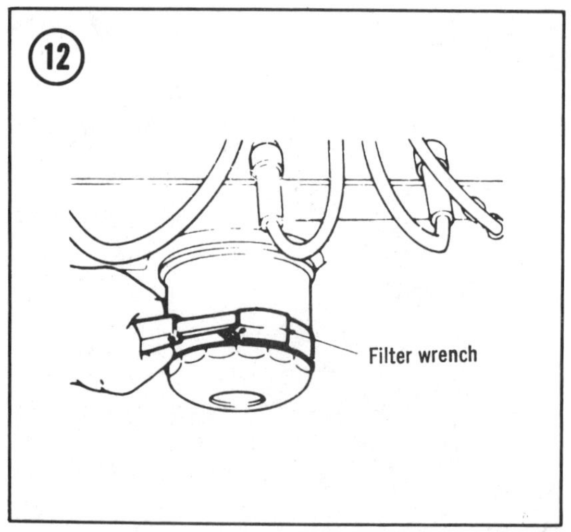

Manual Transaxle Check

Every 7,500 miles, check fluid level in manual transaxle. To do this, remove filler plug (**Figure 18**) and make sure that fluid level reaches to the bottom of the hole. If the level is low, top up with transmission fluid recommended in **Table 4**.

NOTE

Always check transaxle fluid level when transaxle is cold.

Automatic Transaxle Check

At every engine oil change (7,500 miles/6 months), check the automatic transaxle fluid level. The transmission must be thoroughly warmed up, the engine idling, the selector in PARK and the car level. Pull out the dipstick (**Figure 19**) and touch the end of the dipstick cautiously to determine the approximate temperature of the fluid.

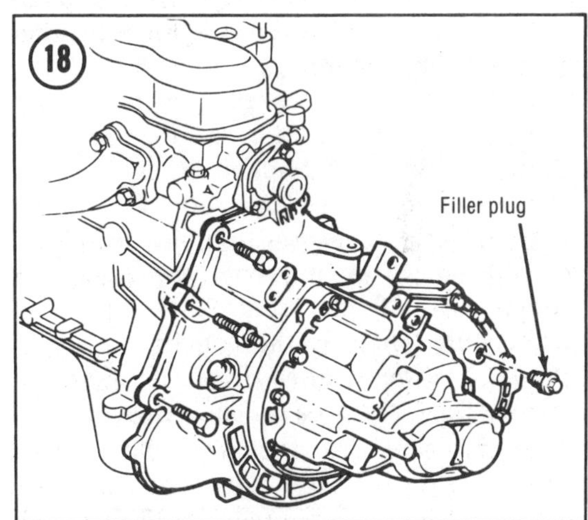

3

Wipe the dipstick with a clean cloth and reinsert it. Pull the dipstick out again and check the level. See **Figure 20**. If the fluid was cool (about room temperature), the level should be between the 2 dimples on the dipstick above the FULL HOT mark. If the fluid was hot (too hot to hold comfortably), the level should be between the ADD and FULL marks.

If necessary, add fluid but do not overfill. If level is above the top mark, fluid must be drained to restore proper level or seals may be damaged.

CAUTION

It takes only one pint to raise level from ADD to FULL with a hot transaxle. Use fluid clearly marked DEXRON-II only.

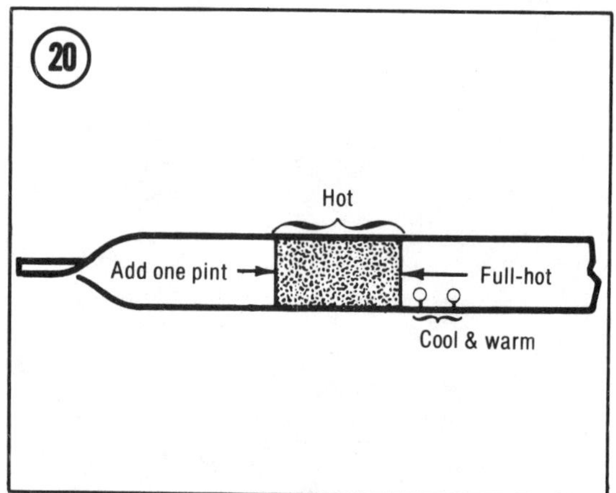

Power Steering Fluid Level

At every engine oil change (7,500 miles/6 months), check power steering fluid level. The power steering fluid level can be checked cold or with the engine and fluid warmed up to operating temperature.

1. Turn the steering wheel to right and left lock positions several times and then turn the wheels straight ahead. Shut off the engine.
2. Remove the dipstick from the pump reservoir, wipe it clean with a lint-free cloth, reinsert it all the way into the tube and withdraw it. If the fluid is at operating temperature (hot to the touch) the level should be between the HOT and COLD marks (**Figure 21**). If the fluid is "cold" (about 70° F or 21° C), the level should be between the

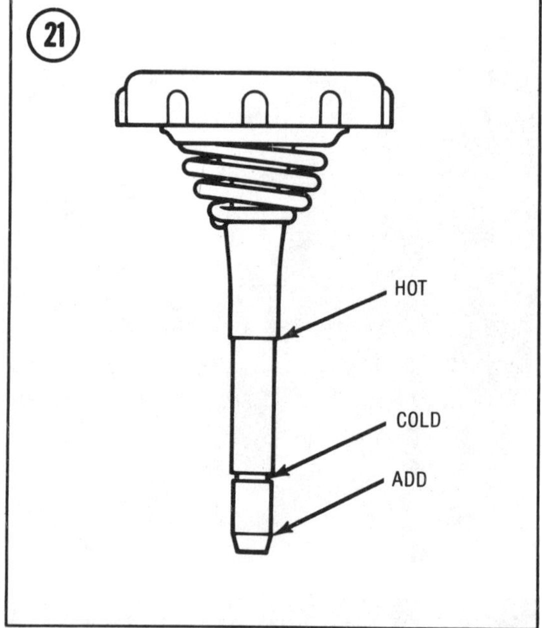

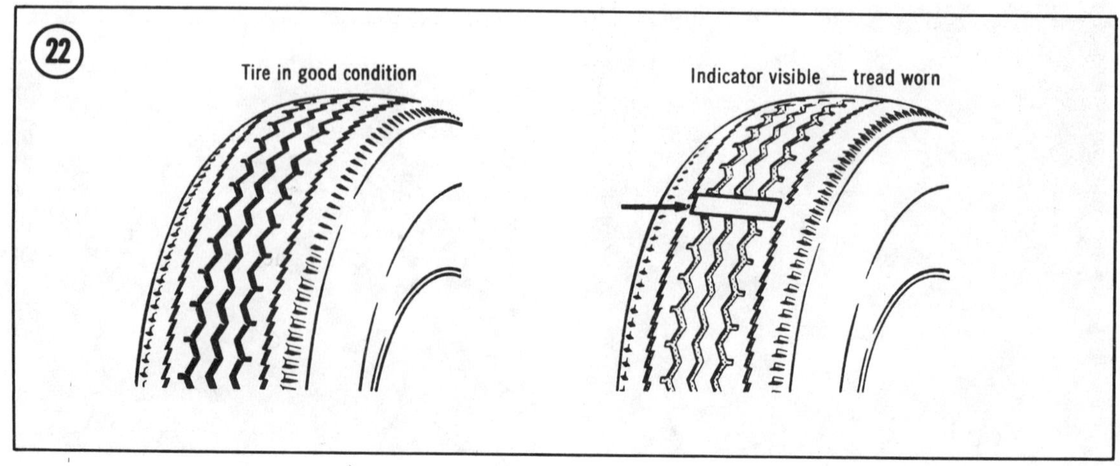

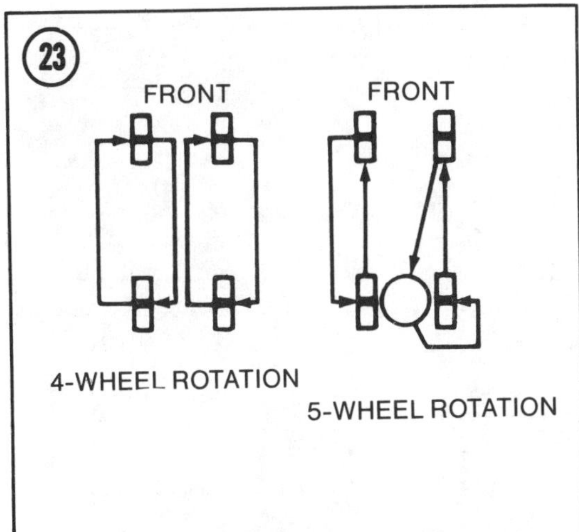

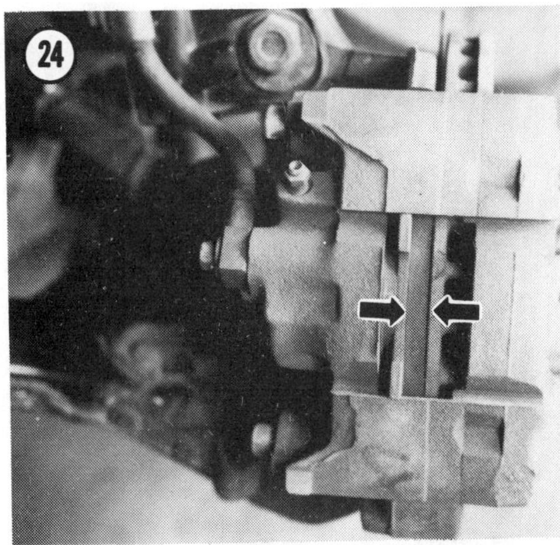

ADD and COLD marks. If the level is not correct, carefully add GM Power Steering Fluid or equivalent automatic transmission fluid and recheck the level. Do not overfill the reservoir. If the level, after filling, is above the FULL mark, fluid must be siphoned off until the level is correct.

Engine Compartment Check

Every 7,500 miles, check entire engine compartment for leaking or deteriorated oil and fuel lines. Check electrical wiring for breaks in insulation caused by deterioration or chafing. Check the radiator and hose connections for coolant residue rust. Check for loose or missing bolts, nuts and screws. On vehicles with automatic transaxles, check oil cooler lines at radiator and transaxle for leakage.

Tire and Wheel Inspection

Every 7,500 miles, check the condition of all tires. Check local traffic regulations concerning minimum tread depth. Most recommend replacing tires when tread depth is less than 1/32 inch. Original equipment tires have tread wear indicators molded into the bottom of the tread grooves. Tread wear indicators appear as 1/2 inch bands (see **Figure 22**). Tires should be replaced at this point.

General Motors recommends rotating radial tires initially at 7,500 miles, then every 15,000 miles. **Figure 23** shows how this should be done. Inspect front disc brakes as described below while the front tires are off for rotation.

Front Disc Brakes

When rotating the tires, check brake pad thickness. See **Figure 24**. Brake pads should be replaced if thickness is less than 1/32 inch (0.8 mm). See Chapter Twelve for replacement procedure. If any pad is worn to the limit, replace all 4 pads to keep braking balanced. Never replace pads on one wheel only.

NOTE

A brake wear indicator is used on each outside brake pad ***(Figure 25)****. When the wear indicator rubs against the brake* *disc, all 4 front brake pads must be replaced.*

Check condition of rotor (brake disc). See **Figure 25**. Minor radial scratches are normal. If they are deep enough to snag your fingernail, have your dealer or a brake specialist determine if replacement is necessary.

Brake Fluid Check

Every 7,500 miles or 6 months, check the fluid level in the master cylinder reservoir. Clean dirt and grime away from edge of cover so that it will not fall into the reservoir. Press upward on 2 side retainers securing cover (**Figure 26**) and lift off. The level should be 1/4 inch (6 mm) below the top edge of the reservoir. See **Figure 27**. Top up if necessary with hydraulic brake fluid clearly marked DOT-3. Install cover.

Parking Brake Lubrication

Every 7,500 miles, apply a small amount of EP Chassis Lubricant to cable guides and equalizer. See **Figure 28**.

Hood Latches

Every 7,500 miles or 6 months, lubricate hood latch and hinges. First wipe off accumulated dirt. Apply white grease (e.g., Lubriplate) to latch pilot bolt and locking

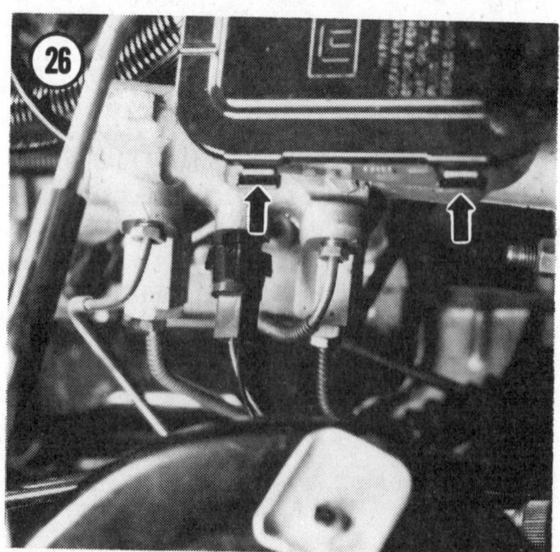

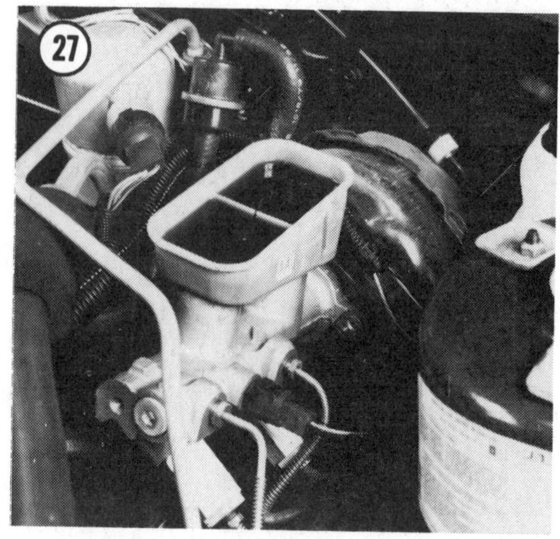

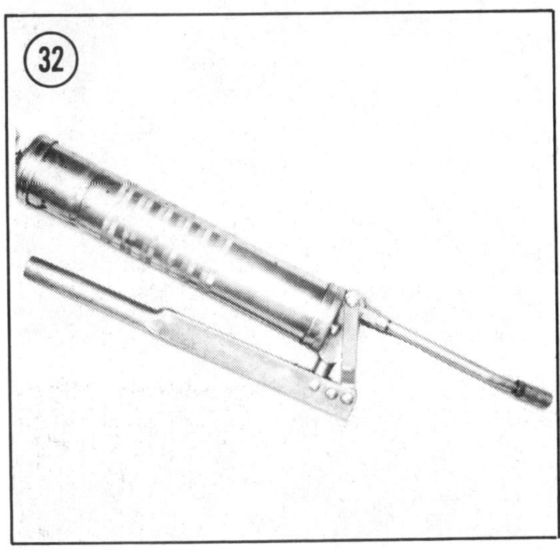

plate. See **Figure 29**. Apply light engine oil to all moving parts of release mechanism and hinges.

Windshield Wiper Blades

Long exposure to weather and road film hardens the rubber wiper blades and destroys their effectiveness. When blades smear or otherwise fail to clean the windshield, they should be replaced. See Chapter Eight.

NOTE
Whenever it is necessary to test the wiper motor, always first wet the windshield to prevent damage to blades or glass surface.

Front Suspension Lubrication

Every 7,500 miles or 6 months, lubricate ball-joint fittings on each front wheel with EP Chassis Lubricant.

1. Locate upper (**Figure 30**) and lower (**Figure 31**) ball-joint fittings.
2. Wipe off the grease fitting with a rag. Position the hose of a grease gun (**Figure 32**) onto the grease fitting. Pump grease into the fitting until the rubber boot begins to expand.
3. Remove grease gun when rubber boots are full. Make sure not to overfill the rubber boots which would cause the boot to tear and allow dirt to enter.

CAUTION
Do not lubricate ball-joints when temperature is below 10° F (-12° C). If necessary, warm them up first by placing vehicle in heated garage.

Clutch Linkage Adjustment

Every 7,500 miles or 6 months, check the clutch linkage adjustment on manual shift cars. See Chapter Nine for adjustment.

Exhaust System

Every 7,500 miles or 6 months, examine mufflers, tailpipes, exhaust header and system fasteners for rust, holes and other damage.

Figure 33 and **Figure 34** show typical exhaust system fasteners. Replace any damaged parts. See Chapter Six.

CAUTION
The replacement of damaged exhaust system components is important to prevent the entry of exhaust fumes into the driving compartment. In addition, damaged fasteners which are not replaced can eventually allow exhaust components to fall off the car and become a potential driving hazard to other vehicles.

15,000 MILE/12 MONTH SERVICE

Drive Belts

The drive belts drive the water pump, alternator, air conditioner compressor and power steering unit. A belt in poor condition or improperly tensioned can cause serious engine cooling and battery charging problems.

Every 12 months or 15,000 miles, check the belts for wear, fraying or cracking. If any of these conditions exist, replace the belt.

To replace a drive belt:

1. Loosen the adjuster bolt and, if necessary, the bracket pivot bolt.
2. Swing the alternator or air conditioner compressor downward to loosen the belt.
3. Remove the belt.
4. Install the new belt around the pulleys.
5. Pull up on the alternator or compressor to tighten the belt. Tighten the adjuster bolt when the belt deflects 1/4 in. (6 mm) under moderate thumb pressure. See **Figure 7** (4-cylinder) or **Figure 8** (V6).

Cooling System Service

Every year, service the cooling system by performing the following:

WARNING
Do not remove the radiator cap when the engine is hot. You could be seriously burned by escaping coolant and steam which is under considerable pressure.

1. When engine is cool, rotate radiator cap (**Figure 35**) counterclockwise without pushing down. When residual pressure (if any) has been relieved (hissing will stop),

33

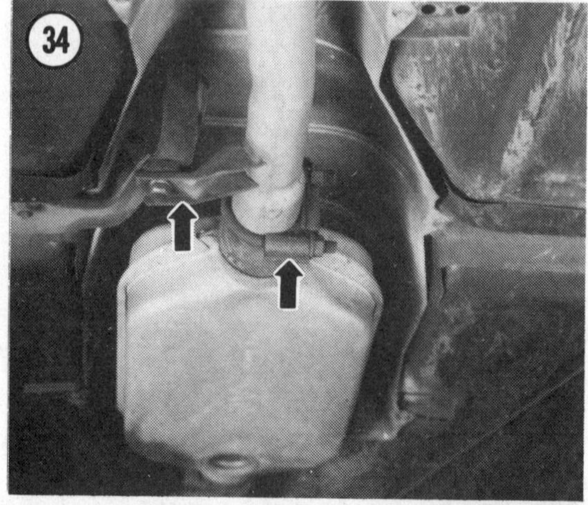
34

35

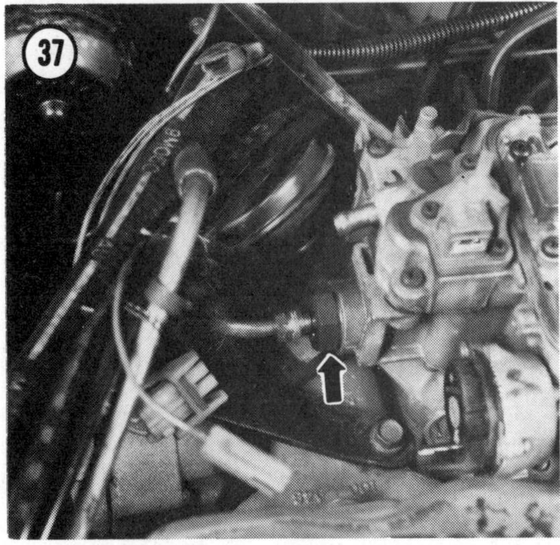

press cap down and rotate counterclockwise until cap can be removed.
2. Wash radiator cap and filler neck with clean water.

NOTE
Steps 3 and 4 require special equipment available at most service stations or your dealer.

3. Test freeze protection with an antifreeze hydrometer. System must be protected to at least -34° F (-37° C) to provide corrosion protection, but protection must exceed lowest anticipated temperature in your area.
4. Test system and radiator cap pressure capacity with appropriate testing device. Both must be able to maintain 15 psi.
5. Check condition of hoses. If there are signs of swelling, cracking or other deterioration, replace them. See Chapter Seven.
6. Check tightness of hose clamps. Replace questionable clamps with adjustable stainless steel clamps.
7. Clean bugs and dirt from front of radiator core and air conditioner condenser by directing compressed air from the back of the radiator.

3

Rear Brake Inspection

Every 15,000 miles, check condition of brake drums and linings while the rear wheels are removed for tire rotation.

Remove rear wheels and pull off drums as described in Chapter Twelve. Brake linings should be at least 1/16 in. (1.5 mm) thick. See **Figure 36**. If any shoe is worn to the limit, replace all 4 shoes at the same time. See Chapter Twelve for procedure.

Brake Pedal Height

With the brakes cold and the engine not running, measure the distance from the top of the brake pedal pad to the floorboard while firmly depressing the brake pedal. Pedal height should be 3 1/2 in. for manual brakes and 2 3/4 in. for power brakes.

NOTE
When depressing brake pedal, an approximate force of 50 lb. must be exerted on manual brakes and 100 lb. on power brakes.

Fuel Filter Replacement

Every 15,000 miles or 12 months, replace the fuel filter. See **Figure 37** (4-cylinder) or **Figure 38** (V6). **Figure 39** shows the fuel filter assembly.
1. Disconnect the fuel line connection at the inlet fuel filter nut.
2. Remove inlet fuel filter nut from carburetor.
3. Remove filter element and spring.

4. Install new spring and filter element in carburetor. Make sure hole in filter faces inlet nut.
5. Install new gasket on inlet fitting nut. Install nut in carburetor and tighten securely.
6. Install fuel line and tighten connector.
7. Start engine and check for leak.

ENGINE TUNE-UP (30,000 MILE SERVICE)

In order to maintain a car in perfect running condition, the engine must receive periodic tune-ups. The procedure outlined here is performed every 30,000 miles. **Table 5** summarizes tune-up specifications. Since different systems in an engine interact to affect overall performance, a tune-up must be accomplished in the following order:

a. Cylinder head bolts tightening
b. Compression test
c. Spark plug replacement
d. Distributor inspection
e. Ignition timing
f. Carburetor adjustment

To perform a tune-up on your vehicle, you will need the following tools and parts:

a. Spark plug wrench
b. Universal joint for socket wrench
c. Socket wrench
d. 12 inch extension for socket
e. Common screwdriver
f. Spark plug gapper tool
g. Compression gauge
h. Ignition timing light
i. Phillips screwdriver
j. 12 mm wrench
k. Torque wrench

Firing Order

The cylinder firing order for engines discussed is:

a. 4-cylinder, 1-3-4-2
b. V6, 1-2-3-4-5-6

CYLINDER HEAD TORQUE

Refer to Chapter Four (4-cylinder) or Chapter Five (V6) and remove the valve cover. On 4-cylinder engines, tighten the cylinder head bolts to 75 ft.-lb. (100 N•m) in the sequence shown in **Figure 40**. On V6

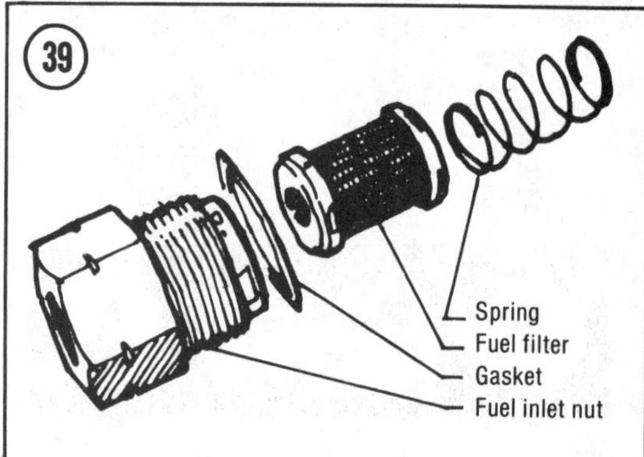

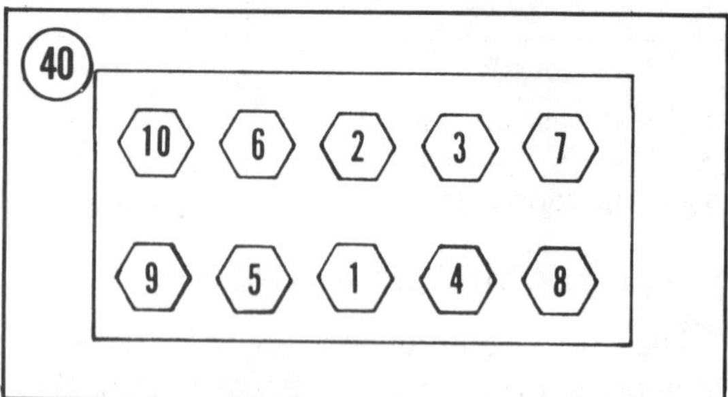

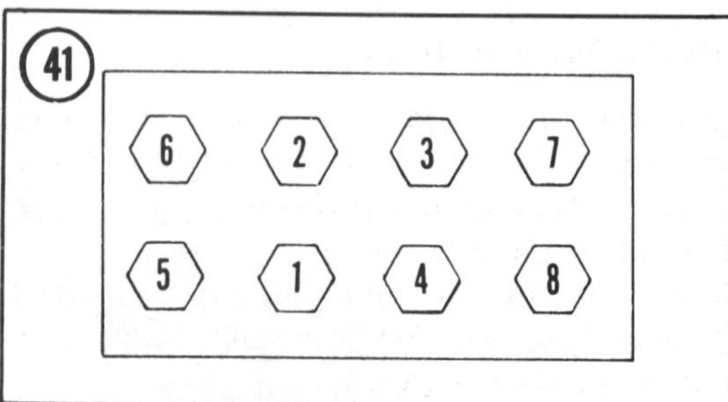

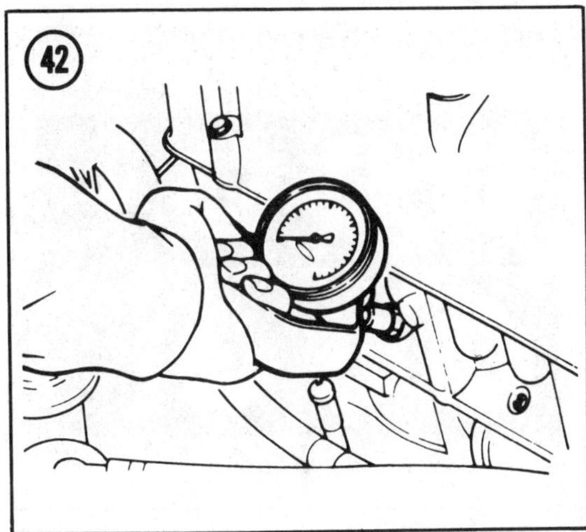

42

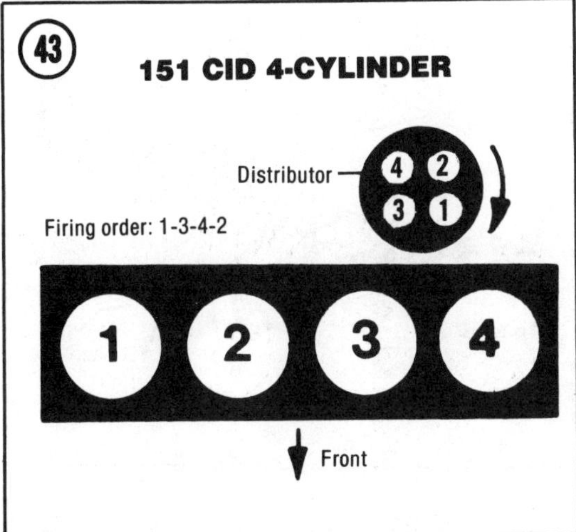

43

engines, tighten the cylinder head bolts to 65-75 ft.-lb. (88-100 N•m) in the sequence shown in **Figure 41**.

COMPRESSION TEST

The "dry" compression test and the "wet" compression test must be interpreted together to isolate the trouble in cylinders or valves.

Dry Compression Test

1. Warm the engine to normal operating temperature. Ensure that the choke valve and throttle valve are completely open.
2. Remove the spark plugs.
3. Connect the compression tester to one cylinder following the tester manufacturer's instructions. See **Figure 42**.
4. Have an assistant crank the engine over until there is no further rise in pressure.
5. Remove the tester and record the reading.
6. Repeat Steps 3 through 5 for each cylinder.

When interpreting the results, actual readings are not as important as the difference between readings. All readings should be about 145 psi (1000 kPa). Readings below 100 psi (690 kPa) indicate that an engine overhaul is due. A maximum difference of 21 psi (145 kPa) between any 2 cylinders is acceptable. Greater differences indicate worn or broken rings, leaky or sticky valves, or a combination of all. Compare with vacuum gauge reading to isolate the trouble more closely.

Wet Compression Test

Add one tablespoon of heavy oil (at least SAE 30) through the spark plug hole of any cylinder which checks low. Repeat the procedure above. If compresson increases noticeably, the rings are probably worn. If adding oil produces no change, the low reading may be caused by a broken ring or valve trouble. If two adjacent cylinders read low, the head gasket may be damaged.

SPARK PLUGS

Removal

1. Blow out any foreign matter from around spark plugs with compressed air.

CAUTION

When spark plugs are removed, dirt around the plug can fall into the spark plug hole. This could cause expensive engine damage.

NOTE

Small cans of compressed, inert gas used to blow off photographic equipment are available at photo supply stores.

2. Mark spark plug wires with cylinder number so that you can reconnect them properly. A small strip of masking tape numbered in sequence works well. See **Figure 43** (4-cylinder) or **Figure 44** (V6).

3

3. Disconnect the spark plug wires. Pull off by grasping the connector, *not* the spark plug wire. See **Figure 45**. If you pull on the wire, it could break.

CAUTION

If the boots seem to be stuck, twist them a half turn by hand to break the seal. Do not pull boots off with pliers. The pliers could cut through the silicone material and permit the spark to arc to ground.

4. Remove the spark plugs. Keep plugs in order so that you know which cylinder they came from.

NOTE

*Spark plugs No. 1, 3 and 5 on the V6 engine (**Figure 44**) are very difficult to reach without a universal joint, 2 3/4 in. short and 11 1/4 in. long extensions, 5/8 in. spark plug wrench with rubber insert, and rachet.*

5. Examine each spark plug and compare its condition to **Figure 46**. Condition of spark plugs is an indication of engine condition and can warn of developing trouble.
6. Discard the plugs. Although they could be cleaned, gapped and reused if in good condition, they rarely last very long; new plugs are not very expensive and will be far more reliable.

Gapping and Installing the Plugs

New plugs should be carefully gapped to ensure a reliable, consistent spark. You must use a special spark plug gapping tool with a wire gauge. See **Figure 47**.

1. Remove new plugs from box and screw on the small end pieces that are loose in each box. See **Figure 48**.

NOTE

*Spark plugs used are of the tapered seat design (**Figure 49**) and do not require the use of a gasket for sealing purposes.*

2. Refer to **Table 5** and insert the proper size gauge wire between the center and side

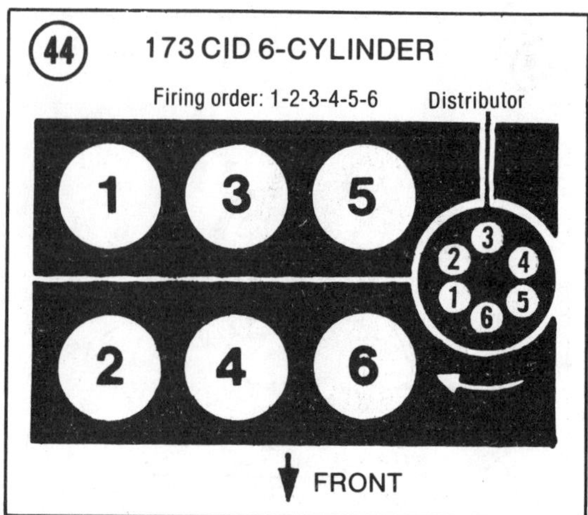

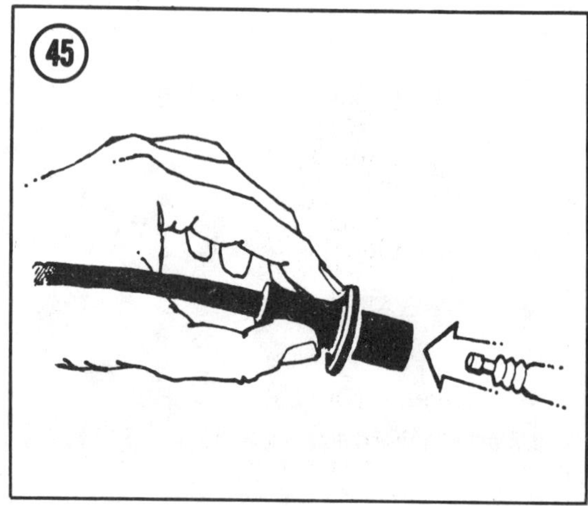

electrode of each spark plug. See **Figure 50**. If the gap is correct, you will feel a slight drag as you pull the wire through. If there is no drag or the gauge won't pass through, bend the side electrode *with the gapping tool* (see **Figure 51**) to set proper gap.
3. Put a *small* drop of oil on the threads of each spark plug.
4. Crank starter for about 5 seconds to blow out any debris around spark plug holes.
5. Screw each spark plug in by hand until it seats. Very little effort is required. If force is necessary, you have the plug cross-threaded; unscrew it and try again.
6. Tighten the spark plugs. If you have a torque wrench, tighten them to 7-15 ft.-lb. (10-20 N•m). If you don't have a torque wrench, an additional 1/4 to 1/2 turn after finger-tight is sufficient.

SPARK PLUG CONDITION

NORMAL

• Identified by light tan or gray deposits on the firing tip.
• Can be cleaned.

GAP BRIDGED

• Identified by deposit buildup closing gap between electrodes.
• Caused by oil or carbon fouling. If deposits are not excessive, the plug can be cleaned.

OIL FOULED

• Identified by wet black deposits on the insulator shell bore electrodes.
• Caused by excessive oil entering combustion chamber through worn rings and pistons, excessive clearance between valve guides and stems, or worn or loose bearings. Can be cleaned. If engine is not repaired, use a hotter plug.

CARBON FOULED

• Identified by black, dry fluffy carbon deposits on insulator tips, exposed shell surfaces and electrodes.
• Caused by too cold a plug, weak ignition, dirty air cleaner, defective fuel pump, too rich a fuel mixture, improperly operating heat riser, or excessive idling. Can be cleaned.

LEAD FOULED

• Identified by dark gray, black, yellow, or tan deposits or a fused glazed coating on the insulator tip.
• Caused by highly leaded gasoline. Can be cleaned.

WORN

• Identified by severely eroded or worn electrodes.
• Caused by normal wear. Should be replaced.

FUSED SPOT DEPOSIT

• Identified by melted or spotty deposits resembling bubbles or blisters.
• Caused by sudden acceleration. Can be cleaned.

OVERHEATING

• Identified by a white or light gray insulator with small black or gray brown spots and with bluish-burnt appearance of electrodes.
• Caused by engine overheating, wrong type of fuel, loose spark plugs, too hot a plug, low fuel pump pressure, or incorrect ignition timing. Replace the plug.

PREIGNITION

• Identified by melted electrodes and possibly blistered insulator. Metallic deposits on insulator indicate engine damage.
• Caused by wrong type of fuel, incorrect ignition timing or advance, too hot a plug, burned valves, or engine overheating. Replace the plug.

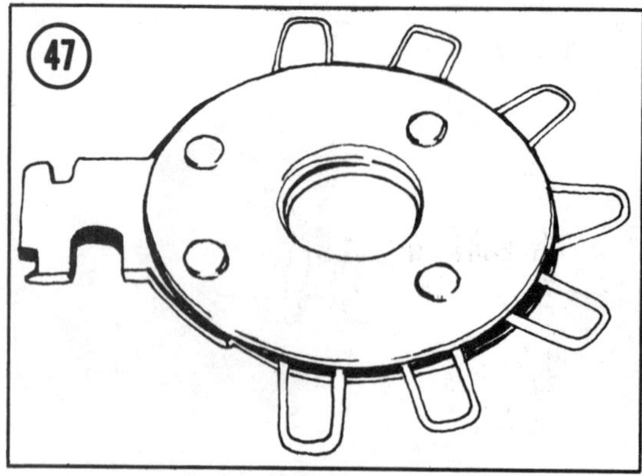

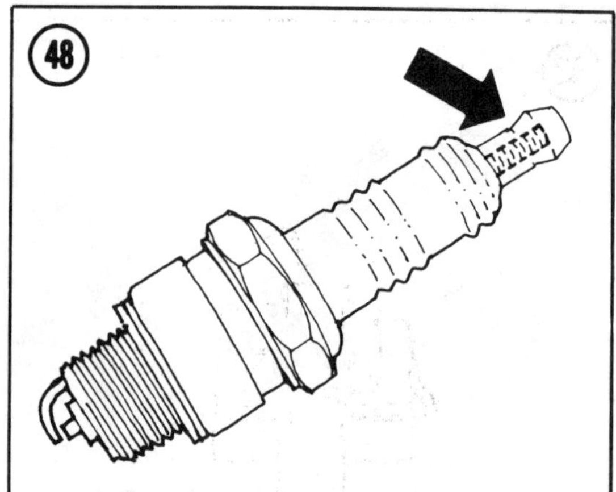

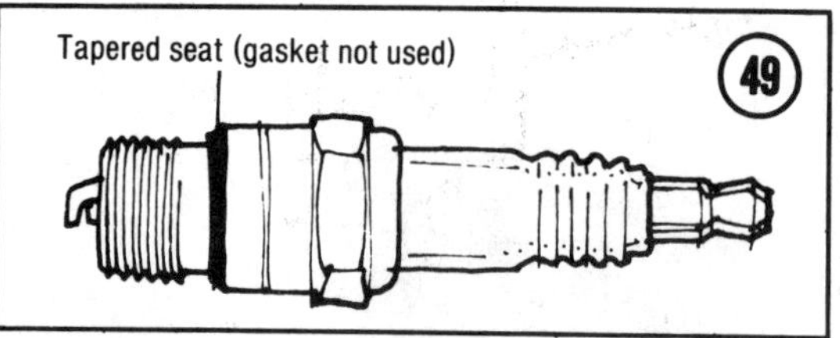

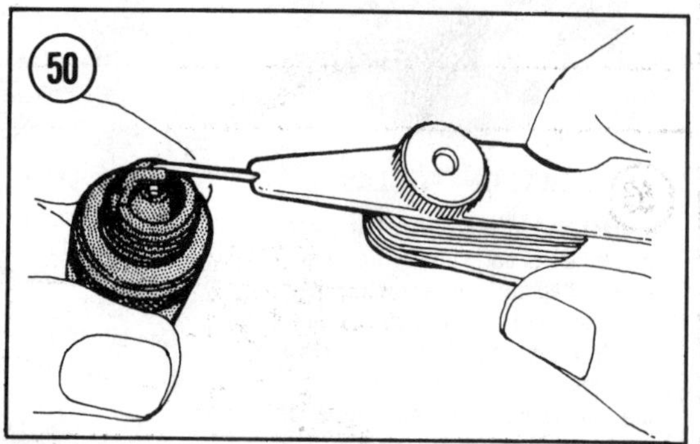

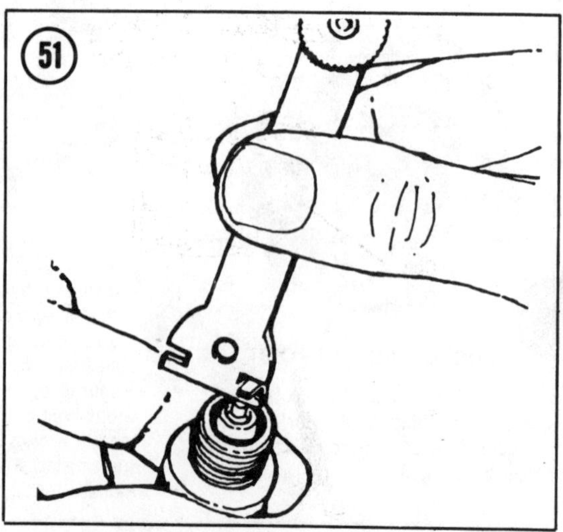

NOTE
Do not overtighten. This prevents the plug from sealing.

7. Install the spark plug wires. Make sure each is connected to the proper spark plug. Refer to **Figure 43** (4-cylinder) or **Figure 44** (V6) for spark plug wire routing.

DISTRIBUTOR

The distributor provides an electrical signal to the ignition coil at the proper time to produce a very high voltage and acts as a rotary switch to route the high voltage to the appropriate spark plug. The High Energy Ignition (HEI) system distributor on the V6 engines combines the distributor, electronic control unit and coil in one assembly (**Figure 52**). The distributor on 4-cylinder engines may have either an integrated coil (**Figure 53**) or a separate coil and connector (**Figure 54**). Although they appear slightly different, all units operate in the same way.

To ensure reliable operation, the distributor must be inspected every 30,000 miles as described below.

Inspection

Refer to **Figures 52-54** for this procedure.

1. Disconnect the ignition switch wires from the distributor cap. See **Figure 54** or **Figure 55**. On 4-cylinder engines with separate coil, disconnect the coil wire from the distributor cap.

NOTE
On 4-cylinder engines, the distributor is located between the firewall and the rear right side of the engine.

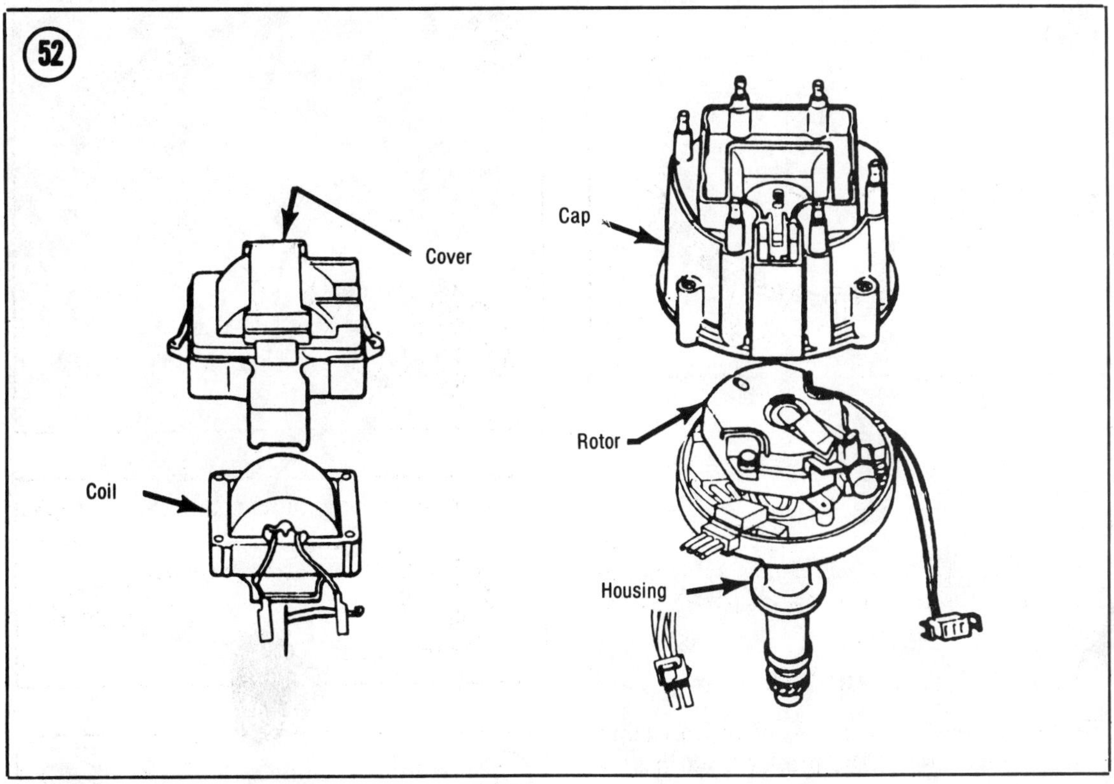

52

Cap
Cover
Rotor
Coil
Housing

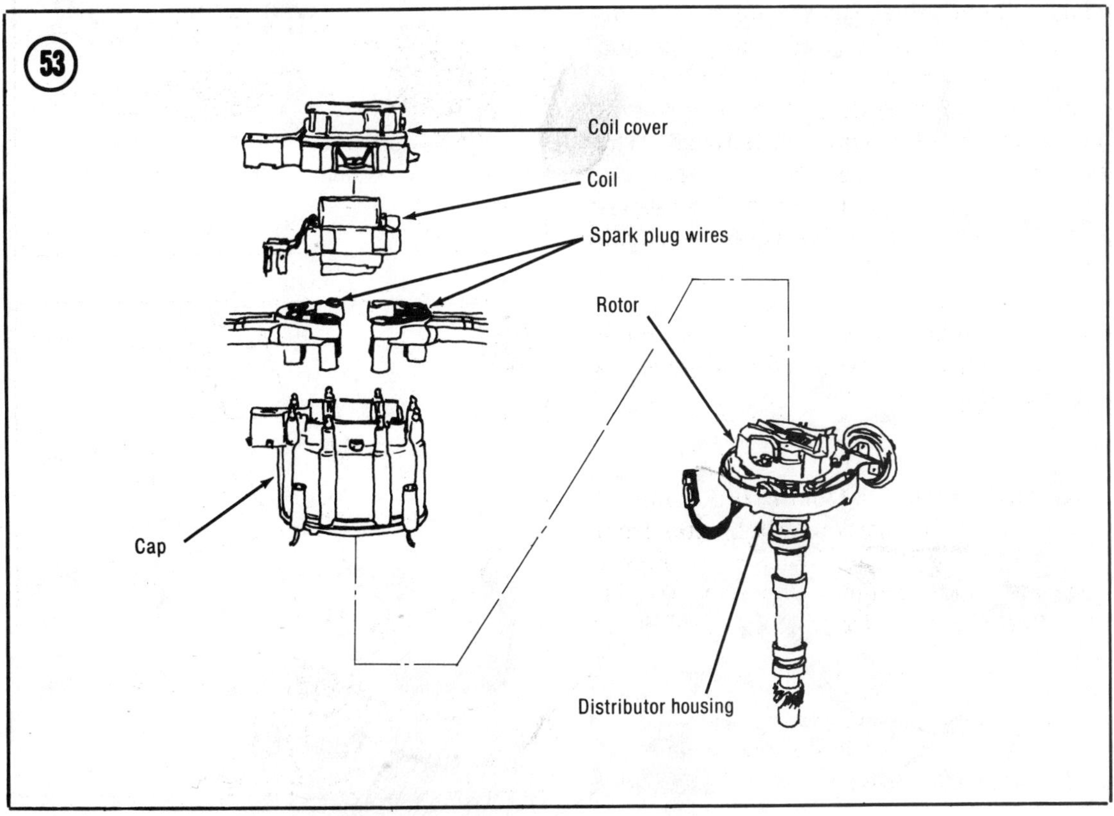

53

Coil cover
Coil
Spark plug wires
Rotor
Cap
Distributor housing

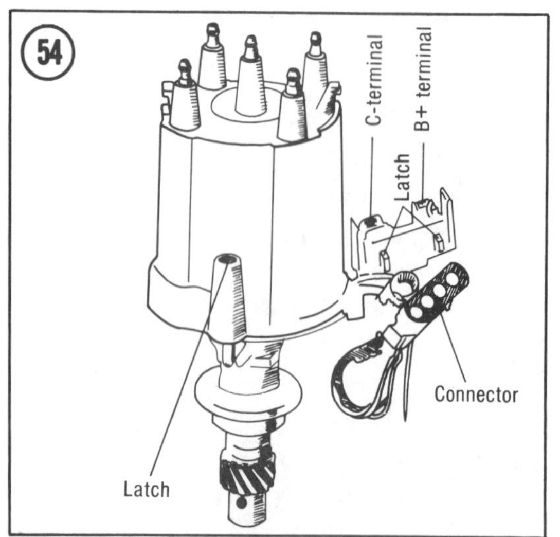
54
C-terminal
B+ terminal
Latch
Connector
Latch

57

55

58

56

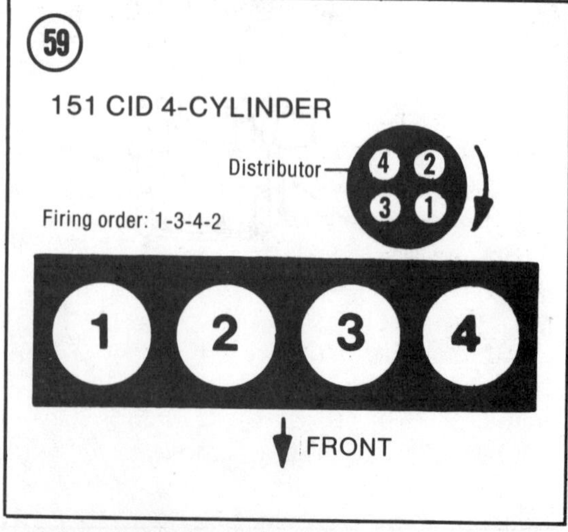
59
151 CID 4-CYLINDER
Distributor
4 2
3 1
Firing order: 1-3-4-2
1 2 3 4
FRONT

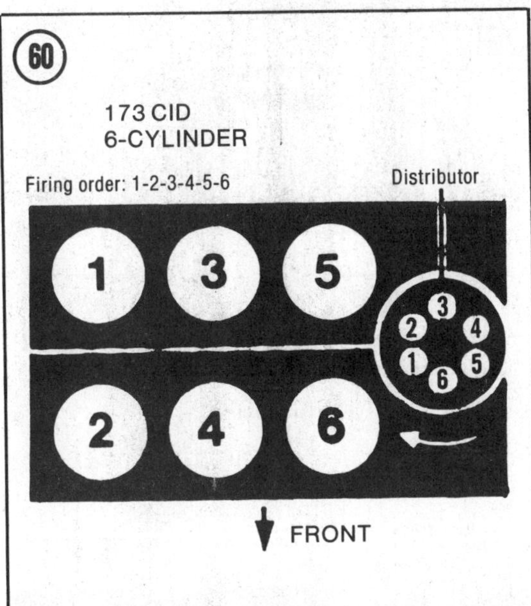

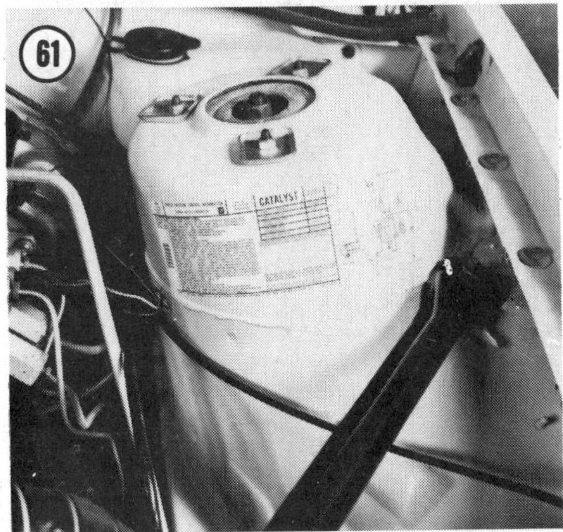

2. If so equipped, remove the spark plug wire connector from the top of the distributor cap by releasing the 2 latch pins. See **Figure 56**. Lay the spark plug connector and spark plug wires aside. On distributors without connectors, label and remove each individual spark plug wire.
3. Remove the distributor cap by turning the 4 lock latches counterclockwise. On 4-cylinder engines, it will be necessary to use a stubby screwdriver to get at the latches due to lack of space. Lift off the distributor cap and move it aside.

NOTE

If the distributor cap on 4-cylinder vehicles cannot be removed from the top side because of air conditioning lines and hoses, refer to Chapter Eight for its removal.

4. Unscrew 2 Phillips screws securing rotor (see **Figure 57**). Lift off rotor.
5. Blow off advance mechanism and inside of rotor with compressed air.
6. Check rotor carefully for cracks and a worn or damaged center electrode. Replace it if questionable.
7. Install rotor. Note cutout on rotor which permits it to be installed only one way (**Figure 58**).
8. Blow off inside and outside of distributor cap with compressed air. Check for cracks and severely burned or worn electrodes. If questionable, replace the distributor cap. Check the carbon button at the center of the cap.

CAUTION

*To prevent mixing up the wires, transfer one wire at a time from the old cap to the corresponding terminal on the new cap. **Figure 59** (4-cylinder) and **Figure 60** (V6) show cylinder number of each terminal, just in case.*

9. Install distributor cap on distributor. It only goes on one way. Try to rotate it slightly; when properly seated, it will lock in place. Push the lock screws down and rotate them until they lock.

IGNITION TIMING

The distributor must be aligned to fire each plug at precisely the right moment. The emission control sticker under the hood gives the correct timing for different combinations of engine and optional equipment and for different locations. See **Figure 61**. Due to varying state and federal regulations, your sticker may differ from the one shown. Always use the specifications on the sticker on your own car.

1. Disconnect distributor vacuum hose at distributor and plug it with a pencil.

3

2. Connect timing light according to the manufacturer's instructions.

NOTE

***Figure 62** shows typical connections if you have no instructions. Refer to **Figure 59** or **Figure 60** for the No. 1 cylinder spark plug location.*

3. Clean off the timing scale and locate the notch on the crankshaft pulley. See **Figure 63**. Rub chalk into the notch and the scale to make them more visible.
4. Connect a tachometer to the unattached TACH connector leading from the distributor TACH terminal. See **Figure 54** or **Figure 55**.

CAUTION

The tachometer terminal on the HEI distributor cap must never be grounded or serious damage to the solid-state module and the ignition coil will result.

5. Make sure the timing light wires are out of the way of the fan belts, then start the engine.
6. Refer to the emission control sticker (**Figure 61**) and set the engine speed to the correct setting. See *Carburetor Adjustments* later in this section for adjustment procedures.
7. Pull the trigger on the timing light and point it at the timing scale. The notch on the pulley will appear to stand still (it may waver occasionally) opposite the scale. If it aligns with the timing mark indicated on your emission control sticker, the timing is correct—no adjustment is necessary. If not, adjust as described in the next step.
8. If adjustment is required, turn off the engine and loosen the distributor hold-down clamp. **Figure 64** shows the clamp used on the 4-cylinder engine. To adjust ignition timing, loosen the outer lockbolt and slide the clamp away from the distributor. The V6 engine uses a round clamp. Start the engine, point the timing light at the scale and slowly rotate the distributor body until the notch on the pulley aligns with the proper timing mark. Stop the engine and tighten the distributor locknut. Repeat Steps 6 and 7 to make sure adjustment has not changed.
9. Turn engine off.
10. Remove pencil from vacuum line and reconnect it to the distributor advance unit.

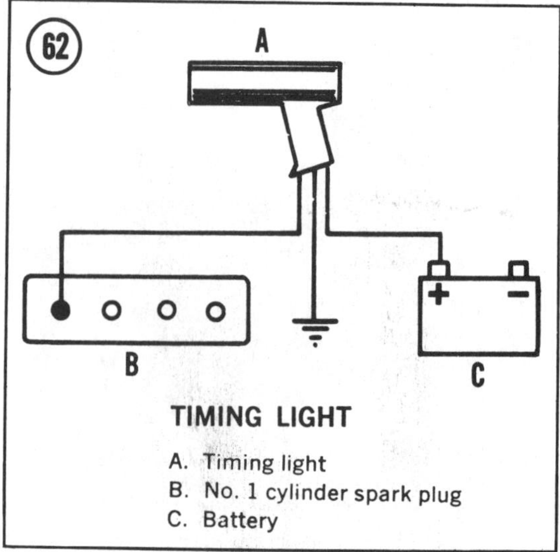

TIMING LIGHT

A. Timing light
B. No. 1 cylinder spark plug
C. Battery

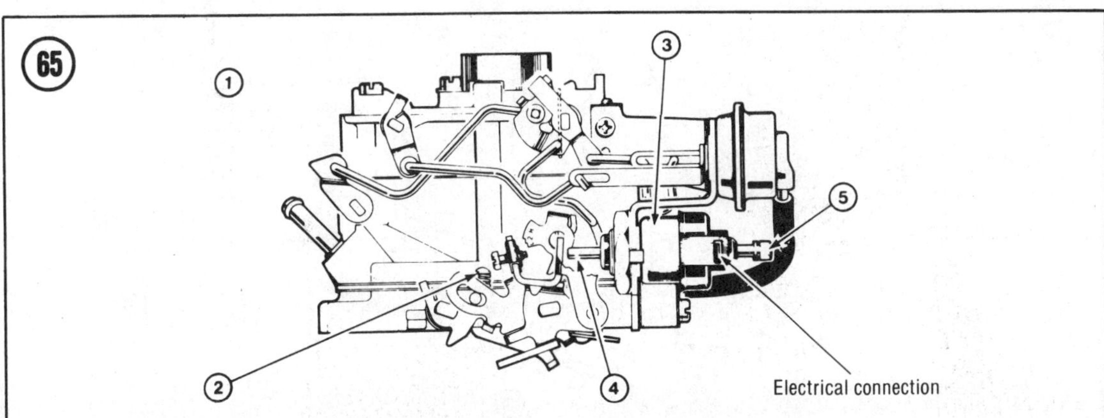

1. Prepare vehicle for adjustments. See emission label on the vehicle. Note: ignition timing set per label.
2. Adjust curb idle speed if required
3. Place fast idle screw on highest step of fast idle cam
4. Turn fast idle screw in or out to obtain specified fast idle R.P.M. (see label.)

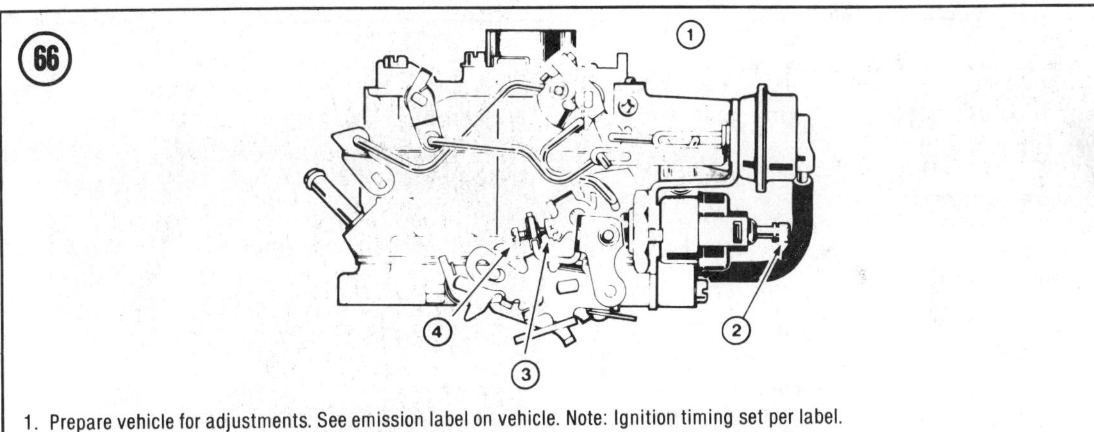

1. Prepare vehicle for adjustments. See emission label on vehicle. Note: Ignition timing set per label.
2. Turn idle speed screw to set curb idle speed to specifications-A/C OFF, (see emission label).
3. Solenoid energized. A/C compressor lead disconnected at A/C compressor. A/C ON, A/T in DRIVE, M/T in NEUTRAL.
4. Open throttle slightly to allow solenoid plunger to fully extend.

11. Disconnect timing light and tachometer.

CARBURETOR ADJUSTMENTS

Carburetor adjustments are limited to setting the fast idle and the idle speed to the values stated on the emission control sticker (**Figure 61**). See **Figure 65** for fast idle adjustment procedures. See **Figure 66** (air conditioned vehicles) or **Figure 67** (non-air conditioned vehicles) for idle speed adjustments.

EXHAUST EMISSION CONTROL CHECK

After every engine tune-up, have a General Motors dealer check carbon monoxide (CO) content of exhaust gas.

30,000 MILE/24 MONTH SERVICE

Steering Gear Inspection

Every 30,000 miles or 2 years, check the steering gear housing seals for leakage. An oil

67

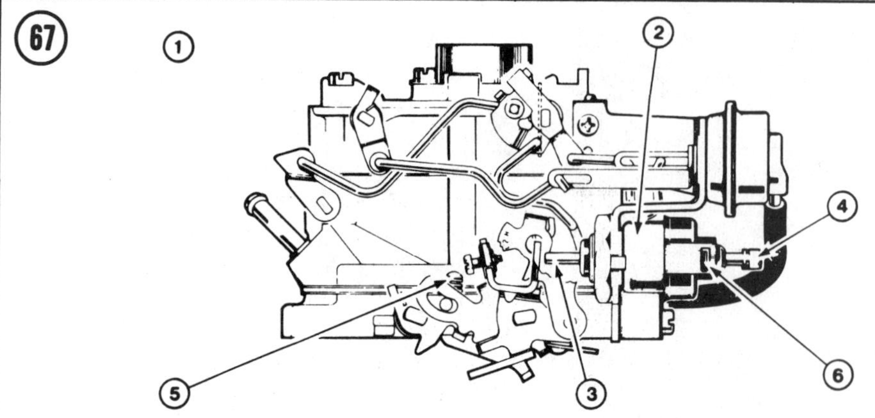

1. Prepare vehicle for adjustments. See emission label on vehicle. Note: Ignition timing set per label.
2. Solenoid energized. A/T in DRIVE, M/T in NEUTRAL.
3. Open throttle slighty to allow solenoid plunger to fully extend.
4. Turn solenoid screw to adjust curb idle speed to specified RPM (solenoid energized).
5. Turn idle speed screw to set basic idle speed to specifications (solenoid de-energized.)
6. Reconnect solenoid electrical lead after adjustment.

film is permissible, but visible solid grease indicates the need for steering gear overhaul. See Chapter Ten.

Coolant Change

Every 30,000 miles or 2 years, change the engine coolant.

WARNING
Do not remove radiator cap when engine is hot. You could be seriously burned by escaping coolant and steam which is under considerable pressure.

1. When engine is cool, rotate radiator cap (**Figure 68**) counterclockwise without pushing down. When residual pressure (if any) has been relieved (hissing will stop), press cap down and rotate counterclockwise until cap can be removed.
2. Run engine until upper radiator hose feels hot, indicating the thermostat has opened.
3. Stop engine and open drain petcock on radiator.
4. Close petcock and fill system through radiator cap opening with plain water.
5. Repeat Steps 2 through 4 until drained water is colorless.
6. Let system drain completely, then tighten drain petcock.
7. Remove cap on recovery tank.
8. Remove recovery tank, pour out coolant and clean inside of tank with detergent. Rinse thoroughly with clean water and install empty tank.
9. Add sufficient ethylene glycol antifreeze to protect system below lowest anticipated temperature in your area.

NOTE
Approximate cooling system capacity on 4-cylinder vehicles is 9 1/2 quarts (non-air conditioned) or 9 3/4 quarts (air conditioned). Cooling system capacity on V6 vehicles is 11 1/2 quarts (non-air conditioned) or 11 3/4 quarts (air conditioned).

10. Fill the radiator with plain water to the base of the radiator filler neck. Fill recovery tank to FULL HOT level and install recovery tank cap.
11. Run engine with radiator cap removed until upper hose feels hot.
12. With engine idling, add coolant to radiator until level reaches bottom of filler neck.
13. Install radiator cap. Make sure arrows line up with overflow tube. See **Figure 68**.

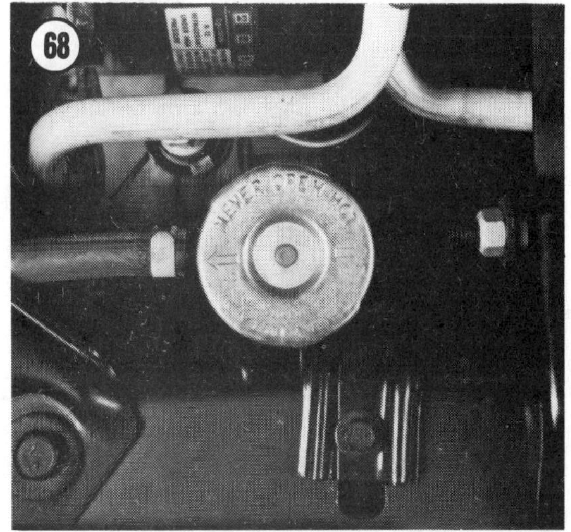

Air Cleaner

Replace the air cleaner element every 30,000 miles or 2 years. If you live in a very dusty area, you may have to change it more often. Check with a local dealer for his recommendation.

1. Either remove the 2 nuts (4-cylinder) or unscrew the wingnut (V6) securing the air cleaner cover to the carburetor air horn stud. See **Figure 69** or **Figure 70**.
2. Detach air cleaner from air horn and housing and discard air cleaner element. Inspect cover gasket and wipe inside of housing with damp cloth. Replace if damaged or cracked.
3. Install new air cleaner element.

Positive Crankcase Ventilation Valve

The positive crankcase ventilation (PCV) system draws blowby crankcase fumes through a regulating valve and into the combustion chamber where they are burned.

The PCV valve must be changed every 24 months or 30,000 miles.

1. Pull PCV valve out of its grommet in the valve cover. See **Figure 71** (4-cylinder) or **Figure 72** (V6).

2. Squeeze the valve retaining clip with pliers and pull the valve out. Discard the valve; it cannot be cleaned.

3. Carefully inspect all hoses associated with the PCV system. Replace any that are cracked or don't fit tightly.
4. Install new PCV valve in hose and push it firmly into the valve cover grommet.

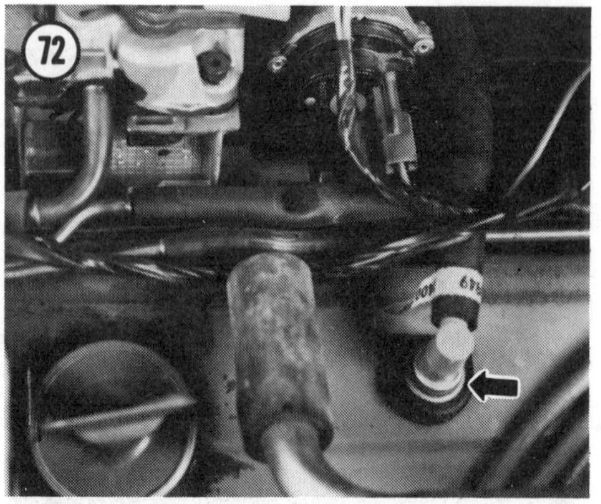

PCV Filter (4-cylinder)

Four-cylinder engines also have a PCV filter located in the air cleaner assembly which must be replaced every 24 months or 30,000 miles.

1. Remove the air cleaner cover and air filter.
2. Remove the PCV filter retaining clip and remove filter. See **Figure 73**.
3. Install a new PCV filter. Replace retaining clip and reinstall air cleaner filter and cover.

Fuel Evaporation Emission Canister

The emission canister reduces fuel vapor that would normally vent to the atmosphere from the fuel tank and carburetor float bowl. See **Figure 74** (4-cylinder) or **Figure 75** (V6).

The canister should be replaced every 30,000 miles.

1. Remove 2 bolts securing the canister to its base in the engine compartment. Remove the canister without detaching any lines.
2. Pull old filter out from the bottom of the canister.

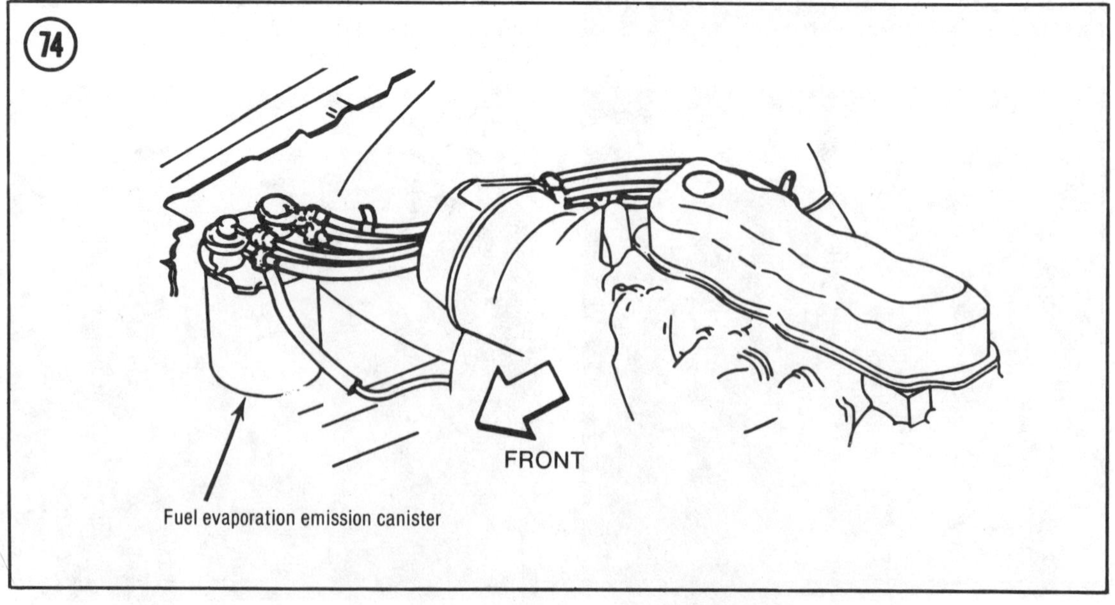

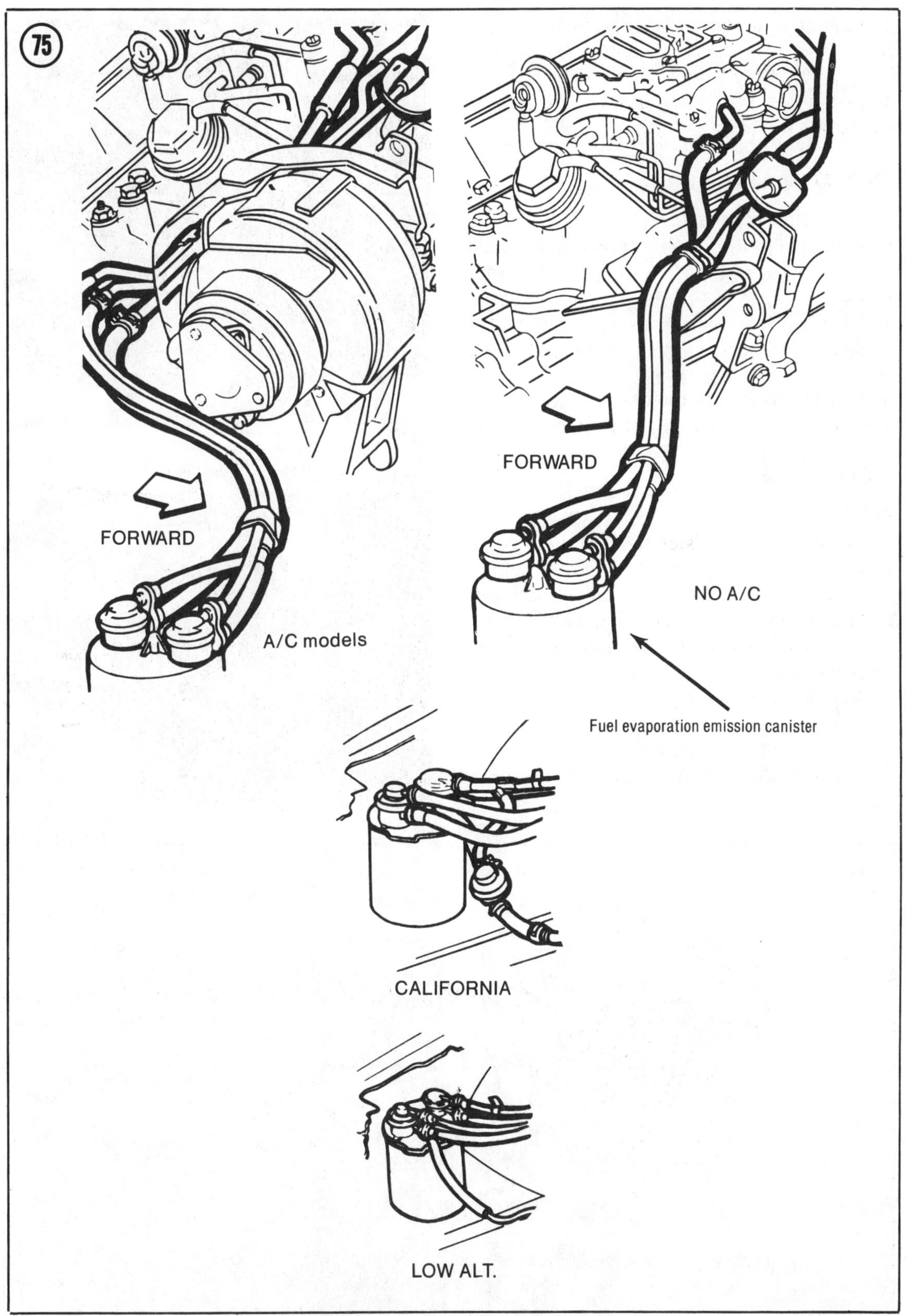
75
FORWARD
A/C models
FORWARD
NO A/C
Fuel evaporation emission canister
CALIFORNIA
LOW ALT.

3. Push a new filter into place with your fingers.
4. Install the canister in its mount and tighten the 2 attaching screws.
5. Check condition of all hoses leading to the canister. Replace any that are cracked or loose.

Catalytic Converter Catalyst Change (V6 only)

At 30,000 mile intervals, the word "Catalyst" may appear in the face of the speedometer. At such time, the catalyst in the catalytic converter must be changed by your local General Motors dealer.

Oxygen Sensor Replacement (California Vehicles)

At 30,000 mile intervals, a "sensor" flag will appear in the instrument panel. At such time, the oxygen sensor must be replaced. See Emission Control Systems, Chapter Six.

Drive Axle Boots and Output Shaft Seal Inspection

At 30,000 miles, inspect the drive axle boots and output shaft seals for damage or leakage. See Chapter Nine.

45,000 MILE SERVICE

Vacuum Fittings and Hoses

Check the vacuum fittings and connections to make sure they are tight and inspect the hoses for cracking, kinking or deterioration. Any unsatisfactory hoses should be replaced.

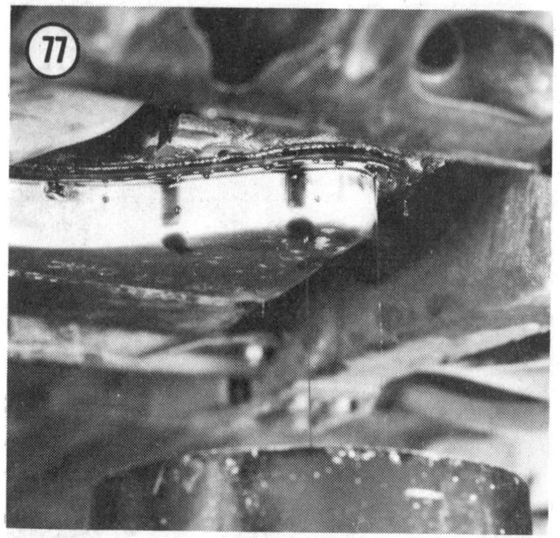

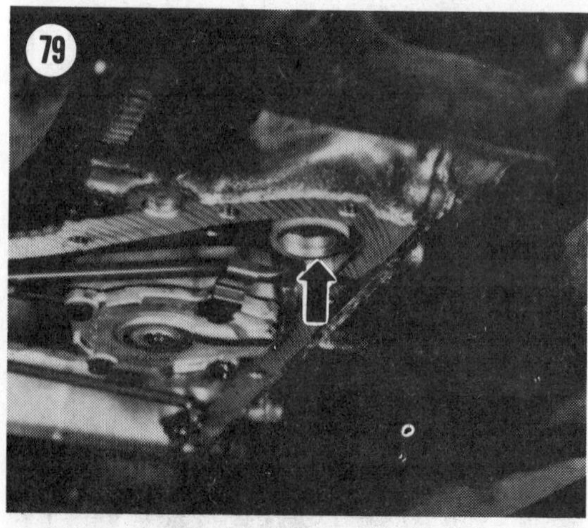

Carburetor Choke

Check the carburetor choke and vacuum break assemblies to make sure they are working properly. Correct any binding due to damage or gum buildup on the choke shaft. Inspect the hoses for cracking, kinking or deterioration.

100,000 MILE SERVICE

Automatic Transaxle Fluid Change

Under normal driving conditions, change the automatic transaxle fluid and filter every 100,000 miles. If the vehicle is used under any of the following conditions, change fluid every 15,000 miles:

a. Primarily heavy city traffic
b. Extended periods with outside temperature regularly at 90° F (32° C) or more
c. Very hilly or mountainous areas
d. Commercial use, e.g., delivery
e. Frequent trailer pulling

To change the fluid, you will need the following:

a. 4 quarts of DEXRON-II ATF
b. Funnel
c. Pour spout
d. New oil pan gasket and strainer

CAUTION

Do not remove sump if you must work outdoors. Cleanliness is very important when working with an automatic transaxle. Blowing dust can settle on internal transaxle parts and cause serious damage. Let your dealer or local repair shop change the oil if you do not have access to a clean garage.

1. Raise front end of car and secure with jackstands.
2. Place a container with at least a 1 1/2 gallon capacity under the transaxle.
3. Clean the oil pan of all oil and dirt (**Figure 76**).
4. Remove oil pan attaching bolts from side and front of oil pan.
5. Carefully pry transaxle oil pan to one side with a screwdriver, allowing fluid to drain. Do not damage the gasket mating surfaces (**Figure 77**).
6. When most of fluid has drained, remove oil pan from transaxle. Discard gasket.
7. Drain fluid trapped in oil pan. Clean oil pan with solvent and blow dry with compressed air.
8. Remove the strainer (filter) securing screw (**Figure 78**) and rotate the clamp away from the strainer. Pull the strainer down and remove. Discard the strainer and O-ring (**Figure 79**).
9. Install new O-ring (**Figure 79**) and strainer. Position clamp against strainer and install attaching screw (**Figure 78**).
10. Clean off all traces of old gasket from transaxle and oil pan.
11. Install oil pan with new gasket. Tighten pan bolts to 12 ft.-lb. (16 N•m).
12. Fill transaxle through the dipstick tube with 4 quarts (3.8 liters) of DEXRON-II automatic transmission fluid. Check fluid level with dipstick as described in this chapter.

Tables are on the following pages.

3

Table 1 SUMMARY OF PERIODIC MAINTENANCE

Interval	Service
Every 7,500 miles/6 months	•Change engine oil •Check transmission oil level •Check power steering fluid level •Inspect engine compartment •Inspect tires and wheels •Check front brake pad thickness •Check front brake fluid level •Lubricate parking brake •Lubricate hood latches •Check windshield wiper blades •Lubricate front suspension •Check clutch linkage •Inspect exhaust system
Every 15,000 miles/12 months	•Inspect and adjust drive belts •Service cooling system •Check rear brake lining thickness •Check brake pedal height •Fuel filter replacement
Every 30,000 miles/24 months	•Perform a complete engine tune-up •Check manual steering gear seal •Change coolant •Replace the air cleaner •Replace the PCV valve •Replace evaporative control canister filter •Replace catalytic converter catalyst (V6 only) •Change oxygen sensor (California only) •Check drive axle boots and output shaft seals
Every 45,000 miles	•Check vacuum fittings and hoses •Check carburetor choke
Every 100,000 miles	•Change the automatic transaxle fluid

Table 2 RECOMMENDED GRADES OF OIL

Oil Grade	Temperature Range
5W-20*, 5W-30	20° F and below
10W, 5W-30, 10W-30, 10W-40	0° to 60° F
20W-20, 10W-30, 10W-40, 20W-40, 20W-50	20° F and above

*If the vehicle is being operated at sustained highway speeds, the next heavier grade of oil should be used.

Table 3 LUBRICANT AND FUEL CAPACITIES

Item	Capacity
Engine oil	
4-cylinder	3.0 qt. (2.8 lit.)
V6	4.0 qt. (3.8 lit.)
Manual transaxle	3.0 qt. (1.5 lit.)
Automatic transaxle	5.0 qt. (4.6 lit.)
Fuel	14.0 U.S. gal. (53 lit.)

Table 4 RECOMMENDED LUBRICANTS

Item	Lubricant
Engine oil	API service SE
Brake fluid	DOT 3
Engine coolant	Ethylene Glycol type
Manual transaxle	ATF (DEXRON-II)
Automatic transaxle	ATF (DEXRON-II)
Power steering system	GM power steering fluid or equivalent
Manual steering gear	GM lubricant #1052182 or equivalent
Chassis lubrication	Chassis grease (GM specification #6031-M) or equivalent
Lock cylinders	WD-40 spray or equivalent
Clutch linkage	
Pivot points	Engine oil
Push rod to clutch fork joint	Chassis grease (GM specification #6031-M or equivalent)
Manual transaxle shift linkage	Chassis grease

Table 5 ENGINE TUNE-UP SPECIFICATIONS

Spark plug type	
4-cylinder	R43TSX
V6	R44TS
Spark plug gap	
4-cylinder	0.060 in. (1.52 mm)
V6	0.045 in. (1.15 mm)
Ignition timing	Varies with location; see Emission Control Sticker.
Idle speed	Varies with location and carburetor type; see Emission Control Sticker.

NOTE: If you own a 1981 or later model, first check the Supplement at the back of the book for any new service information.

CHAPTER FOUR

4

ENGINE (4-CYLINDER)

The standard engine is a 4-cylinder, inline, cast-iron, L-head type design. The engine is mounted transversely between the front driving wheels (see **Figure 1**). **Figure 2** shows a cross section of the engine.

This chapter covers removal and installation of the engine; removal and replacement of subassemblies; and inspection, adjustment and repair of some subassemblies and components. Although the illustrations usually show workbench operations, many single procedures, when not a part of a general overhaul, can be performed successfully with the engine in the vehicle.

Engine specifications are provided in **Table 1** and tightening torques in **Table 2**. Both are located at the end of the chapter.

SERVICE NOTES

WARNING

When working in the engine compartment, keep hands and other objects clear of the radiator fan blades. The fan can start automatically, whether or not the engine is running, due to the underhood temperature at the time of service.

ENGINE REMOVAL

1. Scribe alignment marks directly onto the underside of the hood around the hood hinges, then remove the hood. The alignment marks will ensure that the hood is properly installed and aligned later.

2. Disconnect the negative cable from the battery (**Figure 3**).
3. Drain the engine coolant and engine oil. Engine coolant may be reused if it has not been in the vehicle for more than 24 months and if the coolant is free of dirt and rust.
4. Disconnect the upper and lower radiator hoses at the radiator and the engine, then remove the hoses. Remove the heater hose also.

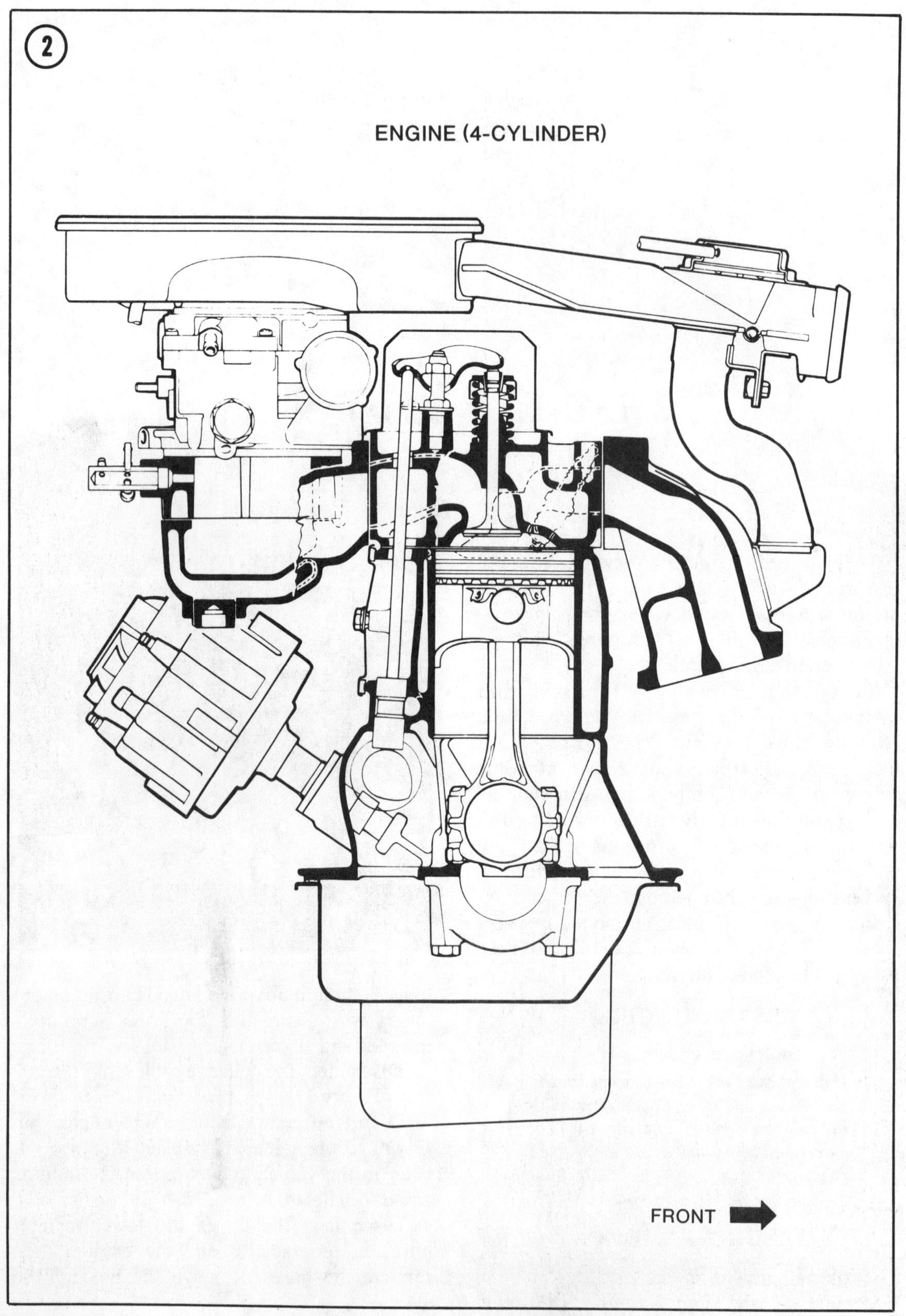
2
ENGINE (4-CYLINDER)
FRONT

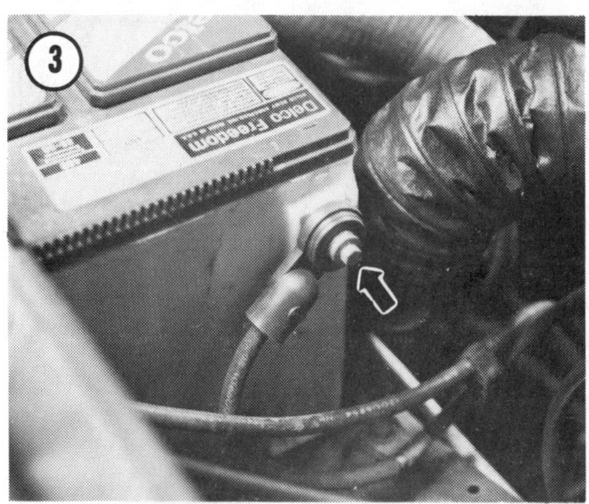

5. Remove the air cleaner. Refer to Chapter Six.

6. Disconnect the electrical wiring from the following items:

   a. Distributor
   b. Starter (**Figure 4**) and alternator (**Figure 5**)
   c. Engine temperature switch leads (**Figure 6**) and the fan switch lead (**Figure 7**) at the fan
   d. Oil pressure switch (1, **Figure 8**)
   e. Oil pressure transducer lead (2, **Figure 8**)
   f. Coil lead (3, **Figure 8**)
   g. Idle stop switch lead (4, **Figure 8**)

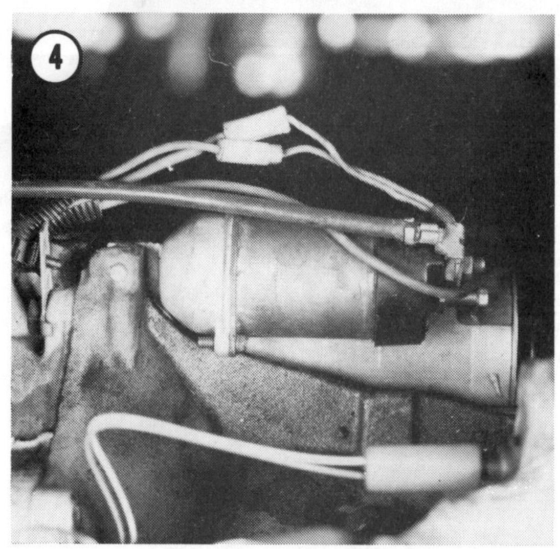

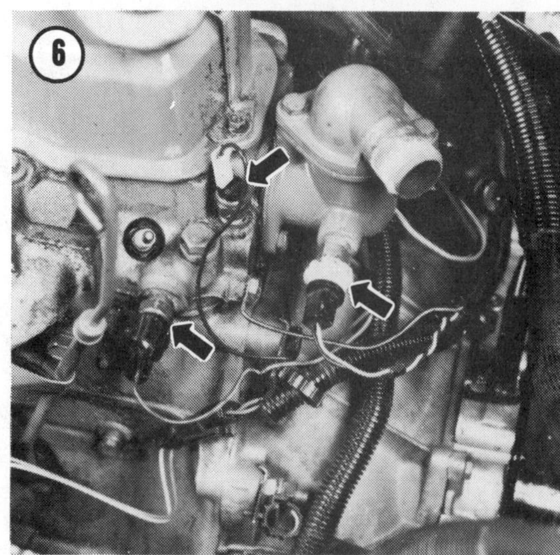

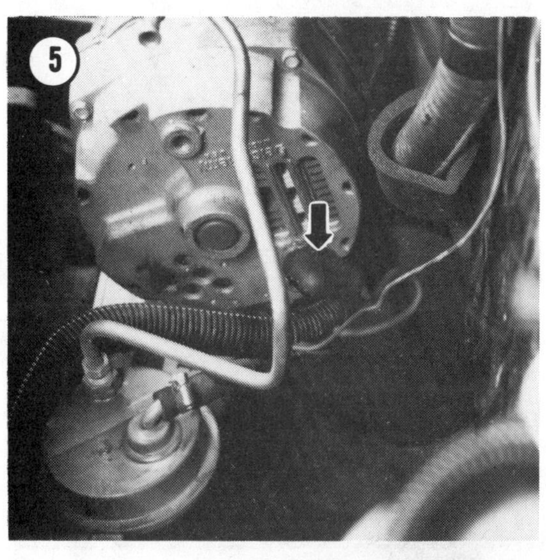

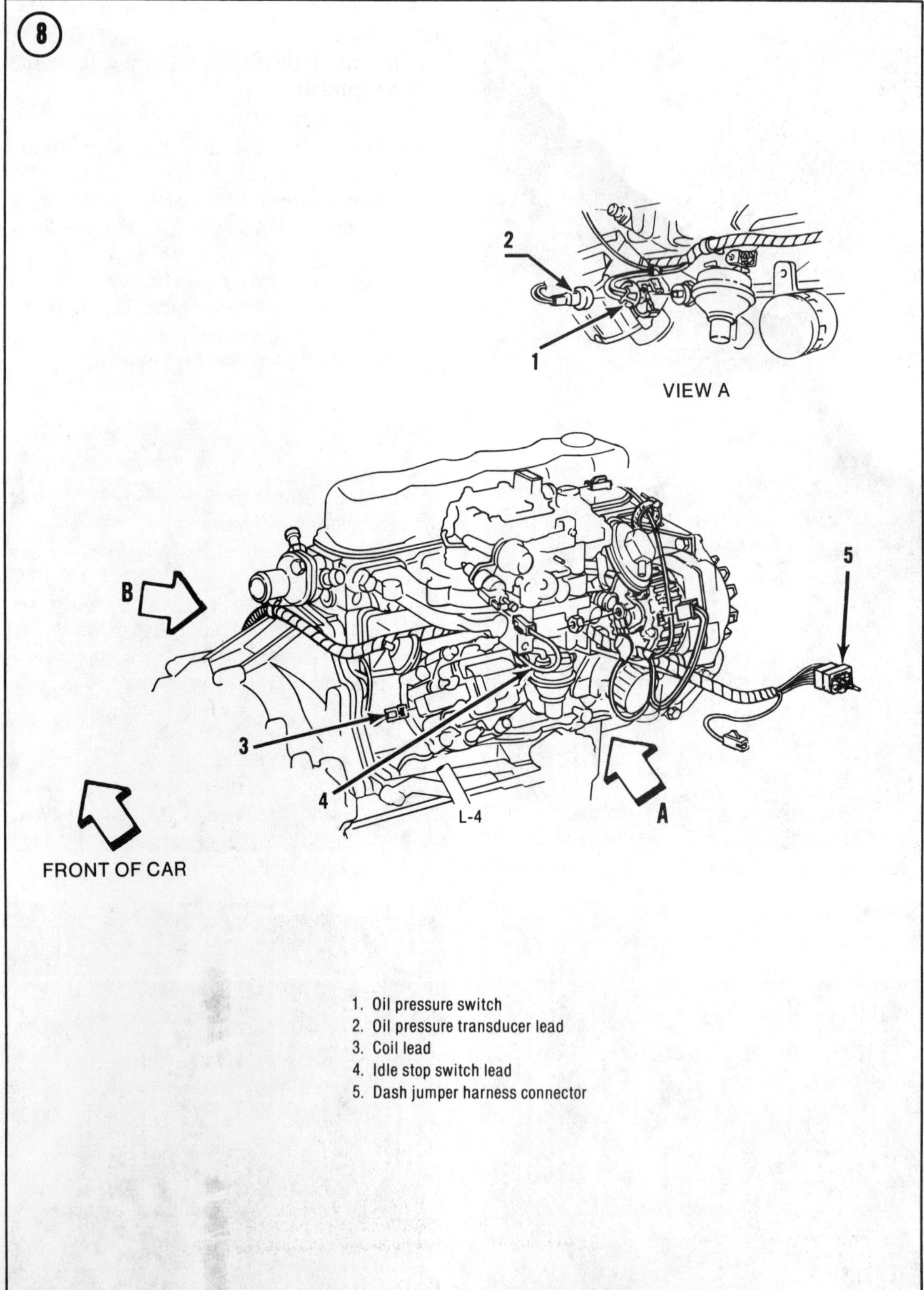
8
2
1
VIEW A
5
B
3
4
L-4
A
FRONT OF CAR
1. Oil pressure switch
2. Oil pressure transducer lead
3. Coil lead
4. Idle stop switch lead
5. Dash jumper harness connector

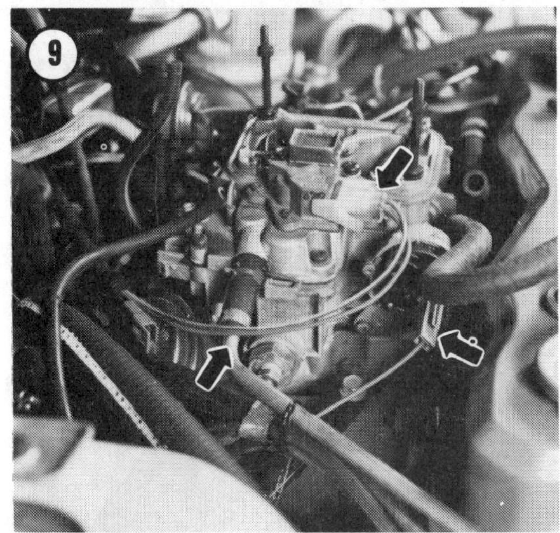

h. Dash harness jumper connector (5, **Figure 8**)
i. Electric choke and choke coil lever lead (**Figure 9**)

7. Label and disconnect all vacuum lines from the engine.
8. Disconnect the engine-to-body ground strap at the transaxle (**Figure 10**).

NOTE
For vehicles equipped with air conditioning, carefully read the air conditioning section in Chapter Seven to acquaint yourself with the system. Then, remove the compressor and position it out of the way. Do not disconnect the lines from the components. Make certain that there is no strain on any of the hoses or lines.

9. Remove throttle and transaxle linkage at the carburetor. See **Figure 11**.
10. Disconnect the fuel feed line (rubber fuel line) at the fuel pump. See **Figure 12**. Plug end of fuel line to prevent fuel leakage (**Figure 13**). The fuel pump is located on the rear of the engine under the intake manifold.
11. Raise vehicle front end and secure with jackstands. Remove the following items:
    a. Front exhaust pipe (Chapter Six)
    b. Starter (Chapter Eight)
    c. Flywheel inspection cover
    d. On automatic transaxle models, bolt attaching torque converter to flywheel (**Figure 14**)

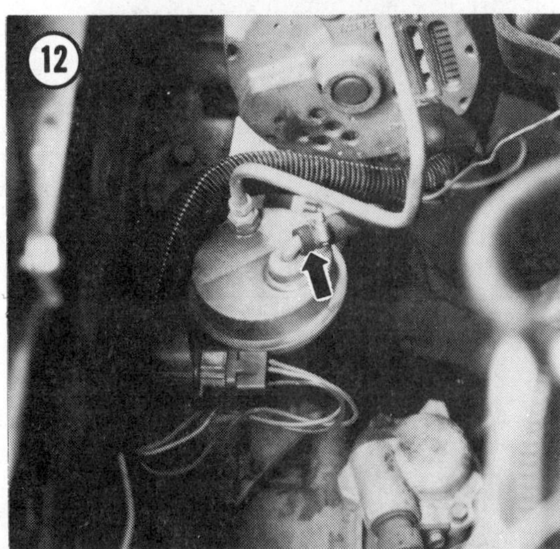

4

12. Lower vehicle and remove the power steering pump with hoses attached. See **Figure 15**. Set unit out of the way.
13. Remove the front engine strut assembly.
14. Remove bolts attaching engine to transaxle, leaving upper 2 bolts attached. See **Figure 16**.
15. Remove front engine mount to cradle nuts (**Figure 17**).
16. Remove the bolts that attach the rear transaxle support bracket to the engine assembly. See **Figure 18**.
17. Support the transaxle with a floorjack and block of wood. Raise engine and transaxle until front engine mount studs clear cradle.
18. Connect a lifting device to the engine lifting eyes (**Figure 19**) and lift engine just enough to allow removal of 2 remaining transaxle bolts (**Figure 16**).

CAUTION

Double check to make sure all electrical leads, vacuum lines and control links between the engine/transaxle assembly and the vehicle have been disconnected or removed. Check also to ensure that air conditioning lines, oil lines and wiring harness will not snag on the engine when it is removed.

19. Slide engine forward. Then raise the engine assembly with the lifting device and remove from the vehicle.
20. If an engine stand is available, mount engine on the stand. If a stand is not available, support the engine on wooden blocks.

ENGINE INSTALLATION

1. To install engine assembly, reverse *Engine Removal* Steps 1-20 noting the following precautions:
   a. Check the wire harness for damage and correct or replace as necessary.
   b. Check the engine mount (**Figure 20**) for looseness or damage and tighten or replace as necessary. Check the support bracket for cracks or damage and replace as necessary.
2. Refill the engine cooling system. See Chapter Seven.

3. Fill the engine crankcase with engine oil. See Chapter Three.
4. Start and let engine run at idle; check for leakage.
5. Adjust the following points by referring to appropriate section in Chapter Three:
   a. Drive belt tension
   b. Ignition timing
   c. Engine idle

DISASSEMBLY

The following sequences are basic outlines that tell how much of the engine needs to be removed and disassembled to perform specific

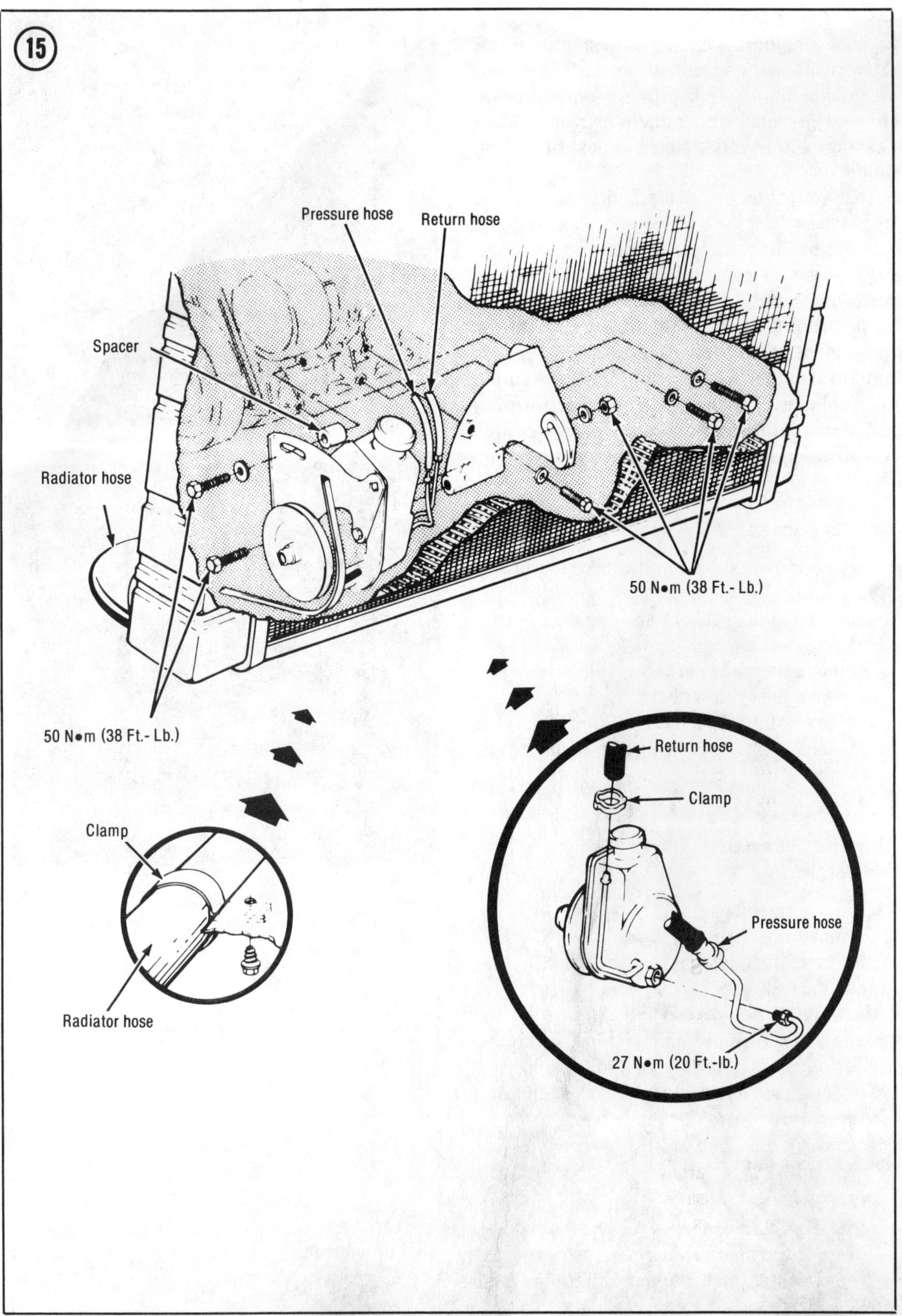
15
Pressure hose
Return hose
Spacer
Radiator hose
50 N•m (38 Ft.- Lb.)
50 N•m (38 Ft.- Lb.)
Return hose
Clamp
Pressure hose
27 N•m (20 Ft.-lb.)
Clamp
Radiator hose

types of service. The sequences are designed to keep engine disassembly to a minimum, thus avoiding unnecessary work. The major assemblies mentioned in these sequences are covered in detail under their own individual headings within this chapter, unless otherwise noted.

To use these sequences, first determine what type of engine service you plan to do (a valve job, for example), then turn to the sequences that cover that type of service. To perform a specific step within a sequence, turn to the heading covering the major assembly or component and the inspection procedures contained under that heading. To reassemble or install, reverse the sequences, performing the installation or assembly procedures contained under that major heading.

Decarbonizing or Valve Service

1. Remove the exhaust and intake manifolds (Chapter Six).
2. Remove the rocker arm and pushrod covers.
3. Remove the rocker arms and pushrods.
4. Remove the cylinder head.
5. Remove and inspect valves. Inspect valve guides and seats, repairing or replacing as necessary.
6. Assemble by reversing Steps 1-5.

Ring and Connecting Rod Service

1. Remove the oil pan.
2. Remove the oil pump.
3. Remove the pistons together with the connecting rods.
4. Remove the piston rings. It is not necessary to separate the pistons from the connecting rods unless a piston, connecting rod or piston pin needs repair or replacement.
5. Assemble by reversing Steps 1-4.

General Overhaul

1. Remove the engine from the car as described in this chapter.
2. Remove the motor mounts.
3. Remove the fuel pump, carburetor and intake and exhaust manifolds (Chapter Six).

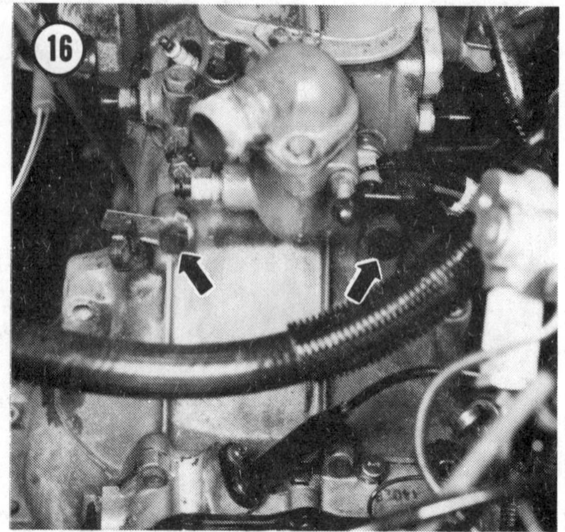

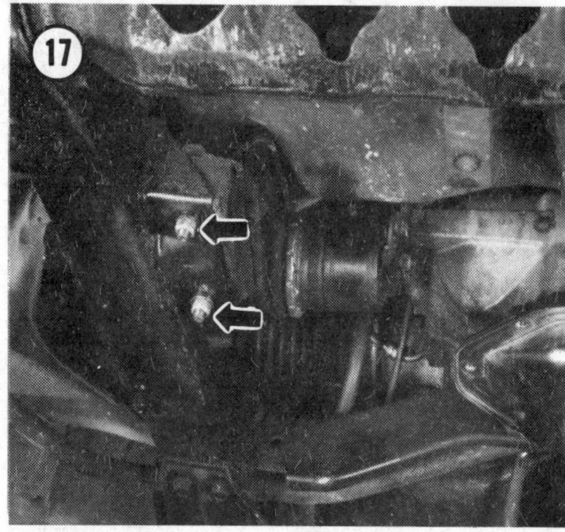

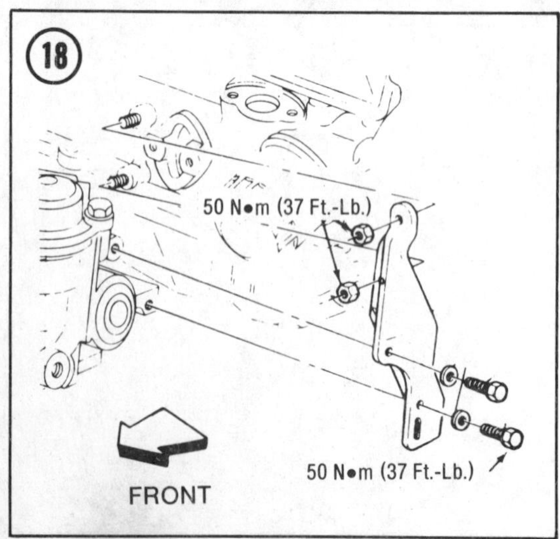

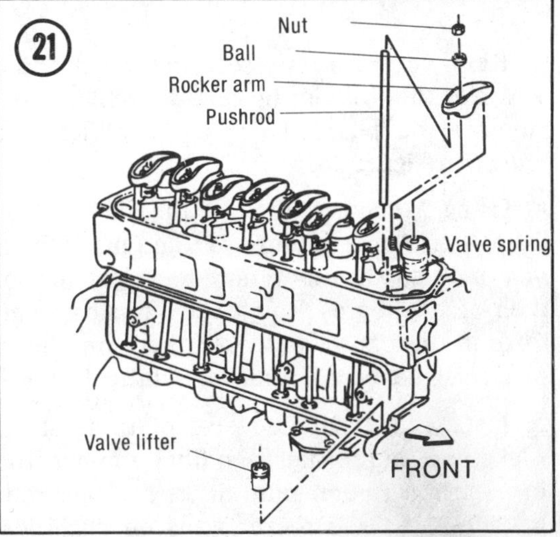

4. Remove the pulley, water pump and thermostat (Chapter Seven).
5. Remove the alternator and the distributor (Chapter Eight).
6. Remove the valve rocker assembly.
7. Remove the cylinder head.
8. Remove the engine timing cover.
9. Remove the oil pan.
10. Remove the oil pump.
11. Remove the camshaft.
12. Remove the pistons together with the connecting rods.
13. Remove the flywheel.
14. Remove the crankshaft and main bearings.
15. Inspect the cylinder block.
16. Assemble by reversing Steps 1-14.

ROCKER ASSEMBLY AND PUSHRODS

Rocker Arm/ Pushrod Removal

Figure 21 shows the rocker arm/pushrod assembly.

1. Remove the air cleaner (Chapter Six).
2. Remove the PCV valve and pulse air rubber hose from the pulse air unit (Chapter Six). Plug hose to prevent entry of dirt and other foreign material.
3. Disconnect the spark plug wires from the spark plugs and the wire looms and lay them back out of the way (Chapter Three).
4. Remove the rocker arm cover attaching bolts, then remove the rocker arm cover.

NOTE

If rocker arm cover is difficult to remove, tap side of cover with plastic hammer to help break RTV gasket seal. Do not pry cover off.

5. Loosen and remove the rocker arm nut and ball (**Figure 22**).
6. Remove the rocker arms. Label the rocker arms in order. The rocker arms must be reinstalled in the same position from which they were removed.
7. Lift the pushrods out of their bores. Make a holder to keep the pushrods in order (**Figure 23**). The pushrods must be reinstalled in the same bores from which they were removed.

NOTE

*If procedure requires removal of pushrods only, loosen the rocker arm nut and swing rocker arm to side. See **Figure 24**. Remove pushrod by lifting up through hole in cylinder head.*

Inspection

1. Clean all parts in solvent.
2. Check the pushrods for wear or damage, particularly at the ends. Check the pushrods for straightness by rolling on a piece of glass. A clicking sound will be heard if the pushrod is bent even slightly. Replace bent, worn or otherwise damaged pushrods.
3. Check the valve stem contact surface on the rocker arm for wear. Replace worn rocker arms. Do not attempt to smooth rocker arm contact surfaces.

Assembly

1. Remove the old RTV sealant from the rocker arm cover and cylinder head mating surfaces.
2. Install each pushrod through the bore in the cylinder head into its valve lifter seat. See **Figure 25**.
3. Install rocker arm together with its ball and nut. Tighten rocker arm nuts to 20 ft.-lb. (27 N•m).
4. Coat the sealing surface of the rocker arm cover with a 3/16 in. bead of RTV gasket sealant. See **Figure 26**.
5. Install the rocker arm cover and all attaching bolts. Tighten all rocker arm cover bolts to 7 ft.-lb. (10 N•m).
6. Install the spark plug wires, ensuring that the wires are properly routed through the wire looms.
7. Install the pulse air hose, PCV valve and air cleaner.
8. Start engine and check for leaks.

Hydraulic Lifter Replacement

1. Remove the intake manifold. See Chapter Six.
2. Remove the rocker arm cover. Loosen rocker arms and rotate to side, then remove the pushrods.

22

23

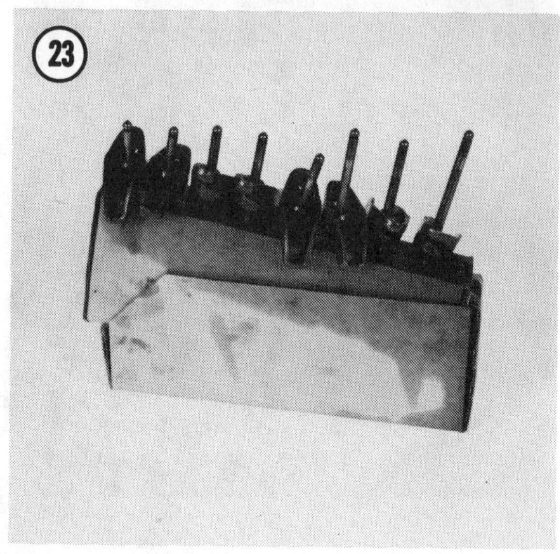

3. Remove the screws securing the pushrod cover to the cylinder block (**Figure 27**), then remove the pushrod cover. The lifters are shown in **Figure 28**.

4. Using a magnet, remove the valve lifters from their bores (**Figure 29**) and place them in a rack so that they may be reinstalled in their original bores. Rotate the lifters back and forth in their bores to loosen them from gum or varnish deposits if removal is difficult.

5. Installation is the reverse of these steps. Make sure to reinstall each lifter and pushrod in its original bore. With lifters and pushrods installed, position rocker arms on pushrods.

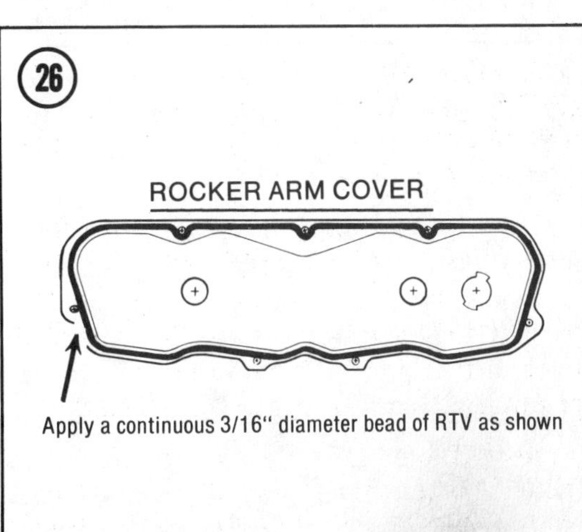
ROCKER ARM COVER
Apply a continuous 3/16" diameter bead of RTV as shown

Rotate the crankshaft with a wrench on the crankshaft pulley and position lifter on base circle of camshaft (**Figure 30**). Tighten the rocker arm nut to 20 ft.-lb. (27 N•m).

6. The pushrod screws have their cap top machined for the placement of O-rings. Remove and discard the old O-rings. Insert a new O-ring on each pushrod cover screw.
7. Coat the sealing surface of the pushrod cover with a 3/16 in. bead of RTV gasket sealant. See **Figure 31**.
8. Install the pushrod cover and all attaching screws. Tighten all pushrod cover screws to 75 in.-lb. (9 N•m).

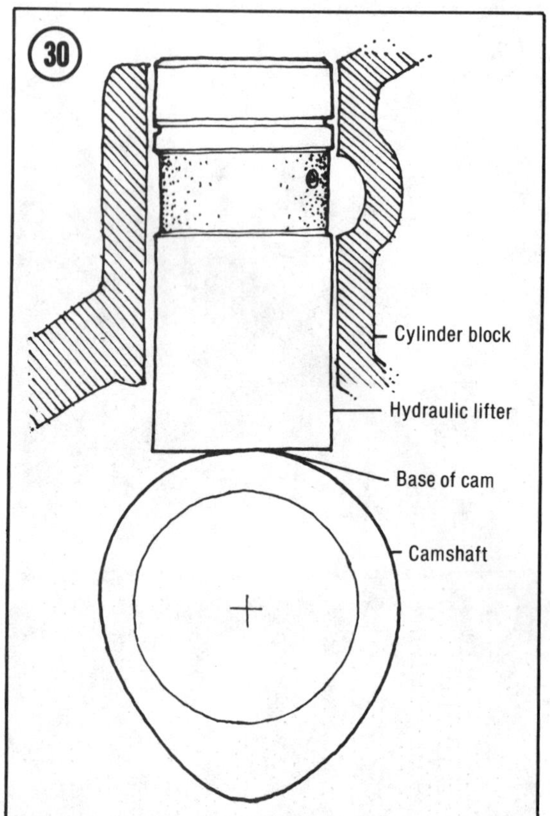

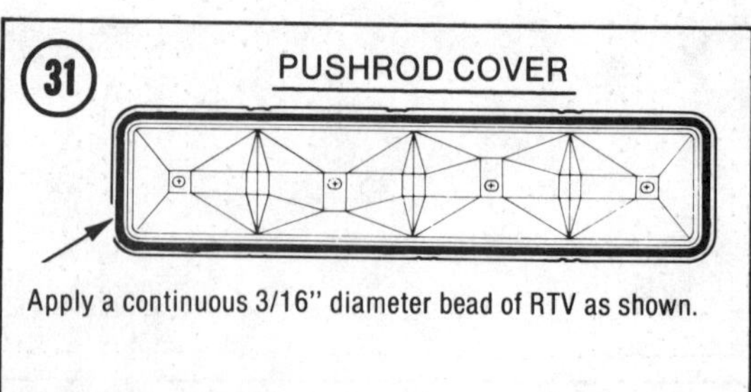

Apply a continuous 3/16" diameter bead of RTV as shown.

Inspection

The hydraulic lifter is assembled with a simple crimped retainer spring which snaps into a groove on the inside of the lifter body. This ring can be removed to permit cleaning of the adjuster parts (**Figure 32**). See **Figure 33** for an exploded view of the hydraulic valve lifter.

CAUTION

The valve lifter body and plunger are a matched set and cannot be interchanged with other lifter assemblies.

1. Disassemble each lifter and thoroughly clean all parts in solvent.

CAUTION

Because of close tolerances in which lifters are assembled, proper handling and cleanliness must be observed. When cleaning lifters, always use approved lubricant and a soft brush. Never use lubricant which has been used to clean other parts. Store lifters in a clean covered box until reinstallation.

2. Check the lifters for wear or scoring. Replace any lifters that show these conditions.
3. Check the bottom surface of each lifter to make sure it is not severely worn. If base of lifter is found to be heavily worn, examine mating camshaft lobe also. Replace parts which are severely worn.
4. After lifters have been cleaned and reassembled, each should be tested by a General Motors dealer for correct leak-down rate.

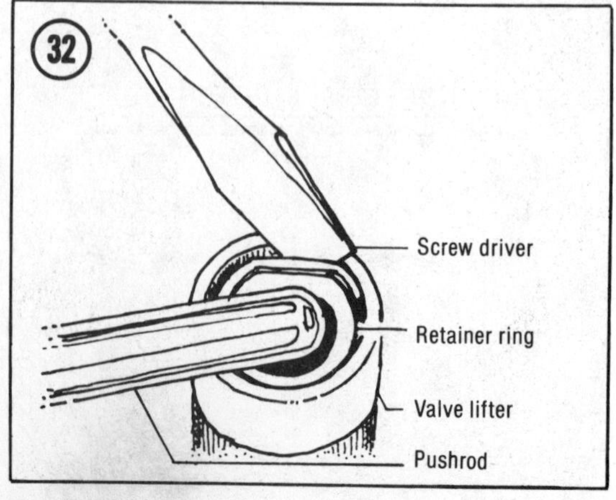

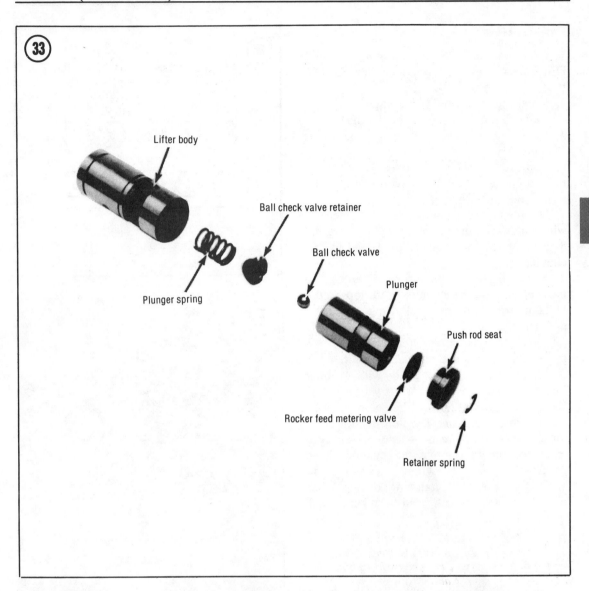

33

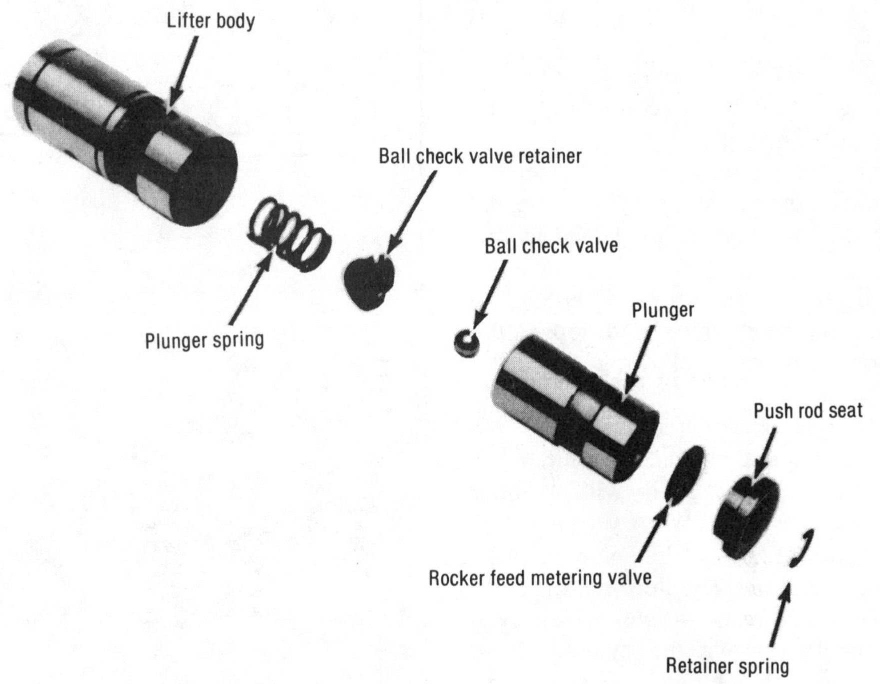

Lifter body
Ball check valve retainer
Ball check valve
Plunger
Plunger spring
Push rod seat
Rocker feed metering valve
Retainer spring

CYLINDER HEAD

Some of the following procedures must be done by a dealer or machine shop, since they require special knowledge and expensive machine tools. Others, while possible for the home mechanic, are difficult and time-consuming. A general practice among those who do their own service is to remove the cylinder head, perform all disassembly except valve removal and take the head to a machine shop for inspection and service. Since the cost is low in relation to the required effort and equipment, this is usually the best approach, even for more experienced owners.

Cylinder Head Removal

1. Completely drain the cooling system. Disconnect the upper radiator hose at the thermostat (**Figure 34**).
2. Label and remove all spark plugs.
3. Remove the air cleaner (Chapter Six).
4. Remove the intake and exhaust manifolds (Chapter Six).
5. Remove the rocker arm cover.
6. Loosen air conditioner compressor and swing aside. See Chapter Seven.
7. Disconnect all vacuum lines and electrical wiring necessary to remove the cylinder head.
8. Remove the pushrods as explained in this chapter.
9. Remove the cylinder head bolts. To prevent warping the cylinder head, loosen the bolts in several stages, following the order given in **Figure 35**.
10. Once the bolts are removed, lift the cylinder head off the engine. If the head is difficult to remove, tap it gently with a rubber mallet. If that does not work, try reinstalling the spark plugs and turning the engine over by hand. The compression should force the head loose. Once the cylinder head is removed from the block, remove the cylinder head gasket, then place the cylinder head on a soft surface to prevent scratching or otherwise damaging the cylinder head-to-engine block mating surface.

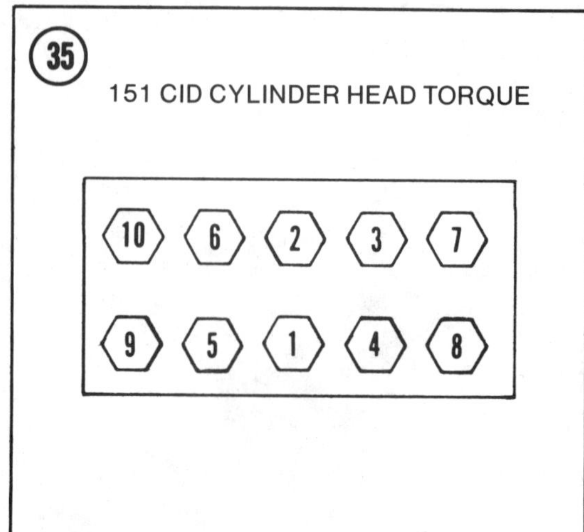

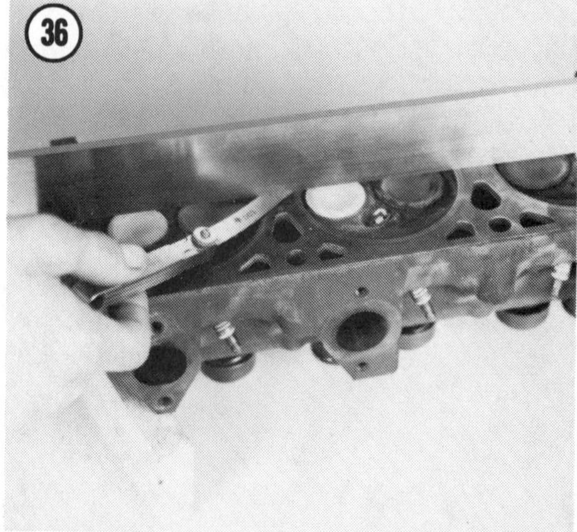

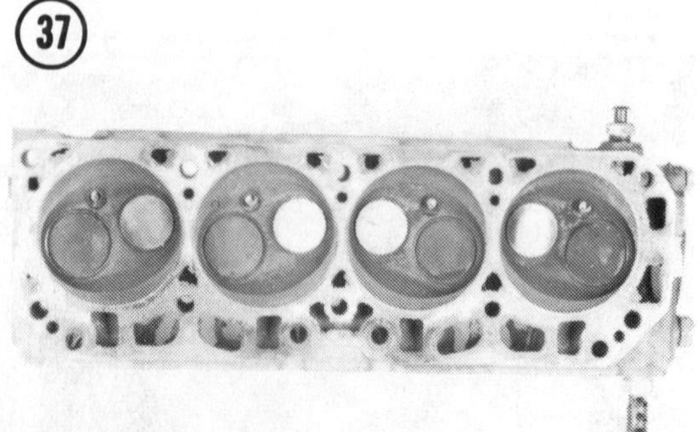

Inspection

1. Check the cylinder head for water leaks before cleaning.
2. Clean the cylinder head thoroughly in solvent. While cleaning, check for cracks in exhaust ports, combustion chambers or water chambers or other visible damage. Look for corrosion or foreign material in oil or water passages. Clean the passages with a stiff spiral brush, then blow them out with compressed air.
3. Check the cylinder head bottom (block mating) surface for flatness. Place an accurate straightedge along the surface. If there is any gap between the straightedge and cylinder head surface, measure it with a feeler gauge (**Figure 36**). Have the cylinder head

resurfaced by a machine shop if the gap exceeds 0.004 in. (0.102 mm).

Decarbonizing

1. Without removing the valves, remove all deposits from the combustion chambers, intake ports and exhaust ports. Use a wire brush dipped in solvent or make a scraper out of hardwood. Be careful not to scratch or gouge the combustion chambers (**Figure 37**).
2. After all carbon is removed from the combustion chambers and ports, clean the entire head in solvent.
3. Clean away all carbon on the piston tops. Do not remove the carbon ridge at the top of the cylinder bore.

Cylinder Head Installation

1. Clean the cylinder head mating surfaces and the engine block, intake manifold and valve rocker arm cover surfaces to which the cylinder head mounts. Be sure that the cylinder bores are clean and check all visible oil and water passages for cleanliness.
2. Clean each cylinder head bolt of sealant and any traces of oil or dirt. Bolts which have unclean threads cannot be torqued correctly and will eventually loosen and cause cylinder head-to-block leakage.

NOTE
Make sure that the cylinder head bolt holes in the block are clean and free of any debris or other foreign material. If they are not clean, it is possible for the cylinder head bolt to bottom on the foreign material. Under such conditions, the bolt cannot be torqued correctly.

NOTE
Return any dowel pin from the cylinder head back to its position in the cylinder block (cylinder head mating surface) to help in aligning the cylinder head gasket.

3. Install a new cylinder head gasket. Make sure the gasket is placed correctly over the dowel pins and does not cover up any fluid transfer holes. Never reuse an old head gasket. *Do not* use gasket sealer on the head gasket. Position the cylinder head onto the block.
4. Apply sealer (GM part No. 1052080 or equivalent) onto the threads of the two 18 mm bolts shown in **Figure 38**. Install these along with the remaining head bolts.
5. With the engine cool, tighten the head bolts in the order given in **Figure 35**. Tighten bolts gradually to final torque.
6. Clean the pushrods in solvent. Check ends of the pushrods for nicks, grooves, roughness or excessive wear. Check all pushrods for straightness as described under *Rocker Assembly, Inspection.*
7. The remainder of the installation procedure is accomplished by performing Steps 1-8 of the *Cylinder Head Removal* procedure in reverse order. After installation is complete run the engine for several minutes, let it cool, then recheck head bolt tightness.
8. Perform the tune-up as described in Chapter Three.

VALVES AND VALVE SEATS

Valve Removal

NOTE
Label all parts so they can be reinstalled in the same location from which they were removed.

1. Remove cylinder head as described in this chapter.

2. Compress each valve spring with a valve spring compressor as shown in **Figure 39**. Remove the valve keepers (**Figure 40**) and release the spring tension. Remove spring retainers, spring shield, springs and dampers. Remove the oil seal from end of valve as shown in **Figure 41**. **Figure 42** shows valve and related parts.

CAUTION

*Remove any burrs from the valve stem (**Figure 43**) before removing valves. Otherwise, the valve guides will be damaged.*

3. Remove the valves through the combustion chamber.

Valve and Valve Guide Inspection

1. Clean the valves with a wire brush and solvent. Discard cracked, warped or burned valves.
2. Measure the valve stems at the bottom, center and top for wear, using a micrometer. A machine shop can do this when the valves are ground. Also measure the length of each valve and the diameter of each valve head. **Figure 44** shows dimensions for valves.

NOTE

When measuring valves, take into account that exhaust valves have tapered stems and are 0.001 in. (0.025 mm) larger at top of stem than at head end.

3. The valve faces and stem ends should be refaced when the valves are ground.
4. Remove all carbon and varnish from valve guides with a stiff spiral wire brush or similar valve guide cleaning tool (**Figure 45**).

NOTE

The next step assumes that all valves have been measured and are within specifications. Replace any valves with worn stems before performing this step.

5. Insert each valve into the guide from which it was removed. Hold valve just slightly off its seat and rock it sideways. See **Figure 46**. If the valve rocks more than slightly, the valve guide is worn and should be reamed for an oversize valve stem as described in this chapter.

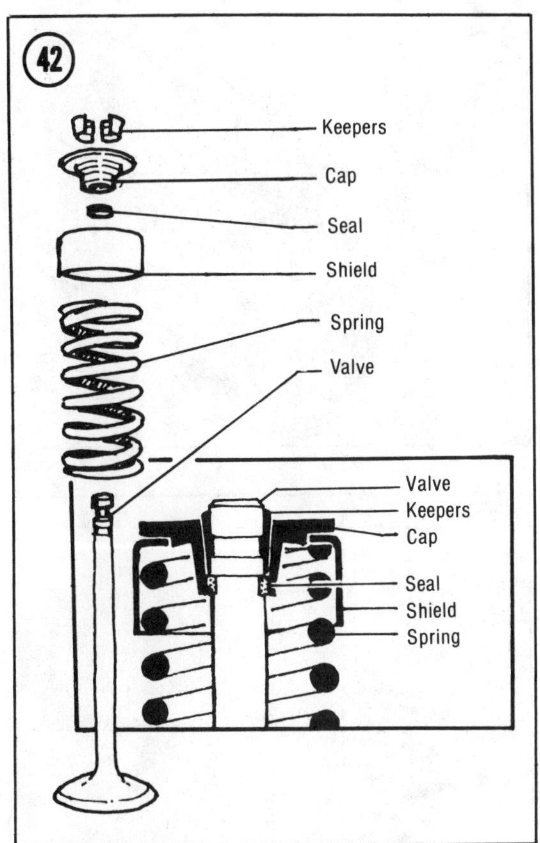

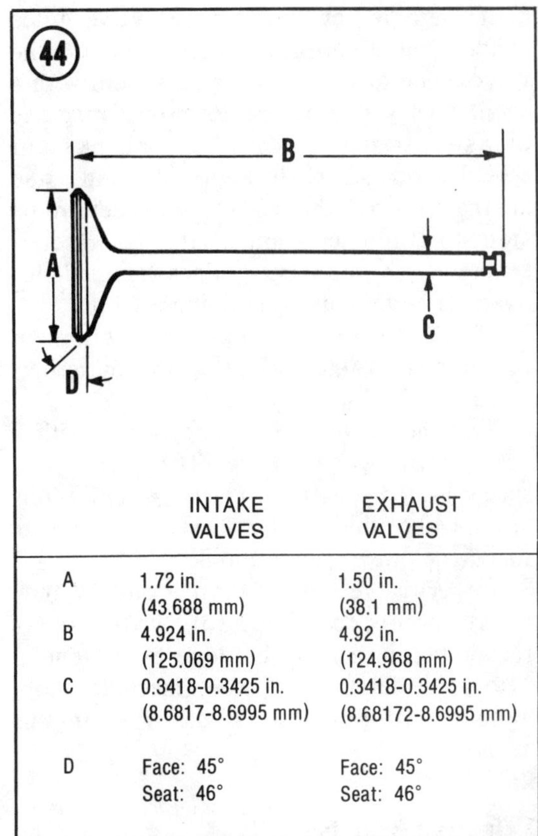

	INTAKE VALVES	EXHAUST VALVES
A	1.72 in. (43.688 mm)	1.50 in. (38.1 mm)
B	4.924 in. (125.069 mm)	4.92 in. (124.968 mm)
C	0.3418-0.3425 in. (8.6817-8.6995 mm)	0.3418-0.3425 in. (8.68172-8.6995 mm)
D	Face: 45° Seat: 46°	Face: 45° Seat: 46°

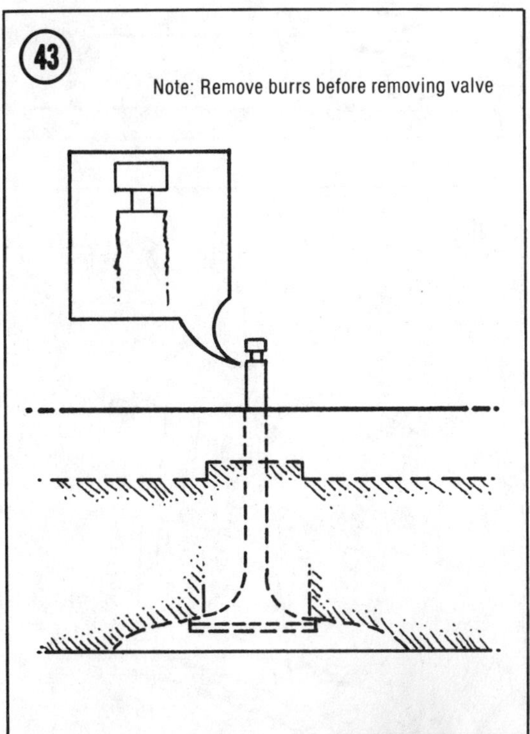

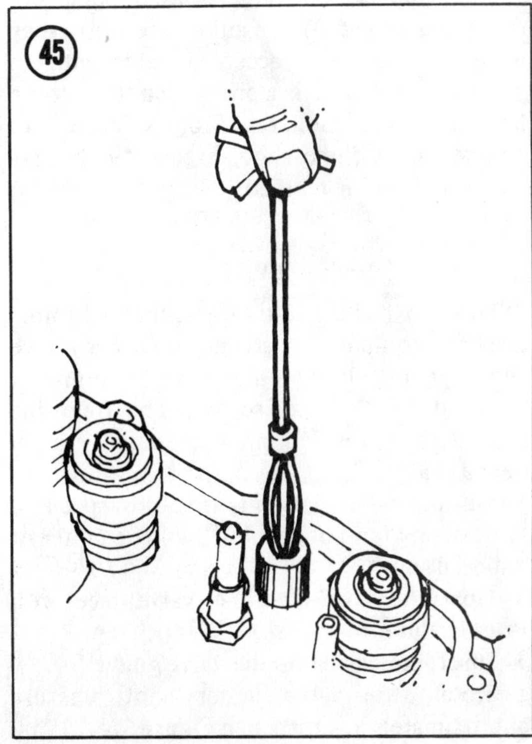

6. If there is any doubt about valve guide condition after perforning Step 5, measure the valve guide at top, center and bottom with a small hole gauge. Compare the valve guide measurements with the valve stem specifications shown in **Figure 44**, and listed at the end of this chapter, to determine stem-to-guide clearance. If clearance is excessive, have valve guides reamed for oversize valve stems by a machine shop.
7. Check the valve springs for deformation with a square (**Figure 47**). Replace any springs more than 1/16 in. out of square.
8. Test the valve springs under load with a spring tester (**Figure 48**). Compare spring loaded lengths with the specifications at the end of this chapter. Replace any springs that do not meet specifications.
9. Inspect valve seats. If worn or burned, they must be reconditioned. Valve seat reconditioning should be done by a General Motors dealer or competent machine shop, although the procedure is described in this section.

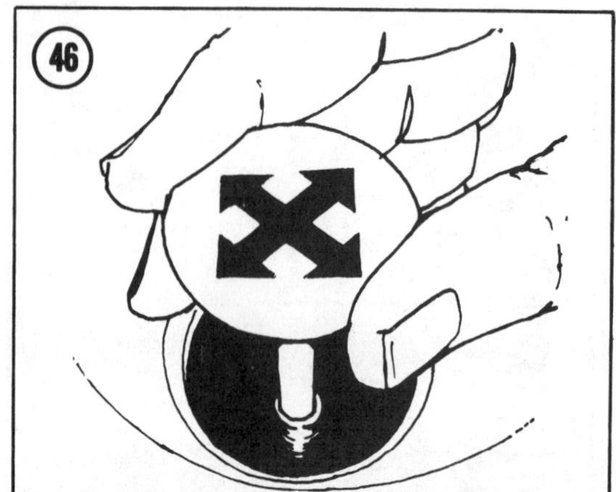

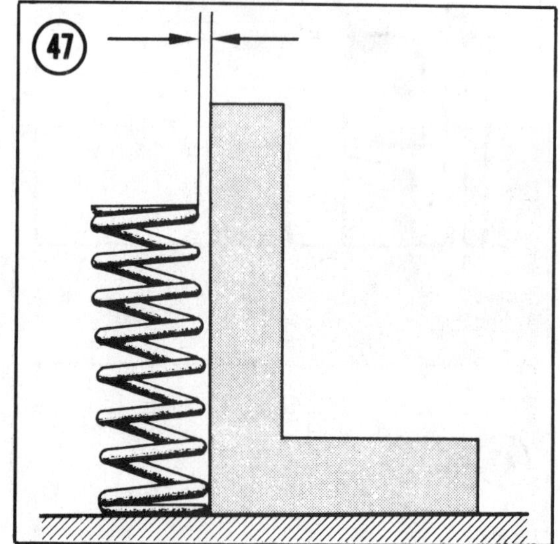

Valve Seat Reaming

Valve guides on all engines are integral with the cylinder head. When guides are worn, they must be reamed to accept a valve with an oversize stem. This is a precise job that should be left to a General Motors dealer or competent machine shop. **Figure 49** shows a valve guide being reamed.

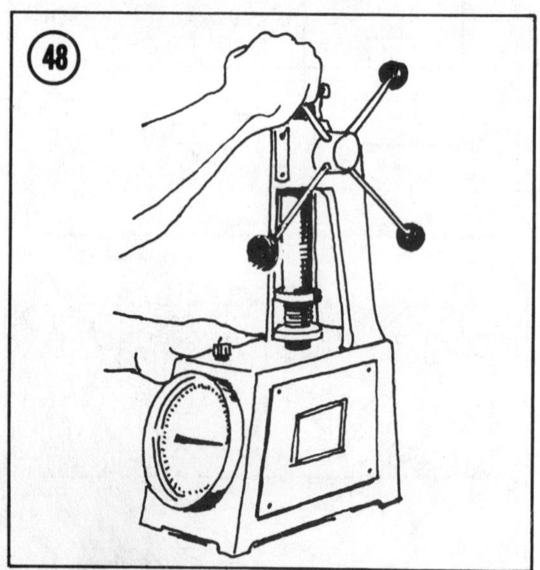

Valve Seat Reconditioning

This job is best left to a General Motors dealer or competent machine shop. They have the special knowledge and equipment required for this precise job. The following procedure is provided in the event you are not near a dealer.

1. Cut the valve seats (**Figure 50**) to specified dimensions (end of chapter), using a cutter or a special stone.
2. Coat the corresponding valve face with Prussian blue.
3. Insert the valve into the valve guide.
4. Rotate the valve under light pressure approximately 1/4 turn. See **Figure 51**.

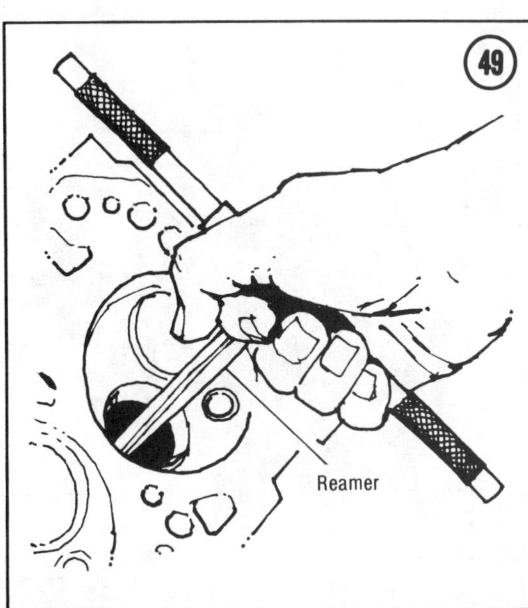

5. Lift the valve out. If it seats properly, the dye will transfer evenly to the valve face.

Valve Installation

1. Coat the valves with oil and insert them in the cylinder head.
2. Install a new oil seal in the lower groove of the valve stem (**Figure 41**).
3. Install the valve spring, damper, shield and retainer in place. Compress the valve with a valve spring compressor (**Figure 39**); ensure that the oil seal is installed flat and not twisted. Install the valve keepers in the upper groove of the valve stem (**Figure 40**) and release the valve spring. Make sure the valve keepers are installed correctly in the valve groove as shown in **Figure 52**.

4

FRONT COVER, FRONT OIL SEAL AND TIMING GEAR

Front Cover Removal

Figure 53 shows the front cover assembly.

1. Remove the drive belts (Chapter Seven).
2. Jack up the vehicle's front end and secure with jackstands. Remove the right front wheel. From inside the wheel well, remove the right front inner splash shield attaching bolts and remove the shield. **Figure 54** shows the crankshaft pulley bolt with the shield removed.

3. Remove the crankshaft pulley attaching bolt, then slide the pulley off the end of shaft. Remove the pulley hub also. If tight, the pulley hub can be removed with a universal gear puller as shown in **Figure 55**.

4. Remove the alternator (Chapter Eight).
5. Remove the alternator lower mounting bracket from the left side of the front cover. See **Figure 53**.
6. Remove the bolts attaching the front engine mount to the frame cradle (**Figure 17**).
7. Install suitable lifting hoist to engine lifting eyes (**Figure 19**) and lift engine slightly to remove weight from engine support bracket bolts.
8. Remove bolts securing the engine support bracket to the cylinder block, then remove the support bracket and engine mount. See **Figure 18**.
9. Remove the front cover-to-oil pan attaching bolts. Note that reinforcement tabs are located at each corner of the oil pan. Remove these also. See **Figure 56**.
10. Withdraw the front cover forward slightly, then cut the oil pan front seal flush with the cylinder block at both sides of the timing cover using a thin-bladed knife. See **Figure 57**.
11. Remove all remaining front cover attaching bolts. If necessary, tap the cover lightly with a plastic hammer to break the gasket seal, then remove the front cover, gasket and the attached portion of the oil pan front seal.

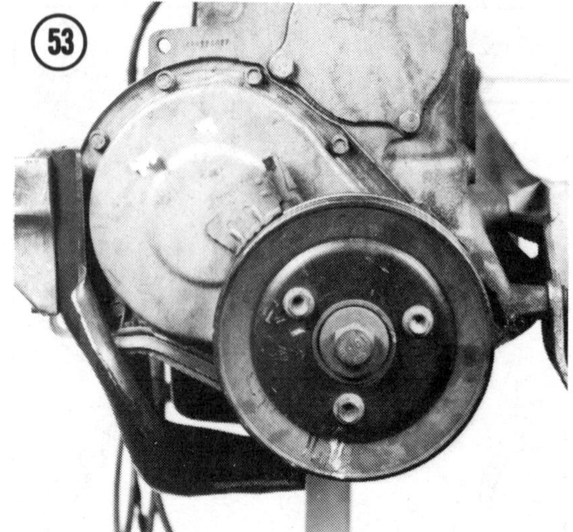
53

54

Front Cover Installation

1. Clean gasket material from all mating surfaces.
2. Use a new oil pan front seal and cut to shape as shown in **Figure 58**. When cutting seal, use a sharp tool to ensure a clean cut.
3. Install the oil pan seal to the front cover, pressing seal tips into holes provided in timing cover.
4. Install a new front cover oil seal as described in the next procedure. This should be done whenever the front cover is removed.
5. Apply sealing compound to the front cover gasket and the back side of the front cover plate, then place the gasket on the front cover plate.
6. Apply RTV sealing compound to the joint formed at the cylinder block and oil pan (**Figure 59**).
7. Install the front cover on the engine and start all retaining screws 2-3 turns. Center the front cover by inserting GM centering tool part No. J-23042 into the front cover opening (**Figure 60**). Tighten front cover attaching bolts to specification listed at the end of this chapter. Remove centering tool.

CAUTION

If the centering tool is not used, it is likely the timing cover will not be aligned correctly and the seal could be damaged by the misalignment of the pulley hub.

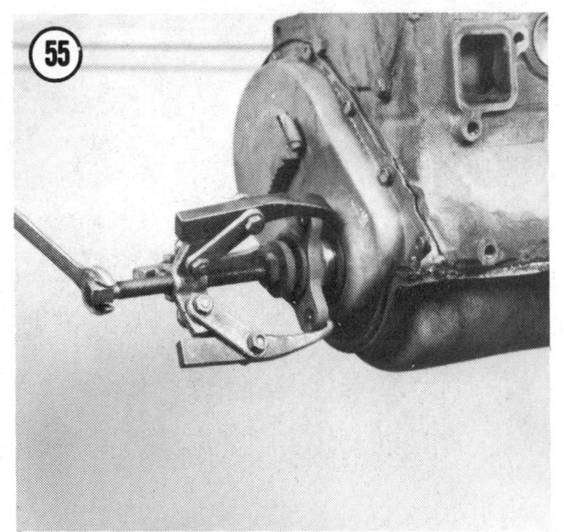
55

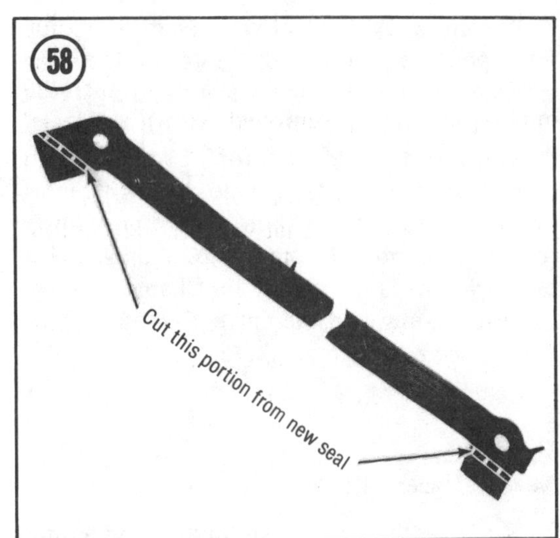
58
Cut this portion from new seal

56

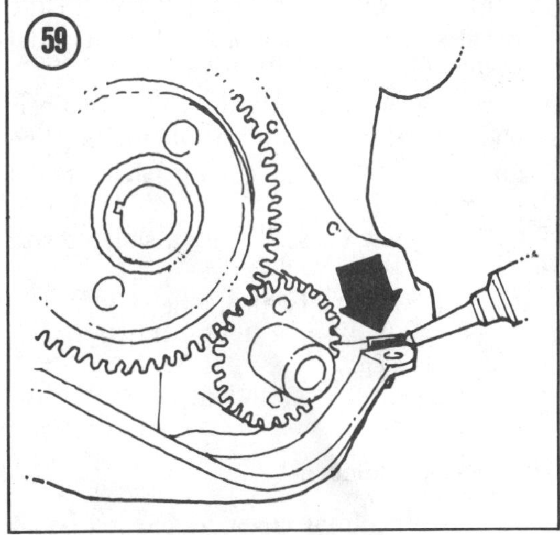
59

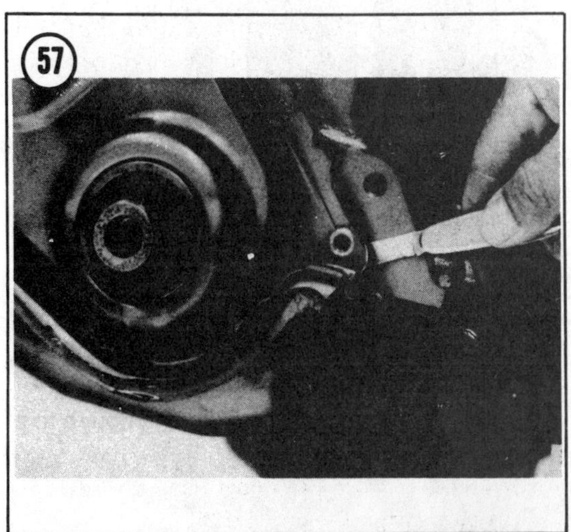
57

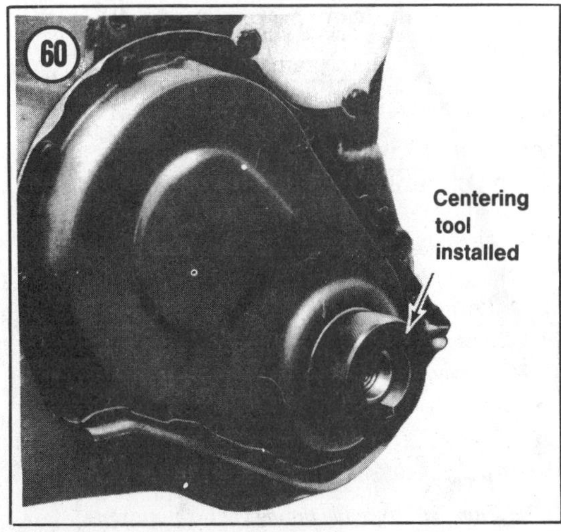
60
Centering tool installed

8. Install pulley hub on crankshaft and slide into position until hub rests against the crankshaft gear. Tighten attaching bolt (**Figure 61**) to 160 ft.-lb. (212 N•m).

9. Install the alternator bracket and alternator, drive belts, engine mount support bracket and any other parts previously removed to provide clearance. Adjust drive belt tension as described in Chapter Three. Fill the engine with the correct amount of oil as described in Chapter Three.

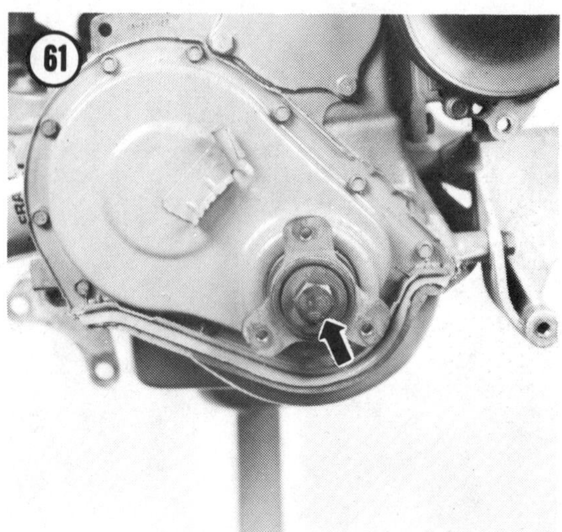

Front Oil Seal Replacement

1. Remove the crankshaft pulley and pulley hub as described under *Front Cover Removal.*
2. With a punch, knock a small hole in the front oil seal. Then install a small sheet metal screw into the hole.
3. Grasping the sheet metal screw with a pair of pliers, carefully pry out the old oil seal. See **Figure 62**. Do not gouge the sheet metal front cover.
4. Tap in a new oil seal using a suitable size drift.
5. Coat the oil seal lip with engine oil.
6. Install the pulley hub and crankshaft pulley as described earlier.

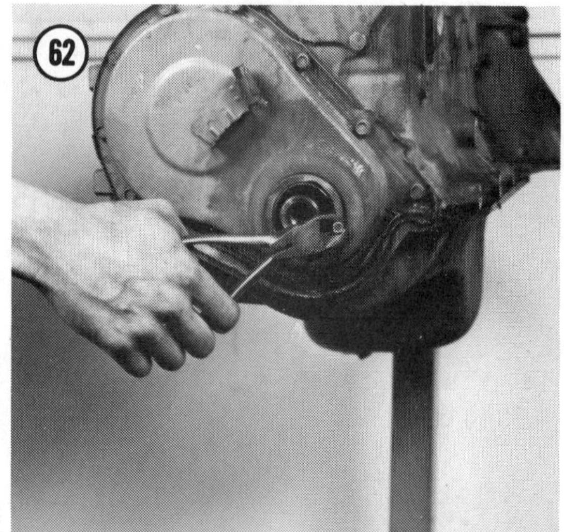

Timing Gear Removal

1. Remove the front cover to gain access to the timing gears. See **Figure 63**.
2. Remove the camshaft as described in this chapter.
3. Place the timing gear and camshaft assembly in a suitable arbor press, and support as shown in **Figure 64**. Then press timing gear off end of camshaft.

CAUTION
Position thrust plate so that Woodruff key does not damage camshaft when gear is pressed off shaft.

NOTE
Prepare suitable means to catch the camshaft once the timing gear is removed.

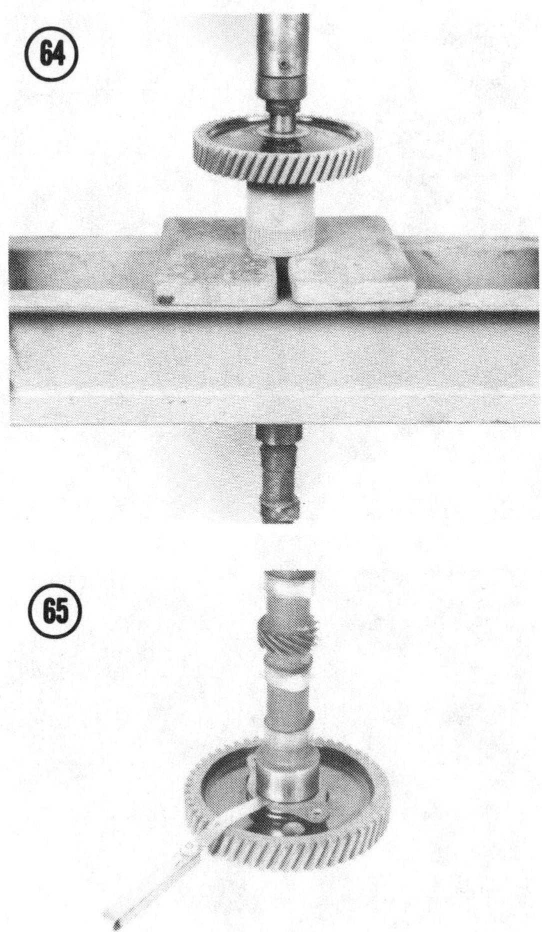

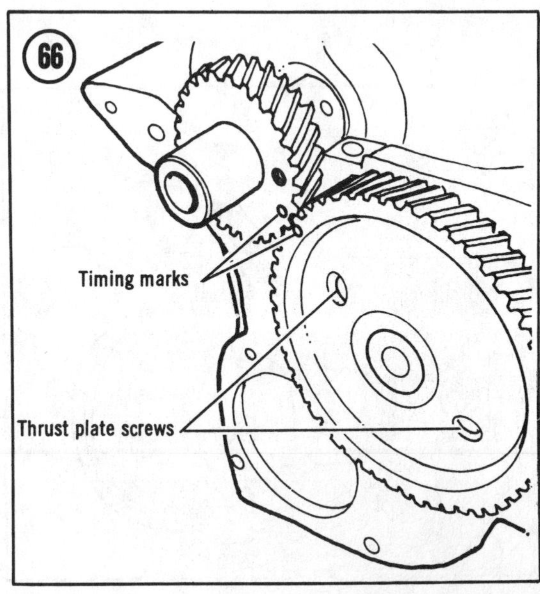

Timing Gear Installation

1. Install camshaft in arbor press and support at back of front journal.
2. Install the gear spacer ring and thrust plate over end of camshaft, then place Woodruff key in the camshaft (if removed previously).
3. Align the keyway in the camshaft sprocket with the key in the camshaft. Press sprocket onto camshaft until it bottoms against the gear spacer ring. Refer to **Figure 65** and measure camshaft end play clearance with feeler gauge. End clearance should be between 0.0015-0.0050 in. (0.0381-0.127 mm). If clearance is less than 0.0015 in. (0.0381 mm) replace the spacer ring. If clearance is more than 0.0050 in. (0.127 mm), replace the thrust plate.
4. Install the camshaft as described in this chapter.
5. Install the front cover and accessory equipment as described under *Front Cover Installation.*

CAMSHAFT

Removal/Installation

1. Remove the engine as described in this chapter.
2. Remove the rocker arm cover and pushrods as described in this chapter.
3. Remove the distributor (Chapter Eight).
4. Remove the fuel pump (Chapter Six).
5. Remove the pushrod cover and hydraulic valve lifters as described in this chapter.
6. Remove the alternator, lower alternator bracket and front engine mount bracket assembly as described in Chapter Eight.
7. Remove the oil pump drive shaft and gear assembly as described under *Oil Pump Removal* in this chapter.
8. Remove the crankshaft pulley hub and timing gear cover as explained under *Front Cover Removal.*
9. Align holes in camshaft timing gear with thrust plate attaching screws, then remove screws. See **Figure 66**.
10. Carefully remove the camshaft and timing gear from the bearings through front of engine block. Rotate the camshaft while removing.

4

Do not let the cam lobes touch or nick the bearings.

11. If timing gear must be removed from camshaft, follow procedures under *Timing Gear Removal* in this chapter.

12. Check camshaft end play as explained under *Timing Gear Installation.*

Camshaft Inspection

The following procedures require precision measuring tools. If you don't have them, have the inspection done by an automotive machine shop.

1. Check all machined surfaces of the camshaft for nicks or grooves. Minor defects may be removed with a smooth oilstone. Severe damage or wear beyond the specifications, listed at the end of this chapter, requires replacement of the camshaft.

2. Measure the inner diameter of the camshaft bearings, being careful not to damage the bearing material. **Figure 67** shows the 3 camshaft bearings. Compare this measurement with the specifications listed at the end of this chapter. If the bearings are excessively worn, grooved, pitted or scored, take the engine block to an automotive machine shop and have the bearings replaced.

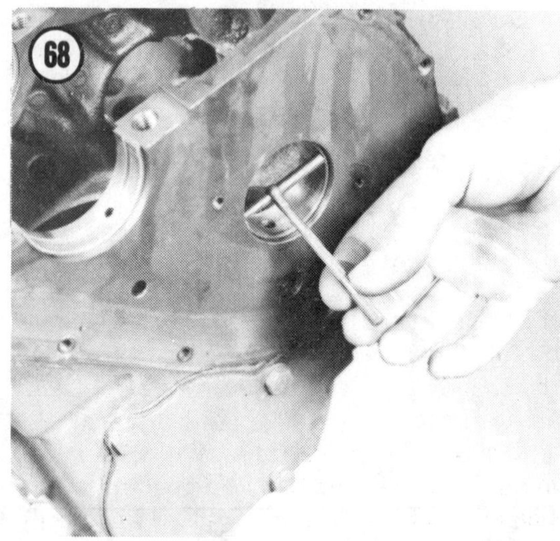

NOTE

*If the crankshaft is removed as shown in **Figure 67**, the camshaft bearings can be measured with a telescoping gauge as shown in **Figure 68**. However, if the crankshaft has not been removed, it will be necessary to have an automotive machine shop equipped with a special measuring device measure the camshaft bearings.*

CAUTION

All camshaft bearings should be replaced, even if only one bearing is worn. Otherwise, the camshaft may be out of alignment when reinstalled.

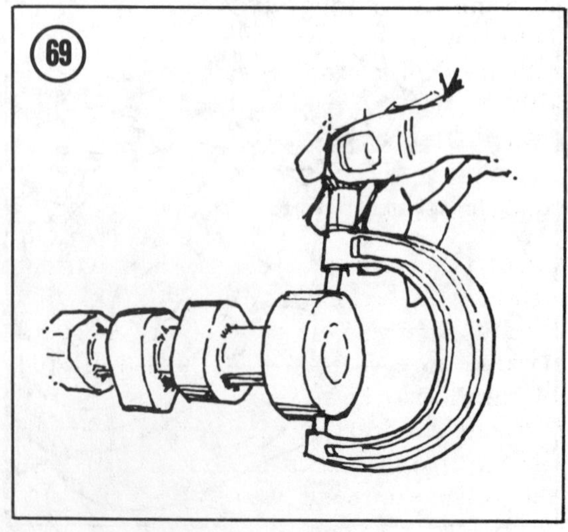

3. Measure the outer diameter of the camshaft journals (**Figure 69**). Compare this measurement with the specifications listed at the end of this chapter. Replace the camshaft

if the journals exceed the wear or out-of-round specification listed at the end of this chapter.

4. Subtract the journal diameter measurement from the bearing diameter measurement to determine the bearing- to-journal clearance. If this clearance exceeds the specifications listed at the end of this chapter, either the camshaft bearings or the camshaft (or both) is worn and must be replaced. Compare both the journal and bearing measurements with the nominal values to determine which must be replaced.

Camshaft Installation

1. Coat the camshaft journals and bearing surfaces with clean engine oil.
2. Carefully install the camshaft in the engine block. Rotate the camshaft slowly while inserting to ease installation.
3. Rotate camshaft and crankshaft timing gears so that the valve timing marks on gear teeth will line up. See **Figure 66**.
4. Install the thrust plate bolts through the holes in the camshaft gear and through the thrust plate. Tighten to 75 in.-lb. (10 N•m).
5. Install the following parts as described in this chapter:

   a. Front cover and gasket
   b. Pulley hub
   c. Valve lifters
   d. Push rods and pushrod cover

6. Install the fuel pump as described in Chapter Six.
7. Install the oil pump shaft and gear assembly as described in this chapter.
8. Install the distributor as described in Chapter Seven.
9. Position rocker arms over pushrods. Tighten rocker arm nuts to 20 ft.-lb. (27 N•m).
10. Install alternator bracket, alternator, and the front engine mount as described in Chapter Eight. Refer to *Engine Installation* and reinstall engine assembly into vehicle.
11. Tune up vehicle as described in Chapter Three.

4

PISTON/CONNECTING ROD ASSEMBLIES

CAUTION
When performing the following procedures, handle the piston assemblies with care. Do not clamp the piston in a vise or allow it to hit against another piston or object. Conditions such as these can ruin the piston.

Piston/Connecting Rod Removal

1. Remove the cylinder head.
2. Remove the oil pan as described in this chapter.
3. Measure connecting rod side play with a feeler gauge (**Figure 70**). Normal clearance is 0.006-0.022 in. (0.152-0.559 mm). If it exceeds specifications (**Table 1**, end of chapter), replace the connecting rod.

4. Check for carbon ridges at the tops of the cylinder bores. If these are present, remove the ridge from the top of the bore with a ridge reamer (**Figure 71**). These are available from tool rental dealers.

CAUTION
Do not cut more than 1/32 in. into the ring travel area when using the ridge reamer.

5. Rotate the crankshaft until the piston is at bottom dead center and the connecting rod is centered in the cylinder bore.
6. Check the rods and bearing caps for cylinder number markings. If there are no marks visible, scribe your own with a sharp tool. Make the marks on the same side of rod and cap so they can be reassembled in their original positions.
7. Unbolt the connecting rod cap (**Figure 72**) and remove the rod cap and bearing from the crankshaft.

NOTE
Wrap the connecting rod studs with tape so the cylinder bores won't be damaged during removal.

8. Free the connecting rod and piston assembly from the crankshaft by tapping gently with a wooden hammer handle (**Figure 73**). Remove the assembly from its bore.
9. Remove the rings using a ring expander tool. See **Figure 74**.

Piston Pin Removal/Installation

Piston pins are press-fitted to the connecting rods and slip fit into the pistons. Removal requires an arbor press, or similar device and a suitable support tool. This is a job for a General Motors dealer or machine shop equipped to fit the pistons and pin as well as align the pistons with the connecting rods.

NOTE
*When having piston pin removal/-installation procedure performed by a General Motors dealer or machine shop, ensure that notch on piston crown and notches on connecting rod and bearing cap match those of the piston assembly as shown in **Figure** 75.*

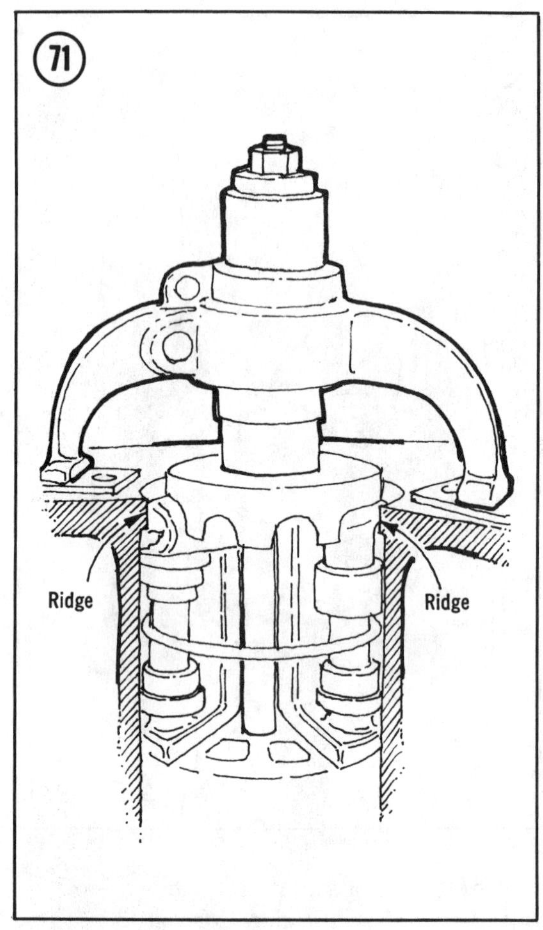

Piston Cleaning and Inspection

1. Clean the pistons thoroughly in solvent. Scrape carbon deposits from the piston's top with a flat blunt-edge scraper. The ring grooves can be cleaned with a piston ring groove cleaner or with a broken piston ring (**Figure 76**).
2. Examine the piston for cracks at the skirts, ring grooves, pin or bushing bosses, and top. Any noticeable fault requires that the piston be replaced.

NOTE
The following procedures should be done at room temperature. The cylinder walls must be clean and dry.

3. Measure the cylinder bore as described under *Cylinder Bore Inspection* in this chapter.
4. Measure the piston diameter at the points shown in **Figure 77**.

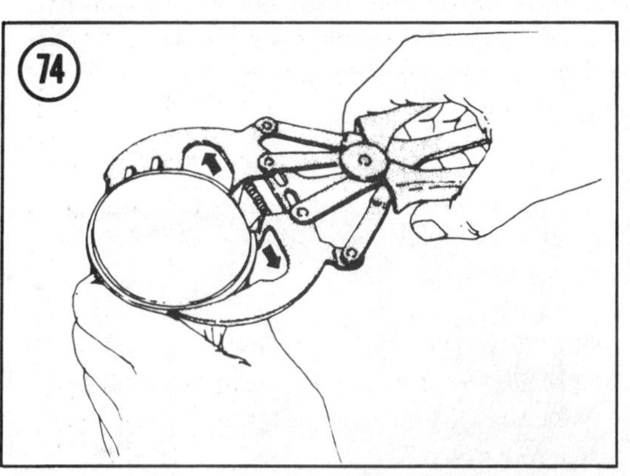

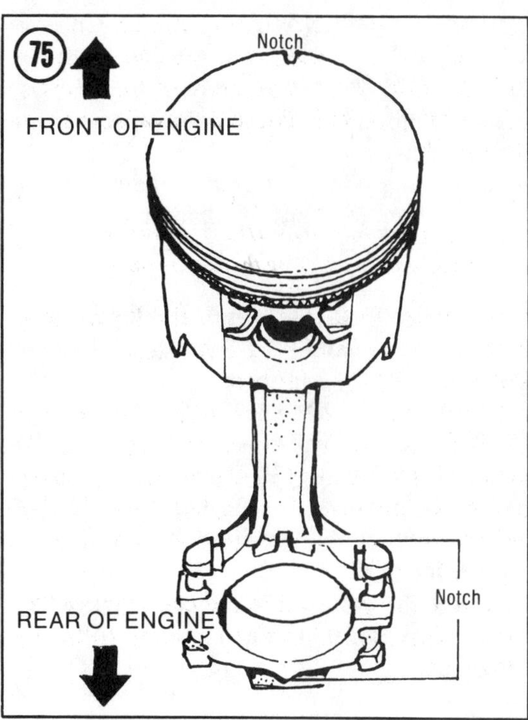

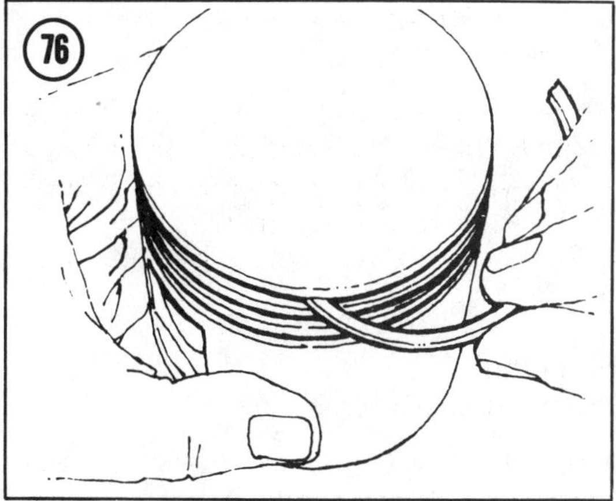

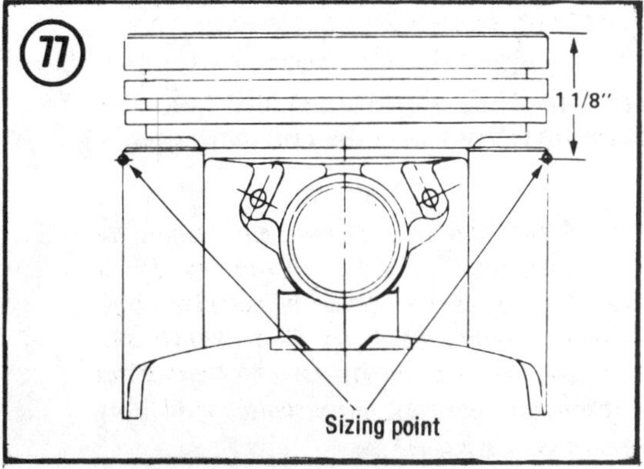

4

NOTE
*The piston must be measured at the point indicated in **Figure** 77 because it is the point of maximum piston wear.*

5. Determine the difference between the cylinder bore and piston diameter taken in Steps 4 and 5. This gives the piston clearance. Compare this figure with the specifications listed at the end of this chapter (**Table 1**).
6. Repeat this procedure for all cylinders and pistons.
7. If the piston clearance is out of specification for any cylinder, all of the cylinders should be bored and oversize pistons installed. This is a job for a General Motors dealer or competent machine shop.

Piston Ring Fitting/Installation

1. Check the ring gap of each piston ring. To do this, first press the ring about one inch down the cylinder bore and square it by tapping gently with an inverted piston.

NOTE
If the cylinders have not been rebored, check the ring gap at the bottom of the ring travel, where the cylinder is least worn.

2. Measure the ring gap with a feeler gauge, as shown in **Figure 78**. Compare the ring gap with the specifications at the end of this chapter. If the ring gap is not within specification, use another set of rings.
3. Check side clearance of the rings as shown in **Figure 79**. Place the feeler gauge beneath the ring and insert all the way into the ring groove. The feeler gauge should slide all the way around the piston without binding. Any wear that occurs will form a step at the inner portion of the ring groove's lower edge. If large steps are discernible (**Figure 80**), the pistons should be replaced. Compare the inserted feeler gauge size with the specification at the end of this chapter.
4. Using a ring expander tool, carefully install the oil control ring assembly, then the compression rings. Distribute the ring gaps around the piston as shown in **Figure 81**.

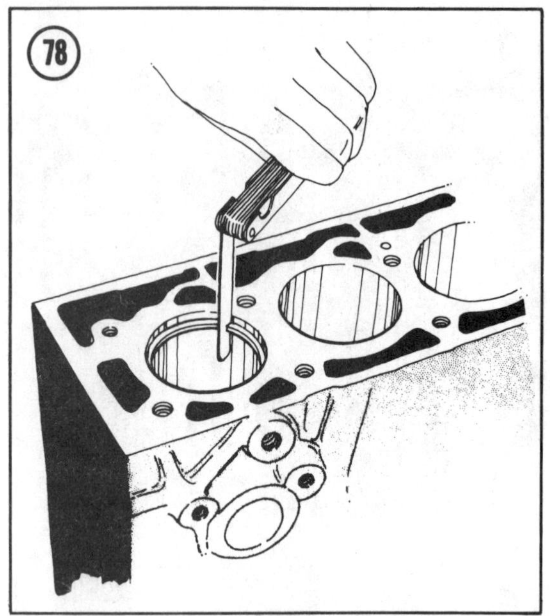

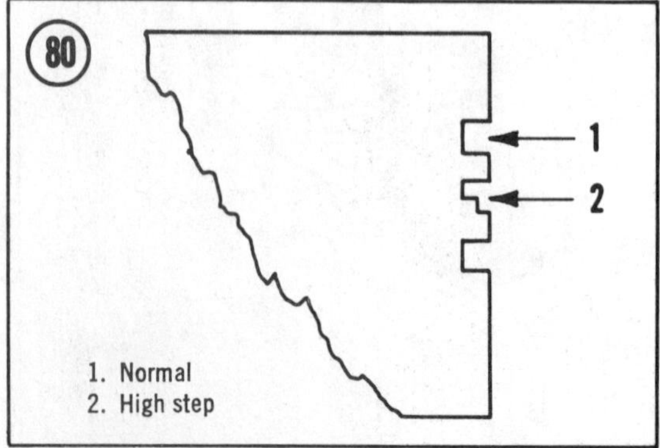

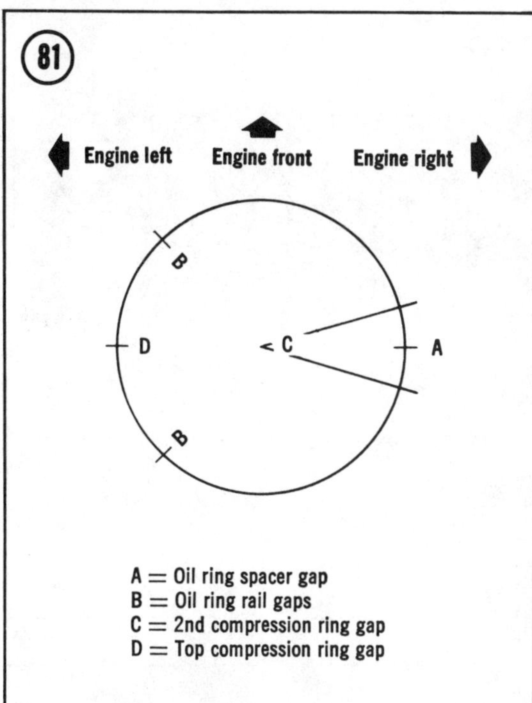

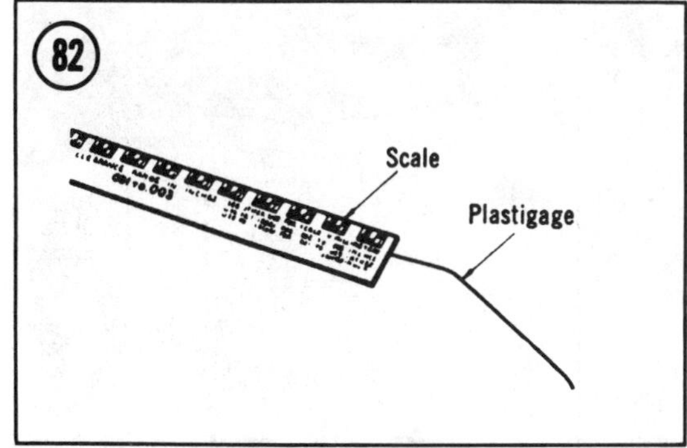

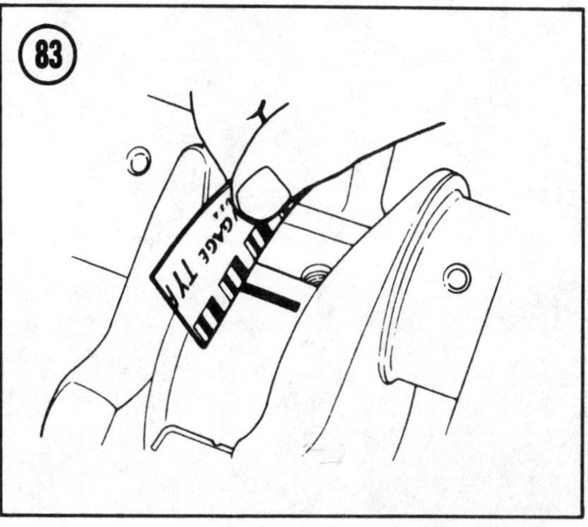

Connecting Rod Inspection

1. Check the pistons for shiny, scuffed areas above the piston pins on one side and below the piston pin on the other. This indicates a bent connecting rod.
2. Have the connecting rods checked by your General Motors dealer or a competent machine shop for twisting, bends and overall straightness and alignment.

Measuring Bearing Clearance

1. Assemble connecting rods with bearings on the proper crankshaft journal. Do not tighten.
2. Cut a piece of Plastigage (**Figure 82**) the width of the bearing. Insert the Plastigage between the crankshaft journal and the connecting rod bearing.

NOTE

Do not place the Plastigage over the crankshaft journal oil hole.

3. Install connecting rod cap and torque to 32 ft.-lb. (44 N•m). Do not rotate the crankshaft while Plastigage is in place.
4. Remove the connecting rod cap. Bearing clearance is determined by comparing width of flattened Plastigage with scale markings on the Plastigage envelope (**Figure 83**). Compare Plastigage measurement with the specifications listed at end of this chapter.

NOTE

If clearance is excessive, replacement bearings are available in standard size and undersizes of 0.001, 0.002 and 0.010 in. for use with new and reconditioned crankshafts.

Piston/Connecting Rod Installation

1. Remove cylinder wall glaze with a hone if new piston rings are to be installed. Follow hone manufacturer's recommendations.
2. Oil piston rings, pistons and cylinder walls with light engine oil. Be sure to install pistons in same cylinders from which they were removed or to which they were fitted.
3. Install piston rings on piston using piston ring expander tool.

4

NOTE

*Pistons are installed with notch facing toward front of engine (**Figure 84**).*

4. Install piston ring compressor on piston. Push piston into the cylinder with a hammer handle until it is slightly below top of cylinder (**Figure 85**). Be sure to guide connecting rods onto the crankshaft to avoid damage to bearings.
5. Check bearing clearance. See *Measuring Bearing Clearance*, this chapter. Apply a light coat of engine oil to the journals and bearings after the bearings have been fitted.
6. Turn crankshaft throw to bottom of its stroke. Push piston down until connecting rod bearing seats on crankshaft journal. Remove tape from connecting rod studs (if required).
7. Install connecting rod cap with notches on rod opposite notch in piston as shown in **Figure 75**. Tighten nuts to 32 ft.-lb. (44 N•m).
8. Recheck side clearance between connecting rods on each crankshaft journal after piston and connecting rod assemblies are installed. See *Piston/Connecting Rod Removal*, this chapter.

84

85

OIL PAN, OIL PUMP AND DRIVE SHAFT

Oil Pan Removal

1. Jack up the front end of the vehicle and place it on jackstands.
2. Drain the engine oil.
3. Remove nuts securing front engine mount to engine cradle (**Figure 86**).
4. Disconnect bolts securing exhaust pipe to manifold and to rear transaxle mount. See Chapter Six.
5. Remove the flywheel inspection cover and remove the starter, if required, to gain access to the oil pan.
6. Remove upper bracket securing alternator to engine block.
7. Connect suitable engine lifting hoist to engine and raise engine slightly to remove weight from rear engine support bracket.
8. From beneath engine, remove the lower alternator bracket and engine support bracket.
9. Remove the oil pan attaching bolts, then remove the oil pan and gasket.

86

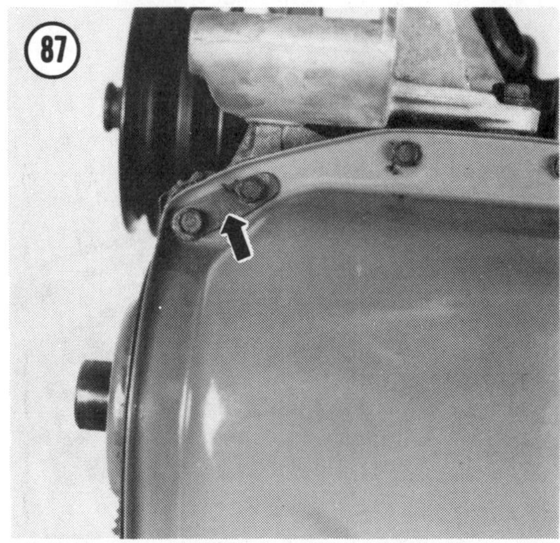

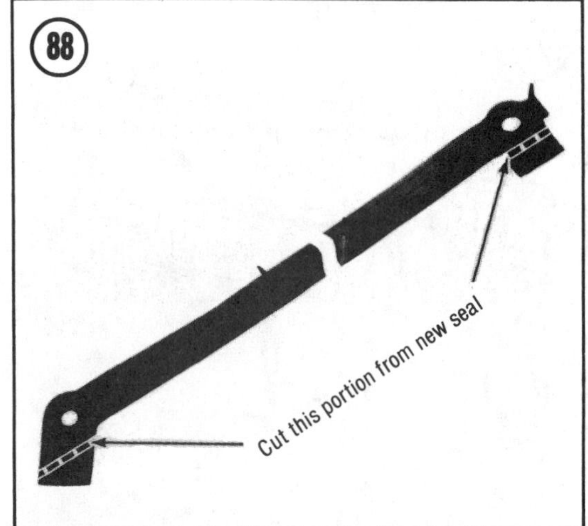

NOTE

*Metal reinforcement tabs are located at every corner around the oil pan. See **Figure 87**. These tabs are used to help seal around the lower front cover and rear oil seal areas. Do not lose these tabs when removing the oil pan.*

Oil Pan Installation

1. Clean the oil pump pickup screen.
2. Clean all traces of old gasket material and sealant from oil pan, cylinder block, front cover and rear main bearing cap. Be sure to clean groove in front cover and rear main bearing cap.
3. Insert rear oil pan gasket into rear main bearing cap. Apply RTV sealant material in depressions where oil pan gasket engages cylinder block.
4. Cut new oil pan seal as shown in **Figure 88** and install seal on timing cover by pressing seal tips into holes in cover.

NOTE

*If the timing cover was removed, it is not necessary to cut the new seal at the points indicated in **Figure 88**.*

5. Install side gaskets along sides of oil pan.
6. Apply RTV gasket sealant along split lines of both front and side gaskets.
7. Position the oil pan against the cylinder block and install the oil pan reinforcement tabs (**Figure 87**) and attaching bolts.

NOTE

Bolts inserted into the timing cover should be installed last.

8. Check the oil pan for proper alignment and install the remaining attaching screws. Tighten all screws evenly, a little at a time, to specification listed at end of chapter.
9. Reverse Steps 1-8 to complete installation. Start engine and check for leaks.

Oil Pump Removal/Installation

1. Remove the oil pan.
2. Remove bolts that attach the oil pump body to the block (**Figure 89**) and the pickup

4

tube to the No. 4 main bearing cap (**Figure 90**). Remove the pump body and pickup tube assembly.

3. Installation is the reverse of these steps. Make sure to align the pump shaft with the oil pump drive shaft tang. Then install oil pump to cylinder block by positioning flange over the oil pump drive shaft lower bushing. Tighten oil pump attaching bolts to 20 ft.-lb. (30 N•m).

Disassembly/Inspection/Assembly

Considering the importance of the oil pump in providing lubrication to the engine, if you do not feel competent to overhaul the oil pump, you should remove the assembly and let your dealer or a competent specialist do it.

Figure 91 is an exploded view of the oil pump.

1. Remove the oil pump cover attaching screws (**Figure 92**), then remove the cover plate.
2. From inside the oil pump assembly, note that the index mark on the idler gear faces up. Then remove the idler gear and drive gear and shaft (**Figure 93**).
3. Using a drift punch, drive out the spring retainer (**Figure 94**) and remove the pressure regulator spring and valve (**Figure 91**).

CAUTION
*Do not remove the pickup tube or screen from the pump body (**Figure 95**).*

4. Thoroughly clean all parts in solvent.
5. Inspect pump body and gears for excessive wear or cracks.
6. Install drive gear and shaft into housing and check for excessive looseness.
7. Inspect the inside cover for excessive wear which would allow oil to leak past the gears.
8. Examine the oil pickup screen for damage (**Figure 96**). If screen is torn, entire oil pump assembly must be replaced.
9. Oil all pump parts thoroughly before beginning assembly.
10. Assembly is the reverse of the removal procedure. Be sure to install idler gear with mark on gear facing up (**Figure 93**). Tighten the cover plate attaching screws to 105 in.-lb. (9 N•m).

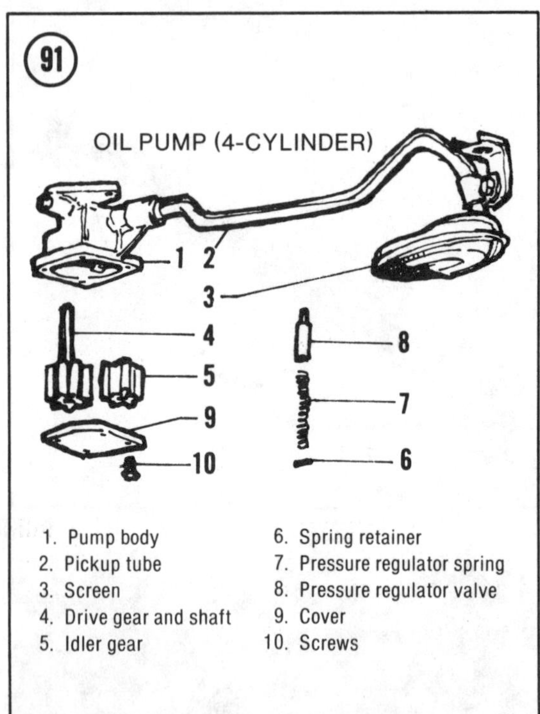

Oil Pump Drive Shaft Replacement

1. Remove the air cleaner (Chapter Six).
2. Remove the carburetor bowl vent line attached at the rocker arm cover.
3. Remove the alternator and upper alternator attaching bracket.
4. Remove 2 drive shaft retainer plate attaching screws (**Figure 97**). Then take out

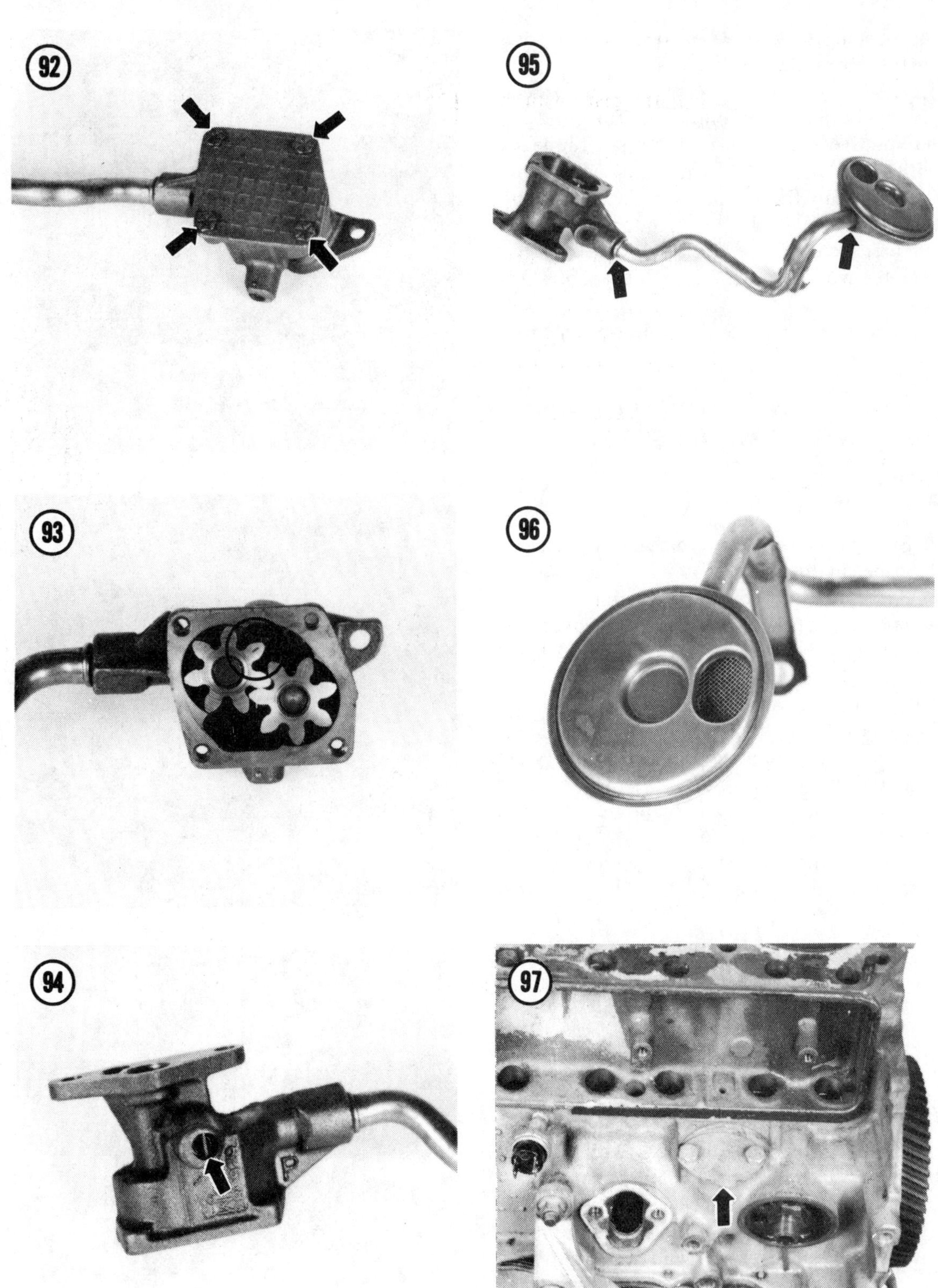
92
95
93
96
94
97

the bushing (**Figure 98**) and oil pump drive shaft (**Figure 99**).

5. Assembly is the reverse of the removal procedure plus the following. Turn the oil pump drive shaft to ensure that shaft indexes with the camshaft drive gear and pilots properly into the oil pump body. Clean the mating surfaces of the cylinder block and retainer plate of all gasket material. Coat the retainer plate with a 1/16 in. bead of RTV gasket sealant and install on cylinder block. Tighten retainer plate attaching screws to 10 ft.-lb. (14 N•m).

CRANKSHAFT, MAIN BEARINGS AND REAR OIL SEALS

Crankshaft/Main Bearing Removal

1. Remove the engine from the vehicle as described in this chapter.
2. Remove the following parts, in order, as described earlier in this chapter:
   a. Fan pulley
   b. Crankshaft pulley and hub assembly
   c. Timing gear cover and timing gear
3. Remove the Woodruff key from end of crankshaft and remove the crankshaft gear (**Figure 100**).
4. Remove the oil pan and oil pump assembly as described in this chapter.
5. Remove the connecting rod bearing caps as described in this chapter.

NOTE

*Check that the main bearing caps are numbered "1" through "5" from the front to rear. Also, caps are marked with an "F" and an arrow to indicate front of engine. See **Figure 101**. Caps must be installed in same position during engine reassembly.*

6. Remove main bearing cap bolts, then remove the main bearing caps with bearing inserts attached. Lay the main bearings and bearing caps in order on a clean surface.
7. Push the connecting rod/piston assemblies toward the top of each cylinder to provide clearance for crankshaft removal and installation.
8. Carefully remove the crankshaft from the main bearing journals in the block so that the

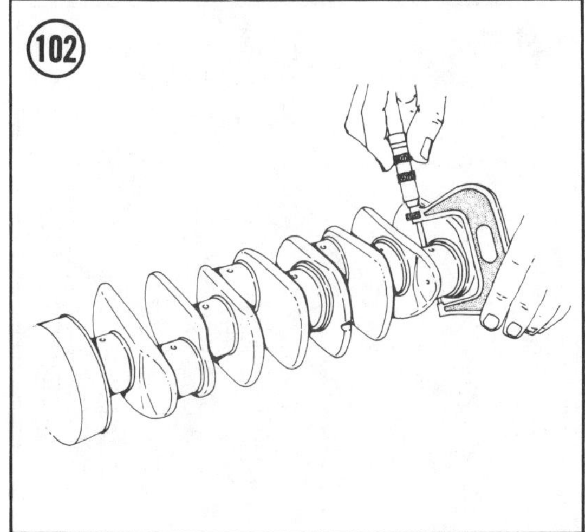

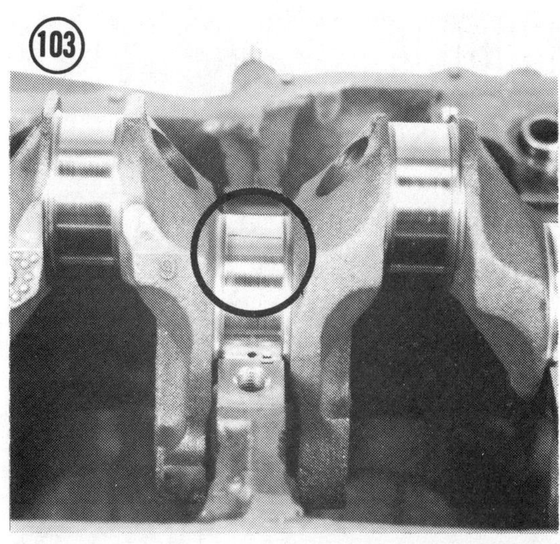

thrust bearing surfaces are not damaged. Handle the crankshaft with care to avoid damage to the crankshaft finished surfaces.

Inspection

1. Clean the crankshaft thoroughly in solvent. Blow out the oil passages with compressed air.

NOTE

If you do not have precision measuring equipment, have a machine shop perform Steps 2 and 3.

2. Examine crankpins and main bearing journals for wear, scoring and cracks. Check all journals against specifications (end of chapter) for out-of-roundness, taper and wear. See **Figure 102**. If necessary, have the crankshaft reground.
3. Check the crankshaft for bending. Mount the crankshaft between accurate centers (such as V-blocks or a lathe) and rotate it one full turn with a dial gauge contacting the center journal. Actual bend is half the reading shown on the gauge. The crankshaft must be reground if bent beyond specifications.
4. Measure crankshaft end play. Install the crankshaft in the block. Install all bearing shells and caps and tighten bolts to 70 ft.-lb. (95 N•m). Rotate crankshaft to make sure drag is not excessive.
5. Force crankshaft as far forward as possible. Insert feeler gauge at the front end of No. 5 main bearing. End play should be 0.0015-0.0085 in. (0.0381-0.216 mm). If not, replace the No. 5 thrust bearing.

Measuring Main Bearing Clearance

1. Install the main bearings previously removed from the cylinder block in their original positions, then install the crankshaft on these bearings taking care not to damage the sides of thrust bearing.
2. Cut a piece of Plastigage the width of the main bearing journal to be measured. Lay the Plastigage on the main bearing journal. See **Figure 103**. Install the main bearing cap, complete with main bearing insert, and tighten to 70 ft.-lb. (95 N•m). See **Figure 104**.

NOTE
Do not place Plastigage across crankshaft oil holes. Do not rotate the crankshaft while the Plastigage is in place.

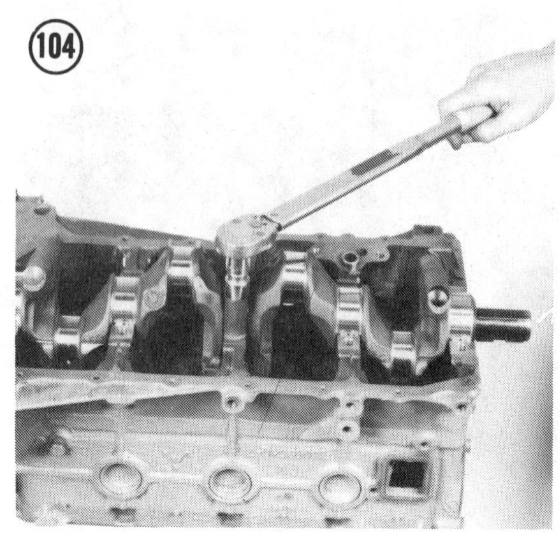

3. Remove the main bearing cap and bearing insert. Compare the width of the flattened Plastigage to the markings on the envelope to determine main bearing clearance (**Figure 105**). Compare the narrowest point on the Plastigage with the widest point to determine journal taper.
4. If wear is greater than the specifications listed at the end of this chapter, a 0.001 or 0.002 in. undersize bearing may be used to produce proper clearance.

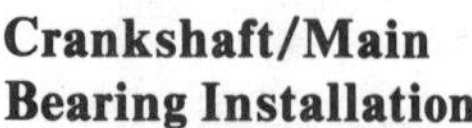

Crankshaft/Main Bearing Installation

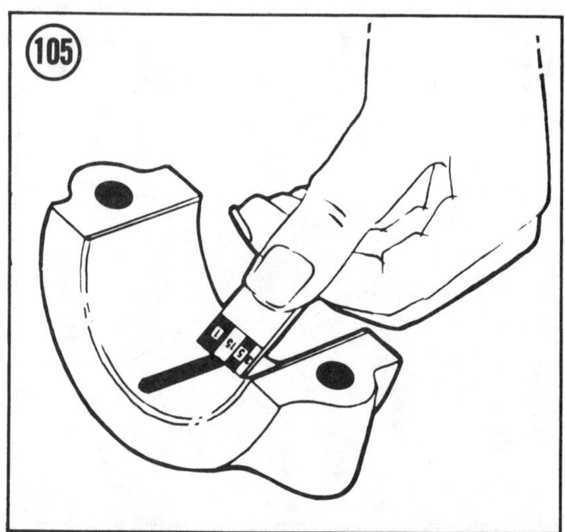

1. With the main bearings removed from the bearing caps and the cylinder block, clean the main bearing bores in the cylinder block, main bearing caps and the main bearing inserts with lacquer thinner to remove all foreign material.
2. If the old main bearings are being reinstalled, be sure that they are reinstalled in the main bearing caps and the cylinder block bores from which they were removed. If new bearings (or undersize bearings) are being installed, be sure that they are installed in the proper location.
3. Coat the main bearing surfaces and the crankshaft journals with clean, heavy engine oil.
4. Carefully lay the crankshaft in the main bearings installed in the cylinder block, being careful not to damage the sides of the thrust bearings.
5. Install all main bearings caps, but do not tighten.
6. Coat the connecting rod and cap journals with oil and reinstall on the crankshaft. Do not tighten.
7. Using a rubber hammer, hit both ends of the crankshaft, to center the thrust bearing.

CAUTION
Do not use a hard metal hammer or the crankshaft may be damaged.

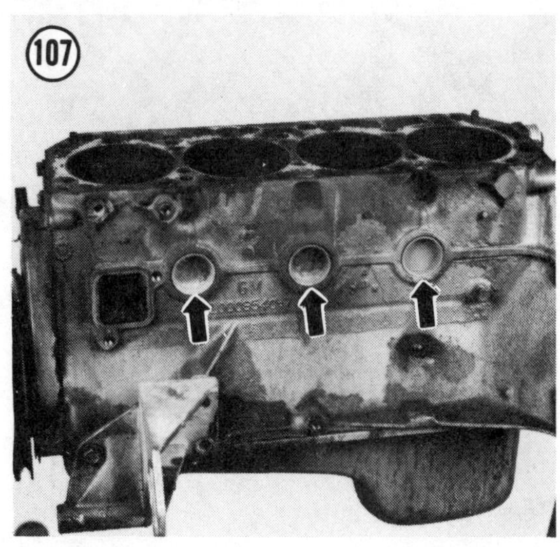

107

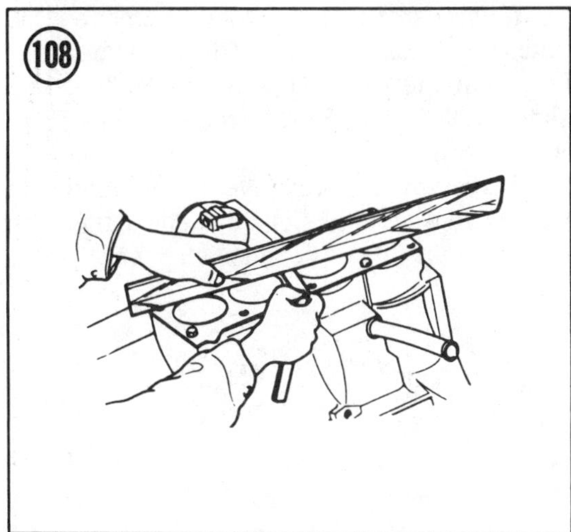

108

8. Torque main bearing cap bolts to 70 ft.-lb. (95 N•m). Next, tighten the connecting rod cap nuts to 32 ft.-lb. (44 N•m).
9. Reverse *Removal* Steps 1-4 to complete engine reassembly.

Rear Main Bearing Oil Seal

1. Remove the engine assembly as described in this chapter.
2. With a punch, knock a small hole in the rear main bearing oil seal.
3. Thread a small sheet metal screw into the seal and, using a pair of pliers, remove the seal by twisting the screw outward. See **Figure 106**.
4. Oil a new seal with engine oil. Install seal by pressing into crankshaft seal flange by hand.

NOTE
Make sure lip of seal faces toward the engine.

5. Install the engine assembly as described in this chapter.

CYLINDER BLOCK INSPECTION

1. Clean the cylinder block thoroughly with solvent and check all freeze plugs for leaks. Replace any plugs that are suspect. It is a good idea, at this level of disassembly, to replace all the freeze plugs. **Figure 107** shows freeze plugs on one side of engine. While cleaning, check oil and water passages for dirt, sludge and corrosion. If the passages are very dirty or clogged, the block should be boiled out by a General Motors dealer or competent automotive shop.
2. Examine the cylinder block for cracks. It is a good idea to take the block to a General Motors dealer or competent automotive shop for Magnafluxing, to locate any hairline cracks that might escape visual examination.
3. Check all machined gasket surfaces for nicks or burrs. If necessary, smooth the surfaces with an oilstone.
4. Check the cylinder head mating surface of the block for flatness. Use an accurate straightedge and feeler gauge as shown in **Figure 108**. Have the block resurfaced if it is warped more than 0.004 in. (0.101 mm).
5. Measure the cylinder bores for out-of-roundness or excessive wear with a bore gauge (**Figure 109**). Measure the bores at top, center and bottom, in front-rear and side-to-side directions. Compare measurements to specifications at the end of the chapter. If the cylinders exceed maximum tolerances, they must be rebored. Reboring is also necessary if the cylinder walls are badly scuffed or scored. Cylinder reboring is a job for a General Motors dealer or competent machine shop.

4

FLYWHEEL

Removal/Installation

1. Remove the engine as described earlier.
2. *Manual transaxle vehicles*: Remove the clutch. See *Clutch Removal*, Chapter Nine.
3. Unbolt the flywheel from the engine. See **Figure 110**. Remove bolts gradually, in a diagonal pattern.
4. Installation is the reverse of removal. Tighten flywheel bolts in a diagonal pattern to specifications (**Table 2**, end of chapter).

Table 1 4-CYLINDER ENGINE SPECIFICATIONS

General Specifications	
Displacement	151 cu. in. (2.5 liter)
Bore	4.00 in. (101.6 mm)
Stroke	3.0 in. (76.2 mm)
Horsepower @ rpm	90 @ 4000
Torque @ rpm	134 @ 2400
Compression ratio	8.3:1
Firing order	1-3-4-2
Cylinder number front to rear	1-2-3-4
Cylinder bore	
Diameter	4.00 in. (101.6 mm)
Out-of-round	0.0005 in. (0.0127 mm) max.
Taper	0.0005 in. (0.0127 mm) max.
Piston	
Clearance in bore	0.0017-0.0041 in. (0.0430-0.1041 mm)
Piston diameter	3.9971-3.9975 in. (101.526-101.536 mm)
Piston Pin	
Diameter	0.938-0.942 in. (23.8252-23.9268 mm)
Length	3.00 in. (76.2 mm)
Pin to piston	
Clearance (loose)	0.0002-0.0004 in. (0.00508-0.01016 mm)
Fit in rod	Press
Piston Compression Ring	
Groove clearance	
Top	0.0030 in. (0.062 mm)
2nd	0.0030 in. (0.062 mm)
Ring width	
Top & 2nd	0.0775-0.0780 in. (1.9685-1.9812 mm)
Gap	
Top	0.015-0.025 in. (0.381-0.635 mm)
2nd	0.009-0.019 in. (0.2286-0.4826 mm)
Piston Oil Ring	
Ring width	0.189 in. (4.8006 mm)
Gap	0.015-0.055 in. (0.3810-1.397 mm)
Camshaft	
Lobe lift, intake & exhaust	0.406 in. (10.3124 mm)
Journal diameter (all)	1.869 in. (47.4726 mm)
Bearing clearance	0.0007-0.0027 in. (0.01778-0.0685 mm)
End Play	0.0015-0.0050 in. (0.0381-0.1270 mm)

(continued)

4

TABLE 1 4-CYLINDER ENGINE SPECIFICATIONS (continued)

Valves (Intake)	
Lash	0
Face angle	45°
Seat angle	46°
Head diameter	1.72 in. (43.688 mm)
Stem diameter	0.3418 - 0.3425 in. (8.68172 - 8.6995 mm)
Overall length	4.924 in. (125.0696 mm)
Stem-to-guide clearance	0.0010-0.0027 in. (0.0254-0.06858 mm)
Seat width	0.353-0.0747 in. (0.897-1.897 mm)
Installed height	1.69 in. (42.926 mm)
Valves (Exhaust)	
Lash	0
Face angle	45°
Seat angle	46°
Head diameter	1.50 in. (38.1 mm)
Stem diameter	0.3418-0.3425 in (8.68172-8.6995 mm)
Overall length	**4.92 in. (124.968 mm)**
Stem-to-guide clearance	
Top	0.0010-0.0027 in. (0.0254-0.06858 mm)
Bottom	0.0020-0.0037 in. (0.0508-0.09398 mm)
Seat width	0.058-0.0971 in. (1.468-2.468 mm)
Installed height	1.69 in. (42.926 mm)
Valve Train	
Rocker arm ratio	1.75:1
Push rod length	9.754 in. (242.316 mm)
Valve lifter	
Leak down rate	12 to 90 seconds with 50 lb. load
Body diameter	0.8420-0.8427 in. (21.3868-21.4046 mm)
Plunger travel	0.125 in. (3.175 mm)
Clearance in boss	0.0025 in. (0.635 mm)
Lifter bore diameter	0.8435-0.8445 in. (21.425-21.450 mm)
Valve Springs	
Pressure @ (lb. @ in.)	
Open	122-180 @ 1.254
Close	78-86 @ 1.66
Crankshaft main journal	
Diameter	2.300 in. (59.182 mm)
Taper	0.0005 in. (0.0127 mm) max.
Out of round	0.0005 in. (0.0127 mm) max.
Clearance limit (new)	0.0005-0.0022 in. (0.0127-0.0558 mm)
End play	0.0035-0.0085 in. (0.0889-0.2159 mm)
Connecting rod bearings	
Diameter	2.000 in. (50.8 mm)
Taper	0.0005 in. (0.0127 mm) max.
Clearance limit (new)	0.0005-0.0026 in. (0.0127-0.0660 mm)
Rod side clearance	0.006-0.022 in. (0.1524-0.5588 mm)
Taper	0.0005 (0.0127 mm) max.

TABLE 2 TIGHTENING TORQUES 4-CYLINDER

Item	Ft.-lb.	N•m
Carburetor to manifold bolt	15	20
Camshaft thrust plate to block bolts	7	10
Connecting rod nuts	32	44
EGR valve bolt	10	14
Cylinder head bolt	75	102
Distributor bolt	22	30
Exhaust manifold bolt	44	60
Flywheel bolt	44	60
Fuel pump to block	18	25
Fan & pulley bolt to water pump	18	25
Harmonic balancer bolt	200	260
Intake manifold bolts	29	40
Intake manifold adapter bolt	15	20
Main bearing bolt	70	95
Oil pan (front, side, and rear bolts)	75 in.-lb.	6
Oil pan drain bolt	25	34
Oil screen support nut	37	50
Oil pump to block bolt	22	30
Oil pump cover bolt	10	14
Push rod cover bolt	90 in.-lb.	10
Rocker arm stud	75	100
Rocker arm nut	20	27
Rocker arm cover bolt	6	8
Thermostat housing bolt	20	27
Timing cover to block bolt	90 in.-lb.	10
Timing cover to oil pan bolt	90 in.-lb.	10
Water pump to block bolt	25	34
Water outlet housing bolt	20	27

NOTE: If you own a 1981 or later model, first check the Supplement at the back of the book for any new service information.

CHAPTER FIVE

ENGINE (V6)

The 173 cid V6 engine is mounted transversely between the front driving wheels. See **Figure 1**. The cylinder block is made of cast alloy iron, with banks of cylinders at a 60 degree angle. The cast iron cylinder heads have integral valve guides. Rocker arms are retained on individual threaded studs. The cast iron crankshaft is supported by 4 steel-backed aluminum main bearings. Cast aluminum pistons are operated by forged steel connecting rods. The camshaft, located between the cylinder banks, is driven by the crankshaft through a chain and sprocket pressed on the end of the crankshaft. The valves are operated by the camshaft through hydraulic valve lifters and pushrods.

The lubrication system consists of a gear type pump mounted at the rear of the crankcase and a full-flow filter mounted on the front side of the block. Oil is drawn up through the pickup screen and tube and passed through the oil pump to the full flow paper oil filter element. The oil pump forces oil though various passages and galleries to the lubrication points in the engine.

This chapter covers removal and installation of the engine, removal and replacement of subassemblies, and inspection, adjustment and repair of some subassemblies and components. Although the illustrations usually show workbench operations, many single procedures, when not a part of a general overhaul, can be performed successfully with the engine in the vehicle.

Engine specifications are provided in **Table 1** and tightening torques are provided in **Table 2**. **Tables 1-3** are located at the end of the chapter.

SERVICE NOTES

WARNING

When working in the engine compartment, keep hands and other objects clear of the radiator fan blades. The fan can start automatically, whether or not the engine is running, due to the underhood temperature at the time of service.

ENGINE REMOVAL

1. Scribe alignment marks directly onto the underside of the hood around the hood hinges, then remove the hood. The alignment marks will ensure that the hood is properly installed and aligned later.

NOTE

When it is necessary to raise vehicle to provide working space beneath the engine, support front of vehicle with jackstands as discussed in Chapter One.

2. Disconnect negative cable from battery (**Figure 2**).

3. Drain the engine coolant and engine oil. Engine coolant may be reused if it has not been in the vehicle for more than 24 months and if the coolant is free of dirt and rust.

4. Disconnect the upper and lower radiator hoses at the radiator and the engine, then remove the hoses. See **Figure 3** and **Figure 4**. Disconnect the heater hose at the water pump (**Figure 5**).

5. Remove the air cleaner. Refer to Chapter Six.

6. Disconnect electrical wiring from the following items:
   a. Distributor (**Figure 6**)
   b. Water temperature sender (1, **Figure 7**)
   c. Water temperature switch (2, **Figure 7**)
   d. Fast idle solenoid (3, **Figure 7**)
   e. Oil pressure switch (4, **Figure 7**)
   f. Electric choke (5, **Figure 7**)
   g. Engine wiring harness at firewall (7, **Figure 7**)
   h. Alternator (8, **Figure 7**)
   i. Cooling fan switch (9, **Figure 7**)
   j. Oil pressure transducer switch (10, **Figure 7**)
   k. Starter (**Figure 8**)

7. Label and disconnect all vacuum lines from the engine.
8. Disconnect the engine-to-body ground straps (**Figure 9**).
9. Disconnect the fuel lines at the fuel pump (**Figure 10**).

NOTE
For vehicles equipped with air conditioning, carefully read the air conditioning section in Chapter Seven to acquaint yourself with the system. Then, remove the compressor (see Chapter Seven) and position it out of the way. Do not disconnect the lines from the components. Make certain that there is no strain on any of the hoses or lines.

10. Remove the following items:
   a. Front exhaust pipe (Chapter Six)
   b. Flywheel inspection cover (Chapter Nine)
   c. Starter (Chapter Eight)
   d. Power steering pump with hoses attached (set out of the way)

NOTE
Steps 11-15 apply to automatic transaxle equipped vehicles only.

11. Disconnect rubber fuel line connections at right side of engine.

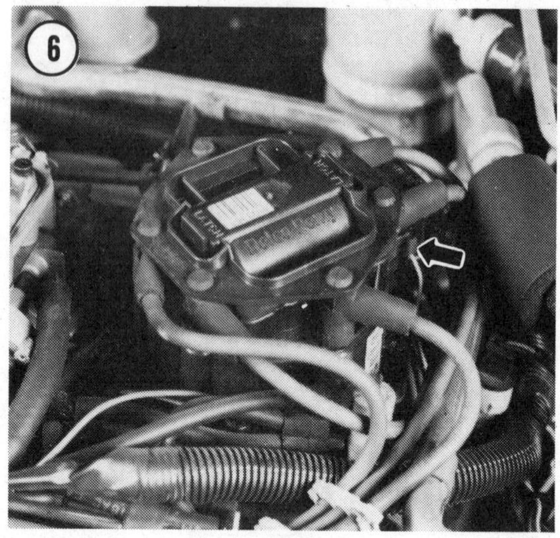

12. Remove the following items:
   a. Engine front mount to cradle retaining mounts at right side of engine (**Figure 11**). See **Figure 12** for view of mount bracket.
   b. Transaxle access cover (**Figure 13**). Then disconnect the torque converter from the flywheel (**Figure 14**).
   c. Transaxle-to-engine support bracket (**Figure 15**).

13. Place a jack and block of wood under the transaxle rear extension housing.
14. Connect a lifting device to the engine (**Figure 16**) and lift the engine just enough to unweight the engine/transaxle mounts. Then remove the engine strut bracket from the radiator support and swing the bracket forward (**Figure 17**).
15. Remove the bolts that attach the transaxle to the cylinder block.

NOTE
Steps 16-25 apply to manual transaxle equipped vehicles only.

16. Disconnect the following items:
   a. Clutch cable from transaxle (Chapter Nine).
   b. Shift linkage from transaxle shift levers (remove cables from transaxle bosses)
   c. Speedometer cable at transaxle

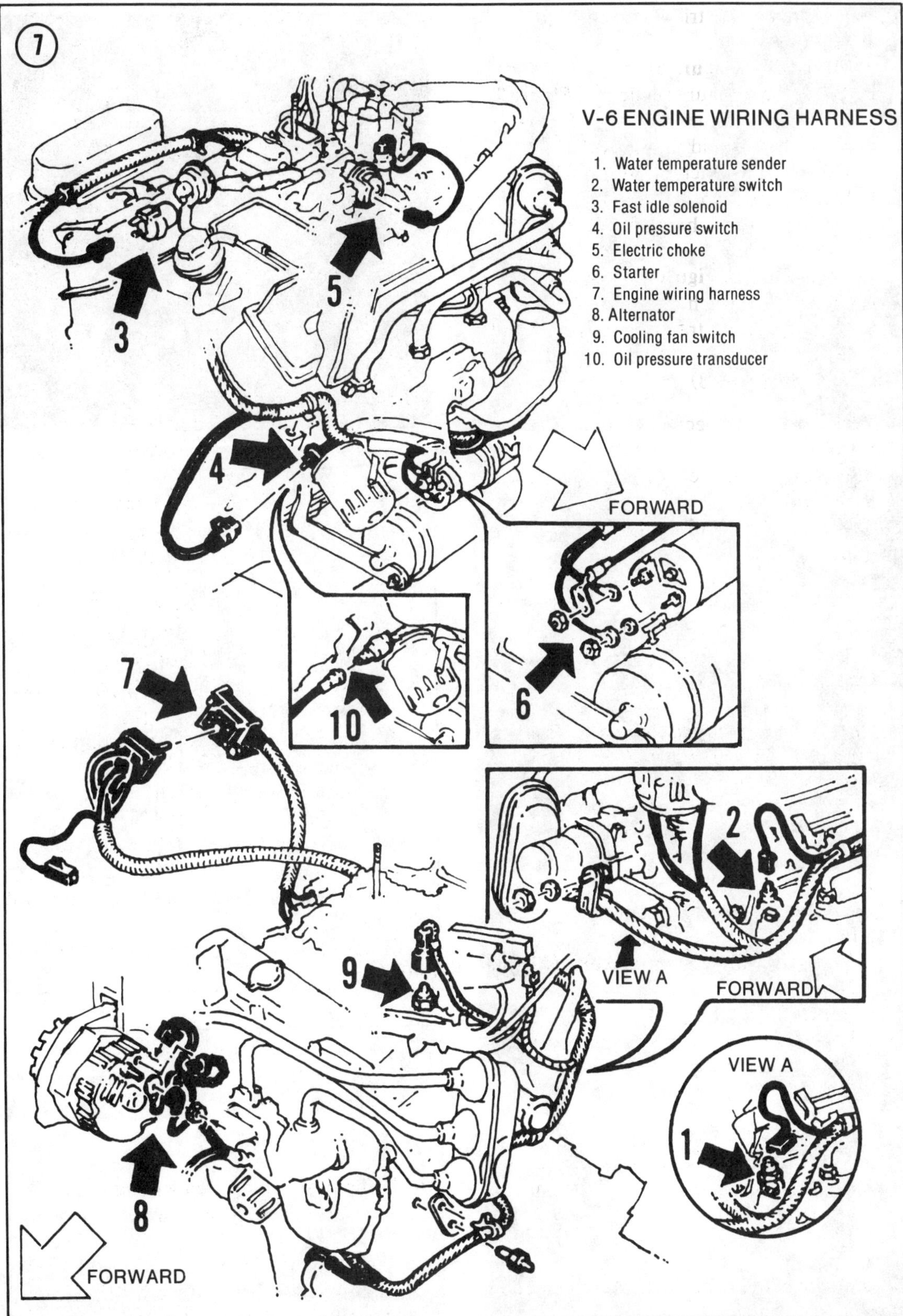
7
V-6 ENGINE WIRING HARNESS
1. Water temperature sender
2. Water temperature switch
3. Fast idle solenoid
4. Oil pressure switch
5. Electric choke
6. Starter
7. Engine wiring harness
8. Alternator
9. Cooling fan switch
10. Oil pressure transducer
3
5
4
FORWARD
10
6
7
2
9
VIEW A
FORWARD
VIEW A
1
8
FORWARD

8

11

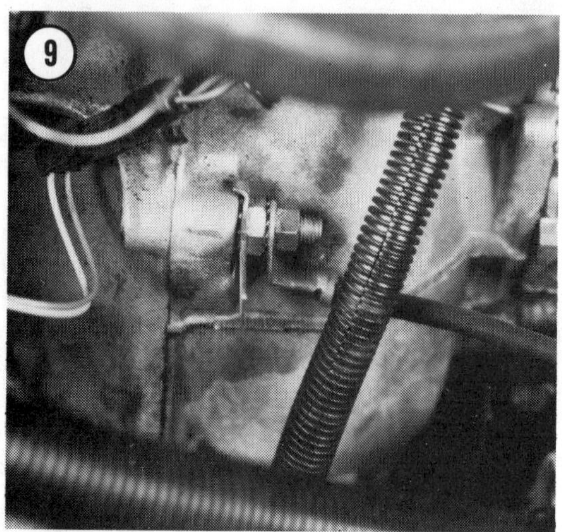
9

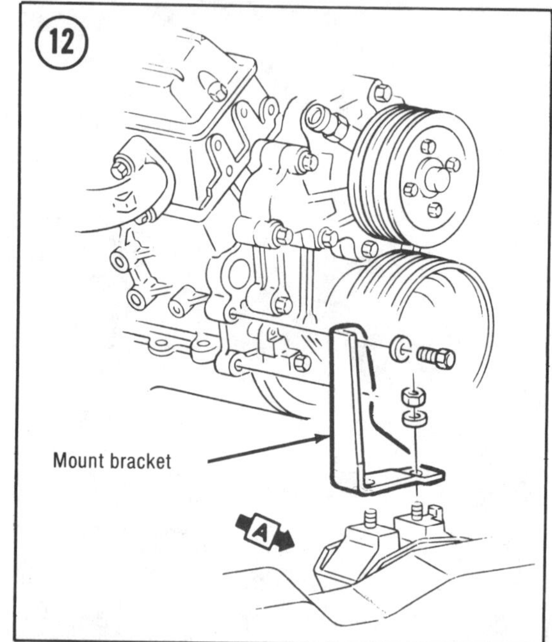
12
Mount bracket
A

10

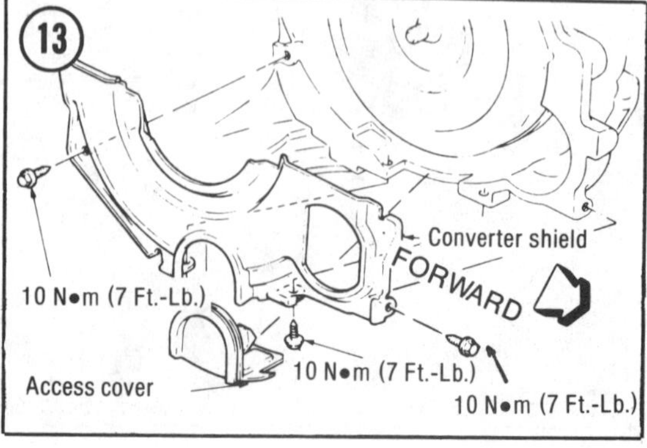
13
Converter shield
FORWARD
10 N•m (7 Ft.-Lb.)
10 N•m (7 Ft.-Lb.)
Access cover
10 N•m (7 Ft.-Lb.)

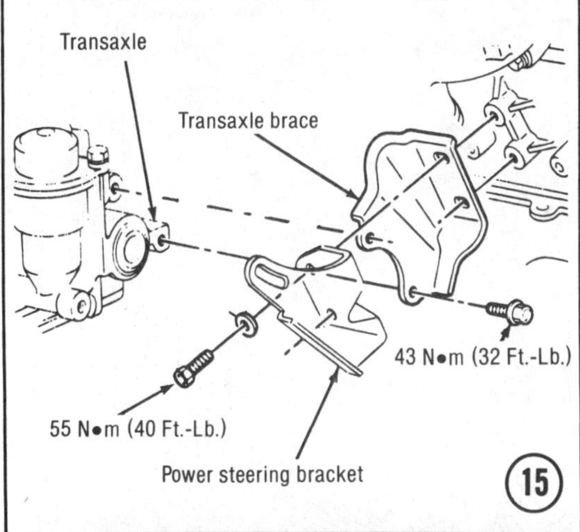

17. Using the engine lifting device, lift the engine just enough to take the weight off the engine transaxle mounts (**Figure 16**).
18. Remove all but one of the engine-to-transaxle attaching bolts.
19. Insert key in ignition switch and turn to unlock steering.
20. Remove the following items:
   a. Left and right side front tire and wheel assemblies
   b. Side and crossmember plate and crossmember assembly attaching bolts (then remove plate from left side — loosen right side plate bolts)
   c. Exhaust crossover pipe at exhaust manifold (Chapter Six)
   d. Powertrain mount to cradle nuts (front, side and rear)
   e. Front crossmember to right side member attaching bolts
21. Pull right and left side drive axle shafts from transaxle assembly (Chapter Nine).
22. Remove left side cradle-to-body mount attaching bolts. See **Figure 18**.
23. Swing the side member and crossmember assembly to the left. Secure outside of the fender well.
24. Loosen the engine support assembly and lower the left side of engine. Place a block of wood beneath transaxle and support transaxle assembly with jack.
25. Remove last transaxle-to-engine attaching bolt, then separate engine from transaxle and lower engine.

CAUTION

Double check to make sure all electrical leads, vacuum lines and control links between the engine/transaxle assembly and the vehicle have been disconnected and removed. Check also to ensure that air conditioning lines, oil lines and wiring harness will not snag on the engine when it is removed.

26. If an engine stand is available, raise the engine with the lifting device (**Figure 16**) and mount it on the stand. If a stand is not available, support the engine on wooden blocks.

5

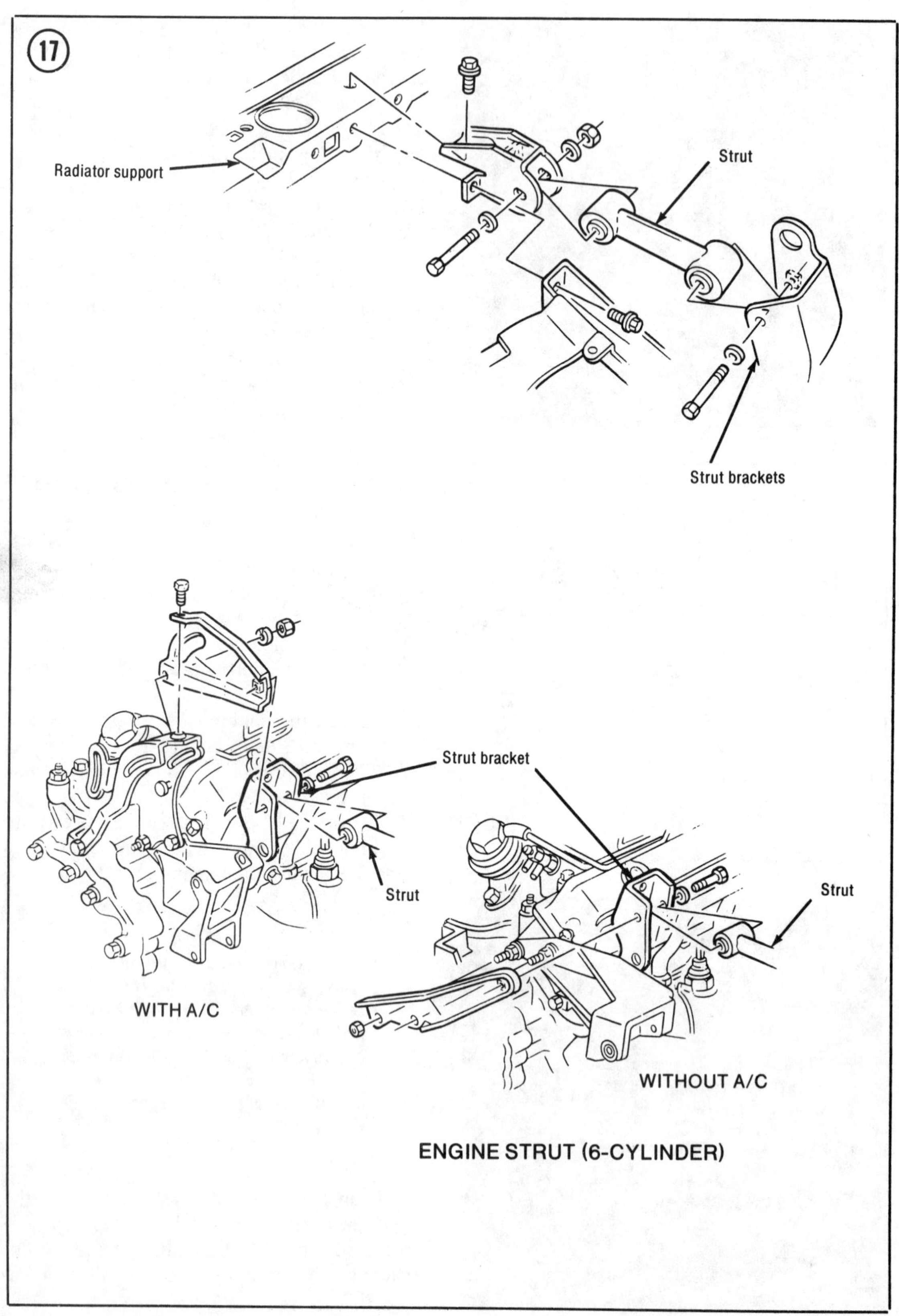

ENGINE STRUT (6-CYLINDER)

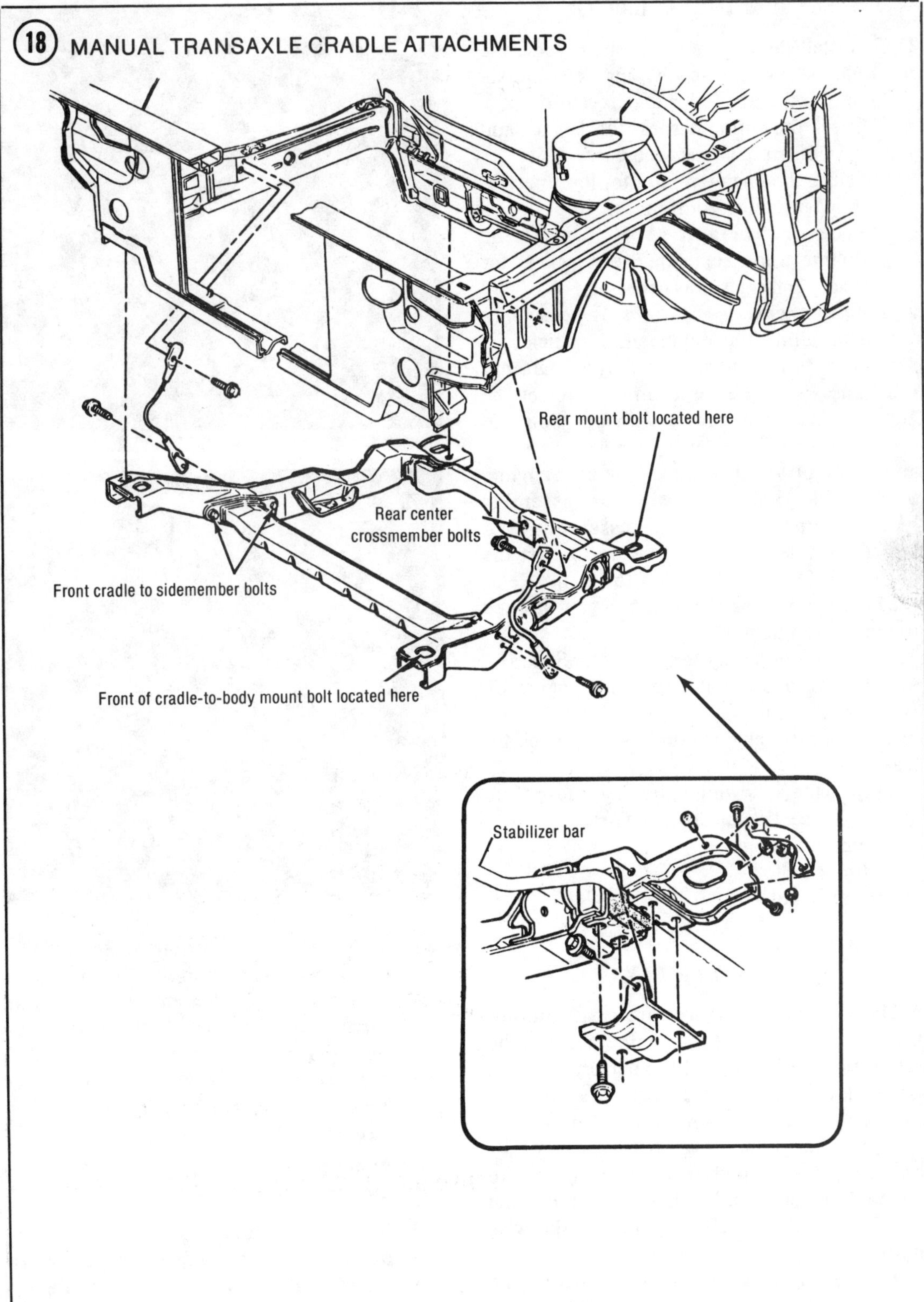
18 MANUAL TRANSAXLE CRADLE ATTACHMENTS
Rear mount bolt located here
Rear center
crossmember bolts
Front cradle to sidemember bolts
Front of cradle-to-body mount bolt located here
Stabilizer bar

ENGINE INSTALLATION

1. To install the engine assembly, reverse the removal steps for each engine/transaxle assembly, noting the following precautions.
   a. Check the wiring harness for damage and correct or replace as necessary.
   b. Check the engine mount for looseness or damage and tighten or replace as necessary (**Figure 19**). Check the engine/transaxle support bracket for cracks and replace as necessary.
2. *Manual transaxle equipped vehicles only*: When installing the engine into vehicle, be sure to start the right side axle drive shaft into the transaxle at the same time. Connect the engine/transaxle assembly with one bolt and secure with a suitable lifting device and a jack and block of wood positioned under engine. Swing side and crossmember assembly beneath engine/transaxle assembly and reinstall cradle assembly. Be sure to start the left side axle drive shaft into the transaxle as the crossmember assembly is being positioned to the cradle assembly.
3. Refill the cooling system (Chapter Seven).
4. Fill the engine crankcase with engine oil (Chapter Three).
5. Start and let engine run at idle. Check for leakage.
6. Adjust the following points by referring to appropriate section in Chapter Three.
   a. Ignition timing
   b. Engine idle
7. Road test vehicle.

DISASSEMBLY

The following sequences are basic outlines that tell how much of the engine needs to be removed and disassembled to perform specific types of service. The sequences are designed to keep engine disassembly to a minimum, thus avoiding unnecessary work. The major assemblies mentioned in these sequences are covered in detail under their own individual headings within this chapter, unless otherwise noted.

To use these sequences, first determine what type of engine service you plan to do (a valve job, for example), then turn to the sequences that cover that type of service. To perform a specific step within a sequence, turn to the heading covering the major assembly or component and the inspection procedures contained under that heading. To reassemble or install, reverse the sequences, performing the installation or assembly procedures contained under that major heading.

Decarbonizing or Valve Service

1. Remove the cylinder head.
2. Remove and inspect valves. Inspect valve guides and seats, repairing or replacing as necessary.
3. Installation is the reverse of these steps.

Ring and Connecting Rod Service

1. Remove the oil pan.
2. Remove the oil pump.
3. Remove the pistons together with the connecting rods.
4. Remove the piston rings. It is not necessary to separate the pistons from the connecting rods unless a piston, connecting rod or piston pin needs repair or replacement.
5. Assemble by reversing Steps 1-4.

General Overhaul

1. Remove the engine from the car.
2. Remove the motor mounts.
3. Remove the fuel pump, carburetor and intake and exhaust manifolds (Chapter Six).
4. Remove the pulley, water pump and thermostat (Chapter Eight).
5. Remove the alternator and the distributor (Chapter Nine).
6. Remove the valve rocker assemblies.
7. Remove the cylinder head.
8. Remove the oil pan.
9. Remove the oil pump.
10. Remove the harmonic balancer and the engine timing cover.
11. Remove the pistons together with the connecting rods.
12. Remove the crankshaft and main bearings.
13. Inspect the cylinder block.
14. Assemble by reversing Steps 1-12.

ROCKER ASSEMBLY AND PUSHRODS

Removal

1. Disconnect the battery negative cable (**Figure 2**).
2. Disconnect the spark plug wires from the spark plugs and the wire looms and lay them back out of the way. See Chapter Three.
3. Remove the air filter assembly (Chapter Six).
4. Disconnect, or move out of the way, any other hoses preventing removal of the rocker arm cover. See **Figure 20** for an overall view of the left and right side rocker arms and vacuum lines.
5. *Left cover only*: Remove the front engine strut-to-bracket bolt (**Figure 21**) and pull the strut forward and away from the rocker arm cover. Then remove the bolts attaching the engine strut bracket to the cylinder head (**Figure 22**) and remove the bracket.
6. *Right cover only*: Detach accelerator linkage cable from the carburetor (**Figure 23**) and pull cable from its mounting bracket (**Figure 24**) and lay aside. Remove cruise control diaphragm acuator mounting bracket (if so equipped). If vehicle is equipped with automatic transaxle, disconnect the TV linkage from the carburetor and rocker arm

cover and lay aside. See **Figure 25**. Also remove the PAIR pipe attaching bolt (**Figure 26**) and position pipe aside.
7. Remove the rocker cover screws. Tap the cover with a rubber mallet to loosen it. Lift the cover(s) off the engine.
8. Remove the nut securing the rocker arm and rocker arm ball to the rocker arm stud (**Figure 27**). Then remove the rocker arms and rocker balls.

NOTE
Lay parts aside in order to ensure reinstallation to same position.

9. Lift the pushrods (**Figure 28**) out of the engine. Place the pushrods with their rocker arms in a numbered holder so they can be reinstalled in their original positions (**Figure 29**).

Inspection and Repair

1. Thoroughly clean all parts in solvent. Make sure all oil passages in the pushrod are clear.
2. Check the pushrods for wear or damage, particularly at the ends (**Figure 30**). Check the pushrods for straightness by rolling on a piece of glass. A clicking sound will be heard if the pushrod is bent even slightly. Replace bent, worn or otherwise damaged pushrods.
3. Check the valve stem contact surface on the rocker arm for wear (**Figure 30**). Replace worn rocker arms. Do not attempt to smooth rocker arm contact surfaces.
4. Inspect rocker arm studs for cracked or damaged threads. See **Figure 31**. Replace studs as necessary.

Installation

1. Coat contact surfaces of rocker arms and rocker arm balls with Molykote or equivalent. Apply a coat of SE type engine oil to the pushrods.
2. Insert the pushrods in the holes from which they were removed. Ensure that pushrods are positioned through the upper guide rod and seated correctly in the lifter (**Figure 32**).
3. Install rocker arms on studs. Insert rocker arm ball and nut in position and tighten rocker arm nut until valve lash is eliminated.

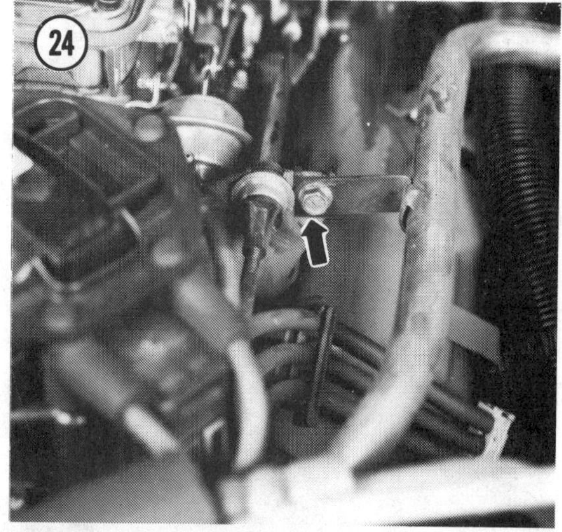

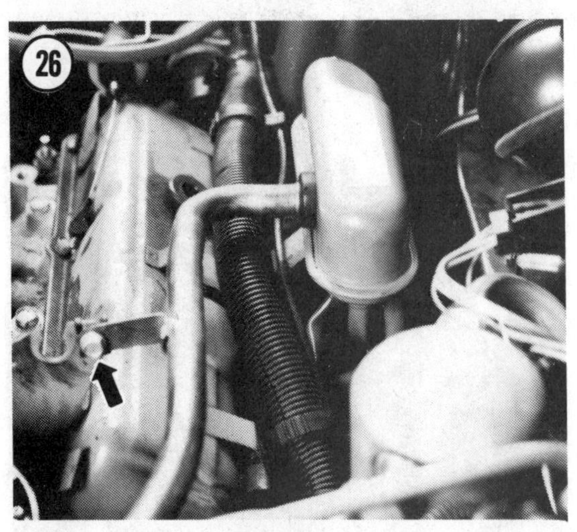
26

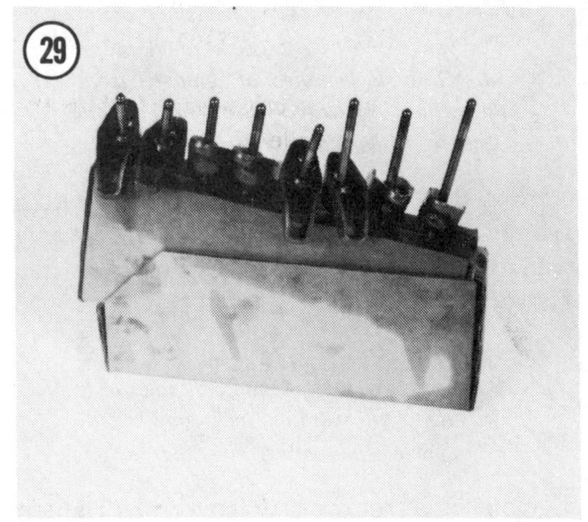
29

5

27

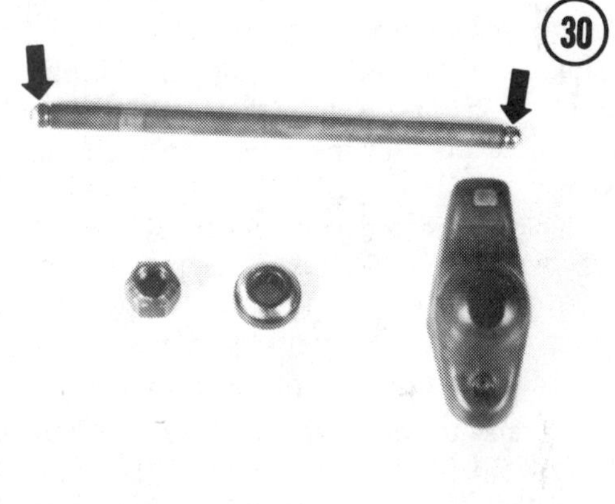
30

28
ROCKER ARMS
ROCKER ARM STUDS
PUSH ROD GUIDE
PUSH RODS
LIFTERS

NOTE
*The valves must be adjusted anytime the valve train is loosened or removed from the engine. Adjust the valve clearances as described under **Valve Adjustment**.*

4. Coat the rocker arm sealing surface with a 1/8 in. bead of RTV gasket sealant. Apply sealant to inside of bolt holes on cover. See **Figure 33**.

CAUTION
Do not let sealant flow into bolt holes or it will create an hydraulic lock condition to the cylinder head casting.

5. Install the rocker arm cover(s). Tighten attaching screws to 8 ft.-lb. (12 N•m).
6. Perform *Removal* Steps 1-6 in reverse order. Install the carburetor, if removed, using a new gasket and tighten attaching bolts to 11 ft.-lb. (14 N•m). Tighten front engine strut bracket-to-cylinder bolts to 35 ft.-lb. (47 N•m).
7. Start engine and check for leaks.

VALVE ADJUSTMENT

The valve adjustment procedures described below are to be performed only when the valve train is loosened or removed from the engine. Valve adjustment is not required during periodic engine tune-up.

1. Place a finger on the exhaust rocker arm for the No. 1 cylinder. **Figure 34** identifies cylinder position and valve alignment. Position your finger so you can feel any rocker arm motion.
2. Turn engine until timing mark on damper lines up with "0" timing mark on timing tab (**Figure 35**). If the exhaust valve did not move, the engine is in the No. 1 cylinder firing position (both valves closed). If valve movement was noticed, however, the engine is in the No. 4 cylinder firing position. Rotate engine one revolution to reach the No. 1 cylinder firing position.
3. With the engine in the No. 1 firing position, adjust the following valves, referring to **Figure 34**:
   a. Exhaust 1, 2, 3
   b. Intake 1, 5, 6

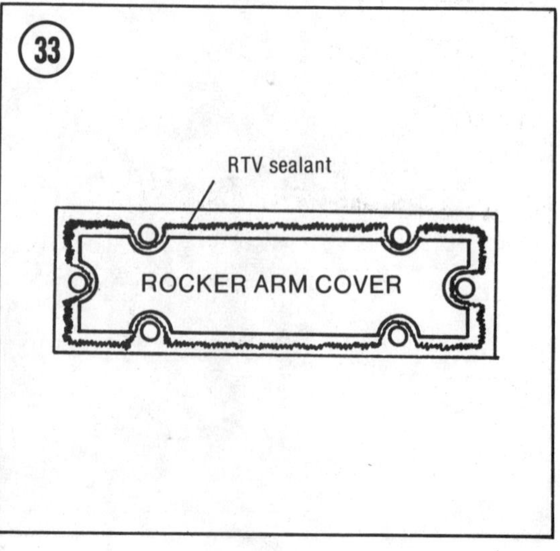

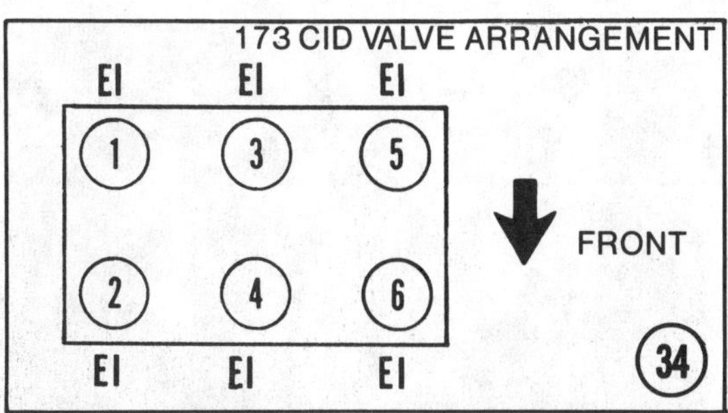

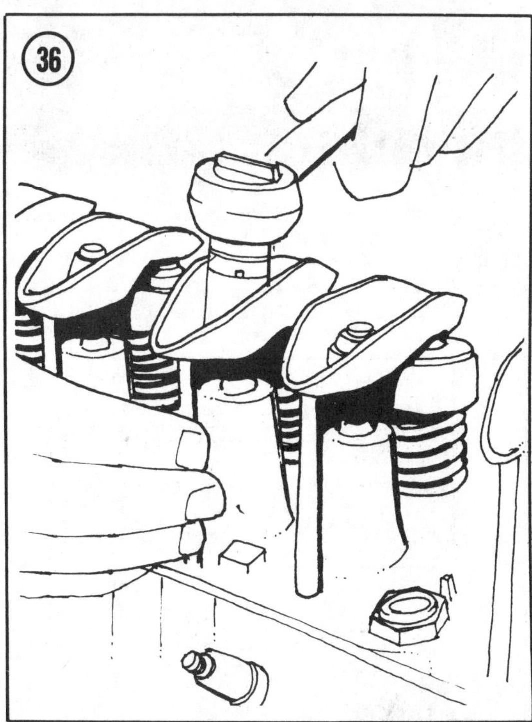

4. Rotate crankshaft one revolution (No. 4 cylinder is in firing position with both valves closed). Adjust the following valves:
   a. Exhaust 4, 5, 6
   b. Intake 2, 3, 4

NOTE

*Valve adjustment is made by backing off the rocker arm adjusting nut until play is felt in the pushrod. See **Figure 36**. Then, slowly tighten the rocker arm adjusting nut until no play can be felt in the pushrod (hold the pushrod while the nut is tightened). When the pushrod cannot be turned, tighten the rocker arm adjusting nut an additional 1 1/2 turns to center the rocker arm with the valve lifter plunger (**Figure 37**).*

5

CYLINDER HEAD

Some of the following procedures must be done by a dealer or machine shop, since they require special knowledge and expensive machine tools. Others, while possible for the home mechanic, are difficult and time-consuming. A general practice among those who do their own service is to remove the cylinder head, perform all disassembly except valve removal, and take the head to a machine shop for inspection and service. Since the cost is low in relation to the required effort and equipment, this is usually the best approach, even for more experienced owners.

Cylinder Head Removal

1. Remove all spark plugs.
2. Remove the air cleaner and carburetor (Chapter Six).
3. *Air conditioned vehicles*: Refer to Chapter Seven and remove the air conditioner compressor. Then remove the compressor bracket from its mounting position (**Figure 38**).
4. Label and disconnect all vacuum lines and electrical wiring as necessary to remove the intake manifold and cylinder head. See **Figure 39** for an overall view of lines and wiring.
5. Remove the intake and exhaust manifolds (Chapter Six).
6. Remove the alternator bracket and strut and the dipstick tube bracket from the left cylinder head.
7. Remove the PAIR pipe from the right and left side cylinder heads. See Chapter Six.
8. Remove the rocker arm covers and pushrods as described in this chapter. Be sure to keep the pushrods in order, so they can be reinstalled in the holes from which they were originally removed.
9. Remove the cylinder head bolts. To prevent warping the cylinder head, loosen the bolts in several stages, following the order given in **Figure 40**.
10. Once the bolts are removed, lift the cylinder head(s) off the engine. If the head is difficult to remove, tap it gently with a rubber mallet. If that does not work, try reinstalling the spark plugs and turning the engine over by hand. The compression should force the head loose. Once the cylinder head is removed from the block, remove the cylinder head gaskets, then place the cylinder head(s) on a soft surface to prevent scratching or otherwise damaging the cylinder head-to-engine block mating surface. If possible, do not lay the cylinder head on its mating surface at all.

Inspection

1. Check the cylinder head for water leaks before cleaning.
2. Clean the cylinder head thoroughly in solvent. While cleaning, check for cracks in exhaust ports, combustion chambers and water chambers or for other visible damage.

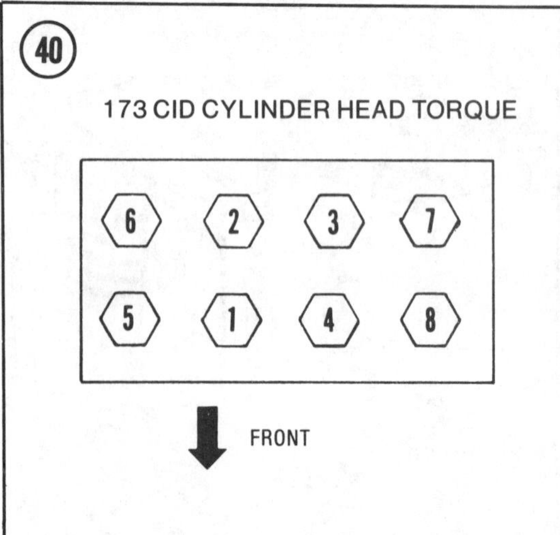

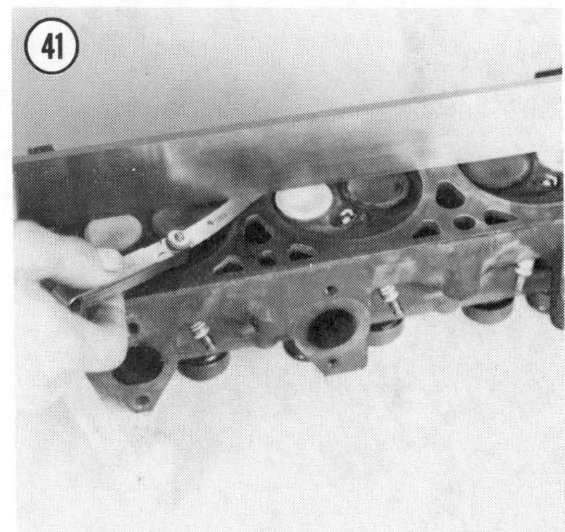

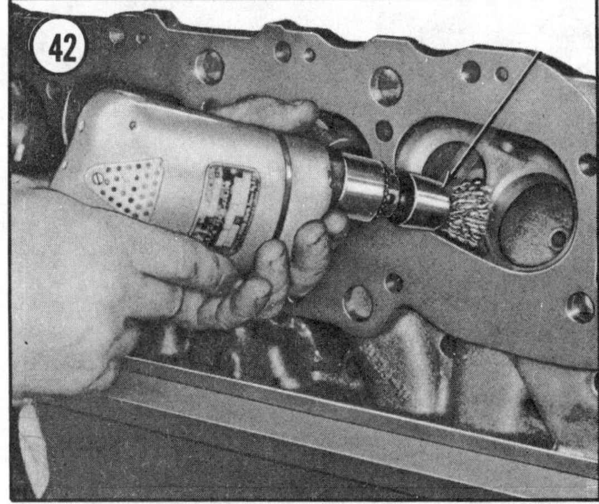

Look for corrosion or foreign material in oil or water passages. Clean the passages with a stiff spiral brush, then blow them out with compressed air.

3. Check the cylinder head bottom (block mating) surface for flatness. Place an accurate straightedge along the surface. See **Figure 41**. If there is any gap between the straightedge and cylinder head surface, measure it with a feeler gauge. Have the cylinder head resurfaced by a machine shop if the gap exceeds 0.004 in. (0.101 mm).

Decarbonizing

1. Without removing valves, remove all deposits from the combustion chambers, intake ports and exhaust ports. Use a power drill with brush attachment (**Figure 42**) or make a scraper out of hardwood. Be careful not to scratch or gouge the combustion chambers.
2. After all carbon is removed from the combustion chambers and ports, clean the entire head in solvent.
3. Clean away all carbon on the piston tops. Do not remove the carbon ridge at the top of the cylinder bore.

Cylinder Head Installation

1. Clean the cylinder head mating surfaces and the engine block, intake manifold and valve rocker arm cover surfaces to which the cylinder head mounts. Be sure that the cylinder bores are clean and check all visible oil and water passages for cleanliness.

NOTE
Make sure to clean all cylinder bolt threads in the cylinder block and the cylinder head bolt threads. Dirt will affect bolt torque.

NOTE
Return any dowel pin from the cylinder head back to its position in the cylinder block to help in positioning the cylinder head gasket.

2. Install new cylinder head gasket(s) with the note "This Side Up" facing upward. Never reuse an old head gasket. *Do not* use gasket sealer on the head gasket(s).
3. Position cylinder head over dowel pins and install on block.
4. Coat cylinder head bolts with GM sealer part No. 1052080 or equivalent.
5. With engine cool, tighten the head bolts in order given in **Figure 40**. Tighten bolts gradually. Final torque is 70 ft.-lb. (90 N•m).
6. Clean the pushrods in solvent. Check end of pushrods for nicks, grooves, roughness or excessive wear. Check all pushrods for straightness as explained in this chapter.
7. The remainder of the installation procedure is accomplished by performing Steps 1-8 of the *Cylinder Head Removal* procedure in reverse order. After installation is complete

run the engine for several minutes, let it cool, then recheck head bolt tightness (**Figure 40**).

8. Perform the tune-up as described in Chapter Three.

VALVES AND VALVE SEATS

Valve Removal

1. Remove cylinder head as described in this chapter.
2. Compress each valve spring with a valve spring compressor like the one shown in **Figure 43**. Remove the valve keepers (**Figure 44**) and release the spring tension. Remove spring retainers, spring shield, springs and dampers.

NOTE
*A rotator shield is used on exhaust valves. See **Figure 45**. Make sure to label and install all valve parts in a rack so they can be reinstalled in the same location from which they were removed. See **Figure 46** for valve parts.*

3. Remove and discard oil seal from end of valve stem (**Figure 47**).

CAUTION
Remove any burrs from the valve stem grooves before removing valves. Otherwise, the valve guides will be damaged as the valve is removed.

4. Remove the valves through the combustion chamber.

Valve and Valve Guide Inspection

1. Clean the valves with a wire brush and solvent. Discard cracked, warped or burned valves.
2. Measure the valve stems at the bottom, center and top for wear, using a micrometer. A machine shop can do this when the valves are ground. Also measure the length of each valve and the diameter of each valve head. See **Figure 48** and **Table 1** (end of chapter).
3. The valve faces and stem ends should be refaced when the valves are ground.
4. Remove all carbon and varnish from valve guides with a stiff spiral wire brush (**Figure 49**).

43

44

45

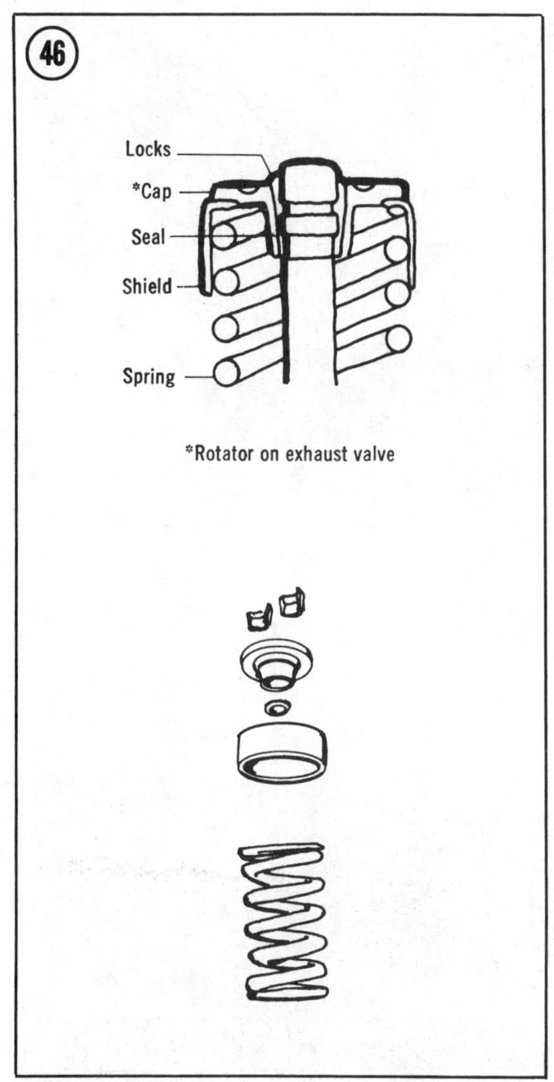
46
Locks
*Cap
Seal
Shield
Spring
*Rotator on exhaust valve

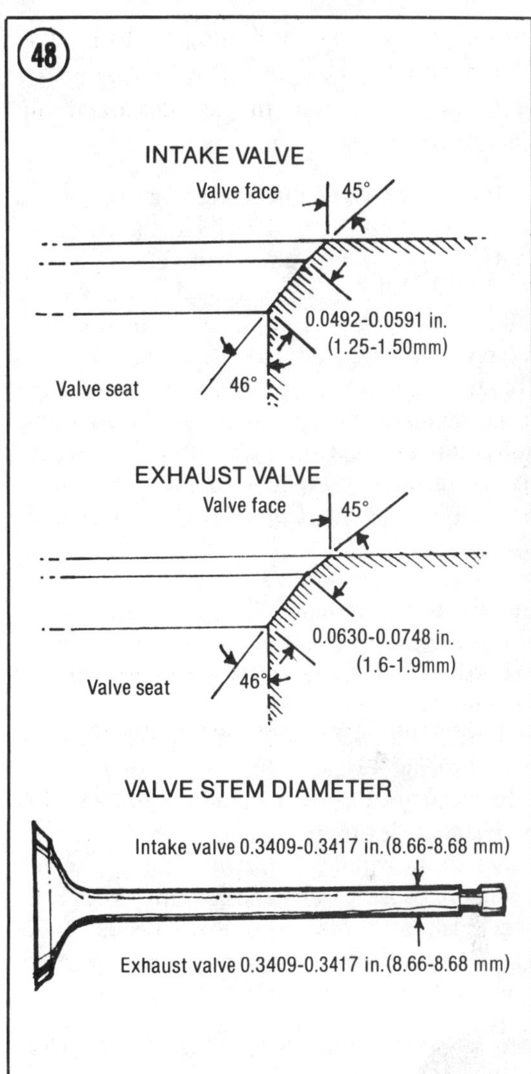
48
INTAKE VALVE
Valve face
45°
0.0492-0.0591 in.
(1.25-1.50mm)
Valve seat
46°
EXHAUST VALVE
Valve face
45°
0.0630-0.0748 in.
(1.6-1.9mm)
Valve seat
46°
VALVE STEM DIAMETER
Intake valve 0.3409-0.3417 in.(8.66-8.68 mm)
Exhaust valve 0.3409-0.3417 in.(8.66-8.68 mm)

47

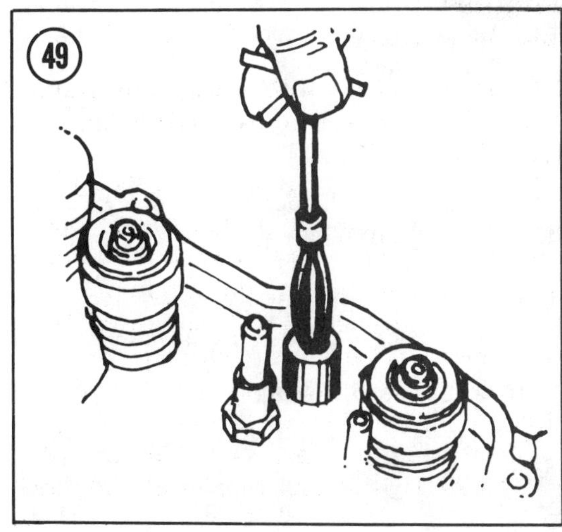
49

5

NOTE
The next step assumes that all valves have been measured and are within specifications. Replace any valves with worn stems before performing this step.

5. Insert each valve into the guide from which it was removed. Hold valve just slightly off its seat and rock it back and forth (**Figure 50**). If the valve rocks more than slightly, the valve guide is worn and should be reamed for an oversize valve stem as described in this chapter.
6. If there is any doubt about valve guide condition after performing Step 5, measure the valve guide at top, center and bottom with a small hole gauge. Compare the valve guide measurements with the valve stem specifications shown in **Figure 48** and listed at the end of this chapter (**Table 1**) to determine stem-to-guide clearance. If clearance is excessive, have valve guides reamed for oversize valve stems.
7. Check the valve springs for deformation with a square (**Figure 51**). Replace any springs more than 5/64 in. out of square.
8. Have a dealer or machine shop test the valve springs under load with a spring tester. Compare spring loaded lengths with the specifications at the end of this chapter (**Table 1**). Replace any springs that do not meet specifications.
9. Inspect valve seats. See **Figure 52**. If worn or burned, they must be reconditioned. Valve seat reconditioning should be done by a General Motors dealer or competent machine shop, although the procedure is described later in this section.

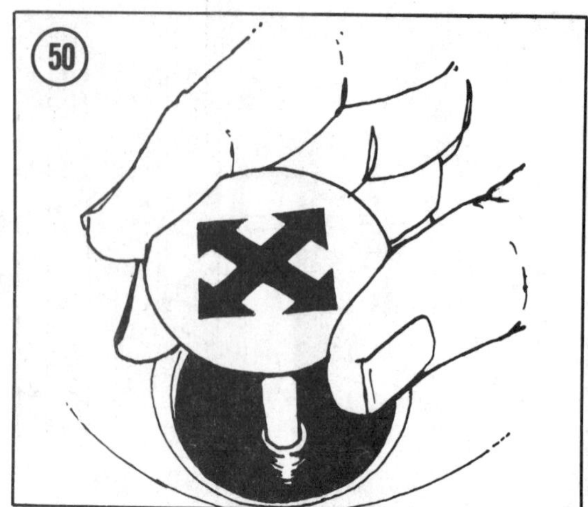

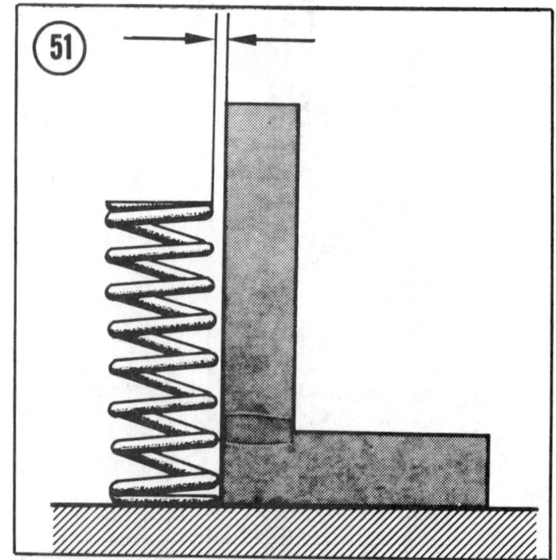

Valve Guide Reaming

Valve guides on all engines are integral with the cylinder head. When guides are worn, they must be reamed to accept a valve with an oversize stem. This is a precise job that should be left to a dealer or competent machine shop.

Valve Seat Reconditioning

This job is best left to a General Motors dealer or competent machine shop. They have the special knowledge and equipment

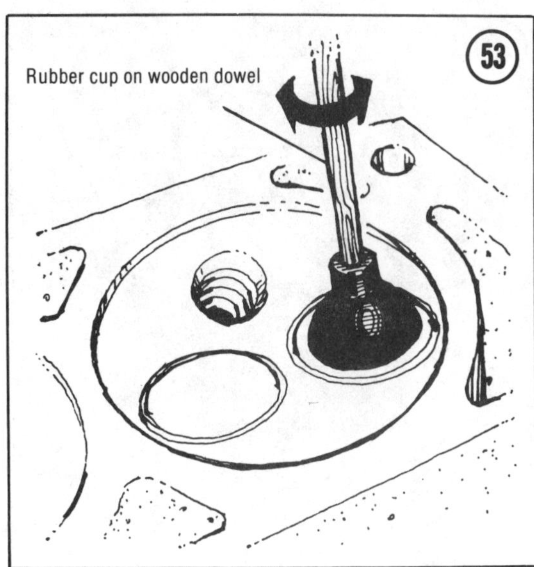

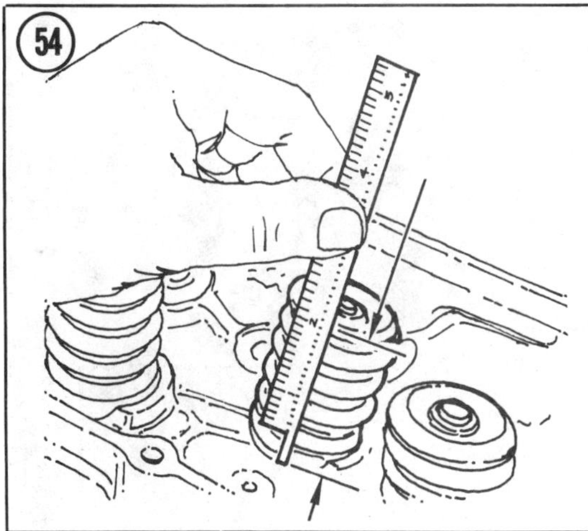

required for this precise job. The following procedure is provided in the event you are not near a dealer.

1. Cut the valve seats (**Figure 52**) to specified dimensions (**Figure 48** and **Table 1**, end of chapter) using a cutter or a special stone.
2. Coat the corresponding valve face with Prussian blue.
3. Insert the valve into the valve guide.
4. Rotate the valve under light pressure with a rubber dowel approximately 1/4 turn (**Figure 53**).
5. Lift the valve out. If it seats properly, the dye will transfer evenly to the valve face. If not, the refacing procedure must be repeated.

Valve Installation

1. Coat the valves with oil and insert them in the cylinder head.
2. Install the valve spring, valve spring damper, shield and valve retainer in place. Compress the valve with a tool like the one shown in **Figure 43** and install the oil seal in the lower groove of the valve stem. Ensure that the seal is installed flat and not twisted. Install the valve keepers in the upper groove of the valve stem (**Figure 44**) and release the valve spring.

NOTE

*Ensure that valve keepers are positioned correctly when the valve spring tension is released. See **Figure 45**.*

3. Measure height of installed springs against specifications. A cutaway scale (**Figure 54**) will help. Measure from the top of the spring seat or shim (if any) to the top of the oil shedder (**Figure 55**). Proper height is 1.57 in. (40 mm). If height exceeds this, disassemble valve and install seat shim of required thickness. These are available from your dealer.

CAUTION

Do not shim any spring so that installed height is less than specifications or coil bind may occur.

TORSIONAL DAMPER AND FRONT COVER

Removal

1. Disconnect negative cable from battery.
2. Remove the drive belts.
3. Remove the radiator hose attached to the timing cover (**Figure 4**) and the heater hose attached to the water pump (**Figure 5**).
4. Remove the water pump as described in Chapter Seven.

> *NOTE*
> *For vehicles equipped with air conditioning, carefully read the air conditioning section in Chapter Seven to acquaint yourself with the system. Then, remove the compressor and its mounting bracket and position it out of the way. Make certain that there is no strain on any of the hoses or lines. Do not disconnect any hoses or lines.*

5. Raise vehicle front end and secure with jackstands. Remove the right front tire and wheel.
6. Remove the right inner fender splash shield.
7. Remove the drive pulley attaching bolts and the pulley (**Figure 56**).
8. Pull the torsional damper from crankshaft with a puller such as the one shown in **Figure 57**.

> *CAUTION*
> *The inertial weight (outside ring) of the torsional damper is secured with rubber (**Figure 58**) and must be removed with a puller on the inside threads. See **Figure 57**. Removing the torsional damper by its outside ring will destroy the outside ring and the tuning of the damper.*

9. Remove the front cover-to-block and front cover-to-oil pan retaining bolts (**Figure 59**). Tap the cover with a rubber mallet to free it, then lift the cover off.

Installation

Installation is the reverse of the removal procedure, plus the following steps:

1. Remove all old sealant from engine block and front cover mating surfaces.

56

57

58

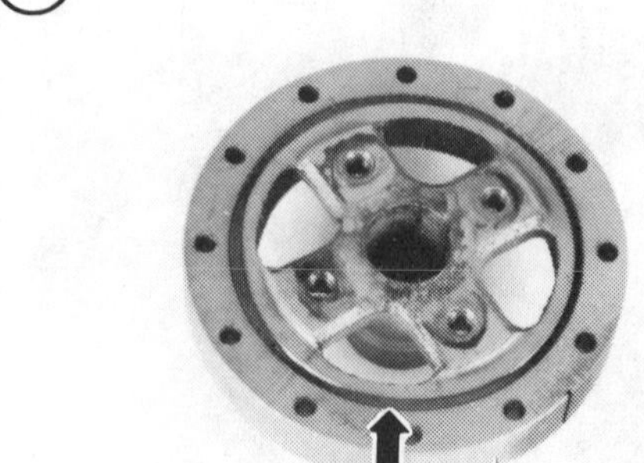

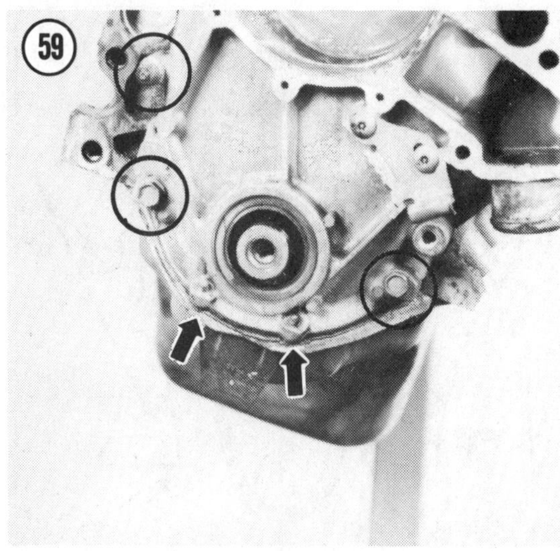

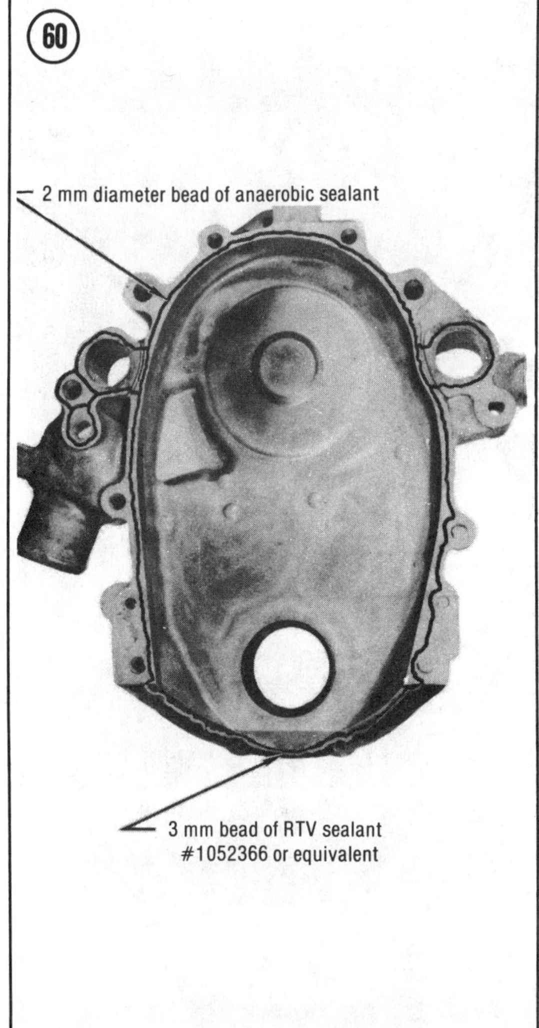

NOTE
A new front cover oil seal should be installed in the front cover each time the front cover is removed. Refer to the ***Timing Cover Oil Seal Replacement*** *procedure described later in this chapter.*

2. Coat the front cover with a continuous bead of anaerobic and RTV sealant at the points indicated in **Figure 60**.
3. Place the front cover on the engine and install the water pump as described in Chapter Seven. Tighten all attaching bolts to specifications (**Table 2**, end of chapter). See **Figure 61**.
4. Coat the front cover seal with engine oil.
5. Install the torsional damper onto crankshaft. Make sure to align with key on crankshaft. Install GM tool part No. J-29113 into end of crankshaft. Ensure that at least 1/4 in. of tool threads are engaged in crankshaft. Pull torsional damper onto crankshaft with tool and tighten attaching bolt to specification listed at end of this chapter.

CAUTION
If the securing tool is not used, the inertial weight section may separate from the hub. This will ruin the torsional damper.

6. Start the engine and operate at a fast idle to check for oil or coolant leaks.

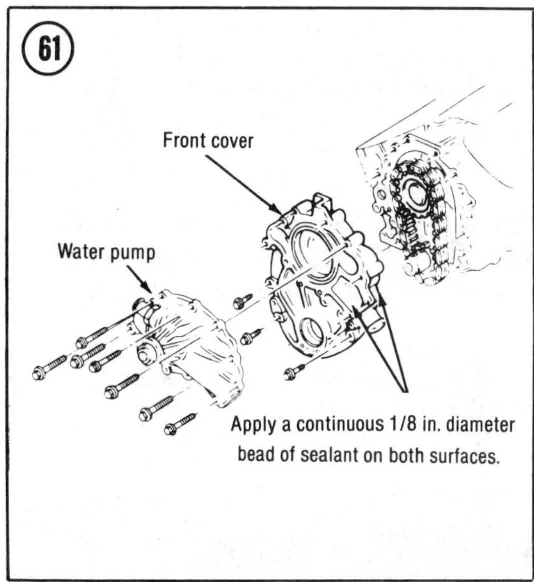

5

TIMING CHAIN AND SPROCKET

Removal/Installation

1. Remove the torsional damper and front cover as described previously.
2. Turn the engine by hand until the timing marks on the camshaft and crankshaft gears are aligned as shown in **Figure 62**. Align marks with the No. 1 piston at top dead center.
3. Remove the camshaft sprocket attaching bolts (**Figure 63**), then lower sprocket from end of camshaft. If sprocket fit is tight, lightly hit sprocket with plastic mallet. Then remove camshaft sprocket and timing chain.
4. Remove the crankshaft gear with a universal gear puller.
5. Installation is the reverse of these steps. Install crankshaft gear with GM tool part No. J-5590 or equivalent. Make sure to align the dowel pin in the camshaft (**Figure 64**) with the dowel hole in the camshaft sprocket and to align the timing sprockets (**Figure 62**). Tighten the camshaft sprocket bolts to 15-20 ft.-lb. (20-27 N•m). Tighten the crankshaft pulley hub bolt to 66-84 ft.-lb. (90-115 N•m).

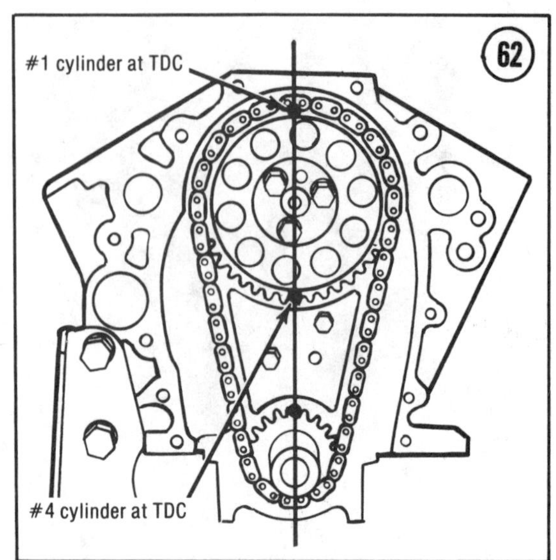

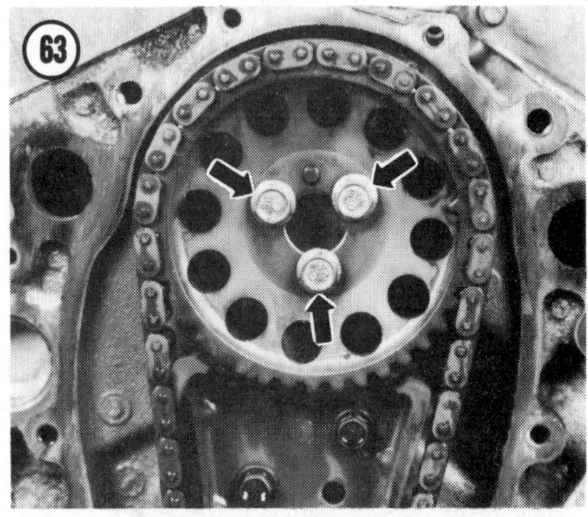

TIMING COVER OIL SEAL REPLACEMENT

The front seal can be replaced with the front cover on or off the engine. If the seal is being replaced with the timing cover installed, remove the torsional damper as described in this chapter to provide access to seal.

1. Remove the cylinder block front cover.
2. Remove seal from cover by prying out with 2 large screwdrivers.
3. Coat the new seal lip with engine oil.
4. Support the front cover around the area of the oil seal. Drive the new seal into place using a suitable size drift.

NOTE
The seal lip faces into the engine.

VALVE LIFTERS

The V6 cid engine is equipped with hydraulic lifters. These seldom require attention and do not require periodic adjustment.

65

66

67

Removal

1. Remove the intake manifold as described in Chapter Six.
2. Remove the rocker arms and pushrods as described in this chapter.
3. Take the lifters out of their bores (**Figure 65**). Place them in a numbered rack so they can be returned to their original positions. See **Figure 66**.

NOTE

*Some engines use both standard and 0.010 in. oversize lifters. If your engine uses the 0.010 in. oversize lifters, the cylinder case where the oversize lifter operates will be marked with a daub of white paint and have "0.25 mm O.S." stamped on the lifter boss. See **Figure 67**.*

Installation

Installation is the reverse of removal, plus the following.

1. Coat the bottoms of the lifters with Molykote or equivalent.
2. Adjust the valves as described under *Valve Adjustment* in this chapter.

CAMSHAFT

Removal/Installation

1. Remove the engine as described in this chapter.
2. Remove the rocker arm cover and pushrods as described in this chapter.
3. Remove the fuel pump (Chapter Six).
4. Remove the valve lifters from their bores (**Figure 65**) and place them in a rack so that they may be reinstalled in their original locations. See **Figure 66**.
5. Turn the engine to align the timing marks (**Figure 62**) and remove the timing chain and sprocket as described in this chapter.
6. Thread one or more of the sprocket bolts into the camshaft. Use the bolt(s) as a handle to pull the camshaft out.
7. Carefully remove the camshaft from the bearings through front of engine block. Rotate the camshaft while removing. Do not let the cam lobes touch or nick the bearings.

5

Camshaft Inspection

The following procedures can be done by a machine shop if you do not have the precision tools.

1. Check all machined surfaces of the camshaft for nicks or grooves. Minor defects may be removed with a smooth oilstone. Severe damage or wear beyond the specifications, listed at the end of this chapter, requires replacement of the camshaft.
2. Measure the outer diameter of the camshaft journals (**Figure 68**). Compare this measurement with the specifications listed at the end of this chapter. Replace the camshaft if the journals exceed the wear or out- of-round specification listed at the end of this chapter.

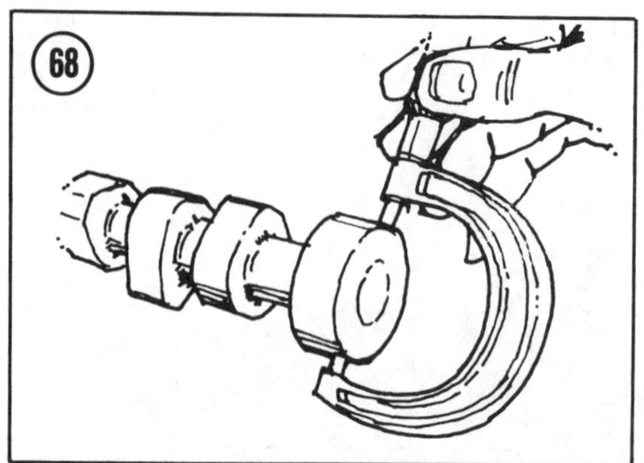

Camshaft Installation

1. Coat the camshaft journals and bearing surfaces with clean engine oil.
2. Carefully install the camshaft in the engine block. Rotate the camshaft slowly while inserting to ease installation.
3. Rotate camshaft and crankshaft timing gears so that the valve timing marks on gear teeth will line up. See **Figure 62**.
4. Install the following parts as described in this chapter:
   a. Front cover and gasket
   b. Water pump
   c. Torsional damper
   d. Valve lifters
   e. Pushrods
   f. Fuel pump
   g. Engine assembly
5. Tune-up vehicle as described in Chapter Three.

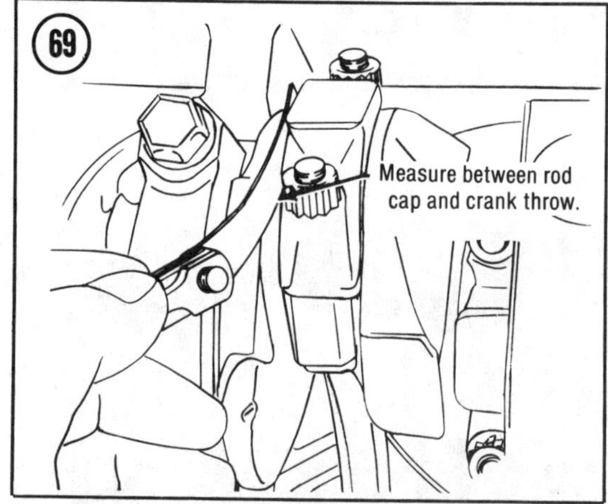

PISTON/CONNECTING ROD ASSEMBLIES

Piston/Connecting Rod Removal

1. Remove the cylinder head as described in this chapter.
2. Remove the oil pan as described in this chapter.
3. Measure connecting rod side play with a feeler gauge (**Figure 69**). Normal clearance is

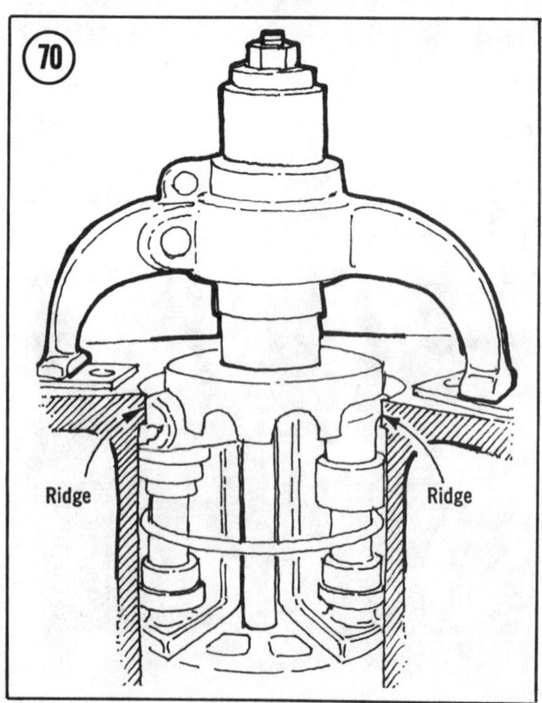

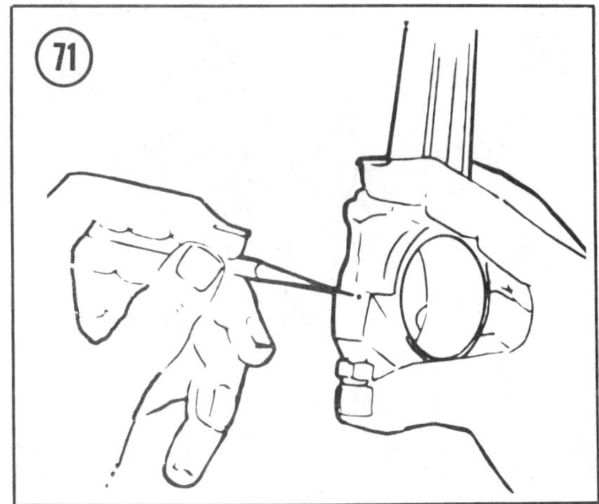

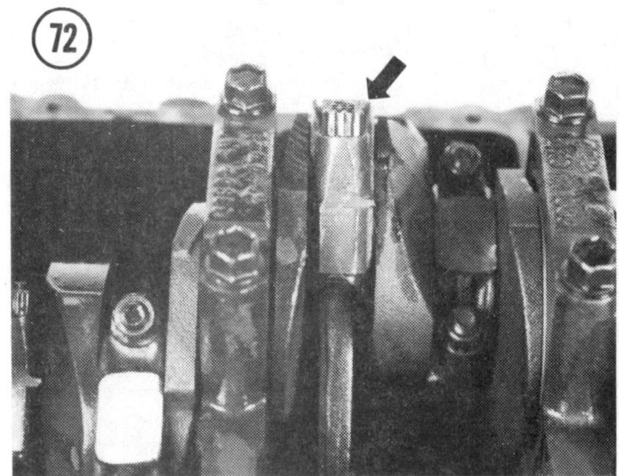

0.006-0.017 in. (0.152-0.439 mm). Replace the connecting rod if it exceeds specifications.

4. Remove the carbon ridge at the top of the cylinder bores with a ridge reamer (**Figure 70**). Do not cut more than 1/32 in. into the ring travel area when using the ridge reamer.

CAUTION

Turn each piston to the bottom of its travel and pack a rag into the cylinder before removing the ridge. Vacuum out all cuttings, then remove the rag.

5. Check rod and bearing caps for cylinder number markings. If there are no marks visible, scribe your own with a sharp tool. See **Figure 71**. Make the marks on the same side of rod and cap so they can be reassembled in their original relationship.

6. Unbolt the connecting rod cap (**Figure 72**) and remove the rod cap and bearing from the crankshaft. Wrap the studs with tape to prevent damage to the cylinder walls when removing the piston/connecting rod assembly.

7. Free the connecting rod and piston assembly from the crankshaft by tapping gently with a hammer (**Figure 73**). Remove the connecting rod bearing, then push the piston and connecting rod assembly out of the cylinder bore using a hammer handle.

NOTE

It will be necessary to rotate crankshaft slightly to remove some of the connecting rods.

Disassembly

1. Remove the piston rings with a ring expander tool (**Figure 74**).

2. Secure the connecting rod in a vise. Rock the piston as shown in **Figure 75**. Any rocking motion (not sliding) indicates wear in the piston, connecting rod bushing, piston pin or all three.

NOTE

Piston pins are press-fitted to the connecting rods and slip fit into the pistons. Removal requires an arbor press, or similar device, and a suitable support tool. This is a job for a General Motors dealer or machine shop, equipped to fit the

5

pistons and pin, as well as align the pistons with the connecting rods.

Piston Clearance Check

This procedure should be done at room temperature. The cylinder walls must be clean and dry.

1. Clean the pistons thoroughly in solvent. Scrape carbon deposits from the piston top with a blunt-edge wood tool (**Figure 76**) and from the ring grooves with a ring groove cleaner or broken piston ring (**Figure 77**). Use a drill of the proper size to clean the oil ring holes in the lower ring groove. Do not remove any metal when cleaning with drill.

CAUTION
Do not use a wire brush to clean the sides of the piston as this could damage the piston skirt finish.

2. Check ring grooves for burrs, dented edges and side wear. Pay particular attention to top compression ring groove, as it usually wears more than the others.
3. Measure the cylinder bore as described under *Cylinder Bore Inspection.*
4. Measure the piston diameter at the piston pin centerline height and 90° to the piston pin axis (**Figure 78**).
5. Determine the difference between the cylinder bore and piston diameter. This gives the piston clearance. Compare this figure with the specifications listed at the end of this chapter (**Table 1**). If greater than specified, select another piston size from **Table 3**.
6. Repeat this procedure for all cylinders and pistons.

Piston Ring Fitting/Installation

1. Check the ring gap of each piston ring. To do this, first press the ring about one inch down the cylinder bore and square it by tapping gently with an inverted piston.

NOTE
If the cylinders have not been rebored, check the ring gap at the bottom of the ring travel, where the cylinder is least worn.

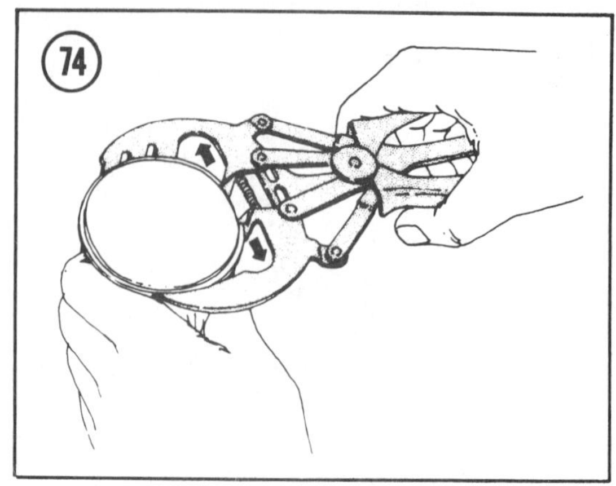

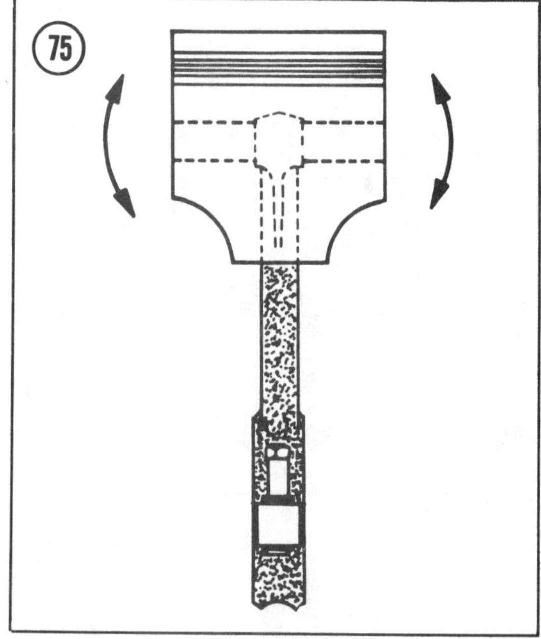

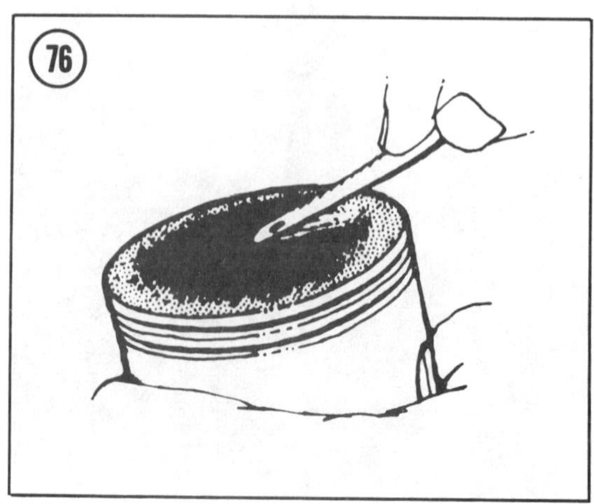

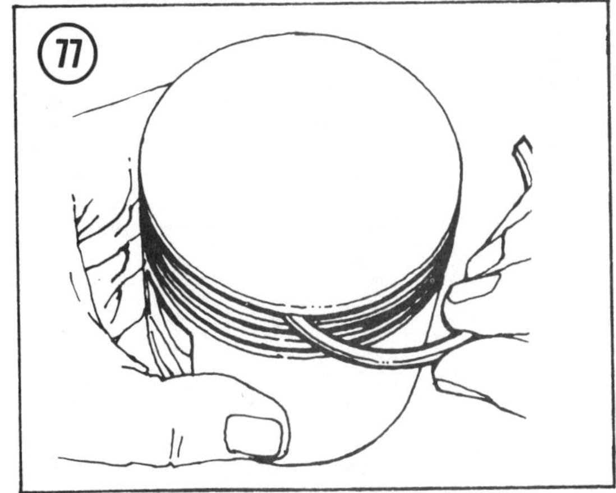

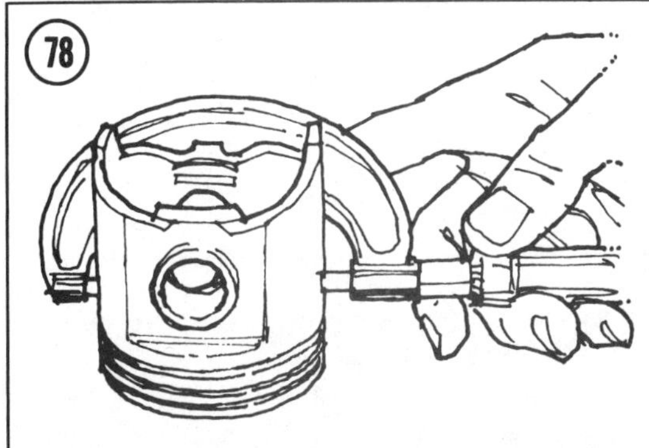

2. Measure the ring gap with a feeler gauge, as shown in **Figure 79**. Compare the ring gap with the specifications at the end of this chapter (see **Table 1**). If the ring gap is not within specification, use another set of rings.

3. Check side clearance of the rings as shown in **Figure 80**. Place the feeler gauge beneath the ring and insert all the way into the ring groove. The feeler gauge should slide all the way around the piston without binding. Any wear that occurs will form a step at the inner portion of the ring groove's lower edge. If large steps are discernible (**Figure 81**), the pistons should be replaced. Compare the inserted feeler gauge size with the specification at the end of this chapter (see **Table 1**).

4. Using a ring expander tool, carefully install the oil control ring assembly, then the compression rings.

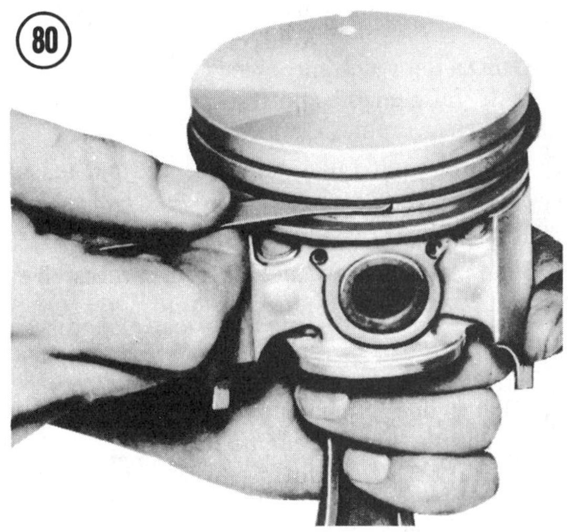

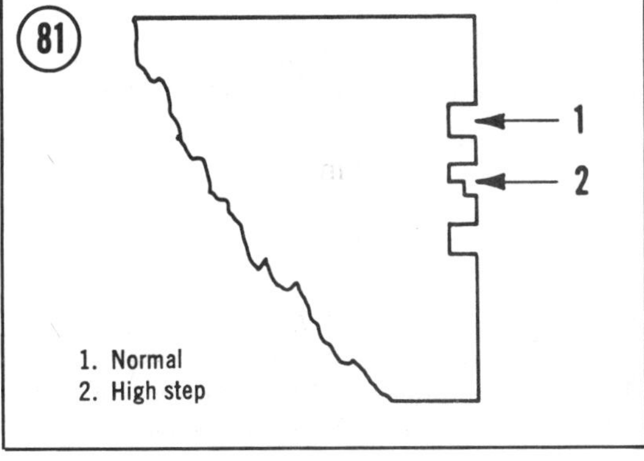

Connecting Rod Inspection

1. Check the pistons for shiny, scuffed areas above the piston pins on one side and below the piston pin on the other. This indicates a bent connecting rod.
2. Have the connecting rods checked by your General Motors dealer or a competent machine shop for twisting, bends and overall straightness and alignment.

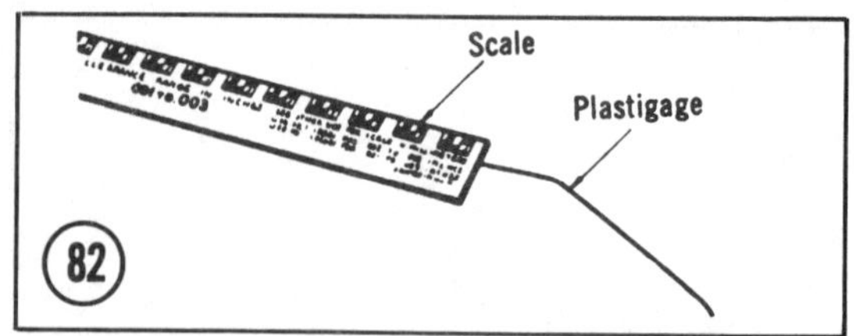

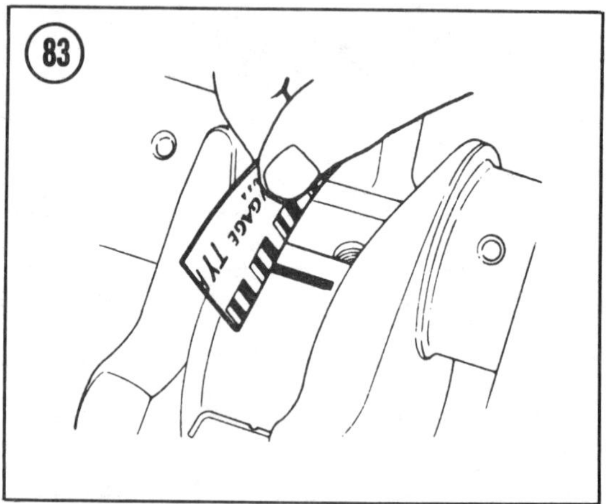

Measuring Bearing Clearance

1. Assemble connecting rods with bearings on the proper crankshaft journal. Do not tighten.
2. Cut a piece of Plastigage the width of the bearing. Insert Plastigage between crankshaft journal and connecting rod bearing. See **Figure 82**.

NOTE
Do not place the Plastigage over the crankshaft journal oil hole.

3. Install connecting rod cap and torque to 37 ft.-lb. (50 N•m). Do not rotate the crankshaft while Plastigage is in place.
4. Remove connecting rod cap. Bearing clearance is determined by comparing width of flattened Plastigage with scale markings on the Plastigage envelope (**Figure 83**). Compare Plastigage measurement with the specifications listed at end of this chapter (see **Table 1**). Replacement bearings are available in standard size and 0.005 in. (0.013 mm) and 0.010 in. (0.026 mm) undersize for use with used and new crankshafts.

Piston/Connecting Rod Installation

1. Remove cylinder wall glaze with a hone if new piston rings are to be installed. Follow hone manufacturer's recommendations.
2. Oil piston rings, pistons and cylinder walls with light engine oil. Be sure to install pistons in same cylinders from which they were removed or to which they were fitted.

NOTE
*Pistons must be installed with hole in piston top (**Figure 84**) facing toward front of engine.*

3. Install piston rings on piston using piston ring expander tool. Position the ring gaps around the piston as shown in **Figure 85**.
4. Install piston ring compressor on piston. Push piston into the cylinder with a hammer handle until it is slightly below top of cylinder (**Figure 86**).

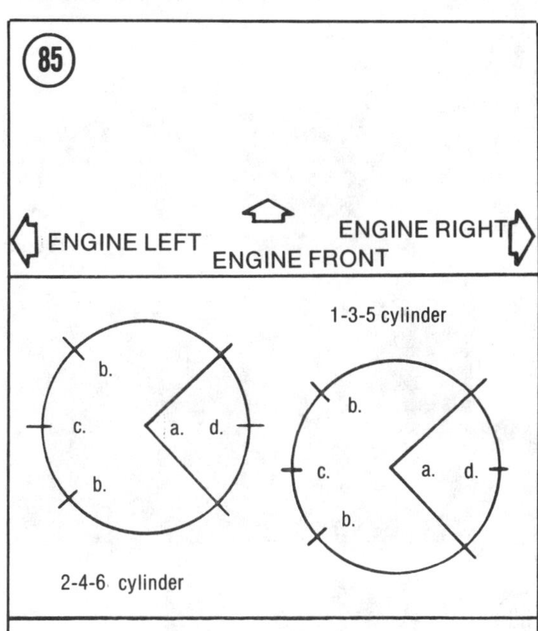

5. Check bearing clearance. See *Measuring Bearing Clearance*, this chapter. Apply a light coat of engine oil to the journals and bearings after the bearings have been fitted.
6. Turn crankshaft throw to bottom of its stroke. Push piston down until connecting rod bearing seats on crankshaft journal. Remove tape from end of connecting rod studs.
7. Install connecting rod cap. Tighten nuts to 37 ft.-lb. (51 N•m).
8. Recheck side clearance between connecting rods on each crankshaft journal after piston and connecting rod assemblies are installed as described in this chapter.

5

OIL PAN AND OIL PUMP

Oil Pan Removal

1. Jack up the front end of the vehicle and place it on jackstands.
2. Drain the engine oil.
3. Remove the front exhaust crosssover pipe (Chapter Six).
4. Remove the transaxle converter/starter shield or clutch housing cover as necessary to provide access to oil pan removal. See Chapter Nine.
5. Remove the starter (Chapter Eight).
6. *Manual transaxle equipped vehicles only*: Install suitable engine lifting hoist to engine.

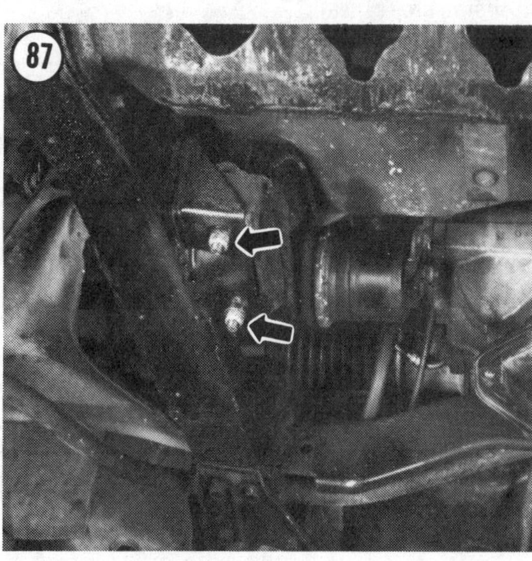

Remove engine mounting bracket-to-engine mount attaching bolts (**Figure 87**) and raise engine approximately 3/4 in. (19 mm).
7. Remove the oil pan attaching bolts, then remove the oil pan and gasket.

Oil Pan Installation

1. Clean the oil pump pickup screen.
2. Clean all traces of old gasket material and sealer from oil pan, cylinder block and front cover. Be sure to remove old sealant from blind attaching holes.
3. Coat a 1/8 in. bead of RTV sealant around the oil pan sealing flange.
4. Install new oil pan rear seal.
5. Position the oil pan against the cylinder block and install the oil pan attaching bolts.
6. Check the oil pan for proper alignment and install the remaining attaching screws. Tighten all screws evenly, a little at a time, to specification listed at end of chapter, to prevent warping the oil pan.
7. Reverse Steps 1-6 of *Oil Pan Removal* to complete installation. Start engine and check for leaks.

Oil Pump Removal/ Installation

1. Remove the oil pan.
2. Remove bolt that attaches the pump body and pickup tube to the rear main bearing cap (**Figure 88**). Remove the pump body and extension shaft assembly. See **Figure 89** for extension shaft location.

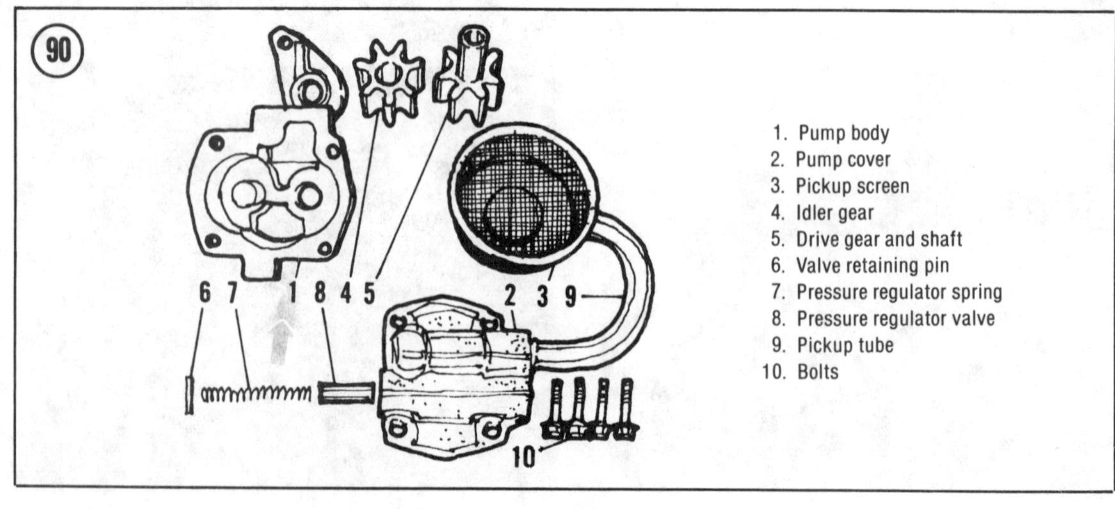

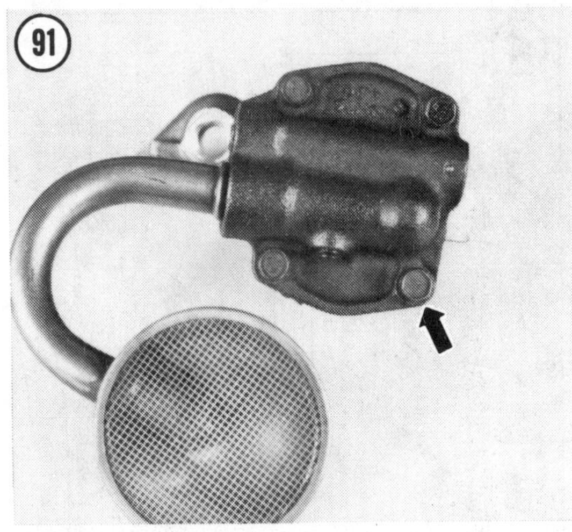

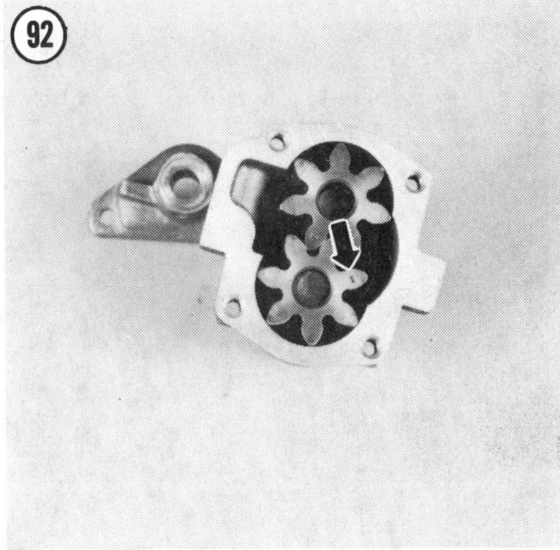

3. Installation is the reverse of these steps. Assemble oil pump and extension shaft with retainer to rear main bearing cap. Align top end of hexagon extension shaft with hexagon socket to the lower end of the distributor drive gear. Tighten oil pump attaching bolts to 26-35 ft.-lb. (35-47 N•m).

Disassembly/Inspection/ Assembly

Refer to **Figure 90** for the following procedure.

1. Remove the oil pump cover attaching screws (**Figure 91**), then remove the cover plate.

NOTE
*Note that mark on idler gear faces up. See **Figure 92**.*

2. Remove the idler gear and drive gear and shaft from the pump body. Drive out the valve retaining pin and remove the pressure spring and valve from inside the pump cover (**Figure 93**).

CAUTION
*Do not separate the pump cover or pickup screen from the pickup tube (**Figure 94**). If removed, pickup screen and pump cover must be replaced as a unit.*

3. Thoroughly clean all parts in solvent.
4. Inspect pump body and gears for excessive wear or cracks.

5

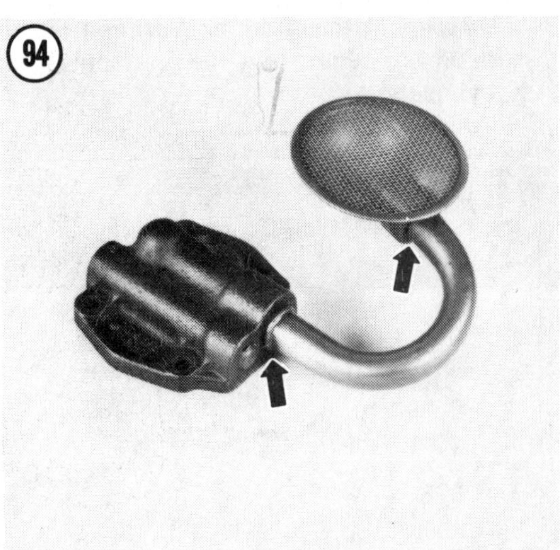

5. Install drive gear and shaft into housing and check for excessive looseness.
6. Inspect the inside cover for excessive wear which would allow oil to leak past the gears.
7. Examine the oil pickup screen for damage. If pickup screen and pipe become separated during cleaning (**Figure 94**), pickup screen and pump cover must be replaced as a unit.
8. Oil all pump parts thoroughly before beginning assembly.
9. Assembly is the reverse of the removal procedure. Be sure to install the idler gear with mark facing up (**Figure 92**). Turn drive shaft by hand and check for smooth operation. Tighten the cover plate attaching screws to 6-9 ft.-lb. (8-12 N•m).

CRANKSHAFT, MAIN BEARINGS AND REAR OIL SEALS

Crankshaft/Main Bearing Removal

Crankshaft, main bearings and rear oil seal removal, inspection and installation procedures may be performed with the engine still in the vehicle. However, this is a job for a General Motors dealer or a competent auto mechanic. The following procedure details removal, inspection and installation procedures once the engine has been removed from the vehicle.

1. Remove the engine from the vehicle as described under *Engine Removal* in this chapter.
2. Disconnect the spark plug wires from the spark plugs, then remove the spark plugs from the cylinders.

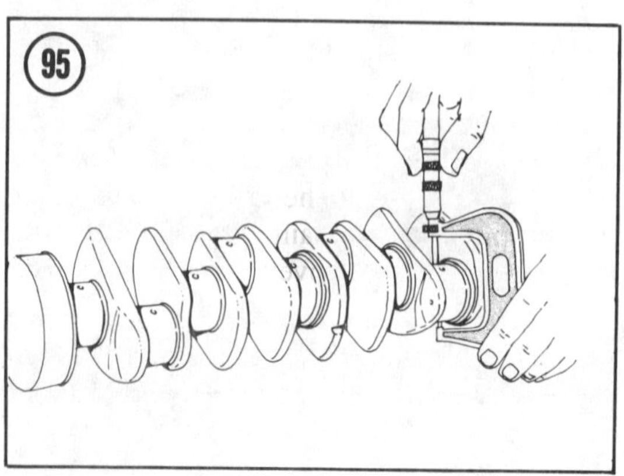

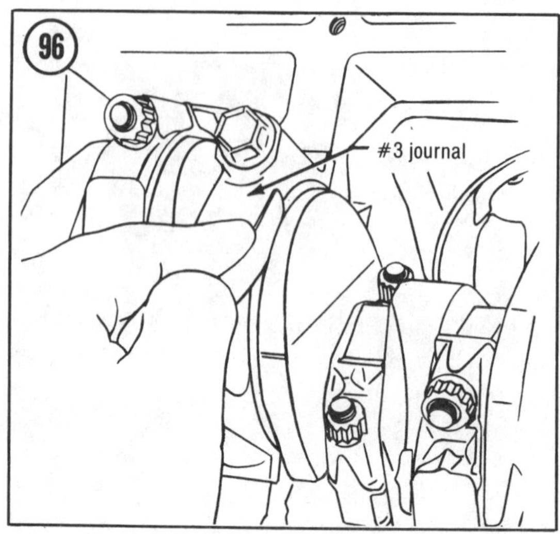

3. Remove the following parts, in order, as described in this chapter:
   a. Crankshaft pulley and torsional damper
   b. Oil pan and oil pump assembly
   c. Water pump and timing gear cover
   d. Timing gears and chain
   e. Connecting rod caps
4. Unbolt the flywheel from the rear end of the crankshaft.
5. Check the main bearing caps for numbers and for arrows pointing to the front of the engine. If none are present, make your own. Then remove the caps.
6. Carefully remove the crankshaft from the main bearing journals in the block so that the thrust bearing surfaces are not damaged. Handle the crankshaft with care to avoid damage to the crankshaft finished surfaces. Lay the main bearings and bearing caps in order on a clean surface.

Inspection

1. Clean the crankshaft thoroughly in solvent. Blow out the oil passages with compressed air.

NOTE

If you do not have precision measuring equipment, have a machine shop perform Steps 2 and 3.

2. Examine crankpins and main bearing journals for wear, scoring and cracks. Check all journals against specifications (**Table 1**, end of chapter) for out-of-roundness, taper and wear (**Figure 95**). If necessary, have the crankshaft reground.
3. Check the crankshaft for bending. Mount the crankshaft between accurate centers (such as V-blocks or a lathe) and rotate it one full turn with a dial gauge contacting the center journal. Actual bend is half the reading shown on the gauge. The crankshaft must be reground if bent beyond specifications.
4. Measure crankshaft end play. Install the crankshaft in the block. Insert a feeler gauge between the crankshaft and the thrust bearing flange (**Figure 96**). Replace the thrust bearing (**Figure 97**) if the end play exceeds specifications.

NOTE

Always replace the upper and lower bearing inserts as a set.

Measuring Main Bearing Clearance

1. Install the main bearings previously removed from the cylinder block in their original positions, then install the crankshaft on these bearings taking care not to damage the sides of thrust bearing (**Figure 97**).
2. Cut a piece of Plastigage the width of the main bearing journal to be measured. Lay the Plastigage on the main bearing journal. Install the main bearing cap complete with main bearing insert and tighten to 70 ft.-lb. (95 N•m).

NOTE

Do not place Plastigage across crankshaft oil holes. Do not rotate the crankshaft while the Plastigage is in place.

3. Remove the main bearing cap and bearing insert. Compare the width of the flattened Plastigage to the markings on the envelope to determine main bearing clearance (**Figure 98**). Compare the narrowest point on the Plastigage with the widest point to determine journal taper.
4. Compare measurement with specifications in **Table 1** (end of chapter). Slight excessive clearance may be corrected with a 0.0006 in. (0.016 mm) or 0.001 in. (0.030 mm) undersize bearing. Greater wear requires that the crankshaft be ground to accept undersize bearings. Refer this service to an automotive machine shop.

Crankshaft/Main Bearing Installation

1. With the main bearings removed from the bearing caps and the cylinder block, clean the main bearing bores in the cylinder block, main bearing caps and the main bearing inserts with lacquer thinner to remove all foreign material.

2. If the old main bearings are being reinstalled, be sure that they are reinstalled in the main bearing caps and the cylinder block bores from which they were removed. If new

5

bearings (or undersize bearings) are being installed, be sure that they are installed in the proper location.
3. Coat the main bearing surfaces and the crankshaft journals with clean, heavy engine oil.
4. Carefully lay the crankshaft in the main bearings installed in the cylinder block, being careful not to damage the sides of the thrust bearing (**Figure 97**).
5. Install the oil seal as described under *Rear Main Bearing Oil Seal Replacement*, in this chapter.
6. Install the main bearing caps with the arrow mark pointing forward.
7. Tighten the rear main bearing cap bolts to 70 ft.-lb. (95 N•m).

NOTE
If the crankshaft was removed to replace the main bearings, perform Step 8 and Step 9.

8. Torque all main bearing caps except the number 3 bearing cap (**Figure 99**) to 70 ft.-lb. (95 N•m).
9. Refer to **Figure 100** and center the thrust bearing. Then, while holding the crankshaft and thrust bearing in position, retorque all main bearing cap bolts to 70 ft.-lb. (95 N•m).
10. The remainder of the installation procedure is accomplished by performing Steps 1-4 of the removal procedure in reverse order.

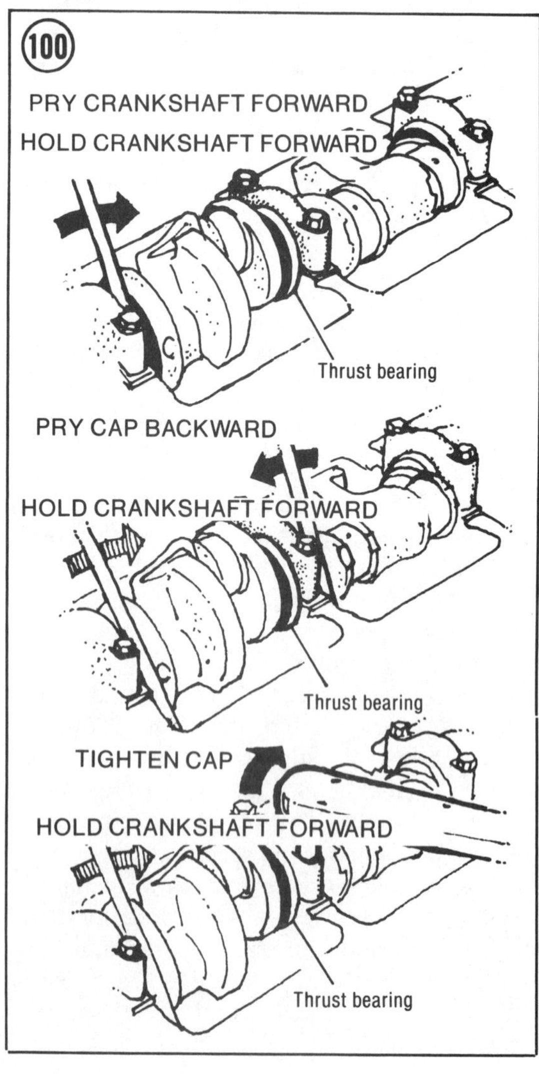

Rear Main Bearing Oil Seal Replacement

The rear main bearing oil seal can be replaced without removing the engine or crankshaft from the car.
1. Remove the oil pan and oil pump.
2. Remove the rear main bearing cap.
3. Pry the bottom seal half out of the cap (**Figure 101**) with a small screwdriver.
4. Tap one end of the upper seal half (in block) with a hammer and brass pin punch until the other end protrudes far enough to be pulled out with pliers.
5. Use a non-abrasive cleaner to remove all traces of sealer and other foreign matter from cylinder block, crankshaft and bearing cup.

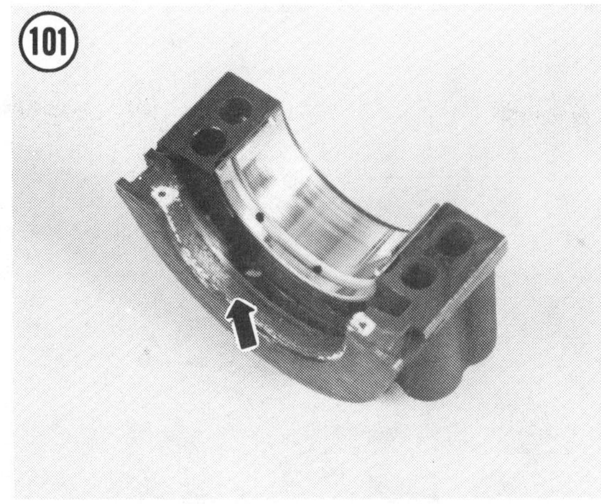

101

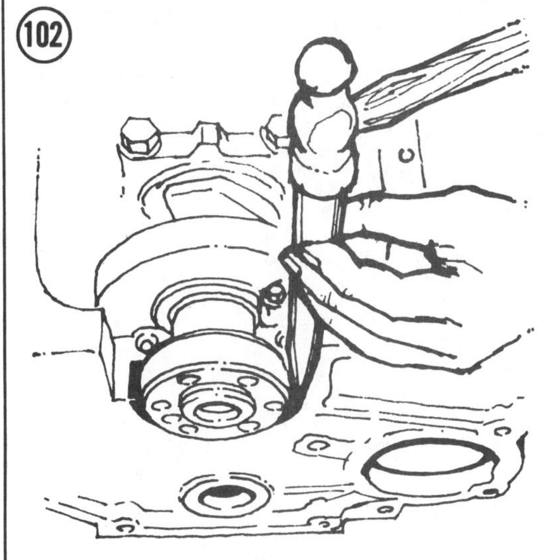

102

103

6. Check for defects on sealing surfaces, cylinder block and crankshaft.

7. Coat the seal lips and bead with engine oil. Keep oil off the mating ends of the seal.

8. Drive the upper seal (in block) into the cap groove approximately 1/4 in. on each side. See **Figure 102**.

9. Measure the amount the seal was driven in on one side and add 1/16 in.

10. Cut this length from the old seal with a sharp knife. Use the rear main bearing cap as a guide. Repeat for other side.

11. Insert piece of cut seal into the seal groove, then pack seal into the cylinder block. See **Figure 103**.

12. Install a new lower seal in the rear main bearing cap.

13. Measure bearing clearance as described under *Measuring Main Bearing Clearance.* If bearing clearance measures out of specification, examine ends of the seal for fraying which may be preventing the cap from seating fully. If seals are not at fault, problem lies with worn main bearings. Repair as necessary. Clean Plastigage from journal surface.

14. Apply a thin film of GM sealant (part No. 1052357) to the mating surfaces of the main bearing cap and cylinder block. Do not let sealant touch the journal or bearing.

15. Install main bearing cap and bolts. Tighten to 70 ft.-lb. (95 N•m). Install oil pump and oil pan to complete procedure.

CYLINDER BLOCK INSPECTION

1. Clean the cylinder block thoroughly with solvent and check all freeze plugs for leaks. **Figure 104** shows freeze plug for one side. Replace any plugs that are suspect. It is a good idea, at this level of disassembly, to replace all the freeze plugs. While cleaning, check oil and water passages for dirt, sludge and corrosion. If the passages are very dirty or clogged, the block should be boiled out by a General Motors dealer or competent automotive shop.

2. Examine the cylinder block for cracks. It is a good idea to take the block to a General Motors dealer or competent automotive shop

for Magnafluxing, to locate any hairline cracks that might escape visual examination.

3. Check all machined gasket surfaces for nicks or burrs. If necessary, smooth the surfaces with an oilstone.

4. Check the cylinder head mating surface of the block for flatness. Use an accurate straightedge and feeler gauge as shown in **Figure 105**. Have the block resurfaced if it is warped more than 0.004 in. (0.102 mm).

5. Measure the cylinder bores for out-of-roundness or excessive wear with a bore gauge (**Figure 106**). Measure the bores at top, center, and bottom, in front-rear and side-to-side directions. Compare measurements to specifications at the end of the chapter (**Table 1**). If the cylinders exceed maximum tolerances, they must be rebored. Reboring is also necessary if the cylinder walls are badly scuffed or scored. Cylinder reboring is a job for a General Motors dealer or competent machine shop.

FLYWHEEL

Removal/Installation

1. If the engine is in the car, remove the transaxle.
2. Remove the clutch. See *Clutch Removal*, Chapter Nine.
3. Unbolt the flywheel from the engine.
4. Installation is the reverse of removal. Tighten the flywheel bolts to specifications (**Table 2**, end of chapter).

Table 1 V6 ENGINE SPECIFICATIONS

General Specifications	
Displacement	173 cid (2.8 liter)
Bore	3.50 in. (89 mm)
Stroke	3.00 in. (76 mm)
Horsepower @ rpm	115 @ 4800
Torque @ rpm	150 @ 2000
Compression ratio	8.6:1
Firing order	1-2-3-4-5-6
Cylinder Bore	
Diameter	3.5036-3.5066 in. (88.992-89.070 mm)
Out-of-round	0.0007 in. (0.02 mm) max.
Taper	0.0007 in. (0.02 mm) max.
Piston	
Clearance	0.0017-0.0027 in. (0.043-0.069 mm)
Diameter	See Table 3
Oversizes available	See Table 3
Piston Pin	
Diameter	0.9052-0.9057 in. (22.9937-23.0015 mm)
Clearance	0.0002-0.0003 in. (0.0065-0.0091 mm)
Fit in rod	Press
Piston Compression Ring	
Groove clearance	
Top	0.0011-0.0027 in. (0.030-0.070 mm)
2nd	0.0015-0.0037 in. (0.040-0.095 mm)
Gap	
Top	0.0098-0.0196 in. (0.25-0.50 mm)
2nd	0.0098-0.0196 in. (0.25-0.50 mm)
Piston Oil Ring	
Groove clearance	0.0078 in. (0.199 mm) max.
Gap	0.020-0.055 in. (0.51-1.40 mm)
Camshaft	
Lobe lift	
Intake	0.231 in. (5.87 mm)
Exhaust	0.262 in. (6.67 mm)
Journal diameter (all)	1.8677-1.8696 in. (47.44-47.49 mm)
Journal clearance	0.010-0.0039 in. (0.026-0.101 mm)
Valves	
Lash	1 1/2 turns from zero lash
Face angle	45°
Seat angle	46°
Seat runout	0.002 in. (0.05 mm)
Seat width	
Intake	0.050-0.060 in. (1.25-1.50 mm)
Exhaust	0.063-0.074 in. (1.60-1.90 mm)
Stem clearance	0.010-0.0026 in. (0.026-0.068 mm)

(continued)

5

Table 1 V6 ENGINE SPECIFICATIONS (continued)

Valve Springs	
Pressure lbs. @ in. (N @ mm)	
Closed	87.90 @ 1.574 (391 @ 40)
Open	194.91 @ 1.181 (867 @ 30)
Free length	1.858 in. (47.2 mm)
Installed height	1.574 in. (40 mm)
Approx. No. of coils	4
Crankshaft main journal	
Diameter	2.4936-2.4946 in. (63.340-63.364 mm)
Taper	0.0002 in. (0.005 mm) max.
Out-of-round	0.0002 in. (0.005 mm) max.
Main bearing	
Clearance (all)	0.0017-0.0029 in. (0.044-0.076 mm)
End play	0.002-0.007 in. (0.05-0.20 mm)
Crankpin	
Diameter	1.992-2.000 in. (50.758-50.784 mm)
Taper	0.0002 in. (0.005 mm) max.
Out-of-round	0.0002 in. (0.005 mm) max.
Rod bearing clearance	0.0014-0.0035 in. (0.036-0.091 mm)
Rod side clearance	0.0063-0.0173 in. (0.16-0.44 mm)

Table 2 TIGHTENING TORQUES, V6 CID ENGINE

Item	Torques	
Camshaft sprocket bolt	15-20 ft.-lb.	(20-27 N•m)
Camshaft rear cover bolt	6-9 ft.-lb.	(8-12 N•m)
Clutch cover to flywheel bolt	13-18 ft.-lb.	(18-24 N•m)
Cylinder head bolt	65-75 ft.-lb.	(88-102 N•m)
Connecting rod cap bolt	34-40 ft.-lb.	(46-54 N•m)
Crankshaft pulley bolt	20-30 ft.-lb.	(27-41 N•m)
Crankshaft pulley hub bolt	66-84 ft.-lb.	(90-115 N•m)
Distributor bolt	20-30 ft.-lb.	(27-41 N•m)
EGR valve bolt	13-18 ft.-lb.	(18-24 N•m)
Engine mounting bracket	70-92 ft.-lb.	(95-125 N•m)
Engine mounting torque strut bracket	30-40 ft.-lb.	(40-54 N•m)
Exhaust manifold	22-28 ft.-lb.	(30-38 N•m)
Flex plate to torque converter bolt	25-35 ft.-lb.	(34-47 N•m)
Flywheel	45-55 ft.-lb.	(61-75 N•m)
Front cover		
M8 x 1.25	13-18 ft.-lb.	(18-24 N•m)
M10 x 1.5	20-30 ft.-lb.	(27-41 N•m)
Fuel pump	13-18 ft.-lb.	(18-24 N•m)
Alternator bracket to cylinder head bolt	30-40 ft.-lb.	(40-54 N•m)
Alternator brace to cover bolt	20-30 ft.-lb.	(27-41 N•m)
Alternator pivot brace	20-30 ft.-lb.	(27-41 N•m)
Alternator adjust bolt	20-25 ft.-lb.	(27-34 N•m)
Intake manifold	20-25 ft.-lb.	(27-34 N•m)
Main bearing caps	63-74 ft.-lb.	(85-100 N•m)
Oil gauge tube	20-30 ft.-lb.	(27-41 N•m)
Oil filter	12-17 ft.-lb.	(16-23 N•m)
Oil filter connector	24-34 ft.-lb.	(32-46 N•m)
Oil pan		
M6 x 1.0	6-9 ft.-lb.	(8-12 N•m)
M8 x 1.25	14-22 ft.-lb.	(19-30 N•m)
Oil pump	26-35 ft.-lb.	(35-47 N•m)
Oil pump cover	6-9 ft.-lb.	(8-12 N•m)
Oil drain plug	15-20 ft.-lb.	(20-27 N•m)
Rocker arm cover	6-9 ft.-lb.	(8-12 N•m)
Rocker arm stud	43-49 ft.-lb.	(58-66 N•m)
Spark plug	7-15 ft.-lb.	(10-20 N•m)
Starter motor	26-37 ft.-lb.	(36-50 N•m)
Starter motor brace to case	13-18 ft.-lb.	(18-24 N•m)
Starter motor brace to motor	25-30 in. lb.	(2.8-3.4 N•m)
Timing chain tensioner	13-18 ft.-lb.	(18-24 N•m)
Water outlet	20-30 ft.-lb.	(27-41 N•m)
Water pump		
M6 x 1.0	6-9 ft.-lb.	(8-12 N•m)
M8 x 1.25	13-18 ft.-lb.	(18-24 N•m)
M10 x 1.5	20-30 ft.-lb.	(27-41 N•m)
Water pump pulley	13-18 ft.-lb.	(18-24 N•m)

5

Table 3 PISTON SIZE CHART, V6

Type	Code	Size
Std.	BG BH	3.5030-3.5034 in. (88.987-88.988 mm) 3.5034-3.5039 in. (88.988-89.001 mm)
High Limit	BJ BK	3.5039-3.5040 in. (89.001-89.014 mm) 3.5040-3.5049 in. (89.014-89.027 mm)
Oversize 0.002 in. (0.05 mm)	BG BH BJ BK	3.5226-3.5231 in. (89.475-89.488 mm) 3.5331-3.5236 in. (89.488-89.501 mm) 3.5236-3.5241 in. (89.501-89.514 mm) 3.5241-3.5246 in. (89.514-89.527 mm)
Oversize 0.040 in. (1.0 mm)	BG BH BJ BK	3.5423-3.5428 in. (89.975-89.988 mm) 3.5428-3.5433 in. (89.988-90.001 mm) 3.5433-3.5438 in. (90.001-90.014 mm) 3.5438-3.5443 in. (90.014-90.027 mm)

NOTE: If you own a 1981 or later model, first check the Supplement at the back of the book for any new service information.

CHAPTER SIX

FUEL AND EXHAUST SYSTEMS

6

This chapter presents repair and replacement procedures for the fuel tank, fuel pump, carburetor, exhaust pipe, muffler and tailpipe. Carburetor adjustments performed on a routine basis are found in the *Tune-up* section of Chapter Three. Your General Motors vehicle uses either a Rochester 2SE or E2SE Varajet II carburetor. Both are of the 2 barrel, 2 stage downdraft type.

The fuel tank incorporates the fuel pick-up, vapor return, filter and fuel level sender. On the V6 models, a fuel return system is used.

Tables 1-3 are at the end of the chapter.

AIR CLEANER

All engines use the Thermostatic air cleaner system (Thermac). The system, which uses a vacuum motor controlled inlet valve assembly in the air cleaner, is used to mix pre-heated and ambient air entering the air cleaner to maintain controlled air temperatures to the carburetor. By pre-heating inlet air, leaner carburetor and choke calibrations are permitted which result in lower emission levels.

Element Replacement

The air cleaner needs servicing at 30,000 mile intervals under normal driving conditions.

When replacement is required, remove either the 2 nuts (4-cylinder) or unscrew the wingnut (V6) securing the air cleaner cover to the carburetor air horn stud. See **Figure 1** or **Figure 2**. Detach air cleaner from air horn and housing and discard air cleaner element. Inspect cover gasket and wipe inside of housing with damp cloth. Replace if damaged or cracked. Install new air cleaner element.

Air Cleaner Assembly Replacement

Attached to the air cleaner assembly on all models are a number of vacuum lines and

hoses. Each plays an important part in the operation and efficiency of the engine. Therefore, it is important that all lines and hoses be tagged before removal of the air cleaner assembly so that each can be returned to its original position.

1. Remove the air cleaner cover and filter. See **Figure 1** (4-cylinder) or **Figure 2** (V6).
2. Remove the hot air duct to intake duct screw (**Figure 3**). Then detach the intake hose clip (**Figure 4**) and remove hose from intake tunnel.
3. Remove the breather hose from the side of air cleaner housing. See **Figure 5** (4-cylinder) or **Figure 6** (V6). On the V6 housing, remove the sensor clip from inside the air cleaner housing (**Figure 7**) and pull the sensor outward to remove.
4. Raise the air cleaner assembly slightly and remove the PCV hose by pulling the tube out of the rubber grommet. **Figure 8** shows the V6 hose. The 4-cylinder hose assembly is similar.
5. Referring to **Figure 9**, remove the hoses from the vacuum sensor.
6. Reverse the removal procedures to install. Check all vacuum lines and hoses, rubber grommet, and intake hoses for damage. Replace parts as required.

Thermac Inspection

The most likely cause of Thermac air cleaner trouble is when the inlet valve is stuck open. This is not apparent in warm weather, but in cold weather, it results in slow acceleration, engine hesitation or stalling. The inlet valve may also be stuck shut, which causes extremely high fuel consumption or loss of power. Refer to **Figure 10**.

1. Check all hoses for proper connection. Replace hoses which appear kinked, plugged or damaged.
2. With the engine off, hold a mirror up to the air inlet and see if the valve is open. See **Figure 11**. If it is closed, check the valve linkage for binding.
3. Disconnect the vacuum hose from the vacuum motor inlet on top of the air cleaner nozzle. See **Figure 10**. Apply vacuum directly to the vacuum motor inlet. (Apply at least 9 in. Hg of vacuum with a vacuum pump).

2

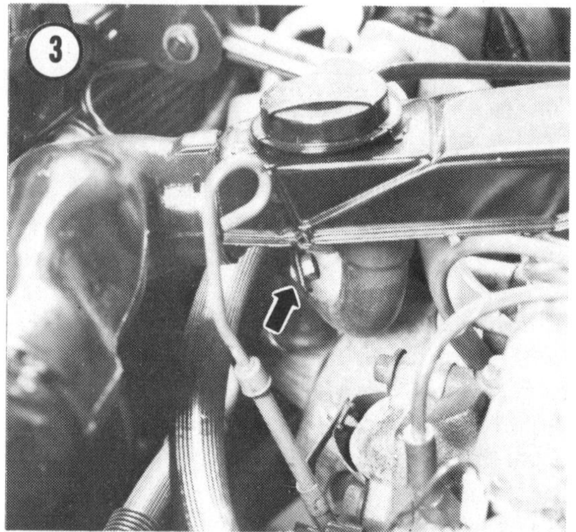

3

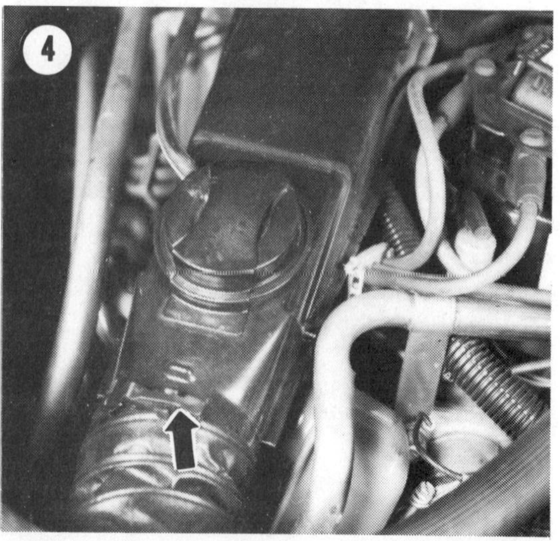

4

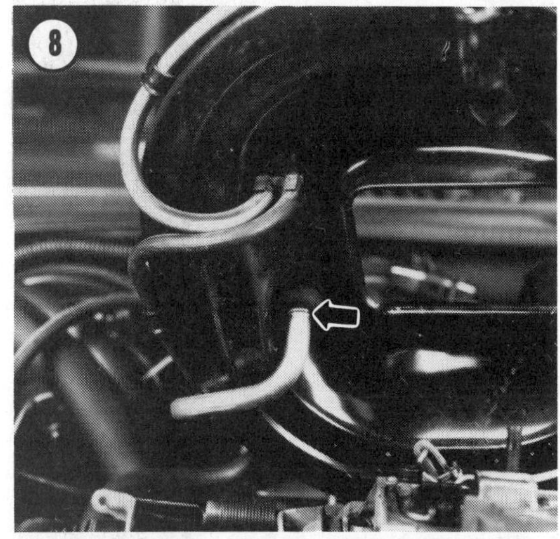

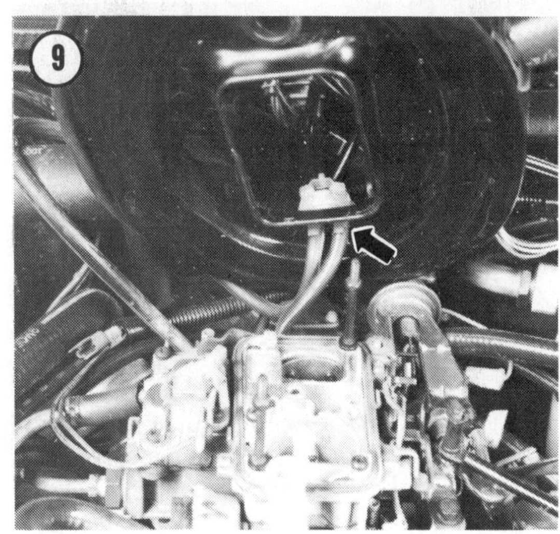

6

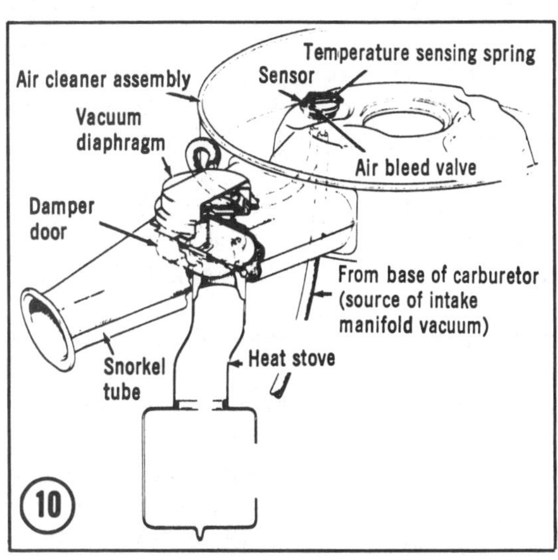
Temperature sensing spring
Air cleaner assembly
Sensor
Vacuum diaphragm
Air bleed valve
Damper door
From base of carburetor (source of intake manifold vacuum)
Snorkel tube
Heat stove
10

Watch the air inlet valve with a mirror while applying vacuum to the vacuum motor inlet. If the valve closes, it is in good condition (**Figure 11**). If the valve does not close, check the linkage for binding. If the linkage is in good condition, the vacuum motor is probably defective and should be replaced as described under *Vacuum Motor Removal/Installation*, in this section.

4. If vacuum motor is good, yet the system does not work properly, perform the *Thermo Sensor Check* as described in this section.

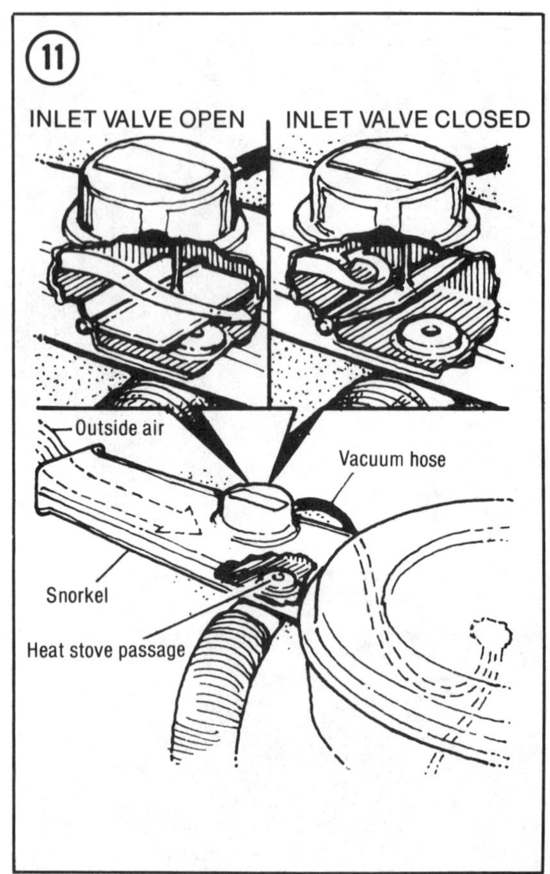

Thermo Sensor Check

Begin this test with the engine cold. The temperature around the sensor must be below 77° F (25° C).

1. Check the air inlet valve with a mirror. Make sure it is open (**Figure 11**).
2. Start the engine and let it idle. If the air inlet valve closes immediately after starting the engine, the valve is in good condition (**Figure 11**).
3. Let the engine idle until it warms up. Watch the air inlet with a mirror as the engine warms. It should open gradually.

NOTE

If this test is conducted at ambient temperatures near 30° F, the valve will take considerable time to open and may open only partially. This does not indicate a defective sensor.

If the valve does not work properly or you are in doubt about the above test results, perform the next 2 steps.

4. Remove the air cleaner cover and tape a small thermometer as close to the sensor as possible (**Figure 12**). Let the air cleaner cool until the thermometer reads below 77° F (25° C). Install air cleaner cover.
5. Start the engine and let it idle for several minutes, until the valve is partially open. Remove the air cleaner cover and note the thermometer reading. It should read 103-143° F (34-46° C). If the reading is obviously outside this range, replace the sensor. See *Sensor Replacment*, in this section.

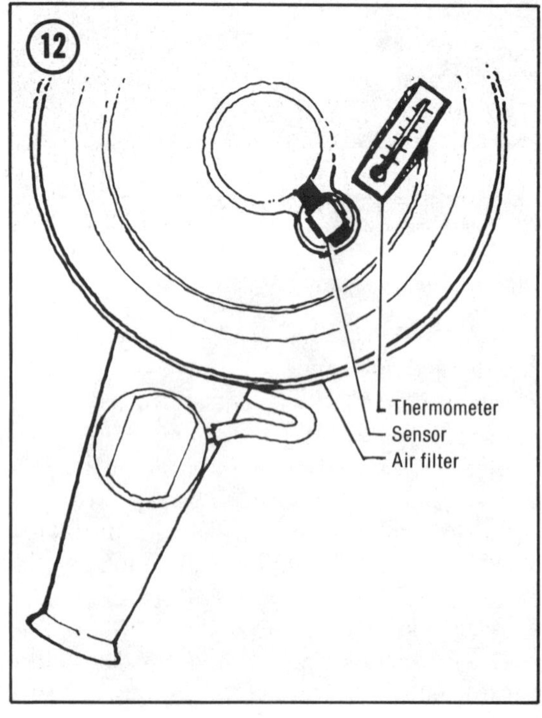

13

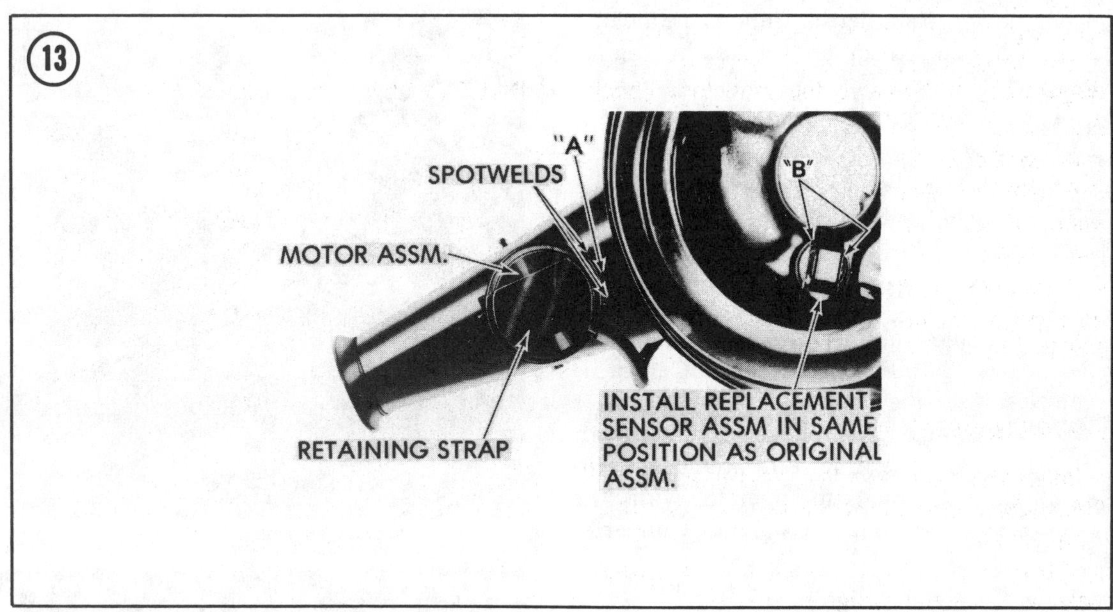

Vacuum Motor Removal

1. Remove the air cleaner assembly as described in this section.
2. Disconnect the vacuum hose from the motor (**Figure 10**).
3. The motor assembly is secured to the snorkel by 2 spotwelds (**Figure 13**). Drill out both spotwelds with a 1/16 in. drill and enlarge holes as required to remove the vacuum motor retaining strap.
4. Raise up vacuum motor and turn to one side. This will unhook motor linkage at the control damper assembly. Remove the vacuum motor.

Vacuum Motor Installation

1. Drill a 7/64 in. hole at point "A" indicated in **Figure 13**.
2. Insert the vacuum motor linkage into the control damper assembly. Secure vacuum motor with retaining strap and screw to the snorkel tube. The retaining strap and screw are provided in the vacuum motor replacement kit.

NOTE
Make sure, once screw is installed, that it does not interfere with operation of the inlet valve. If inlet valve cannot open fully, shorten screw as required.

3. Connect vacuum hose to vacuum motor (**Figure 10**). Install air cleaner and check operation of vacuum motor.

Sensor Replacement

1. Remove the air cleaner.
2. Remove hoses at sensor unit. See **Figure 9**.

NOTE
Note position of sensor for installation. New sensor must be installed in same position.

3. Loosen sensor by prying up retaining clip with screwdriver (**Figure 14**).

6

4. Remove clip and sensor from air cleaner.
5. Install new sensor and gasket in original position.
6. Press retainer clip on hose connectors to secure sensor.
7. Connect vacuum hoses to sensor (**Figure 10**). Install air cleaner.

CARBURETOR

All 49-state vehicles use the model 2SE Rochester Varajet carburetor. California vehicles use the model E2SE Rochester Varajet. The E2SE carburetor is an electronically controlled air/fuel ratio carburetor designed to operate with the Computer Controlled Catalytic Converter (C-4) system.

The Rochester 2SE and E2SE models are a 2 barrel, 2 stage, downdraft design. The primary stage has a triple venturi with a 35 mm bore. The secondary stage has a 46 mm bore. Aluminum die castings are used primarily to reduce the carburetor's overall weight. However, a zinc die-cast choke housing is used on 4-cylinder vehicles to reduce heat transfer for optimum engine warm-up operation.

To facilitate carburetor service, alphabetical code letters are included on the air horn, float bowl and throttle body castings at external tube locations to identify air and vacuum hose connections.

NOTE
Carburetors on the 4-cylinder and V6 engines are slightly different and are not interchangeable.

Removal

Attached to the carburetor assembly on all models are a number of vacuum lines and hoses. Each play an important part in the operation and efficiency of the engine. Therefore, it is important that all lines and hoses be tagged before removal of the carburetor assembly so that each can be returned to its original position.

1. Remove the air cleaner assembly as described under *Air Cleaner Assembly Removal.*

NOTE
Steps 2-4 describe 4-cylinder carburetor removal. Steps 5-8 describe V6 carburetor removal.

2. Referring to **Figure 15**, remove the vapor return line, mixture control solenoid connector and the choke wire. Then disconnect and remove the fuel line (**Figure 16**).

3. At rear of carburetor, remove the vacuum lines (**Figure 17**). If lines are tight, it may be necessary to pry lines to remove.
4. Remove the throttle linkage return spring, then pry the throttle lever clip away from the linkage stud. See **Figure 18**.

NOTE
Steps 5-8 describe carburetor removal procedures unique to the V6 engine.

5. Referring to **Figure 19**, remove the vapor return line, mixture control solenoid connector and the choke wire. Then disconnect the throttle position sensor connector (**Figure 20**).
6. Disconnect and remove the fuel line.
7. Disconnect the vacuum lines from the right side of the carburetor (**Figure 21**).
8. From rear of carburetor, disconnect the accelerator linkage and return springs.
9. Remove the carburetor mounting nuts. Then check the carburetor for other attached

hoses or electrical connectors. Pull the carburetor up and remove.

10. Remove the insulator.

Installation

1. Make sure carburetor and intake manifold sealing surfaces are clean.
2. Install carburetor insulator.
3. Place carburetor on manifold studs. Install mounting nuts and tighten to 145 in.-lb. (16 N•m).
4. Install vacuum lines to carburetor.
5. Install fuel line to carburetor and tighten. See **Figure 16** (typical).
6. Connect accelerator linkage.
7. Connect choke and solenoid electrical connectors. See **Figure 15** (4-cylinder) or **Figure 19** (V6).
8. Install air cleaner housing.
9. Adjust idle speeds as described under *Carburetor Adjustments*, Chapter Three.

Disassembly

The following procedures describe disassembly and reassembly procedures for the 2SE carburetor.

NOTE

Because the E2SE carburetor is an integral part of the emission control system, overhaul should be entrusted to a General Motors dealership or mechanic familar with GM emission controls.

NOTE

*It is recommended that carburetors be exchanged with a new or rebuilt equivalent model rather than rebuilding them. The exchange price of a rebuilt unit is little more than the price of a kit. Kit savings are hardly worth the time involved. In addition, the rebuilt unit will be correctly adjusted to ensure good operation and compliance with emission control standards. To obtain the correct replacement carburetor, copy the part number stamped on the carburetor float bowl (**Figure 22**) and take it with you to purchase a new or rebuilt unit. However, in the event you cannot obtain a new or rebuilt carburetor, service procedures are provided where practical to help take you through disassembly and reassembly.*

Before disassembling carburetor, clear a large work area to allow placement of all parts in order of removal. Do not interchange any

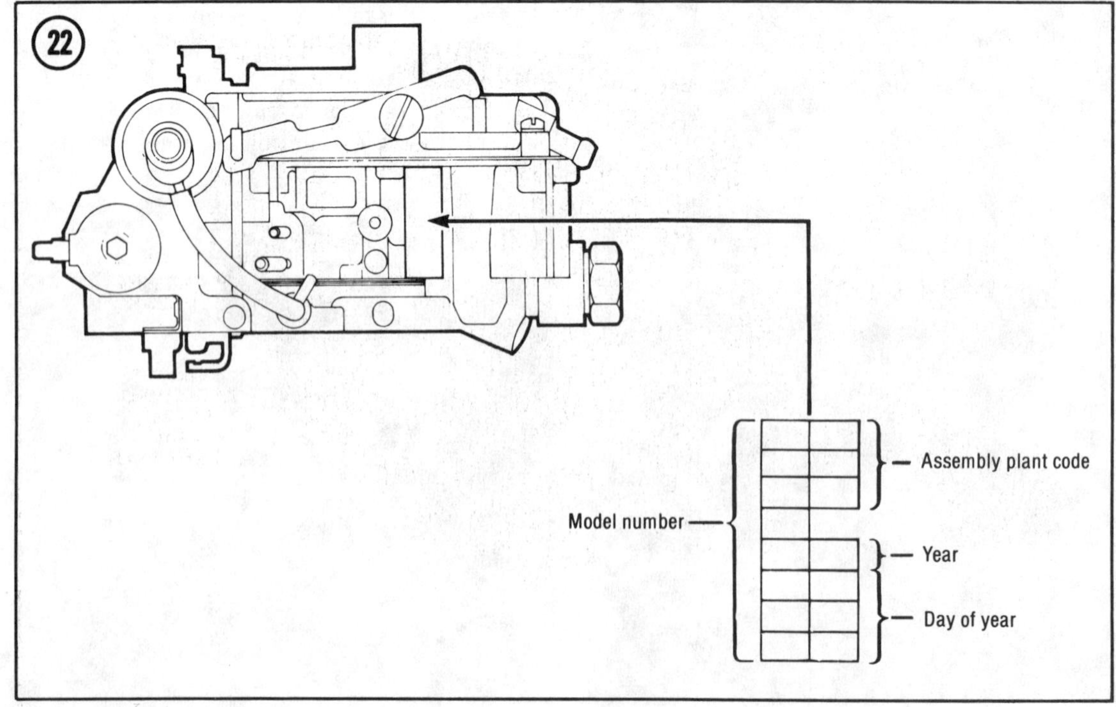

parts. When removing jets, note their location and the number stamped on each jet. When disassembling and assembling carburetors, use proper sized tools.

NOTE

Before disassembling carburetor, purchase a carburetor rebuild kit to ensure discarded retaining clips, screws, etc., can be replaced with correct size parts.

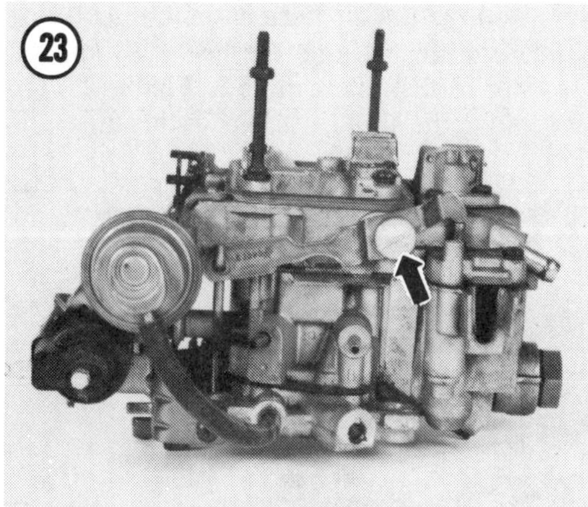

CAUTION

Idle mixture screws have been preset at the factory and sealed with a cap plug. During carburetor disassembly, do not remove the plugs and or alter the screw setting.

Steps 1-11 describe air horn removal.

1. Remove the pump rod attaching screw (**Figure 23**). Then rotate the pump and remove.
2. Detach hose from vacuum break assembly.
3. Remove screws attaching the idle speed solenoid vacuum break bracket to the air horn and throttle body. See **Figure 24** (4-cylinder) or **Figure 25** (V6).
4. *4-cylinder engines only*: Remove the vacuum break rod and air valve rod from the vacuum break diaphragm plunger by rotating the idle speed solenoid vacuum break bracket. Then remove the bracket assembly from the float bowl (**Figure 24**).
5. *V6 engines only*: Rotate vacuum break and bracket assembly to detach rods from vacuum break and air valve levers (**Figure 25**).

24

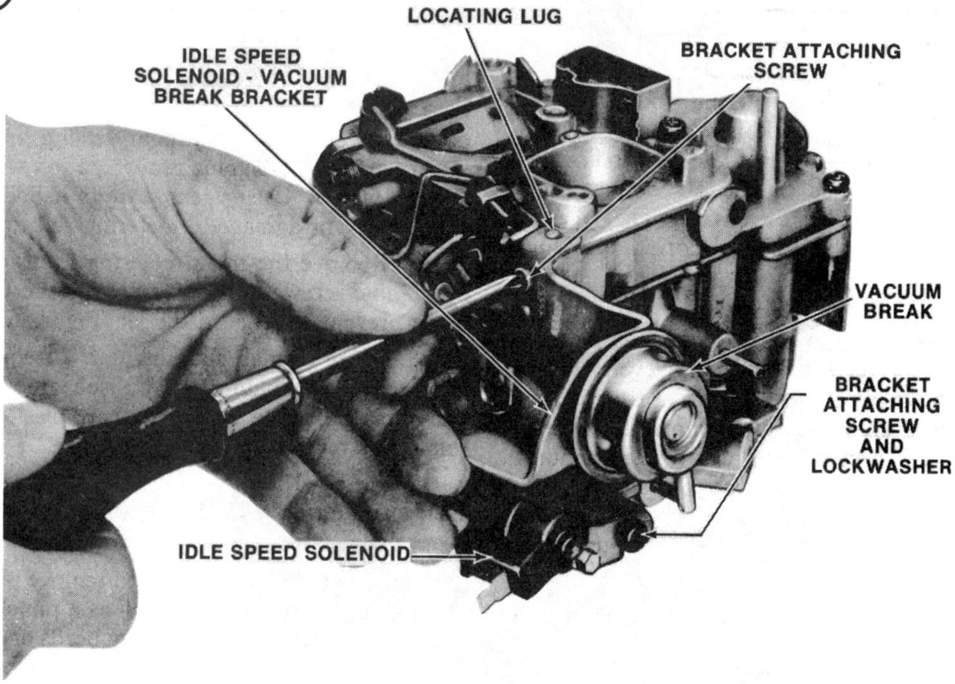

LOCATING LUG

IDLE SPEED SOLENOID - VACUUM BREAK BRACKET

BRACKET ATTACHING SCREW

VACUUM BREAK

BRACKET ATTACHING SCREW AND LOCKWASHER

IDLE SPEED SOLENOID

NOTE
Unless replacement of rods or vacuum break unit is necessary, removal of vacuum break or air valve rods from the vacuum break plunger is not required (all carburetor models). If rod or vacuum break replacement is necessary, proceed to Step 6. If not, proceed to Step 7.

6. Remove and discard retaining clips from ends of rods. New retaining clips are provided in carburetor kit. Also remove plastic bushings from rods and set aside for reuse.
7. Remove retaining clip from the intermediate choke rod at the choke lever (**Figure 26**). Discard clip, then remove choke rod and plastic bushing from choke lever.
8. Remove screws attaching the hot idle compensator valve to the carburetor body and remove the valve (if so equipped). See **Figure 27**.
9. Remove the air horn mounting screws (**Figure 28**), then remove the vent and screen assembly.
10. Rotate fast idle cam to the *up* position. Then remove the air horn assembly by tilting to side and disengaging the fast idle cam rod from slot in fast idle cam. See **Figure 29**. Do not remove the air horn gasket at this time.

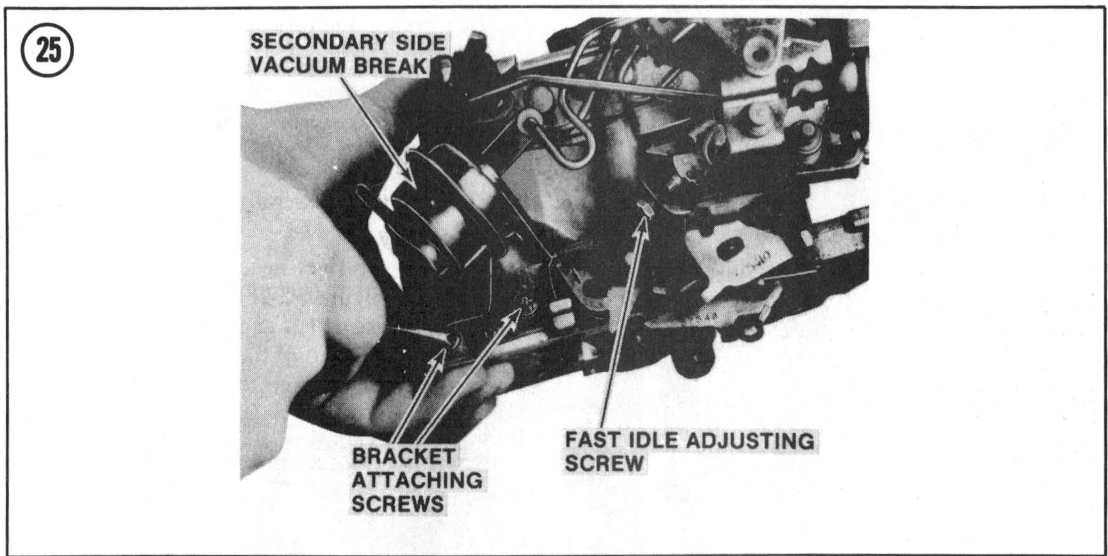

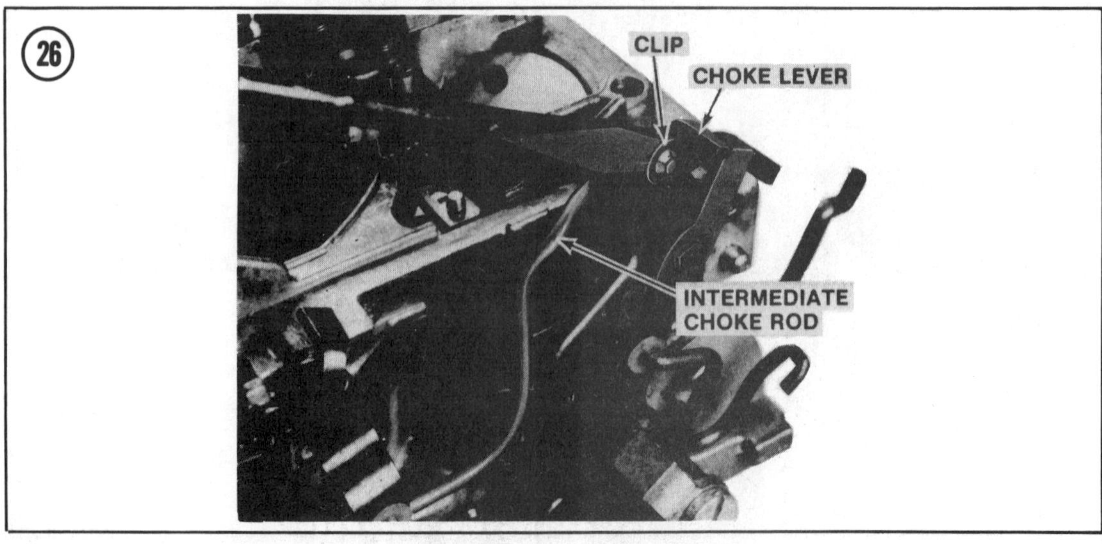

CAUTION
Do not remove the fast idle cam and screw from their position in the float bowl. If replacement is required, float bowl assembly must be replaced.

11. Remove fast idle cam rod from choke lever.

NOTE
Further disassembly of air horn is not required. If air horn is to be replaced, however, remove staking on choke valve attaching screws. Then remove screws, choke valve and shaft from air horn and set aside for assembly on new air horn.

Steps 12-22 describe float bowl disassembly.

12. Remove the air horn gasket (**Figure 30**).

13. Remove the pump plunger from the pump well.

14. Remove the pump return spring from the pump well.

15. Remove plastic filler block positioned over the float valve.

16. Remove float assembly and float needle by pulling up on retaining pin.

17. Remove the float needle seat and gasket using GM tool part No. J-22769 or equivalent. See **Figure 31**.

18. Remove the power piston and metering rod assembly by pressing down on the piston stem with your finger and releasing quickly (**Figure 32**). Spring will then snap piston up against plastic retainer. Do not remove piston with pliers.

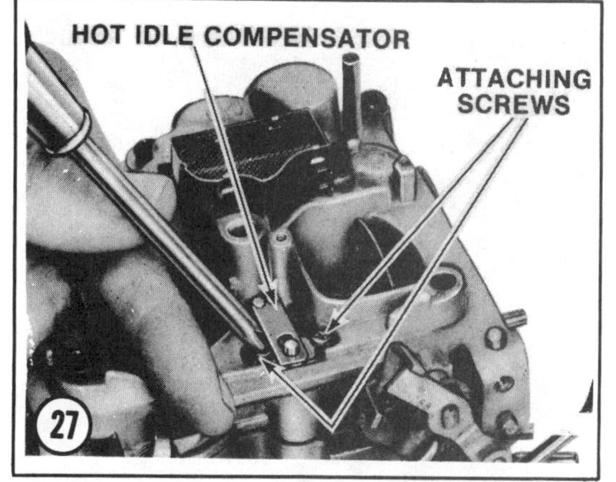

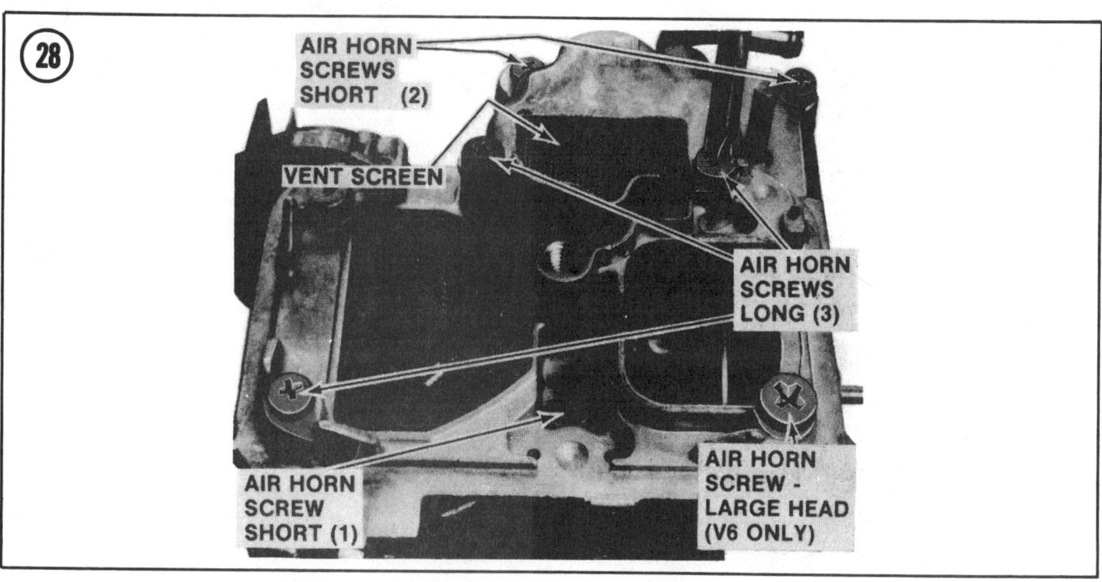

6

19. Remove the piston spring from inside the piston bore.

NOTE
*If metering rod must be replaced, remove from piston hanger by compressing spring on top of metering rod and aligning groove on rod with slot in holder. See **Figure 33**.*

CAUTION
Be extremely careful when handling or replacing the metering rod to prevent damage to rod tip. If the rod tip is damaged, it must be replaced.

20. Remove the main metering jet with GM tool part No. J-22769 or an equivalent size screwdriver. See **Figure 34**.
21. Using a small slide hammer as shown in **Figure 35**, remove the plastic retainer securing the pump discharge spring and check ball to the carburetor body. Discard the plastic retainer.

CAUTION
Do not remove plastic retainer by prying with screwdriver or similar tool, as damage to sealing beads will require replacement of the float bowl.

Turn bowl upside down and catch pump discharge spring and check ball.

NOTE
Steps 22-24 describe choke disassembly.

NOTE
*The choke unit has been installed with a tamper-resistant choke cover to prevent removal and readjustment. See **Figure 36**. Steps 22-24 should be used only when the carburetor is being disassembled for cleaning and overhaul.*

22. Remove the 3 pop rivets from choke housing using a No. 21 drill bit (**Figure 37**). Drill rivet only enough to remove rivet head. Then remove choke retainers and choke cover from choke housing.
23. Refer to **Figure 38** and remove the choke coil lever from the intermediate choke shaft.

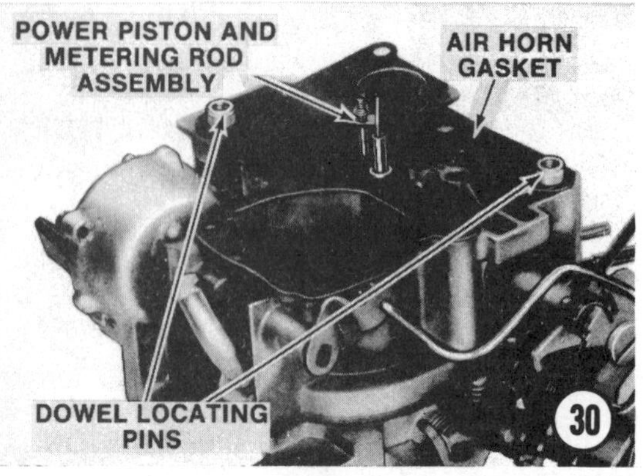

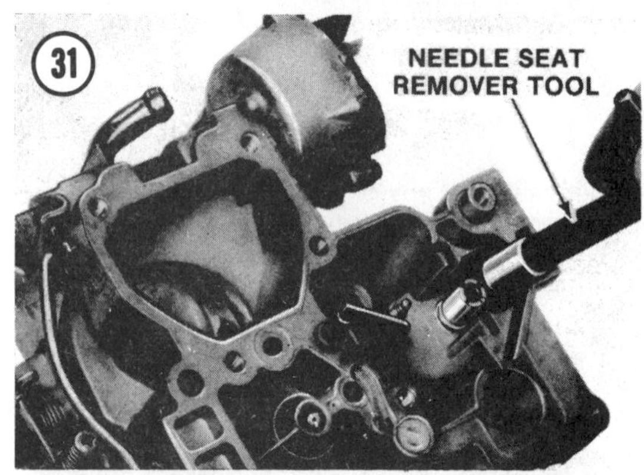

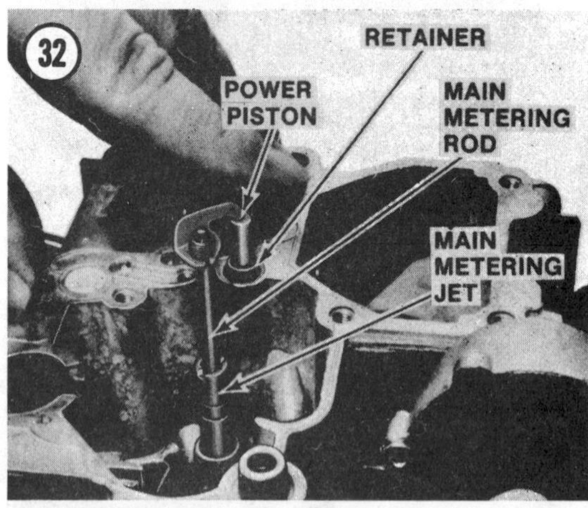

Slide the intermediate choke shaft rearward from the throttle lever side and remove from carburetor (**Figure 39**).
24. Remove the choke housing attaching screws and choke housing. See **Figure 40**.

NOTE
Steps 25 and 26 describe disassembly of remaining float bowl parts.

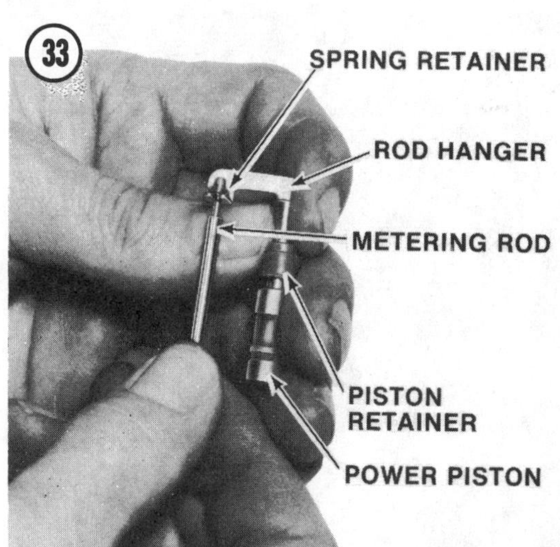
33
SPRING RETAINER
ROD HANGER
METERING ROD
PISTON
RETAINER
POWER PISTON

36

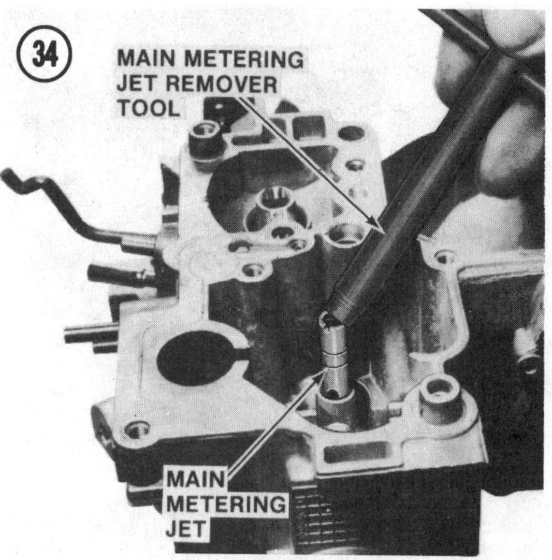
34
MAIN METERING
JET REMOVER
TOOL
MAIN
METERING
JET

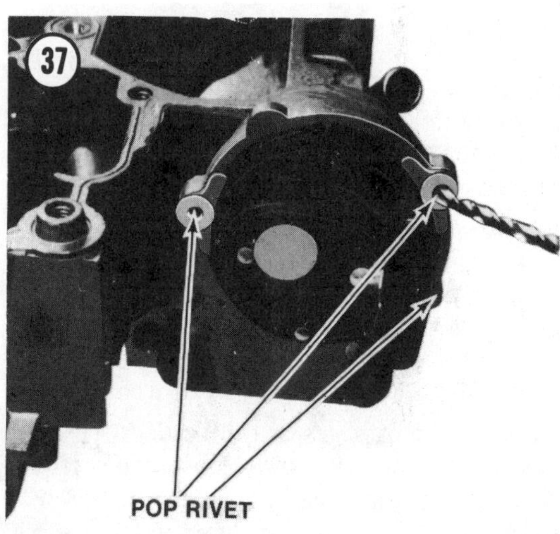
37
POP RIVET

6

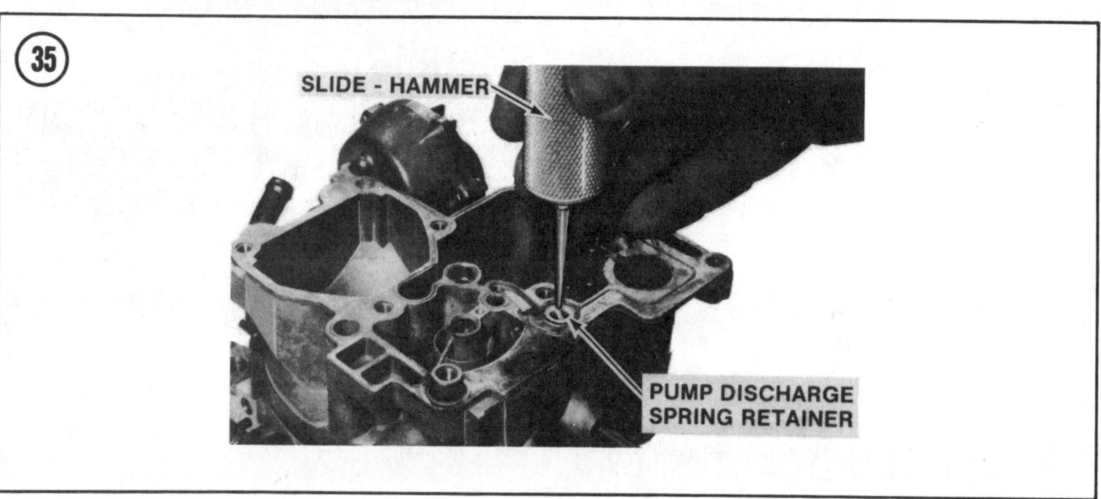
35
SLIDE - HAMMER
PUMP DISCHARGE
SPRING RETAINER

25. Remove the fuel inlet nut, gasket, check filter/valve assembly and spring.
26. Remove throttle body-to-float bowl attaching screws and remove throttle body assembly and gasket. See **Figure 41**.

NOTE
Disassembly of throttle body is not required. If throttle valves are damaged, throttle body must be replaced.

Cleaning and Inspection

1. Thoroughly clean all metal parts (except solenoid and electric choke) in a suitable carburetor cleaning solvent such as Carbon X (X-55). O-rings, gaskets and diaphragms should be replaced if they are included in the repair kit. If not, clean them with a lint-free cloth.

CAUTION
Do not insert objects such as drill bits or pieces of wire into jets and passages while cleaning them. These openings are carefully calibrated and scratching them may seriously affect carburetor performance.

2. If jets and passages are difficult to clean, blow them out with compressed air. If a compressor is not available, use a spray-on carburetor cleaner. These often come with plastic tubes that fit into the can's nozzle, making it easy to spray the cleaner through jets and passages.
3. Examine the needle valve and seat for wear. Replace as needed.
4. Check all castings for cracks.
5. Test the solenoids as described in this chapter.

Assembly

NOTE
Steps 1-12 describe float bowl and choke assembly procedures. If new float bowl assembly is being installed, stamp the model number on side of new bowl (see ***Figure 22****).*

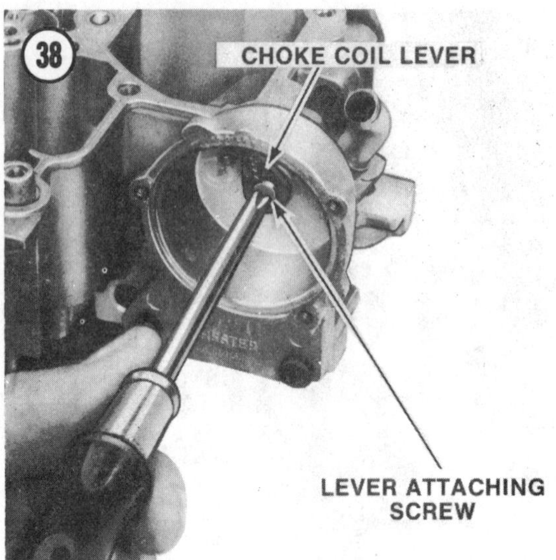

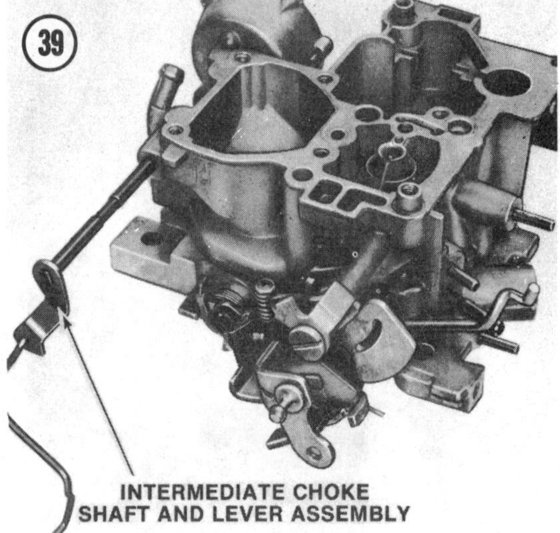

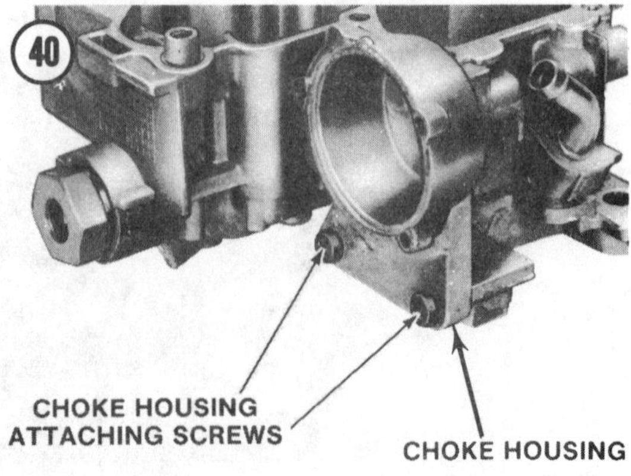

41

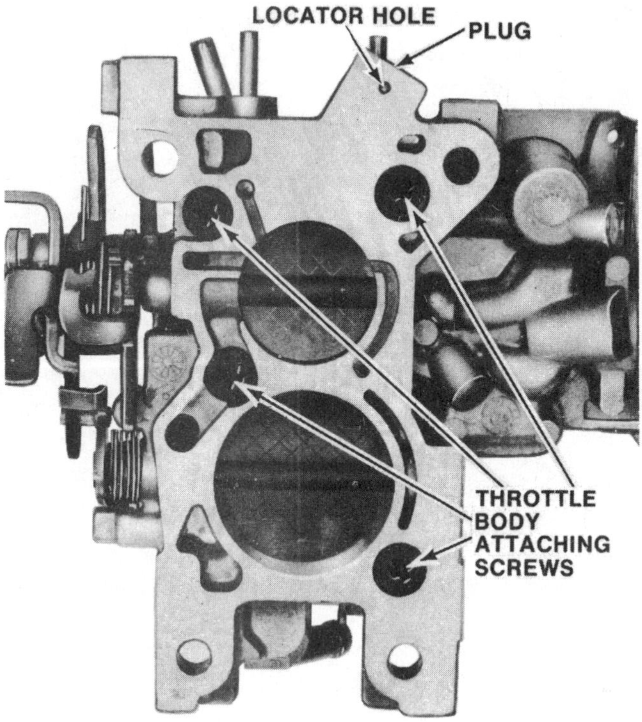

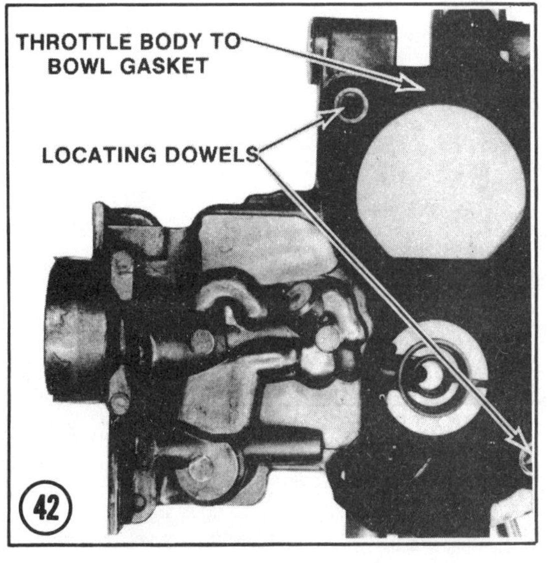

NOTE

When installing new gaskets, make sure all holes are properly punched and that there is no loose material on the gasket.

1. Install a new throttle body-to-bowl insulator gasket on the float bowl. Make sure gasket fits over 2 locating dowels. See **Figure 42**.
2. Install the float bowl and attaching screws. Start the 4 screws and tighten them in rotation. Make sure the linkage lockout tang is located so it engages the slot in secondary lockout lever and that the linkage moves freely.
3. Reassemble fuel inlet filter spring, check valve/filter assembly, gasket and inlet nut. Tighten nut to 18 ft.-lb. (24 N•m).

4. Install choke housing and secure with 2 attaching screws. Make sure raised boss and locating lug on rear of choke housing fit into recesses in float bowl casting (**Figure 40**).
5. Install intermediate choke shaft and lever assembly (**Figure 39**).
6. Position intermediate choke lever straight up. Install thermostatic coil lever inside choke housing onto flats on intermediate choke shaft. Coil is properly aligned when coil pick-up tang is at the top position. See **Figure 43**. Install intermediate lever attaching screw and tighten.

NOTE
*Thermostatic choke cover and coil assembly are not installed until coil lever is adjusted. This procedure is described under **Choke Coil Lever Adjustment** in this chapter.*

7. Refer to **Figure 35** and insert pump discharge check ball and spring in passage and secure with new plastic retainer. Tap retainer in position until flush with casting surface.
8. Install main metering jet (**Figure 34**).
9. Refer to **Figure 31** and install needle seat assembly, using GM tool part No. J-22769 or equivalent.
10. Install float needle onto float arm by sliding float lever under the needle pull clip. Make sure to hook clip over edge of float arm facing the float pontoon.

NOTE
To ease installation, carefully bend the float arm upward at the notch in arm.

11. Insert float retaining pin into float arm (end loop of pin must face pump well). Install float assembly by aligning needle in seal and float retaining pin into locating channels in float bowl. Adjust float level as described under *Float Adjustments* in this chapter.
12. Insert power piston spring into piston bore. Then install pump return spring and pump plunger assembly in pump well.

NOTE
Steps 13 and 14 describe air horn assembly procedures.

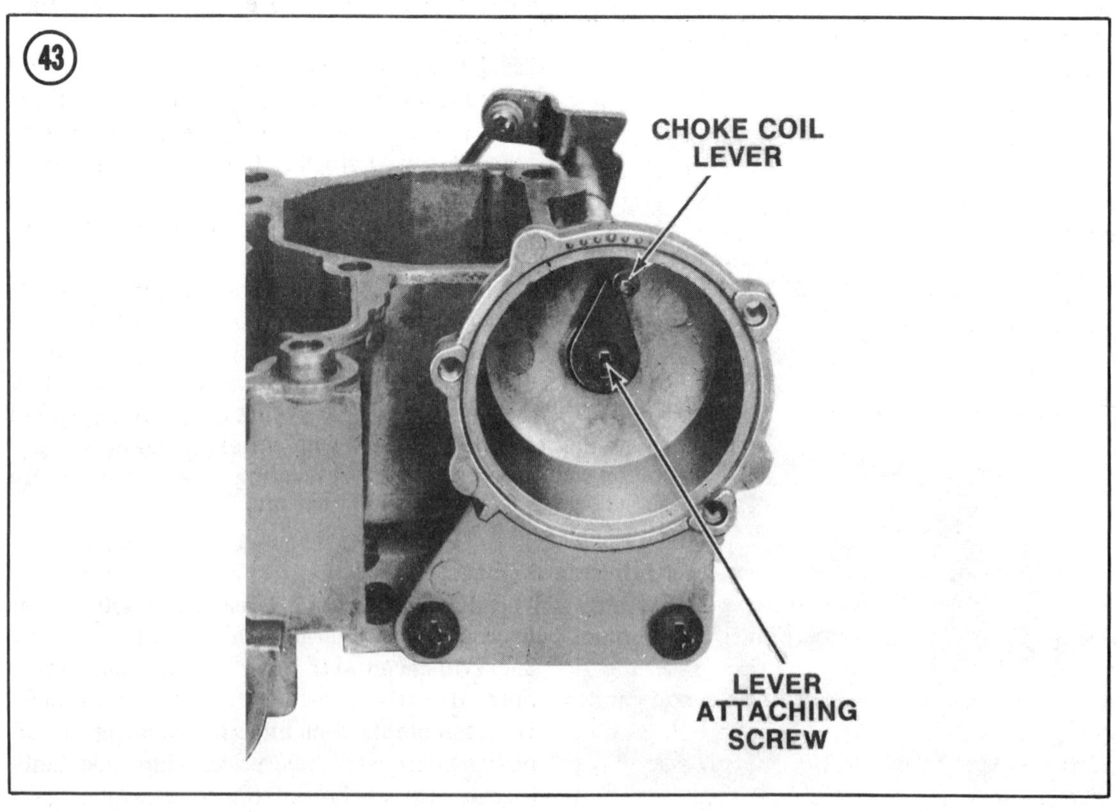

13. Install choke shaft and valve if removed. Tighten attaching screws and stake lightly.

NOTE
Check choke valve for proper movement before staking attaching screws.

14. Install fast idle cam rod in lower hole of choke lever and align squirt on rod with small slot in lever.

NOTE
Perform Steps 15 and 16 to reinstall vacuum break or air valve rods removed from the vacuum break plunger during disassembly. If vacuum break or air valve rods were not removed, proceed to Step 17.

15. *4-cylinder vehicles only*: Install plastic bushing in hole in vacuum break lever. Make sure small end of bushing faces retaining clip when installed. Then pass end of vacuum break rod through bushing in lever. Secure rod with new retaining clip. Make sure locking lugs face end of rod. Tighten clip by pressing ends with needlenose pliers. Measure rod to bushing clearance. Clearance of 0.030 in. (0.762 mm) must be maintained to ensure adequate rod movement.
16. *4-cylinder vehicles only*: Install plastic bushing in hole in air valve lever. Make sure small end of bushing faces retaining clip. Then pass end of air valve rod through bushing in lever. Secure rod with new retaining clip. Make sure locking lugs face end of rod. Tighten clip by pressing ends with needlenose pliers. Measure rod to bushing clearance. Clearance of 0.030 in. (0.762 mm) must be maintained to ensure adequate rod movement.

NOTE
Check that clip engages rod fully and is not distorted.

17. Turn fast idle cam to full *up* position, then tilt air horn assembly and engage fast idle cam rod in slot in fast idle cam (**Figure 29**). While holding down on pump plunger assembly, lower air horn assembly onto float bowl and guide pump plunger stem through hole in air horn casting. Do not force air horn assembly into position.
18. Install vent and screen assembly (**Figure 28**). Install air horn attaching screws. Tighten screws in rotation (**Figure 44**).
19. Install new float bowl seal in float bowl recess (if so equipped). Install hot idle compensator valve.
20. Insert plastic bushing in hole in choke lever. Make sure small end of bushing faces retaining clip when installed. Position inner choke coil lever at 12 o'clock position, then install intermediate choke rod in bushing. Secure rod with new retaining clip. Make sure locking lugs face end of rod. Tighten clip by pressing ends with needlenose pliers. Measure rod to bushing clearance. Clearance of 0.030 in. (0.762 mm) must be maintained to ensure adequate rod movement.
21. *V6 vehicles only*: Install plastic bushing in secondary side vacuum break plunger hole. Make sure small end of bushing faces retaining clip when installed. Secure rod with new retaining clip. Make sure locking lugs face end of rod. Tighten clip by pressing ends with needlenose pliers. Measure rod to bushing clearance. Clearance of 0.030 in. (0.762 mm) must be maintained to ensure adequate rod movement.
22. *V6 vehicles only*: Install end of secondary side vacuum break rod into upper slot of vacuum break lever. See **Figure 25** and install bracket on throttle body. Secure with attaching screws.
23. Install solenoid if removed during disassembly.
24. *4-cylinder vehicles only*: Insert end of vacuum break rod into solenoid bracket inner slot and end of air valve rod into outer slot of the vacuum break diaphragm plunger. See **Figure 24**. Install bracket over locating lugs on air horn, then install attaching screws in air horn and throttle body.

NOTE
Do not attach vacuum break hose until vacuum break adjustment is complete.

25. *V6 vehicles only*: Insert plastic bushings in holes in vacuum break plunger vacuum side (if removed). Make sure small end of bushings face retaining clips when installed. Insert vacuum break rod in plunger upper

6

(44)

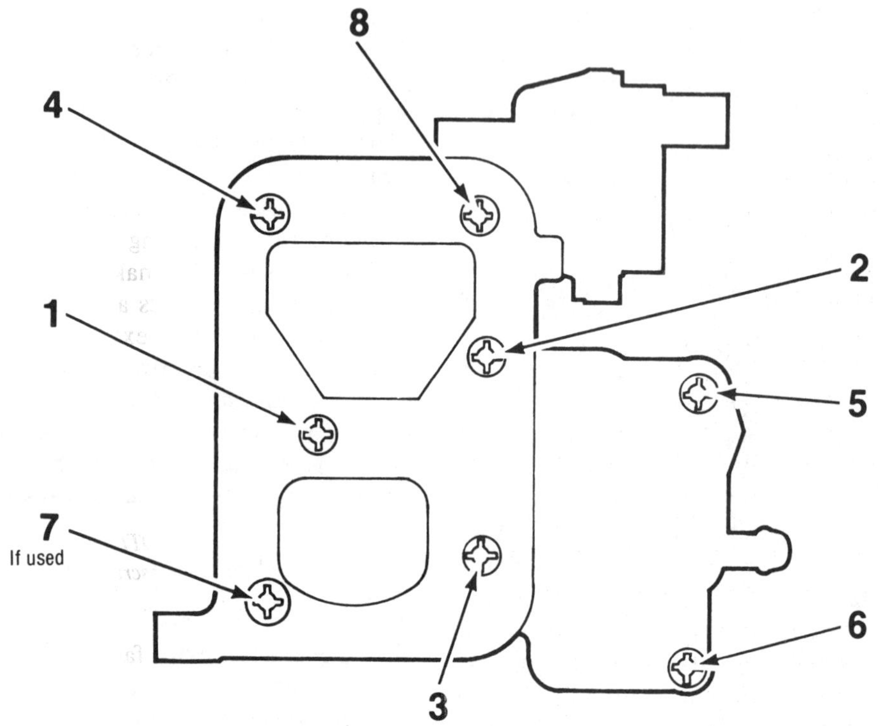

8
4
2
1
5
7
If used
6
3

hole and air valve rod in plunger lower hole. Secure rod with new retaining clip. Make sure locking lugs face end of rod. Tighten clip by pressing ends with needlenose pliers. Measure rod to bushing clearance. Clearance of 0.030 in. (0.762 mm) must be maintained to ensure adequate rod movement.

26. Engage vacuum break and air valve rods in vacuum break and in air valve lever by rotating primary side vacuum. Position bracket over locating lug on air horn and secure with attaching screws (see **Figure 24** or **Figure 25**).

27. Refer to **Figure 23** and insert pump rod in pump lever. Secure with attaching screw. Then hold down on pump plunger stem and install pump lever on carburetor air horn.

(45)

Make sure screw seats in hole in lever and washer fits between lever and air horn casting.

28. Install thermostatic coil and cover assembly. Make sure coil tang engages the inside choke coil lever.

NOTE

The vacuum break and choke rod adjustments must be performed and the thermostatic coil lever indexed before the choke thermostatic coil and cover assembly is installed. Refer to ***Carburetor Adjustments*** *in this chapter.*

29. Install the choke cover and coil assembly into the choke housing. Install 3 self-tapping screws included with carburetor kit (**Figure 45**). Once screws are properly aligned, remove screws and set aside.

30. Position fast idle screw on highest step of fast idle cam. Place the thermostatic cover and coil assembly in the choke housing, aligning notch in choke cover with raised casting on housing cover flange. Check to see that coil tang engages the inside choke coil lever.

NOTE

On V6 vehicles, the tang on the thermostatic coil is formed to completely encircle the coil pickup lever. When installing choke cover and coil assembly, make sure coil pickup lever is positioned inside the coil tang.

31. Install 3 choke cover self-tapping screws and tighten securely (**Figure 45**).

CAUTION

Do not install choke cover gasket between the electric choke assembly and the choke housing. Choke will not operate.

32. After installing carburetor on vehicle, check the CO exhaust content with an exhaust emission analyzer. Your dealer can do this for you.

Choke Inspection

The choke mechanism and vacuum break should be checked for proper operation at intervals specified in Chapter Three. Refer to **Figure 46** (4-cylinder) or **Figure 47** (V6) for the following procedure.

1. Remove the air cleaner assembly.
2. Check choke hoses for proper connections and for cracking or deterioration. Replace as necessary.
3. With engine turned off, open and close choke several times. Check to see that all linkage arms are connected and operating properly. If linkage arms appear sluggish or dirty, spray choke linkage assembly with United Delco Choke Cleaner X-20-A or equivalent. Follow manufacturer's instructions on can. If cleaning fails to repair problem, replace binding parts.
4. With engine off, make sure the vacuum break diaphragm shafts are fully extended. If shafts are not fully extended, replace the vacuum break assembly.
5. With engine running, the vacuum break diaphragm shafts should retract into the diaphragm housing. If shafts fail to retract into housing, replace the vacuum break assembly.

NOTE

Steps 6 and 7 describe electric choke inspection procedures.

6. If the electric choke fails to open, check the voltage at the choke heater connection (**Figure 48**) with a voltmeter, with the engine running. If voltage reads between 12 and 15 volts, replace the electrical choke unit. If voltage reads low or zero, check all wires and connections leading from the choke heater.

NOTE

The oil pressure switch is important to operation of electric choke. If the oil pressure switch connection is faulty, the temperature pressure warning light will fail to operate with the ignition key turned on. Check and repair connections as required.

7. If Step 6 checks okay, replace the oil pressure switch.

Solenoid Replacement

Refer to **Figure 49** (4-cylinder) or **Figure 50** (V6) for this procedure.

1. Bend back retaining tabs on lockwasher. Then remove large solenoid retaining nut using wrench. Remove lockwasher and solenoid from bracket.
2. Reverse to install.

6

46

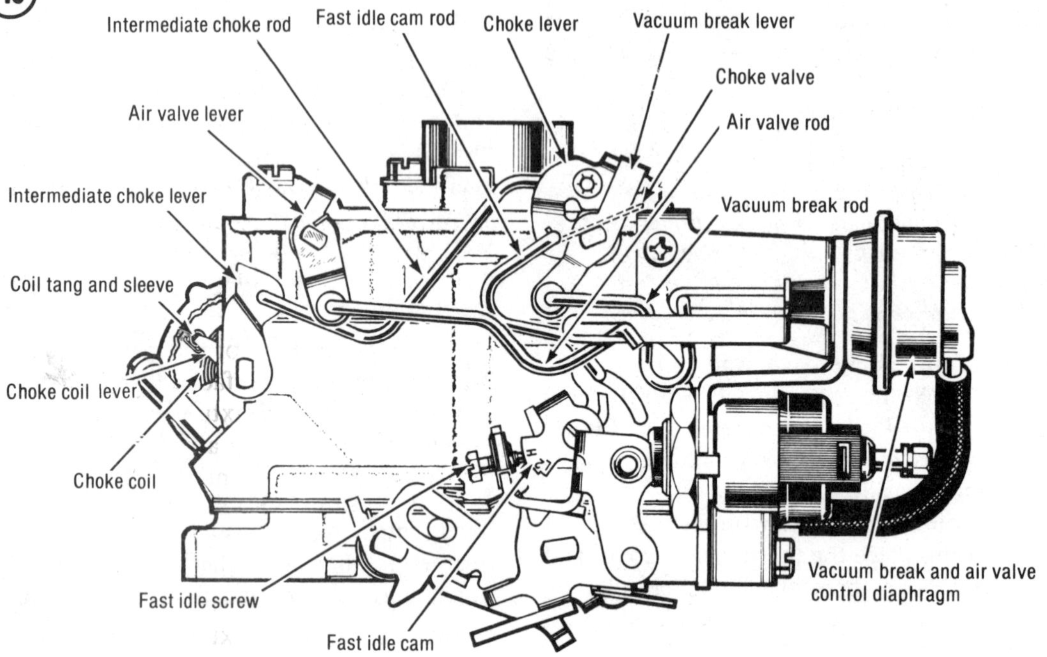

Intermediate choke rod
Fast idle cam rod
Choke lever
Vacuum break lever
Choke valve
Air valve lever
Air valve rod
Intermediate choke lever
Vacuum break rod
Coil tang and sleeve
Choke coil lever
Choke coil
Fast idle screw
Fast idle cam
Vacuum break and air valve control diaphragm

47

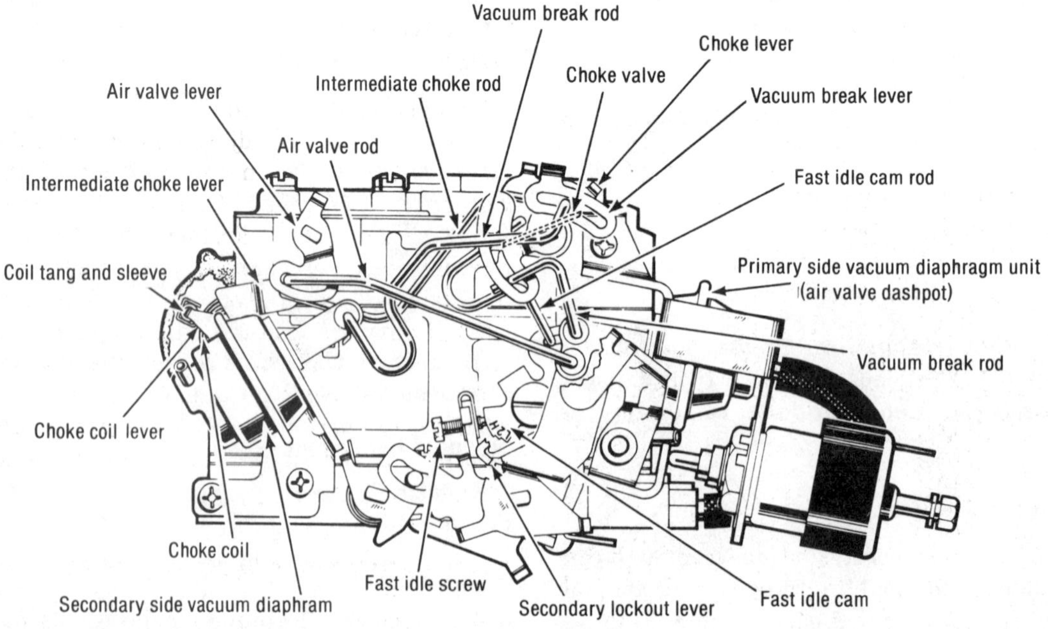

Vacuum break rod
Choke lever
Air valve lever
Intermediate choke rod
Choke valve
Vacuum break lever
Air valve rod
Intermediate choke lever
Fast idle cam rod
Coil tang and sleeve
Primary side vacuum diaphragm unit (air valve dashpot)
Vacuum break rod
Choke coil lever
Choke coil
Fast idle screw
Secondary side vacuum diaphram
Secondary lockout lever
Fast idle cam

48

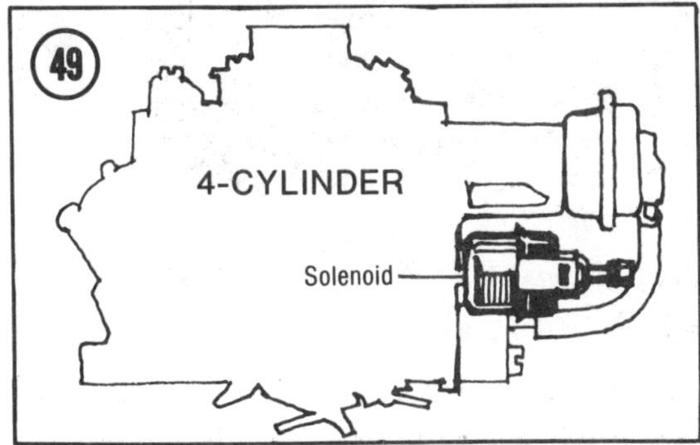

49

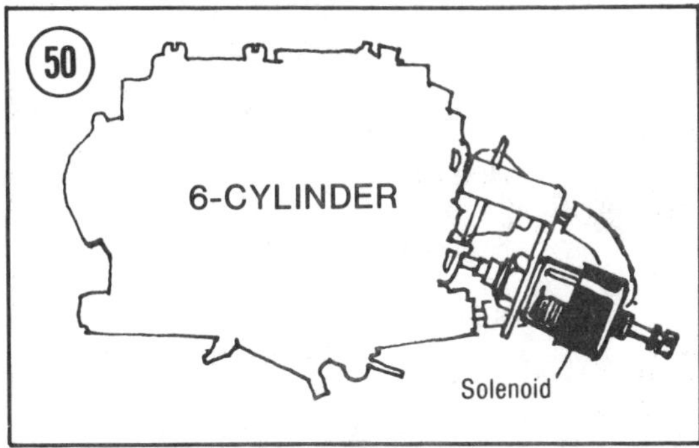

50

51

Idle Mixture Plug (Model 2SE)

The idle mixture needle is factory adjusted and sealed to prevent adjustment. During carburetor cleaning and overhaul, do not remove the tamperproof plug and adjust the idle mixture unless it is necessary to replace the idle mixture needle or normal cleaning procedures fail to clean the idle mixture passages.

1. Remove the carburetor as described in this section.
2. Place the carburetor on the workbench with the throttle valves facing upward.
3. Locate the idle mixture locator point in **Figure 51**. Then, using a punch, drive punch through locator point until the hardened steel plug shatters. Continue to break out the throttle body casting until the idle mixture plug is reached. The idle mixture screw can then be removed with a socket.
4. Install a new idle mixture screw and spring. Install carburetor as described in this chapter.
5. Adjust the idle mixture as described in this chapter.
6. After adjusting the idle mixture, have a General Motors dealer check the content of CO in the vehicle's exhaust.

Idle Mixture Plug (E2SE)

The idle mixture needle is factory adjusted and sealed to prevent adjustment. Because the E2SE carburetor is an integral part of the Computer Controlled Catalytic Converter (C-4) system, any adjustment to the idle mixture needle can prevent the system from maintaining proper control of carburetor air/fuel mixtures. If at any time you feel there is a problem with the idle mixture system, refer your vehicle to a General Motors dealer where he can perform a "System Performance Check" to determine the cause of your complaint.

CARBURETOR ADJUSTMENTS

The following carburetor adjustments can be performed with the carburetor mounted on the vehicle, unless noted otherwise in

6

procedure. Adjustment procedures are for both the 2SE and E2SE carburetors. Carburetor adjustment specifications are found in **Table 1**. Make sure that replacement parts are available from dealer (if necessary) before beginning procedure.

Float Adjustment

Refer to **Figure 52** for the following procedure.

1. Remove air cleaner assembly from carburetor.
2. Hold float retainer in place with finger, then push float down against needle.
3. Remove carburetor gasket and measure distance from toe of float (furthest from hinge) to top of carburetor.
4. Compare float measurement with specifications in **Table 1**. If the float measurement is incorrect, remove the float from the carburetor. Bend float arm slightly up or down to specification.
5. Inspect float alignment after adjustment.
6. Install carburetor gasket and air filter cleaner assembly. Road test vehicle.

Fast Idle Adjustment (Bench Setting)

Refer to **Figure 53** for fast idle adjustment. See **Table 1** for specifications.

NOTE
On-vehicle fast idle adjustment procedures are found in Chapter Three.

Choke Coil Lever Adjustment

Refer to **Figure 54** (4-cylinder) or **Figure 55** (V6) for choke coil lever adjustment. See **Table 1** for specifications.

NOTE
A choke stat cover retainer kit is necessary to perform this procedure. Make sure your dealer has kit available before beginning adjustment.

Fast Idle Cam (Choke Rod) Adjustment

Refer to **Figure 56** (4-cylinder) or **Figure 57** (V6) for fast idle cam (choke rod) adjustment. See **Table 1** for specifications.

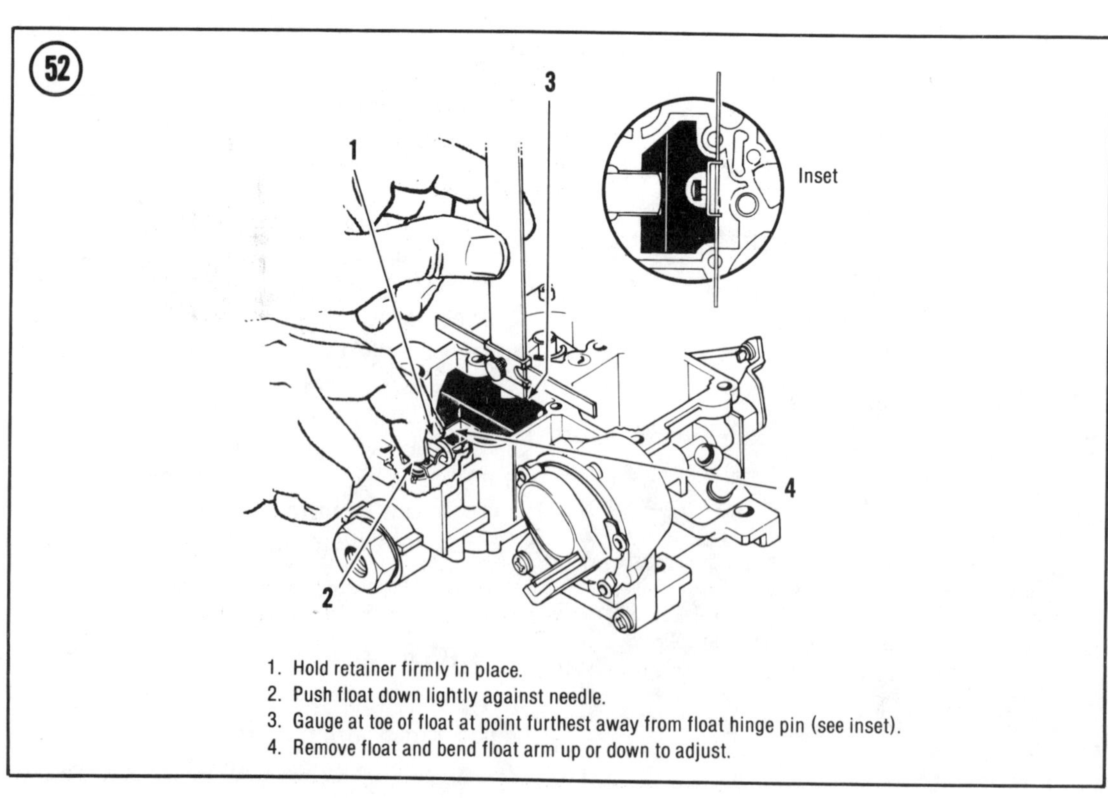

1. Hold retainer firmly in place.
2. Push float down lightly against needle.
3. Gauge at toe of float at point furthest away from float hinge pin (see inset).
4. Remove float and bend float arm up or down to adjust.

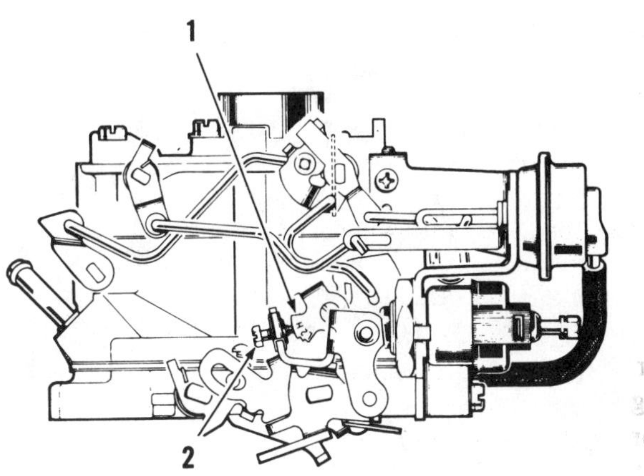

1. Place fast idle screw on highest step of fast idle cam
2. Turn fast idle screw in or out to specified number of turns. (See decal).

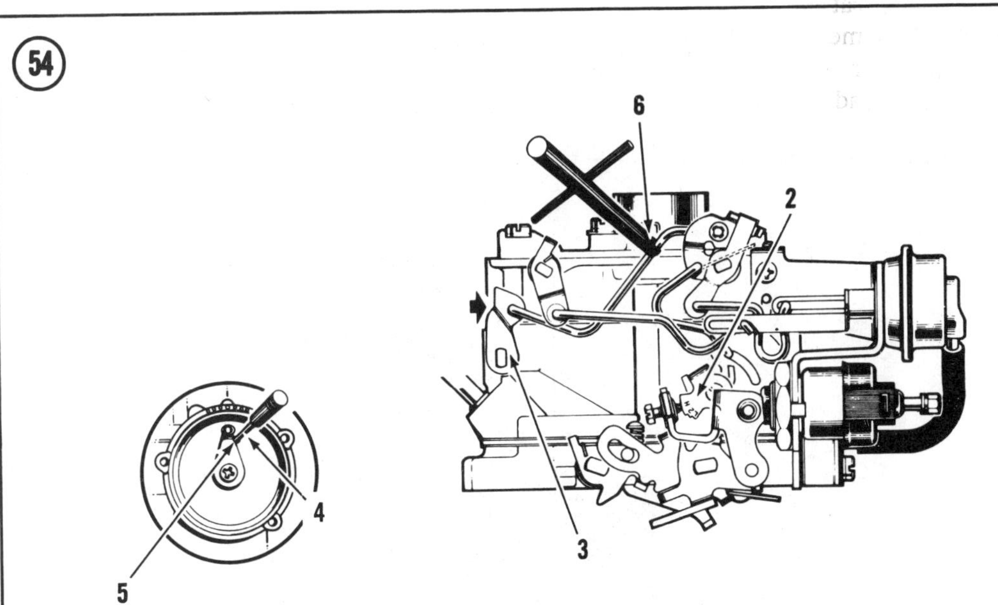

1. Remove rivets, choke cover and coil assembly following instructions in choke stat cover retainer kit (see note).

Note: *Do not* remove pop-rivets and retainers holding choke cover and coil assembly in place unless necessary to check the choke coil lever adjustment. If rivets and cover are removed, a choke stat cover retainer kit is required for reassembly.

2. Place fast idle screw on high step of fast idle cam.
3. Push on intermediate choke lever until choke valve is closed.
4. Insert specified plug gauge into hole provided.
5. Edge of lever should just contact side of plug gauge as shown.
6. Bend intermediate choke rod at this point to adjust.

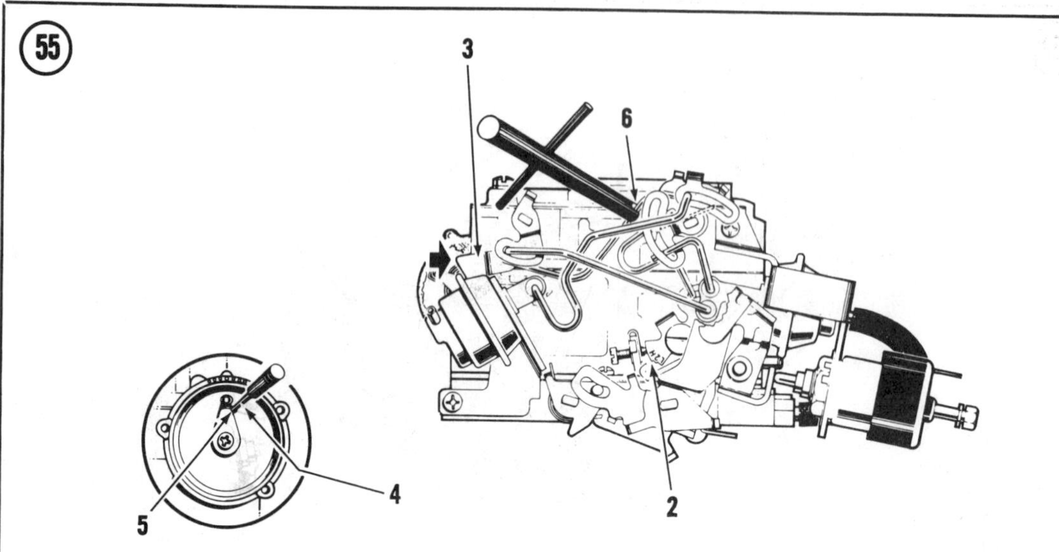

1. Remove rivets and choke cover and coil assembly following instructions in choke stat cover retainer kit (see note).
Note: *Do not* remove pop-rivets and retainers holding choke cover and coil assembly in place unless necessary to check the choke coil lever adjustment. If rivets and cover are removed, a choke stat cover retainer kit is required for reassembly.
2. Place fast idle screw on high step of fast idle cam.
3. Push on intermediate choke lever until choke valve is closed.
4. Insert specified plug gauge into hole provided.
5. Edge of lever should just contact side of plug gauge as shown.
6. Bend intermediate choke rod at this point to adjust.

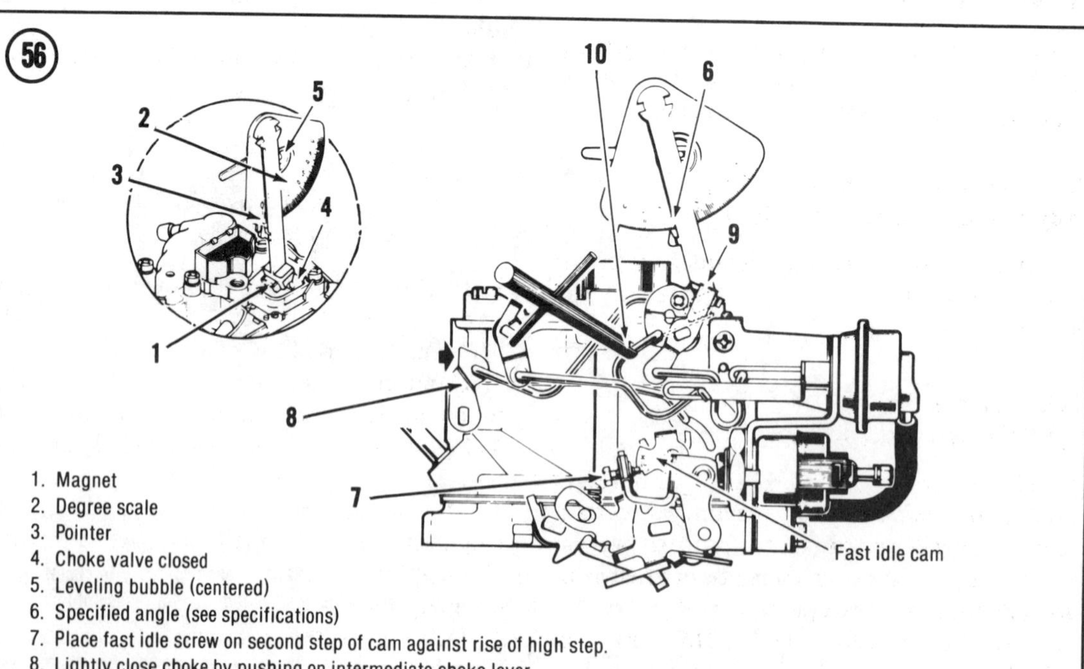

1. Magnet
2. Degree scale
3. Pointer
4. Choke valve closed
5. Leveling bubble (centered)
6. Specified angle (see specifications)
7. Place fast idle screw on second step of cam against rise of high step.
8. Lightly close choke by pushing on intermediate choke lever.
9. Push on vacuum break lever toward open choke until lever is against rear tang on choke lever.
10. Bend rod to adjust
11. Remove gauge.

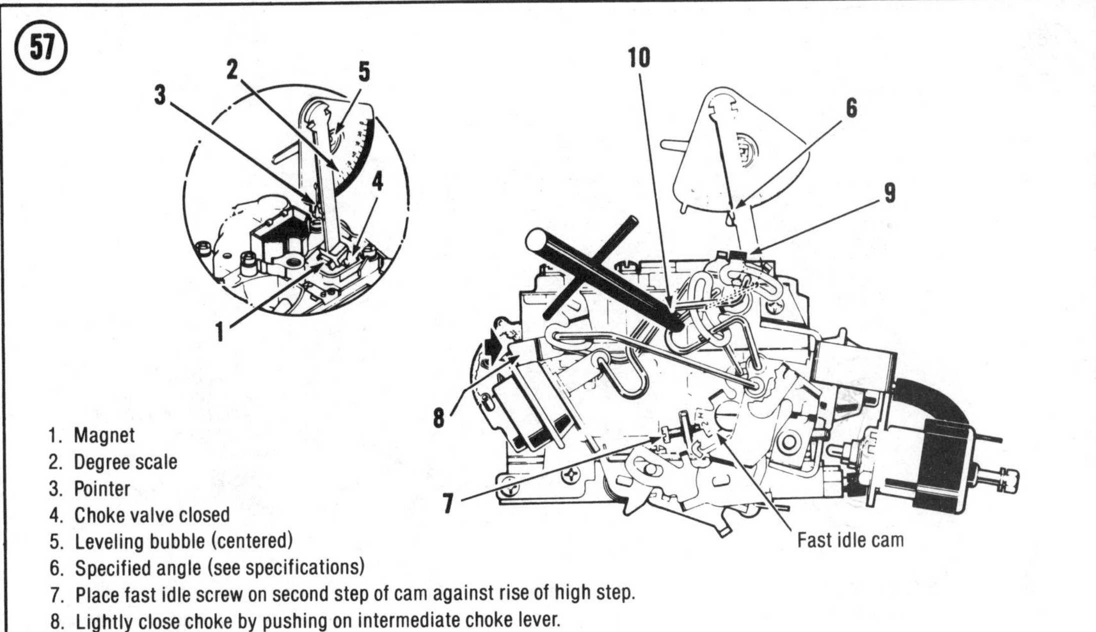

1. Magnet
2. Degree scale
3. Pointer
4. Choke valve closed
5. Leveling bubble (centered)
6. Specified angle (see specifications)
7. Place fast idle screw on second step of cam against rise of high step.
8. Lightly close choke by pushing on intermediate choke lever.
9. Push on vacuum break lever toward open choke until lever is against rear tang on choke lever.
10. Bend rod to adjust.

Primary Side Vacuum Break Adjustment

Refer to **Figure 58** (4-cylinder) or **Figure 59** (173) for primary side vacuum break adjustment. See **Table 1** for specifications.

Secondary Vacuum Break Adjustment (V6 Vehicles Only)

Refer to **Figure 60** for secondary vacuum break adjustment. See **Table 1** for specifications.

Idle Mixture (2SE Carburetors Only)

Vehicles equipped with 2SE carburetors cannot be adjusted rich beyond a certain limited range. In order to properly adjust them, they must be artificially enriched with propane using a special procedure.

A special propane tool (GM part No. J-26911) is required for this procedure. See **Figure 61**. You may be able to find a suitable substitute at an auto supply or parts store. If the tool is not available, do not try to adjust the idle speed mixture. Before attempting to adjust the idle mixture, read this entire procedure. If there is any doubt about your ability to perform this adjustment, have your General Motors dealer perform it for you.

NOTE

The 2SE carburetor does not usually require propane adjustment unless the carburetor has been overhauled.

1. Run engine to bring it to normal operating temperature. Make sure the choke is fully open and turn the air conditioner off.
2. Connect a tachometer to the engine, following the manufacturer's instructions.
3. Set the parking brake and block the rear wheels.
4. Disconnect and plug other hoses (if required) as explained on the Emission Control Information label in the engine compartment.
5. Disconnect the vacuum advance at the distributor and plug the hose. Check the ignition timing as described under *Ignition Timing* in Chapter Three. Reconnect the vacuum hose.

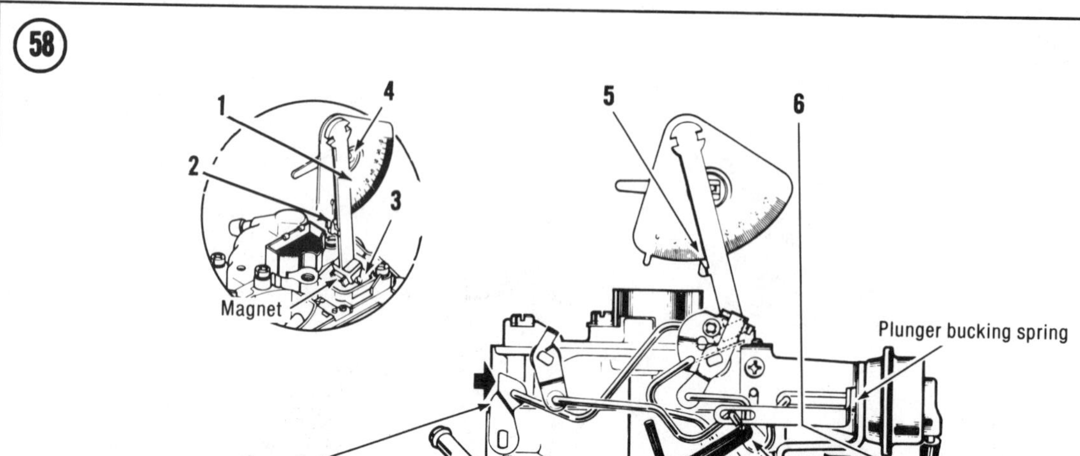

1. Degree scale
2. Pointer
3. Choke valve closed
4. Leveling bubble (centered)
5. Specified angle (see specifications)
6. Seat diaphragm using vacuum source.

Note: On delay models with air bleed, plug end cover with piece of 1" square masking tape. Remove tape after adjustment.

7. Lightly close choke by pushing on intermediate choke lever. Make sure plunger bucking spring (if used) is compressed and seated.
8. To adjust, bend vacuum break rod until bubble is centered.

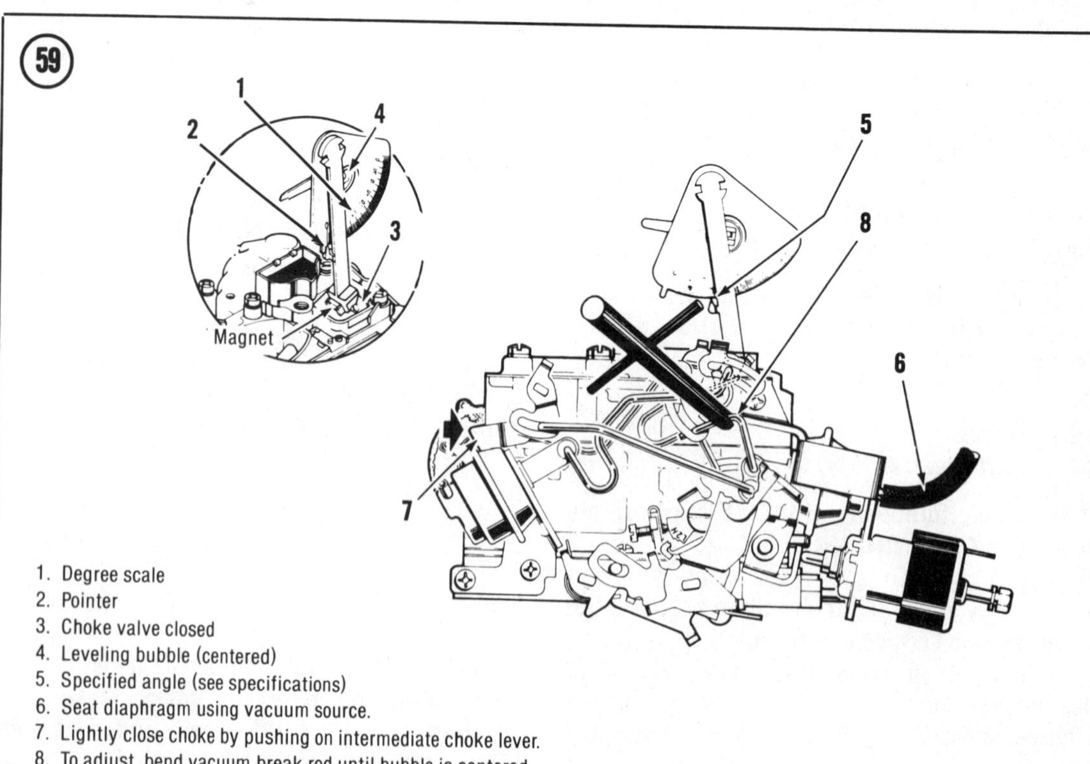

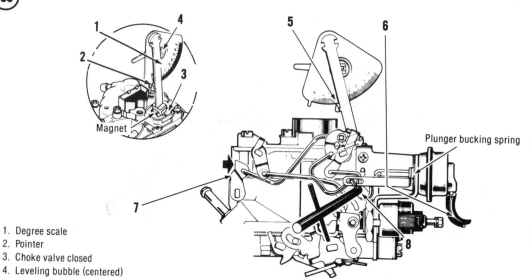

1. Degree scale
2. Pointer
3. Choke valve closed
4. Leveling bubble (centered)
5. Specified angle (see specifications)
6. Seat diaphragm using vacuum source.
7. Lightly close choke by pushing on intermediate choke lever.
8. To adjust, bend vacuum break rod until bubble is centered.

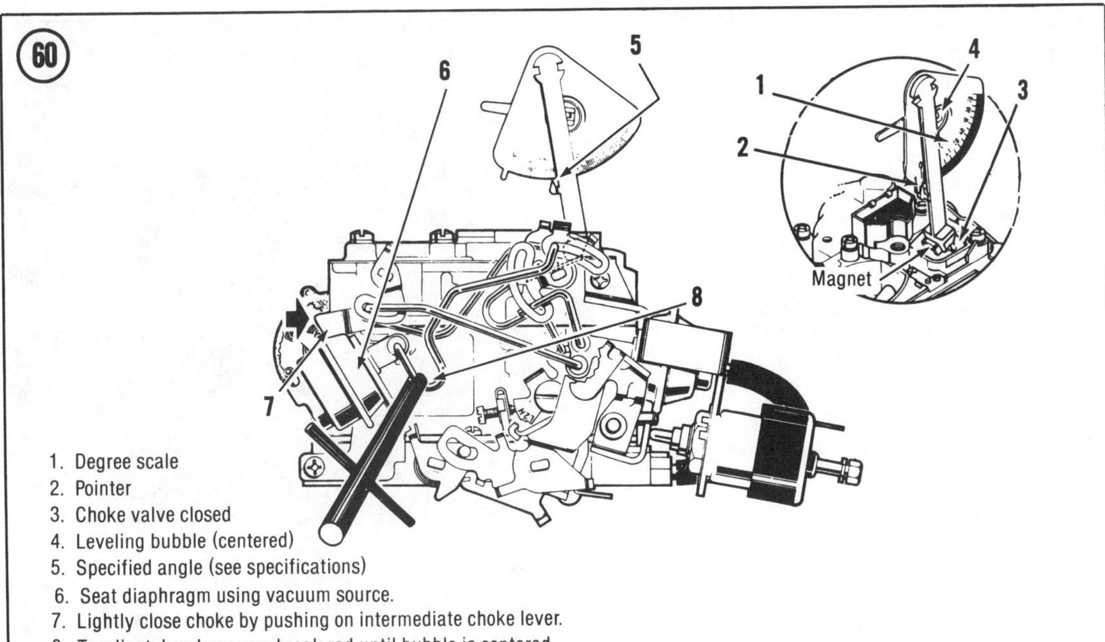

1. Degree scale
2. Pointer
3. Choke valve closed
4. Leveling bubble (centered)
5. Specified angle (see specifications)
6. Seat diaphragm using vacuum source.
7. Lightly close choke by pushing on intermediate choke lever.
8. To adjust, bend vacuum break rod until bubble is centered.

Note: On delay models with air bleed, plug end cover with piece of 1" square masking tape. Remove tape after adjustment.

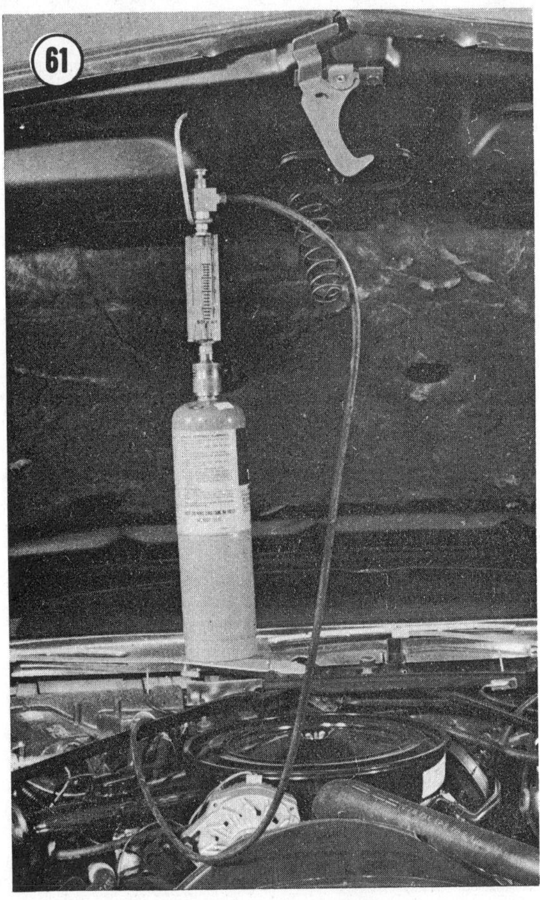

6. Disconnect the crankcase ventilation tube from the air cleaner. See **Figure 62**.

7. With tool part No. J-26911, insert the hose with the rubber stopper from the propane valve into the positive crankcase ventilation tube opening in the air cleaner.

8. Hold the propane cartridge vertical. See **Figure 61**.

9. Start the engine. Place the transmission in DRIVE (automatic) or NEUTRAL (manual).

10. Slowly open the propane control valve until engine speed is maximum. Too much propane will cause engine speed to drop.

11. With propane flowing, adjust idle speed screw (**Figure 63**) to enriched rpm shown in **Table 2**. Readjust the propane flow to be sure that you still have maximum engine speed, then readjust idle speed if necessary.

12. Turn off the propane. Put transmission in DRIVE (automatic) or NEUTRAL (manual) and run the engine at approximately 2,000 rpm for about 30 seconds.

13. Check the idle speed. If it is the same as that specified on the Emission Control Information label in the engine compartment, then the idle mixture is correct. Proceed to Step 20. If not, proceed to Step 14.

14. If the speed is not correct, gently remove the plug from the idle mixture screw. The idle mixture plug is shown in **Figure 64**.

NOTE

To remove the plug from the screw, first try to center punch the plug. Then drill a small hole in the plug; be careful not to damage the screw. Remove the plug using a screw extractor. Rotate the extractor counterclockwise and pull outward until the plug is free. If the plug cannot be removed by this method, the carburetor must be removed and idle mixture screw removed as described under ***Idle Mixture Screw*** *in this chapter.*

NOTE

It will be necessary to remove the air cleaner to reach the idle mixture screw. However, make sure to install air cleaner when checking the idle speed.

15. If the speed is too low, back out the screw 1/8 turn at a time until the speed on the Emissions label is reached.
16. If the speed is too high, turn in the screw 1/8 turn at a time until the speed on the Emissions label is reached.
17. Turn the propane on again to check the maximum idle speed. If the speed is different from the enriched rpm in **Table 2**, readjust the idle speed screw (**Figure 63**) to specifications with the propane flowing.
18. Turn off the propane. Put transmission in NEUTRAL and run the engine at approximately 2,000 rpm for about 30 seconds. Put the transmission in DRIVE (automatics) or NEUTRAL (manuals).
19. Check the idle speed. If it is the same as that specified on the Emission Control Information label in the engine compartment, the idle mixture is correct. If not, repeat Steps 13-19.
20. If rough idle persists, turn the mixture screw in until it seats lightly. Repeat the whole procedure.
21. When adjustment is complete, turn off the engine, disconnect the propane and connect the crankcase ventilation tube to the air cleaner.

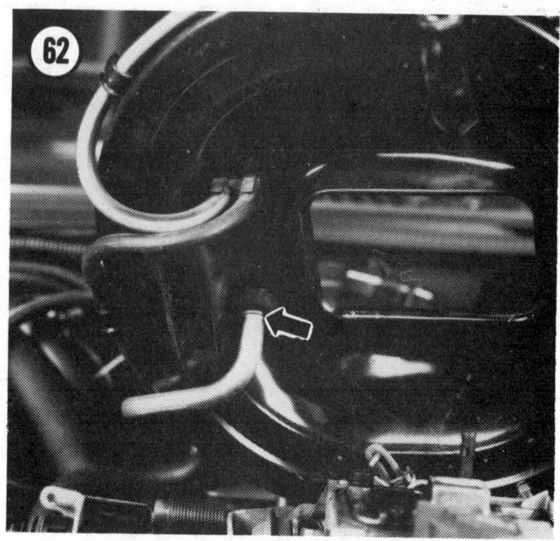

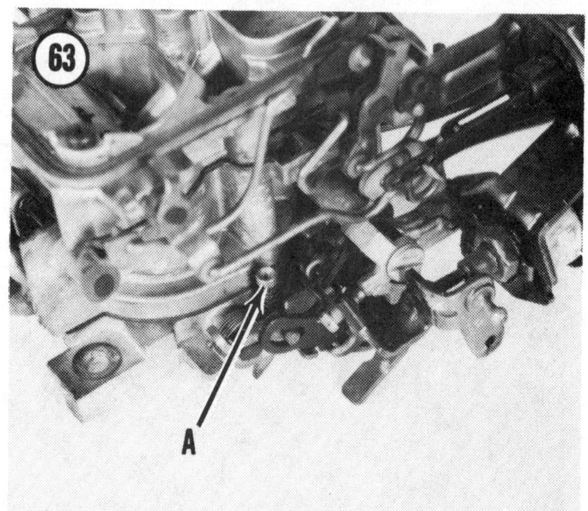

A. Idle speed screw

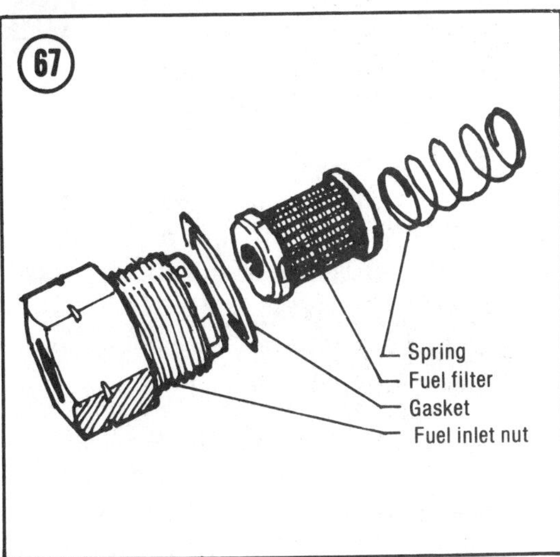

FUEL FILTER REPLACEMENT

Refer to **Figure 65** (4-cylinder) or **Figure 66** (V6) for fuel filter location. The fuel filter assembly is shown in **Figure 67**.

1. Disconnect fuel line connection at inlet fuel filter nut.
2. Remove inlet fuel filter nut from carburetor.
3. Remove filter element and spring.
4. Install new spring and filter element in carburetor. Make sure hole in filter faces inlet nut.
5. Install new gasket on inlet fitting nut. Install nut in carburetor and tighten securely.
6. Install fuel line and tighten connector.

ACCELERATOR CONTROL CABLE

Figure 68 (4-cylinder) and **Figure 69** (V6) show the accelerator control cable connection at the carburetor. **Figure 70** shows passenger compartment accelerator control cable routing for all models. On all models, there are no cable linkage adjustments. If any binding is felt, check routing of cable. Check for correct carburetor opening and closing positions by having an assistant operate the accelerator cable while you observe the carburetor.

Replacement

Accelerator control cable replacement is performed by removing old cable and installing new cable in exact same position.

CAUTION
Flexible components, such as hoses, wires, conduits, etc., must not be routed within 2 in. of any accelerator cable moving part unless routing is positively controlled.

CAUTION
On V6 vehicles, the braided portion of the accelerator cable assembly must not contact the front of the dash sealer during replacement.

FUEL PUMP

A mechanical fuel pump is used on both the 4-cylinder and V6 engines. If troubleshooting procedures in Chapter Two indicate a defective fuel pump, it must be replaced. See **Table 3** for fuel pump test specifications.

Fuel Pump Replacement

Figure 71 (4-cylinder) and **Figure 72** (V6) show the fuel pumps used. The fuel pump on the 4-cylinder engine is mounted at the rear of the engine under the intake manifold. The V6 fuel pump is mounted on the right front of the engine next to the oil filter.

1. Disconnect negative battery cable.

2. Raise vehicle front end and secure with jackstands. On 4-cylinder vehicles, remove the right front wheel to provide access to the fuel pump.

3. On V6 vehicles, remove the pump shield (**Figure 73**) and oil filter.

4. Disconnect the fuel inlet hose at the fuel pump. Disconnect the vapor return hose, if so equipped.

5. Loosen fuel line at carburetor (see **Figure 65** or **Figure 66**), then disconnect the fuel outlet pipe at the pump.

6. Remove the 2 bolts securing the fuel pump to the engine block, then lift the pump away from the engine.

7. Installation is the reverse of these steps. Remove all gasket material from the fuel pump and mounting pad. Install new gasket and pump. Tighten attaching bolts to 13-18 ft.-lb. (18-24 N•m).

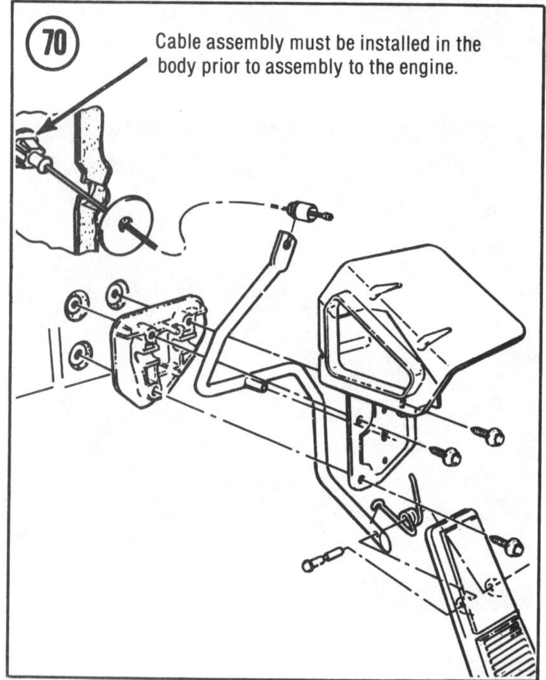

70
Cable assembly must be installed in the body prior to assembly to the engine.

FUEL TANK

Inspection

The fuel tank, cap and lines should be periodically inspected for road damage. Replace any damaged or malfunctioning parts.

WARNING
Before servicing the fuel tank, always: place "no smoking" signs near work area; be sure to have a CO^2 fire extinguisher handy; wear safety glasses; disconnect negative cable from battery; siphon or pump fuel into an explosion-proof container.

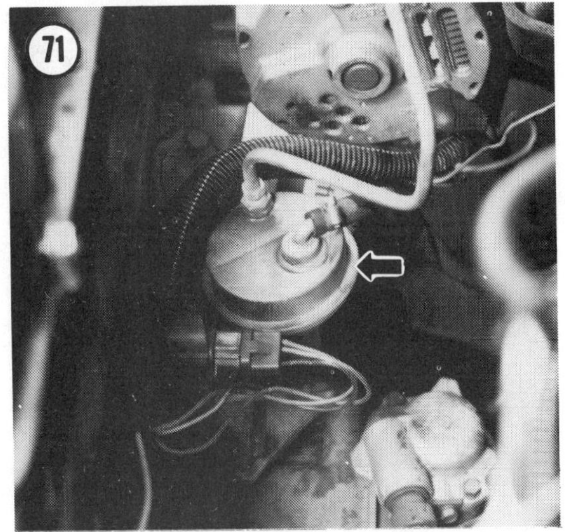

Draining Fuel Tank

If a car is to be stored for any length of time, the gasoline should be drained from the complete system, including carburetor, fuel pump, fuel lines and fuel tank, to prevent gum formation.

There is no fuel tank drain plug. Therefore, fuel must be siphoned or pumped from the fuel tank through the fuel feed line to drain fuel tank. Disconnect fuel feed line at the fuel pump.

Replacement

1. Drain the fuel tank as described above.
2. Raise vehicle on hoist or jack.
3. Disconnect fuel hose and vapor return hose from the fuel level sender.
4. Remove ground wire screw.
5. Disconnect sender wire at fuel level sender.
6. Disconnect fuel filler and vent hoses at the fuel tank (**Figure 74**).
7. Remove fuel tank strap bolts. See **Figure 75**. Lower and remove fuel tank.
8. Installation is the reverse of these steps.

Fuel Line Replacement

CAUTION

When necessary to replace portions of steel fuel line, use only brazed seamless steel tubing meeting General Motors Specification 123M or its equivalent.

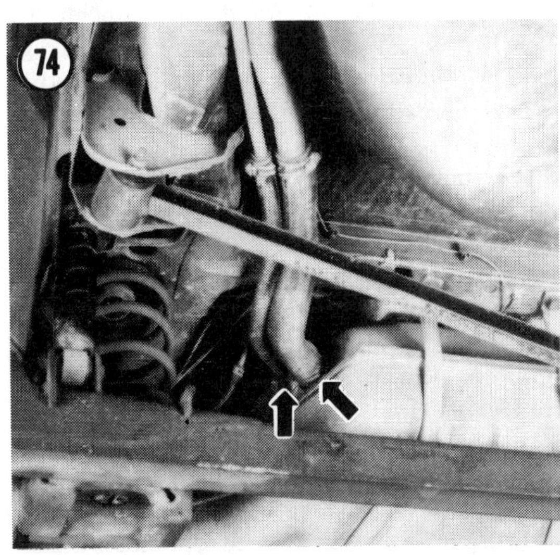

Under no conditions use copper or aluminum tubing to replace steel tubing. Those materials cannot withstand normal vehicle vibrations.

Remove fuel line from vehicle and replace by observing the following guidelines.

1. Do not use rubber hose within 4 in. (101 mm) of any part of the exhaust system.
2. In repairable areas, cut new fuel hose 4 in. (101 mm) longer than portion of fuel line removed.
3. If more than 6 in. (152 mm) of fuel pipe is removed, use a new combination of steel pipe and hose to ensure that new hose lengths will not be longer than 10 in. (254 mm).
4. Slide clamps onto pipe and push hose 2 in. (51 mm) onto each portion of fuel pipe. Tighten clamps on each side of repair.

INTAKE MANIFOLD

Intake Manifold Removal/ Installation (4-cylinder)

1. Drain the radiator below the level of the intake manifold by opening the drain tap at the bottom of the radiator. If the coolant is clean, it should be drained into a clean container and reused.
2. Remove the air cleaner assembly.
3. If the carburetor is to be removed from the intake manifold, perform the *Carburetor Removal/Installation* procedure described in this chapter. If the carburetor is to be removed with the intake manifold, disconnect the throttle linkage, transaxle downshift linkage and the cruise control linkage (if required) from the carburetor. Disconnect all vacuum lines, emission hoses and the fuel line from the carburetor.
4. Disconnect the PCV valve or hose.
5. Remove the carburetor/EGR spacer bolts (**Figure 76**) and lift the spacer up and remove from the manifold. Leave the vacuum lines and emission hoses attached to spacer.
6. Remove the heater hose attached to the intake manifold (**Figure 77**).
7. Remove the bell crank and throttle linkage brackets from the intake manifold (**Figure 78**). Set aside to provide clearance. If the carburetor is being removed together with the

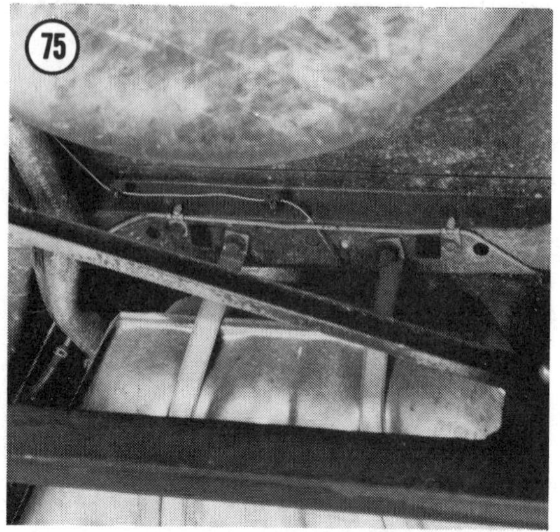

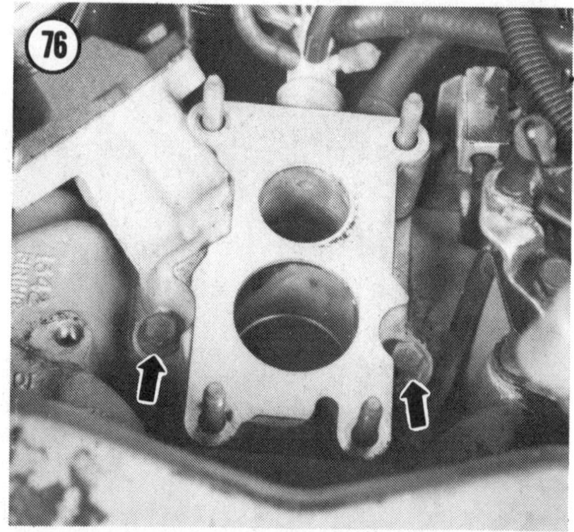

manifold, refer to *Carburetor Removal*, to remove the throttle linkage assembly.

8. Remove the pulse air check valve bracket at the manifold.

9. Remove the bolts attaching the intake manifold to the cylinder head (**Figure 79**) and remove the intake manifold from the cylinder head.

NOTE

When lifting the intake manifold up to remove, make sure not to damage the steel fuel line at rear of manifold.

10. Remove all gasket material from the manifold and cylinder head mating surfaces. Check manifold for cracks or damaged gasket surfaces.

11. Installation is the reverse of these steps. Install new intake manifold-to-cylinder head gasket, then install the intake manifold and tighten all attaching bolts finger-tight. Tighten the intake manifold attaching bolts to 25 ft.-lb. (34 N•m) in the sequence shown in **Figure 79**.

Intake Manifold Removal (V6)

1. Drain the radiator below the level of the intake manifold by opening the tap at the bottom of the radiator. If the coolant is clean, drain it into a clean container and reuse.
2. Remove the rocker arm covers as described in Chapter Five.
3. Remove the distributor as described in Chapter Eight.
4. Disconnect the heater and radiator hoses from the intake manifold. See **Figure 80**.
5. Remove the air cleaner assembly.
6. Remove the power brake vacuum pipe and bracket.

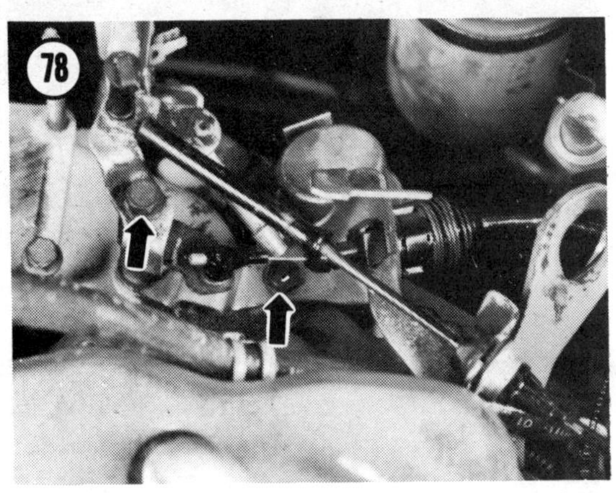
78

80

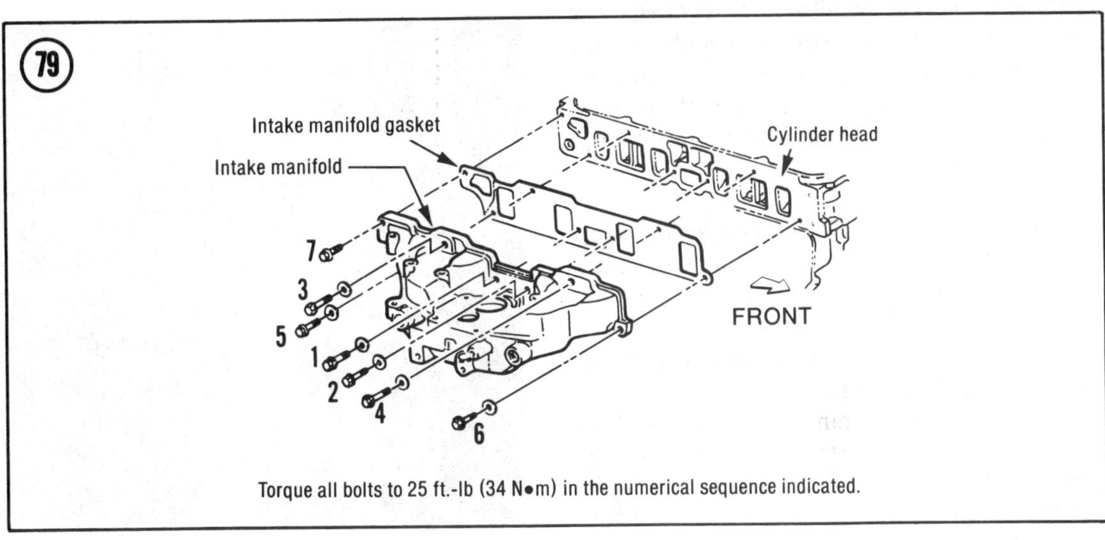

Torque all bolts to 25 ft.-lb (34 N•m) in the numerical sequence indicated.

7. Remove external EFE pipe at rear of manifold.
8. If the carburetor is to be removed from the intake manifold, perform the *Carburetor Removal/Installation* procedure described in this chapter. If the carburetor is to be removed with the intake manifold, disconnect the throttle linkage and the cruise control linkage (if required) from the carburetor. Disconnect all vacuum lines, emission hoses and the fuel line from the carburetor.
9. Remove all vacuum lines and emission hoses from the intake manifold.
10. Remove the bolts attaching the intake manifold to the cylinder head (**Figure 81**), then remove the intake manifold from the engine.

CAUTION
The intake manifold is made of aluminum and should not be pried upon when removing.

11. Remove all gasket material from the manifold and cylinder head mating surfaces. Check manifold for cracks or damaged gasket surfaces.

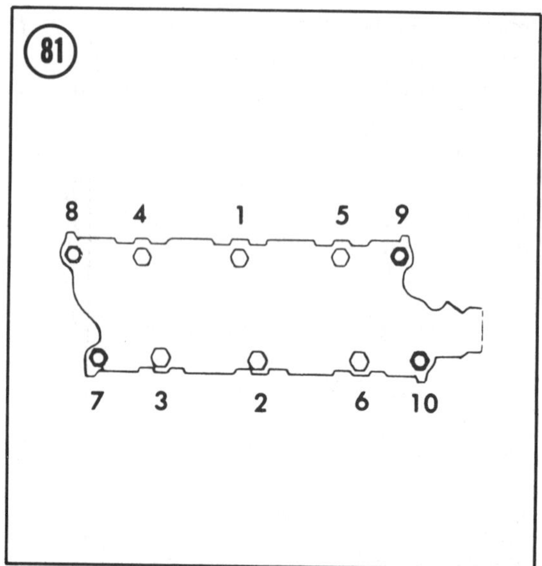

Intake Manifold Installation (V6)

1. Ensure that the intake manifold-to-cylinder head mating surfaces are clean of all gasket material. Use a solvent such as lacquer thinner or engine degreaser.

NOTE
*Before installing sealer to gasket surfaces, cut the intake manifold gaskets as shown in **Figure 82** to allow installation around pushrods. Note also that manifold gaskets are marked "Right Side" and "Left Side". Make sure to install gasket on correct side.*

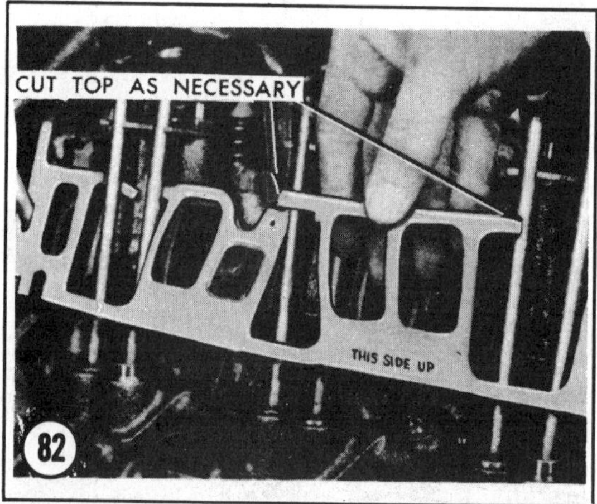

2. Apply a 3/16 in. bead of silicone rubber sealer to the cylinder case front and rear sealing ridges.
3. Install new intake manifold gaskets on the cylinder head. Hold gasket in place by extending ridge of silicone rubber sealer bead up 1/4 in. onto ends of gasket.
4. Install intake manifold on engine. Make sure areas between engine case ridges and intake manifold are sealed completely. Tighten

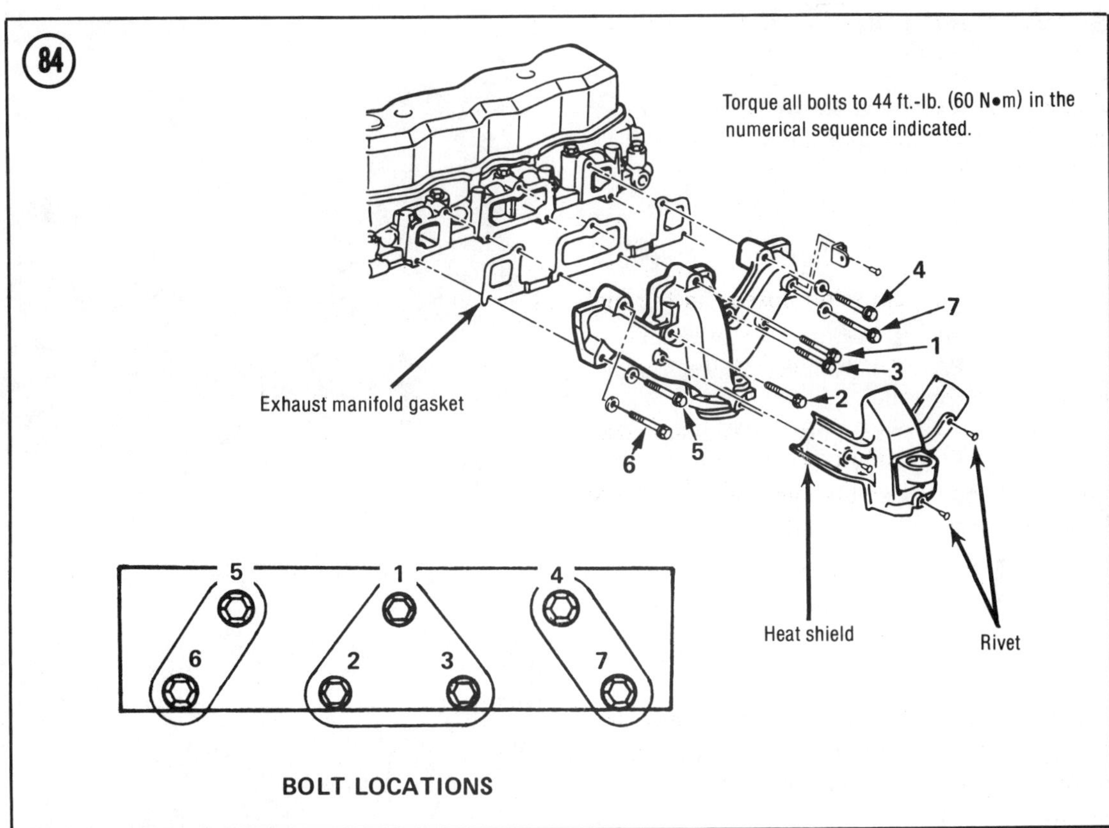

6

the intake manifold attaching bolts to 23 ft.-lb. (31 N•m) in the sequence shown in **Figure 81**.

5. Reverse Steps 1-9 to complete installation. Make sure to fill radiator with a 50/50 mixture of ethylene glycol antifreeze and water. Check ignition timing as described in Chapter Three.

EXHAUST MANIFOLD

Exhaust Manifold Removal/ Installation (4-cylinder)

1. Raise vehicle and support with jackstands.

2. Disconnect the nuts attaching the exhaust manifold to the down pipe. Remove jackstands and lower vehicle.

3. Remove air cleaner assembly as described in this chapter. Then turn the pre-heat tube sideways and remove from the top of the exhaust manifold.

4. Remove torque strut bolts at radiator support panel and at cylinder head.

NOTE

For vehicles equipped with air conditioning, carefully read the air conditioning section in Chapter Seven to acquaint yourself with the system. Then remove the compressor and position it out of the way. Do not disconnect lines from the compressor. Make sure that there is no strain on any of the hoses or lines.

5. Remove engine oil dipstick tube attaching bolt.
6. Disconnect the oxygen sensor lead at the sensor (**Figure 83**).
7. Remove the exhaust manifold-to-cylinder head attaching bolts (**Figure 84**) and lift the exhaust manifold from the engine.
8. Clean the exhaust manifold-to-cylinder head and down pipe mating surfaces of all gasket material and check for cracks or other damage.
9. Install new gaskets then install exhaust manifold by reversing the above steps. Tighten the attaching bolts to 44 ft.-lb. (60 N•m) in the sequence shown in **Figure 84**.

Exhaust Manifold Removal/ Installation (V6)

1. Remove the air cleaner assembly.
2. Disconnect the spark plug wires from the spark plugs.

NOTE

Steps 3-6 describe removal of the left side manifold.

3. Remove the carburetor heat stove pipe.
4. Remove PAIR plumbing from the exhaust manifold (**Figure 85**).
5. Raise vehicle and support with jackstands.
6. Remove the left exhaust manifold-to-cylinder head attaching bolts, then lift the left side manifold from the engine.

NOTE

Steps 7-9 describe removal of right side manifold.

7. With vehicle raised and supported with jackstands, remove the exhaust manifold to EFE valve flange bolts (**Figure 86**). Then remove exhaust pipe from manifold.
8. Remove the PAIR bracket bolt from the rocker arm cover (**Figure 87**) and at the manifold.
9. Remove the exhaust manifold-to-cylinder head attaching bolts, then lift the right side manifold from the engine.
10. Clean the exhaust manifold-to-cylinder head and down pipe mating surfaces of all gasket material and check for cracks or other damage.
11. Installation is the reverse of these steps. Place the exhaust manifold gaskets in position, then install the exhaust manifolds and tighten the attaching bolts finger-tight. Tighten the exhaust manifold attaching bolts to 25 ft.-lb. (34 N•m). Install new exhaust manifold flange bolts (**Figure 86**).

EXHAUST SYSTEM

Muffler and Tailpipe Replacement

The muffler inlet and outlet pipes are welded to the muffler to maintain alignment. Therefore, the muffler and both the inlet and outlet tailpipe assemblies must be replaced together. **Figure 88** represents a typical

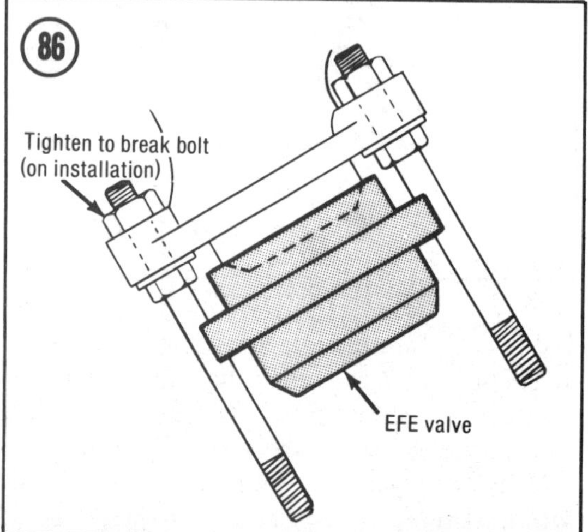

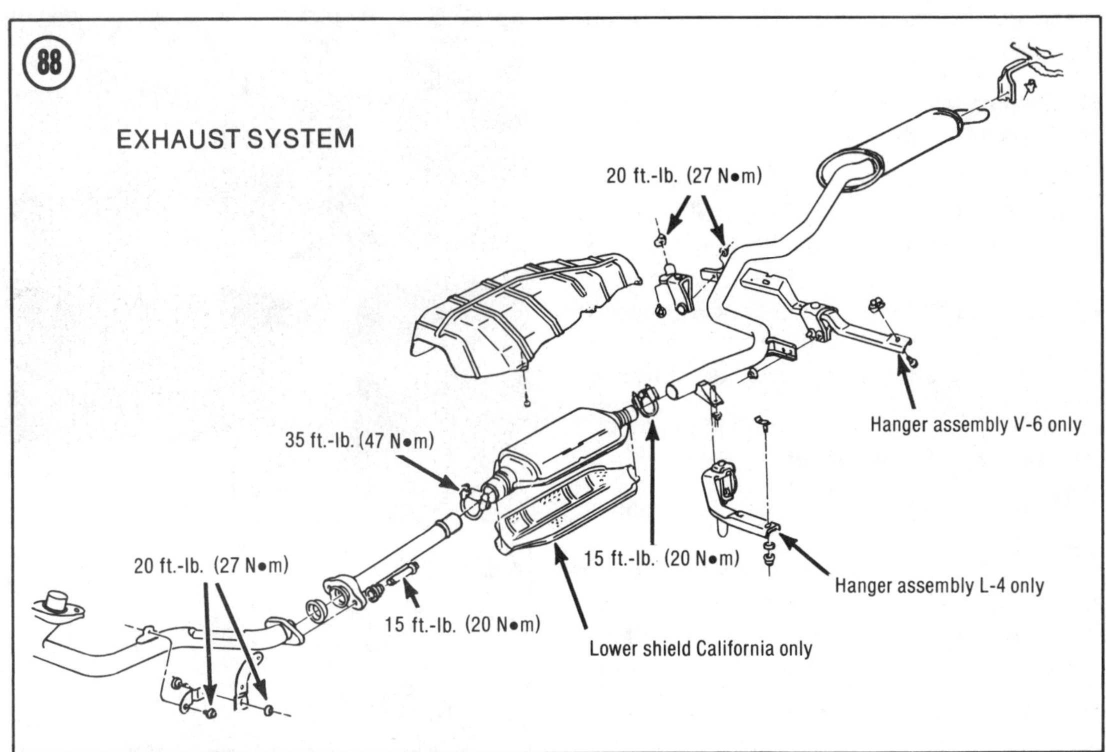

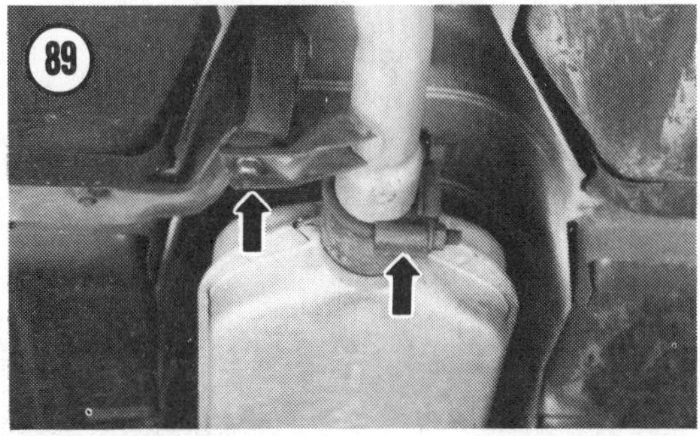

exhaust system found on your General Motors vehicle. Your actual exhaust system will depend on the state in which the vehicle was purchased and its emission controls.

1. Raise the vehicle to provide working space, then support the vehicle with jackstands.
2. Remove bolts securing muffler and tailpipe to the catalytic converter (**Figure 89**).
3. Disconnect the tailpipe (**Figure 90**) and muffler hangers (**Figure 91**). Remove the muffler and tailpipe.
4. Installation is the reverse of these steps. Make sure there is adequate clearance around muffler and tailpipe before tightening tailpipe to the converter.

Exhaust Pipe Replacement

1. Raise the vehicle to provide working space, then support the vehicle with jackstands.
2. Disconnect front of exhaust pipe at manifold. See **Figure 92** (4-cylinder) or **Figure 93** (V6). Then disconnect rear of exhaust pipe as shown in **Figure 88** and remove exhaust pipe.
3. Installation is the reverse of these steps. Make sure the catalytic converter- to-

6

underbody clearance is 1 in. (25 mm) before tightening bolts.

Renewing the Catalyst in Converter (V6)

At 30,000 mile intervals, a flag will appear in the speedometer face on cars with certain emission control systems. When the flag appears, the catalyst in the converter must be replaced. The job requires very special equipment and must be done by your dealer. It is not necessary to remove the converter from your car.

Bottom Cover Replacement

If the bottom cover of the catalytic converter is torn or severely damaged, your dealer can replace it with a bottom cover repair kit. This is cheaper than a new converter. However, if the inner shell of the converter is damaged, the inner shell must be replaced.

EMISSION CONTROL SYSTEMS

There are a number of emission control systems used on your General Motors vehicle:

a. Positive crankcase ventilation (PCV)
b. Exhaust gas recirculation (EGR)
c. Early fuel evaporation (EFE)
d. Pulse Air Injection Reaction (PAIR)
e. Catalytic converter
f. Computer controlled catalytic converter (C-4 system)
g. Distributor calibration
h. Carburetor calibration

The following sections describe each system briefly and provide service information where applicable.

POSITIVE CRANKCASE VENTILATION

The positive crankcase ventilation system draws blowby gases from the crankcase into the intake manifold so that they can eventually be reburned in the normal combustion process. See **Figure 94**.

A PCV valve restricts the ventilation system flow whenever intake manifold vacuum is high.

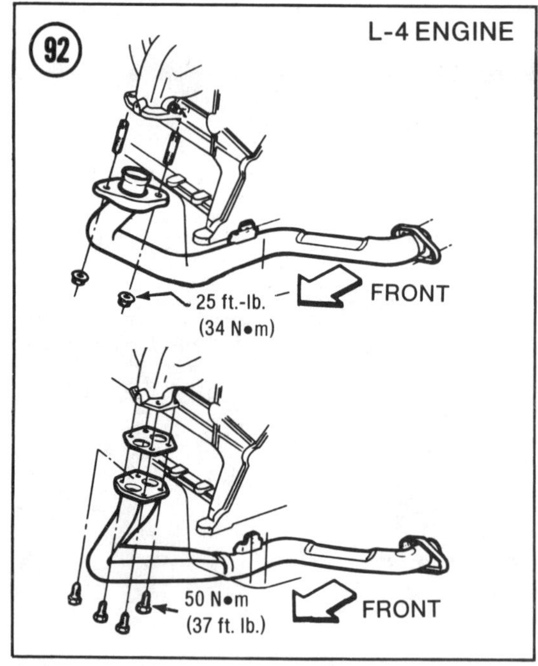

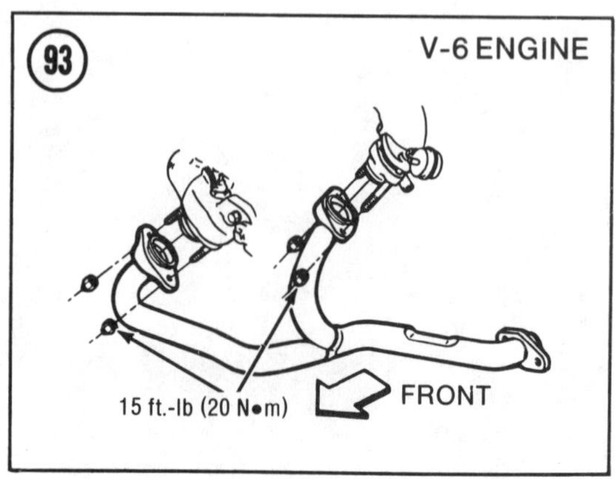

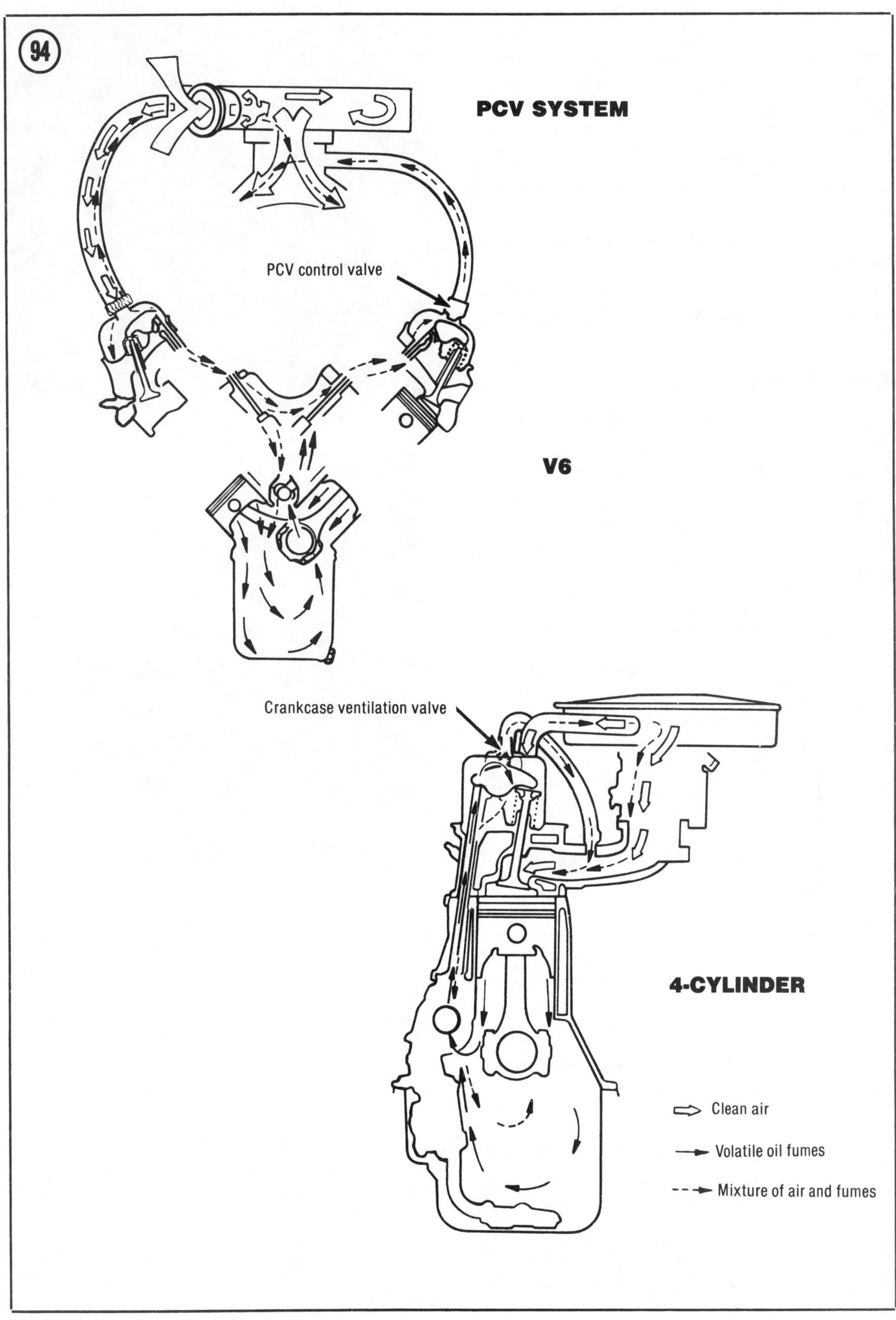
94
PCV SYSTEM
PCV control valve
V6
Crankcase ventilation valve
4-CYLINDER
Clean air
Volatile oil fumes
Mixture of air and fumes

PCV System Check

Check the valve as follows every 12 months or 15,000 miles. Replace it every 24 months or 30,000 miles.

1. Pull PCV valve out of the rocker arm cover. See **Figure 95**.
2. Shake valve. If valve does not rattle, replace valve.
3. Start engine. Place thumb over end of valve and check for vacuum.
4. If no vacuum is felt, check for plugged hoses or valve. The valve must be replaced if plugged.

PCV Filter (4-cylinder)

Four-cylinder engines also have a PCV filter located in the air cleaner assembly which must be replaced every 24 months or 30,000 miles.

1. Remove the air cleaner cover.
2. Remove the PCV filter retaining clip and remove filter (**Figure 96**).
3. Install new filter. Replace retaining clip and reinstall air cleaner cover.

EXHAUST GAS RECIRCULATION

The exhaust gas recirculation (EGR) system reduces oxides of nitrogen in the exhaust. A portion of the exhaust gas is tapped off and recirculated through the intake manifold or carburetor to intake manifold spacer. The gases dilute the air/fuel mixture in the combustion chambers and lower the combustion temperature.

There are 2 types of EGR systems used: vacuum modulated and exhaust backpressure modulated. Both types, while similar in function, differ mainly due to the method used to control how far each valve opens.

On the vacuum modulated EGR, a vacuum signal (ported vacuum) controlled by throttle position controls the amount of exhaust gas admitted to the intake manifold. During idle or deceleration (when throttle is closed) there is no vacuum signal emitted to the EGR valve because the EGR vacuum port is positioned above the closed throttle valve. As throttle is applied, a ported vacuum signal is supplied to the EGR valve admitting exhaust gas to the intake manifold. See **Figure 97**.

The exhaust backpressure modulated EGR uses a transducer located inside the EGR valve to control the operating vacuum signal. The vacuum signal is generated in the same manner as for the vacuum modulated EGR system. The integral transducer uses exhaust gas pressure to control an air bleed within the valve to modify the vacuum signal from the carburetor. See **Figure 98**.

The EGR valve on all vehicles is mounted on the intake manifold. See **Figure 99** (4-cylinder) or **Figure 100** (V6).

An EGR valve malfunction usually causes a rough idle. Eliminate the ignition system as a source of trouble before suspecting the EGR valve.

VACUUM MODULATED EGR SYSTEM

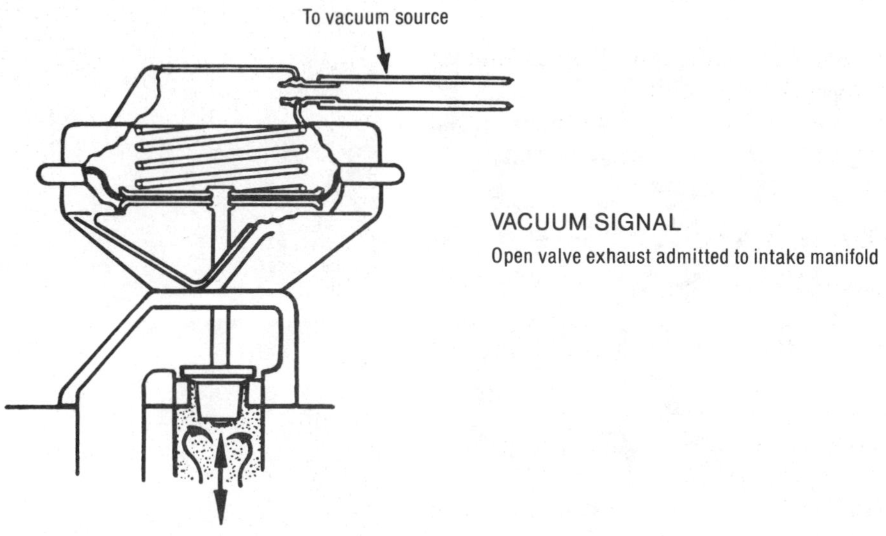

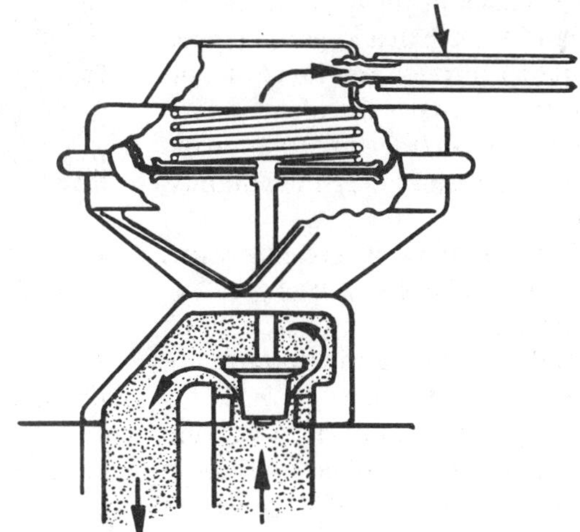

NO VACUUM SIGNAL
Closed valve

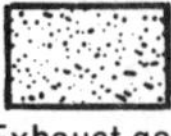

EXHAUST BACKPRESSURE MODULATED EGR SYSTEM

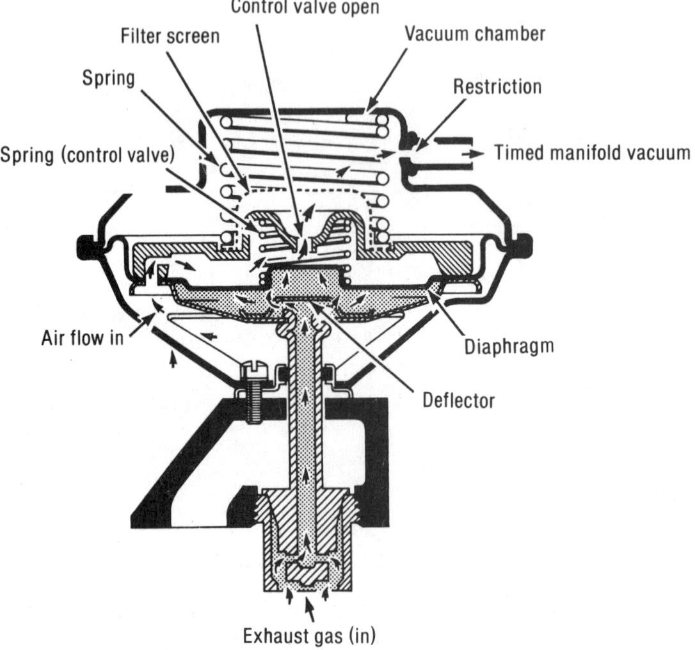

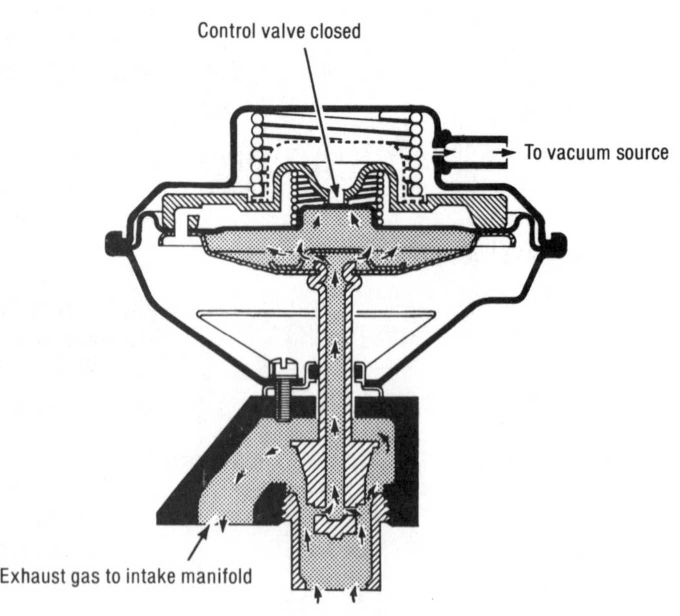

Exhaust gas

EGR Valve Removal/Installation

1. Disconnect the vacuum line from the valve.
2. Remove bolts securing valve to manifold.
3. Remove EGR valve from manifold.
4. Install new valve on manifold, using a new gasket. Install spacer (if used).
5. Tighten valve and install vacuum line to tube at top of valve.

EGR Valve Cleaning

CAUTION

Do not wash valve assembly in solvents or degreaser or the valve diaphragm may be permanently damaged.

1. Remove all traces of old gasket from mounting surface.
2. Insert valve and pintle into opening in spark plug cleaning machine and blast for approximately 30 seconds.

NOTE

Many service stations have this type of spark plug cleaner and will clean the valve for a small charge.

3. Compress the diaphragm spring so that valve is fully unseated and blast for another 30 seconds.
4. Inspect valve to ensure that exhaust deposits have been removed. Repeat cleaning procedure as required to remove all deposits.
5. Clean valve seat and pintle area with compressed air to ensure that abrasive material is thoroughly removed from valve.

EGR Valve Inspection

1. Remove EGR valve from intake manifold.
2. Depress the diaphragm plate. Diaphragm should move freely from open to closed position. If not, clean as described in this section.
3. Apply about 5 in. of vacuum to the vacuum tube on top of valve. Engine coolant must be at normal operating temperature.

NOTE

If you do not have any means to produce the vacuum, take the valve to your dealer for testing.

4. Remove vacuum hose from tube at top of EGR valve. Increase engine speed. Diaphragm should move downward.
5. Reinstall vacuum hose and increase engine speed. Diaphragm should move upward.

NOTE

Diaphragm plate vibration may be noticed on backpressure EGR valves. This does not indicate a bad valve or diaphragm.

NOTE

If diaphragm doesn't move while performing Steps 1-5, perform Steps 6-8. If diaphragm moves with no change in engine speed, proceed to Step 9.

6. Check engine vacuum. It should be at least 5 in. at EGR valve with engine running and throttle open. Make sure engine is operating at normal engine operating temperature.
7. Check for vacuum at EGR hose. If no vacuum is present, check for incorrect hose routing, plugged or leaking hose or carburetor port.
8. On backpressure EGR valves, have dealer check transducer control valve operation.
9. Check EGR manifold passages for blockage and clean if necessary.
10. If the cause of the problem is not found by performing above steps, refer EGR valve to dealer for further functional checks.

EGR Thermal Switch Replacement

1. Drain engine coolant.
2. Disconnect vacuum lines from the thermal vacuum switch.
3. Wrap threaded portion of switch with Teflon tape sealer.
4. Install switch and torque to 15 ft.-lb. (20 N•m).
5. Rotate switch head as required for proper hose routing and install the vacuum hoses. Replace engine coolant and check for leaks.

NOTE
The thermal vacuum switch is non-repairable. If defective, replace it.

EARLY FUEL EVAPORATION SYSTEM (EFE)

The early fuel evaporation (EFE) system, used on V6 engines, provides heating to the intake manifold while the engine is cold to promote fuel vaporization. This helps cut down on choke time and also promotes more thorough burning of the fuel. This, in turn, reduces the amount of pollutants released into the air. The heart of the system is the EFE valve, which controls the amount of heat (exhaust gas) directed under the intake manifold. The valve is controlled by a thermal vacuum switch that applies or removes vacuum to the EFE valve according to the temperature of the engine coolant. Use the following procedure to check operation of the EFE system.

EFE System Check

Check the valve initially at first 6 months or 7,500 miles, then every 24 months or 30,000 miles.

Figure 101 shows the EFE valve disconnected from the exhaust manifold and exhaust pipe. In **Figure 101**, the valve is open.

1. With the engine cold, place the transmission in NEUTRAL (manual) or PARK (automatic), apply the handbrake and start the engine. Observe movement of EFE actuator rod. The actuator rod should be pulled into the diaphragm housing (EFE valve closes).

2. If the valve does not close, remove the vacuum hose from the EFE valve and apply an external vacuum source in excess of 8 in. The valve should close. If the valve does not close, lubricate the valve with manifold heat valve lubricant (GM part No. 1050422 or equivalent), then recheck or replace as required. If valve closes, the EFE valve is not at fault. Check for damaged vacuum hoses and replace as required. Recheck with external vacuum supply or proceed to Step 3.

3. If the valve closes, allow the engine to warm up to normal operating temperature. The valve should move to the open position. If not, remove hose from EFE valve and see if valve opens. Valve should open. If valve opens, there is no air bleed for the diaphragm. Replace the thermal vacuum switch.

PULSE AIR INJECTION REACTION (PAIR)

A pulse air injection reaction system (PAIR) is used on some vehicles. Consisting of distribution pipes and check valves, the PAIR system creates a pulsating pressure flow of positive or negative exhaust gas. Negative pressure at the pulse air valve forces a flow of fresh air into the exhaust system. If positive pressure gas is present, the check valves close and no exhaust gas can flow past the valve and into the fresh air supply line.

During normal operation, the pulse air valves will operate quietly. However, a hissing noise may indicate a defective pulse air valve or a loose manifold bolt.

CAUTION

If one or more pulse air valves fail, exhaust gas will enter the engine through the air cleaner and cause engine surge and poor performance. As the exhaust gas passes through the pulse air valve, excessive heat is transmitted to the rocker arm plenum. This buildup of heat will cause premature hose and grommet wear.

Pulse Air Valve Replacement

1. Remove air cleaner and disconnect hose(s) from pulse air valves. **Figure 102** shows typical hose to valve connection.

CAUTION

When removing hoses, inspect for cracks.

2. Disconnect PAIR pipes from exhaust manifold (**Figure 85**).
3. Disconnect PAIR support bracket if present. On V6 engines, remove PAIR solenoid and bracket from PAIR unit if necessary.
4. Remove PAIR attaching nuts, then lift PAIR air valves away from engine.
5. Install in the reverse order. Apply a light coat of engine oil to mouth of pulse air valve tubes. Tighten pulse air valve attaching nuts to 10-13 ft.-lb. (7-10 N•m).

CATALYTIC CONVERTER

The catalytic converter mounts between the engine exhaust manifold and the muffler. It contains catalysts (usually platinum and palladium) which speed up the combination of oxygen with unburned hydrocarbons and carbon monoxide. This significantly reduces emissions of these harmful pollutants. Catalytic converter replacement is covered in this chapter.

6

COMPUTER CONTROLLED CATALYTIC CONVERTER SYSTEM (C-4)

A computer controlled catalytic converter system is used on all California models. The C-4 system reduces harmful emissions by constantly controlling the air/fuel ratio and by using a 3-way catalytic converter and electronic carburetor. A schematic diagram of the C-4 system is shown in **Figure 103**.

The essential components of the system are an oxygen sensor in the exhaust system (OS), a 3-way catalytic converter (ORC), an electronically-controlled carburetor (model E2SE) and an electronic control module (ECM).

Oxygen Sensor

The oxygen sensor is a cone-shaped device placed in the engine's exhaust system. The oxygen sensor produces a voltage which is determined by the amount of oxygen in the exhaust gases compared to the amount of oxygen in the outside air. As the oxygen content increases, indicating a lean air/fuel mixture, the voltage drops. As the oxygen

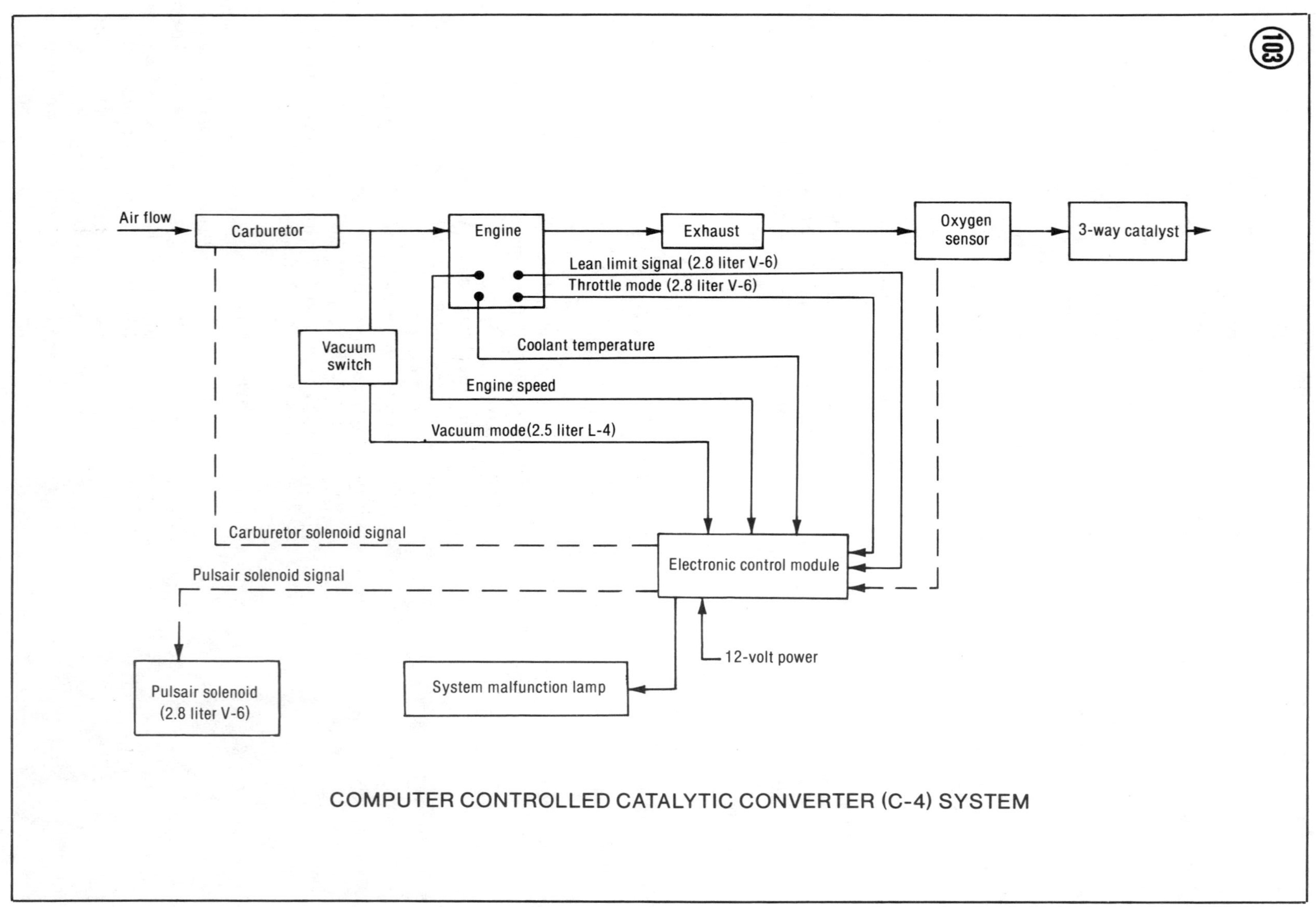

COMPUTER CONTROLLED CATALYTIC CONVERTER (C-4) SYSTEM

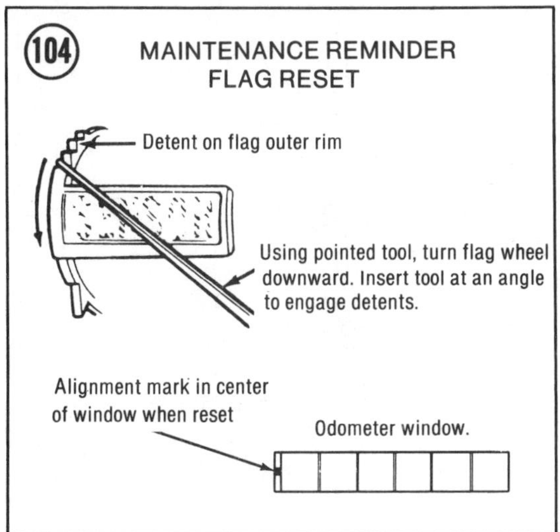

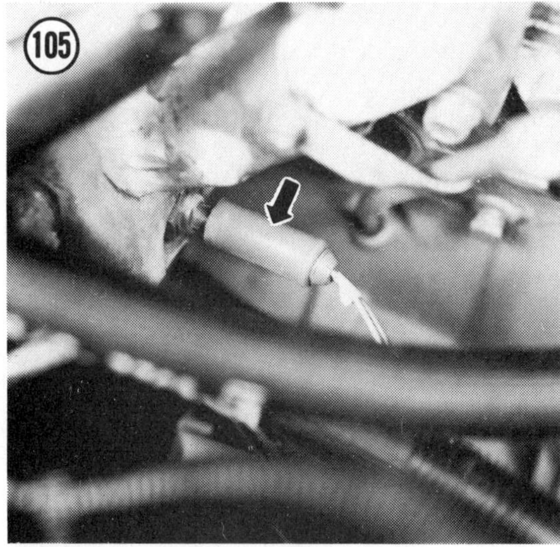

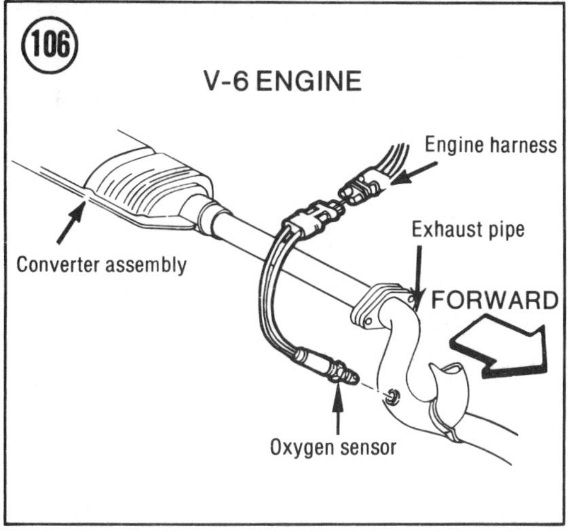

content decreases, indicating a rich air/fuel mixture, the voltage from the sensor rises.

This voltage output from the sensor is constantly monitored by the ECM and recorded with information from other system input signals. From the input information, a signal is created and sent from the ECM to the carburetor solenoid which is continually cycling between *on* (lean command) and *off* (rich command).

When a lean air/fuel mixture is burned, the control signal turns the solenoid off and the spring-loaded metering rod returns to its up position, thus increasing fuel flow. When a rich air/fuel mixture is burned, the solenoid is energized. The metering rod is then pulled down, reducing fuel flow.

Maintenance

Normal routine maintenance requires that the oxygen sensor be replaced at the specified service intervals listed in Chapter Three. On all cars with the C-4 system, a flag stating either "Sensor" or "Emissions" will appear in a window in the speedometer face. This is a reminder that the oxygen sensor must be replaced. After replacing the oxygen sensor, the reminder flag must be reset.

Oxygen Sensor Flag Reset

Refer to **Figure 104** for this procedure.

1. Remove the instrument panel bezel and cluster lens as described in Chapter Eight.
2. Locate the flag wheel and place a pointed tool on one of the flag detents. It will be necessary to angle the tool tip upward to engage the flag detent.
3. Lightly force the flag wheel downward with tool until the flag alignment mark rests in the center of the window. This indicates that the flag is properly reset.
4. Reinstall instrument cluster lens and panel bezel.

Oxygen Sensor Replacement

The oxygen sensor is located in the exhaust manifold on the 4-cylinder engine (**Figure 105**) and in the exhaust pipe on the V6 engine (**Figure 106**).

CAUTION
The oxygen sensor may be difficult to replace when the engine temperature is below 120° F. Excessive force may damage threads in the exhaust manifold or exhaust pipe. Therefore, the engine should be started and run for approximately 10 minutes before attempting to remove the oxygen sensor.

1. *V6 engines*: Raise vehicle front end and secure with jackstands.
2. Disconnect the electrical connector from the oxygen sensor.

CAUTION
The oxygen sensor uses a permanently attached wiring pigtail and connector. No attempt should be made to remove the wiring pigtail from the sensor. Damage to the sensor or wiring could affect operation of sensor. See ***Figure 107****.*

3. Spray a heat lube, such as GM part No. 105422, onto the oxygen sensor threads and allow to soak for 5 minutes.
4. Carefully unscrew the oxygen sensor and remove.
5. Coat the oxygen sensor threads with anti-seize compound (GM part No. 5613659 or equivalent). Screw sensor into position. Torque to 30 ft.-lb. (42 N•m). Reconnect the electrical connector at the oxygen sensor.

Fuel Type

Unleaded gasoline must be used in a C-4 equipped car. Leaded gasoline will damage the oxygen sensor and consequently affect fuel economy and emission control.

Troubleshooting

When troubleshooting your vehicle for causes of poor engine operating conditions, the C-4 system should be considered as a source of possible trouble. However, while dealer service is required to perform in depth troubleshooting, the C-4 self-diagnostic system will enable the experienced enthusiast to determine at which condition the system is operating and thus save both time and money.

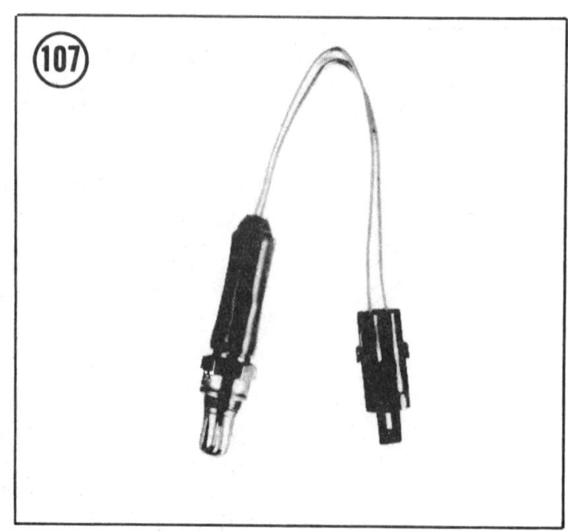

Check Engine Light

When the vehicle is first started, a CHECK ENGINE lamp will come on to let you know that the bulb is working properly. The light will stay on for a short time (3-5 seconds) and then go out. During engine operation the ECM is constantly monitoring the C-4 system. If the CHECK ENGINE lamp should come on when the engine is running, a malfunction has occured in the C-4 system.

When the light comes on, a trouble code is set in the memory of the ECM. If the malfunction is continuous, the CHECK ENGINE lamp will stay on. If the malfunction is intermittent, the CHECK ENGINE lamp will go out when the trouble stops and come on again if the trouble is repeated. During engine operation, the malfunction is stored in the computer's temporary memory as a trouble code. However, when the engine is turned off, the trouble code is lost. When troubleshooting the C-4 system, consider the following:

a. When a malfunction has occured and the ignition switch has been left on, the trouble code is locked into the ECM memory.

b. When a malfunction has occured and the ignition switch is turned off, the trouble code is lost. It is then necessary to restart the engine to allow the ECM to relocate and store the trouble code.

C-4 TROUBLE CODES	
Trouble Code	Problem Area
12	No tachometer signal to the ECM.
13	Oxygen sensor circuit. The engine has to operate approximately 5 minutes for this code to show.
14	Shorted coolant sensor circuit. The engine has to run 2 minutes for this code to show.
15	Open coolant sensor circuit. The engine has to run 5 minutes for this code to show.
21	Throttle position sensor circuit (V6 engine only).
21 & 22	(At same time) Grounded wide open throttle switch circuit (4-cylinder engine only).
22	Grounded closed throttle or wide open throttle switch circuit (4-cylinder engine only).
23	Carburetor solenoid circuit.
44	Lean oxygen sensor.
45	Rich oxygen sensor.
51	On service replacement ECM, check the calibration (PROM) unit. On original equipment ECM, replace ECM.
52, 53	Replace the ECM.
54	Faulty carburetor solenoid and/or ECM.
55	4-cylinder: Replace ECM.
55	V6: Faulty throttle position sensor or ECM.

108

6

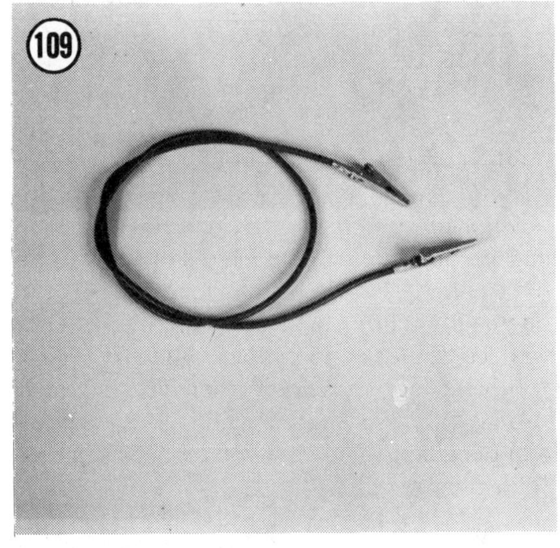

109

c. When a malfunction occurs only intermittently, the "CHECK ENGINE" light will flash on and off as the problem occurs and stops. However, when the malfunction first occurs, its trouble code is locked into the ECM and will remain on as long as the ignition key is not turned off.

It is important to have the trouble code stored in the ECM. By grounding a test lead from the ECM, the stored trouble code will flash across the CHECK ENGINE lamp as a series of long and short light flashes. For example, the code may read as one long flash, followed by 5 short flashes. This indicates trouble code 15. The trouble code can then be compared to a listing of problem areas which will indicate the cause of the C-4 system malfunction. See **Figure 108**.

See *System Test* on reading C-4 operating codes.

System Test

A basic test can be made to determine if the C-4 diagnostic system is operating correctly. A set of jumper wires is required (**Figure 109**).

1. From inside the passenger compartment, remove the fuse panel cover from underneath the right side dash panel and locate the diagnostic ground test lead (green connector—white wire with black stripe). Attach one end of the jumper wire to the green connector. Leave the opposite jumper wire end unattached at this time.

2. Start the engine. The CHECK ENGINE lamp should light for approximately 3-4 seconds and then go out. Turn engine off with ignition key, then turn key back to RUN position. The CHECK ENGINE light will come on and stay on.

NOTE

If the CHECK ENGINE light does not come on, check the 20 amp gauge fuse in the fuse block. If the fuse is blown, replace it. If the fuse is okay, refer further service to a General Motors dealer.

3. Connect the unattached jumper wire end (see Step 1) to a good ground and immediately observe the CHECK ENGINE lamp. The lamp will go out. Then the lamp should flash a code 12. This consists of one long flash followed by a slight pause and then 2 more flashes. The system will repeat the series of code 12 flashes until the engine is started or the ignition switch turned off. A code 12 flash indicates that the diagnostic system is working properly. If the light does not flash code 12, but some other code listed in **Figure 108**, it is necessary to have your dealer perform a "Diagnostic Circuit Check" and a "Systems Performance Check".

4. After completing test, remove jumper wire and install the fuse panel cover.

Long Term Memory

Because the ECM has a temporary memory when the engine is running, the trouble code is lost once the ignition key is turned off. However, some trouble codes cannot be located until the engine is run for 5 minutes at part throttle. Furthermore, malfunctions which occur intermittently can be difficult to locate. For this reason, the ECM can be made to have a long term memory. When the ignition switch is turned off and the long term memory activated, the trouble code is locked into the ECM. To activate the long term memory, perform the following:

1. Remove the fuse block front cover. Locate the orange connector (with orange wire) from the ECM hanging beside the fuse block.

2. With a voltmeter or test light, find a fuse terminal that remains hot when the ignition switch is turned off. Two of the 3 BATT terminals located at the bottom of the fuse panel will work.

3. Connect one end of a jumper wire to the orange ECM connector and the other end to a hot terminal at the fuse panel. Current is now continuously supplied to the ECM memory.

4. Drive the vehicle until you notice that the CHECK ENGINE light has flashed during engine operation. A very slight flash of the CHECK ENGINE light will store the trouble code into the ECM memory. To read the trouble code, ground the green connector (white wire with black stripe) test lead as described in the *Systems Test.*

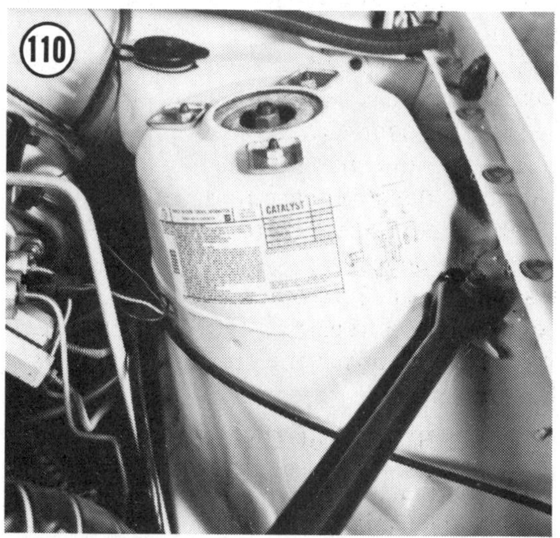

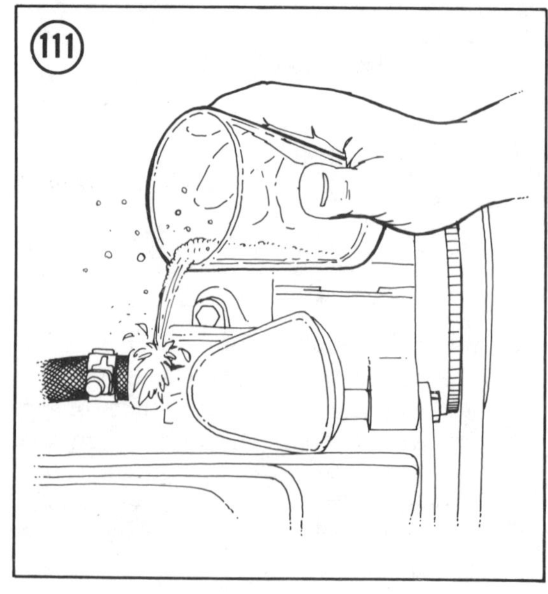

NOTE
The orange connector (orange wire) wire is not normally connected because it causes a small current drain when the ignition switch is turned off. However, if the engine is started and run daily, the battery will not run down.

5. When the trouble code is recorded, remove the jumper wire.
6. Record the trouble code on paper and refer further service to a General Motors C-4 specialist.

DISTRIBUTOR CALIBRATION

Distributor calibration consists of adjusting initial timing, centrifugal advance and vacuum advance to obtain the best combination of engine performance, fuel economy and exhaust emission level control. Timing specifications for each engine are given on the Vehicle Emission Control Information (VECI) decal located in the engine compartment. See **Figure 110**. See *Ignition Timing Adjustment*, Chapter Three, for instructions on how to set the initial timing. Adjustment or repair of the centrifugal and vacuum spark advance systems should be left to an expert.

CARBURETOR CALIBRATION

In addition to providing the engine with a combustible mixture of air and fuel, the carburetor is also calibrated to maintain proper emission levels. The idle, off-idle, power enrichment and accelerator pump systems are calibrated to provide the best combination of performance, economy and exhaust emission control. Carburetor adjustments and services must be performed using the procedures given in this chapter.

EMISSION CONTROL VACUUM LINES AND HOSES

Inspect all hoses for deterioration and check the hoses and tubes for cracks. Replace any that are not satisfactory. Check the connections to make sure they are tight and leak free. Test the pressure side of the lines with a soapy water solution applied to each of the connections with the engine idling (**Figure 111**). Bubbling and foaming are indications that a connection is not tight. Correct any leaks that are found.

If a hose or tube is to be replaced, pay careful attention to the routing of the piece being removed and route the new piece in the same manner. Vacuum hose schematics are included on the VECI decal (**Figure 110**) and should be referred to when replacing hose connections. Tighten all the connections securely and check for leaks as described above.

Tables are on the following pages.

6

Table 1 CARBURETOR SPECIFICATIONS

Carb No.	Float Level (in.)	Fast Idle Screw (turns)	Choke Coil Lever (in.)	Fast Idle Cam (angle)	Primary Vacuum Break (angle)	Secondary Vacuum Break
17059614	3/16	3	0.085	18	17	—
17059615	3/16	3	0.085	18	19	—
17059616	3/16	3	0.085	18	17	—
17059617	3/16	3	0.085	18	19	—
17059650	3/16	3	0.085	27	30	38
17059651	3/16	3	0.085	27	22	23
17059652	3/16	3	0.085	27	30	38
17059653	3/16	3	0.085	27	22	23
17059714	11/16	3	0.085	18	23	—
17059715	11/16	3	0.085	18	25	—
17059716	11/16	3	0.085	18	23	—
17059717	11/16	3	0.085	18	25	—
17059760	1/8	3	0.085	17.5	20	33
17059762	1/8	3	0.085	17.5	20	33
17059763	1/8	3	0.085	17.5	20	33
17059618	3/16	3	0.085	18	17	—
17059619	3/16	3	0.085	18	19	—
17059620	3/16	3	0.085	18	17	—
17059621	3/16	3	0.085	18	19	—

Table 2 IDLE MIXTURE WITH PROPANE ENRICHMENT

Engine	Curb Idle	Enriched rpm
4-cylinder low altitude manual trans.		1150 rpm (N)
4-cylinder low altitude automatic trans.		700 (D)
4-cylinder California manual transmission		*
4-cylinder California automatic transmission	See: Vehicle emission control information label	*
V6 California manual transmission		*
V6 California automatic transmission		*
		*

* See vehicle emission control information label. N-Neutral D-Drive

Table 3 FUEL PUMP PRESSURE

Engine	Pressure
4-cylinder	6.5-8.0 psi (45-55 kPa)
V6	6.0-7.5 psi (41.5-51.7 kPa)

NOTE: If you own a 1981 or later model, first check the Supplement at the back of the book for any new service information.

CHAPTER SEVEN

COOLING, HEATING, AND AIR CONDITIONING

All vehicles use pressurized cooling systems, sealed with a pressure type radiator cap. The higher operating pressure of the system raises the boiling point of the coolant.

Tables 1-3 are at the end of the chapter.

COMPONENTS

Cooling system components are the radiator, pressure cap, reservoir, water pump, cooling fan, thermostat and associated hoses and water passages.

Radiator

The radiator is a cross-flow type. The cross-flow radiator is shown in **Figure 1**.

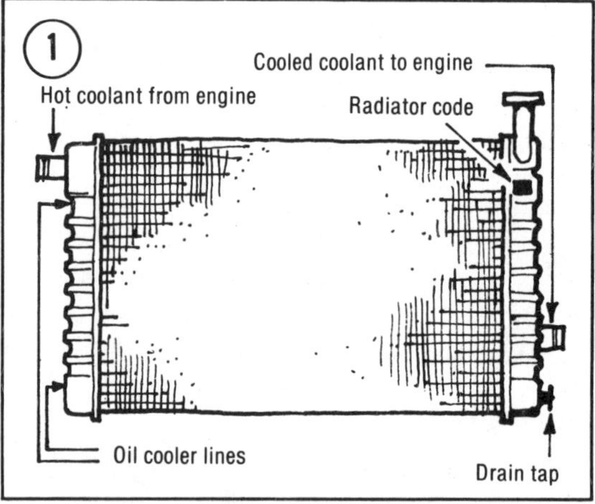

On automatic transaxle equipped vehicles, oil coolers are built into the left hand tank with inlet and outlet fittings for transmission fluid circulation. Manual transaxle equipped vehicles use radiators without oil coolers. Air conditioned vehicles use a larger radiator to provide extra cooling capability.

Radiator Cap

The pressure-type radiator cap (**Figure 2**) allows the cooling system to operate at higher atmospheric pressure, thus raising the boiling point of the coolant to approximately 262° F (125° C). The pressure cap has a pressure

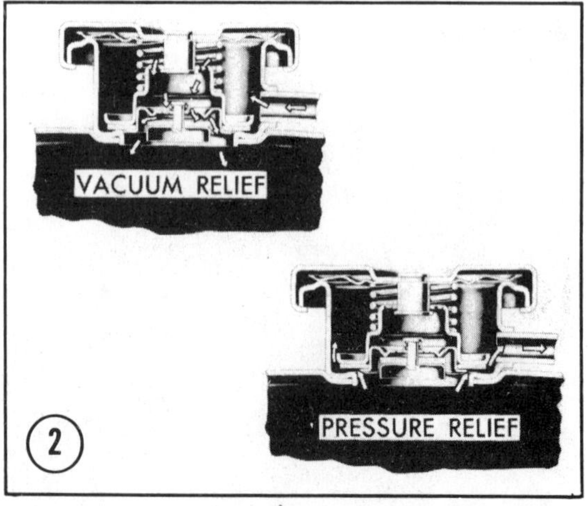

relief valve which allows excessive pressure to be vented. It also has a vacuum valve which opens to relieve the vacuum created when the system cools.

Recovery Bottle

The plastic see-through recovery bottle (**Figure 3**) ensures that the radiator is kept filled with coolant to the desired level at all times. As the coolant is heated and expands during vehicle operation, fluid flows from the radiator into the recovery bottle through a connecting hose. When the vehicle is stopped and the coolant temperature lowers, the displaced coolant is drawn back into the radiator by vacuum.

Water Pump

The centrifugal type water pumps used on the 4-cylinder and V6 engines have sealed bearings and require no periodic maintenance. The pump inlet is connected to the bottom of the radiator by a hose. The pump causes the water to circulate through the water passages in the engine block and cylinder head, where engine heat is transferred to the water. The engine and cylinder head passages are connected and terminate at the water outlet of the thermostat housing, which is connected to the top of the radiator by a hose.

Cooling Fan

The cooling fan increases cooling system efficiency by drawing air through the radiator.

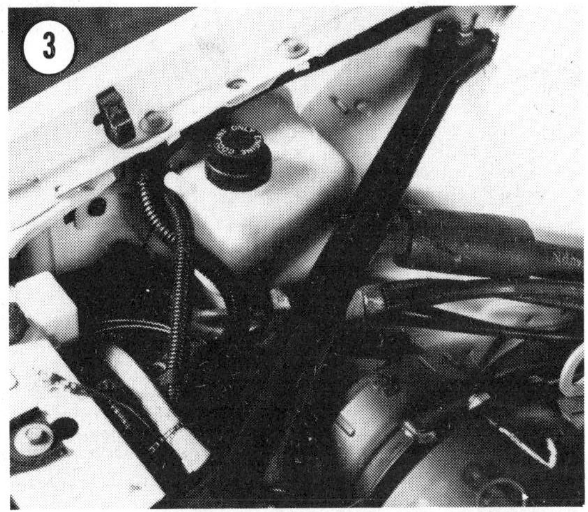

The 12 in. diameter fan is driven by an electric motor attached to the radiator support. The fan motor is activated by a coolant temperature switch which ensures adequate cooling at reduced engine speeds and eliminates overcooling, excessive noise and power loss at high speeds. On air conditioner equipped vehicles, a second switch can activate the fan, depending upon the air conditioner compressor head pressure at the condensor.

Thermostat

The thermostat is a heat-controlled valve in the cooling system, located in the engine water passage outlet to the radiator. When the engine and coolant are cold, the valve remains closed, preventing the circulation of coolant through the radiator. When the engine and coolant approach normal operating temperature, the thermostat opens to allow coolant to flow to the radiator for cooling.

Coolant

Only ethylene glycol-based coolant meeting the requirements of GM Specification 1899-M should be used.

The coolant should be mixed with water in accordance with the coolant manufacturer's instructions to provide freeze protection to -34° F. Even if your climate does not require this degree of protection, the antifreeze makes an excellent rust inhibitor.

DRIVE BELT TENSION ADJUSTMENT

The water pump/fan drive belt, as well as the belts which drive the alternator, power steering pump and air conditioning, should be inspected every 15,000 miles for adjustment and condition.

Worn, cracked or glazed belts should be replaced at once. The components to which they direct power are essential to the safe and reliable operation of the vehicle. If correct adjustment is maintained on the belts, they will usually all enjoy the same service life. For this reason, and because of the labor involved in replacing an inboard belt on a front wheel drive vehicle, it is a good idea to replace all belts as a set. The low added expense is well

7

worth the time involved in doing the job twice, to say nothing of the consequences of a failed belt.

In addition to being in good condition, it is important that the drive belts be correctly adjusted. A belt that is too loose will not permit the driven components to operate at maximum efficiency. In addition, the belt will wear rapidly because of increased friction caused by slipping. A belt that is adjusted too tight will be overstressed and tend to be pulled apart and it in turn will overstress bearings in driven components resulting in their premature wear or possible failure.

Drive belt tension (adjustment) is measured by deflection of the belt between 2 pulleys at the belt's longest run (**Figure 4**). For maximum belt life and component efficiency, General Motors recommends that the belt tension should be checked with a tester like that shown in **Figure 5**.

To check tension with a gauge, attach the gauge to the drive belt and pull the adjusting arm component away from the engine until the desired tension is reached. See **Table 1** for drive belt tension specifications. Tighten all bolts securely and repeat the tension check. See **Figure 6** (4-cylinder) or **Figure 7** (V6) for drive belt and pulley diagrams.

Pulley Inspection

Before installing new drive belts, inspect the pulleys for the following conditions:

a. Oil or grease: Contaminants on the pulley surface will cause the belt to slip. Clean each pulley before installing new drive belts.
b. Pulley damage: Wear spots in the pulley belt groove will cause a new belt to wear quickly. A cracked (see **Figure 8**) or damaged pulley could possibly break and cause damage in the engine compartment. Inspect and replace any pulley as required.
c. Pulley wear: During normal operations, drive pulleys will ride on the sides of the pulley. This is indicated by a polished appearance on the pulley's side. However, if the bottom of the pulley groove appears polished, the belt is

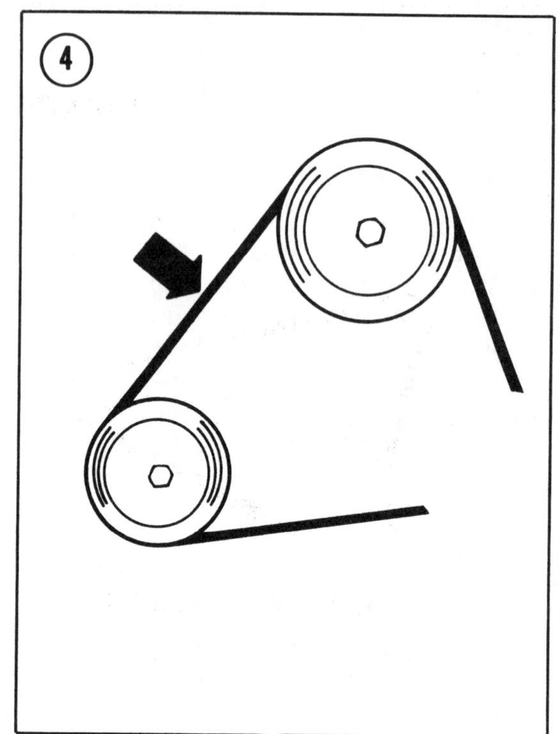

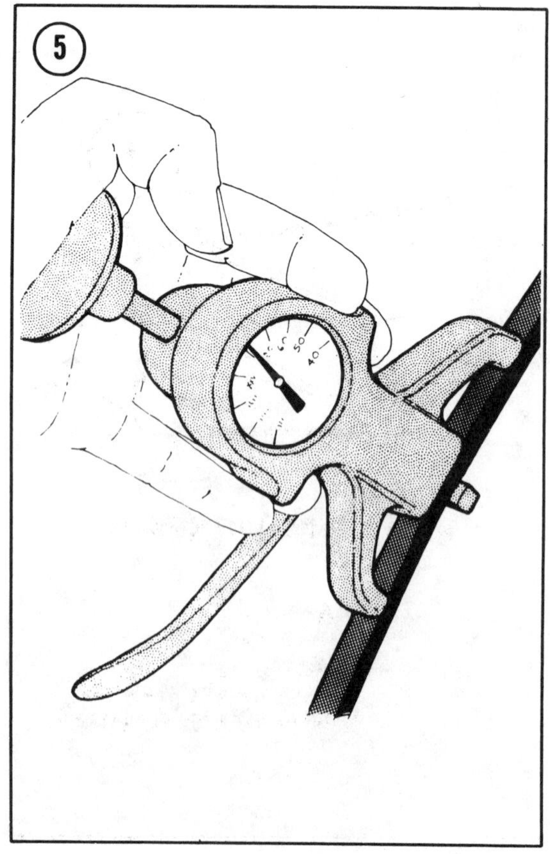

4-CYLINDER DRIVE BELTS

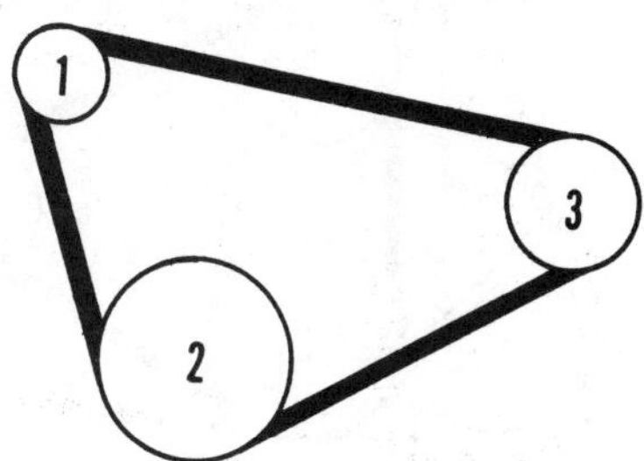

ALTERNATOR ONLY

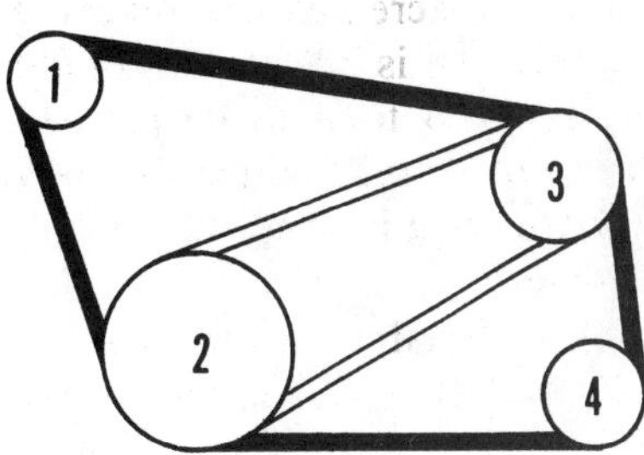

WITH POWER STEERING

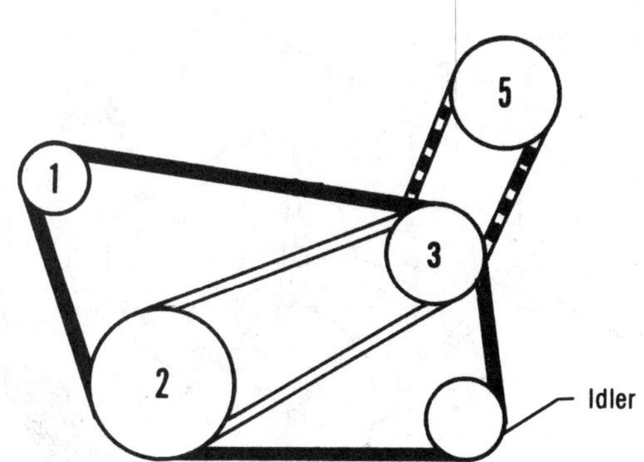

WITH AIR CONDITIONING

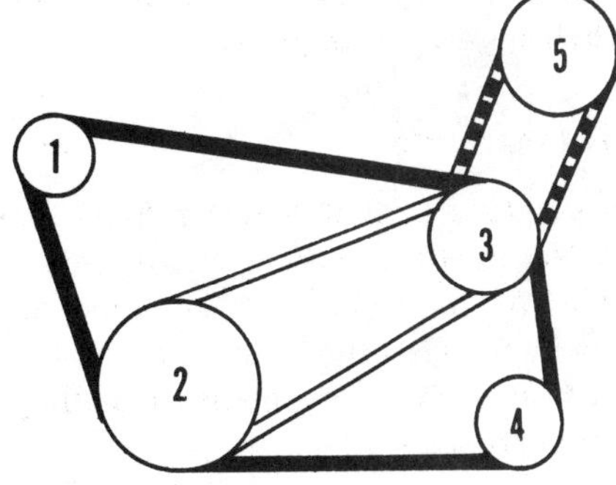

WITH POWER STEERING AND AIR CONDITIONING

1. Alternator
2. Crankshaft
3. Water pump
4. Power steering pump
5. Air conditioning compressor

(7)

6-CYLINDER DRIVE BELTS

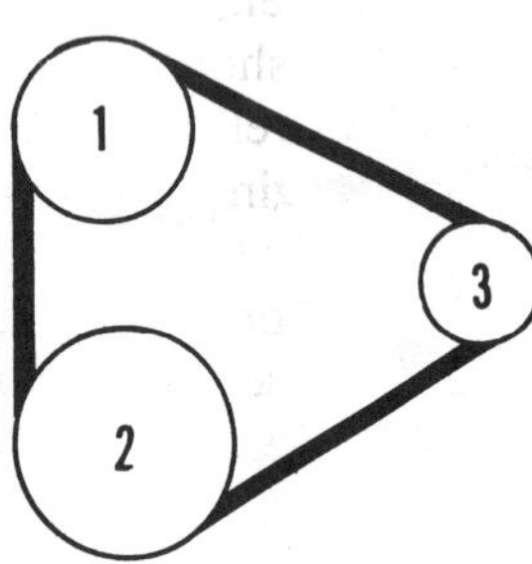

ALTERNATOR ONLY

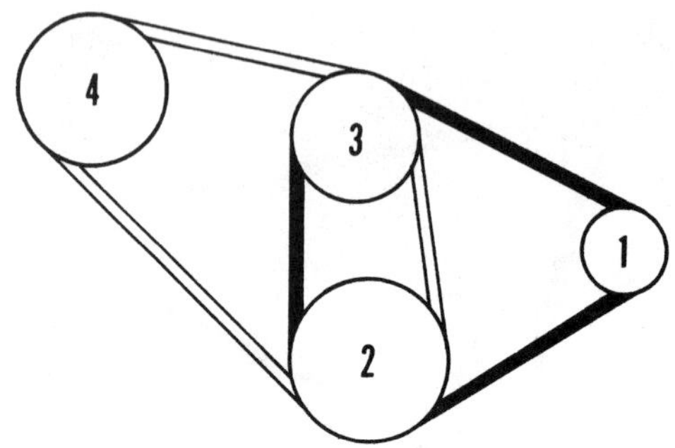

WITH POWER STEERING

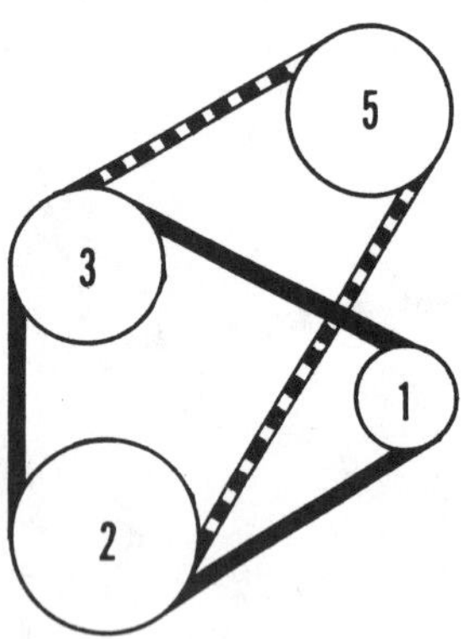

WITH AIR CONDITIONING

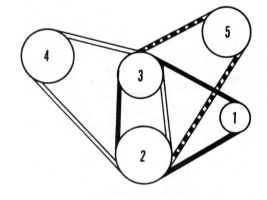

WITH POWER STEERING AND AIR CONDITIONING

1. Alternator
2. Crankshaft
3. Water pump
4. Power steering pump
5. Air conditioning compressor

either adjusted too tight or the pulley is worn. Replace a pulley that seems worn. Make sure to adjust drive belt tension drive belts as described in this chapter.

COOLING SYSTEM FLUSHING

A mixture of ethylene glycol-based antifreeze and water protects the cooling system from freezing to -34° F. The system should be inspected every 15,000 miles or 12 months. If the coolant appears dirty or rusty, the system should be cleaned with a chemical cleaner, drained, flushed with clean water and refilled. Severe corrosion may require pressure flushing, a job for a dealer or radiator shop. Flushing and coolant replacement are required every 30,000 miles or 24 months.

Cooling System Checks

1. Check coolant level by observing the liquid in the recovery system reservoir. The radiator cap should not be removed. If additional coolant is required, it should be added to the recovery reservoir. Level should be at COLD FULL mark when engine is cool or at HOT FULL when engine is hot. See **Figure 3**.
2. Check water pump operation by squeezing the upper radiator hose while the engine is running at normal operating temperature. If pressure surge is felt, the water pump is functioning. If not, check for a plugged vent hole in the pump.
3. Check for exhaust leaks into the cooling system by draining coolant until level is just above top of cylinder head. Disconnect upper radiator hose and remove thermostat and fan belt. Start the engine and accelerate it several times while observing the coolant. If the level rises or bubbles appear, chances are that exhaust gases are leaking into the cooling system.

Flushing

1. Remove the radiator cap. See **Figure 9**.

WARNING
Do not remove the radiator cap while the engine and radiator are hot. Scalding fluid and steam may be blown out under pressure and cause serious injury.

2. Drain the cooling system by opening the radiator drain tap on the lower right side of the radiator (**Figure 1**) and removing the engine block drain plugs. Drain block plugs are located on front side of engine. See **Figure 10**.

3. Once system is drained, reinstall engine block drain plugs and close the radiator drain tap. Add a sufficient amount of water to fill the system and run engine to circulate the water.

4. Repeat Steps 1-3 as required until drained water is clear of rust and other debris. When

drained water appears clean, reinstall engine drain plugs and close the radiator drain tap.
5. Remove screws securing the recovery tank (**Figure 3**) to side of vehicle, flush thoroughly with water and reinstall.

Refilling

Before refilling cooling system, check coolant hoses for damage and replace as described under *Hose Replacement.*

1. Be sure all hoses are connected and the radiator and recovery tank caps are removed.
2. Fill the cooling system with a 50/50 mixture of ethylene glycol-based antifreeze and water to the base of the radiator fill neck and add sufficient coolant to the recovery tank to raise fluid level to the FULL mark. Install the recovery tank cap. See **Table 2** for cooling system capacity.

NOTE

Even if you live in a climate that does not require this degree of freeze protection, the 50/50 mixture of antifreeze and water will provide a good corrosion inhibitor.

3. Run the engine at a fast idle and recheck the coolant level in the radiator and the recovery tank. Add coolant if level falls below base of radiator fill neck or FULL mark in recovery tank. Also check system for leaks.
4. Install radiator cap, ensuring arrows line up with overflow tube (**Figure 9**).
5. Drive vehicle for several miles and recheck coolant level. It takes some time for all the air to be removed from the system. Maintain fluid level between COLD FULL and HOT FULL marks.

PRESSURE CHECK

This test requires a reliable pressure tester and can be performed quickly and economically by your General Motors dealer or a radiator shop. Service stations also may be equipped to perform the test. Perform the test if frequent additions of coolant are necessary to keep the cooling system topped up and your radiator is known to be in good condition.

To check the system:

1. Remove the radiator cap (**Figure 9**).
2. Dip the cap in water and attach to a cooling system pressure tester, using suitable adapter supplied with instrument.

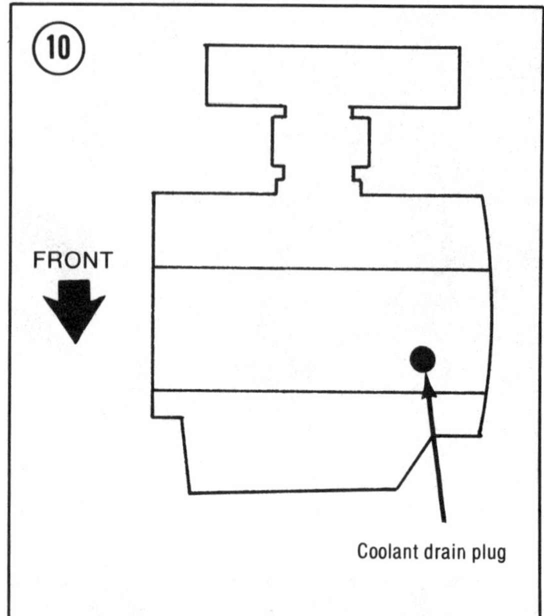

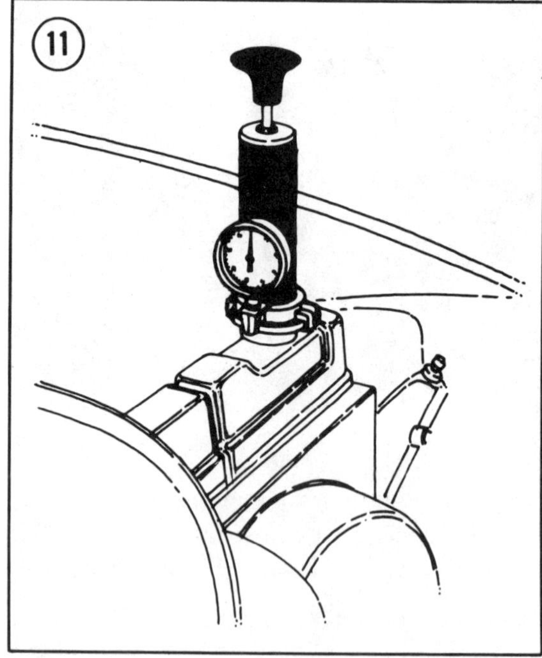

3. Pump pressure to 14 psi. If the cap fails to hold pressure, replace it.
4. Attach the pressure tester to the filler hole on the radiator (**Figure 11**).
5. Pump the system to 14 psi. There should be no noticeable pressure drop in 30 seconds. If pressure falls off, there is a leak which must be found and sealed.

RADIATOR

Removal

1. Disconnect the battery ground cable.
2. Remove the radiator cap (**Figure 9**). Make certain the engine and cooling system are cool. Drain the radiator by opening the drain tap on the lower right side of the radiator (**Figure 1**).
3. Remove engine forward strut brace at radiator and swing strut toward engine. See **Figure 12**. Loosen bolt before swinging strut to prevent damage to rubber bushing.
4. Remove the fan as explained in this chapter.
5. Scribe alignment marks from hood latch to the radiator support, remove screws securing hood latch to radiator support and remove hood latch.
6. Disconnect the upper and lower radiator hoses at the radiator.
7. On automatic transmission models, disconnect the upper and lower transmission oil cooler lines from radiator. See **Figure 13** (upper) and **Figure 14** (lower). Plug both the lines and the fittings on the radiator.
8. Lift the radiator out.

NOTE

On air conditioned vehicles, it may be necessary to raise the right side of the radiator to clear the radiator neck from the air conditioner compressor before the radiator can be removed from the engine compartment. Do not remove the compressor or air conditioning hoses.

Installation

1. Position radiator in vehicle, locating bottom of radiator in lower mounting pad. Install radiator support attaching clamp and bolts and tighten to 7 in.-lb. (10 N•m).
2. On automatic transmission models, unplug and connect the oil cooler lines to the radiator (**Figure 13** and **Figure 14**) and tighten attaching nuts to 6 ft.-lb. (9 N•m).
3. Connect upper and lower hoses to radiator and attach coolant recovery hose to radiator neck.
4. Attach hood latch to radiator support and tighten bolts to 6 ft.-lb. (9 N•m).

5. Install fan as explained in this chapter.
6. Position engine forward strut and brace forward until brace contacts the radiator support (**Figure 12**). Attach brace to radiator support with attaching bolts and tighten to 11 ft.-lb. (15 N•m).
7. Fill cooling system as explained in this chapter.
8. Connect battery negative terminal. Run the engine until it reaches normal operating temperature, then recheck the coolant level. Check the cooling system for leaks.

FAN

Removal/Installation

1. Disconnect the negative battery terminal.
2. Disconnect forward lamp wiring harness from fan motor and remove harness from fan frame. See **Figure 15**.
3. Remove fan frame to radiator support attaching bolts (**Figure 16**) and remove fan.
4. Installation is the reverse of these steps. Tighten the fan bolts to 85 in.-lb. (9.5 N•m).

THERMOSTAT

Removal

1. Drain the coolant until the level is slightly below the thermostat housing base.
2. Remove the upper radiator hose at the thermostat. See **Figure 17** (4-cylinder) or **Figure 18** (V6).
3. On vehicles equipped with cruise control, remove the vacuum modulator mounting bracket at the thermostat housing.
4. Remove the thermostat housing bolts (**Figure 19**, typical) and then remove the water outlet and gasket from the thermostat housing.
5. Remove and inspect the thermostat valve.

Testing

1. Submerge the thermostat in water with a thermometer (**Figure 20**).
2. Heat the water until the thermostat valve begins to open, then check the water temperature. It should range from 190-195° F (85-87° C). If the valve opens at the wrong temperature or fails to open, replace the thermostat.

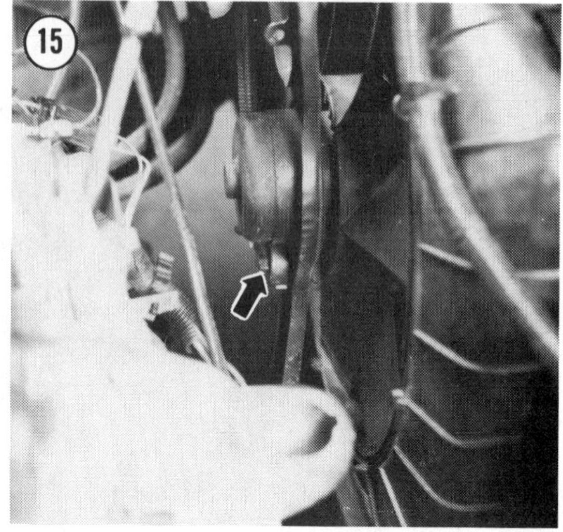

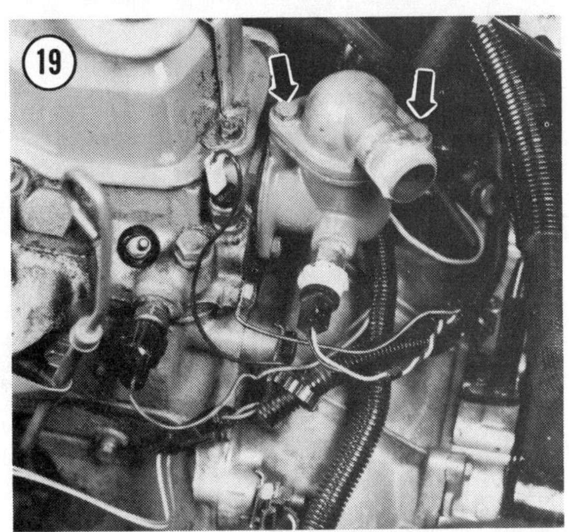

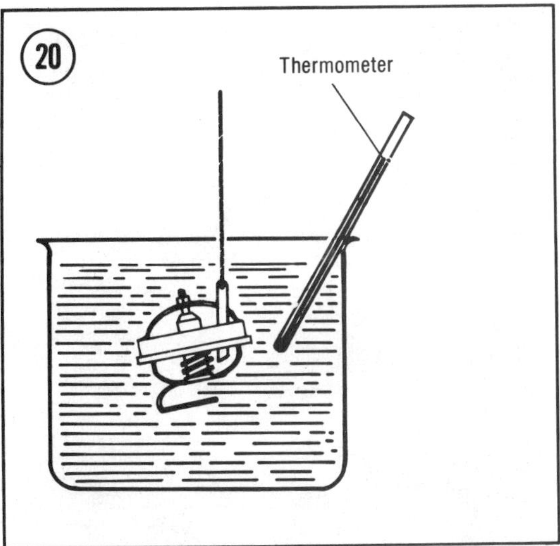

Installation

1. If a new thermostat is being installed, test as described under *Testing*.
2. Install the thermostat in the housing.
3. Position the thermostat housing on the engine using a new gasket coated with RTV sealer. Install the housing bolts and tighten to 6 ft.-lb. (8 N•m).
4. If vehicle is equipped with cruise control, install vacuum modulator bracket to thermostat housing.
5. Install the radiator hose and fill the system with coolant.
6. Start engine and check thermostat housing and radiator hose for leaks.

WATER PUMP

A defective water pump is usually the problem when the engine overheats and no other cause can be found. A water pump will often warn of impending failure by making noise.

Water pumps on both the 4-cylinder and V6 engines are non-rebuildable. If damaged or inoperative, they must be replaced.

Removal/Installation (4-cylinder)

The water pump is shown in **Figure 21**.

1. Drain the cooling system by opening the tap at the lower right side of the radiator (**Figure 1**).

2. Remove the air conditioning compressor (if so equipped). See *Compressor Removal*, in this chapter.
3. Remove all drive belts as necessary to remove the water pump.
4. Loosen the pump-to-bracket attaching bolts (**Figure 21**) until bolts stop against drive pulley (**Figure 22**). Tap the pulley lightly with a rubber-tipped hammer until the pump to bracket seal is broken (**Figure 23**). Remove the water pump.
5. Clean the water pump bracket sealing surface (**Figure 24**) of all old sealant.
6. If a new water pump is to be used, remove pulley and bolts from old pump. Install bolts in new pump first, then install pulley.
7. Installation is the reverse of these steps. Apply a 1/8 in. bead of sealer along water pump mating surface. Use sealer meeting GM requirement No. 1052289. Tighten water pump attaching bolts to specifications listed in **Table 3**. Tighten drive belts to specifications as described earlier in this chapter.

Removal/Installation (V6)

Both the water pump and timing chain covers are fastened to the block with the same bolts (except for a few bolts at the bottom of the timing cover). Because the water pump and timing chain covers are sealed by an anaerobic sealer instead of a gasket, removing the water pump may break the seal between the timing chain cover and the block. Coolant can then leak unnoticed into the crankcase and cause engine damage. Should a water pump failure occur on your engine, it is necessary to perform the following steps to replace the water pump, making sure to use the required fabricated tool to prevent breaking the timing cover to engine seal.

1. Disconnect the negative battery terminal.
2. Open the radiator drain plug (**Figure 1**) and drain the cooling system.
3. Disconnect the upper (**Figure 25**) and lower (**Figure 26**) coolant hoses at the water pump.
4. Remove the water pump pulley attaching bolts and remove the pulley.
5. Referring to **Figure 27**, mount the pump clamping tool against the water pump boss.

22

23

24

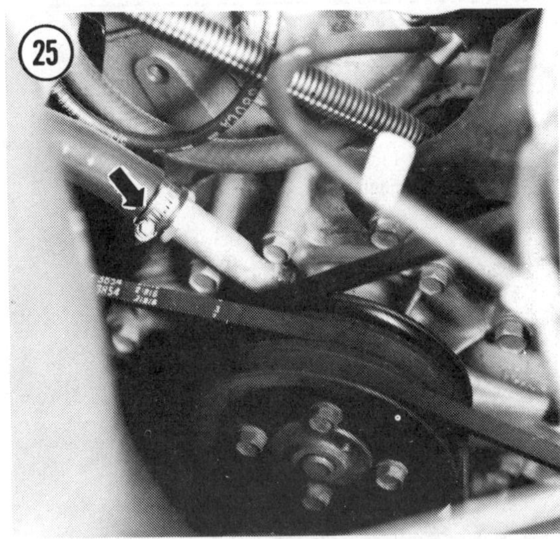

Secure tool with a 10 mm bolt threaded into unused thread hole in cylinder head. Tighten to 10 ft.-lb. (12 N•m).

NOTE
*Specifications for fabricating the water pump clamp tool are found in **Figure 28**.*

6. Remove the water pump attaching bolts and remove the water pump.
7. Clean the water pump and engine sealing surfaces of all old sealant.
8. Coat the water pump sealant surface with a 2 mm bead of anaerobic sealant (GM part No. 1052357 or equivalent). Install pump before sealant dries. Install pump attaching bolts and tighten to specifications in **Table 3**.
9. Remove clamping tool (**Figure 27**).
10. Reverse Steps 1-3 to complete installation. Fill cooling system. Start engine and check for leaks.

COOLING FAN

Fan operation is controlled by an engine coolant temperature switch (at the top front of the engine) and a cooling fan relay (on the inside right front fender). When coolant temperature reaches a specified level, the coolant switch closes and current flows through the fan relay coil. The relay points close, allowing current to flow to the electric cooling fan.

In addition, on air conditioned models the fan is controlled by the compressor pressure switch. This switch closes and allows current flow through the fan relay coil when air conditioning refrigerant pressure exceeds a specified level.

Troubleshooting

If the fan doesn't run at all, check all fuses and fusible links. Disconnect the wire from the engine coolant temperature switch and ground the wire. Turn the ignition ON; if the fan runs, the coolant temperature switch is bad. If the fan still doesn't run, connect a jumper wire across the fan relay points terminals. If the fan now runs, the relay is defective. If the fan still doesn't run, its motor is faulty.

If the car overheats when the air conditioning is on, troubleshoot the cooling

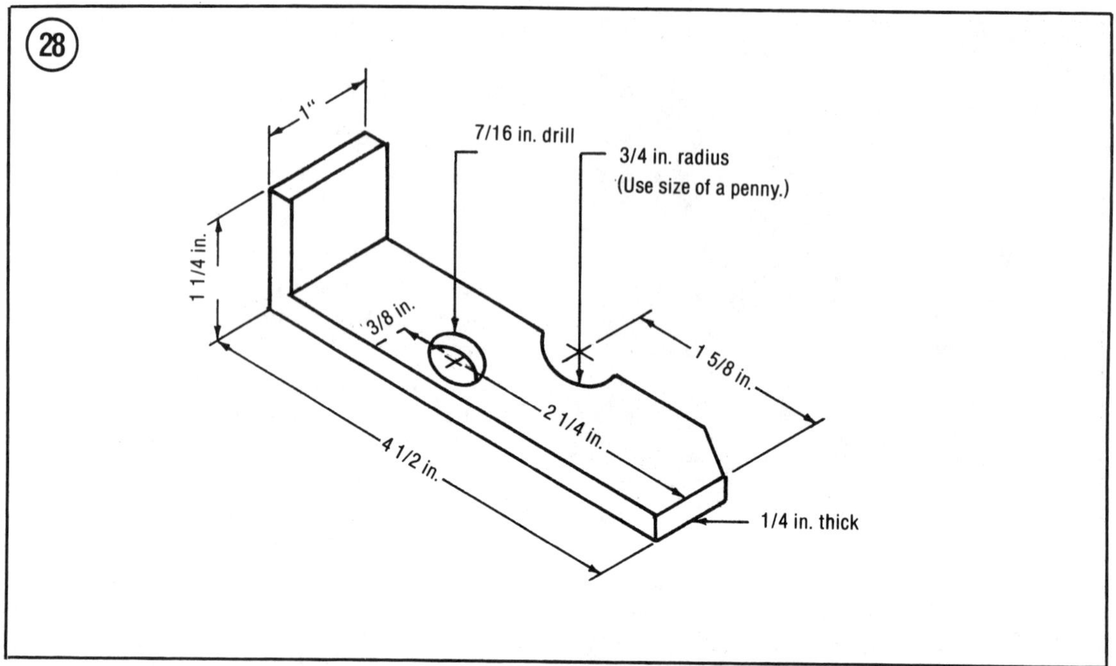

and air conditioning systems as described in this chapter. If they check out okay, disconnect the wire from the air conditioning compressor switch and ground the wire. Turn the ignition ON; the fan should run. If it does, the compressor switch is defective.

If the fan runs whenever the ignition is ON, check the switches to see if they are permanently closed. Check the fan relay contacts to see if they have fused closed.

COOLANT HOSES

A ruptured or broken coolant hose will cause a sudden loss of engine coolant. Before this happens, check the coolant hoses at least once a year and anytime the coolant is replaced.

Inspection

1. With the engine cool, check the coolant hoses for brittleness or hardness. A hose in this condition will usually show cracks and must be replaced.
2. With the engine hot, examine for portions of swelling hose along the entire hose length. Eventually the hose will rupture at this point.
3. Check area around hose clamps. Signs of rust around clamps indicate possible hose leakage.

Replacement

Hose replacement should be performed when the engine is cool.

1. Drain the cooling system.
2. Loosen the hose clamps from the hose to be replaced. Slide the clamps along the hose and out of the way.
3. Twist the hose end and remove from connecting joint. If the hose has been on for some time, it probably has become fused to the joint. If so, cut the hose parallel to the joint connection with a knife. The hose can then be carefully pried loose with a screwdriver.

CAUTION

If coolant hose is difficult to remove, it is necessary to cut hose as described in Step 3, or there is a possibility of damaging the connecting joint.

4. Examine the connecting joint for cracks or other damage. Repair or replace part as required. If the joint is okay, clean it of any hose sealant and rust with sandpaper.
5. Inspect hose clamps and replace as necessary.
6. Slide hose clamps over outside of hose and install hose to inlet and outlet connecting

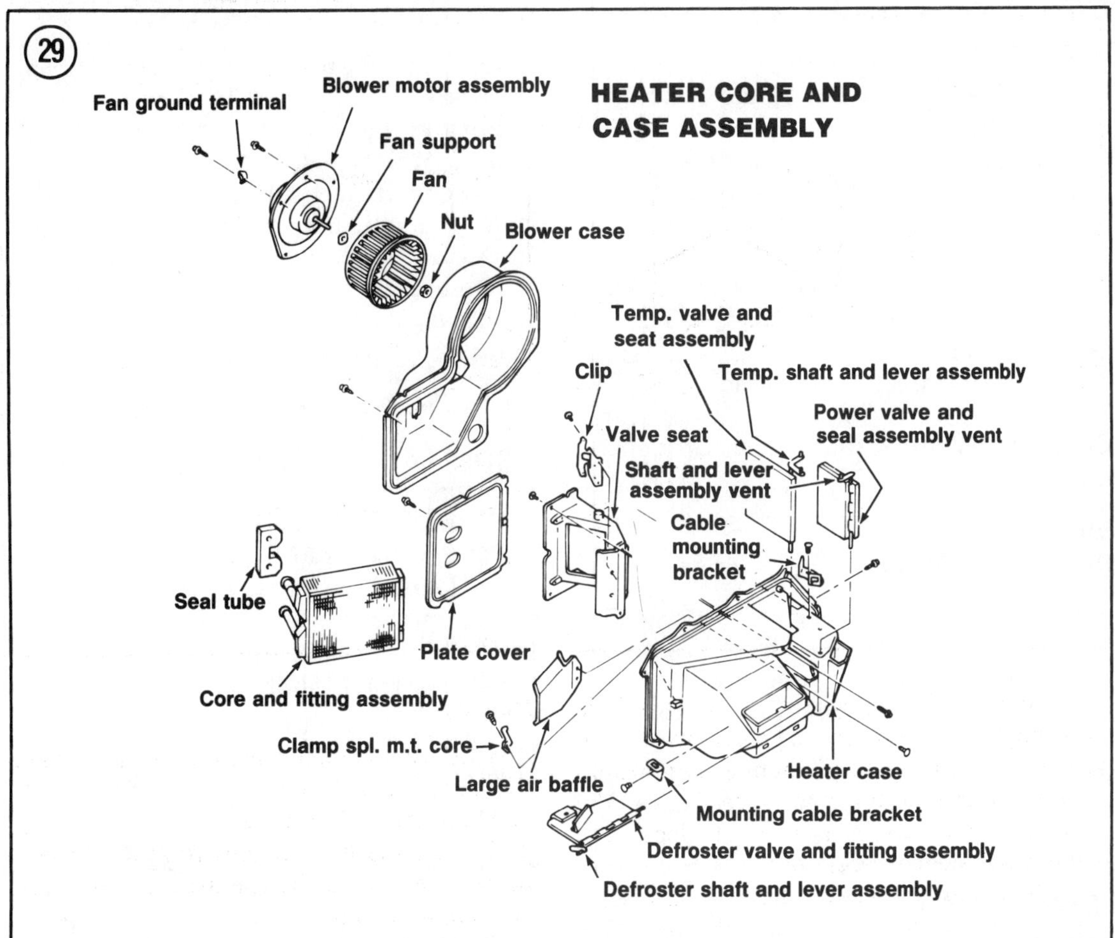

joint. Make sure hose clears all obstructions and is routed properly.

NOTE
If it is difficult to install on inlet or outlet joint, soak end of hose in hot water for approximately 2 minutes. This will soften the hose.

7. With hose positioned correctly on joint, position clamps back away from end of hose approximately 1/4 to 1/2 in. Tighten clamps securely, but not so much that hose is damaged.

8. Refill cooling system. Start engine and check for leaks. Retighten hose clamps as necessary.

HEATER

Blower Motor Removal/Installation

Refer to **Figure 29** for the following procedure.

1. Disconnect the battery ground cable and blower electrical lead wires.
2. Remove the screws securing the blower to the heater core and remove the blower motor assembly.
3. Remove the blower wheel nut, washer and spacer. Separate the blower and wheel.
4. Assemble the blower wheel to the motor shaft using a washer to maintain proper clearance. Install the nut and washer and tighten securely.
5. Install the blower assembly into the heater case and install the attaching screws.
6. Connect the blower electrical leads and battery ground cable.

Heater Control Assembly and Blower Switch Removal/Installation

Refer to **Figure 30** and **Figure 31** for the following procedures.

1. Disconnect the battery ground cable.
2. Remove screws securing heater control and blower switch assembly to instrument panel. Remove assembly.
3. Remove electrical connectors and control cables from heater control head at rear of control assembly.
4. Remove the heater control head.
5. Install by reversing the removal steps. Check the switch operation after installation.

Blower Resistor Removal/Installation

The resistor is attached to the left side of the heater case at the inlet duct (**Figure 32**).

1. Disconnect the battery ground cable.
2. Disconnect the resistor wiring harness.
3. Remove the screws attaching the resistor to the heater case.
4. Install by reversing the removal steps.

Blower Case Removal/Installation

Refer to **Figure 29** for the following procedure.

1. Remove the blower motor as described earlier in this chapter.
2. Disconnect the blower resistor, blower motor and ground strap electrical connectors. See **Figure 32** for connector positions.
3. Remove screws securing blower case to panel and remove blower case.
4. Install by reversing the removal steps.

Heater Core Removal/Installation

Refer to **Figure 29** for the following procedure.

1. Disconnect the battery ground cable.
2. Place a drain pan under the heater core tubes. Loosen the hose clamps and remove hoses from the core tubes. Secure the hoses in a raised position and plug or tape core tubes to prevent coolant spillage during removal.
3. Remove radio suppression strap from top side of heater core cover (**Figure 32**).
4. Remove screws attaching heater core cover to heater core and remove cover.

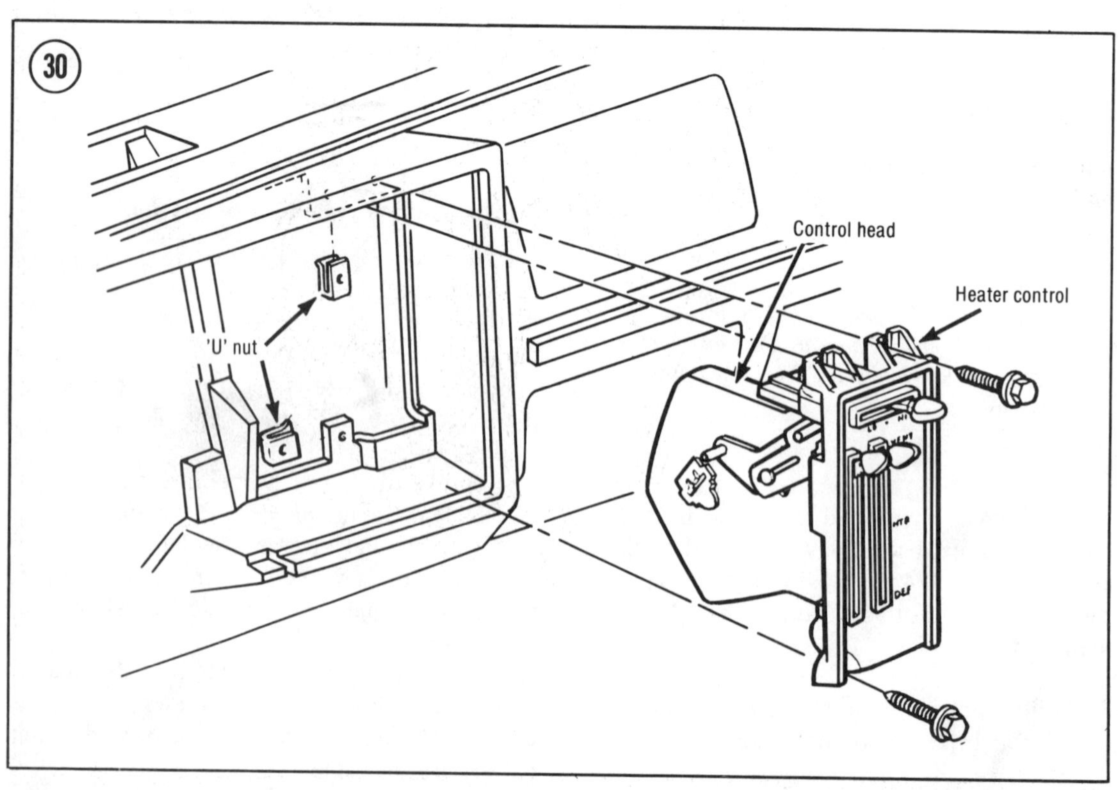

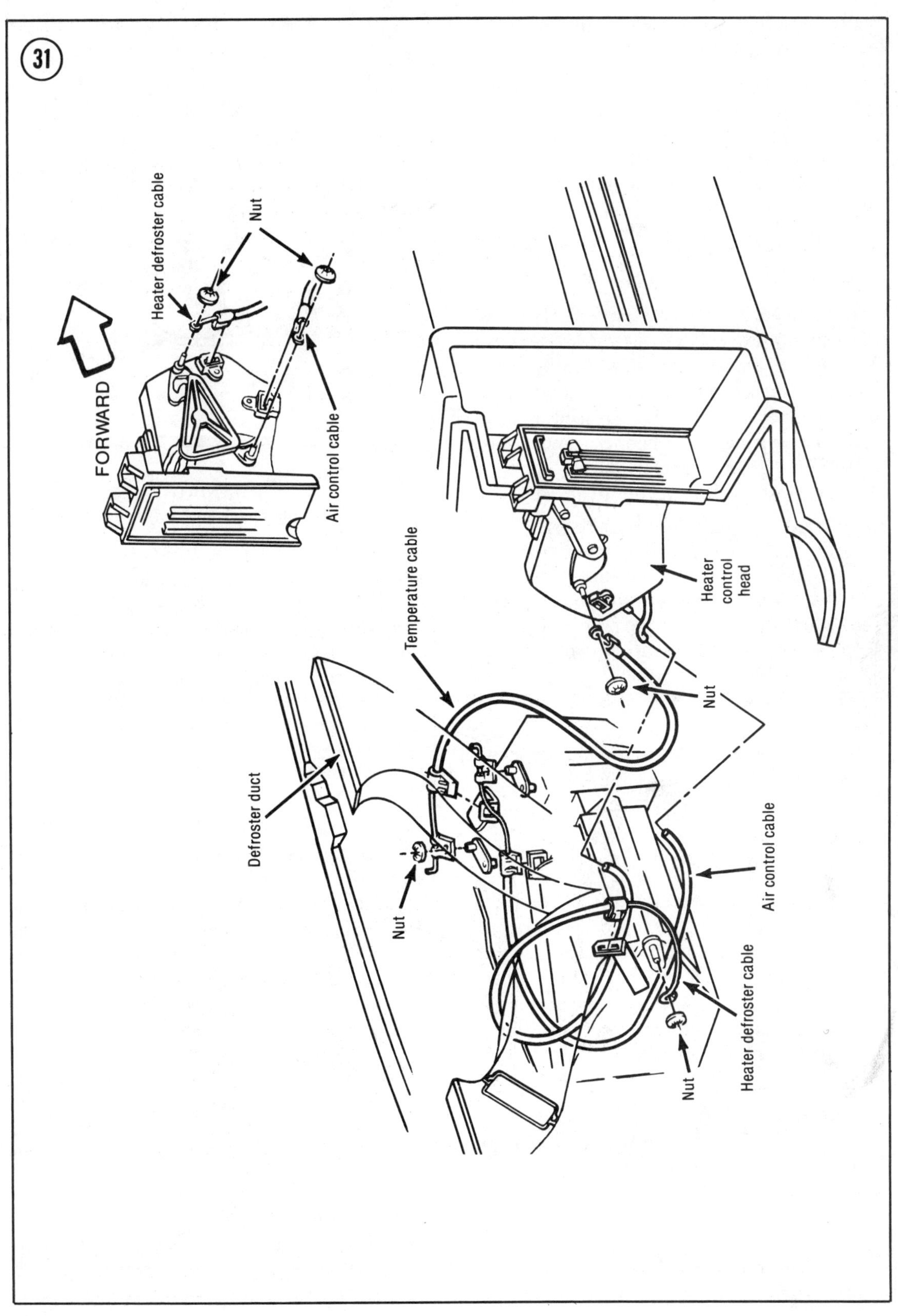
31
FORWARD
Heater defroster cable
Nut
Air control cable
Temperature cable
Heater control head
Nut
Defroster duct
Nut
Air control cable
Heater defroster cable
Nut

5. Remove the heater core from the case.
6. Install by reversing the removal steps.

NOTE
Be sure that all core seals are repositioned and are intact.

7. Start engine and check for leaks.

Temperature Control, Power Vent and Heater Defroster Control Cable Removal/Installation

Refer to **Figure 31** and **Figure 33** for the following procedure.

1. Remove heater control assembly as explained in this chapter.
2. Disconnect cable to be replaced at heater control and module component and remove cable from inside instrument panel.
3. Install by reversing the removal steps.

Vent Control Cable Removal/Installation

Refer to **Figure 34** (left vent) and **Figure 35** (right vent) for the following procedures.

1. Remove screws securing vent control assembly to instrument panel.
2. Detach cable from side of cable outlet and remove cable.
3. Install new vent control cable by reversing the removal steps.
4. Check operation of vent cable.

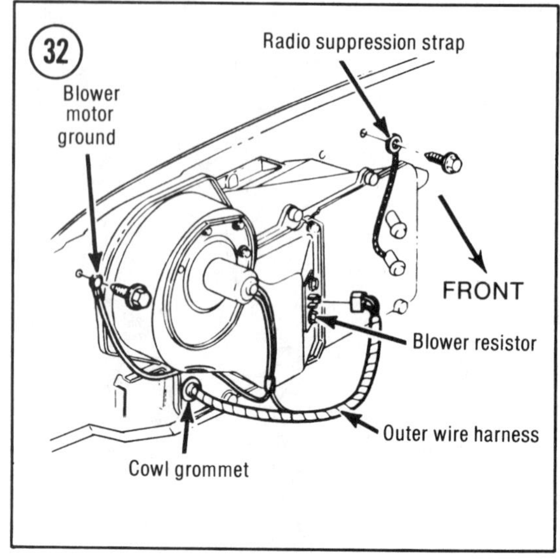

WARNING
The components, connected with high-pressure hoses and tubes, form a closed loop. A refrigerant, dichlorodifluoromethane (more commonly referred to as R-12) circulates through the system under high pressure—as much as 300 psi. As a result, work on the air conditioning system is potentially hazardous if certain precautions are ignored. For safety's sake, read this entire section before attempting any troubleshooting checks or working on the system.

AIR CONDITIONING

Major service and repair to the air conditioning system requires specialized training and tools. However, most air conditioning problems do not involve major repair; they are well within the ability of an experienced hobbyist mechanic, armed with an understanding of how the system works.

SYSTEM OPERATION

The air conditioning system consists of the following 5 basic components:

a. Compressor
b. Condenser
c. Receiver/drier
d. Expansion valve
e. Evaporator

A typical system is shown schematically in **Figure 36**. For practical purposes, the cycle begins at the compressor. The refrigerant, in a warm, low-pressure vapor state, enters the low-pressure side of the compressor. It is compressed to a high-pressure hot vapor and pumped out of the high-pressure side to the condenser.

Air flow through the condenser removes heat from the refrigerant and transfers the heat to the outside air. As the heat is removed, the refrigerant condenses to a warm, high-pressure liquid.

The refrigerant then flows to the receiver/drier where moisture is removed and impurities are filtered out. Thr refrigerant is stored in the receiver/drier until it is needed. Generally,

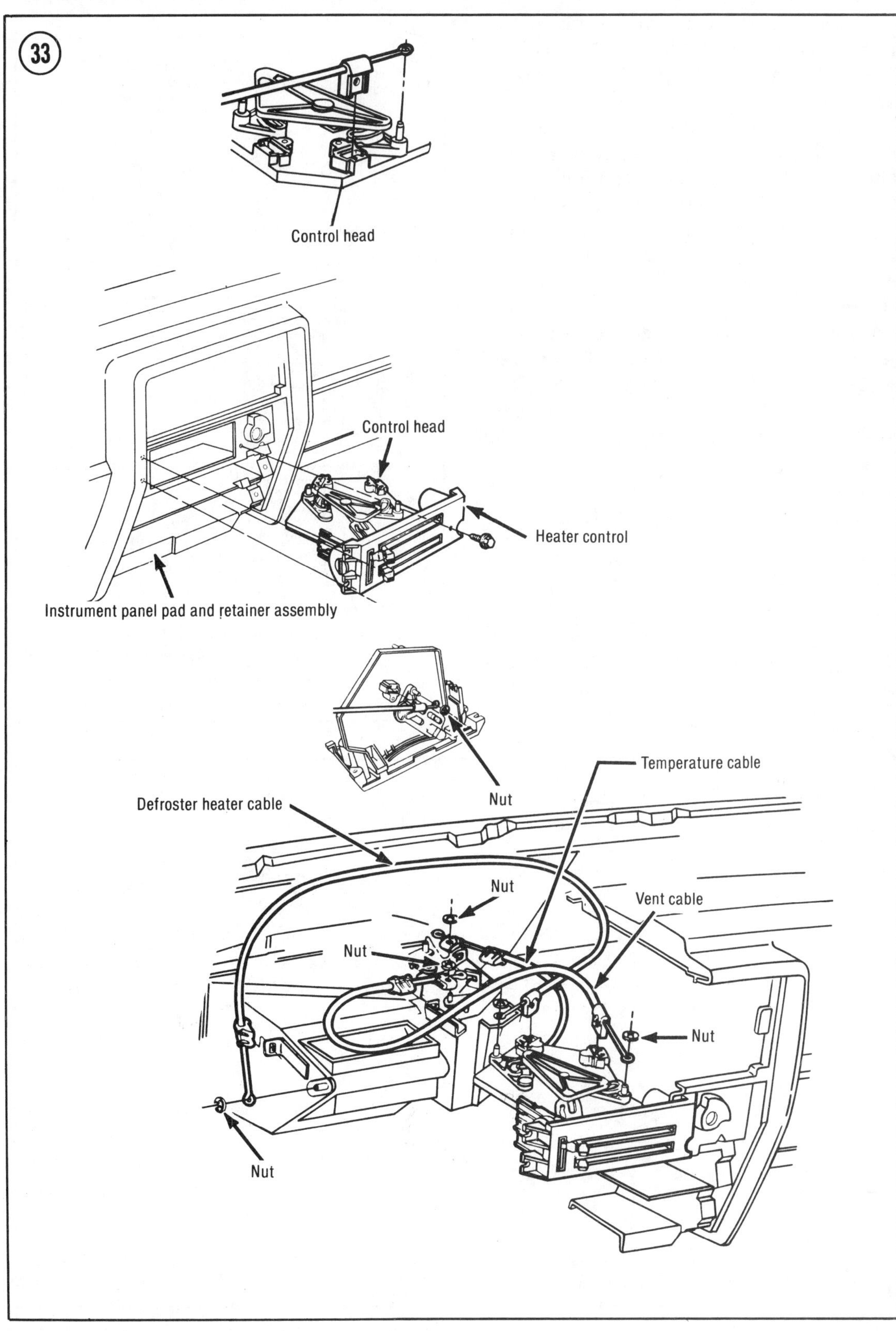
33
Control head
Control head
Heater control
Instrument panel pad and retainer assembly
Temperature cable
Nut
Defroster heater cable
Nut
Vent cable
Nut
Nut
Nut

the receiver/drier incorporates a sight glass that permits visual monitoring of the condition of the refrigerant as it flows. This is discussed later.

From the receiver/drier, the refrigerant flows to the expansion valve. The expansion valve is thermostatically controlled and meters refrigerant to the evaporater. As the refrigerant leaves the expansion valve it changes from a warm, high-pressure liquid to a cold, low-pressure liquid.

In the evaporator, the refrigerant removes heat from the cockpit air that is blown across the evaporator's fins and tubes. In the process, the refrigerant changes from a cold, low-pressure liquid to a warm, high-pressure vapor which flows back to the compressor where the refrigeration cycle began.

ROUTINE MAINTENANCE

Preventive maintenance for your air conditioning system couldn't be simpler; at least once a month, even in cold weather, start your engine and turn on the air conditioner and operate it at each of the switch and control settings. Allow it to operate for about 5 minutes. This will ensure that the compressor

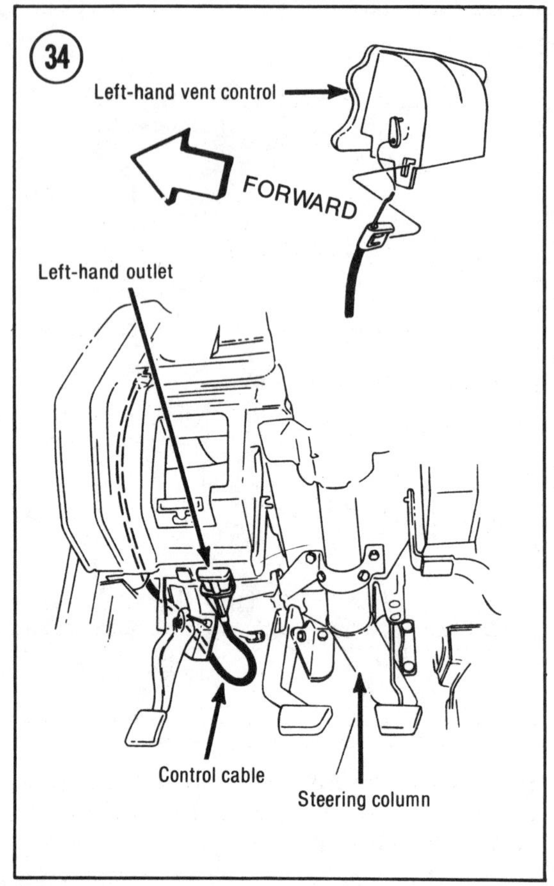

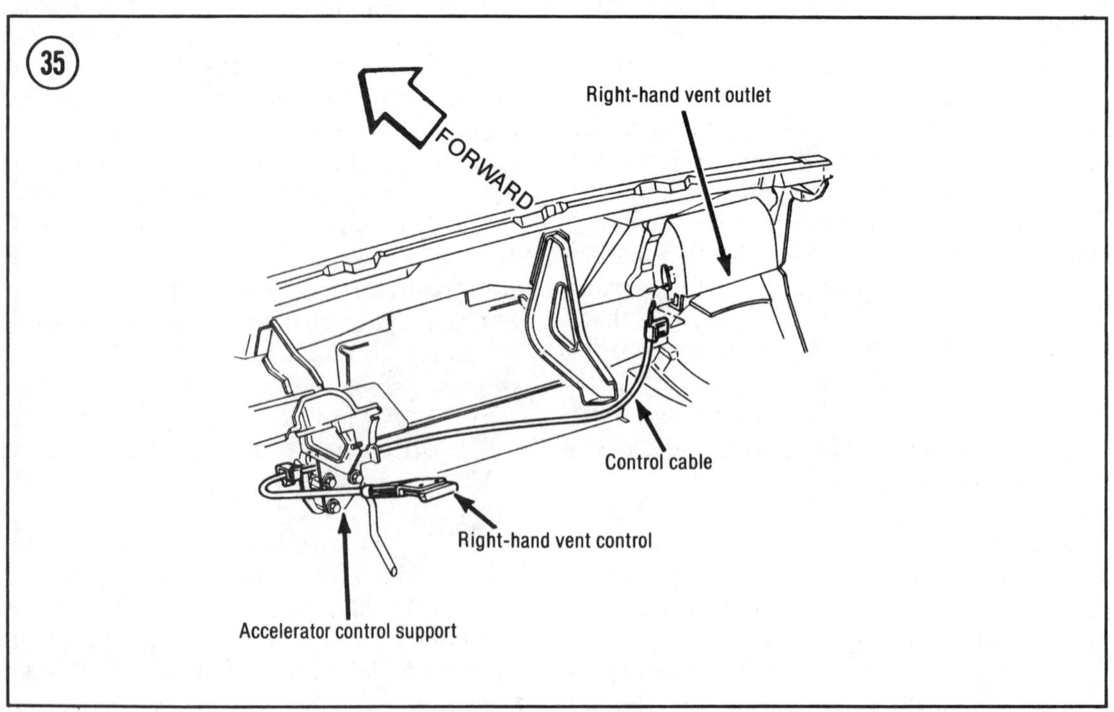

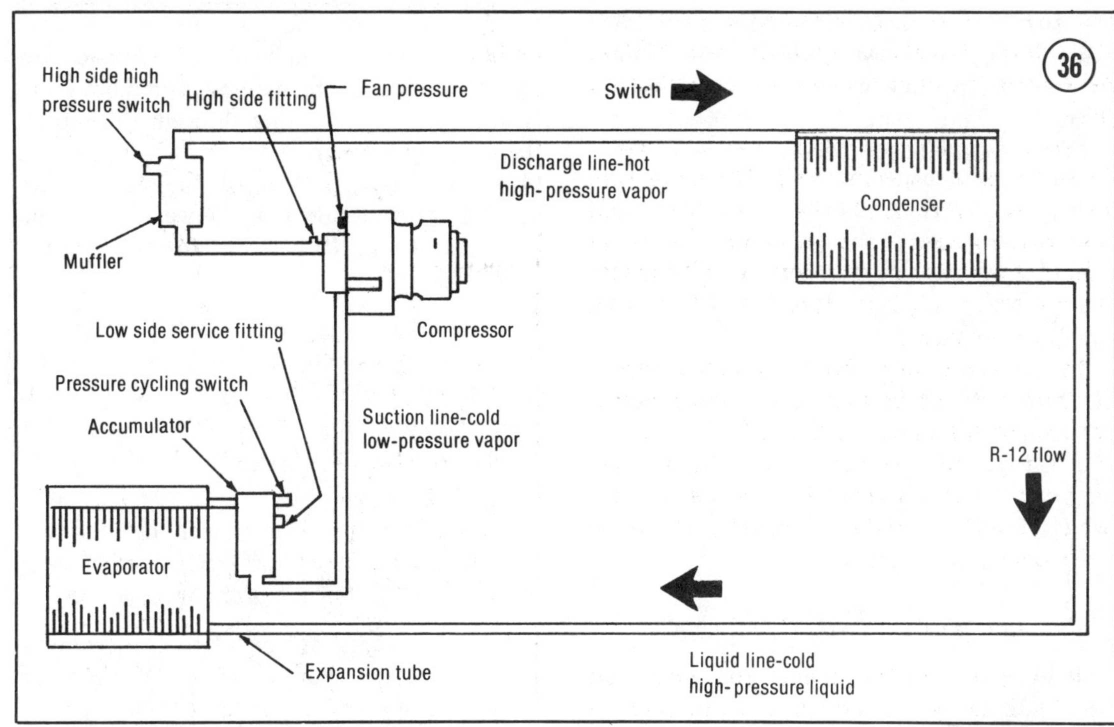

seal will not deform from sitting in the same position for a long period of time. If this occurs, the seal is likely to leak.

The efficiency of your air conditioning system depends in great part on the efficiency of your engine cooling system. Periodically check the coolant for level and cleanliness. If it is dirty, drain and flush the system and fill it with fresh coolant and water, following the coolant manufacturer's instructions for coolant/water ratio. Have your radiator cap pressure tested and replace it if it will not maintain 14 psi pressure. If the system requires repeated topping up and the radiator cap is in good condition, it is likely that there is a leak in the system. Pressure test as described earlier in this chapter.

With an air hose and a soft brush, clean the radiator fins and tubes to remove bugs, leaves and any other imbedded debris.

Check and correct drive belt tension as described earlier.

If the condition of the cooling system thermostat is in doubt, check it as described earlier and replace it if it is faulty.

When you are confident that the engine cooling system is working correctly, you are ready to inspect and test the air conditioning system.

Inspection

1. Clean all lines, fittings and system components with solvent and a clean rag. Pay particular attention to the fittings; oily dirt around connections almost certainly indicates a leak. Oil from the compressor will migrate through the system to the leak. Carefully tighten the connection, taking care not to overtighten and risk stripping the threads. If the leak persists it will soon be apparent once again as oily dirt accumulates.
2. Clean the condenser fins and tubes with a soft brush and air hose or with a high-pressure stream of water from a garden hose. Remove bugs, leaves and other imbedded debris. Carefully straighten any bent fins with a screwdriver, taking care not to dent or puncture the tubes.
3. Check the condition and tension of the drive belts and replace or correct as necessary.
4. Start the engine and check the operation of the blower motor and the compressor clutch by turning the controls on and off. If either the blower or the clutch fails to operate, shut off

the engine and check the condition of the fuses. If they are blown, replace them. If not, remove them and clean the fuse holder contacts. Then recheck to ensure that the blower and clutch operate.

Testing

1. With the transmission in PARK (automatic) or NEUTRAL (manual) and the handbrake set, start the engine and run it at a fast idle.
2. Set the temperature control to its coldest setting and turn the blower to high. Allow the system to operate for 10 minutes with the doors and windows open. Then close them and set the blower on its lowest setting.
3. Place a thermometer in a cold-air outlet. Within a few minutes, the temperature should be 35-45° F. If it is not, it's likely that the refrigerant level in the system is low.

REFRIGERANT

The majority of automotive air conditioning systems use a refrigerant designated R-12. However, a commercial grade, designated R-20, is used in heavy-duty systems. The two are not compatible. Your General Motors vehicle uses R-12 only. The charging capacity is 2.75 lb. (1.246 kg).

TROUBLESHOOTING

Preventive maintenance like that just described will help to ensure that your system is working efficiently. Still, trouble can develop and while most of it will invariably be simple and easy to correct, you must first locate it. The following sequence will help to diagnose system troubles when your air conditioning ceases to cool the passenger compartment.

1. First, stop the vehicle and look at the control settings. One of the most common sources of air conditioning trouble occurs when the temperature control is set for maximum cold and the blower is set on low. This arrangement promotes ice buildup on the fins and tubes of the evaporator, particularly in humid weather. Eventually, the evaporator will ice over completely and restrict air flow. Turn the blower on high and place a hand over an air outlet. If the blower is running but there is little or no air coming through the outlet, the evaporator is probably iced up. Leave the blower on high and turn off the temperature control or turn it down to its lowest setting and wait; it will take 10 or 15 minutes before the ice begins to melt.

2. If the blower is not running, the motor may be burned out, there may be a loose connection or the fuse may be blown. First, check the fuse panel for a blown or incorrectly seated fuse. Then, check the wiring for loose connections.

3. Shut off the engine and check the condition and tension of the compressor drive belt. If it is loose or badly worn, tighten or replace it.

4. Start the engine and check the condition of the compressor clutch by turning the air conditioner on and off. If the clutch does not energize, it may be defective, its fuse may be blown or the evaporator temperature-limiting switches may be defective. If the fuse is defective, replace it. If the clutch does not energize, refer the problem to an air conditioning specialist.

5. If all components checked so far are okay, start the engine, turn on the air conditioner and watch the refrigerant through the sight glass; if it's filled with bubbles after the system has been operating for a few seconds, the refrigerant level is low. If the sight glass is oily or cloudy, the system is contaminated and should be serviced by an expert as soon as possible. Corrosion and deterioration occur rapidly and if not taken care of at once will result in a very expensive repair job.

6. If the system still appears to be operating satisfactorily but the air flow into the passenger compartment is not cold, check the condenser and cooling system radiator for debris that could block the air flow. Recheck the cooling system as described under *Inspection.*

7. If the above steps do not uncover the difficulty, have the system checked and corrected by a specialist as soon as possible.

Table 1 DRIVE BELT TENSION

Belt	Torque*
Alternator belt	
New	135 ft.-lb. (605 N•m)
Used	55 ft.-lb. (205 N•m)
Power steering belt	
New	135 ft.-lb. (605 N•m)
Used	55 ft.-lb. (205 N•m)
Air conditioning belt	
New	150 ft.-lb. (605 N•m)
Used	80 ft.-lb. (360 N•m)
*Do not adjust any used belt if initial reading is 50 ft.-lb. (205 N•m)	

Table 2 COOLING SYSTEM CAPACITY

Engine	Capacity
4-cylinder	
With air conditioning	9 3/4 quarts (9.3 liters)
Without air conditioning	9 1/2 quarts (9.0 liters)
V6	
With air conditioning	11 3/4 quarts (11.2 liters)
Without air conditioning	11 1/2 quarts (10.8 liters)

Table 3 WATER PUMP TIGHTENING TORQUES

Engine	Bolt Size	Torque
4-cylinder	M10 x 1.5	25 ft.-lb. (30 N•m)
V6	M6 x 1	8 ft.-lb. (10 N•m)
	M8 x 1.25	16 ft.-lb. (21 N•m)
	M10 x 1.5	25 ft.-lb. (30 N•m)

NOTE: If you own a 1981 or later model, first check the Supplement at the back of the book for any new service information.

CHAPTER EIGHT

ELECTRICAL SYSTEMS

The X-cars are equipped with a 12-volt, negative-ground electrical system. Included in this chapter are service and repair procedures for the battery, starter, charging system, lighting system, ignition, instruments and windshield wipers. Making repairs to electrical components such as the alternator or starter motor is usually beyond the capability of the inexperienced mechanic and his tool box. Such repairs are best left to the professional mechanic who is equipped with specialized tools.

By using the troubleshooting procedures given in Chapter Two it is possible to isolate problems in a specific component, thus saving money in costly troubleshooting bills.

In most cases, it will be faster and more economical to obtain new or rebuilt components instead of making repairs. Make certain, however, that the new or rebuilt part is an exact replacement. Also, make sure that the cause of the failure has been isolated and corrected before installing a replacement. For instance, an uncorrected short in a wiring harness will in all probability burn out a new alternator as quickly as it damaged the old one. If in doubt, always consult an expert.

Tables 1-4 are at the end of the chapter.

BATTERY MAINTENANCE

Maintenance free batteries are standard on all models (**Figure 1**). Except for a small vent hole in the side, the battery is completely sealed.

Sealed batteries have the following advantages over conventional batteries:

1. It is unnecessary to service the battery water level.
2. There is reduced self-charge when battery is left standing for long periods of time.

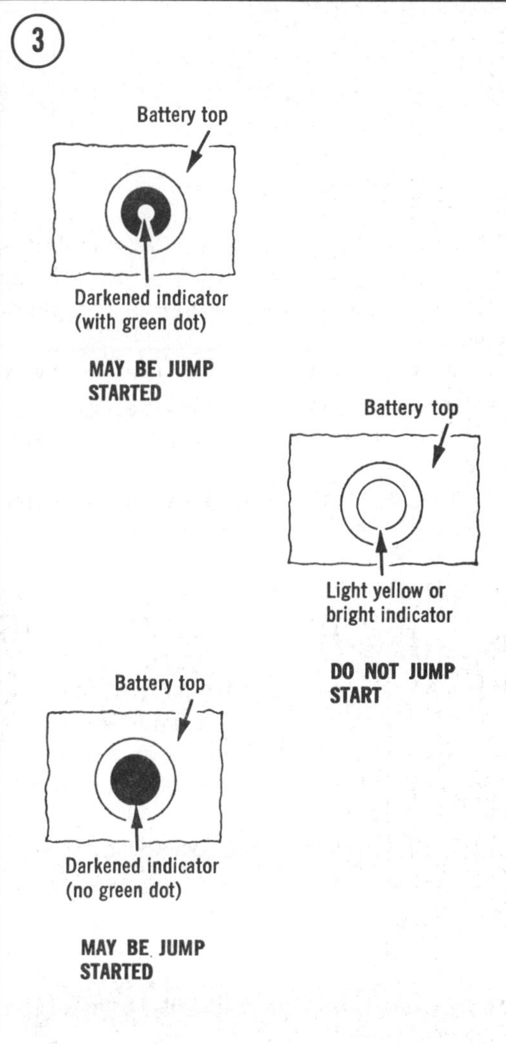

3. The battery is protected against overcharge. Sealed batteries will not accept as much current, compared to conventional batteries, if a too high voltage level is applied.
4. The battery case is lighter and smaller due to the battery's overall design.

Common Causes of Battery Failure

All batteries eventually fail. Their life can be prolonged, however, with a good maintenance program. Some of the reasons for premature failure are listed below.

1. Vehicle accessories left on overnight or longer cause a discharged condition.
2. Slow driving speeds on short trips cause an undercharged condition.
3. Vehicle electrical load exceeds the alternator capacity due particularly to after-market accessory equipment.
4. There are charging system defects, such as high resistance, slipping belt or faulty alternator or regulator.
5. The battery has been abused, e.g., the battery terminals have not been kept clean or the battery has been allowed to become too loose in the battery hold-down box.

8

Battery Hydrometer

To determine the battery's charge, a built-in hydrometer indicator is located in the battery's top (**Figure 2**). By observing the hydrometer indicator, it can be determined whether the battery is good and usable, requires recharging or should be replaced.

NOTE

Before observing the hydrometer, ensure that the battery top is clean. In poorly lit conditions, an accessory light may be required to see the hydrometer indicator.

In reading the built-in hydrometer, 3 different hydrometer color indications are possible. Refer to **Figure 3** for an example of each.

1. ***Green dot visible***—battery is in good condition and can be tested if necessary.
2. ***Dark color visible***—battery charge condition is low, battery should be load tested.
3. ***Clear or yellow color visible***—battery must be replaced.

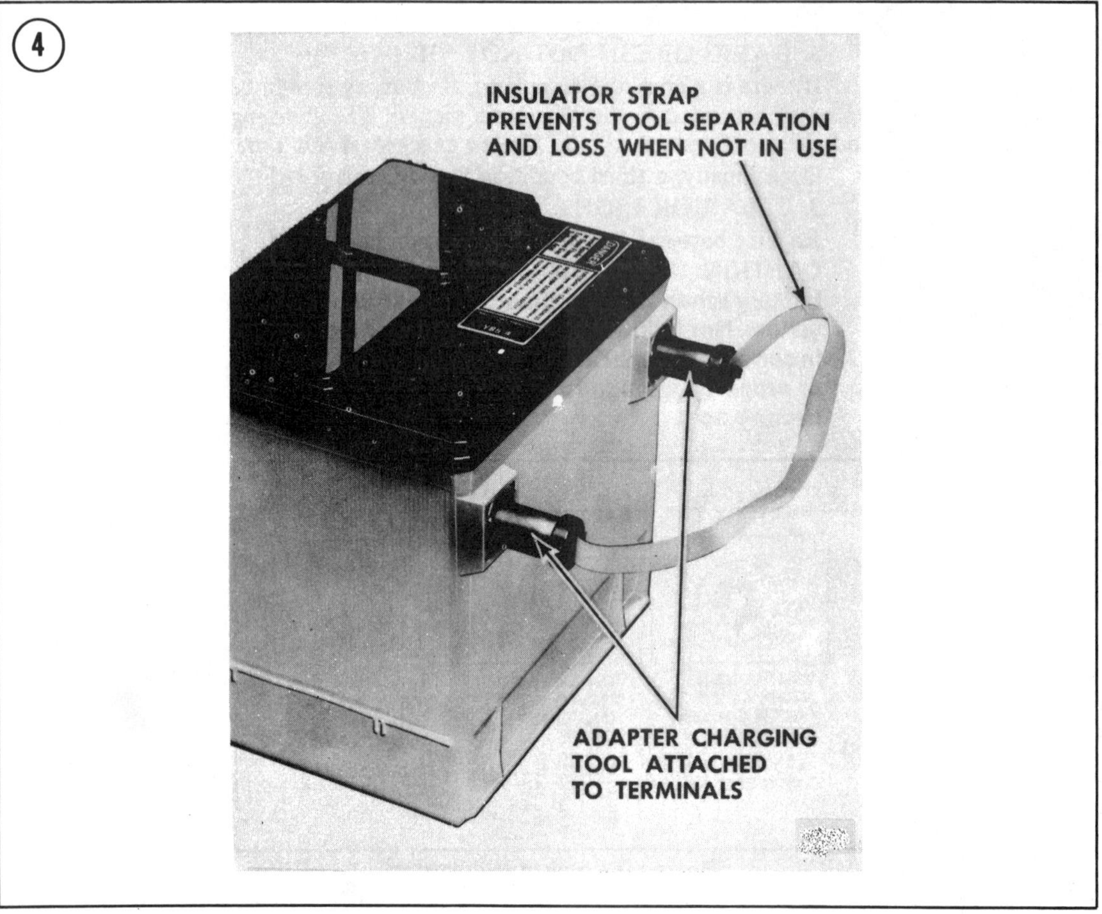

WARNING
When the hydrometer displays a clear or yellow color, do not charge or load test the battery or jump start the vehicle. Failure to observe this warning could result in personal injury or vehicle damage from battery explosion.

BATTERY TESTING

Use of the following test procedures will provide a basis for deciding whether a battery is good and usable, requires recharging or should be replaced. A complete analysis of battery condition requires a visual inspection, a hydrometer check and a battery load test.

Visual Inspection

1. Inspect the battery case for damage, chafing and cracks. Pay particular attention to moisture on the outside of the case; often this is an indication that the case is damaged to the extent that the battery is leaking electrolyte. If any such damage is present, replace the battery.
2. Check for loose cable connections. If necessary, clean and tighten the connections before proceeding.

Hydrometer Check

If it is necessary to test the battery, first observe the battery's built-in hydrometer to determine its condition. Refer to guidelines previously discussed under *Battery Hydrometer.* See **Figure 2**.

1. ***Green dot visible***—load test the battery as discussed under *Load Test* later in this section.
2. ***Dark dot visible***—charge the battery as discussed under *Charging*, then load test the battery as discussed under *Load Test.*
3. ***Clear or yellow dot visible***—replace the battery.

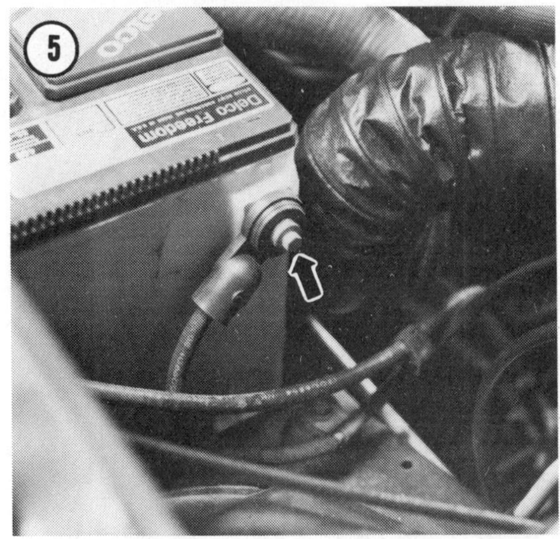

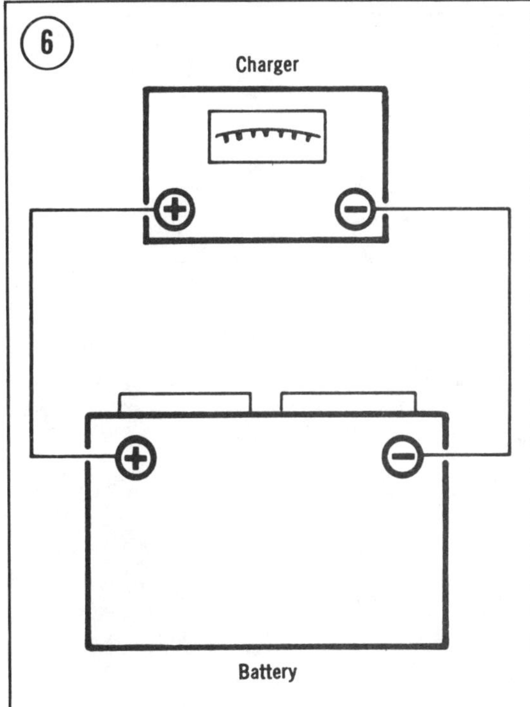

Load Test

Load testing will require the use of an instrument with battery testing capabilities. Side terminal adapters should be used when load testing the battery to provide a larger conductive surface for the tester leads. See **Figure 4**. To use adapters, remove the battery side terminals with a 7 mm wrench. Then screw on the adapters.

NOTE
*Before performing the following procedures, locate the recommended battery replacement number on the decal fixed to the battery's top. See **Figure 2**. This number will be used to direct you to your battery's specifications during testing. See **Table 1** and **Table 2** for battery testing specifications.*

1. Disconnect the battery ground and positive cables and connect battery side terminal adapters (**Figure 4**) to the battery terminals.
2. Connect a battery load tester and voltmeter across the battery terminals following manufacturer's instructions.
3. Apply a 300 amp load to the battery for 15 seconds to remove surface charge, then remove the amp load.
4. Wait 15 seconds, then apply load to the battery as outlined in **Table 1**. Read voltage after 15 seconds and remove load. Interpret results as follows:
   a. Refer to **Table 2** and estimate outside temperature battery has been exposed to before testing.
   b. Refer to **Table 2** and determine minimum voltage as corrected for temperature. If battery voltage is less than the minimum voltage listed in **Table 2**, battery should be replaced.

For example, if estimated battery temperature is 70° F (21° C) and the minimum battery voltage is 9.6 volts, battery can be considered good. However, if minimum battery voltage is 9.5 volts or less, battery condition is bad and must be replaced.

Charging

There is no need to remove the battery from the vehicle to charge it. Just make certain that the area is well-ventilated and that there is no chance of sparks or open flames being in the vicinity of the battery; during charging, highly explosive hydrogen is produced by the battery.

Disconnect the ground lead from the battery (**Figure 5**). Connect the charger to the battery—negative to negative, positive to positive. See **Figure 6**.

The sealed battery can be charged in the same manner as unsealed batteries. If the charger output is variable, select a low setting (5-10 amps), set the voltage selector to 12 volts and plug the charger in.

WARNING

Do not charge battery if the charge indicator is clear or light yellow. Replace the battery.

Charge the battery until the green ball appears in the charge indicator. It may be necessary to tip the battery from side to side to make the green ball appear after a suitable charging time.

Jump Starting

Jump starting procedures for sealed batteries are similar to procedures for unsealed batteries. However, do not connect a jumper cable to the negative battery terminal of the dead battery. Instead, after connecting one end of the negative jumper cable to the negative terminal of the booster battery, connect the other negative jumper cable end to a engine ground at least 18 in. (500 mm) from the battery of the vehicle being started.

CAUTION

Because the positive battery terminal is positioned extremely close to the left fender, the factory has installed a plastic shield in line with the positive battery terminal. This shield is used to prevent accidental grounding of a positive jumper cable to the fender when it is attached to the positive battery terminal. If it is necessary to jump start your vehicle, first check to see that the plastic shield is in position. Without the shield, if the positive jumper cable touches both the positive terminal and the fender (ground), the battery could explode.

Start engine of vehicle providing the jump start. Then start car with discharged battery. Reverse directions exactly to remove jumper cables.

Removal/Installation

1. Referring to **Figure 7**, remove the cross piece and disconnect the fresh air duct.

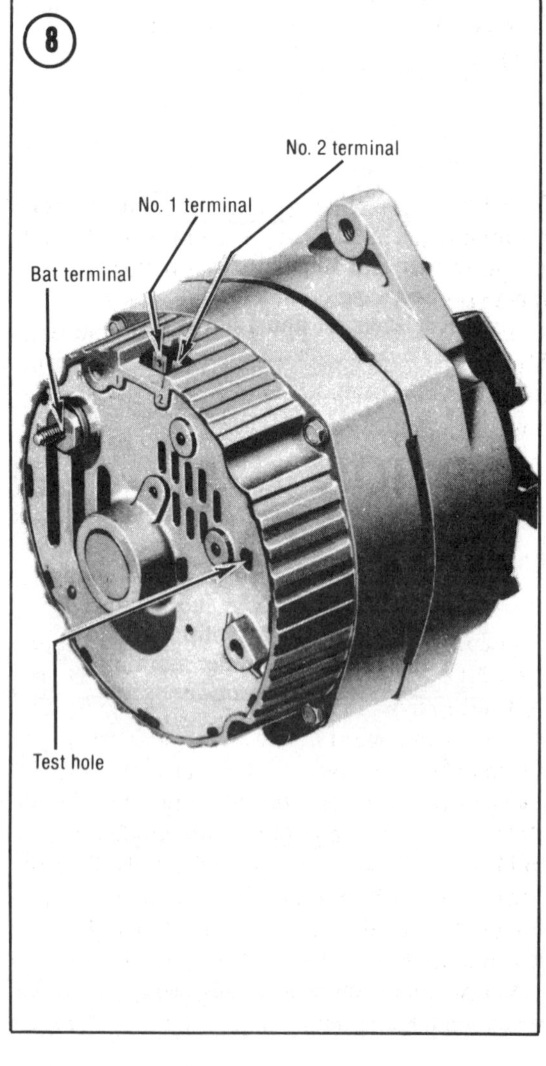

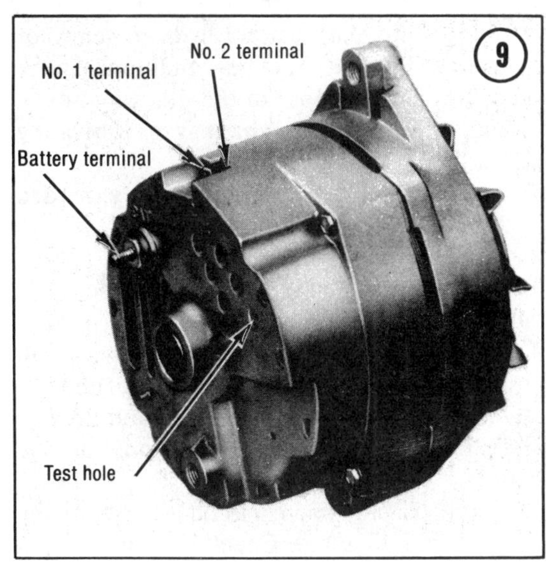

2. Disconnect the battery terminals from side of battery.

NOTE

*Always remove the negative terminal first **(Figure 5)**.*

3. With a 14 inch extension and rachet, remove the battery attaching bolt from the top of the radiator support. Lift the battery out of the engine compartment.
4. Reverse these steps to install the battery. Make certain the battery is seated squarely in the battery box before tightening the attaching bolt. Install the positive lead first.

CAUTION

Do not overtighten the battery side terminals.

CHARGING SYSTEM

The charging system consists of the battery, the alternator, the "tell-tale" lamp or voltmeter and the wiring necessary to connect these components. Two basic types of alternators are used. They are the 10-SI Delcotron (see **Figure 8**) and the 15-SI Delcotron (see **Figure 9**). Both models use a solid state regulator mounted inside the alternator. All regulator components are enclosed in a solid mold with the brush holder attached to the slip ring end frame.

Neither type of alternator requires periodic maintenance, other than a check for loose mounting bolts and belt tension. Certain precautions should be observed, however, since the alternator and regulator are designed for use only on negative systems. These precautions are as follows:

a. Do not attempt to "polarize" the alternator.
b. Do not short across or ground any of the terminals in the charging system except as specifically instructed in these procedures.
c. Never operate the alternator with the output terminal open-circuited.
d. Make sure the alternator and battery are of the same ground polarity.
e. When connecting a charger or booster battery to the vehicle battery, connect the positive cable to the positive terminal and negative terminal to the frame ground 18 inches (500 mm) away from the dead battery.
f. Whenever a lead is disconnected from the alternator, the battery ground cable should also be disconnected.

Static Checks

Before making any electrical checks on the charging system, visually inspect all connections to make sure they are clean and tight. Verify that the battery is serviceable and charged. Inspect all wiring for frayed, broken or cracked insulation. Check for loose mounting bolts and proper belt tension.

8

ALTERNATOR TROUBLESHOOTING

NOTE

*If voltmeter is used instead of indicator lamp, proceed to **Undercharged Battery Condition Check**.*

Indicator Lamp Circuit Check

Check the indicator lamp for normal operation as shown in **Table 3**.

If the indicator lamp operated normally, use procedures described under *Undercharged Battery* or *Overcharged Battery*. Otherwise, make the appropriate abnormal condition checks below:

1. ***Switch off, lamp on***: Disconnect the leads from alternator No. 1 and No. 2 terminals. See

Figure 8 or **Figure 9**. If the lamp remains on, there is a short circuit between the 2 leads. If the lamp goes out, the rectifier bridge is faulty. The alternator must be replaced, as this condition will result in an undercharged battery.

2. ***Switch on, lamp off, engine stopped***: This defect can be caused by the defects listed in Step 1 above, by reversal of the No. 1 and No. 2 leads at these 2 terminals or by an open circuit. To determine where the open exists, proceed as follows:

   a. Connect a voltmeter between alternator No. 2 terminal and ground. If any reading above zero is obtained, proceed to Step b. If the reading is zero, repair open circuit between No. 2 terminal and battery. If lamp comes on, no further check is required.

   b. Disconnect the leads from No. 1 and No. 2 terminals on the alternator and turn the ignition switch on. Momentarily ground the No. 1 terminal lead. Do not ground the No. 2 lead. If the lamp does not come on, check for a blown fuse or fusible link, burned out lamp bulb, defective bulb socket or open in No. 1 lead circuit between the alternator and ignition switch. If the lamp lights, remove the ground at No. 1 terminal and reconnect No. 1 and No. 2 wires to the alternator. Insert a screwdriver in test hole (see **Figure 8** and **Figure 9**) to ground the wiring. If the lamp does not go on, check connection between wiring harness and alternator No. 1 terminal. If the wiring is okay, replace the alternator. If the lamp lights, repeat voltmeter check in Step a. If a reading is obtained, have the regulator replaced.

3. ***Switch on, lamp on, engine running***: Check for a blown fuse (where used) between the indicator lamp and switch and also in the air conditioning circuit. If these circuits check out okay, see *Undercharged Battery Condition Check* for further possible causes.

Undercharged Battery Condition Check

Symptoms of this condition are slow cranking and a dark battery hydrometer color indication (**Figure 3**). The condition can be caused by one or more of the following, even though the indicator light may be operating properly.

1. Accessories have been left on for extended periods.
2. Belt tension is incorrect.
3. Battery is defective or discharged (see battery tests above).
4. There are wiring defects. Check all connectors for tightness and cleanliness, including connectors at alternator and firewall and the battery cable connections at the battery.
5. There is an open circuit between the alternator and battery. Check by connecting a voltmeter between BAT terminal on the alternator and ground, No. 1 terminal and ground, and No. 2 terminal and ground. A zero reading indicates an open between the voltmeter connection point and the battery. If alternator checks out okay and battery undercharged condition persists, refer alternator to General Motors dealership for further testing.

CAUTION

An open in the alternator No. 2 lead circuit will cause uncontrolled voltage, battery overcharge and possible damage to the battery and accessories. Both alternator models have a built-in feature to prevent overcharge and accessory damage by preventing the Delcotron from turning on if there is an open in the No. 2 lead circuit. Such an open could occur between terminals, at the crimp between the harness wire or terminal or in the wire itself.

Overcharged Battery Condition Check

1. Verify that the battery is in serviceable condition and fully charged.
2. If an obvious overcharge condition exists, such as excessive spewing of electrolyte through vent hole, have the following items checked by a General Motors dealership:
   a. Field windings (for shorts)
   b. Brushes and brush leads (for grounding or defective regulator)

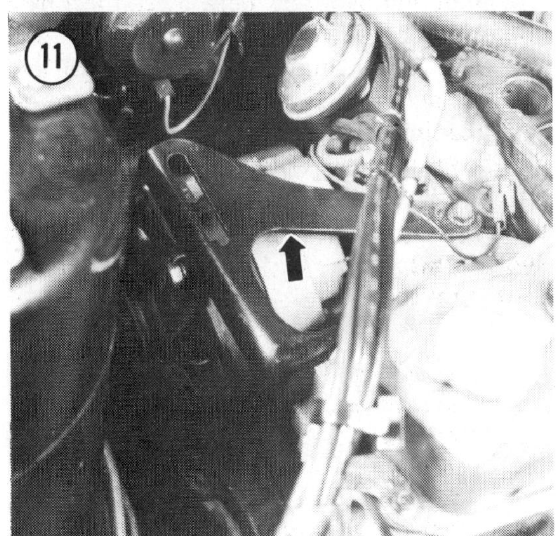

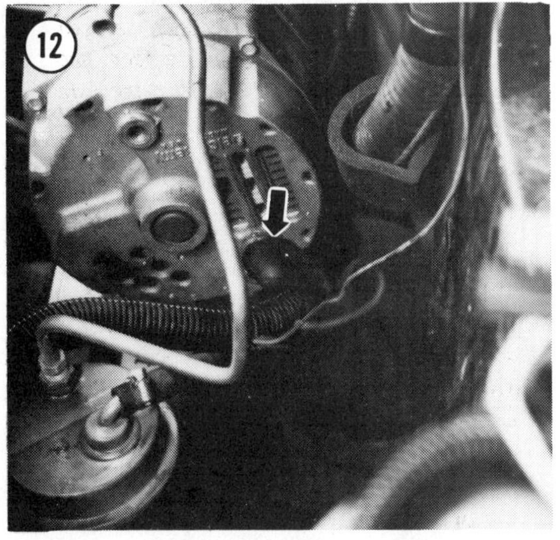

Removal/Installation

1. Disconnect the battery ground cable at the battery to prevent damage to diodes (**Figure 5**).
2. ***V6 with air conditioning***: Remove the air conditioning compressor without disconnecting any hoses or lines. Then remove the compressor/alternator mounting bracket (**Figure 10**) to provide access to the alternator.
3. On all 4-cylinder and those V6 engines without air conditioning, remove the alternator bracket. The bracket used on 4-cylinder vehicles is shown in **Figure 11**.
4. Disconnect the battery cable (**Figure 12**) and field leads (**Figure 13**) from the alternator.
5. Loosen and remove the lower alternator brace brackets.
6. Remove the drive belt.
7. Support the alternator and remove bolts. Remove the alternator from the vehicle.
8. Reverse the procedure to install alternator and then adjust drive belt tension as described in Chapter Seven.

STARTER

The cranking circuit consists of the battery, starting motor, ignition switch and the wiring necessary to connect these components. The cranking circuit is shown in **Figure 14**. The 5MT starter motor is used on both 4-cylinder and V6 vehicles. Periodic lubrication or other maintenance is not required for either the starter motor or the solenoid.

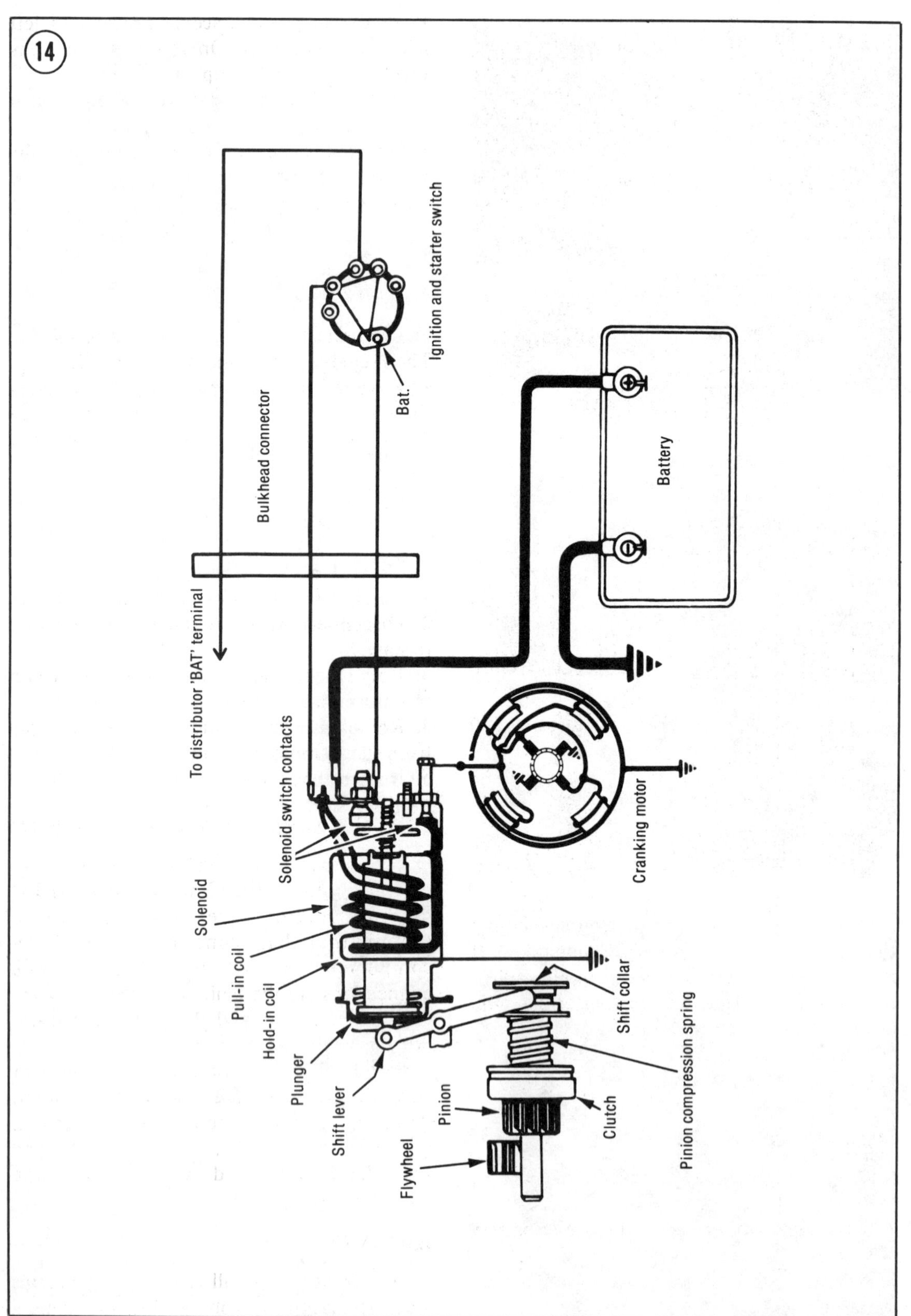
14
Ignition and starter switch
Bat.
Bulkhead connector
Battery
To distributor 'BAT' terminal
Solenoid switch contacts
Solenoid
Pull-in coil
Hold-in coil
Plunger
Shift lever
Pinion
Flywheel
Cranking motor
Shift collar
Pinion compression spring
Clutch

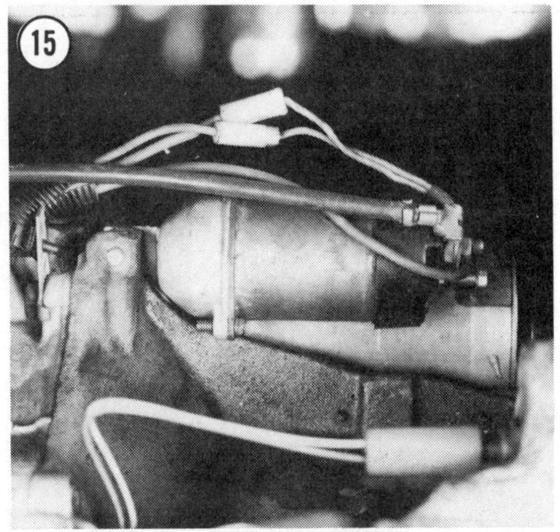

Diagnostic procedures for troubleshooting the starter motor are given in Chapter Two. If it is determined that the starter motor and/or solenoid are defective, the starter/solenoid assembly should be removed from the engine and repaired or replaced. Refer starter motor to General Motors dealership for repair.

Starter Motor Replacement

Refer to **Figure 15** (4-cylinder) or **Figure 16** (V6) for the following procedure.

1. Disconnect battery ground cable at battery (**Figure 5**).
2. Remove brace securing starter to engine from inside engine compartment. On 4-cylinder engines, brace is attached to left side of cylinder block. On V6 engines, brace is attached to the fuel pump heat shield.
3. Jack up the front end of the car and place it on jackstands.
4. Working beneath vehicle, remove bolts securing starter motor to engine and allow starter motor to drop down.

CAUTION
Do not allow starter motor weight to rest on attached wiring.

5. Disconnect all wires at solenoid terminals. Then remove starter motor from vehicle.
6. Reverse the removal procedure to install the starter motor. Tighten mount bolts first to 33 ft.-lb. (40 N•m), then tighten bracket fasteners. Make sure all electrical connections are tight.
7. Check starter operation.

Solenoid Replacement

1. Remove the starter as described earlier.
2. Disconnect wiring running from solenoid to starter.
3. Remove 2 solenoid attaching screws and motor terminal bolt(s).
4. Remove the solenoid by twisting away from starter motor housing.
5. Install in the reverse order.

8

HIGH ENERGY IGNITION SYSTEM

All General Motors vehicles discussed are equipped with the High Energy Ignition (HEI) system. Engines are equipped with a distributor that contains all ignition components in one unit. External wire connections are the ignition switch feed wire, tachometer pickup and the spark plug leads. See **Figure 17**.

The HEI is a pulse-triggered, transistor controlled inductive discharge system. Principal system elements are the ignition coil, electronic module, pick-up assembly and the centrifugal and vacuum advance mechanisms.

Ignition Coil

The HEI coil is small in size and generates very high secondary voltage when the primary circuit is broken. The coil is built into the cap and secured with 4 screws (**Figure 17**).

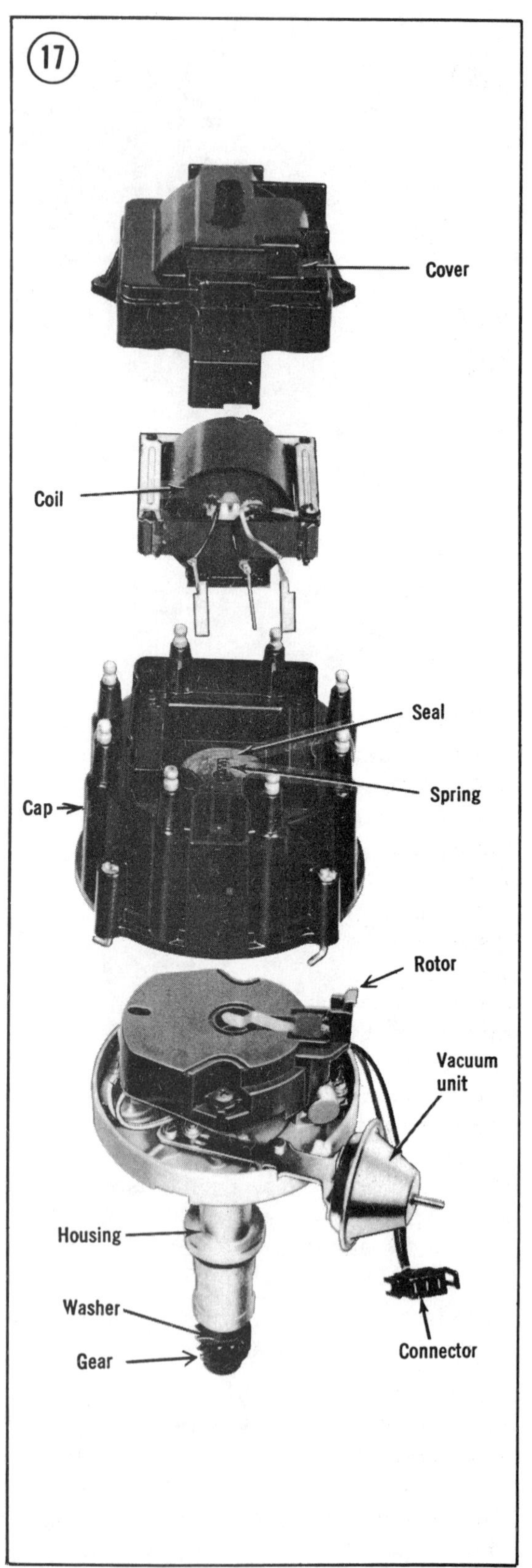

Electronic Module

Circuits within the electronic module perform 5 functions. These are spark triggering, switching, current limiting, dwell control and distributor pickup.

Pickup Assembly

The pickup assembly consists of a rotating timer core with external teeth (turned by the distributor shaft), a stationary pole piece with internal teeth and a pickup coil and magnet located between the pole piece and the bottom plate.

Centrifugal and Vacuum Advance

The centrifugal and vacuum advance mechanisms are similar to units used in breaker point ignition systems.

HEI Operation

As the distributor shaft turns the timer core teeth out of alignment with the pole piece teeth, a voltage is created in the magnetic field of the pickup coil. The pickup coil sends this voltage to the electronic module, which determines from the rotational speed of the distributor shaft when to start building current in the ignition coil primary windings. When the timer core teeth are again aligned with the pole piece teeth, the magnetic field is changed, creating a different voltage. This signal is sent to the electronic module by the pickup coil and causes the module to shut off the ignition coil primary circuit. This collapses the coil magnetic field and induces a high secondary voltage to fire one spark plug.

The electronic module limits the 12-volt current to the ignition coil to 5-6 amperes. The efficiency of the triggering system allows up to approximately 35,000 volts to be delivered through the secondary wiring system to the spark plugs.

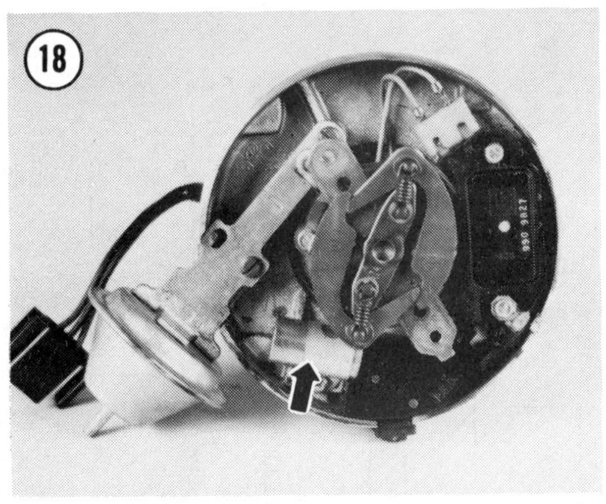

18

Periodic Maintenance

No periodic lubrication is required with the HEI system. The upper bushing is lubricated by an oil-filled reservoir and the lower bushing is lubricated by engine oil.

Corrective Maintenance

If a part in the HEI system fails, it must be replaced. See *Troubleshooting*, this chapter, for diagnostic procedures. Other than ignition timing adjustment described in Chapter Three, the HEI system is not adjustable.

Although a capacitor is present in the HEI system, it is used only as a radio noise suppressor (see **Figure 18**). On the 4-cylinder engine, if the replacement of a part is necessary (other than ignition coil), it will be more convenient to remove the distributor from the engine. Because the distributor is located between the engine and firewall, it is difficult to see exactly how each component is located in the distributor. Replacing a distributor part on a V6 engine can be accomplished with the distributor left in the engine.

Troubleshooting

The test procedures for troubleshooting the HEI system are found in the diagnostic charts in **Figure 19** (engine cranks but will not start) and **Figure 20** (engine runs rough or cuts out). An ohmmeter (described in Chapter One), test light (**Figure 21**) and jumper cables (**Figure 22**) are required to perform the test procedures.

Before beginning actual troubleshooting read the entire test procedure (**Figure 19** or **Figure 20**). Then refer to **Figure 23** and locate the distributor test points. When required, the diagnostic charts will refer you back to a certain chapter and procedure for special service information. Basic ignition system and spark plug troubleshooting information can be found in Chapter Two.

DISTRIBUTOR

Figure 17 shows an exploded view of a typical distributor used on the 4-cylinder and V6 vehicles.

Removal

NOTE

*The distributor on the 4-cylinder engine is located between the engine and firewall. Because of this location, it is difficult to see during service. The distributor was photographed (**Figure 24**) with the engine removed to help serve as an aid during distributor service. The distributor on the V6 engine is located up front.*

1. ***V6 vehicles***: Remove the air cleaner assembly to provide easier access to the distributor. See Chapter Six.
2. Remove the ignition switch battery feed wire and tachometer lead wire from the distributor cap. See **Figure 25**.
3. With a piece of masking tape applied to each spark plug wire, number the wire as shown in **Figure 26** (4-cylinder) or **Figure 27** (V6).
4. On 4-cylinder engines, remove the spark plug wire connector from the top of the distributor cap. Lay the connector and spark plug wires aside. On V6 engines, release the spark plug wires from the distributor cap by releasing the 2 latch levers on top of the spark plug connector ring (**Figure 28**). Lift the connector ring and spark plug wires up and lay aside.
5. Remove the distributor cap by releasing the 4 offset screws securing the cap to the distributor body. On 4-cylinder vehicles, it will be necessary to use a stubby screwdriver to remove the cap screws.

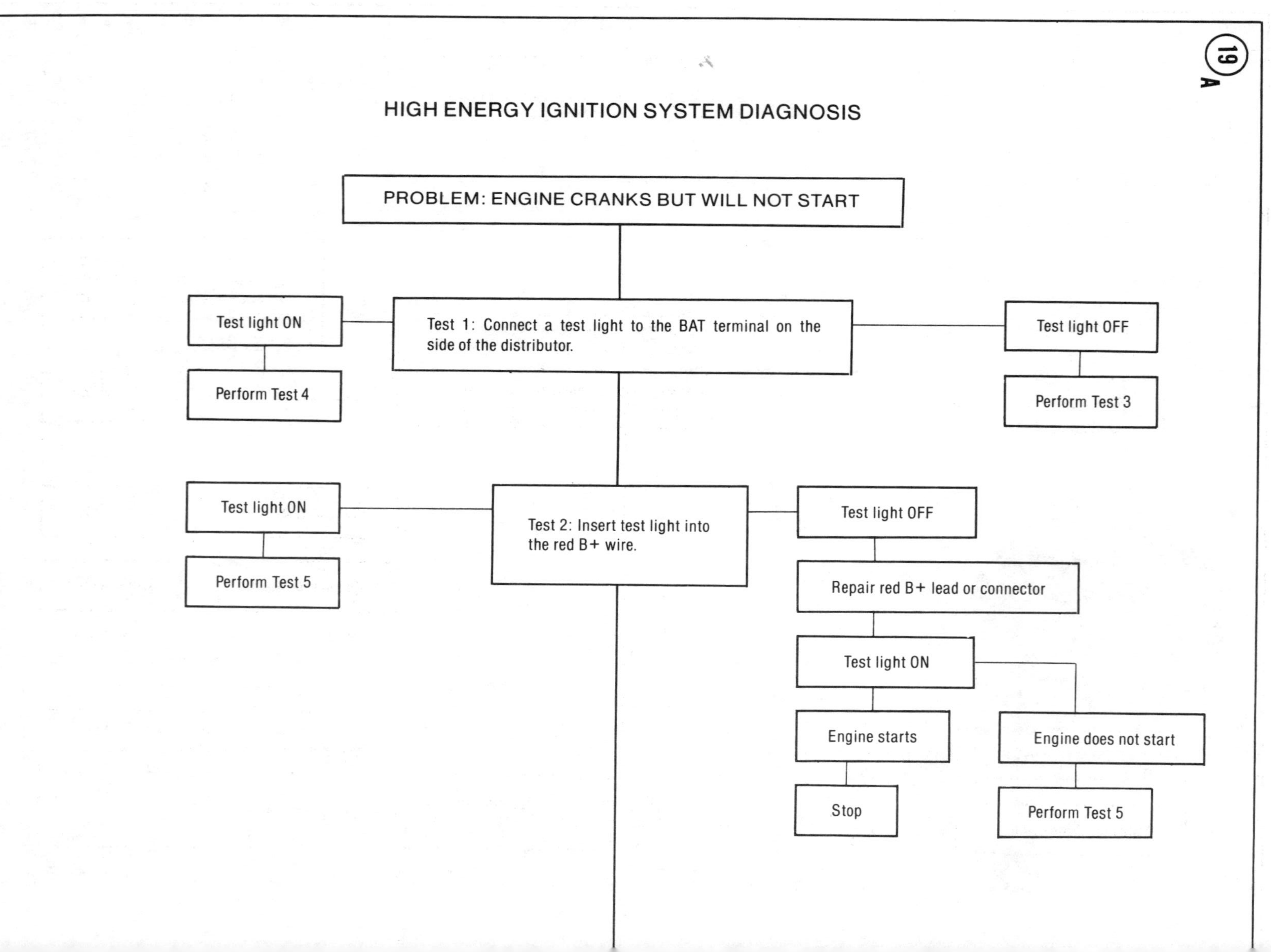
19 A
HIGH ENERGY IGNITION SYSTEM DIAGNOSIS
PROBLEM: ENGINE CRANKS BUT WILL NOT START
Test 1: Connect a test light to the BAT terminal on the side of the distributor.
Test light ON
Perform Test 4
Test light OFF
Perform Test 3
Test 2: Insert test light into the red B+ wire.
Test light ON
Perform Test 5
Test light OFF
Repair red B+ lead or connector
Test light ON
Engine starts
Stop
Engine does not start
Perform Test 5

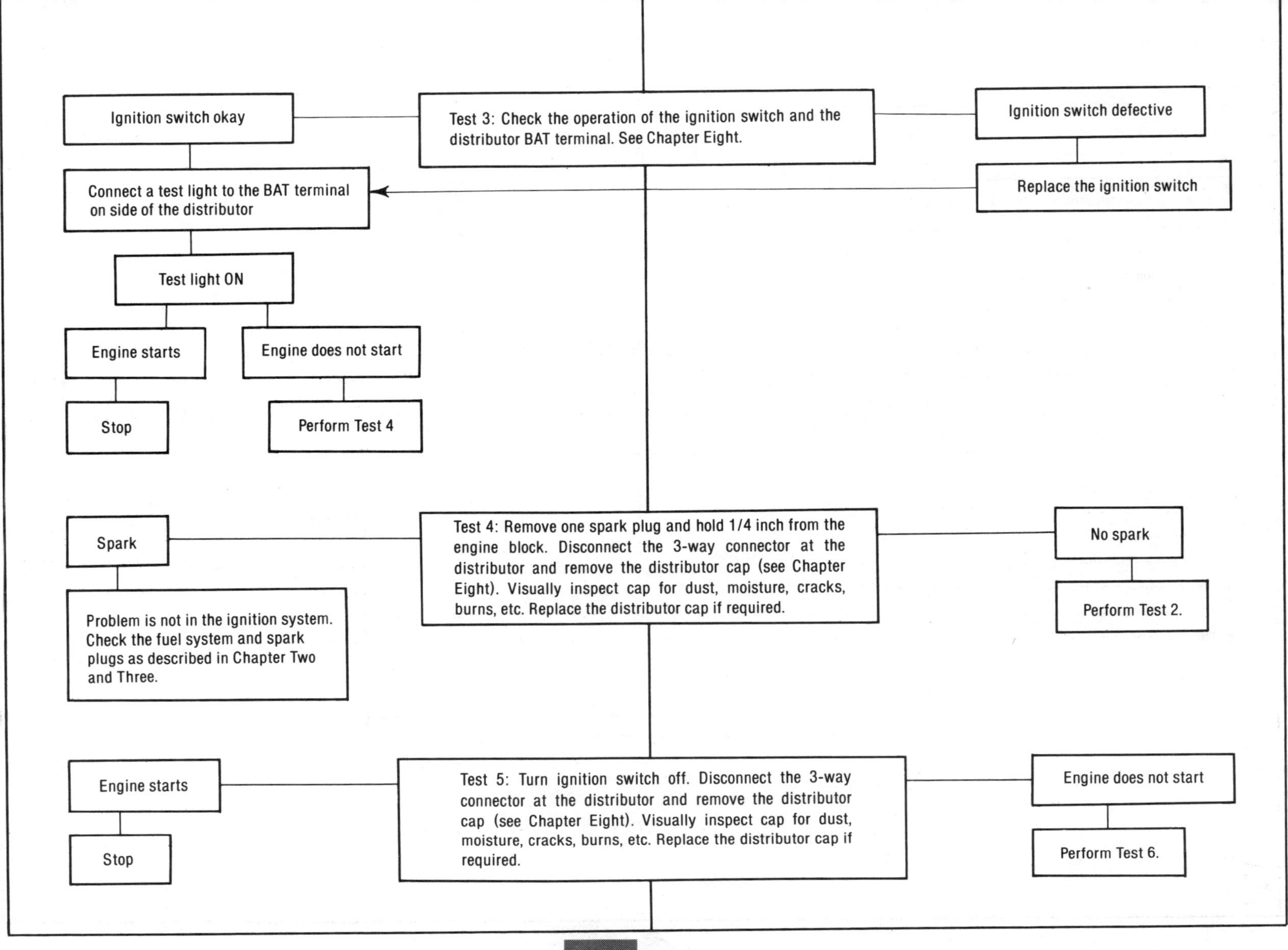
Test 3: Check the operation of the ignition switch and the distributor BAT terminal. See Chapter Eight.
Ignition switch okay
Connect a test light to the BAT terminal on side of the distributor
Test light ON
Engine starts
Stop
Engine does not start
Perform Test 4
Ignition switch defective
Replace the ignition switch
Test 4: Remove one spark plug and hold 1/4 inch from the engine block. Disconnect the 3-way connector at the distributor and remove the distributor cap (see Chapter Eight). Visually inspect cap for dust, moisture, cracks, burns, etc. Replace the distributor cap if required.
Spark
Problem is not in the ignition system. Check the fuel system and spark plugs as described in Chapter Two and Three.
No spark
Perform Test 2.
Test 5: Turn ignition switch off. Disconnect the 3-way connector at the distributor and remove the distributor cap (see Chapter Eight). Visually inspect cap for dust, moisture, cracks, burns, etc. Replace the distributor cap if required.
Engine starts
Stop
Engine does not start
Perform Test 6.
8

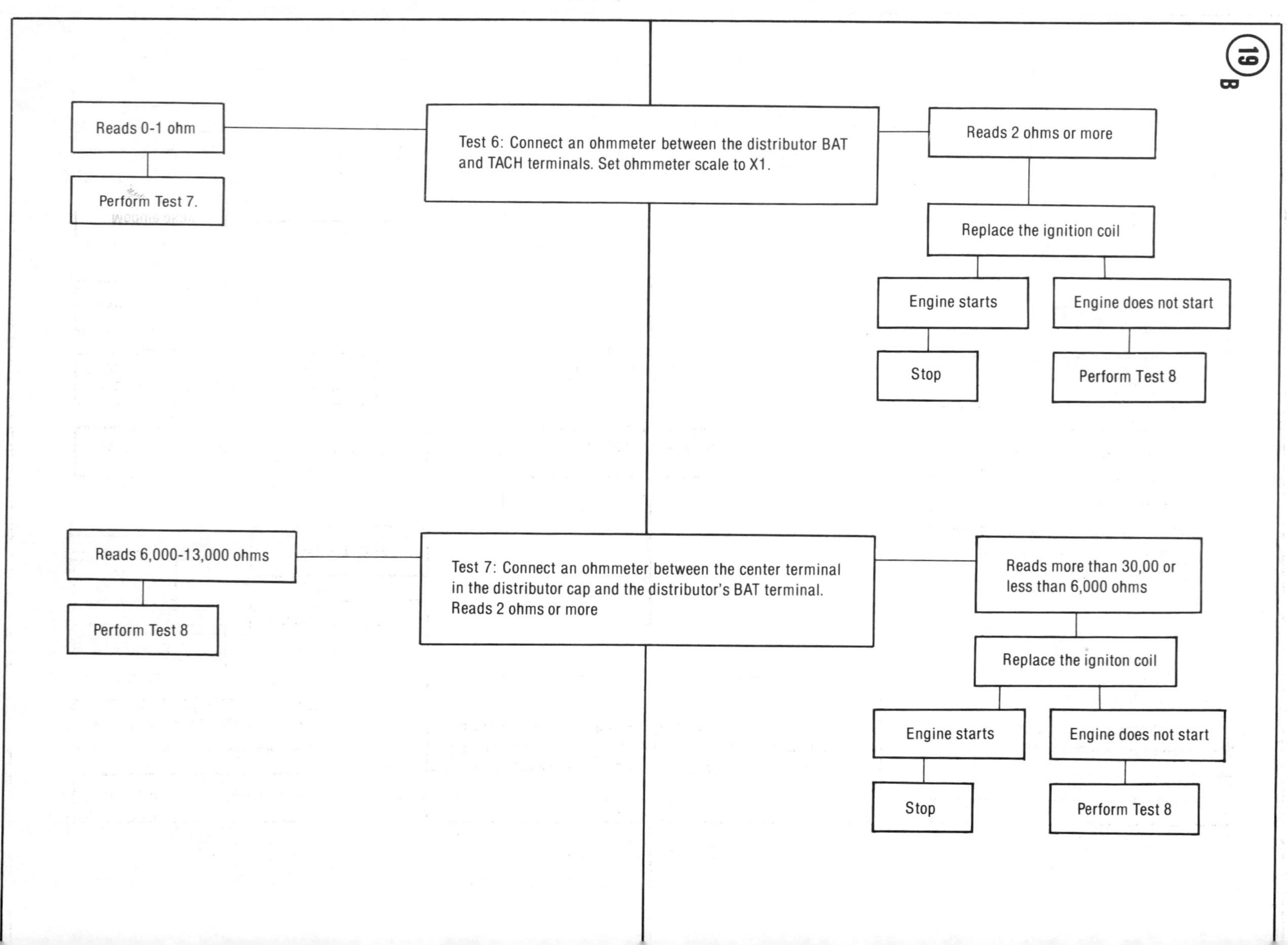
19
B
Test 6: Connect an ohmmeter between the distributor BAT and TACH terminals. Set ohmmeter scale to X1.
Reads 0-1 ohm
Perform Test 7.
Reads 2 ohms or more
Replace the ignition coil
Engine starts
Stop
Engine does not start
Perform Test 8
Test 7: Connect an ohmmeter between the center terminal in the distributor cap and the distributor's BAT terminal. Reads 2 ohms or more
Reads 6,000-13,000 ohms
Perform Test 8
Reads more than 30,00 or less than 6,000 ohms
Replace the igniton coil
Engine starts
Stop
Engine does not start
Perform Test 8

Test 8: Remove the green and white leads from the distributor module. Connect an ohmmeter between either lead to ground. Set ohmmeter scale to X1000.

Reads less than infinity

Replace the pick-up coil

Engine starts

Stop

Engine does not start

Perform Test 10

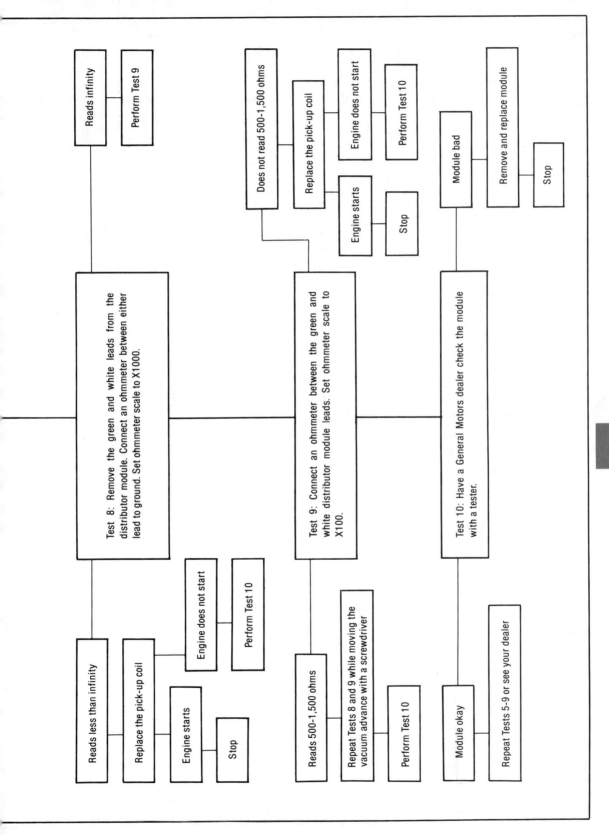

Reads infinity

Perform Test 9

Test 9: Connect an ohmmeter between the green and white distributor module leads. Set ohmmeter scale to X100.

Reads 500-1,500 ohms

Repeat Tests 8 and 9 while moving the vacuum advance with a screwdriver

Perform Test 10

Does not read 500-1,500 ohms

Replace the pick-up coil

Engine starts

Stop

Engine does not start

Perform Test 10

Test 10: Have a General Motors dealer check the module with a tester.

Module okay

Repeat Tests 5-9 or see your dealer

Module bad

Remove and replace module

Stop

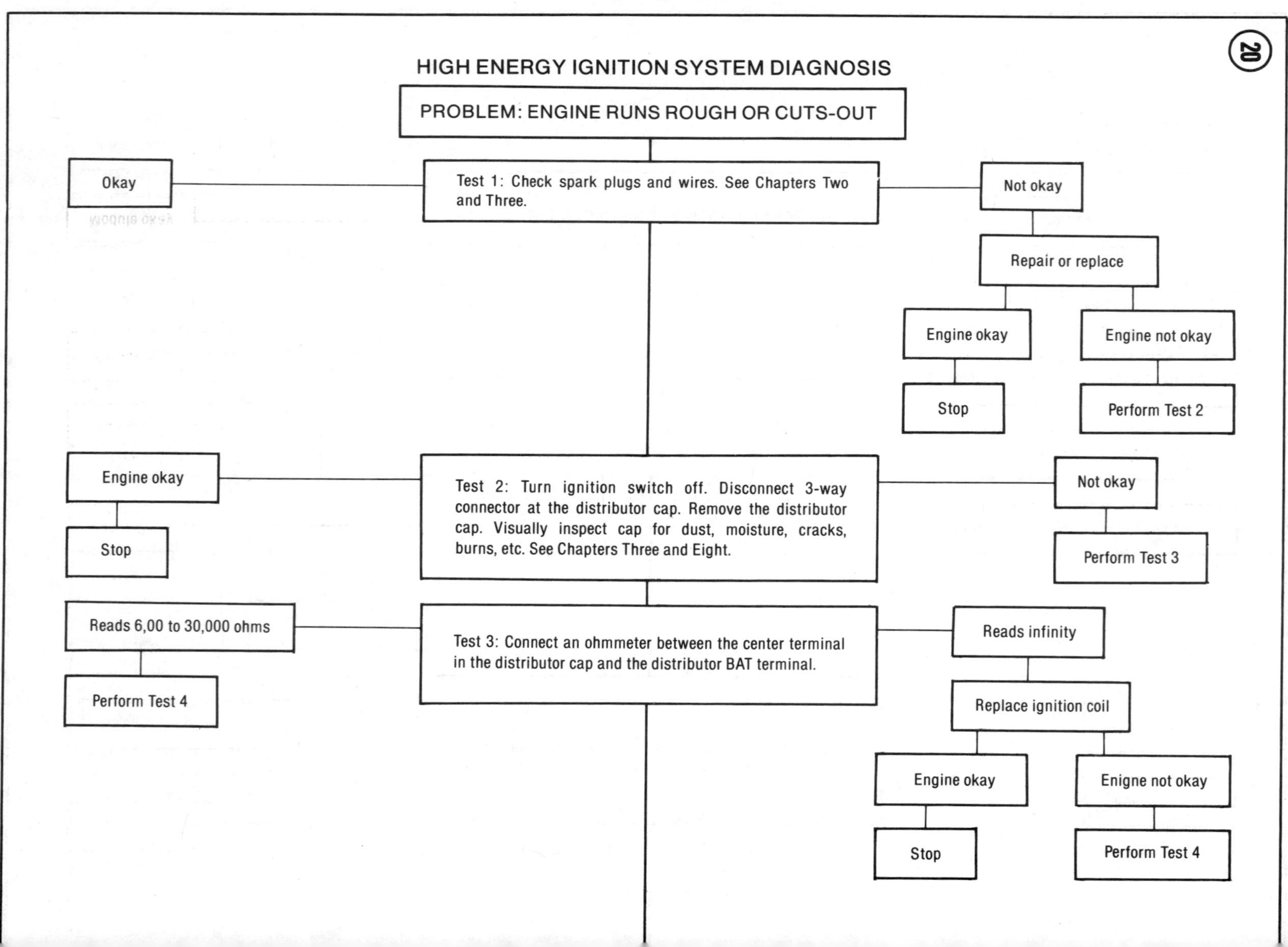
20
HIGH ENERGY IGNITION SYSTEM DIAGNOSIS
PROBLEM: ENGINE RUNS ROUGH OR CUTS-OUT
Okay
Test 1: Check spark plugs and wires. See Chapters Two and Three.
Not okay
Repair or replace
Engine okay
Engine not okay
Stop
Perform Test 2
Engine okay
Stop
Test 2: Turn ignition switch off. Disconnect 3-way connector at the distributor cap. Remove the distributor cap. Visually inspect cap for dust, moisture, cracks, burns, etc. See Chapters Three and Eight.
Not okay
Perform Test 3
Reads 6,00 to 30,000 ohms
Perform Test 4
Test 3: Connect an ohmmeter between the center terminal in the distributor cap and the distributor BAT terminal.
Reads infinity
Replace ignition coil
Engine okay
Enigne not okay
Stop
Perform Test 4

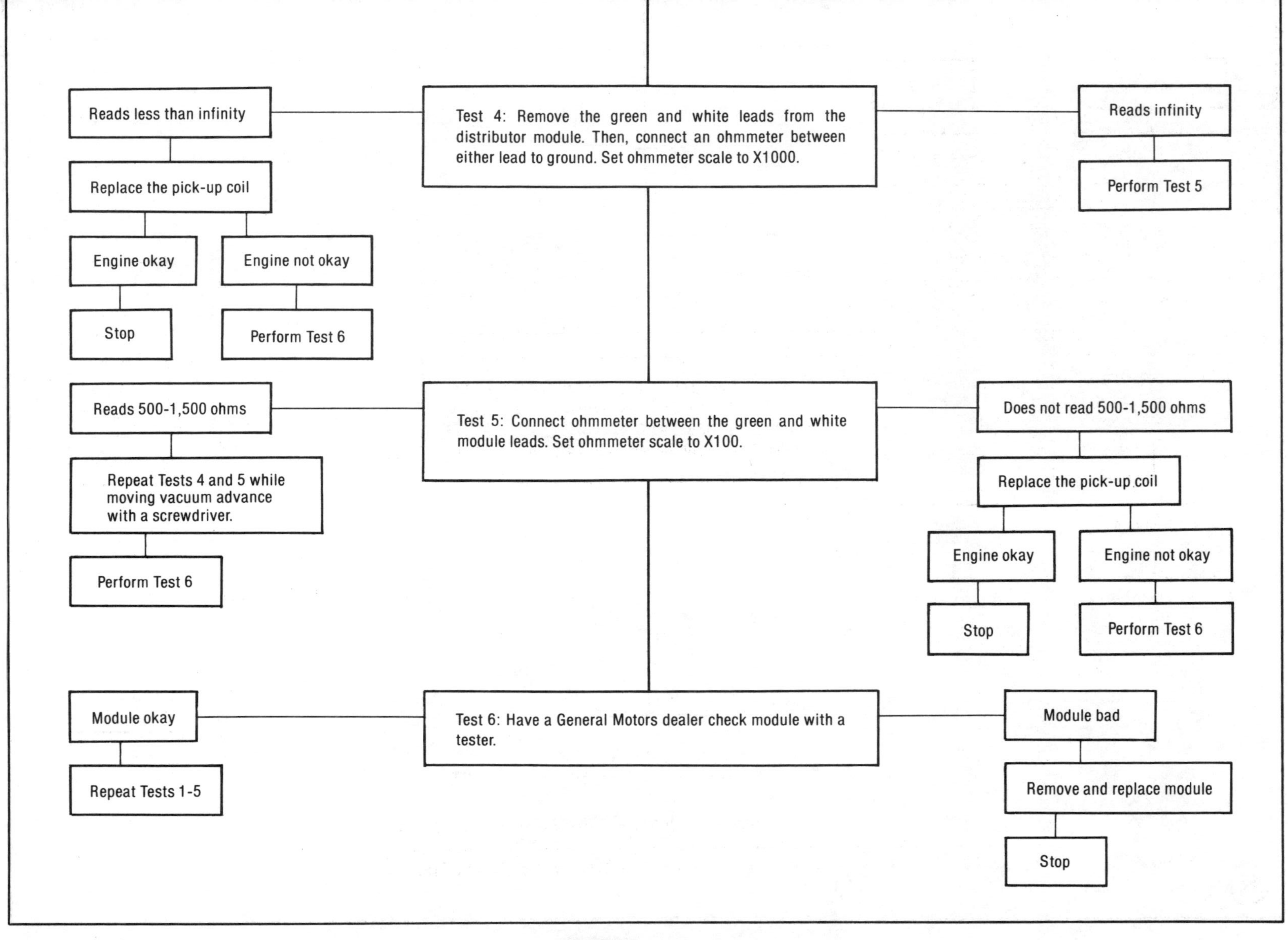

Test 4: Remove the green and white leads from the distributor module. Then, connect an ohmmeter between either lead to ground. Set ohmmeter scale to X1000.
Reads less than infinity
Replace the pick-up coil
Engine okay
Stop
Engine not okay
Perform Test 6
Reads infinity
Perform Test 5
Test 5: Connect ohmmeter between the green and white module leads. Set ohmmeter scale to X100.
Reads 500-1,500 ohms
Repeat Tests 4 and 5 while moving vacuum advance with a screwdriver.
Perform Test 6
Does not read 500-1,500 ohms
Replace the pick-up coil
Engine okay
Stop
Engine not okay
Perform Test 6
Test 6: Have a General Motors dealer check module with a tester.
Module okay
Repeat Tests 1-5
Module bad
Remove and replace module
Stop

8

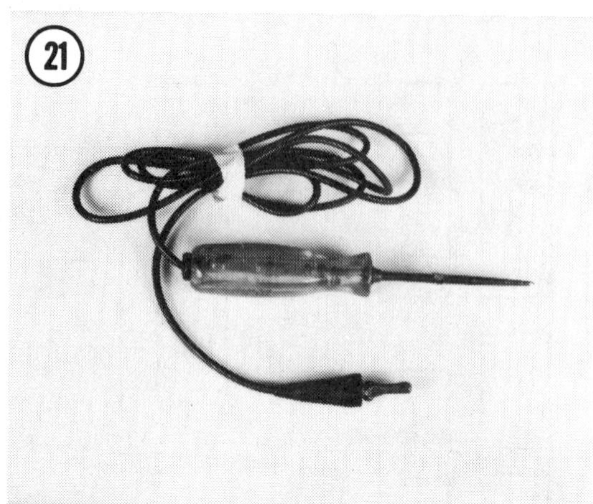
21

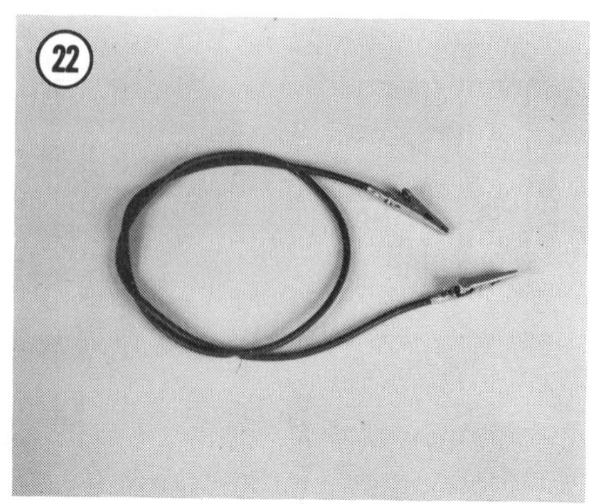
22

23
HEI DISTRIBUTOR TEST POINTS
Coil
TACH terminal
BATT terminal
B + terminal
Ground
C- terminal
Module leads
Module

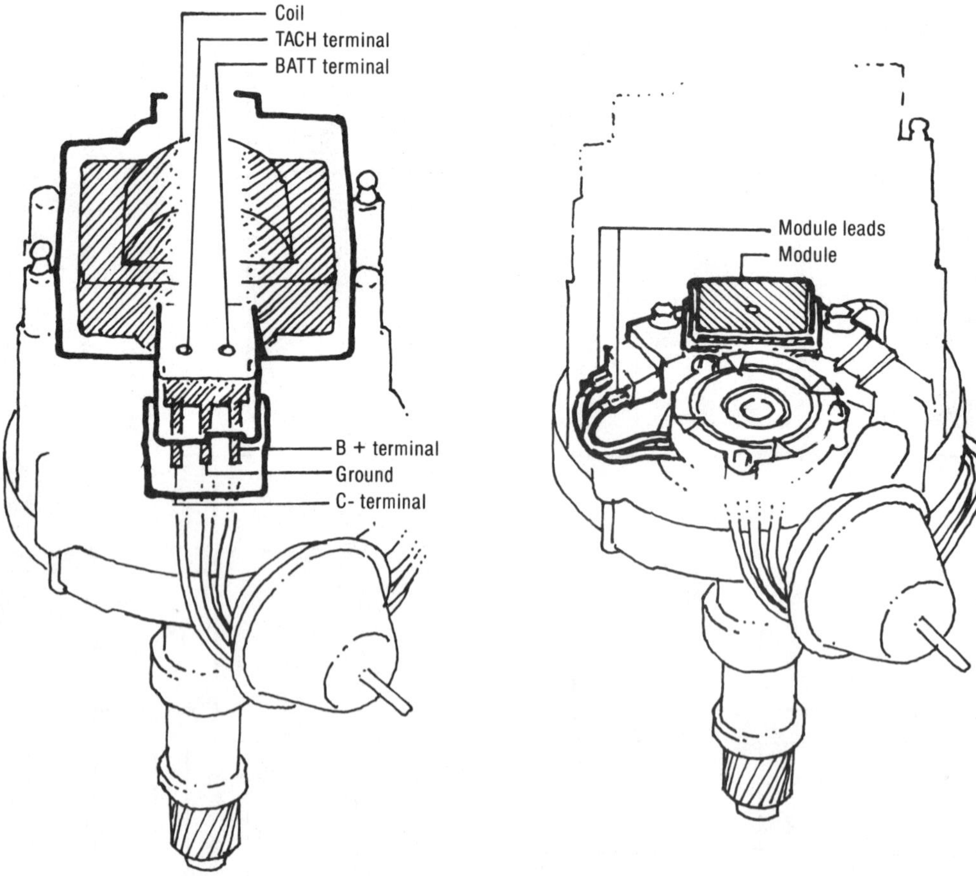

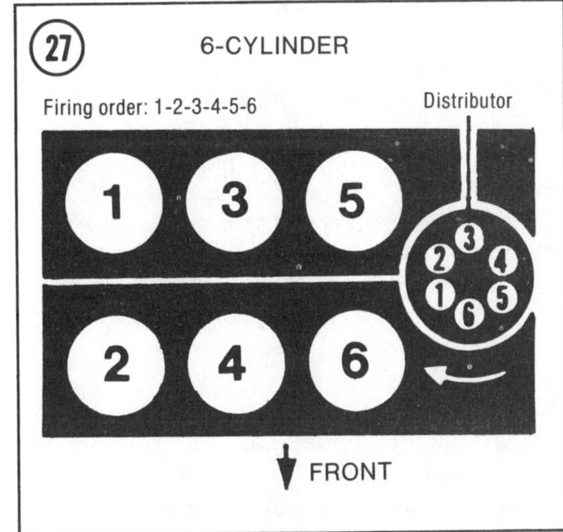
27
6-CYLINDER
Firing order: 1-2-3-4-5-6
Distributor
1
3
5
2
4
6
FRONT

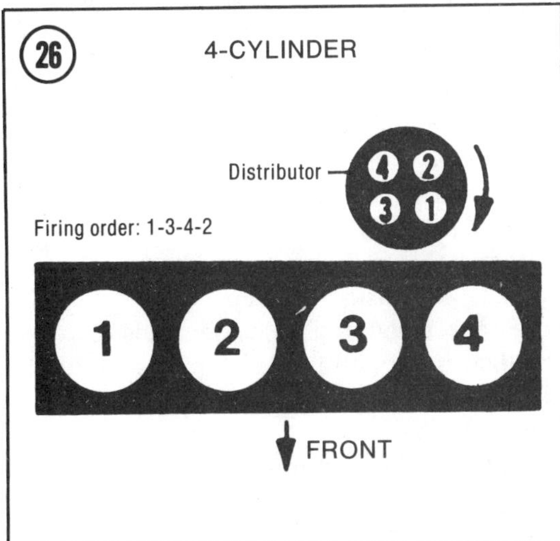
26
4-CYLINDER
Distributor
Firing order: 1-3-4-2
1
2
3
4
FRONT

8

NOTE

To remove the distributor cap and distributor on 4-cylinder engines, it is necessary to jack up the vehicles front end (secure with jackstands) and remove the right front wheel. Once the cap is free from the distributor, it can then be removed by lowering it from the distributor and passing it from the rear side of the engine and out through the right side wheel well. Remove the distributor by the same method.

6. Remove ignition coil retaining screws on top of the distributor cap and remove the ignition coil (**Figure 17**).
7. Scribe an alignment mark on the distributor and the engine, in line with the rotor.
8. Disconnect the vacuum line(s) at the distributor.
9. Unscrew the distributor clamp bolt and remove the clamp. **Figure 29** shows the hold-down clamp for the 4-cylinder engine. The V6 engine distributor is secured with a round clamp.
10. Note the position of the rotor for reference during installation and remove the distributor from the engine.

NOTE

Distributor on 4-cylinder vehicle must be removed through the right fender well as was the distributor cap.

NOTE

If possible, avoid cranking the engine with the distributor out. Installation will be easier if the engine is not turned.

Distributor Installation (Engine Not Turned)

1. Install the distributor in the engine. Make sure the alignment marks on distributor, engine and rotor are lined up.
2. Install the distributor hold-down nut or bolt and clamp.
3. Install the distributor cap and ignition coil, reversing the steps in the removal procedure.
4. Refer to *Tune-up* in Chapter Three and check and adjust timing.

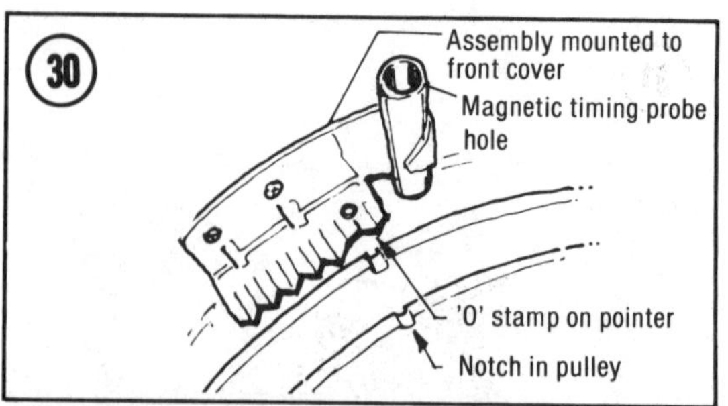

Distributor Installation (Engine Turned)

If the engine was turned with the distributor out, the following steps are necessary to align the distributor with the crankshaft and camshaft.

1. Crank the engine to bring the No. 1 piston to TDC in firing position. See **Figure 26** (4-cylinder) or **Figure 27** (V6) for No. 1 cylinder position. Both the intake and exhaust valves must be closed. Slowly continue rotating the crankshaft until the timing mark on the pulley lines up with the "0" stamp on pointer (**Figure 30**).
2. Start the distributor shaft into the engine but do not push it all the way in.

3A. On 4-cylinder engines, turn the rotor so it points between No. 1 and No. 3 plug towers (**Figure 26**).

3B. On V6 engines, turn the rotor so it points between No. 1 and No. 6 plug towers (**Figure 27**).

4. Carefully push the distributor down into place. Check by feel to make sure the distributor drive gear engages the camshaft gear. It may be necessary to rock the rotor slightly to obtain engagement.
5. Press the distributor down firmly and turn the engine over several times by hand to ensure that the distributor drive shaft is engaged properly.
6. Install the hold-down clamp and bolt or nut.
7. Install the distributor cap.
8. Connect the high-tension leads between the distributor and the spark plugs. Route the wires as shown in **Figure 31** (4-cylinder) or **Figure 32** (V6).
9. Connect the vacuum line and the primary electrical lead. Install coil and coil cover to top of distributor cap (if necessary).

Wires must be routed below cruise control and above throttle cable

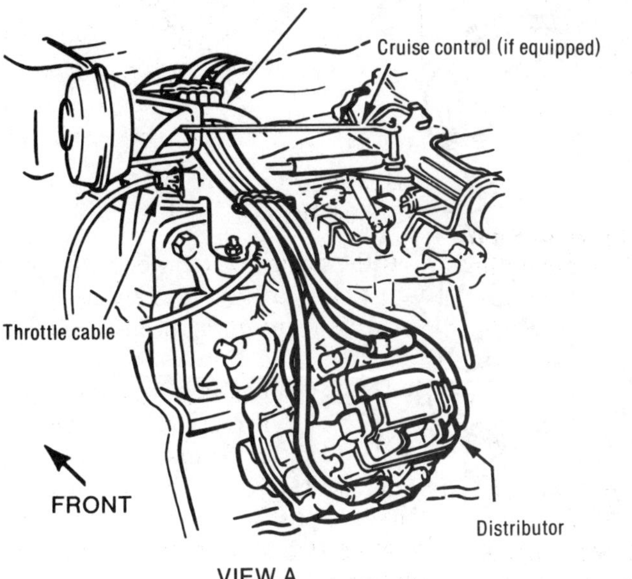

4-CYLINDER

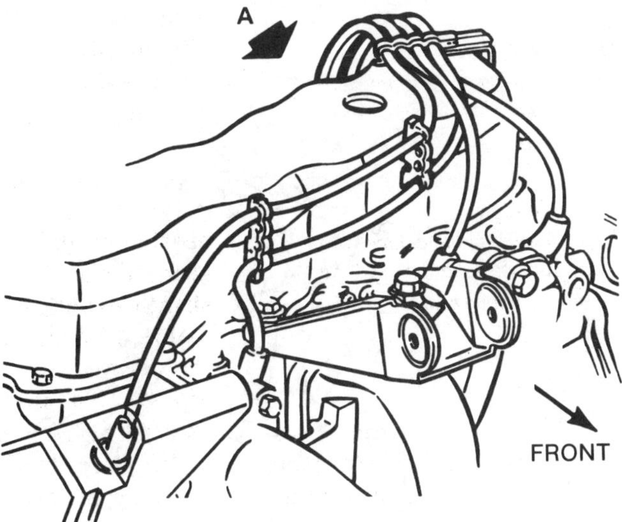

Spark plug wires to be routed to avoid contact or rubbing against each other or some object wherever possible.

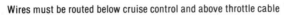

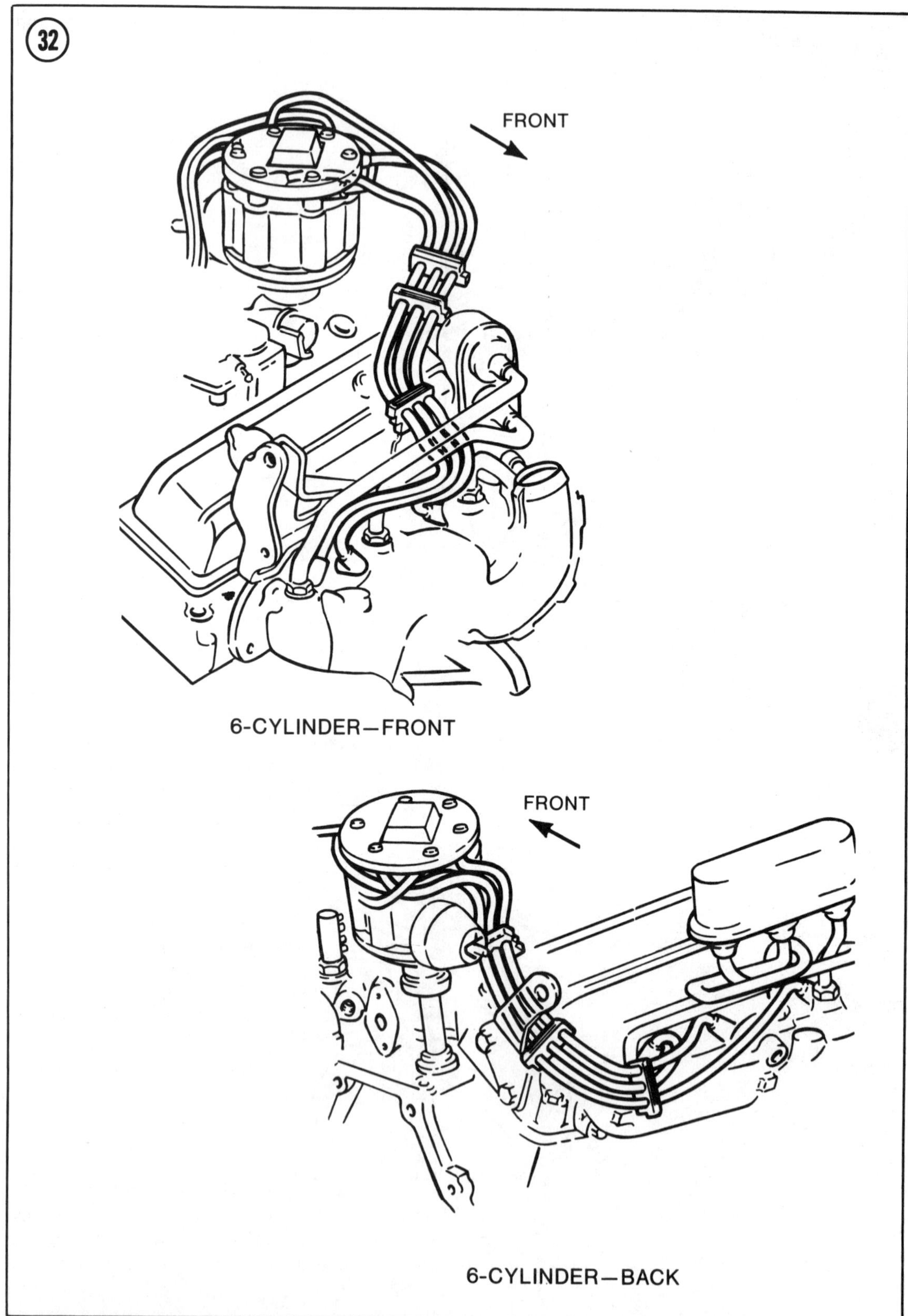

6-CYLINDER—FRONT

6-CYLINDER—BACK

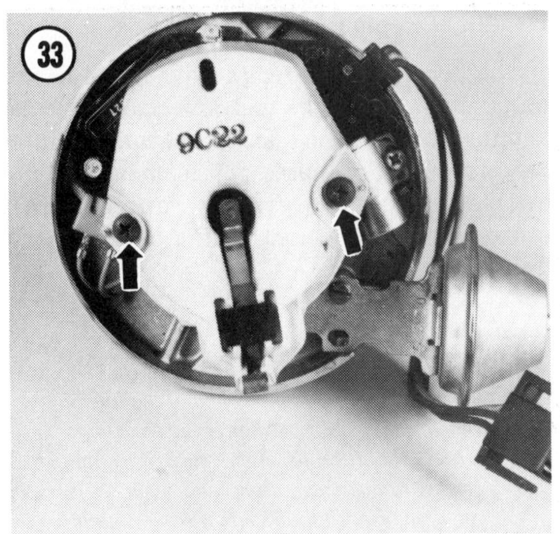

(33)

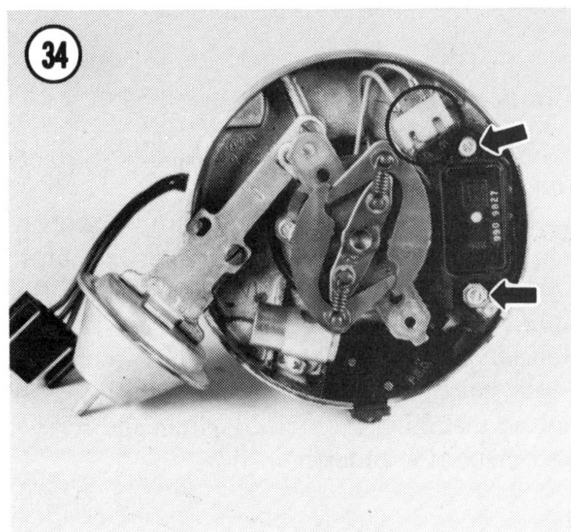

(34)

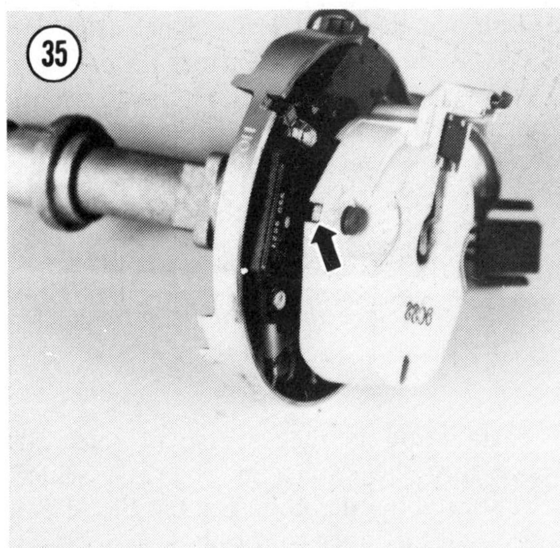

(35)

10. Refer to Chapter Three, *Tune-up*, and adjust the ignition timing.

Rotor/Electronic Module Replacement

1A. On 4-cylinder engines, remove distributor cap and distributor from engine as described in this chapter.
1B. On V6 engines, remove distributor cap.
2. Remove the screws securing the rotor to the centrifugal advance mechanism (**Figure 33**). Then remove the rotor.
3. Pry 2 pickup coil leads away from the module (**Figure 34**) and remove the 2 module attaching screws. Lift module up to remove.

NOTE
Grease found on bottom of module and distributor-module base surface is used for module cooling. If original module is to be reused, do not remove grease from either module or distributor-to-module base surface. If a new module is to be installed, a package of grease will be included in the module replacement kit. Wipe grease from distributor-to-module base surface and spread new grease on metal face of new module and on distributor-to-module base surface.

4. Install in the reverse order. When installing rotor, align cut-out in rotor with tang on centrifugal advance (see **Figure 35**). If installing a new module, make sure to replace with correct part number, as different module models are used.

IGNITION COIL

The ignition coil on all models is an integral part of the distributor. See **Figure 17** (typical). To remove the ignition coil, perform Steps 1-6 as described under *Distributor Removal.* Reverse to install.

SPARK PLUG WIRES

Special 8 mm silicone spark plug wires are used to withstand the higher voltage generated by the HEI system. Do not replace these wires with ordinary spark plug wires or with silicone wires with less than 8 mm insulation.

When disconnecting a spark plug wire, give the boot a 1/2 turn twist to break the seal before pulling the wire loose.

WARNING
Never disconnect any of the high voltage silicone wires with the engine running. The HEI system produces extremely high voltages and could produce a fatal shock.

When replacing the spark plug wires, remove and replace one wire at a time. Make sure, when replacing with new or reinstalling the old plug wires, to route the wires correctly. See **Figure 31** (4-cylinder) or **Figure 32** (V6). Incorrectly routed spark plug wires can cause radio ignition noise, spark plug crossfiring or possible shorting of wire leads to ground.

BODY ELECTRICAL SYSTEM

Instructions and pointers for troubleshooting the electrical wiring system are given in Chapter Two. Service which the owner/-mechanic can be expected to perform includes isolation and repair of short and open circuits, wire connector and fuse replacement, switch replacement and sealed beam and other bulb replacement.

Maintenance of the lighting and wiring systems consists of an occasional check to see that wiring connections are tightly mounted and that headlights are properly adjusted. The latter task should be performed by a qualified mechanic having access to the specialized equipment required.

Loose or corroded connectors can result in a discharged battery, dim lights and possible damage to the alternator or voltage regulator. Should insulation become burned, cracked, abraded, etc., the affected wire or wiring harness should be replaced. Rosin core solder—never use acid core solder on electrical connections—must always be used when splicing wires. Splices should be covered with insulating tape.

Replacement wires must be of the same gauge as the replaced wire—never use a smaller gauge. All harnesses and wires should be held in place with clips, cable ties or other holding devices so that chafing and abrasion can be avoided.

Headlight Replacement

The headlights are replaceable sealed-beam units. Both the high- and low-beam circuits and filaments are included in one unit. Failure of one circuit requires replacement of the entire unit. Individual replacement procedures follow, along with a bulb chart in **Table 4**.

NOTE
If both filaments in the lamp unit fail at the same time, it is possible that there is a short in the wiring to that particular lamp. Check the fuse to make sure it is the correct amperage rating and replace if required. Carefully inspect the wiring and connector too for chafing or damage and correct any breaks in the insulation.

Citation, Phoenix, Skylark

1. Remove screws holding headlight trim ring in place. Remove the ring.
2. Loosen the 4 headlight retaining screws. Pull bulb forward and remove the unit. Unplug the connector from the rear of the light.
3. Installation is the reverse of removal. Make sure the connector is firmly seated before installing the unit. Tighten the screws and install the outer trim ring.

Omega

1. Remove the front grille panel attaching screws. Remove the grille panel.
2. Loosen the 4 headlight retaining screws. Pull bulb forward and remove the unit. Unplug the connector from the rear of the light.

NOTE
Do not move the headlight aiming screws.

3. Installation is the reverse of removal. Make sure the connector is firmly seated before installing the unit. Tighten the screws and install the outer trim ring.

Parking/Turn Signal Bulb Replacement

Citation

To replace bulbs, open the hood and locate the parking/turn signal light bulb socket. Turn the bulb counterclockwise until released from the light body, then remove. Installation is the reverse of removal.

Omega

To replace bulbs, remove the front grille panel and locate the parking/turn signal light bulb socket. Remove the socket from the back of grille and turn bulb counterclockwise until released from the light body, then remove. Installation is the reverse of removal.

Phoenix, Skylark

To replace bulbs, reach inside the front wheel well and locate the parking/turn signal light bulb socket. Turn the bulb socket and remove from housing. Remove bulb from socket. Installation is the reverse of removal.

Front Side Marker Bulb Replacement

Citation

Remove the screws holding the headlight trim ring in place and remove the ring. Turn the bulb socket until released from the light body, then remove the bulb and socket from the light body. Depress bulb and rotate counterclockwise to remove from socket. Installation is the reverse of removal.

Omega, Phoenix, Skylark

To replace bulbs, reach inside the front wheel well and locate the front side marker light bulb socket. Turn the bulb socket and remove from housing. Remove bulb from socket. Installation is the reverse of removal.

Rear Light Replacement (All)

The rear light assembly contains a number of bulb elements. These elements provide the functions of tail/stoplights, back-up lights, rear turn lights, hazard warning lights, rear marker lights and license plate lights. To replace bulbs, open the trunk and remove the wing nuts holding the rear light assembly to rear of trunk. Then remove light assembly by pulling outward. Turn the bulb socket until released from the light body, then remove the bulb and socket from the light body. Depress the bulb and rotate counterclockwise to remove it from the socket. Installation is the reverse of removal.

Dome Light Replacement (All)

To replace the dome light bulb, release the 3 retaining tabs holding the dome light lens and remove lens. Remove bulb from socket. Installation is the reverse of removal.

Rear Compartment Light Replacement (All)

The rear compartment light is accessible through the trunk. To replace bulbs, open the trunk lid, then remove bulb from light assembly located to right of trunk latch in lid. Installation is the reverse of removal.

Instrument Panel Light Replacement (All)

1. Remove the instrument cluster as described in this chapter.
2. Remove the indicator and/or illumination lights by twisting socket and pulling rearward from cluster.

CAUTION

Use care when remove the sockets from the printed circuit board. Do not scratch any of the surrounding circuits as they will be damaged, causing an open circuit; the board would then have to be replaced.

3. Installation is the reverse of removal. Be sure that no electrical wires are caught between the instrument cluster and instrument panel.

SWITCHES

Headlight Switch Replacement

Citation

Refer to **Figure 36** for this procedure.

1. Disconnect the negative battery cable.

2. Pull headlight switch out to last detent position.
3. Remove instrument cluster attaching screws to provide access to headlight switch as discussed under *Instrument Cluster Removal* in this chapter.
4. Pull instrument cluster part way out, depress headlight switch shaft retaining button and remove shaft/knob assembly.
5. Disconnect all accessory switch connectors and remove instrument cluster from instrument panel.
6. Remove nut holding headlight switch to instrument panel. Push switch from mounting hole and lift upward through opening above switch mounting base.
7. Disconnect wiring connector at switch. Remove switch.
8. Installation is the reverse of removal. Make sure no electical wires are caught between instrument panel cluster and panel. Check headlights for proper operation.

Omega

Refer to **Figure 37** for this procedure.

1. Disconnect negative battery cable.
2. Pull headlight switch out to last detent.
3. Depress retaining clip behind headlight switch knob and remove knob from end of shaft.
4. Remove left side trim plate attaching screws. Remove trim plate.
5. Remove screws holding switch to terminal block. Pull switch outward to disconnect from terminal block and remove.
6. Installation is the reverse of removal. Check headlights for proper operation.

Phoenix

Refer to **Figure 38** for this procedure.

1. Disconnect negative battery cable.
2. Remove steering column trim cover attaching screws. Remove trim cover.
3. Pull headlight switch out to last detent.
4. Depress headlight switch knob retaining button behind knob. Remove shaft and knob assembly.
5. Remove left side trim plate attaching screws. Remove trim plate.

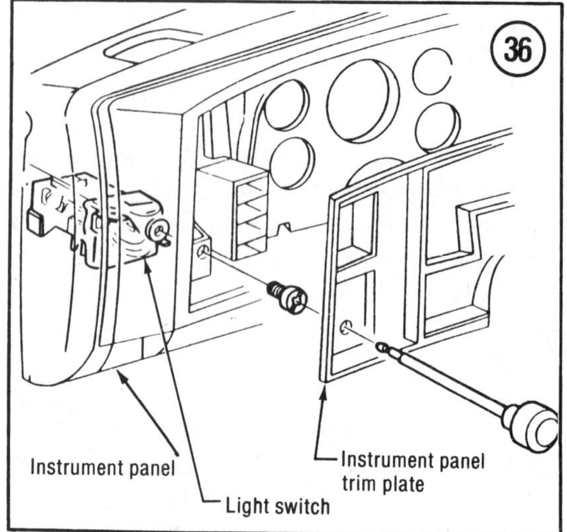

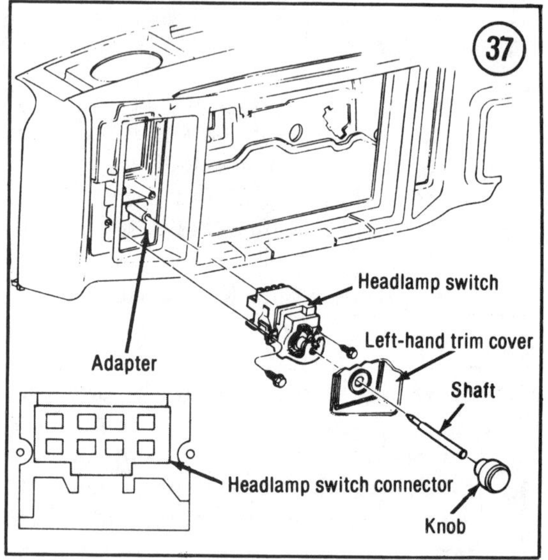

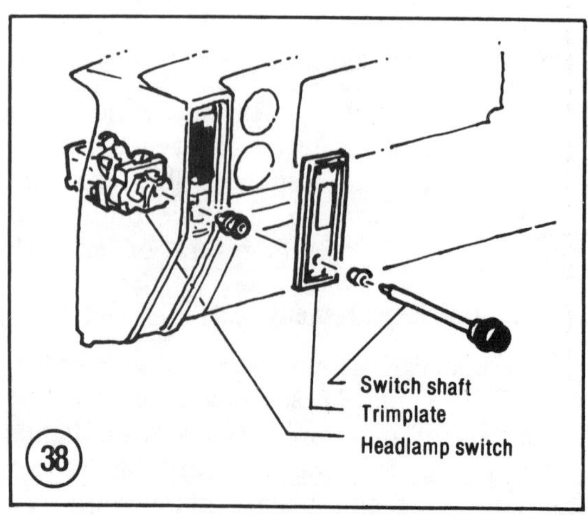

6. Disconnect switch wiring connector. Remove switch.
7. Installation is the reverse of removal. Check headlights for proper operation.

Skylark

Refer to **Figure 39** for this procedure.

1. Disconnect negative battery cable.
2. Pull headlight switch out to last detent.
3. Depress retaining clip behind headlight switch knob and remove from end of shaft.
4. Remove escutcheon from switch shaft.
5. Remove the instrument panel trim plate as described in this chapter.
6. Remove screws holding headlight switch to terminal block. Pull switch outward to unplug from terminal block and remove.
7. Installation is the reverse of removal. Check headlights for proper operation.

Headlight Troubleshooting

Incorrect headlight operation can be diagnosed by determining the complaint and then following the flow chart in **Figure 40**.

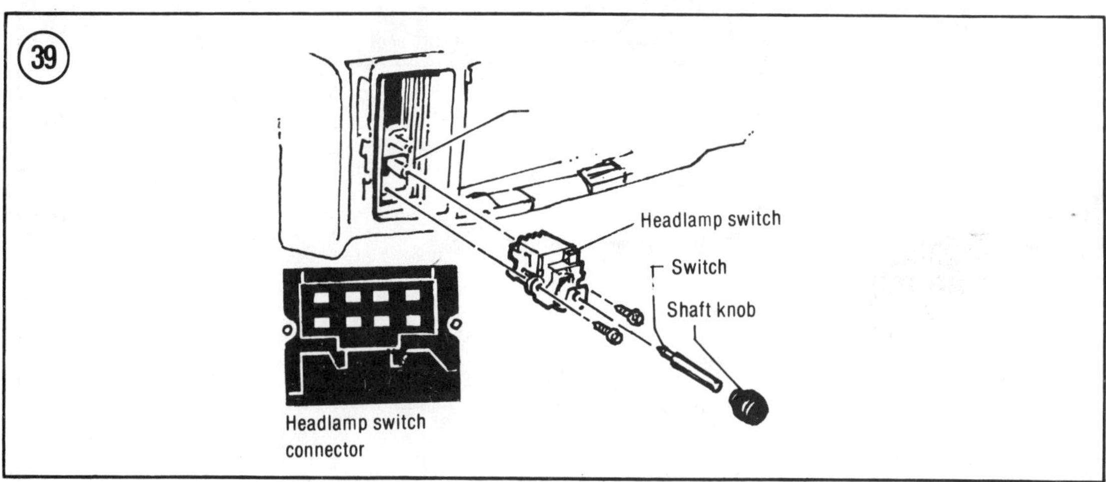

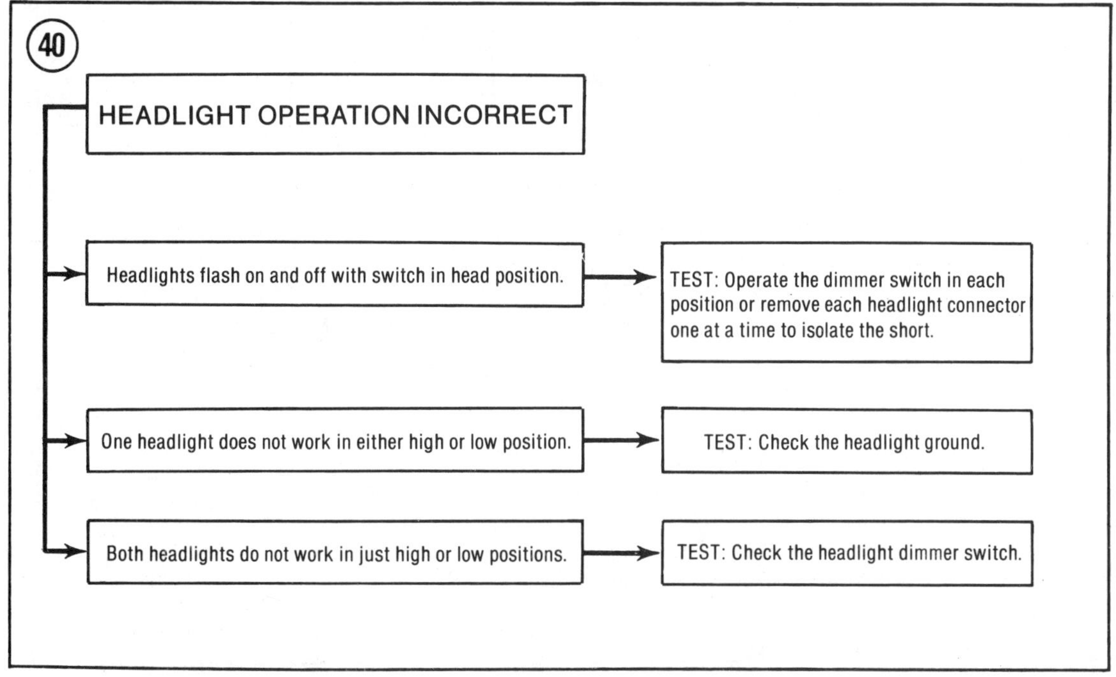

40
HEADLIGHT OPERATION INCORRECT
Headlights flash on and off with switch in head position.
TEST: Operate the dimmer switch in each position or remove each headlight connector one at a time to isolate the short.
One headlight does not work in either high or low position.
TEST: Check the headlight ground.
Both headlights do not work in just high or low positions.
TEST: Check the headlight dimmer switch.

8

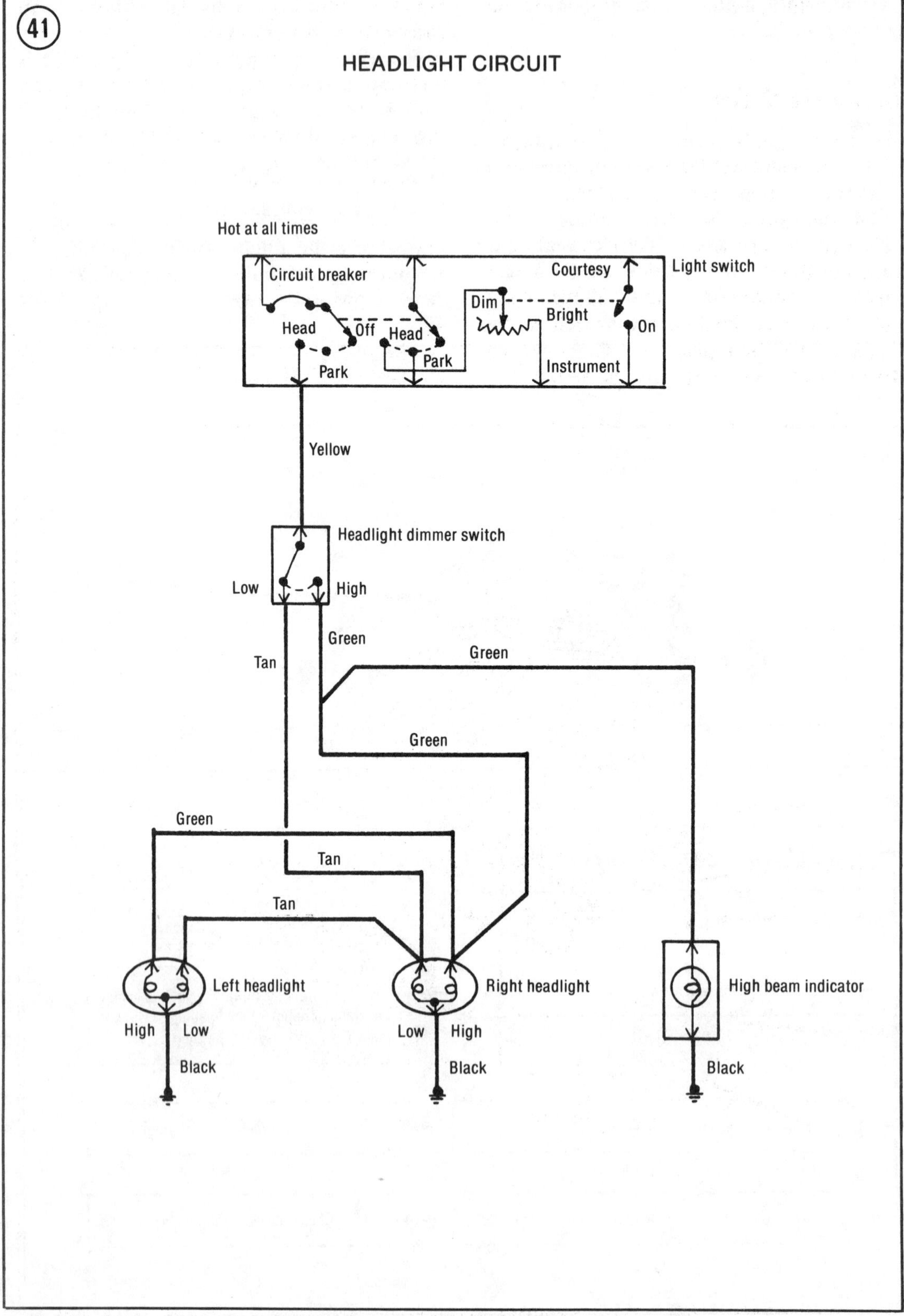
41
HEADLIGHT CIRCUIT
Hot at all times
Circuit breaker
Courtesy
Light switch
Dim
Bright
Head
Off
Head
On
Park
Park
Instrument
Yellow
Headlight dimmer switch
Low
High
Green
Tan
Green
Green
Green
Tan
Tan
Left headlight
Right headlight
High beam indicator
High
Low
Low
High
Black
Black
Black

The headlight operational circuit is shown in **Figure 41**.

Dimmer Switch Test

The switch can be tested with an ohmmeter or a self-powered test lamp. **Figure 41** shows the dimmer switch operation system.

With the switch off, there should be no continuity between any of the terminals. An ohmmeter should show infinite resistance and a test lamp should remain unlit. If any of the terminals are connected, the switch has a short and must be replaced. With the switch activated to the ON position, the yellow and tan (low) terminals should be connected. An ohmmeter should show little or no resistance. A test lamp should light. If not, the switch is bad and must be replaced. Repeat the test with an ohmmeter or test light connected to the yellow and green (high) terminals.

Dimmer Switch Replacement

1. Remove the dashboard trim panel underneath the steering column jacket. On vehicles equipped with air conditioning, remove the sound absorber also. See **Figure 42**.
2. Disconnect the electrical connector at the dimmer switch (**Figure 43**).

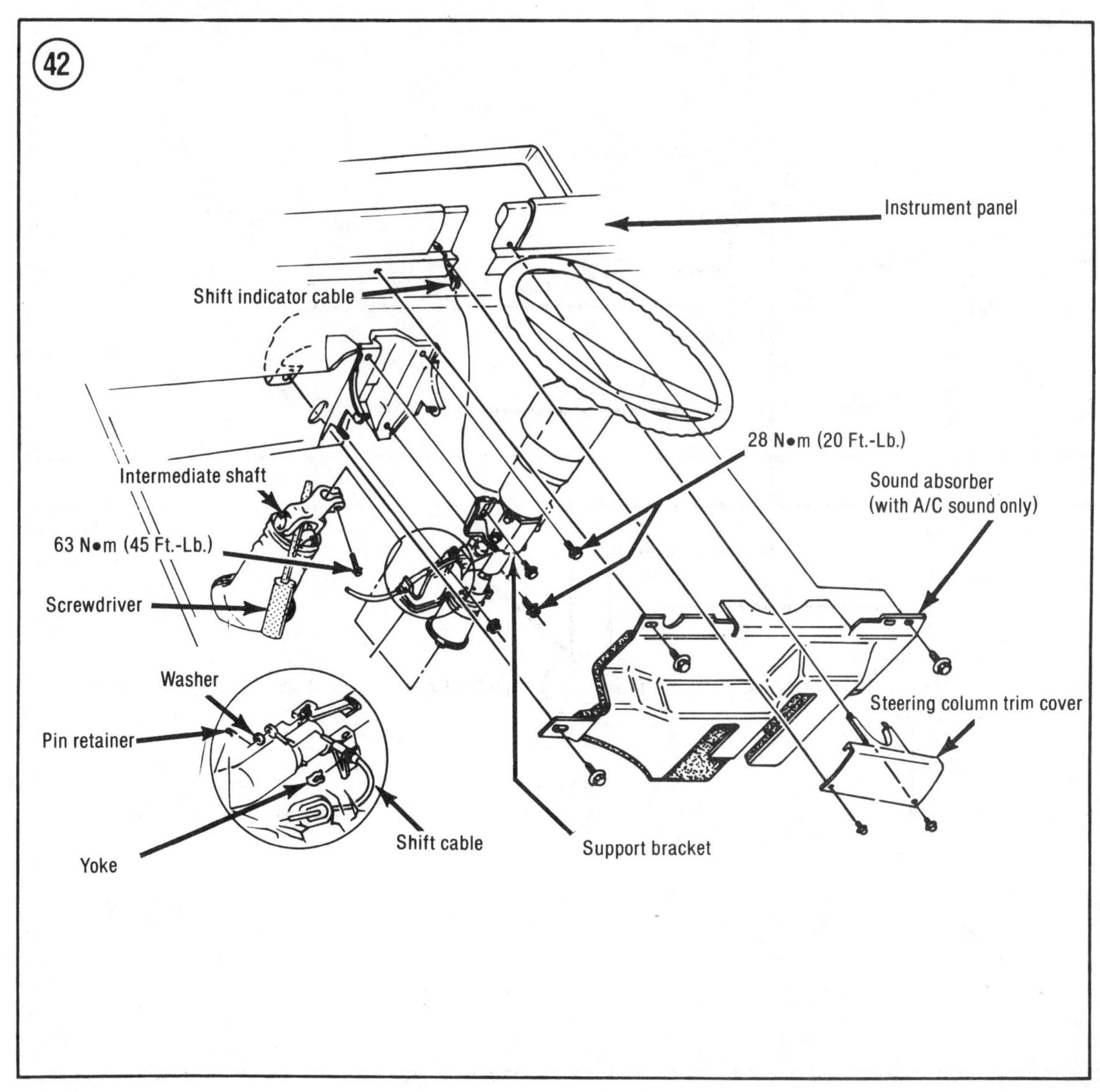

3. Remove the steering column strap nuts (**Figure 42**) and lower the steering column slightly.
4. Remove the nut and screw securing the dimmer switch to the steering column (**Figure 44**).
5. Position new dimmer switch onto the steering column stud. Then insert actuator rod into dimmer switch.
6. Depress the dimmer switch slightly and insert a 3/32 in. drill into the switch as shown in **Figure 45**. Then force the dimmer switch up slightly to remove free play and tighten the screw and nut.
7. Connect the dimmer switch electrical connector (**Figure 43**).
8. Reposition the steering column and tighten the strap nuts. Tighten nuts to 20 ft.-lb. (28 N•m). Install the sound absorber (air conditioning models) and the steering column trim cover.
9. Check the dimmer switch operation.

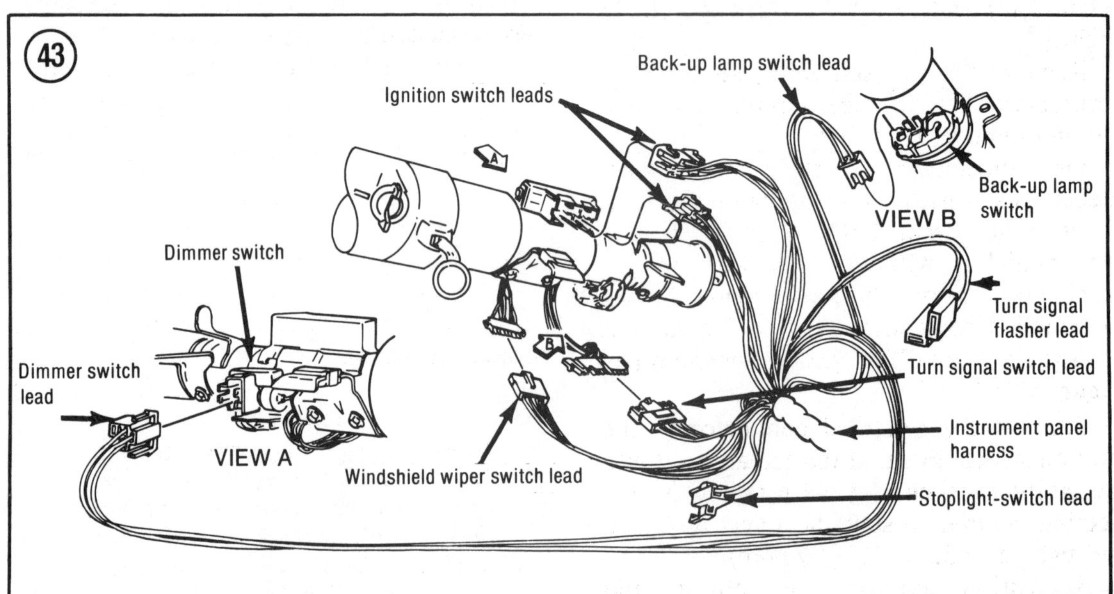

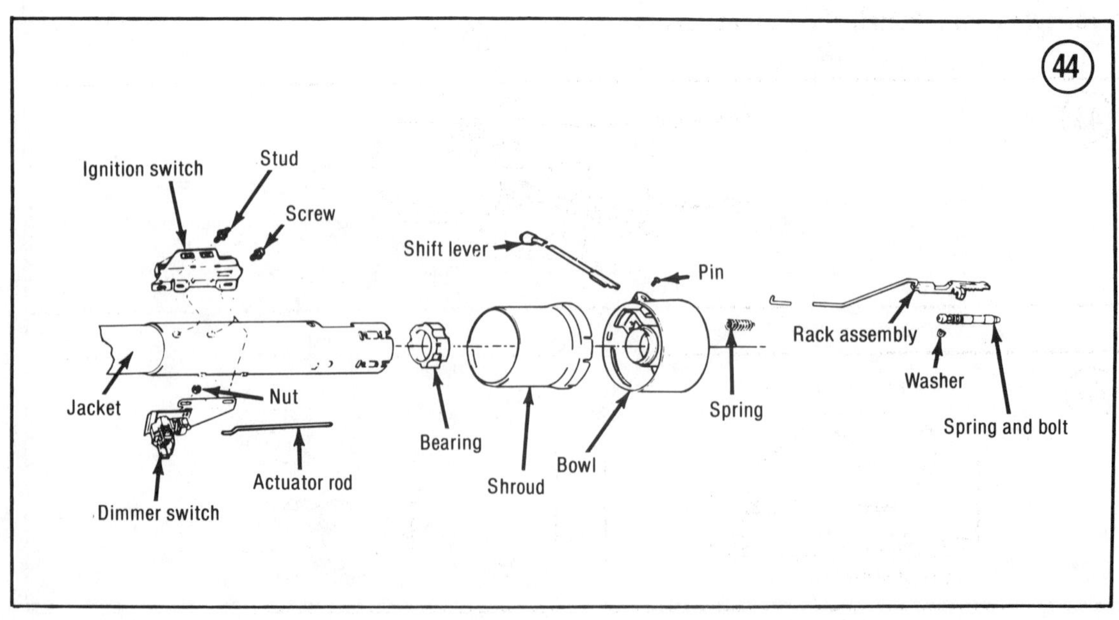

Ignition Switch Replacement

The ignition switch is located at the base of the steering column.

1. Remove the dashboard trim panel underneath the steering column jacket. On vehicles equipped with air conditioning, remove the sound absorber also. See **Figure 42**.
2. Disconnect the electrical connector at the ignition switch (**Figure 43**).
3. Remove the steering column strap nuts (**Figure 42**) and lower the steering column slightly.
4. Remove the nut and screw securing the ignition switch to the steering column (**Figure 44**) and remove the switch.
5. On vehicles in which a key release mechanism is used, move the ignition switch slider to the extreme left position (**Figure 46**). On vehicles without the key release mechanism, move the switch slider to the extreme left position, then move 2 detents to the right to the OFF UNLOCK position (see **Figure 47**).
6. Connect the electrical connector to the ignition switch. Position the actuator rod into the ignition switch and place switch on the steering column. Install the screw and stud and tighten to 35 in.-lb. (3.9 N•m).
7. Reposition the steering column and tighten the strap nuts. Tighten nuts to 20 ft.-lb. (28 N•m). Install the sound absorber (air conditioning models) and the steering column trim cover.
8. Check the ignition switch operation.

FUSES/CIRCUIT BREAKERS

Whenever a failure occurs in any part of the electrical system, always check the fuse box to see if a fuse has blown. If one has, it will be evident by blackening of the fuse or by a break in the metal link in the fuse. Usually the trouble can be traced to a short circuit in the wiring connected to the blown fuse. This may be caused by worn-through insulation or by a wire which has worked loose and shortened to ground. Occasionally, the electrical overload which causes the fuse to blow may occur in a switch or motor.

A blown fuse should be treated as more than a minor annoyance; it should serve also as a warning that something is wrong in the electrical system. Before replacing a fuse, determine what caused it to blow and then correct the trouble.

WARNING
Never replace a fuse with one of a higher amperage rating than that of the one originally used. Never use tinfoil or other metallic material to bridge fuse terminals. Failure to follow these basic rules could result in heat or fire damage to major parts or loss of the entire vehicle.

8

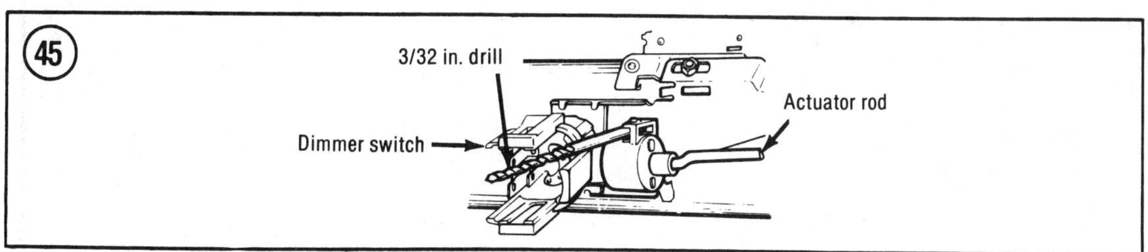

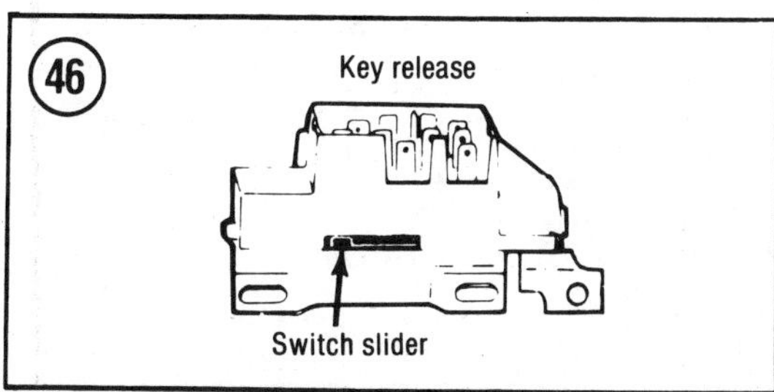

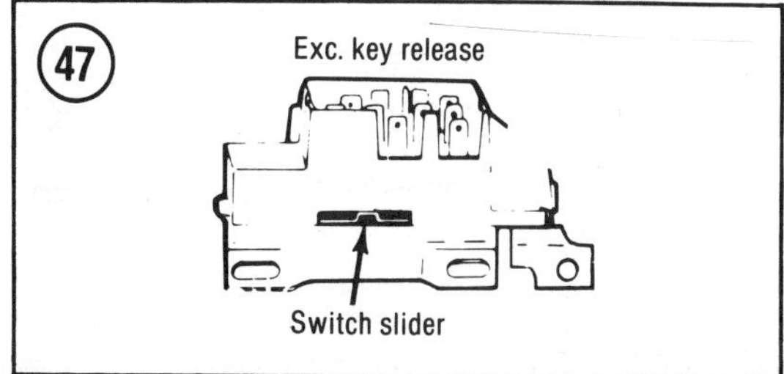

The fuse panel is located at the right end of the firewall, beneath the dashboard. See **Figure 45**.

To replace or inspect a fuse, simply pull it out of its holder and snap a new one into place. No special tools are required to replace or install fuses.

Fusible Links

Fusible links provide protection to circuits which are not protected by the circuit breakers and fuses. The links are short pieces of wire smaller than the wiring in the circuit they are protecting. Fusible links are covered with a special high-temperature insulation. If a link burns out, the cause must be isolated and corrected. A new fusible link must then be spliced into the circuit. Fusible links are located at the following positions:

a. Fusible link A—at starter solenoid (**Figure 49**)
b. Fusible link B—at starter solenoid (**Figure 49**)
c. Fusible link C—at the right side cowl terminal block in the engine compartment (**Figure 50**)

The following procedure should be used to replace fusible links.

1. Disconnect the battery ground cable.
2. Disconnect old fusible link from components to which it is attached.

48

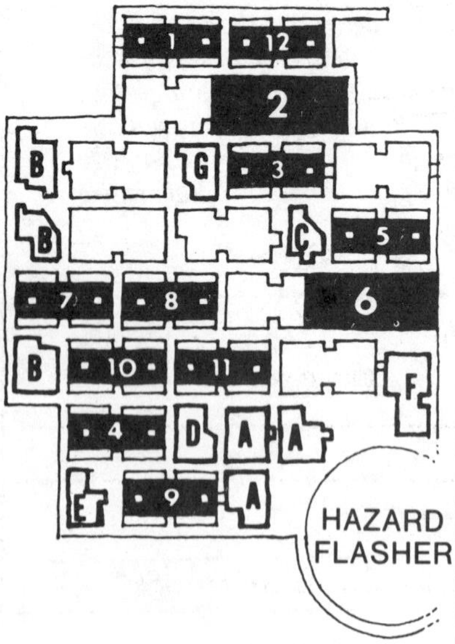

Type	Color/ Size (Amps)	Circuits Protected	Fuse/ CB Loc.	Loc.
Fuse	WHT (25)	Air Conditioner Blower and Compressor (L4 and V6); Heater; Idle Stop Solenoid (L4 and V6)		
Fuse	YEL (20)	Choke Heater (Gauges and No Gauges); Cooling Fan	12	E
Fuse	YEL (20)	Air Conditioner Anti-Dieseling Relay; Cigar Lighter; Clock; Computer Controlled Catalytic Converter System (L4 and V6); Courtesy Lights; Horn; Ignition Key Warning; Light-On Reminder; Power Door Locks (2 and 4 DR); Radio Capacitor	11	A
Fuse	YEL (20)	Air Conditioner Anti-Dieseling Relay (L4); Brake Warning Indicator; Choke Heater (Gauges and No Gauges); Computer Controlled Catalytic Converter System (L4 and V6); Defogger; Fuel Gauge; Gauges; Idle Stop Solenoid; Ignition; Light-On Reminder; Map Light; Seatbelt Warning; Warning Indicators	7	B
Fuse	TAN (5)	Lights: Instrument Panel; Light-On Reminder	1	G
CB	(30)	Defogger: Power Door Locks (2 and 4 DR)	6	F
Fuse	RED (10)	Cruise Control; Radio	9	D
Fuse	YEL (20)	Idle Stop Solenoid (V6); Lights: Hazard Stop/Front Park/Front Marker	5	
Fuse	YEL (20)	Lights: Hazard/Stop/Front Park/Front Marker		
		Lights: Front Park/Front Marker; Lights: License/Rear Park/Rear Marker	8	
Fuse	YEL (20)	Backup Lights: Lights: Turn/Hazard/ Front Park/Front Marker	10	
CB	(30)	Power Windows (2 and 4 DR)	2	
Fuse	WHT (25)	Wiper/Washer; Wiper/Washer (Delay)	4	

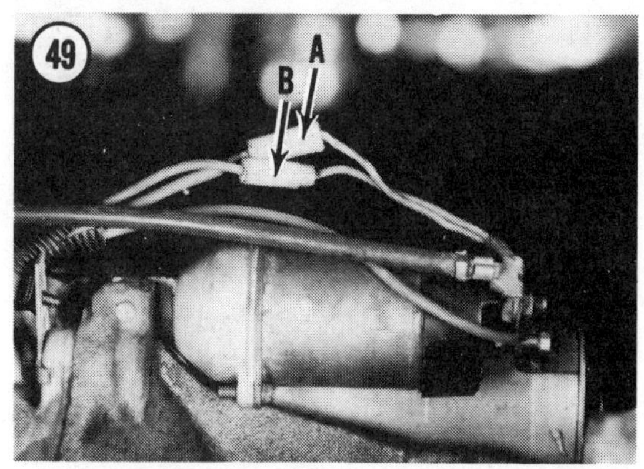

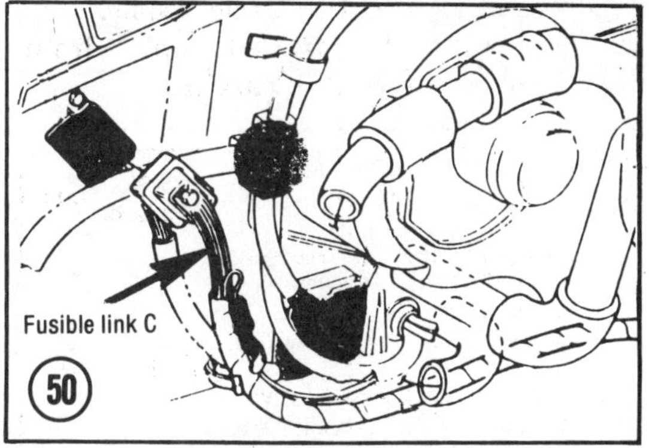

3. Cut harness behind connector (**Figure 51**) to remove the damaged fusible link.

4. Strip harness wire insulation approximately to 1/2 inch.

5. Position clip around ends of new fusible link (**Figure 52**) and harness wire and crimp so that both wires are securely fastened.

6. Solder the connection, using rosin core solder. Use sufficient heat to obtain a good solder joint, but do not overheat.

7. Tape all exposed wires with insulating tape.

8. Connect fusible link to component from which it was removed.

NOTE
*When replacing a fusible link at the starter solenoid, make sure to place the fusible link connection under the battery cable connection at the solenoid terminal. See **Figure 49**.*

9. Reconnect the battery ground cable.

8

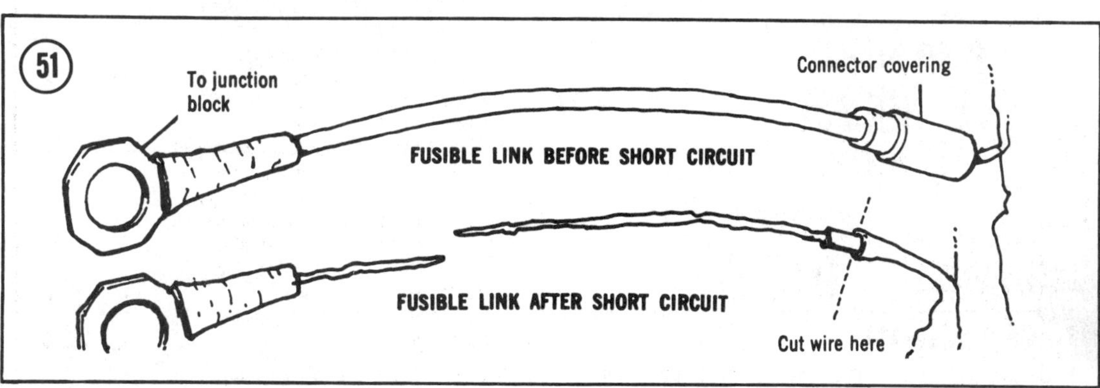

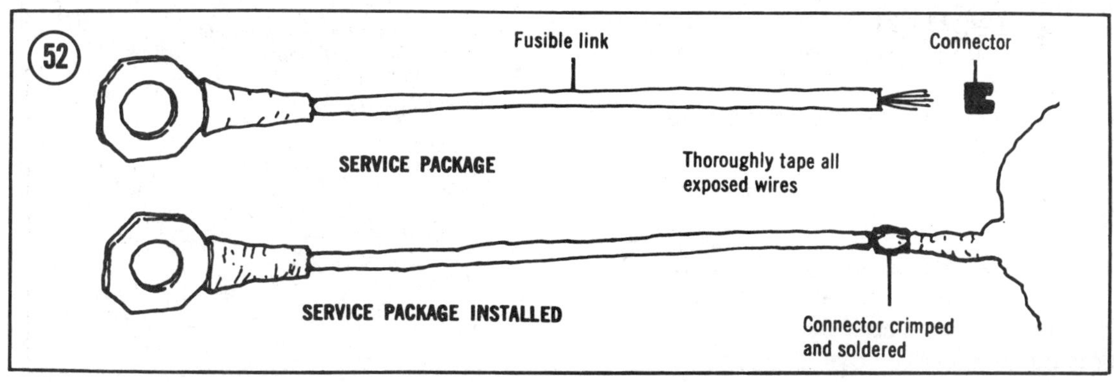

FLASHER UNITS

The hazard flasher unit is located in the fuse box, located under the right hand side of the instrument panel (**Figure 48**). To remove the hazard flasher, pull the old flasher out of fuse box and replace.

The turn flasher unit is attached to the base of the steering column support. See **Figure 53**. To remove, disconnect the flasher unit wire lead and unsnap the flasher from the wire clip. Install in the reverse order

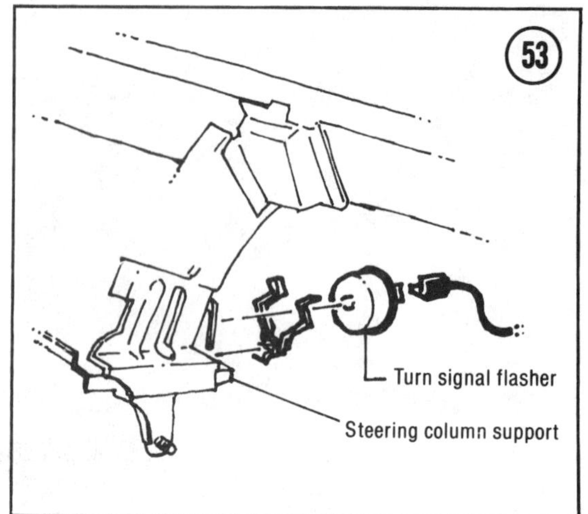

INSTRUMENT PANEL GAUGES

Instrument Panel Trim Plate Replacement

Citation

Refer to **Figure 54** for this procedure.

1. Disconnect the negative battery cable.
2. Remove radio and clock hand control knobs by pulling knobs away from instrument panel.
3. Remove screws holding instrument panel trim plate to front of instrument panel. Pull trim plate rearward slightly to provide access to headlight switch.

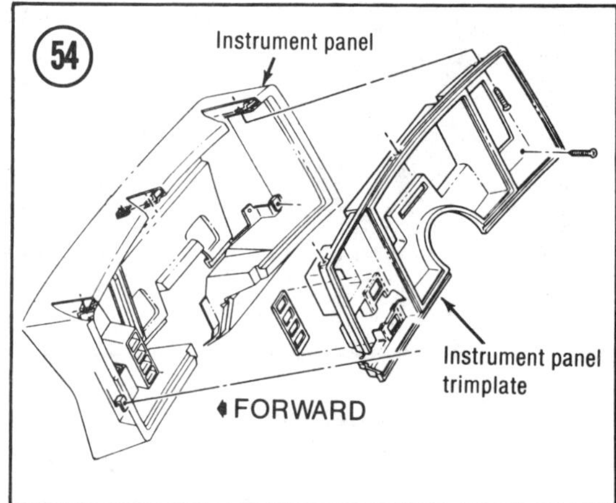

CAUTION
Make sure you have removed all the fasteners. If the trim plate is unusually difficult to remove, check for fasteners you may have missed.

4. Remove headlight knob and shaft as described in this chapter.
5. Pull trim plate outward and disconnect any accessory switch wiring connected to rear of plate. Remove instrument panel trim plate.
6. Installation is the reverse of removal. Make sure no electrical wires are caught between instrument panel trim plate and instrument panel.

Omega

Refer to **Figure 55** for this procedure.

1. Disconnect negative battery cable.
2. Remove lower steering column trim cover attaching screws. Remove trim cover.

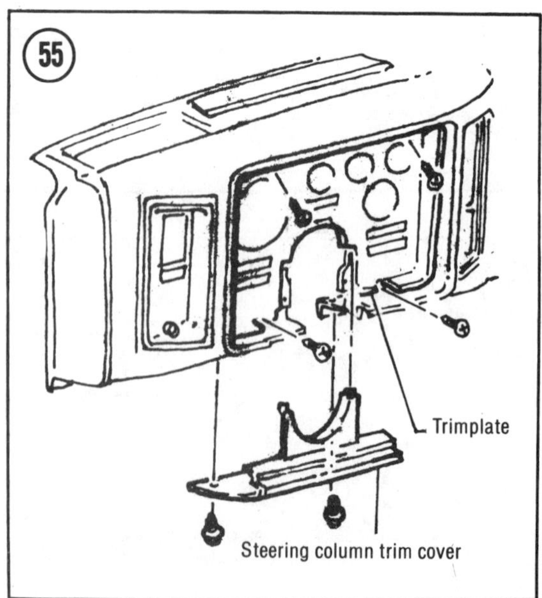

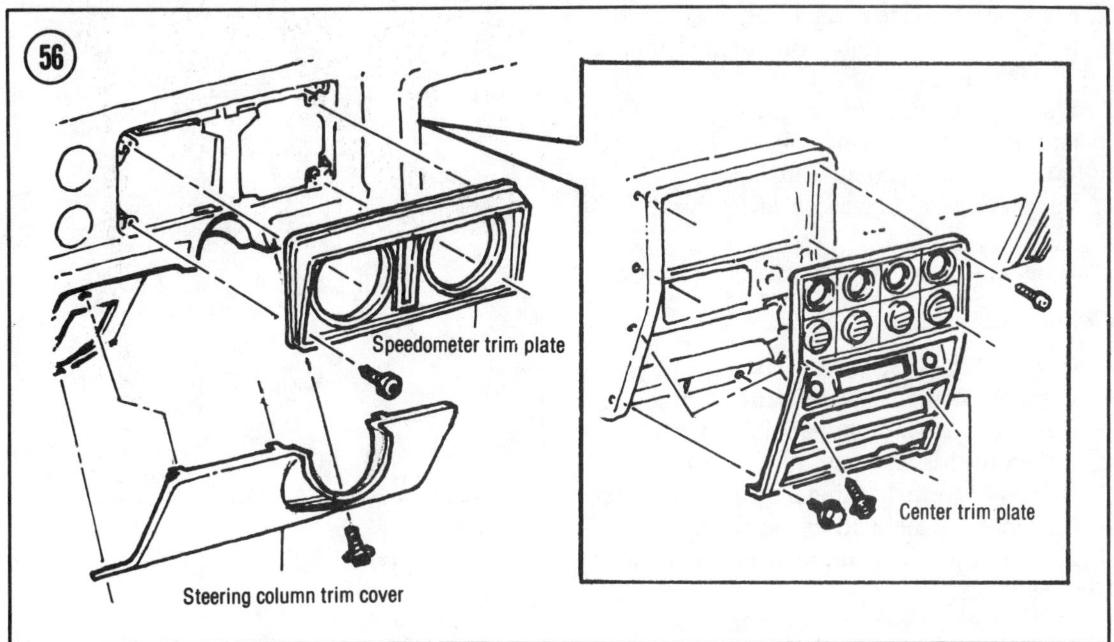

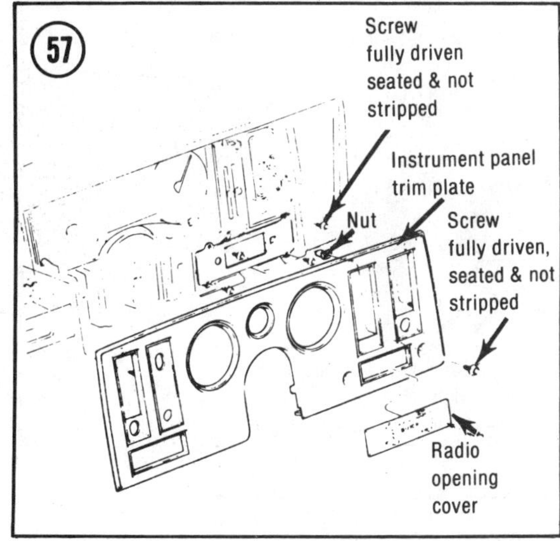

3. Remove bolts holding steering column to instrument panel. Lower steering column slightly.

CAUTION

Use care when lowering steering column. If possible, allow steering wheel to rest on front seat or support steering column with wood blocks.

4. Remove screws holding instrument panel trim plate to instrument panel. Pull trim plate partway out.

5. Disconnect accessory switch wiring. Remove mirror control cable (if so equipped) from rear of plate. Remove trim plate.

6. Installation is the reverse of removal.

Phoenix

Refer to **Figure 56** for this procedure.

1. Disconnect negative battery cable.
2. Remove screws holding speedometer trim plate to front of instrument panel. Remove speedometer trim plate.
3. Remove screws holding center trim plate to front of instrument panel. Remove center trim plate.
4. Installation is the reverse of removal.

Skylark

Refer to **Figure 57** for this procedure.

1. Disconnect the negative battery cable.
2. Remove control knobs from the following items:
   a. Radio.
   b. Rear window defogger.
   c. Pulse windshield wiper.
3. Pull headlight switch out to last detent. Depress retaining clip behind knob and remove knob from switch shaft.
4. Remove headlight switch emblem from light switch shaft.

8

5. Remove radio stem retaining nuts.
6. Remove screws at bottom of instrument panel trim plate.
7. Place gear selector in low gear. Pull instrument panel trim plate down and remove from instrument panel.
8. Installation is the reverse of removal.

Instrument Cluster Replacement

Citation

Refer to **Figure 58** for this procedure.

1. Disconnect the negative battery cable.
2. Remove instrument panel trim plate as described in this chapter.
3. Remove screws holding instrument cluster to instrument panel pad and carrier.
4. Disconnect shift indicator cable from steering column shift bowl.
5. Pull cluster assembly out part way and disconnect speedometer cable and all electrical wiring from back side of instrument cluster. Remove instrument cluster.
6. Installation is the reverse of removal. Make sure no electrical wires are caught between cluster and panel. Speedometer cable must be inserted all the way into speedometer and fastened securely.

Omega

Refer to **Figure 59** for this procedure.

1. Disconnect negative battery cable.
2. Remove center instrument panel trim cover attaching screws. Remove trim cover.
3. Remove screws holding cluster assembly to instrument panel pad.
4. Disconnect shift indicator cable from steering column shift bowl.
5. Pull instrument cluster partway out to disconnect speedometer and electrical connectors. Remove cluster assembly.
6. Installation is the reverse of removal.

Phoenix

Refer to **Figure 60** for this procedure.

1. Disconnect negative battery cable.

NOTE
Steps 2-7 describe replacement of speedometer cluster.

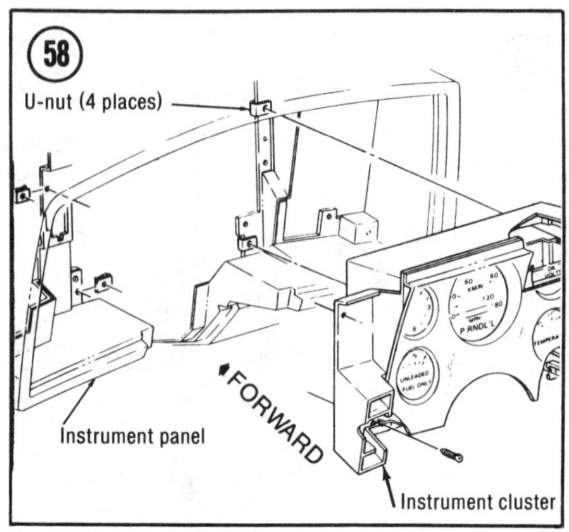

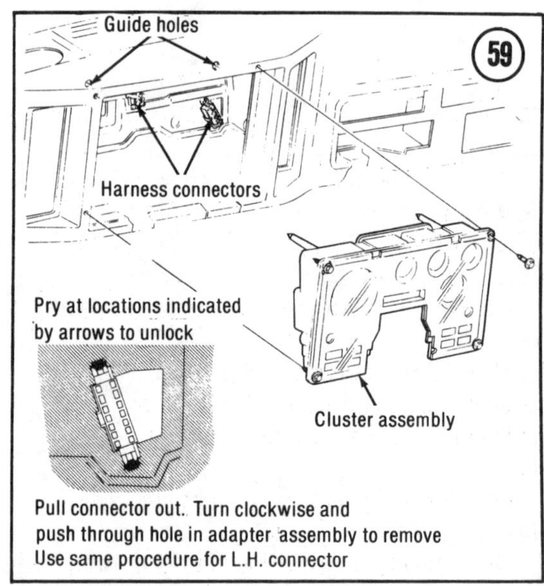

Pull connector out. Turn clockwise and push through hole in adapter assembly to remove
Use same procedure for L.H. connector

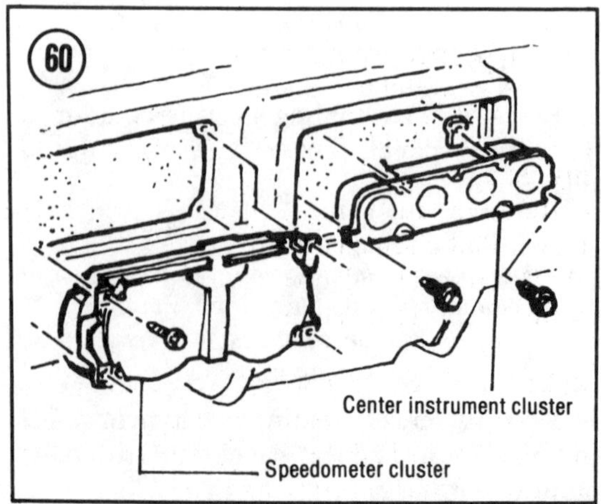

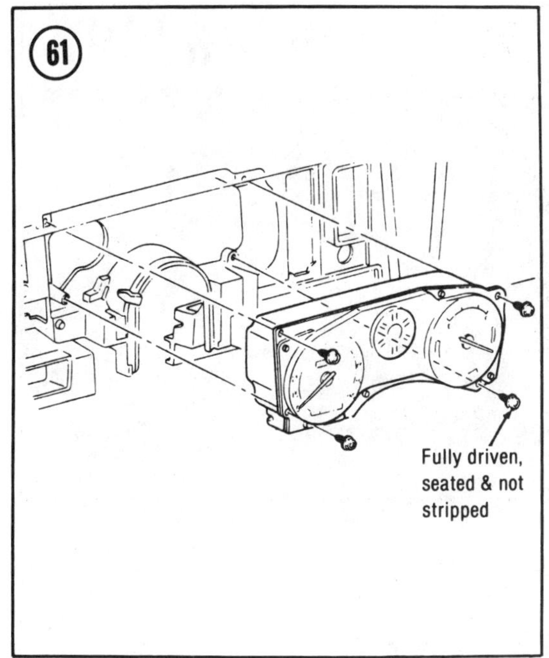

2. Remove speedometer cluster trim plate as described in this chapter.
3. Remove steering column trim cover attaching screws. Remove trim cover.
4. Remove speedometer cluster attaching screws.
5. Mark shift indicator detent cable location on steering column shift bowl prior to cable removal. Disconnect shift indicator detent cable.
6. Disconnect speedometer cable from rear of cluster.
7. Disconnect electrical harness at connector. Remove cluster.

NOTE
Steps 8-10 describe replacement of center instrument cluster.

8. Remove center trim plate as described in this chapter.
9. Remove instrument cluster attaching screws. Pull cluster partway out.
10. Disconnect electrical connectors at cluster. Remove cluster.
11. Installation is the reverse of removal. Make sure no electrical wires are caught between cluster and panel. Speedometer cable must be inserted all the way into speedometer and cable collar securely tightened.

Skylark

Refer to **Figure 61** for this procedure.
1. Disconnect the negative battery cable.

NOTE
If equipped with cruise control, disconnect speedometer cable at cruise control transducer in Step 2.

2. Disconnect the speedometer cable.
3. Remove trip meter reset knob retaining screw at front of instrument cluster. Pull knob from meter.
4. Remove instrument panel trim plate as described in this chapter.
5. Remove instrument cluster lens plate screws. Remove lens plate.
6. Remove screws holding instrument cluster to front of instrument panel.
7. Disconnect gear selector indicator spring below speedometer. Slide indicator needle to the right and remove.
8. Pull instrument cluster outward. Disconnect speedometer cable from rear of cluster by pushing cable retaining clip toward cluster and pulling cable away from speedometer.
9. Disconnect electrical harness at cluster. Remove cluster.
10. Installation is the reverse of removal.

Fuel and Speedometer Gauge Replacement

1. Remove instrument cluster as described in this chapter.
2. Disconnect the speedometer cable from the backside of the instrument cluster.
3. For speedometer removal, remove screws securing cluster lens to instrument cluster, then remove lens and faceplate.
4. Disconnect the electrical harness at the connector of the gauge being removed.
5. Remove the attaching screws securing the gauge to the instrument cluster.
6. For fuel gauge removal, pull fuel gauge out to disengage spring clip.

7. Gauges can now be removed. Make sure that all wiring has been disconnected before removing gauge.

CAUTION
Be careful when removing the sockets from the printed circuit board. Do not scratch any of the surrounding circuits as they will be damaged, causing an open circuit; the board would then have to be replaced.

8. Install by reversing the removal steps. Be sure that there are no electrical wires caught between the instrument cluster and the instrument panel.
9. Be sure that the speedometer cable is inserted all the way into the speedometer and fastened securely.

WINDSHIELD WIPER SYSTEM

Wiper Motor Replacement

The windshield wiper motor is located in the engine compartment on the center of the firewall (**Figure 62**) and is replaced as follows.
1. Disconnect the negative battery cable.
2. Remove both wiper arm assemblies as discussed under *Wiper Arm Replacement.*
3. Remove lower windshield reveal molding, front cowl panel and cowl screw.

CAUTION
Before removing front cowl panel, cover hood corners with rags or towels to prevent possible damage to vehicle paint.

4. Disconnect the washer hose at the wiper motor.
5. Loosen nuts attaching transmission drive link to the motor crank arm. Then remove drive link from the motor crank arm. See **Figure 63**.
6. Disconnect the electrical wiring at the wiper motor.
7. *Air conditioned vehicles only*: Support the wiper motor and remove bolts attaching wiper motor to panel. Then remove motor crank arm nut by holding crank arm with vise

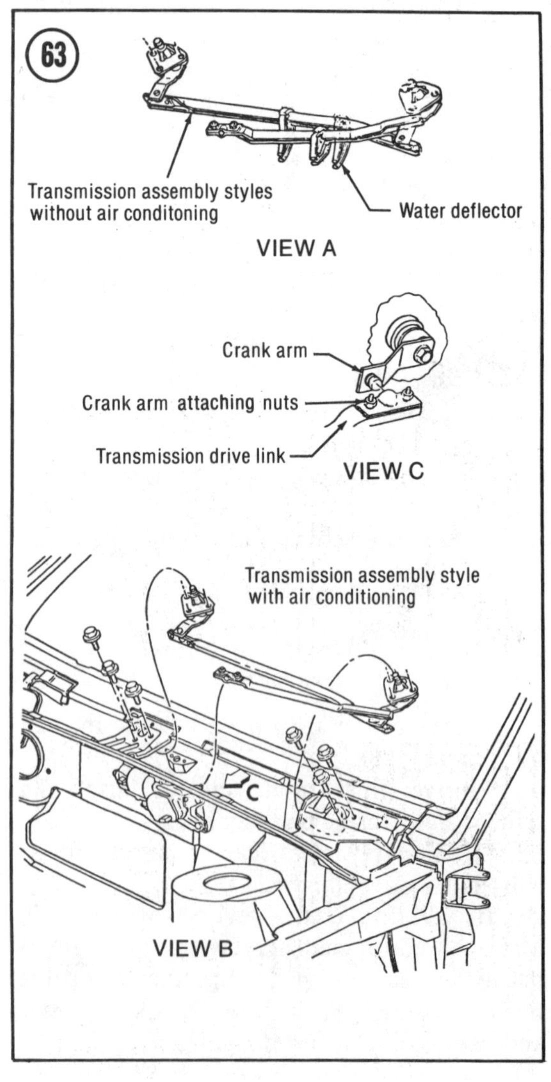

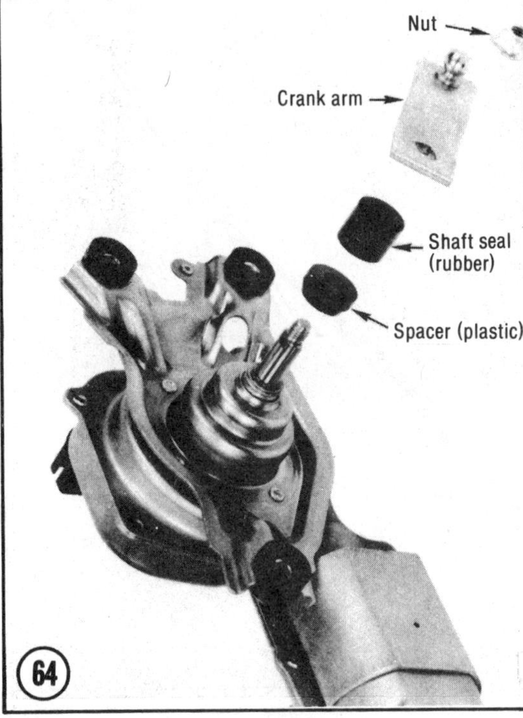

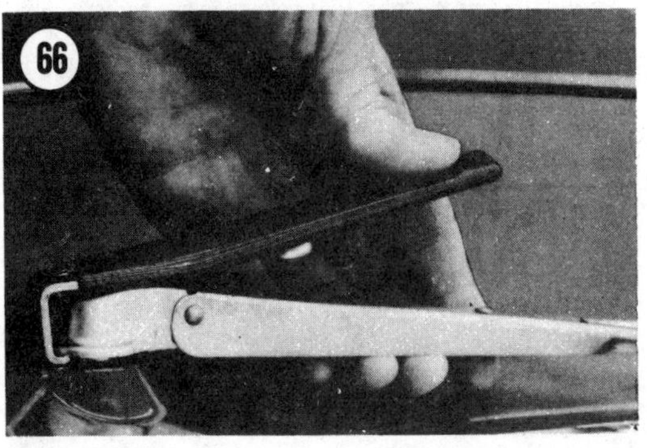

grip pliers and removing nut with box-end wrench. See **Figure 64**.

CAUTION

Bolts securing wiper motor to panel must be removed prior to removing crank arm retaining nut to prevent damage to wiper motor internal nylon gear.

CAUTION

The crank arm on air conditioned vehicles is removed to provide additional removal clearance to prevent damage to air conditioner evaporator unit and tubing. If additional clearance is needed, remove plastic cover and park switch assembly from wiper motor as discussed under ***Park Switch Removal***.

8. *Non-air conditioned vehicles only*: Remove bolts attaching wiper motor assembly to panel.
9. Remove wiper motor by rotating motor assembly up and outward from panel.
10. Inspect all the linkage points for wear, looseness or binding. Stiff linkage may be the cause for the motor's failure. Replace the linkage if its condition is doubtful.
11. Install by reversing the removal steps. On air conditioned vehicles, install the crank arm attaching nut after the wiper motor is positioned through front end of panel and the park switch and cover (if necessary). On all vehicles, make sure that the motor is in the park position (**Figure 65**) and that the linkage is not reversed (**Figure 63**). Tighten wiper motor attaching bolts to 31-44 in.-lb. (35-44.3 N•m).

CAUTION

Make sure the windshield is wet during the testing so it will not get scratched.

Wiper Arm Replacement

To replace the wiper arm and blade assembly, pry the wiper arm off the wiper motor transmission shaft as shown in **Figure 66**. On vehicles equipped with a wet blade system, remove the washer hose from the wiper arm (**Figure 67**). To install, reverse the removal proecedures. The proper park position of the wiper arm and blade assembly

8

is 2 in. (50 mm) above the windshield lower reveal molding. When the installation is complete, check the operation of the wipers.

CAUTION
Make sure the windshield is wet during the testing so it will not get scratched.

HORN

Horn System Check

If the horn does not sound when the horn button is depressed or if the sound is abnormal, check all electrical connections, horn fuse and battery condition. If the fuse and wiring connections are satisfactory, but the horn still does not operate correctly, perform the horn system tests in **Figure 68** (Citation and Phoenix) or **Figure 69** (Skylark and Omega). The horn operating system is shown in **Figure 70** (Citation and Phoenix) and **Figure 71** (Skylark and Omega) and should be used with the appropriate system tests (**Figure 68** or **Figure 69**). The horn relay is located at the right side of the fuse box.

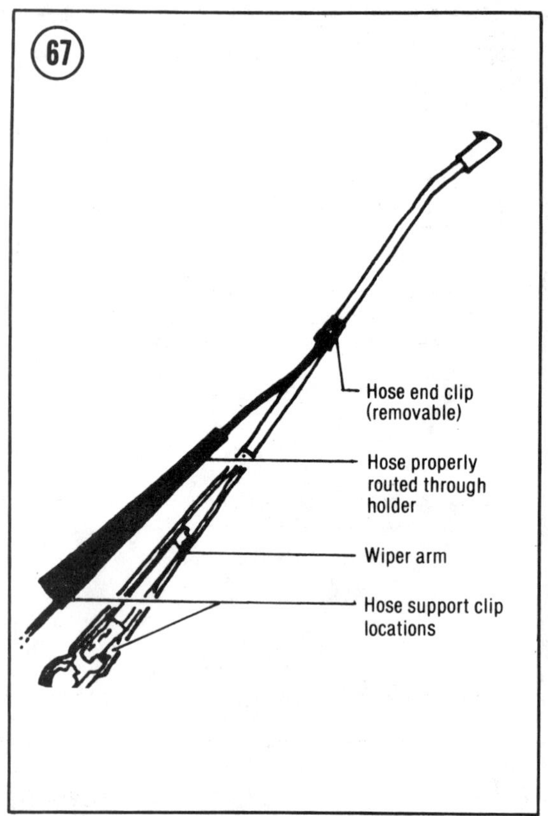

68

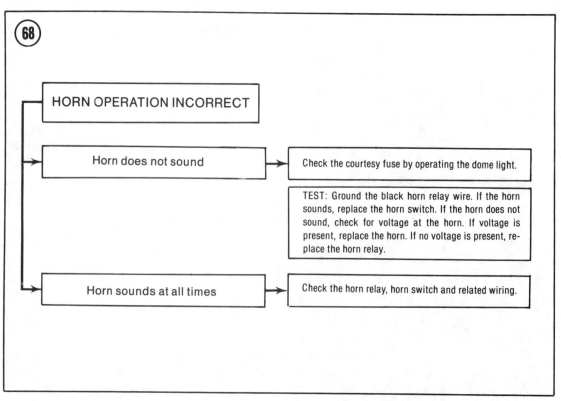

HORN OPERATION INCORRECT

Condition	Action
Horn does not sound	Check the courtesy fuse by operating the dome light.
	TEST: Ground the black horn relay wire. If the horn sounds, replace the horn switch. If the horn does not sound, check for voltage at the horn. If voltage is present, replace the horn. If no voltage is present, replace the horn relay.
Horn sounds at all times	Check the horn relay, horn switch and related wiring.

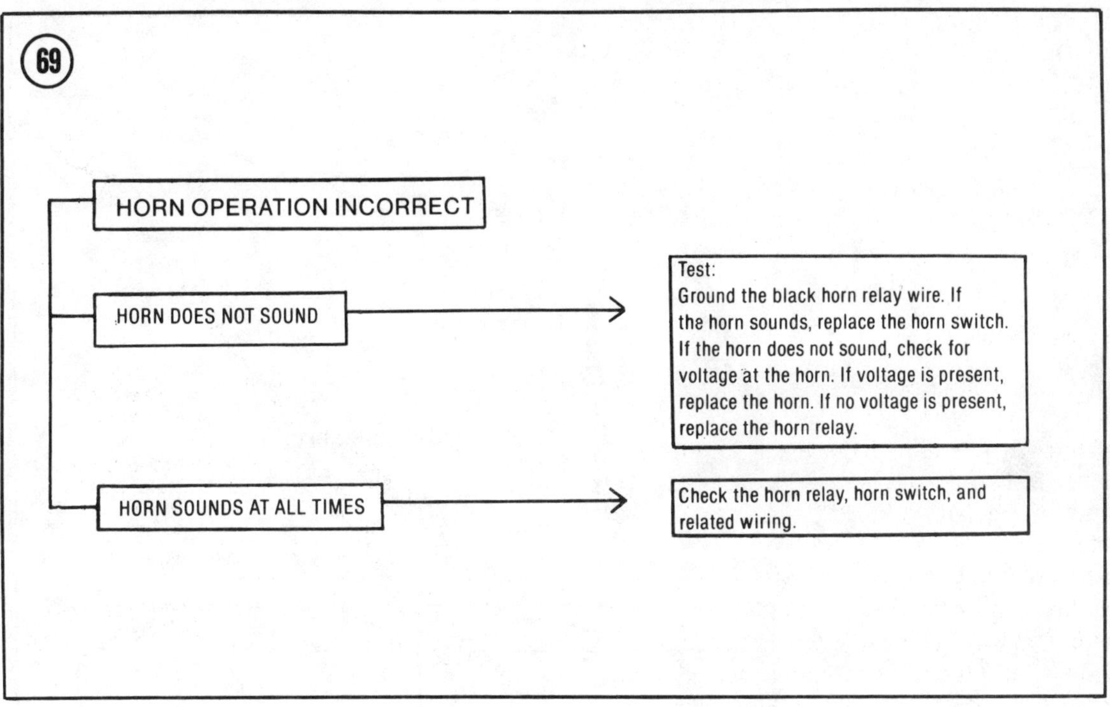
69
HORN OPERATION INCORRECT
HORN DOES NOT SOUND
Test:
Ground the black horn relay wire. If the horn sounds, replace the horn switch. If the horn does not sound, check for voltage at the horn. If voltage is present, replace the horn. If no voltage is present, replace the horn relay.
HORN SOUNDS AT ALL TIMES
Check the horn relay, horn switch, and related wiring.

70

HORN

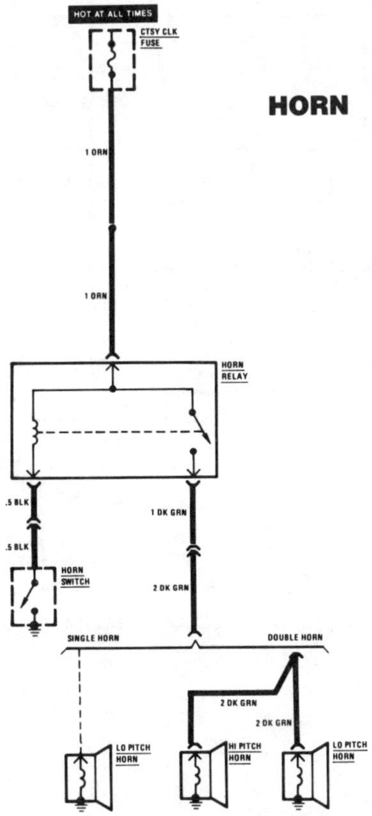

HOT AT ALL TIMES
CTSY CLK FUSE
1 ORN
1 ORN
HORN RELAY
.5 BLK
.5 BLK
HORN SWITCH
1 DK GRN
2 DK GRN
SINGLE HORN
DOUBLE HORN
2 DK GRN
2 DK GRN
LO PITCH HORN
HI PITCH HORN
LO PITCH HORN

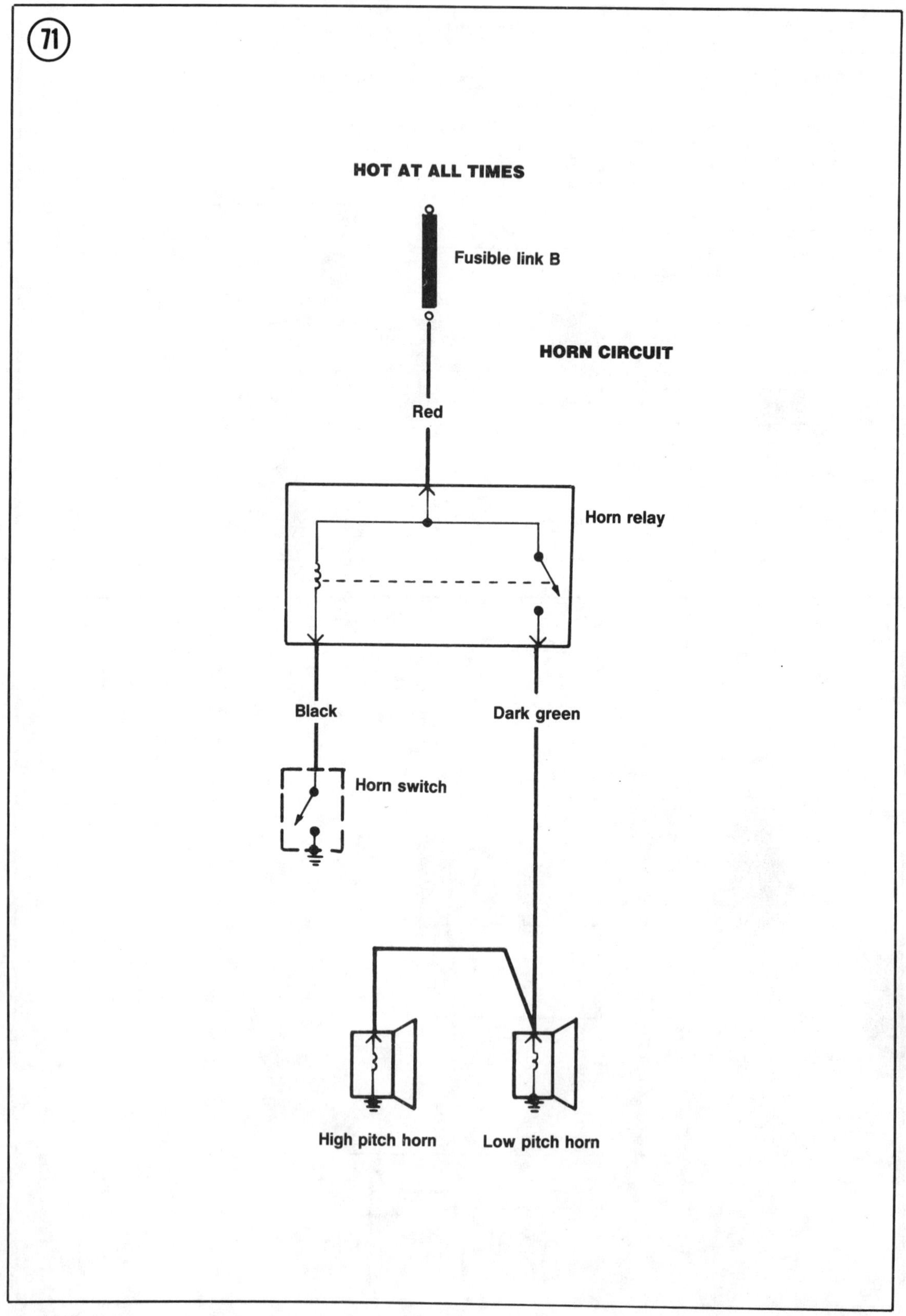
71
HOT AT ALL TIMES
Fusible link B
HORN CIRCUIT
Red
Horn relay
Black
Dark green
Horn switch
High pitch horn
Low pitch horn

Table 1 BATTERY LOAD TEST

Battery Type*	Test Load
85-60	170 amps
87-60	210 amps
89-60	230 amps

* See information on battery top.

Table 2 TEMPERATURE VS. VOLTAGE DROP

Estimated Temperature	Minimum Voltage
70° F (21° C)	9.6
50° F (10° C)	9.4
30° F (0° C)	9.1
15° F (-10° C)	8.8
0° F (-18° C)	8.5
0° F (below:-18° C)	8.0

Note: If voltage does not drop below minimum, the battery is good.

Table 3 INDICATOR LAMP CIRCUIT CHECK

Switch	Lamp	Engine
Off	Off	Stopped
On	On	Stopped
On	Off	Running

Table 4 BULB SPECIFICATIONS

Bulb	SAE No.
Headlamp	6052
Front park and directional signal	1157NA
Front side marker	194
Rear side marker	194
Tail & stop light	1157
License plate	194
Backup	1156
Directional signal (rear)	1156
Luggage compartment	1003
Indicator lamps	194 (1)
Instrument panel	194
Radio dial	1893
Header map lamp	211-2
Underhood lamp	631
Courtesy	906
Dome	561 (2)
Reading lamp	1004

(1) Headlamp Hi Beam indicator lamp 161
(2) Dome with reading lamp 212

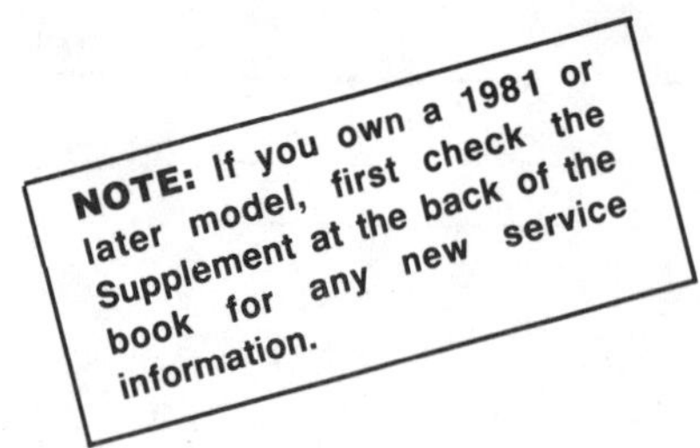

NOTE: If you own a 1981 or
later model, first check the
Supplement at the back of the
book for any new service
information.

CHAPTER NINE

TRANSAXLE SYSTEM

This chapter covers removal, installation and, where practical, the repair of the clutch and manual and automatic transaxle components.

CLUTCH

Major clutch components are the driving members, the driven members and the operating members. See **Figure 1**. The driving members consist of the engine flywheel and the pressure plate; both are machined flat surfaces. The pressure plate is located in a steel cover bolted to the flywheel. The driven member is the clutch disc. A splined hub is free to slide lengthwise along the input shaft splines. Both the driving and driven members are held in contact by spring pressure. The clutch operating members consist of the clutch pedal, clutch adjusting pawl/quadrant, clutch cable, clutch fork lever, clutch shaft-and-fork assembly and the release bearing.

Table 1 and **Table 2** are at the end of the chapter.

CLUTCH LINKAGE

A self-adjusting clutch mechanism is attached to the clutch pedal and bracket assembly. See **Figure 2**.

Adjustment

The clutch should be adjusted every 5,000 miles. To adjust the clutch, pull the clutch pedal up to its rubber bumper and then release. This disengages the pawl from the quadrant ratchet teeth and changes the effective cable length.

Inspection

Before checking major clutch components for cause of failure or malfunction, check the clutch linkage to make sure the clutch is releasing properly.

1. Start engine and place gear selector in NEUTRAL. Apply the parking brake.
2. Press clutch pedal in approximately 1/2 in. (13 mm) from floor mat. Move shift lever between FIRST and REVERSE several times. If shifting is accomplished without clashing into REVERSE, clutch is fully releasing. If shift is not smooth, clutch is not fully releasing and clutch linkage should be inspected for loose or damaged parts and corrected as necessary.
3. Have an assistant sit inside vehicle and press clutch pedal to floor mat. Observe the clutch fork lever travel at the transaxle. The end of the clutch fork lever should travel approximately 1 39/64-1 13/16 in. (40.88-46.00 mm.)

NOTE
Steps 4 and 5 describe inspection of clutch self-adjusting mechanism.

4. Depress the clutch pedal and look for the shift pawl to firmly engage with the teeth in the ratchet assembly (**Figure 2**).

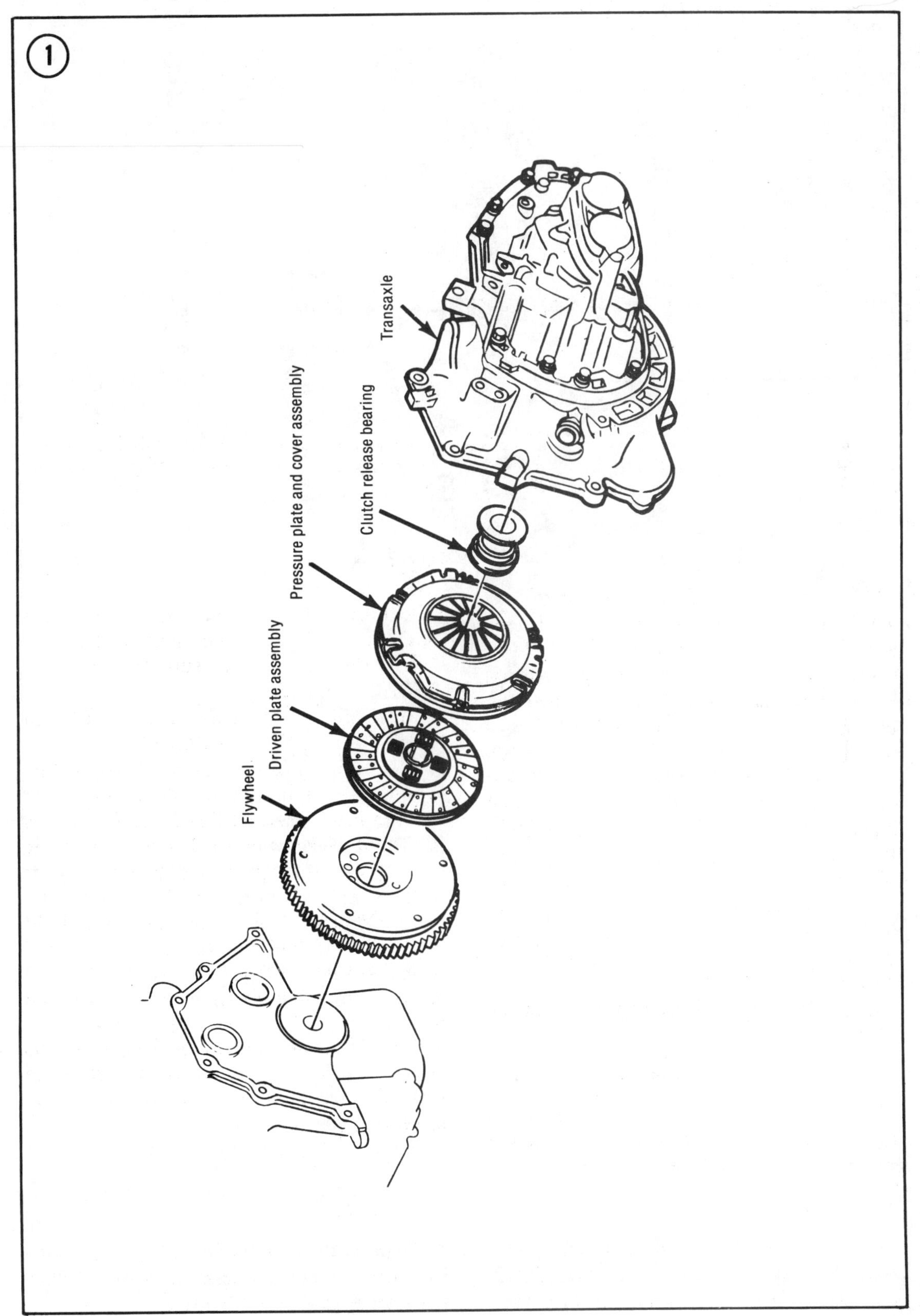
1
Transaxle
Pressure plate and cover assembly
Clutch release bearing
Driven plate assembly
Flywheel

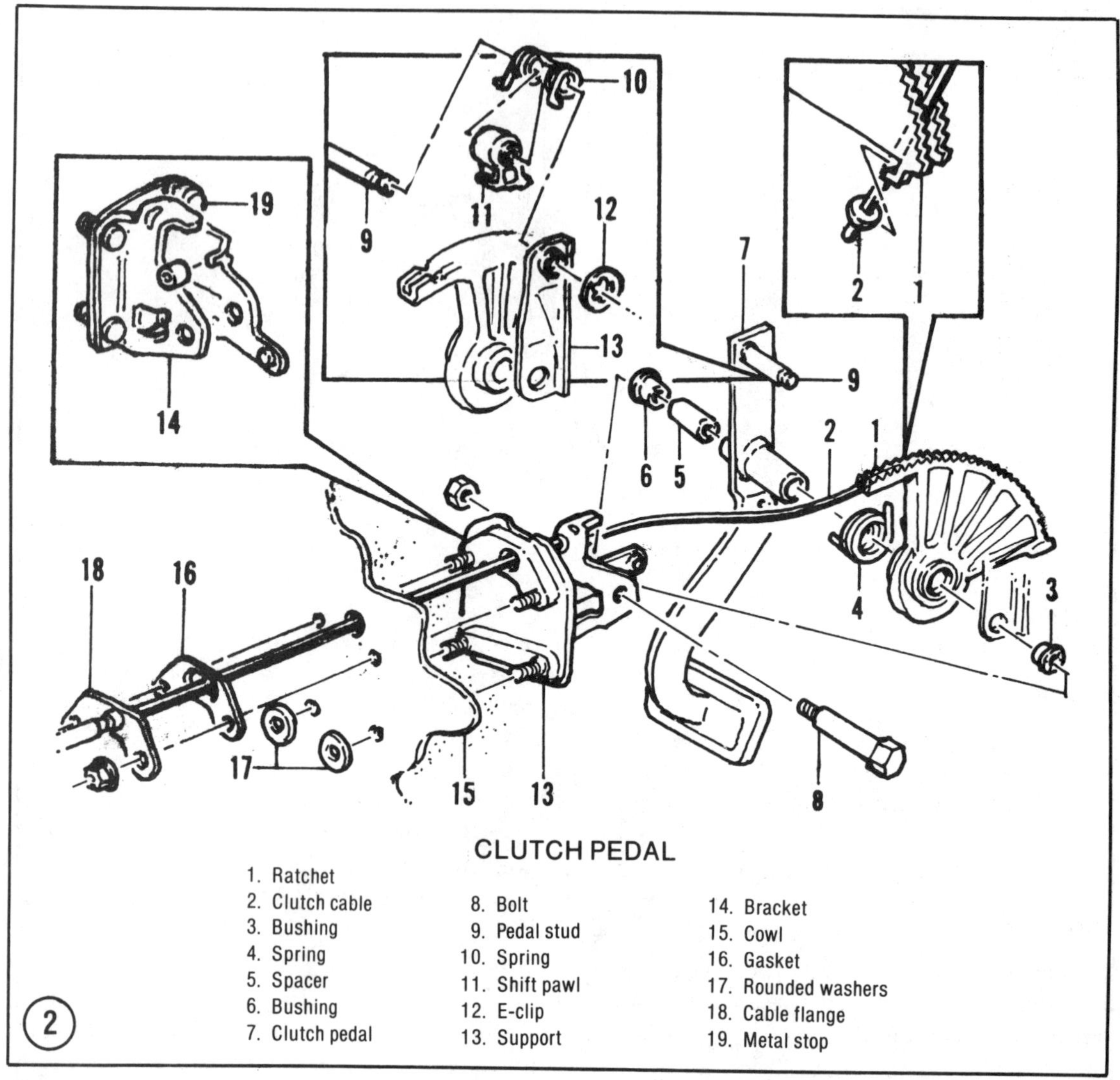

2

CLUTCH PEDAL

1. Ratchet
2. Clutch cable
3. Bushing
4. Spring
5. Spacer
6. Bushing
7. Clutch pedal
8. Bolt
9. Pedal stud
10. Spring
11. Shift pawl
12. E-clip
13. Support
14. Bracket
15. Cowl
16. Gasket
17. Rounded washers
18. Cable flange
19. Metal stop

5. Release the clutch. The shift pawl should disengage from the rachet teeth by the metal stop on the bracket (**Figure 2**).

CLUTCH CABLE REPLACEMENT

Refer to **Figure 3** for this procedure.

1. Disconnect end of clutch cable from the clutch release lever at the transaxle.

CAUTION
When disconnecting the clutch cable, do not allow the cable to snap rapidly toward rear of vehicle or damage to teeth on ratchet assembly could occur.

2. Refer to **Figure 2** and disconnect the clutch cable from the ratchet assembly. Lift the locking pawl away from ratchet assembly and slide cable out on right side.
3. Remove bracket(s) attaching clutch cable to transaxle assembly. Remove clutch cable from vehicle.
4. Install bracket gasket on 2 upper studs where bracket is attached to transaxle assembly. Install new clutch cable with the retaining flange against the bracket.
5. Attach the end of the cable to the ratchet assembly. Make sure to route cable underneath the shift pawl.
6. Attach 2 upper retainer mounting studs and tighten to 25 ft.-lb. (40 N•m).
7. Attach cable to bracket mounted on transaxle.

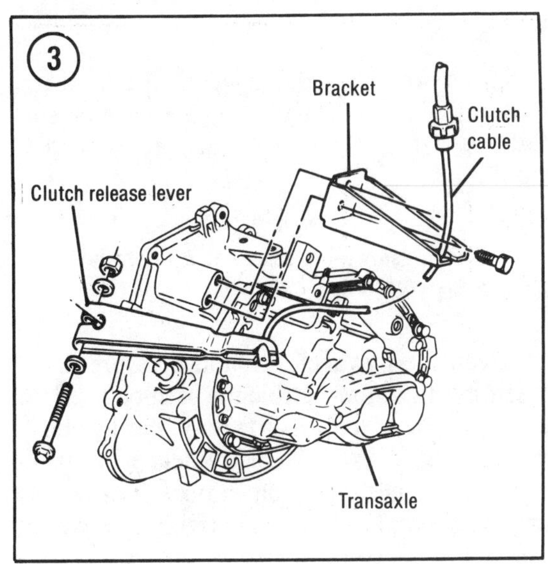

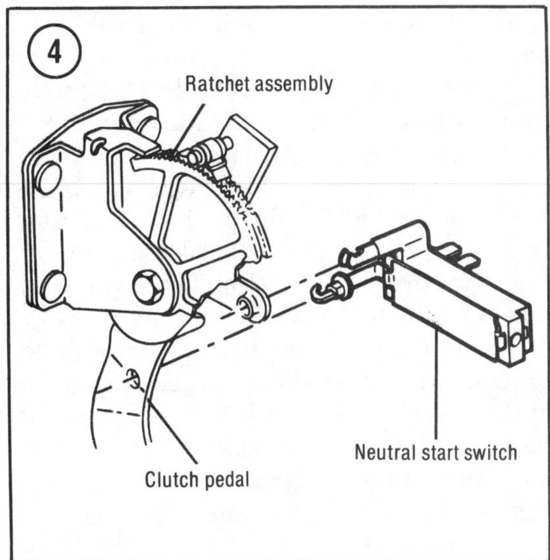

8. Attach the outer end of the cable to the clutch release lever.

CAUTION
When attaching cable to clutch release lever, do not pull on cable excessively or damage may occur to stop on ratchet.

CLUTCH PEDAL

Removal

Refer to **Figure 2** for this procedure.

1. Disconnect the clutch cable at the clutch release lever (**Figure 3**).

CAUTION
When disconnecting the clutch cable, do not allow the cable to snap rapidly toward rear of vehicle or damage to teeth on ratchet assembly could occur.

2. Disconnect the clutch cable from the ratchet assembly. Lift the locking pawl away from ratchet assembly and slide cable out on right side.
3. Remove the nuts attaching the clutch pedal mounting bracket to the engine side of cowl. Remove the gasket.
4. Remove the neutral start switch connector at the switch. Remove pedal assembly from vehicle.
5. Disconnect the neutral start switch from the clutch pedal and bracket. See **Figure 4**.
6. Remove the bolt securing the self-adjusting mechanism to the pedal and bracket assembly. Remove the following parts from the mechanism:
   a. Spacer
   b. E-clip
   c. Pawl and spring
   d. Support plate
   e. Bushing (2)
   f. Rachet assembly

Inspect and replace each part as required.

9

Installation

Refer to **Figure 2** for the following procedure.

1. Install the ratchet spring onto the pedal. Make sure the tang end of the spring is inserted into the pedal. Then rotate the ratchet into the installed position, and seat the ratchet against the pedal. The ratchet must seat against the pedal with the ratchet stop against the back side of the pedal.
2. Install the locking pawl and spring onto the stud at the top of the pedal. Make sure the spring forces the pawl toward the ratchet.
3. Insert the support onto the clutch pedal. Secure with new E-clip. Check operation of ratchet and pawl to ensure assembly is installed correctly at this point.
4. Lubricate the bushings with a coating of SAE 10 engine oil and install bushings onto the pedal assembly.

5. Insert spacer into end of right side bushing.
6. Secure the pedal to the bracket assembly by installing bolt and nut. Make sure the bushing flanges on each side of the pedal assembly contact the bracket housing.
7. Check the operation of the pawl and ratchet to ensure that the pawl disengages from the ratchet in the released position, and that the ratchet rotates fully from stop to stop.
8. Mount the pedal and bracket assembly to the cowl. Insert the gasket into position on the upper studs. Install the 2 special rounded-edge washers underneath the nuts on the lower studs. Tighten the lower nuts finger-tight. Leave upper nuts off.
9. Attach end of clutch cable to ratchet.

NOTE
When attaching end of clutch cable to ratchet, make sure to route cable underneath the shift pawl.

10. Attach the cable flange against gasket on cowl. Install the upper nuts, then tighten all 4 attaching nuts.
11. Attach the outer end of the cable to the clutch release lever (**Figure 3**). Make sure not to pull on the cable, since overloading the cable could damage the ratchet stop.

CLUTCH REPLACEMENT

Removal

Refer to **Figure 1** for this procedure.

1. Remove the transaxle assembly as described under *Transaxle Removal* in this chapter.
2. Mark the flywheel and the edge of the pressure plate so that they may be reassembled in the same relative positions.
3. Loosen pressure plate assembly-to-flywheel attaching bolts one turn at a time. Unscrew bolts diagonally opposite one another rather than working directly around the clutch pressure plate. This insures that heavy spring pressure will not warp the pressure plate.
4. Remove the clutch.

Inspection

Never replace damaged clutch parts without giving thought to the reason for failure. To do this only invites repeated trouble.

NOTE
The pressure plate assembly is not to be disassembled. If defective, it must be replaced.

1. Clean the flywheel face and pressure plate assembly in a non-petroleum base cleaner.
2. Check the friction surface of the flywheel for scoring, roughness or evidence of heat. Slight roughness may be removed with fine emery cloth. If surface is deeply scored or grooved, replace it.
3. Check the pressure plate for cracked or broken springs, evidence of heat, cracked or scored friction surface and looseness. Check spring fingers for wear.
4. Check the clutch disc lining for wear, cracks, oil and burns. Check for loose rivets and cracks in the spring leaves and carrier plate. Ensure that the disc slides freely on the transaxle spline without excessive radial play. If the disc is defective, replace it with a new one. If the lining is oily, check the pilot bushing, engine rear main bearing and transaxle seal for oil leakage.
5. Check the release bearing for wear to determine if it caused the original trouble. Never reuse a release bearing unless necessary. When other clutch parts are worn, the bearing is probably also worn. If necessary to reinstall the old bearing, do not wash it in solvent; wipe it with a clean cloth.
6. Check clutch, fork and pivot shaft for wear.

Clutch Installation

1. Clean the flywheel and pressure plate surface with non-petroleum solvent.

CAUTION
Do not use petroleum-based solvents such as gasoline.

2. Wash your hands *clean* with soap and water before proceeding.

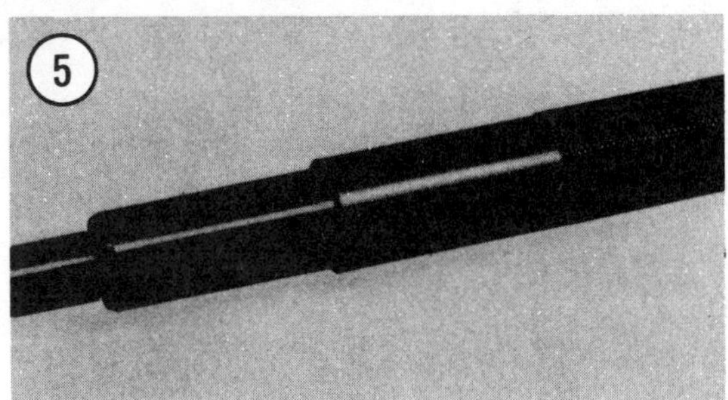

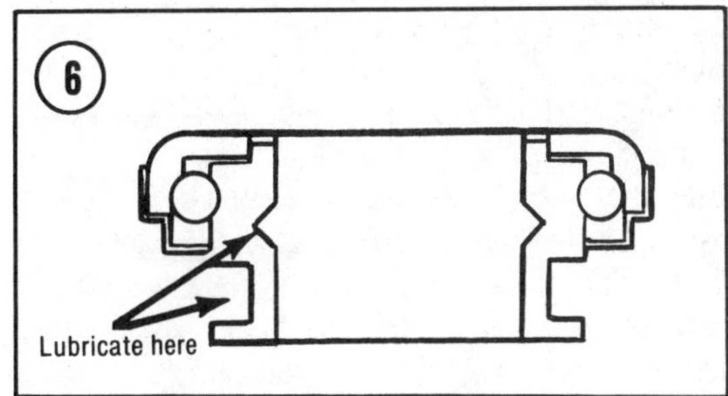

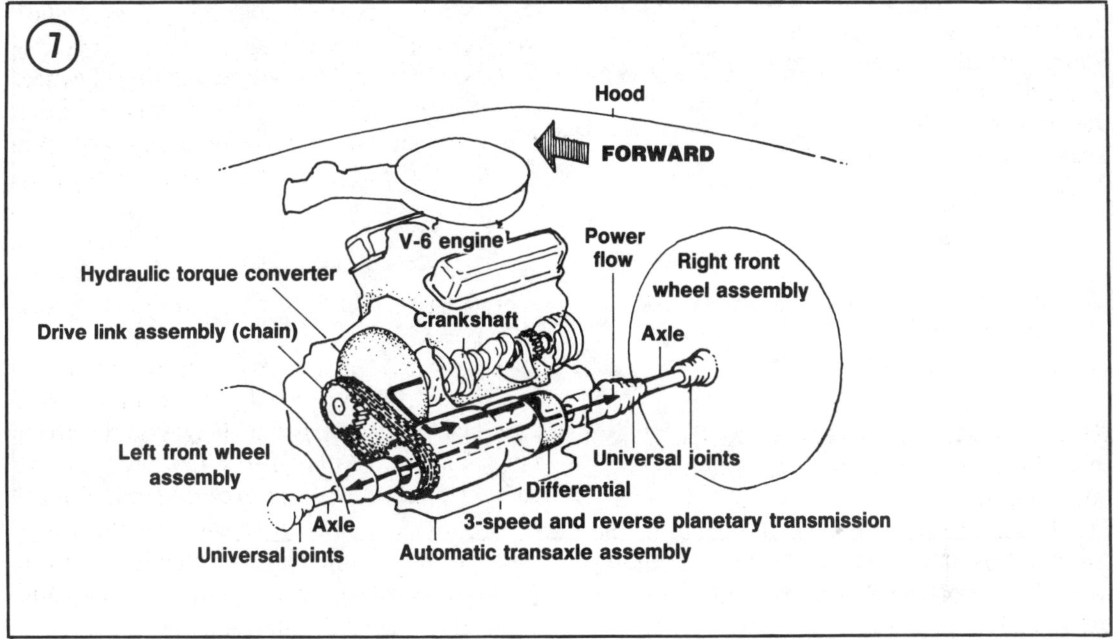

3. Place the clutch disc and pressure plate in position on the flywheel and support with GM tool part No. J-29074 (**Figure 5**). If the original pressure plate is being reused, line up the alignment marks made during removal.

NOTE
*The driven disc is installed with the damper springs offset toward the transaxle. Stamped letters on the driven disc identify **"Flywheel Side"**.*

4. Install the pressure plate cover bolts. Tighten gradually in a diagonal pattern to prevent warping the clutch cover, then remove the aligning tool. Correct torque is 13-18 ft.-lb. (18-24 N•m).
5. Lubricate the release bearing outside diameter and inside diameter recess. See **Figure 6**.
6. Install transaxle as described under *Transaxle Installation.*

TRANSAXLE

All engine assemblies are transversely mounted on the right side of the vehicle (e.g., the engine sits sideways in the engine compartment). A transaxle is transversely mounted on the left side of the vehicle and connects directly to the engine. A transaxle is a complete unit consisting of all transmission components—clutch, gearbox, gears, and final drive—connected directly to the drive axles. **Figure 7** shows the V6 engine/transaxle assembly. The 4-cylinder engine is similar.

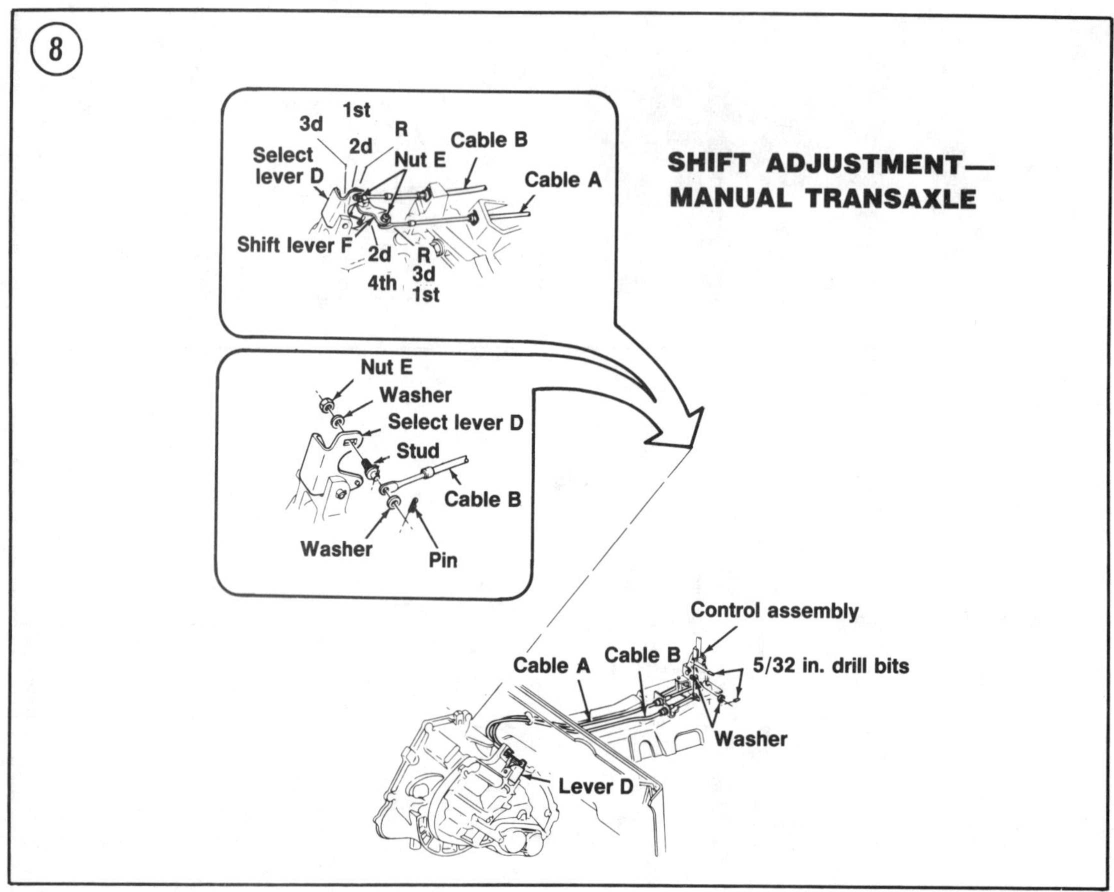

MANUAL TRANSAXLE

The MT-125 manual constant mesh transaxle is standard equipment on all vehicles. Components of the MT-125 transaxle consist of the aluminum transaxle case, aluminum clutch cover, input shaft, output shaft, and the differential assembly. The differential is an arrangement of gears which divides the torque between the drive axle shafts and allows them to rotate at different speeds. Manual transaxle tightening torques are found in **Table 1**.

Shift Cable Adjustment

Two cable assemblies are used to shift the gear assembly. Place the transaxle into first gear before making adjustments. Refer to **Figure 8** for the following procedures.

NOTE

Steps 1-3 describe adjustments performed at the control assembly.

1. Remove the shifter boot and retainer from inside the passenger compartment.
2. Insert two 5/32 in. drill bits into the alignment holes in the control assembly. Drill bits will ensure transaxle assembly is held in first gear.
3. Attach the 2 shift cables to the control assembly. Secure with studs and pin retainers. Make sure cables are routed correctly and operate freely with studs and pins installed.

NOTE

Steps 4-7 describe adjustments performed at transaxle housing. Do not remove 2 drill bits previously installed at the control assembly.

4. Place the transaxle into first gear by pushing the rail selector shaft down to the point where resistance of the inhibitor spring is felt.
5. Rotate the shift lever fully counterclockwise.

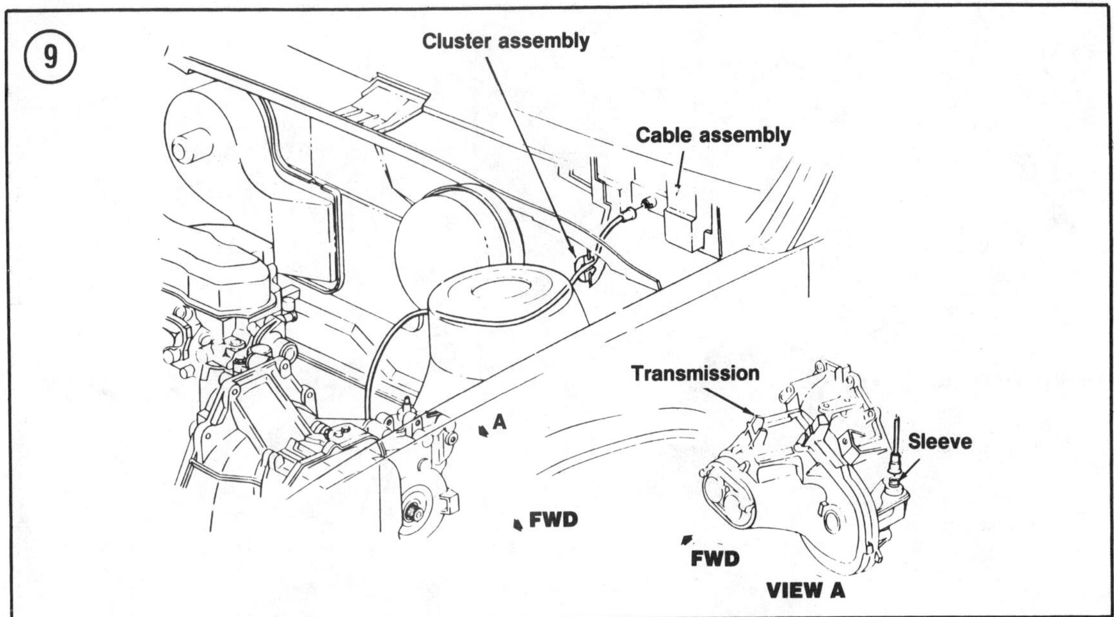

6. Install stud with cable "A" attached into the slotted area in shift lever "F".
7. Pull on lever "D" to remove lash and install stud with cable "B" attached into the slotted area of the select lever "D".
8. Remove the 2 drill bits installed at the control assembly. Install the shifter boot and retainer.
9. Road test vehicle.

NOTE
Because the shift cable adjustment range is minimal, it may be necessary to fine tune the adjustment after road testing.

Transaxle Removal

The transaxle assembly has been designed to be removed from underneath the vehicle. This procedure requires that the engine/transaxle cradle assembly be partially removed while the engine is held in position by a support fixture. However, it is recommended that the home mechanic not attempt this removal method without the use of a hydraulic lift and the required engine support fixture. Jackstands, the normal home mechanic support fixture (described in Chapter Two), would not provide the mechanic with the necessary room or *safety* to remove the transaxle. Therefore, to remove the manual transaxle assembly, it will be necessary to first remove the engine, then lift out the transaxle.

1. Disconnect battery ground cable from transaxle case.
2. Remove the engine assembly as described in Chapter Four (4-cylinder) or Chapter Five (V6).
3. Remove the speedometer cable at the transaxle. See **Figure 9**. For vehicles equipped with cruise control, remove the transaxle speedometer cable at the cruise control transducer.
4. Remove the retaining clip and washer from the transaxle shift linkage at the transaxle. Remove clips securing shift cables to mounting bosses on transaxle housing. See **Figure 8**.
5. Unlock steering column with ignition key.
6. Raise vehicle and place on jackstands.
7. Drain transaxle oil.
8. Disconnect the front and rear transaxle mounts. Refer to **Figure 10**.
9. Remove top bolt from the lower front transaxle damper, if so equipped.
10. Remove front wheels.
11. Remove both the left and right side drive shafts from the transaxle as described under *Drive Shaft Removal* in this chapter.
12. Attach an engine lifting hoist to the transaxle and remove the transaxle from the engine compartment.

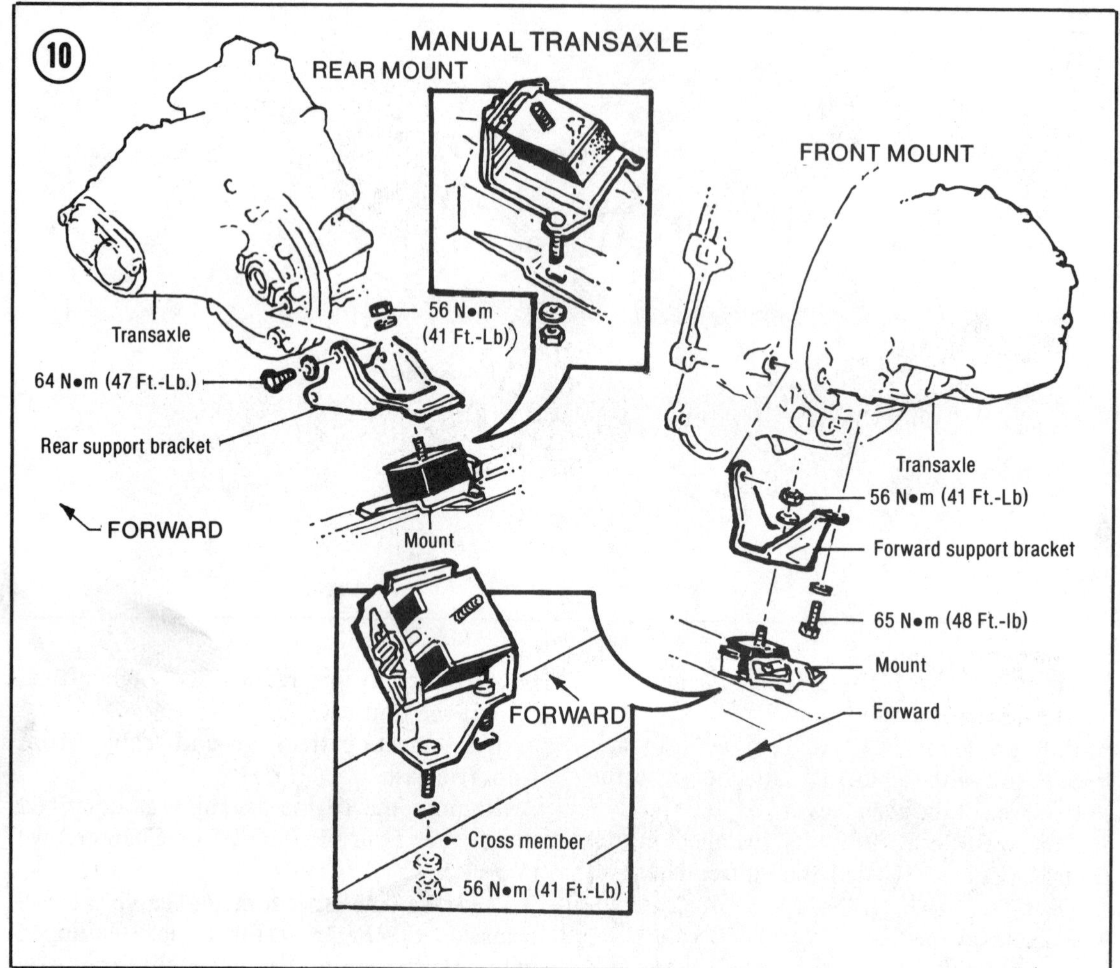

Transaxle Installation

1. Reverse removal procedure to install, plus the following.
2. Fill transaxle to proper level as described in Chapter Three.
3. Drive vehicle and check operation of transaxle.

TRANSAXLE CASE DISASSEMBLY

The special tools required to perform these procedures are shown in **Figure 11**. If you do not have these tools or suitable substitutes, and/or if you are not absolutely sure of your mechanical ability, you should not try to perform the procedures. If you have the necessary tools and skills, read this procedure and the assembly procedure, which follows and make sure you understand every step before starting. If there is any portion of the procedure that you do not understand and you cannot clear it up by studying the steps and illustrations, it is advisable not to start, but to refer service work to your General Motors dealership.

Refer to **Figure 12** while performing the following procedures.

1. Thoroughly clean the outside of the transaxle before disassembly. Place it on a workbench or stand.
2. Remove the bolts securing the clutch cover to the transaxle case.

NOTE

It may be necessary to tap the clutch cover with a plastic hammer to loosen it from the clutch/differential housing. Anaerobic sealant is used between the case and cover instead of a gasket.

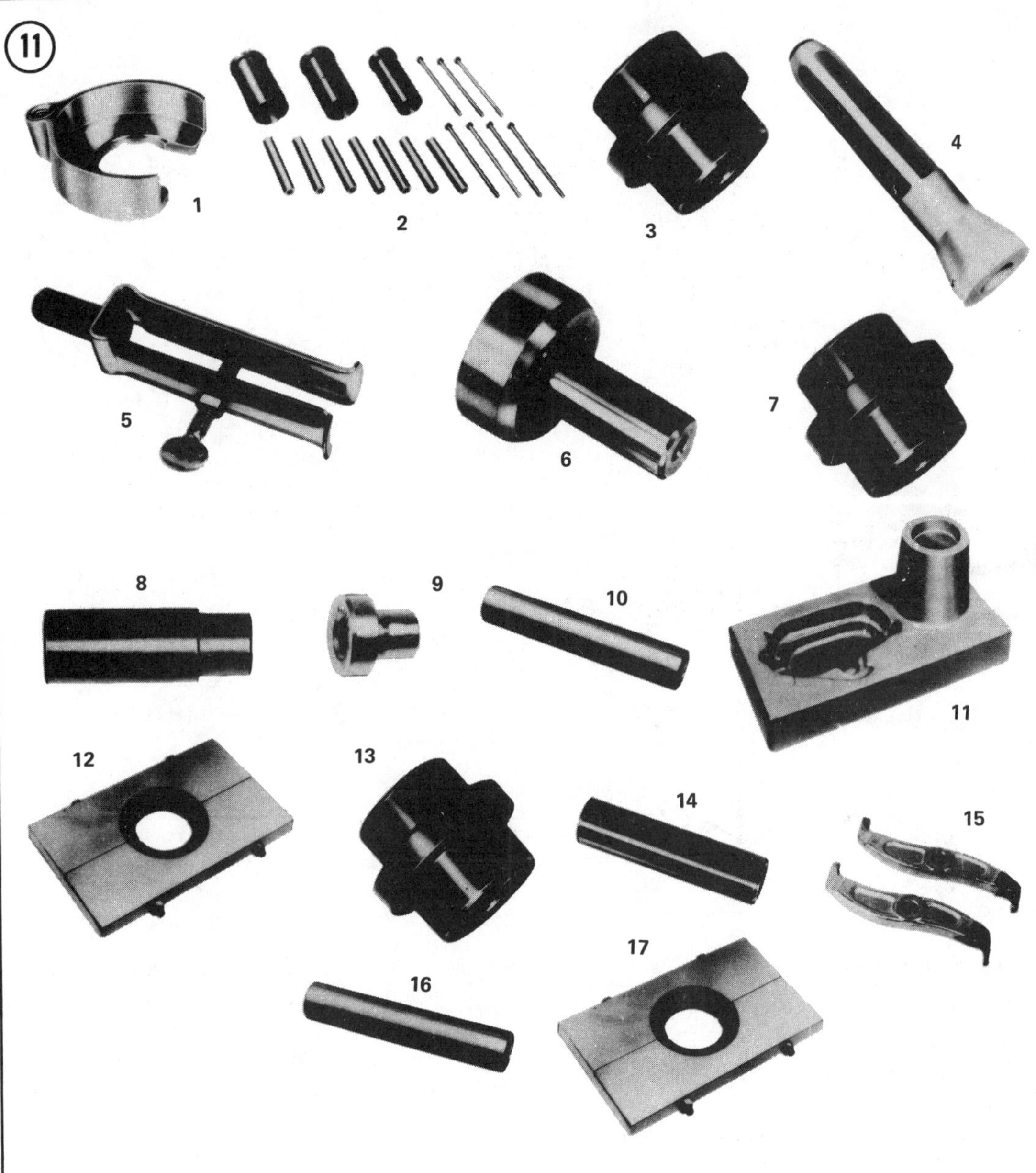

1. J28468 Axle Shaft Remover
2. J26935 Shim Selector Set
3. J26936 Installer, R.H. Input Shaft Seal and R.H. Bearing Cup
4. J26937 Shifter Shaft Seal Installer
5. J26941 Transaxle Case Bearing Cup Remover
6. J26942 Input & Output Shaft, Inner Race Installer
7. J26938 Axle Shaft Seal & Bearing Cup Installer
8. J26943 Input & Output Shaft, Pilot For Bearing Removal
9. J22919 Differential Inner Bearing Installer
10. J28406 Input Shaft R.H. Bearing Installer
11. J28408 Holding Fixture
12. J26946 Input Shaft R.H. Bearing Remover
13. J23423-A Transaxle Case Bearing Cup Remover
14. J28411 Shifter Shaft Alignment Pin
15. J22888-20 Differential Side Bearing Puller Legs
16. J28412 Clutch Shaft Bushing Installer/Remover
17. J22912-01 Input Shaft L.H. Bearing Remover

J22227-A Output Shaft R.H. Bearing Remover (Not Shown)

J28410 Gasket Remover (Not Shown)

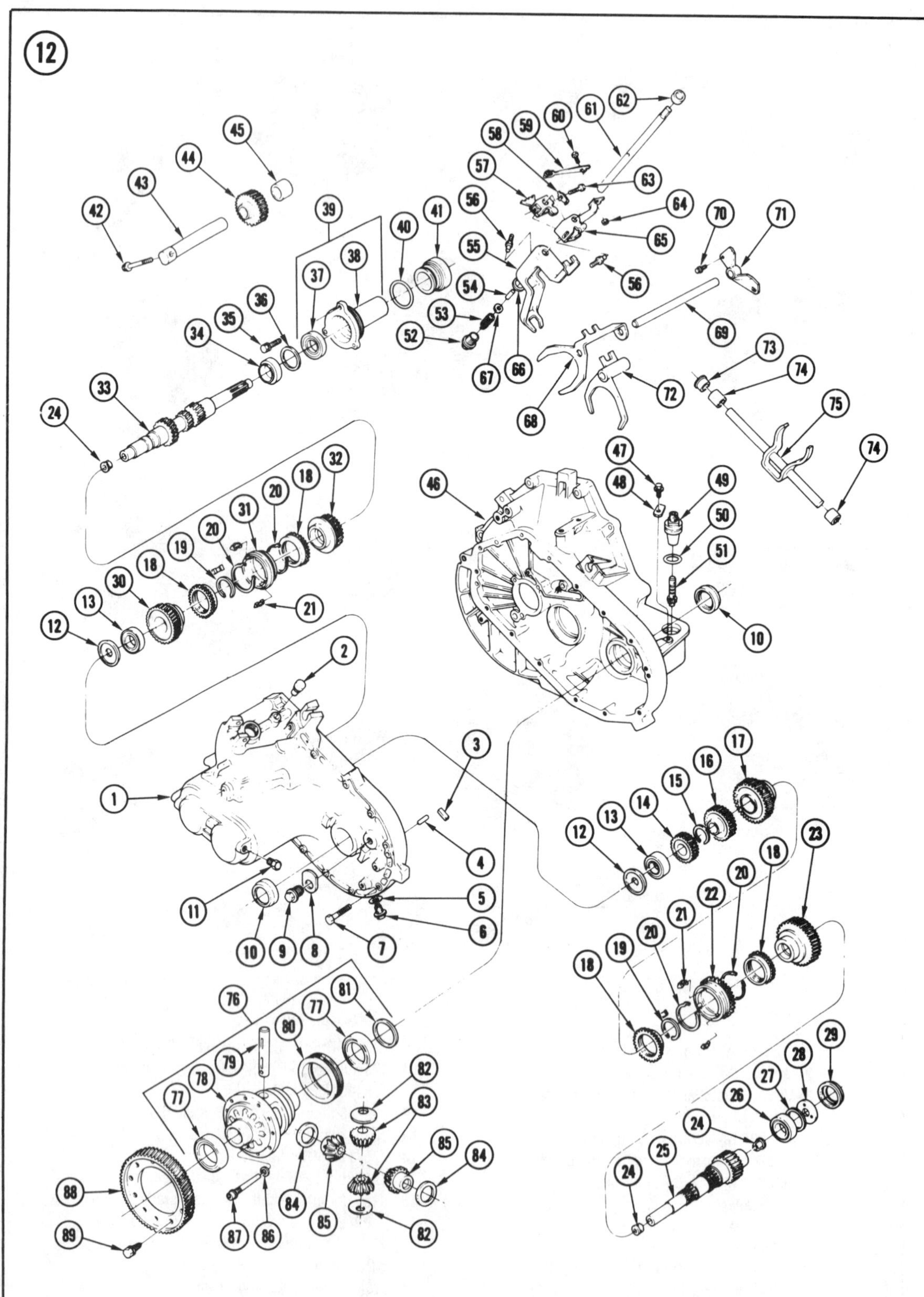
12
1
2
3
4
5
6
7
8
9
10
11
12
13
14
15
16
17
18
19
20
21
22
23
24
25
26
27
28
29
30
31
32
33
34
35
36
37
38
39
40
41
42
43
44
45
46
47
48
49
50
51
52
53
54
55
56
57
58
59
60
61
62
63
64
65
66
67
68
69
70
71
72
73
74
75
76
77
78
79
80
81
82
83
84
85
86
87
88
89

TRANSAXLE CASE

1. Case assembly
2. Vent assembly
3. Magnet
4. Pin
5. Drain screw washer
6. Drain screw
7. Bolt
8. Fill plug washer
9. Fill plug
10. Axle shaft seal assembly
11. Plug
12. Oil shield
13. Bearing assembly
14. 4th speed output gear
15. 3rd speed output gear retaining ring
16. 3rd speed output gear
17. 2nd speed output gear
18. Synchronizer blocking ring
19. Synchronizer retaining ring
20. Synchronizer key retaining spring
21. Synchronizer key
22. Synchronizer assembly
23. 1st speed output gear
24. Oil shield sleeve
25. Output gear
26. Output bearing assembly
27. Output gear bearing oil shield retainer
28. Output bearing oil shield
29. Output gear bearing oil shield retainer
30. 4th speed input gear
31. Synchronizer assembly
32. 3rd speed input gear
33. Input cluster gear
34. Input bearing assembly
35. Screw
36. Input gear bearing adjustment shim
37. Input gear seal assembly
38. Input gear retainer
39. Input gear bearing retainer assembly
40. Input gear bearing retainer seal
41. Clutch release bearing assembly
42. Reverse idler screw & washer
43. Reverse idler shaft
44. Reverse idler gear assembly
45. Reverse idler shaft spacer
46. Clutch & differential housing assembly
47. Screw
48. Speedo gear fitting retainer
49. Speedo driven gear sleeve
50. Speedo gear sleeve seal
51. Speedo driven gear
52. Reverse inhibitor spring seat
53. Reverse inhibitor spring
54. Pin
55. Reverse shift lever
56. Reverse lever locating stud
57. Detent lever assembly
58. Lock detent lever washer
59. Detent spring
60. Bolt
61. Shift shaft
62. Shift shaft seal assembly
63. Bolt
64. Nut
65. Shift interlock
66. Shift shaft shim
67. Reverse inhibitor spring washer
68. 3rd & 4th shift fork
69. Shift fork shaft
70. Screw
71. Oil guide
72. 1st & 2nd shift fork
73. Clutch fork shaft seal assembly
74. Clutch fork shaft bearing
75. Clutch fork shaft assembly
76. Differential assembly
77. Differential bearing assembly
78. Differential case
79. Differential pinion shaft
80. Speedo drive gear
81. Differential bearing adjustment shim
82. Pinion thrust washer
83. Differential pinion gear
84. Side gear thrust washer
85. Differential side gear
86. Lockwasher
87. Pinion shaft screw
88. Differential ring
89. Bolt

3. Remove the ring gear/differential assembly from the clutch/differential housing (**Figure 13**).

4. Place the shifter shaft in neutral so that the shifter moves freely and does not engage any drive gear.

5. Pry back tab on shift shaft lock and remove bolt from the shifter shaft. Then, referring to **Figure 14**, remove the shift fork shaft from the synchronizer forks.

6. Disengage the reverse shift fork from the guide pin and interlock bracket and remove the shift fork. See **Figure 15**.

7. Remove the reverse idler gear, shaft and spacer assembly by removing the attaching lock bolt from outside of case housing. See **Figure 16**.

8. Refer to **Figure 17** and remove the detent shift lever and interlock assembly. Make sure to leave the shift forks engaged with the synchronizers.

9. Remove the input and output shaft from the case housing as an assembly (**Figure 18**). Make sure to note position of shift fork on shafts, then remove shift forks.

NOTE

Steps 10-14 describe main shaft disassembly procedures.

10. Install main shaft in a press (**Figure 19**). Press the fourth gear and left-hand bearing off the main shaft.

11. Remove the brass blocker ring from the main shaft.

12. Remove the snap ring from the 1-4 synchronizer.

13. Place main shaft in press with third gear supported as shown in **Figure 20**. Press third gear and the 3-4 synchronizer off the main shaft.

14. Using GM tool part No. J-26946 or equivalent to support the right-hand bearing, press the right-hand bearing off the main shaft (**Figure 21**).

NOTE

Steps 15-20 describe countershaft disassembly procedures.

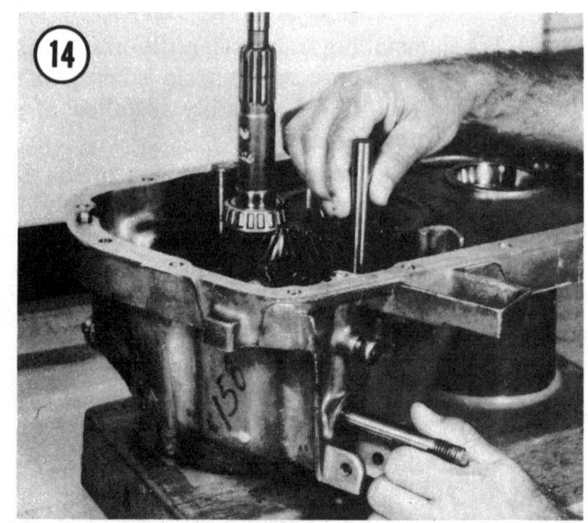

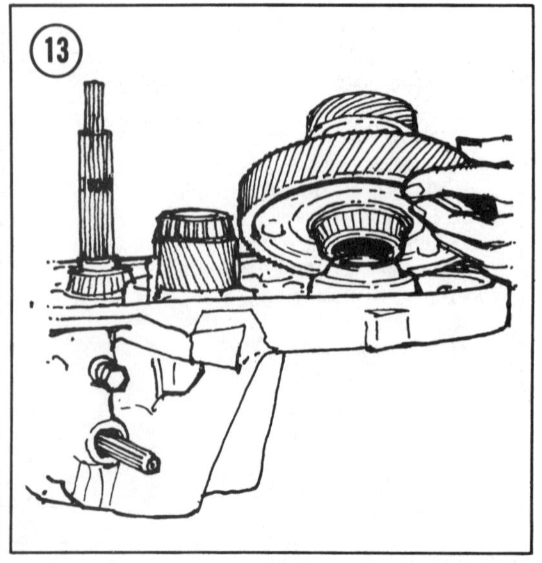

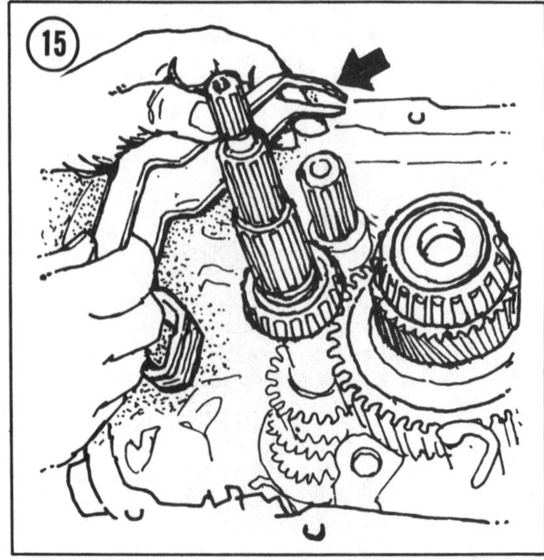

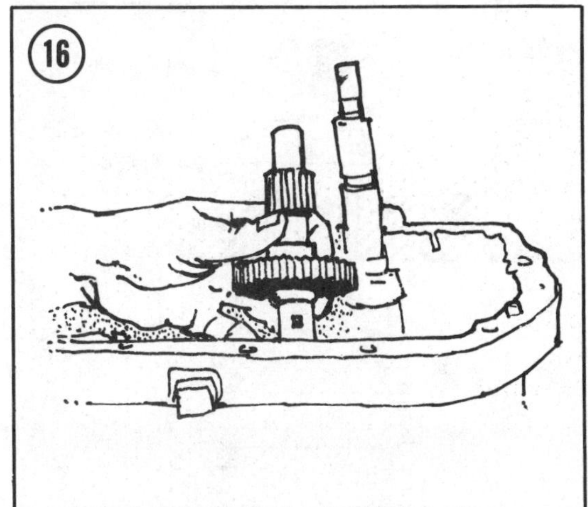
16

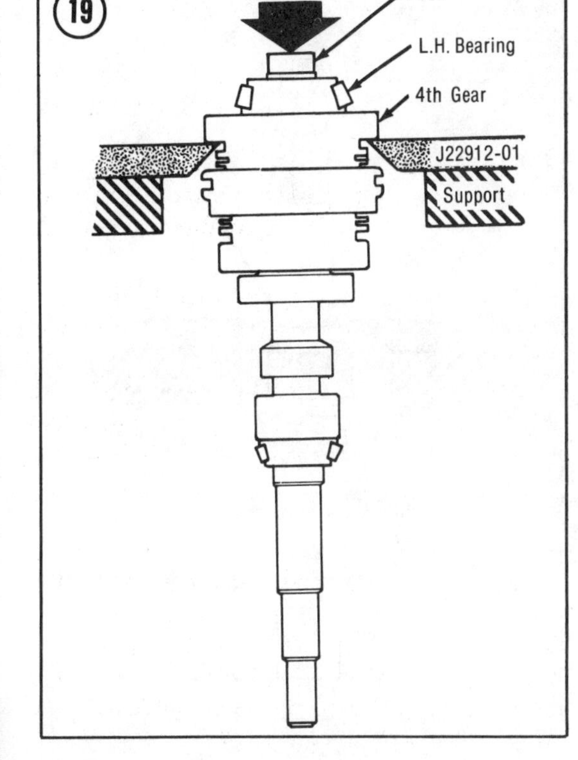
19
Press
Pilot
L.H. Bearing
4th Gear
J22912-01
Support

17

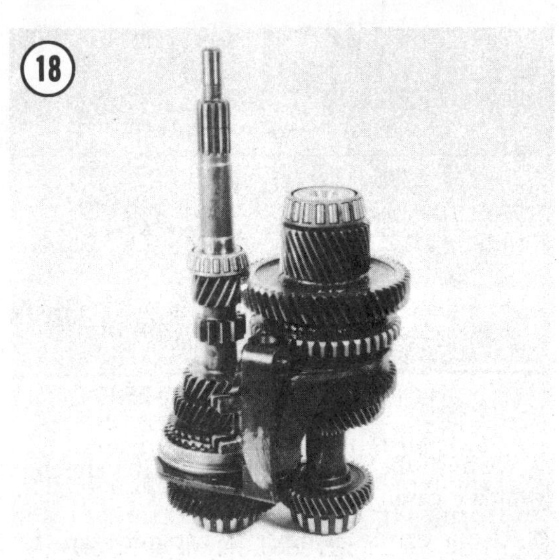
18

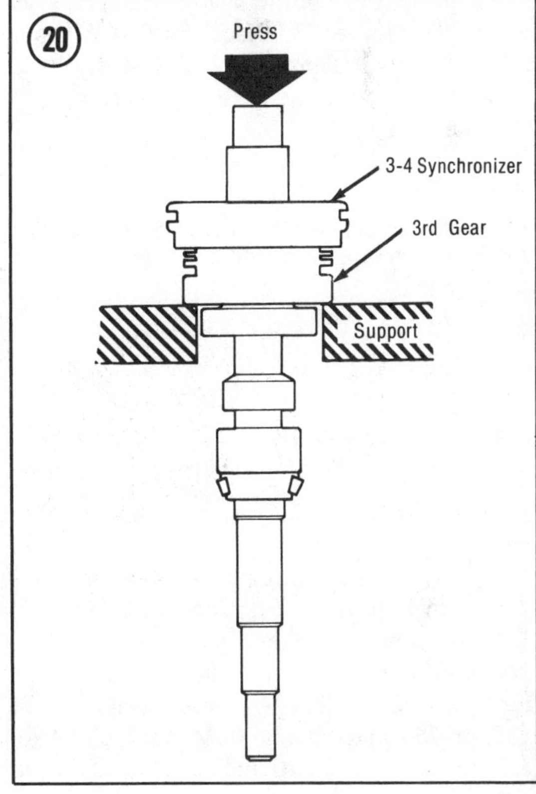
20
Press
3-4 Synchronizer
3rd Gear
Support

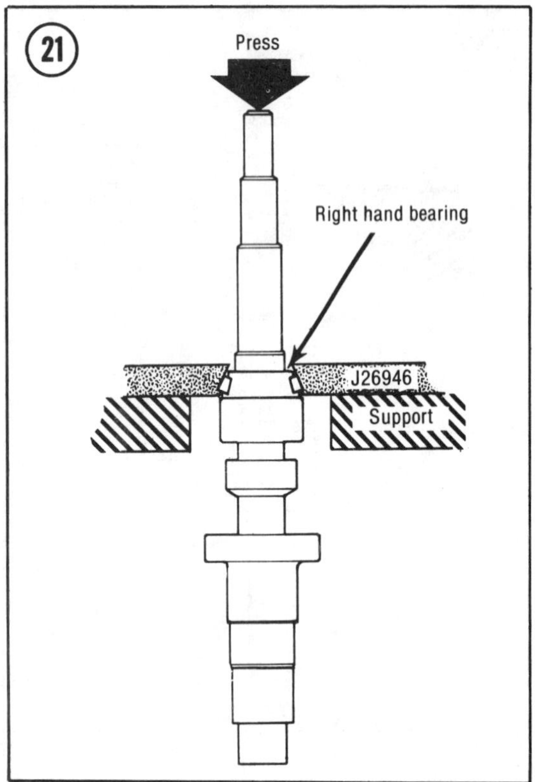

15. Support the countershaft in a press as shown in **Figure 22**. Place pilot (GM tool J-26943 or equivalent) into end of shaft. Press off fourth gear and the left-hand bearing from the countershaft.
16. Remove the third gear snap ring from the countershaft.
17. Support second gear in press. See **Figure 23**. Press second gear and third gear off the countershaft.

NOTE
It will be necessary to slide the 1-2 synchronizer assembly into first gear to allow positioning of second gear in the press.

18. Remove the 1-2 synchronizer snap ring from the countershaft.
19. Support the countershaft in a press as shown in **Figure 24**. Press the first gear and 1-2 synchronizer off the countershaft.
20. Support the right-hand bearing using GM tool part No. J-22227-A or equivalent. See **Figure 25**. Place pilot (GM tool part No. J-26953 or equivalent) into end of shaft and

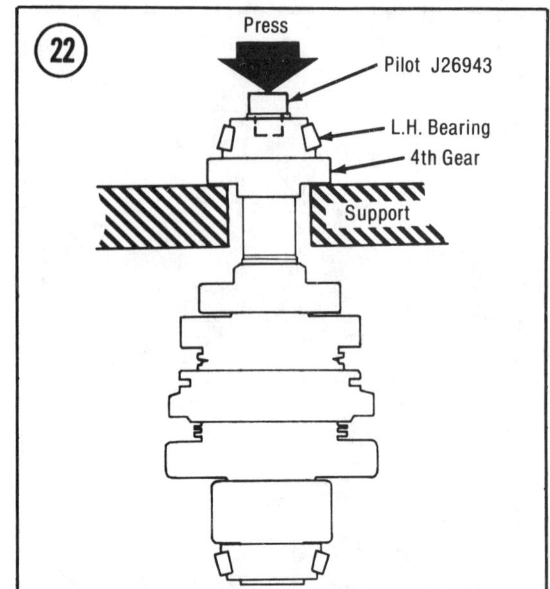

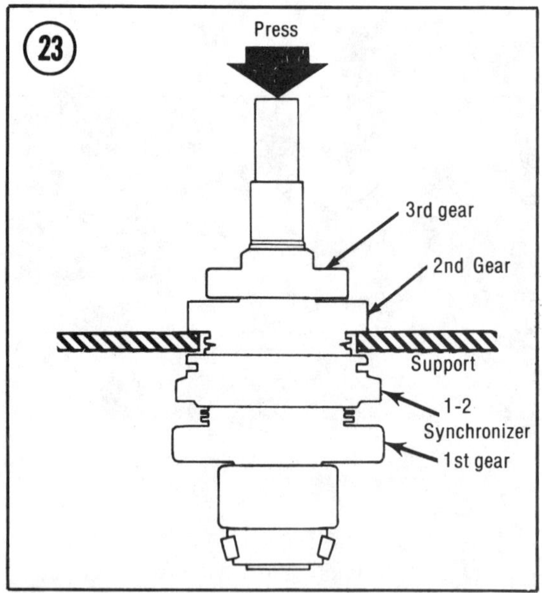

press the right-hand bearing off the countershaft.

NOTE
Step 21 describes synchronizer disassembly.

21. Scribe alignment marks on the synchronizer hub and sleeve to ensure exact reassembly. Disassemble both synchronizers, referring to **Figure 26**. Keep each synchronizer's parts separate from the other's.

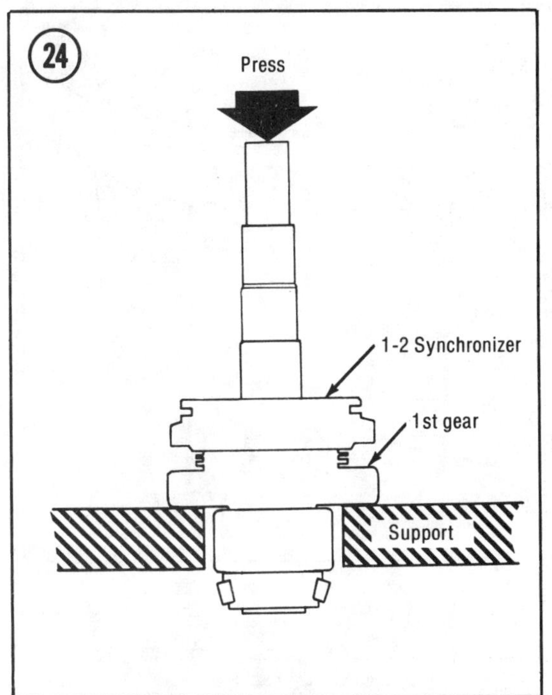
24
Press
1-2 Synchronizer
1st gear
Support

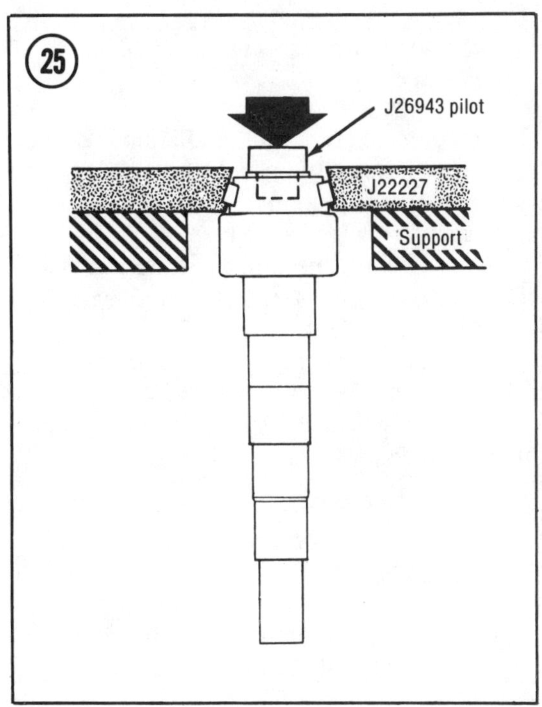
25
J26943 pilot
J22227
Support

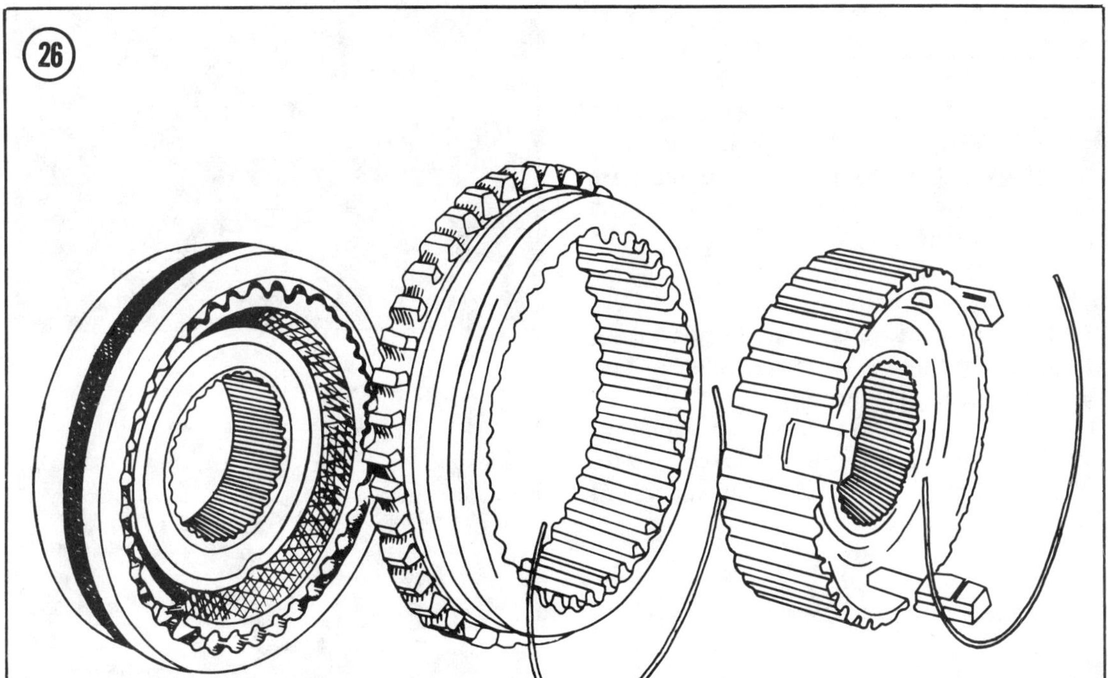

26

9

NOTE
Step 22-25 describe disassembly of the transaxle case.

22. Refer to **Figure 27** and remove the reverse inhibitor fitting from outside of the transaxle case. Remove the spring and pilot/spacer from inside the case.
23. Remove both the input and output shaft left-hand bearing cups using GM tool part No. J-26941 or equivalent.
24. Lift out oil slingers from side of case (**Figure 28**).
25. Remove interlock bracket, reverse shift fork and guide pins.

NOTE
Step 26-30 describe disassembly of the clutch cover.

26. Remove the differential side bearing cup and shim using GM tool part No. J-26941 or equivalent.
27. Remove both the input and output shaft right-hand bearing cups using GM tool part No. J-26941 or equivalent. Remove shim from back of input bearing cup. Remove oil shield, shim and retainer from back of output shaft bearing cup.
28. Remove bolts securing the input gear bearing retainer, then remove bearing retainer and sleeve (**Figure 29**).
29. Remove external oil ring and internal oil seal from sleeve (**Figure 30**).
30. Remove screws attaching the plastic oil scoop to the inside of the clutch cover. Remove oil scoop (**Figure 31**).
31. If the clutch fork shaft is damaged, remove it from inside of the clutch cover with GM tool part No. J-28412 or an equivalent. size drift. See **Figure 32**.

NOTE
Steps 32-34 describe differential case/ring gear disassembly.

32. Remove bolts securing the ring gear to the differential case assembly.
33. Remove the pinion shaft lock bolt from the differential case. Then remove the pinion shaft, gears and thrust washers from the transaxle case.

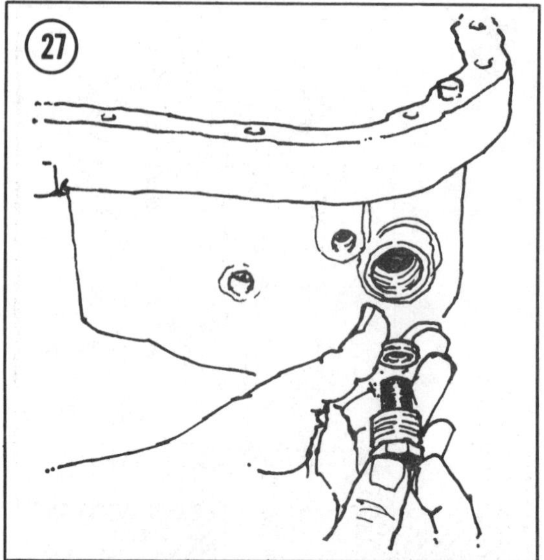

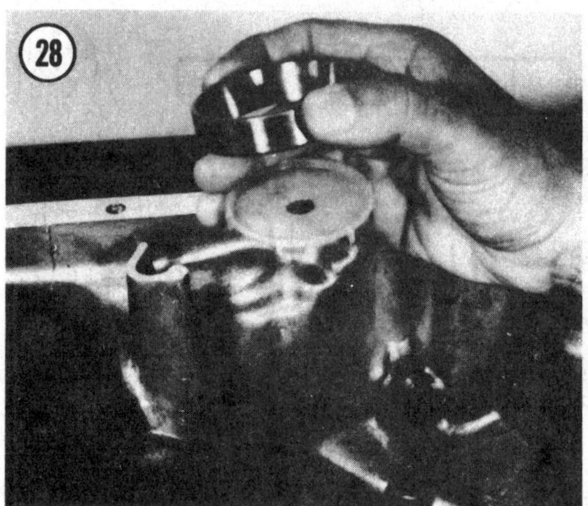

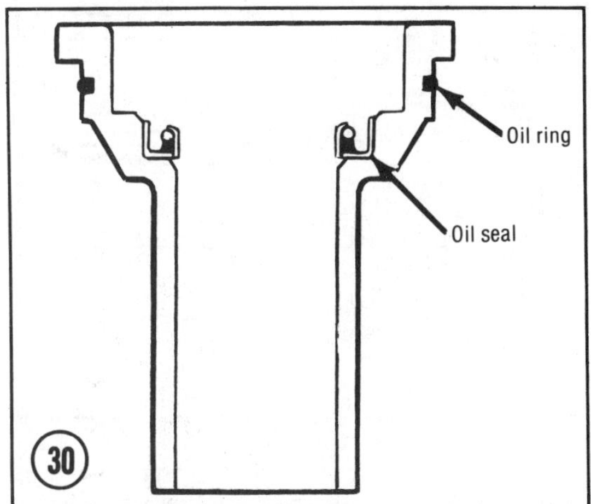

34. If the differential side bearings are to be replaced (see *Inspection*) remove bearings using GM tools part No. J-22888 and part No. J-22888-20 or an equivalent bearing removal tool.

Inspection

1. Thoroughly clean all parts in solvent. Remove all traces of old gasket and sealer. Inspect all parts while cleaning and replace any that show obvious wear or damage.
2. Check the case and housing for cracks. Check all gasket surfaces for gouges or roughness which could cause an oil leak. Replace if these conditions are found.
3. Inspect bearings for wear and damage. Hold the outer race with one hand and rotate the inner race with the other. See **Figure 33**. Check for excessive noise, roughness or looseness. Replace any suspect bearings.
4. Check all seals for wear or damage. Replace if there is any doubt about its condition.
5. Check the shafts for signs of bending, twisting or damaged splines. **Figure 34** shows examples of defective splines.
6. Inspect all gears for chipped, broken or badly worn teeth. Replace any gears with these conditions.
7. Inspect both synchronizer assemblies for wear or damage. Check springs for deformation or weakness. Replace as needed.

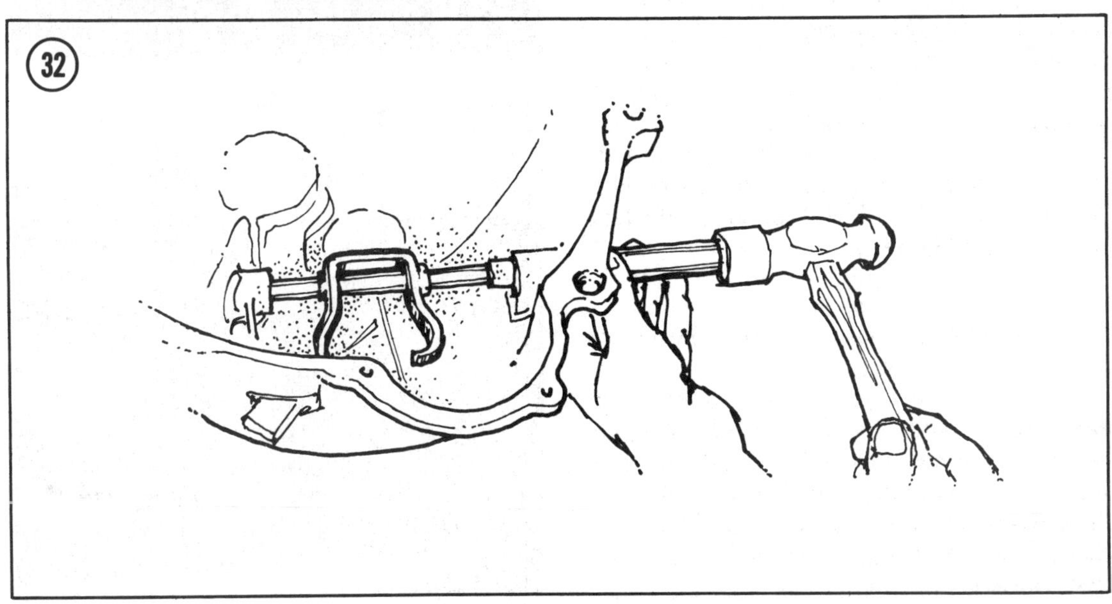

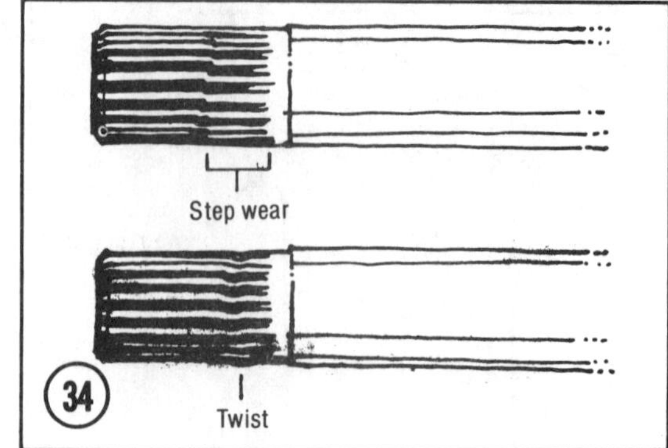

Assembly

Cleanliness is essential for transaxle assembly. Work in a dust-free area and handle parts in clean hands.

During assembly, coat all friction points with gear oil.

NOTE

Steps 1-3 describe synchronizer assembly.

1. Assemble the synchronizers. Make sure to assemble the hub to the sleeve with the extruded lip on the hub facing away from the shift fork groove in the sleeve. Align previous alignment marks. See **Figure 26**.
2. Install one retaining ring. Then, pry the ring back with a screwdriver and insert shifting keys in position, one at a time (**Figure 26**).
3. Install the ring on the opposite side, with the open segment of the ring *not aligned* with the open segment on the other side.

NOTE

Steps 4-8 describe main shaft assembly.

4. Place the main shaft assembly into a press as shown in **Figure 35**. Place GM tool part No. J-28406 or equivalent onto shaft and press the right-hand bearing onto the main shaft.
5. Press third gear on main shaft, then place the brass blocker ring onto the gear cone and press the 3-4 synchronizer onto the main shaft. Make sure to use correct size press tool to contact the hub near the shaft. Do not press on the sleeve portion of synchronizer. See **Figure 36**.
6. Install snap ring on main shaft to position the 3-4 synchronizer. Make sure to install snap ring with beveled edges away from the synchronizer for later access with snap ring pliers. See **Figure 37**.

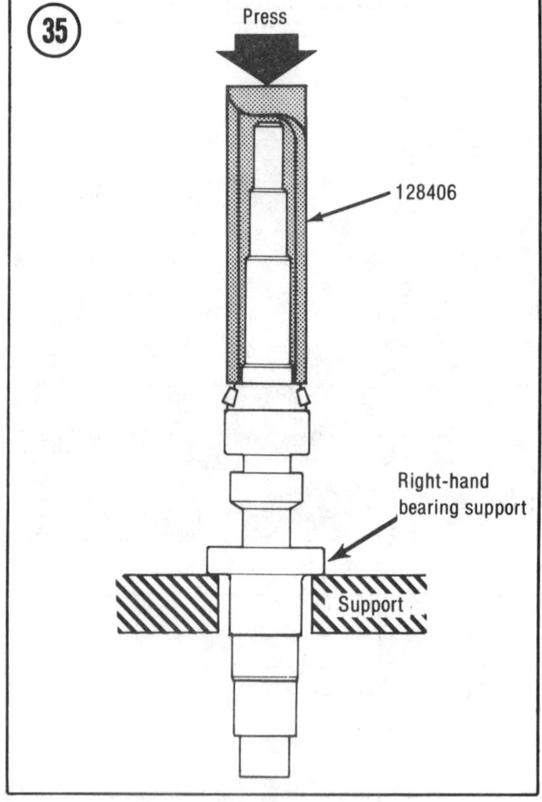

7. Install the brass blocker ring onto the main shaft.
8. Support the main shaft as shown in **Figure 38**. Press fourth gear onto shaft, oriented toward the 3-4 synchronizer. Then Place pilot (GM tool part No. J-26942 or equivalent) into end of shaft and press left-hand bearing onto main shaft.

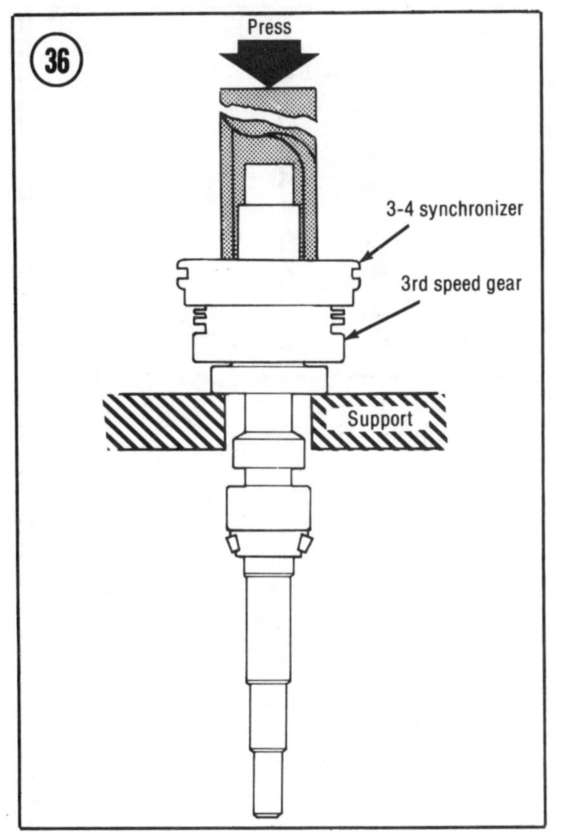

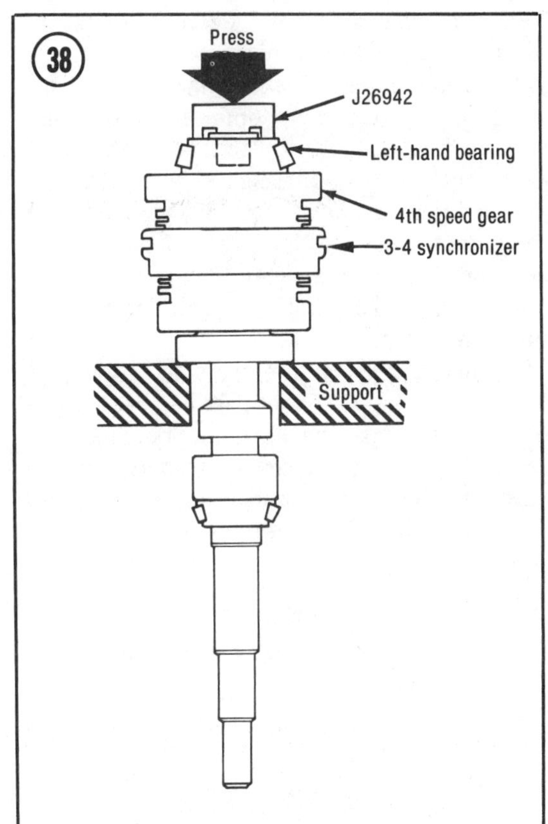

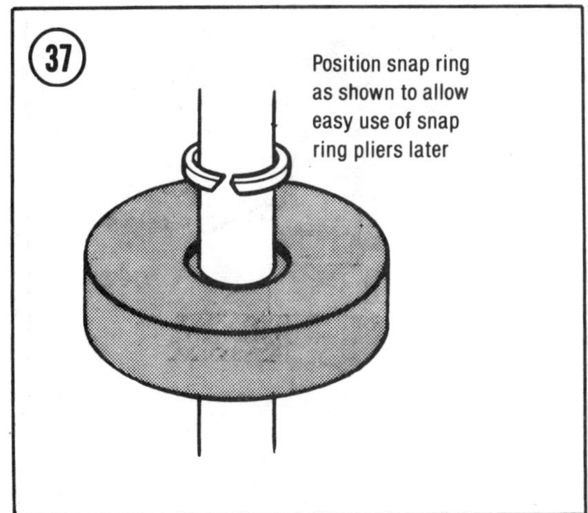

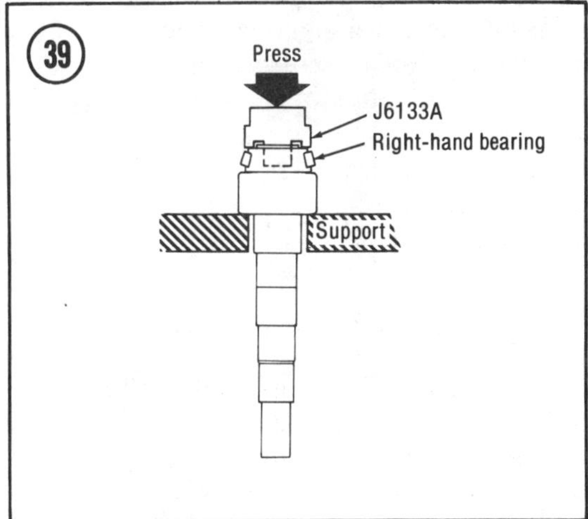

NOTE

Steps 9-15 describe countershaft assembly.

9. Place the countershaft onto a press with the right-hand bearing. Install GM tool part No J-6133A or equivalent onto shaft end and press the right-hand bearing onto shaft. See **Figure 39**.

10. Press first gear on countershaft, then place the brass blocker ring onto gear cone and press the 1-2 synchronizer onto the countershaft. Make sure to use the correct size press tool to contact hub near shaft. Do not press sleeve on countershaft. See **Figure 40**.

11. Install snap ring onto the countershaft to position the 1-2 synchronizer.
12. Install the brass blocker ring.
13. Press second gear onto shaft oriented toward the 1-2 synchronizer. Press the third gear onto the countershaft with its hub directed towards fourth gear. Make sure to use the correct size press tool when pressing third gear on shaft. See **Figure 41**.
14. Install snap ring on countershaft to position third gear.
15. Support the countershaft as shown in **Figure 42** using GM tool part No. J-6133a or equivalent. Press the left-hand bearing onto shaft. Press fourth gear onto shaft, making sure the fourth gear hub is directed toward third gear when pressing onto shaft using GM tool part No. J-26942.

NOTE

Steps 16-20 describe transaxle case reassembly.

16. Install the differential side bearing cup using an equivalent size drift.
17. Install oil slingers into case.

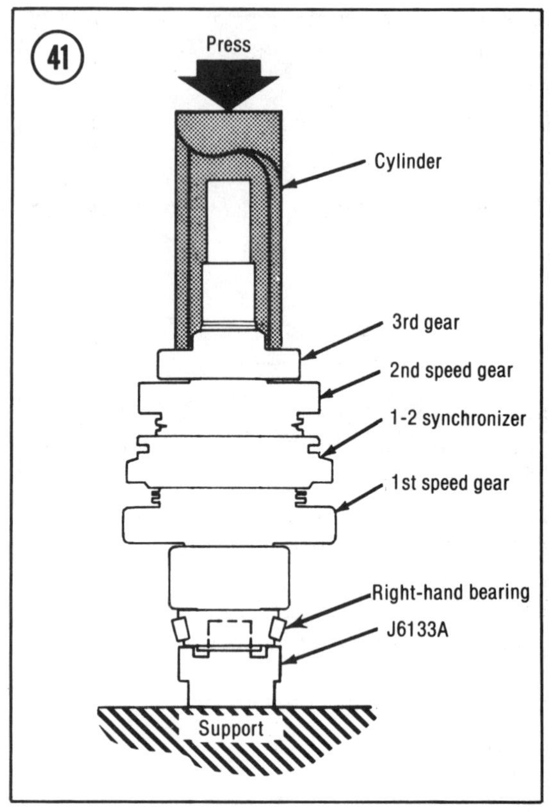

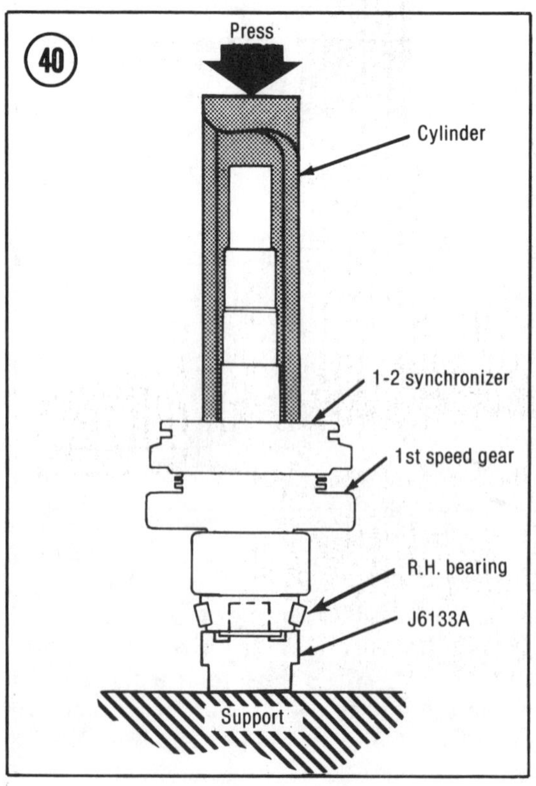

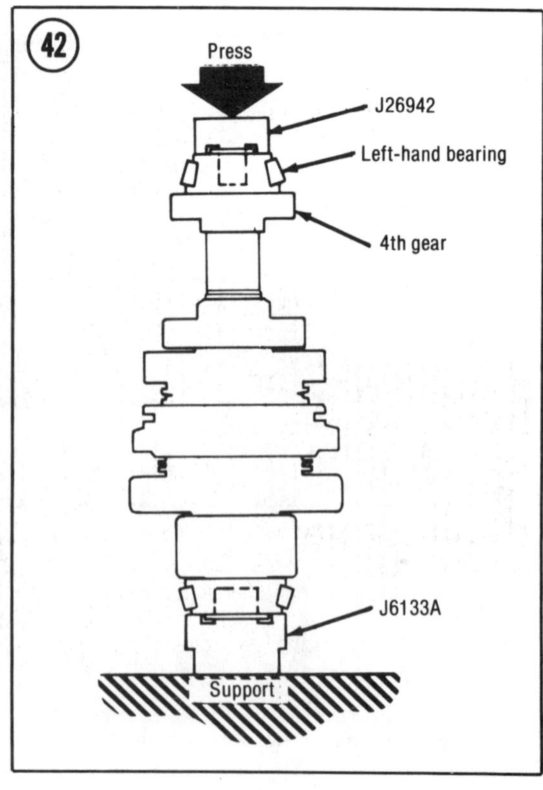

18. Drive the input and output left-hand bearing cups into the transaxle case using an equivalent size drift.

19. Insert the reverse inhibitor spring and pilot/spacer into case, then secure with the reverse inhibitor fitting (**Figure 27**). Tighten the reverse inhibitor fitting to 26 ft.-lb. (35 N•m).

NOTE
Steps 20-22 describe clutch cover reassembly.

20. Install the plastic oil scoop to side of clutch cover and secure with attaching screws (**Figure 31**).

21. Replace the external square-cut ring on sleeve. Install input bearing retainer and secure with attaching bolts.

22. Drive new internal oil seal into clutch cover using a suitable size drift.

NOTE
Steps 23-25 describe differential case/ring gear reassembly.

23. Drive new differential side bearings into side of transaxle case using an equivalent size drift.

24. Install the differential side and pinion gears and thrust washers into case. Then install the pinion shaft and lock bolt. Tighten to 7 ft.-lb. (9 N•m).

25. Attach the ring gear to the differential case and tighten bolts to 54 ft.-lb. (73 N•m).

NOTE
*Before completing transaxle reassembly, the transaxle assembly must be referred to a General Motors dealer for proper selection of preload shims. Once proper size shims are selected, transaxle reassembly can be completed. **Figure 43** shows the gauges used to select shims.*

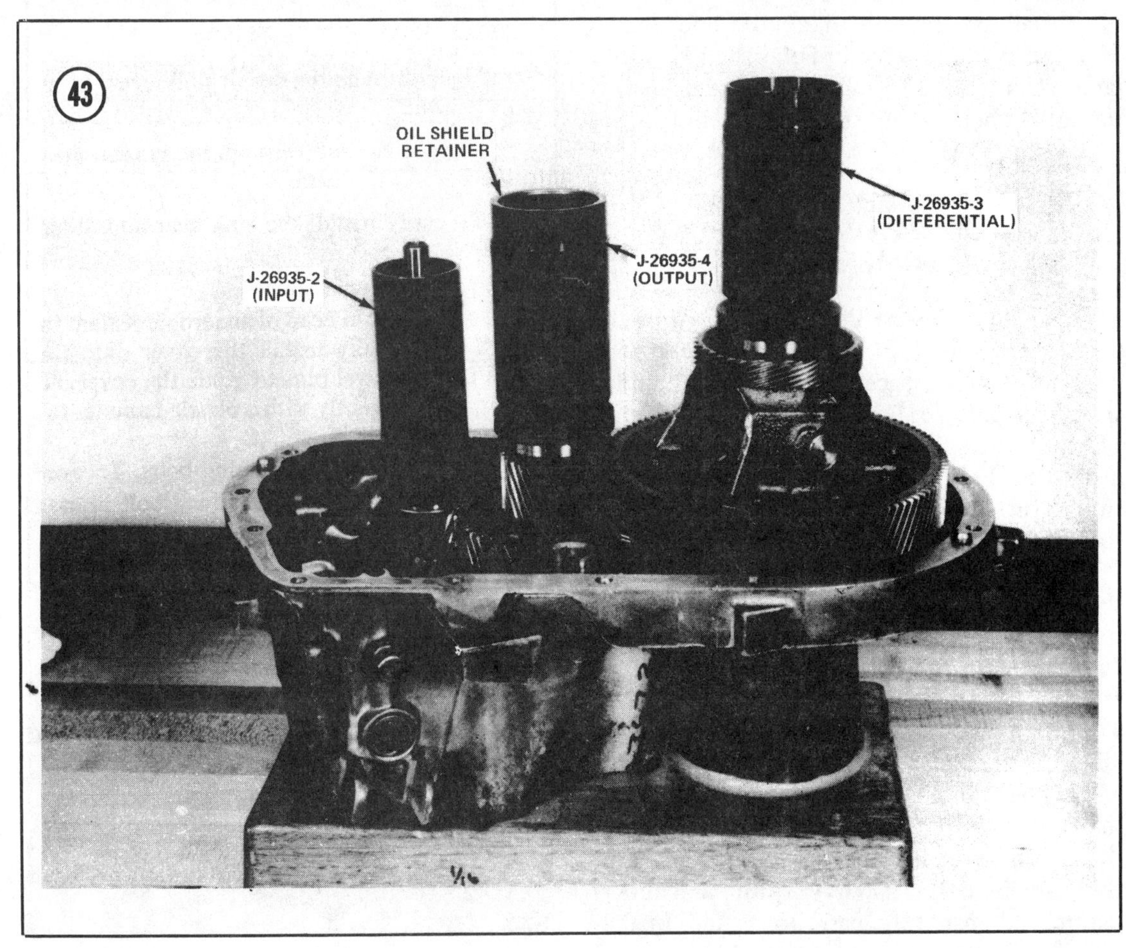

9

NOTE
Steps 26-40 complete transaxle reassembly.

26. Assemble the shift forks to the input and output shafts (**Figure 18**).
27. Install the input shaft, output shaft and shift forks into the transaxle case. Make sure shafts and shift forks fit into case as an assembly.
28. Place the interlock bracket onto guide pin (GM part No. J-28411) and insert into case. Make sure the bracket engages the finger on the shift forks.
29. Place the detent shift lever into the interlock (**Figure 17**).
30. Insert the shift shaft through the interlock bracket and the detent lever. Do not extend further at this point.
31. Install the reverse shift fork onto the guide pin. Make sure the reverse shift fork engages the interlock bracket.
32. Install the reverse idler gear and shaft. Make sure the long end of the shaft and the large chamfered ends of the gear teeth point upward. Then install the spacer onto the reverse idler gear shaft. See **Figure 16**.

NOTE
Make sure the flat on the reverse idler gear shaft faces the input gear shaft.

33. Completely insert the shift shaft through the reverse shift fork until it pilots into the inhibitor spring spacer. Remove the guide shaft (GM part No. J-28411).
34. With the shifter shaft in neutral position, install the bolt and lock through the detent shift lever. Bend lock tab over bolt head to secure.
35. Install fork shaft through the synchronizer forks and into the bore in the transaxle case.
36. Insert the ring gear and differential case assembly into the case housing.
37. Install the magnet if previously removed.
38. Coat the clutch cover sealing surface with a small bead of anaerobic sealant, then install the cover onto the transaxle case. Make sure the clutch cover fits over the guide pins. Tap the clutch cover slightly with a rubber hammer to ensure the parts are seated. Install

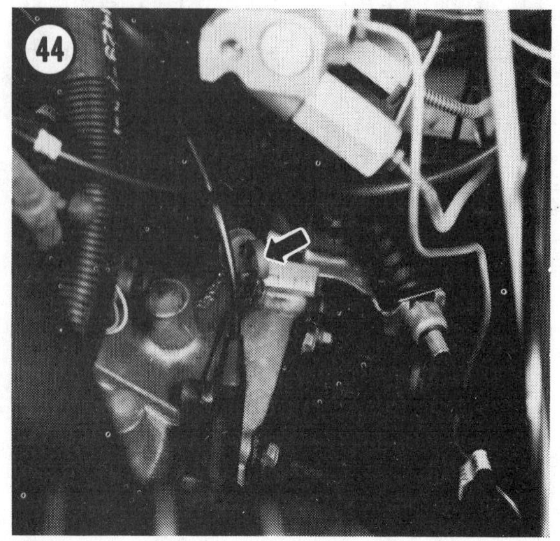

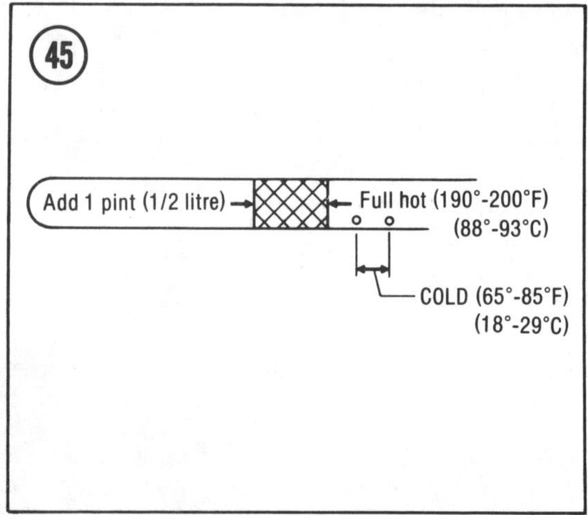

39. Tighten the idler shaft retaining bolt in the case to 16 ft.-lb. (21 N•m).
40. Shift through all the gears to make sure transaxle gear assemblies are not binding.

AUTOMATIC TRANSAXLE

The 125 Turbo Hydra-matic transaxle is a fully automatic unit consisting of a 3-element hydraulic torque converter, compound planetary gear set and dual sprocket and drive link assembly. This section includes checks and adjustment procedures to be performed with the transaxle in the car. Many problems can be corrected with the adjustment procedures described here. Automatic transaxle overhaul, however, requires professional skills, many special tools and extremely high standards of cleanliness. Although procedures for removal and installation are included in this section, disassembly and overhaul should be left to a General Motors dealer or competent automatic transmission repair shop.

Torque specifications for the automatic transaxle are found in **Table 2**.

Fluid Level Check

With the car on a level surface, start the engine and let idle until the transaxle fluid warms to normal operating temperature: 200° F (90° C). Proper operating temperature may be obtained by driving the vehicle 15-20 miles under normal city type driving conditions. When normal operating temperature is obtained, park the vehicle and apply the parking brake. Place transaxle selector in PARK. *Do not* move the shift lever through the gears. With the engine running, check the transaxle fluid level on the dipstick (**Figure 44**). Maintain transaxle fluid level between the ADD and FULL marks at *normal operating temperature.* Do not top up if the fluid level is between the ADD and FULL marks.

NOTE
If transaxle fluid level is checked when ***engine*** *temperature is between 65°-85° F (18°-29° C), the fluid level should be 1/4 in. (7 mm) above the FULL mark or between the 2 dimples on the dipstick* ***(Figure 45)****.*

CAUTION
Do not overfill the transaxle. An excessive fluid level can cause the fluid to become foamy, resulting in wear or damage to the transaxle.

Road Test

1. Place the gear selector in DRIVE and accelerate. There should be a 1-2 and a 2-3 upshift. The shift points will vary with the throttle openings.
2. Run at a speed of 30 mph, then quickly accelerate to three-fourths throttle. A 3-2 downshift should occur at 50 mph when the accelerator is depressed fully.
3. Place the gear selector in INTERMEDIATE and accelerate. There should be a 1-2 upshift.
4. Place the gear selector in LO and accelerate. There should be no transaxle upshift.
5. Place the gear selector in DRIVE and accelerate to 50 mph. Remove foot from accelerator and move gear selector to INTERMEDIATE. There should be a downshift to 2nd with a noticeable increase in engine rpm and engine braking.
6. Place the gear selector in INTERMEDIATE and accelerate to 40 mph. Remove foot from accelerator and move gear selector to LO. There should be a 2-1 downshift in the speed range of 40 to 25 mph. There should be a noticeable increase in engine rpm and engine braking.
7. Place the gear selector in REVERSE and check for reverse vehicle operation.

Leak Inspection

Oil leaking from the engine and transaxle is generally carried toward the rear of the car due to the air stream present during vehicle operation. In trying to determine the location of a leak at some point on the transaxle, first clean the affected area with solvent to remove all traces of oil. Then, with the engine running, begin inspection.

1. Check the transaxle oil pan (**Figure 46**). If leaking is evident, tighten the bolts to 12

ft.-lb. (16 N•m). If necessary, remove the oil pan and replace the mating gasket.

2. Check the speedometer cable connection (**Figure 47**). Replace the O-ring if damaged.

3. Check the transaxle fluid cooler lines and fittings. If a leak cannot be stopped by tightening the fittings, replace the damaged parts.

4. Remove the radiator cap and look at the engine coolant. If transaxle fluid is present in the coolant, the transmission fluid cooler in the radiator is probably leaking. Consult your General Motors dealer or other competent repair shop.

5. Check the connection between the transaxle fluid filler (dipstick) tube and the transaxle case. Replace the multi-lip seal if damaged or missing. Make sure the filler tube attaching bracket is not loose, allowing the filler tube to cock sideways and allow fluid leakage.

6. Check for oil leaks at the following case locations:

   a. TV cable seal (**Figure 48**)
   b. Governor cover and O-rings
   c. Manual valve bore plug
   d. Axle oil seals
   e. Parking pawl shaft cup plug
   f. Line pressure pickup pipe plug
   g. Turbine shaft oil seal

7. Remove the torque converter access cover at the front of the flywheel housing. Check the converter seal for damage. Replace as required. See **Figure 49** (4-cylinder) or **Figure 50** (V6).

Throttle Valve Control Cable Adjustment

The throttle valve (TV) cable should be adjusted any time the transaxle or carburetor assemblies are removed. Refer to **Figure 51** while performing the TV adjustment.

1. Depress and hold the metal lock tab (**Figure 52**).

2. Move the slider through the TV fitting in the readjustment direction (**Figure 51**) until the slider stops against the TV fitting.

3. Open the carburetor idler lever to its wide open throttle position. The idler lever must touch the idler lever stop (**Figure 53**).

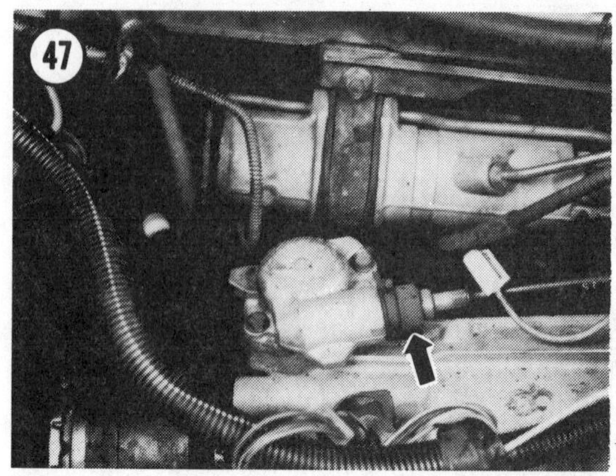

4. Release the metal lock tab. Adjustment is complete.

Transaxle Removal

The transaxle assembly has been designed to be removed from underneath the vehicle—a procedure requiring that the engine/transaxle cradle be partially removed while the engine is held in position by a support fixture. However, for the mechanic working at home, removal of the transaxle from underneath is not recommended. Jackstands, the normal home mechanic's support fixture (described in Chapter Two) would not provide the mechanic with the necessary room or *safety* to remove the transaxle. Therefore, the following recommended procedure is to first remove the engine, then lift out the transaxle.

1. Disconnect the battery ground cable at the transaxle case (**Figure 54**).

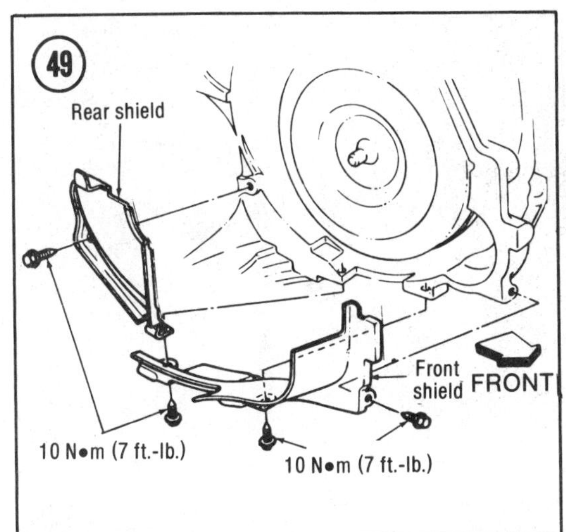
49
Rear shield
Front shield
FRONT
10 N•m (7 ft.-lb.)
10 N•m (7 ft.-lb.)

52

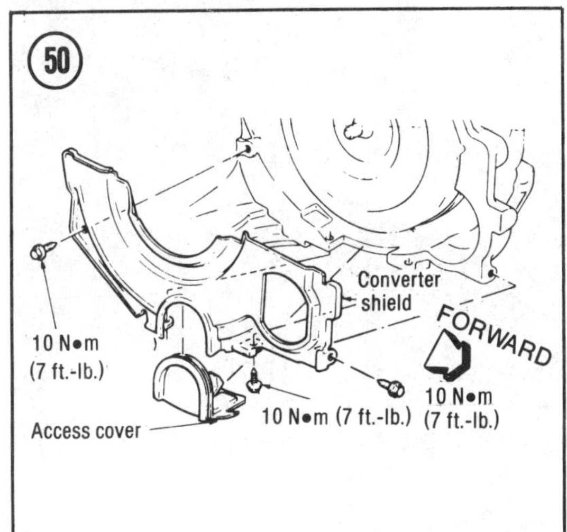
50
Converter shield
FORWARD
10 N•m (7 ft.-lb.)
10 N•m (7 ft.-lb.)
10 N•m (7 ft.-lb.)
Access cover

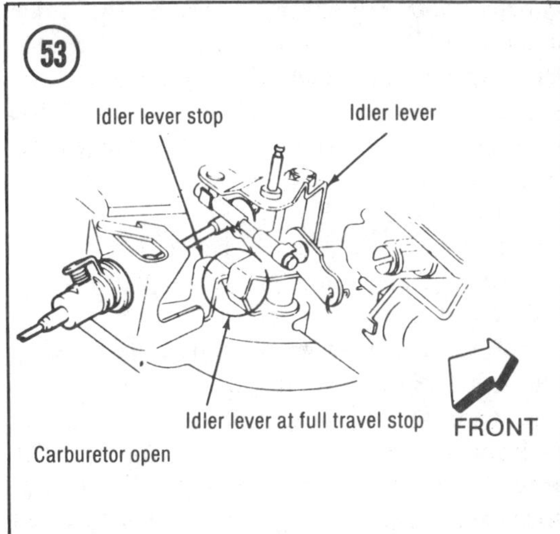
53
Idler lever stop
Idler lever
Idler lever at full travel stop
FRONT
Carburetor open

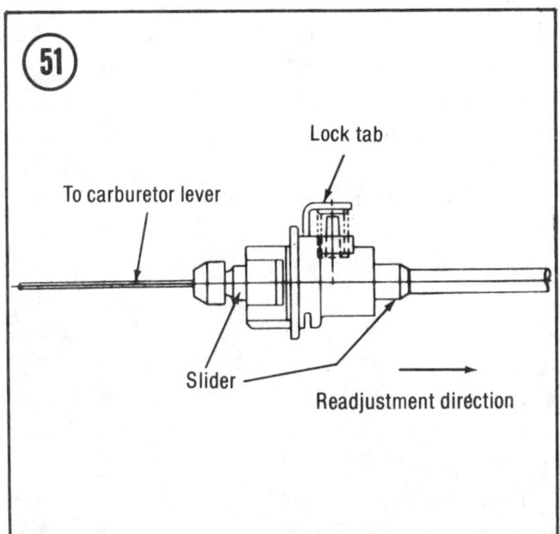
51
Lock tab
To carburetor lever
Slider
Readjustment direction

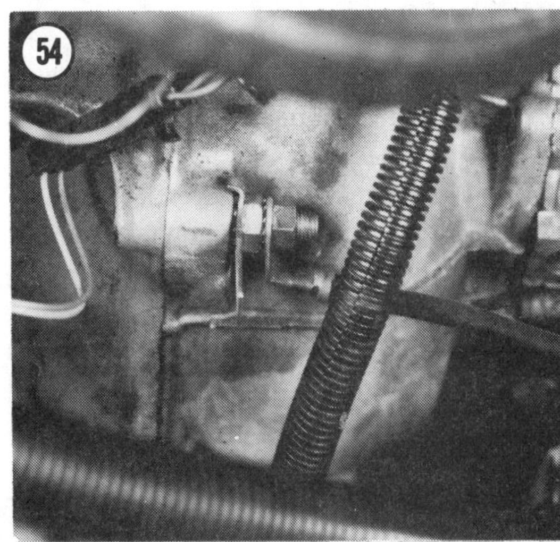
54

9

2. Remove the engine assembly as described in Chapter Four (4-cylinder) or Chapter Five (V6).
3. Disconnect the speedometer cable at the transaxle. See **Figure 47**. For vehicles equipped with cruise control, remove the transaxle speedometer cable at the cruise control transducer (**Figure 55**).
4. Disconnect the shift cable bracket bolt at the transaxle (**Figure 56**). Then remove the bracket and shift cable assembly.
5. Disconnect and plug the 2 oil cooler lines at the transaxle (**Figure 57**).
6. Raise vehicle front end and secure with jackstands. Remove both front wheels.
7. Remove both the left and right side drive shafts from the transaxle as described in this chapter under *Drive Shaft Removal.*
8. Disconnect the front and rear transaxle mount bolts. See **Figure 58**.
9. Attach an engine lifing hoist to the transaxle and remove the transaxle from the engine compartment.

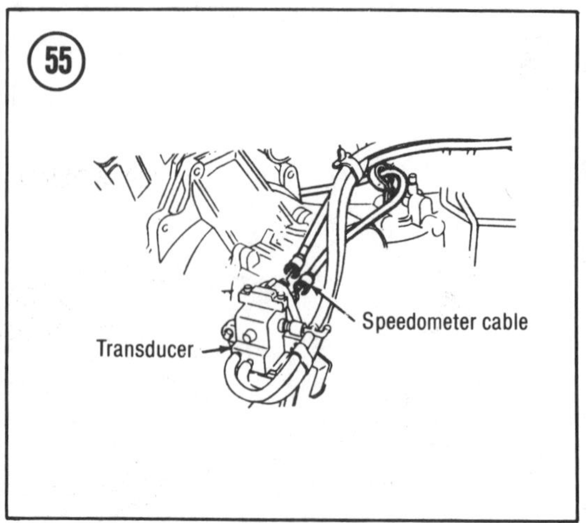

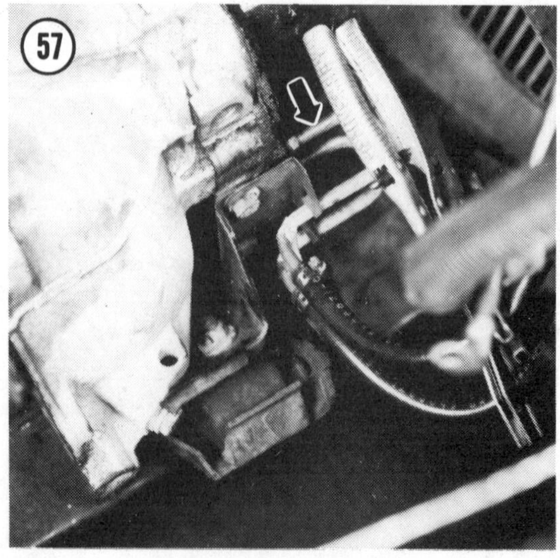

Transaxle Installation

1. Removal is the reverse of installation, plus the following.
2. Fill transaxle to proper level as described in Chapter Three.
3. Check the transaxle, torque converter and all lines and points of attachments for leaks.
4. Perform the TV cable adjustment as described in this section.
5. Drive vehicle and check transaxle operation.

DRIVE AXLE

Drive axles are flexible assemblies which carry the power directly from the transaxle to the front wheels. Each drive axle assembly consists of an inner and outer constant velocity joint connected by an axle shaft. All drive shaft assemblies except the left-hand inboard joint on automatic transaxles use a male spline which interlocks with the transaxle gears through barrel type snap rings. The left-hand inboard shaft on automatic transaxles uses a female spline which inserts over a stub shaft protruding from the transaxle. The inner axle joint is completely

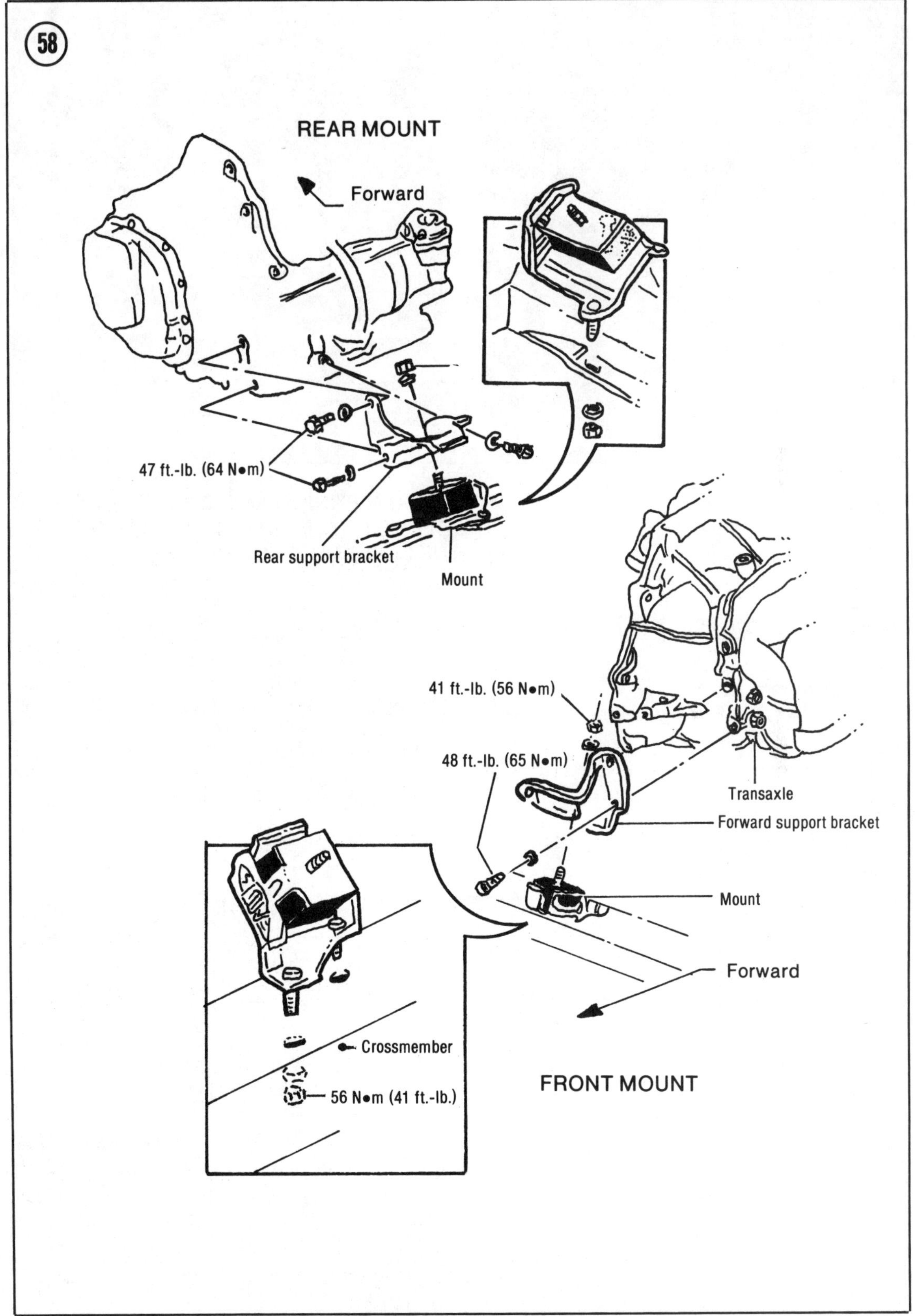
58
REAR MOUNT
Forward
47 ft.-lb. (64 N•m)
Rear support bracket
Mount
41 ft.-lb. (56 N•m)
48 ft.-lb. (65 N•m)
Transaxle
Forward support bracket
Mount
Forward
Crossmember
56 N•m (41 ft.-lb.)
FRONT MOUNT

60

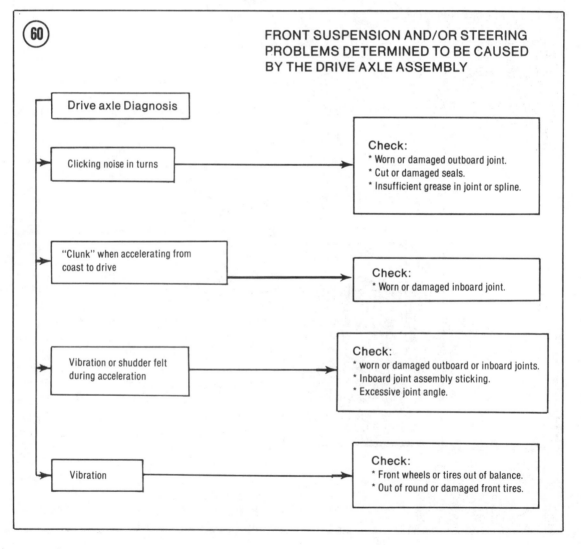

FRONT SUSPENSION AND/OR STEERING PROBLEMS DETERMINED TO BE CAUSED BY THE DRIVE AXLE ASSEMBLY

Drive axle Diagnosis

Clicking noise in turns	Check: * Worn or damaged outboard joint. * Cut or damaged seals. * Insufficient grease in joint or spline.
"Clunk" when accelerating from coast to drive	Check: * Worn or damaged inboard joint.
Vibration or shudder felt during acceleration	Check: * worn or damaged outboard or inboard joints. * Inboard joint assembly sticking. * Excessive joint angle.
Vibration	Check: * Front wheels or tires out of balance. * Out of round or damaged front tires.

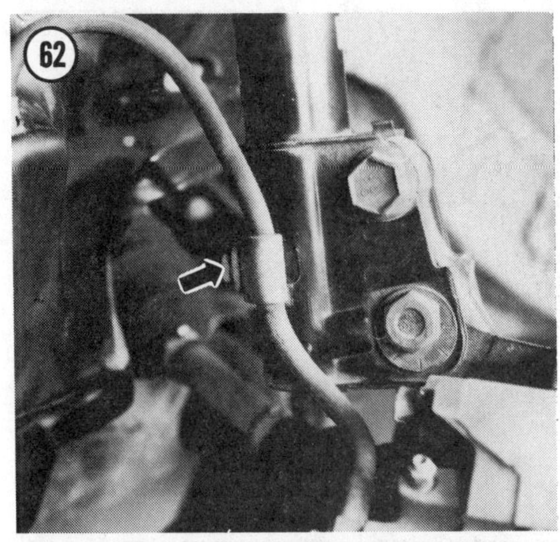

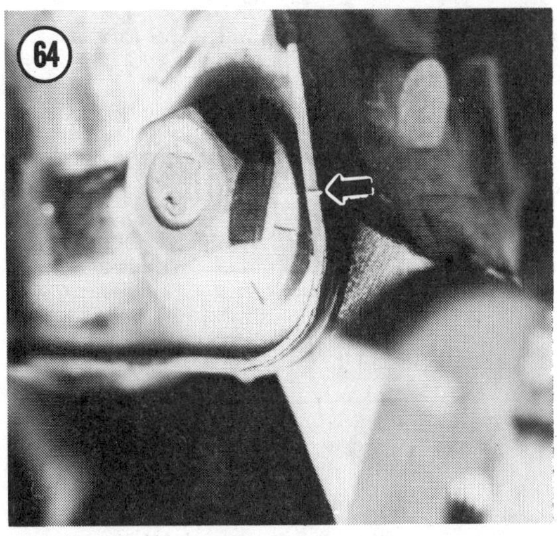

flexible and can move in and out. The outer joint, while also flexible, cannot move in and out. A typical drive axle is shown in **Figure 59**.

CAUTION
All fasteners used in the drive axle assembly must be replaced with parts of the same type. Do not use a replacement part of lesser quality or substitute design, as it may affect the performance of vital components and systems or result in major repair expenses.

Troubleshooting

The drive axle assemblies should be considered as a potential problem area when troubleshooting the front suspension and steering for an unknown steering noise or driving complaint. **Figure 60** lists potential drive axle problem areas which can help you to diagnose the drive axle assemblies.

Removal

1. Jack up the front end of the car and place it on jackstands. Remove the front wheels.
2. Remove the hub nut (**Figure 61**).
3. Disconnect the brake hose clip at the MacPherson strut. See **Figure 62**.

NOTE
Do not disconnect the brake line connection or it will be necessary to bleed the brakes.

4. Remove the brake caliper as described in Chapter Twelve and hang from a wire as shown in **Figure 63**. Do not allow caliper to hang from brake hose.
5. Remove the brake disc assembly as described in Chapter Twelve.
6. Remove the front wheel hub/bearing assembly as described in Chapter Ten.
7. Scribe alignment marks on the camber alignment cam bolt and the MacPherson strut for reassembly (**Figure 64**). Remove the cam bolt and the upper attaching bolt from the MacPherson strut and spindle. The steering knuckle can then be pulled from the strut bracket and drive axle. See **Figure 65**.
8. Position GM tool part No. J-28468 or equivalent (**Figure 66**) behind the drive axle,

65

66

Slide hammer
J-28468

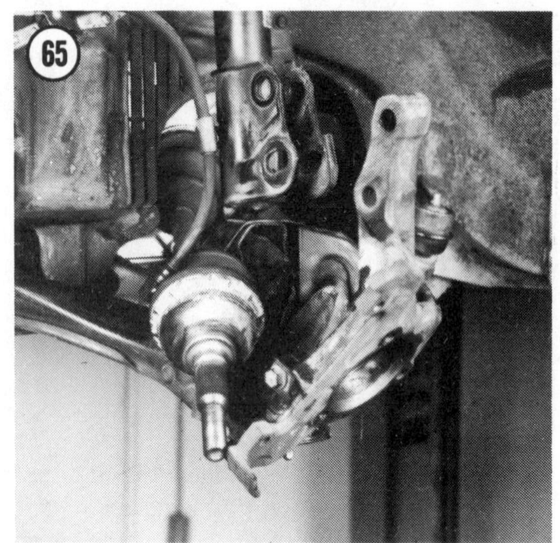

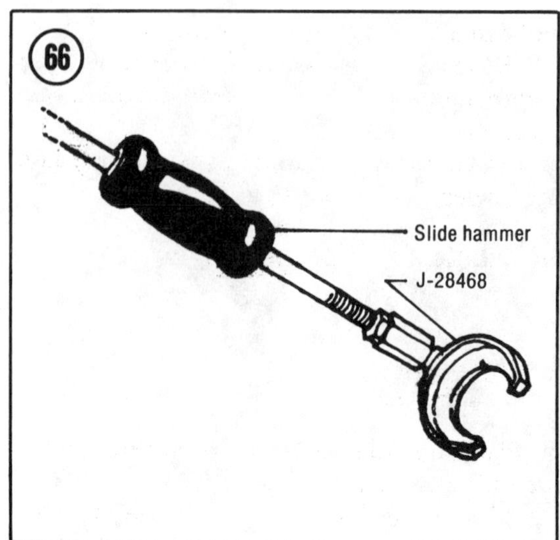

67

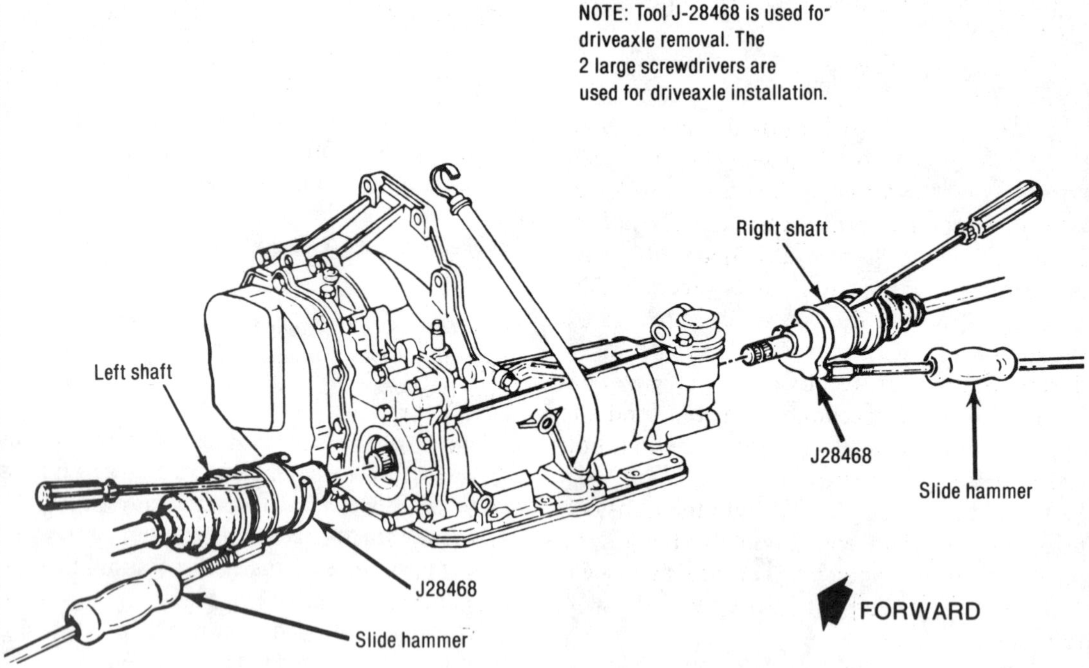

NOTE: Tool J-28468 is used fo-
driveaxle removal. The
2 large screwdrivers are
used for driveaxle installation.
Right shaft
Left shaft
J28468
Slide hammer
J28468
Slide hammer
FORWARD

and install a slide hammer as shown in **Figure 67**. Have an assistant support the drive axle and then pull the drive axle from the transaxle assembly.

9. Inspect and replace the transaxle/drive axle seal as described later in this section.

Installation

NOTE

If the drive axle is being replaced, replace the knuckle seal first, as described in Chapter Ten.

1. Place the outer drive axle joint through the steering knuckle.
2. Attach the steering knuckle to the MacPherson strut and install upper attaching bolt finger-tight.
3. Install the front hub/bearing assembly as described in Chapter Ten.
4. Install the brake disc assembly as described in Chapter Twelve.
5. Install the brake caliper as described in Chapter Twelve.
6. Install the hub nut (**Figure 61**) and tighten to 70 ft.-lb. (100 N•m) to seat the axle shaft into the steering knuckle. Insert a screwdriver into slot in rotor to prevent the axle shaft from turning while tightening nut (**Figure 68**).
7. Load the hub assembly by lowering it onto a jackstand. Install the cam bolt, making sure to align bolt with alignment marks made during Step 6 of removal. See **Figure 64**. Tighten both the eccentric cam bolt and the upper steering knuckle-to-strut attaching bolt to 140 ft.-lb. (190 N•m).
8. Insert the drive axle shaft into the transaxle using a screwdriver positioned into the groove provided on the inner retainer. See **Figure 67**. Tap the screwdriver until the drive axle seats into the transaxle.
9. Connect the brake hose clip to the MacPherson strut bracket (**Figure 62**).

NOTE

If the brake line was disconnected, bleed the brakes as described in Chapter Twelve.

10. Install the wheels and remove the jackstands. Lower the vehicle.
11. Torque the hub nut (**Figure 61**) to 225 ft.-lb. (305 N•m).

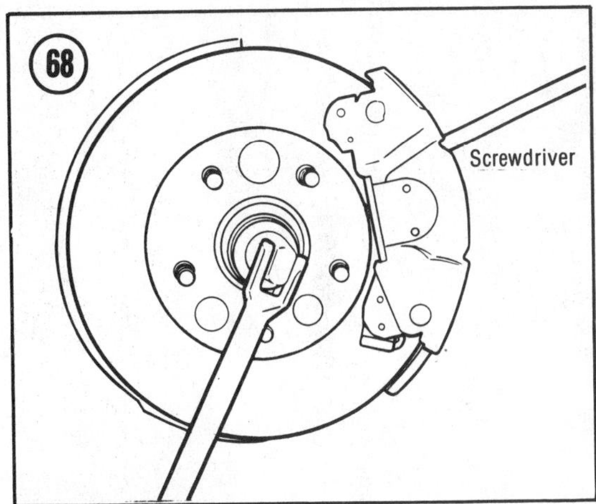

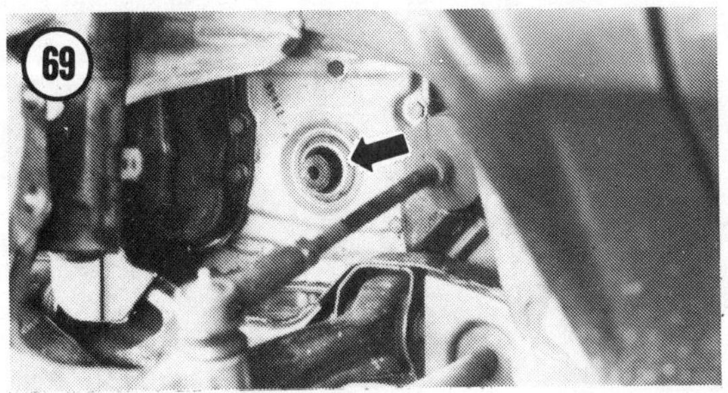

Transaxle Drive Axle Seal Replacement

It's a good idea to replace the transaxle drive axle seal (**Figure 69**) any time the drive axles are removed from the transaxle.

1. Using a punch, knock a hole in the axle seal. Then thread a seal puller (**Figure 70**) into the punched hole. Remove the seal.
2. Coat the seal with lubricating oil and drive into position into the transaxle.

Outer Joint Disassembly

Consider your safety and, if you do not feel competent to overhaul the drive axle assembly, remove the assembly and let your dealer do it. **Figure 71** shows an exploded view of the drive axle assembly. Refer to it as needed.

9

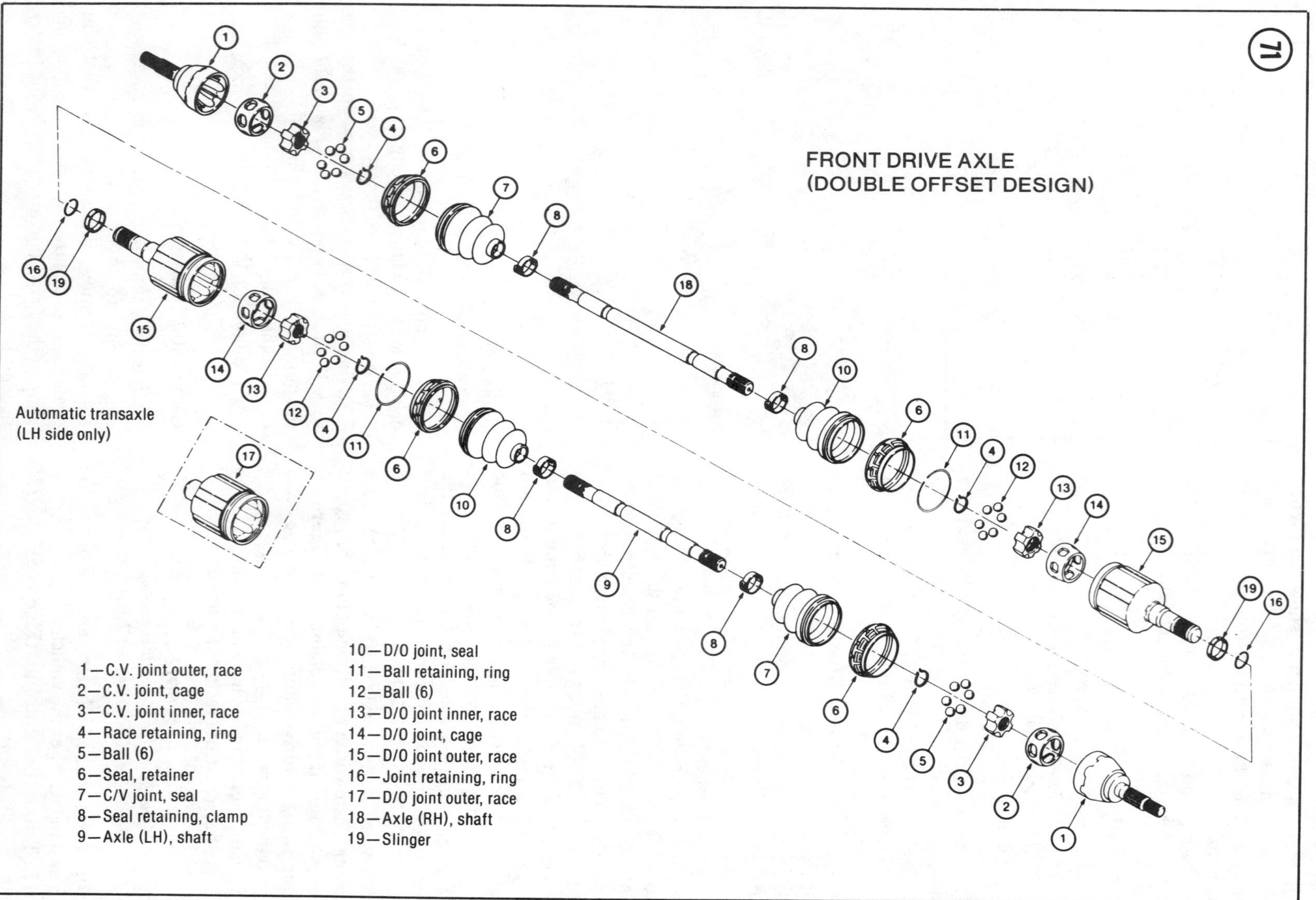
71
FRONT DRIVE AXLE
(DOUBLE OFFSET DESIGN)
Automatic transaxle
(LH side only)
1—C.V. joint outer, race
2—C.V. joint, cage
3—C.V. joint inner, race
4—Race retaining, ring
5—Ball (6)
6—Seal, retainer
7—C/V joint, seal
8—Seal retaining, clamp
9—Axle (LH), shaft
10—D/O joint, seal
11—Ball retaining, ring
12—Ball (6)
13—D/O joint inner, race
14—D/O joint, cage
15—D/O joint outer, race
16—Joint retaining, ring
17—D/O joint outer, race
18—Axle (RH), shaft
19—Slinger

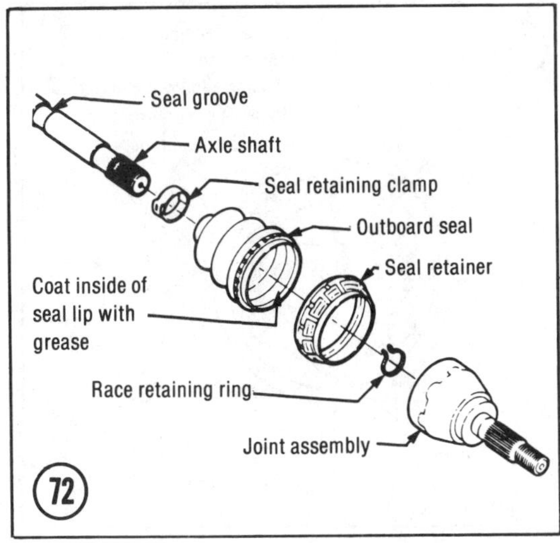

72

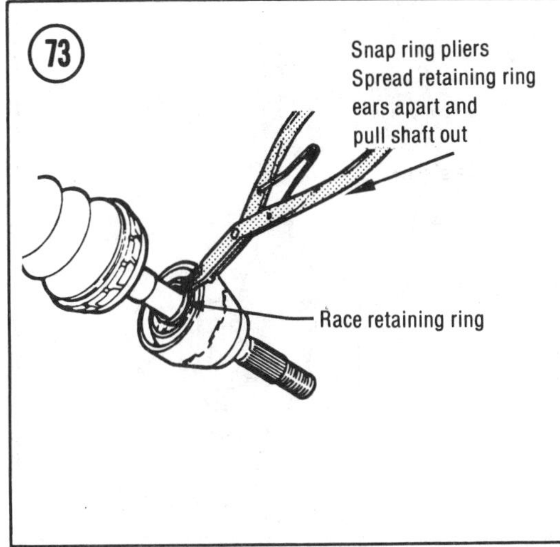

73

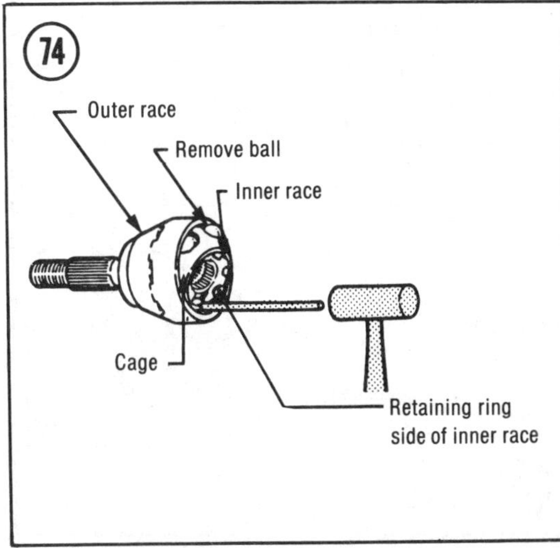

74

NOTE

Before disassembling the drive axle, first purchase a drive axle rebuild kit from a General Motors dealer.

Refer to **Figure 72**.

1. Cut off the seal retaining clamp securing the outboard seal.
2. Lightly tap the seal retainer with a brass drift to detach the retainer from the joint assembly.
3. Remove the retaining ring from the axle shaft by spreading the ring with a pair of snap ring pliers. Remove the joint assembly from the axle. See **Figure 73**.
4. Place the joint assembly on wooden blocks. Using a brass drift and a hammer, gently tap on the bearing cage until it has tilted enough to remove one of the 6 balls. Keep tapping bearing cage in same manner to remove all balls. See **Figure 74**.
5. Referring to **Figure 75**, pivot the cage and inner race 90°. Then, with the cage windows aligned with the lands of the outer race, lift out the cage and inner race.

Outer Joint Reassembly

1. Thoroughly clean all parts in solvent. Replace those parts which are included in the drive axle rebuild kit.
2. With all parts cleaned and placed on a clean work surface, lightly grease the inner and outer race ball grooves. Repack the joint assembly with half of grease provided in rebuild kit. Apply remainder of grease in the outboard seal.
3. Insert the inner race into the cage.
4. Referring to **Figure 75**, insert the cage and inner race assembly into the outer race of the joint assembly.
5. Place the joint assembly on wooden blocks for support. Rotate the inner race, using a brass drift and hammer and insert all 6 balls. See **Figure 74**.
6. Install the seal retaining clamp, outboard seal, seal retainer, race retaining ring and joint assembly onto the axle shaft. Push the joint assembly onto the drive axle by hand until the retaining ring is seated in its groove. See **Figure 72**.

9

NOTE

Coat the inside of the outboard seal lip with grease supplied in drive axle rebuild kit.

7. Place the axle shaft assembly in an arbor press and support the seal retainer as shown in **Figure 76**. Press the axle shaft until the seal retainer seats on the outer joint.
8. Secure rear of outboard seal with retaining clamp.

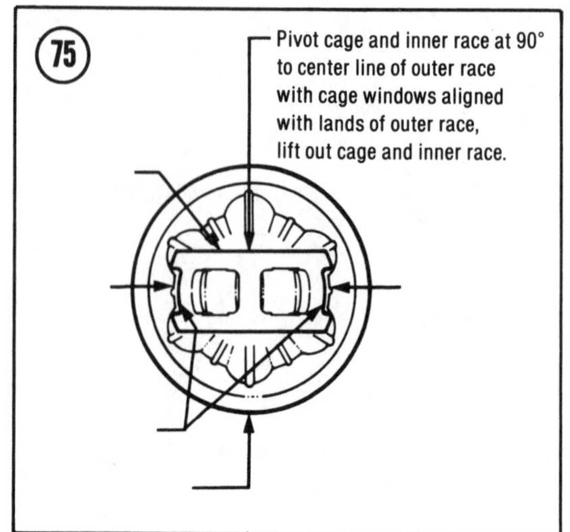

75
Pivot cage and inner race at 90° to center line of outer race with cage windows aligned with lands of outer race, lift out cage and inner race.

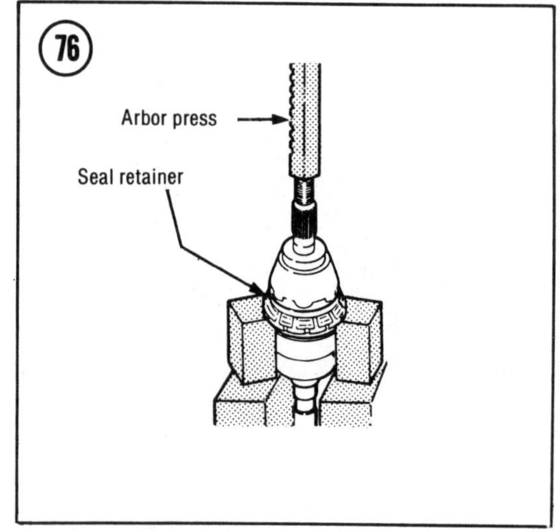

Inner Joint Disassembly

Consider your safety and, if you do not feel competent to overhaul the drive axle assembly, remove the assembly and let your dealer do it. **Figure 77** shows an exploded view of the drive axle assembly. Refer to it as needed.

Refer to **Figure 77**.

1. Cut off the seal retaining clamp securing the outboard seal.
2. Lightly tap the seal retainer with a brass drift to detach the seal retainer from the joint assembly.
3. Remove the retaining ring from the axle shaft by spreading the ring ears with a pair of snap ring pliers. Remove the joint assembly from the axle.
4. Disassemble the inner joint by removing the retaining ball from the joint. Pull the cage, inner race and balls out. See **Figure 78**.
5. Center the inner race lobes in windows of cage (**Figure 79**). Rotate the inner race 90° and lift from cage.

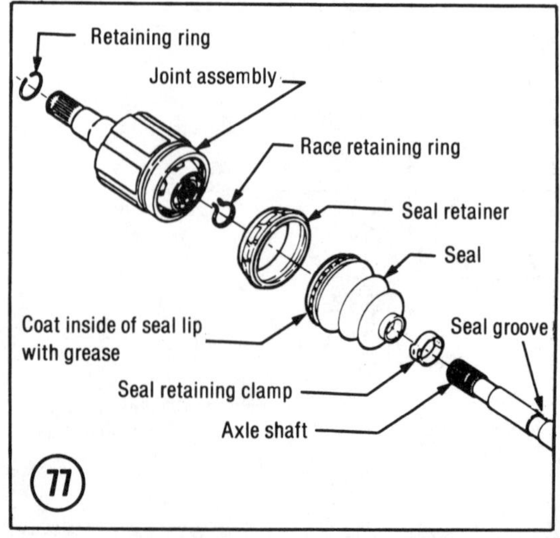

Inner Joint Reassembly

1. Thoroughly clean all parts in solvent. Replace those parts which are included in the drive axle rebuild kit.

CAUTION

On automatic transaxles, the right-hand inboard boot is exposed to extremely high temperatures. During reassembly, a special silicone-rubber boot and high temperature grease must be used. Consult your General Motors dealer for the correct parts.

2. With all parts cleaned and placed on a clean work surface, lightly grease the inner and outer race ball grooves. Repack joint assembly with half of grease provided in rebuild kit. Apply remainder of grease in the seal.

3. Insert the inner race into the cage. Make sure the retaining ring on the inner race faces the small end of the cage before installing balls. See **Figure 80**.

4. Insert the cage and inner race assembly into the outer race of the joint assembly. Secure with a new ball retaining ring.

5. Referring to **Figure 77**, install the seal retaining clamp, seal, seal retainer, ball retaining ring and joint assembly onto the axle shaft. Push the joint assembly onto the drive axle by hand until the retaining ring is seated in its groove.

NOTE
Make sure the retaining ring side of the inner race and small end of cage face the axle shaft.

NOTE
Coat the inside of the outboard seal lip with grease supplied in drive axle rebuild kit.

6. Place the axle shaft assembly in an arbor press and support the seal retainer as shown in **Figure 81**. Press the joint assembly until the seal retainer seats on the outer joint.

7. Secure rear of seal with seal retaining clamp.

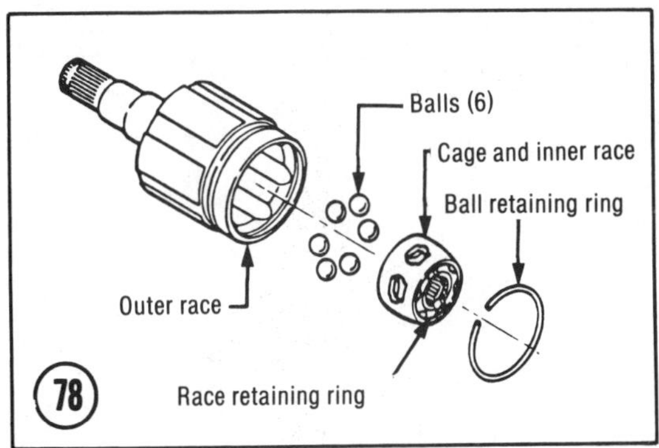

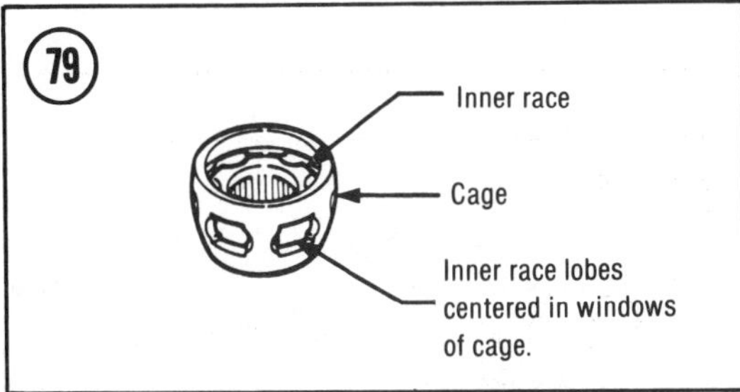

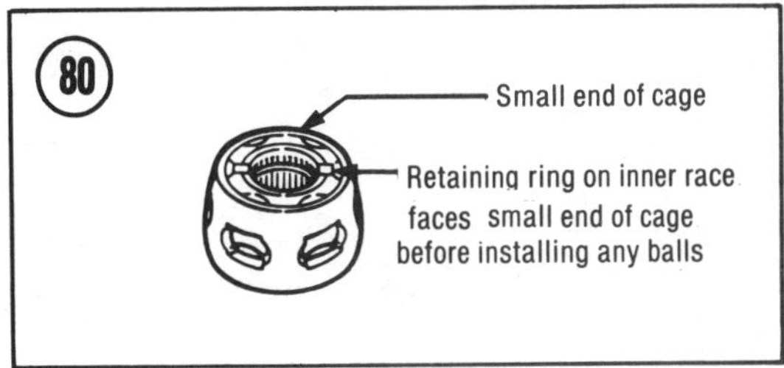

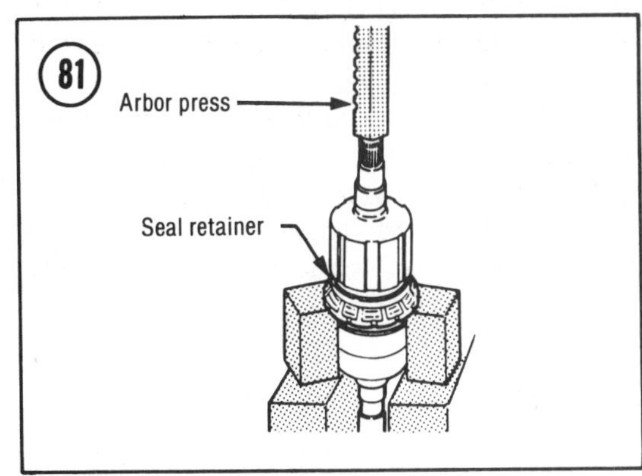

Table 1 TIGHTENING TORQUES, MANUAL TRANSAXLE

Item	Torque	
Input shaft R.H. bearing retainer	7 ft.-lb.	(9 N•m)
Reverse idler shaft lock bolt	16 ft.-lb.	(21 N•m)
Pinion shaft lock bolt	7 ft.-lb.	(9 N•m)
Ring gear bolt	54 ft.-lb.	(73 N•m)
Reverse inhibitor fitting	26 ft.-lb.	(35 N•m)
Case-to-cover bolts	16 ft.-lb.	(21 N•m)

9

Table 2 TIGHTENING TORQUES, AUTOMATIC TRANSAXLE

Item	Torque	
Oil pan and valve to body cover	12 ft.-lb.	(16 N•m)
Cooler connector	23 ft.-lb.	(38 N•m)
Detent spring	8 ft.-lb.	(11 N•m)
Speedometer gear to governor cover	75 in.-lb.	(9 N•m)
T.V. cable to case	75 in.-lb.	(9 N•m)

NOTE: If you own a 1981 or later model, first check the Supplement at the back of the book for any new service information.

CHAPTER TEN

FRONT SUSPENSION AND STEERING

A MacPherson strut front suspension is used in which the shock absorbers and springs are combined into a single unit. The lower control arms pivot from the engine cradle. The cradle is mounted to the body by isolation mounts. Rubber bushings are used for the lower control arm pivots.

Rack-and-pinion steering is used. The steering mechanism is controlled through a 2-section steering column, the upper half of which is collapsible. The lower half of the column is a rigid shaft with universal joints.

Refer to **Figure 1** for the major front suspension components. Additional components are shown throughout this chapter.

Tightening torques are found in **Table 1**. Wheel alignment specificaions are found in **Table 2**. Both tables are at the end of the chapter.

CAUTION

All fasteners used in the front suspension and steering must be replaced with parts of the same type. ***Do not*** *use a replacement part of lesser quality or substitute design, as it may affect the performance of vital components and systems or result in major repair expense.*

WHEEL ALIGNMENT

Front end alignment should be checked at 12,000 mile intervals by a General Motors dealer or a front end specialist (see **Table 2**, end of chapter). Front tire wear patterns can indicate several alignment problems. These are discussed and illustrated under *Tire Wear Analysis*, Chapter Two.

Of the 3 principal factors affecting front end alignment and geometry—caster, camber and toe-in—only camber and toe-in are adjustable.

Front Suspension Inspection

The steering and various suspension angles previously mentioned are affected by several factors. Perform the following steps before checking or adjusting wheel alignment.

1. Check the air pressure in the tires and correct as necessary. Maximum tire pressures are found on the side of each tire. Recommended tire pressures are listed on the left front door panel.
2. Check the operation of the shock absorbers by bouncing the car at both front and rear. When released, the car should not bounce more than twice. Excessive bouncing is an indication that the front struts are no longer serviceable.

1

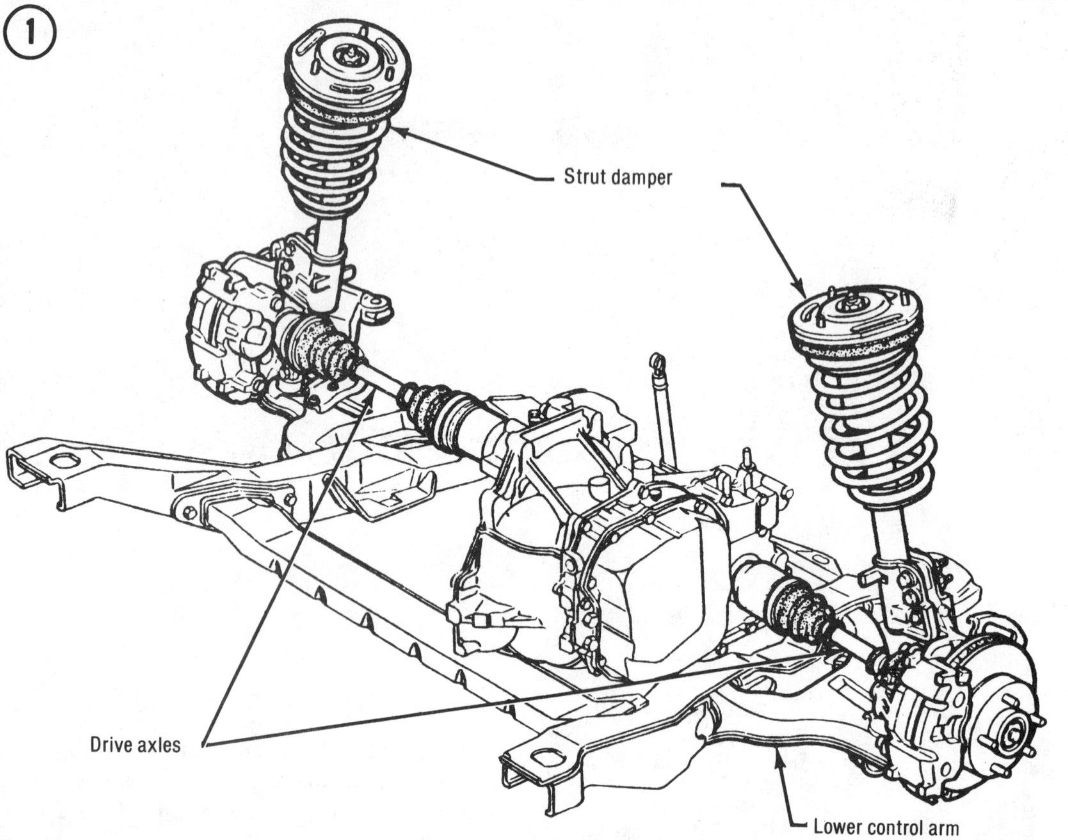

Strut damper

Drive axles

Lower control arm

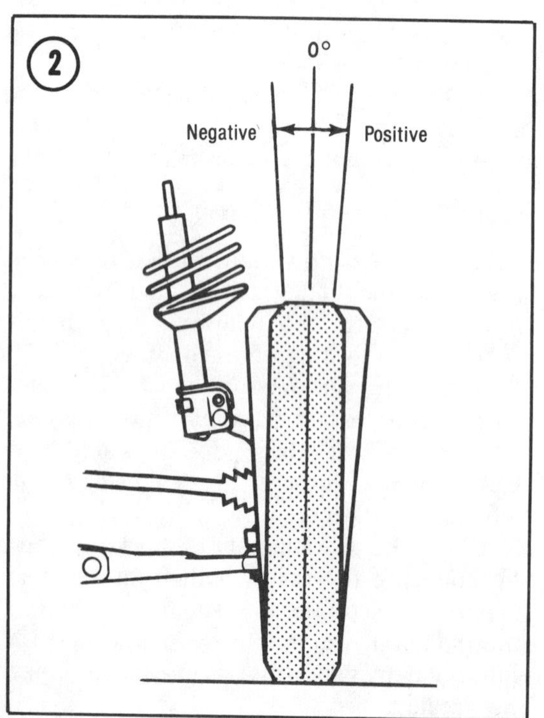

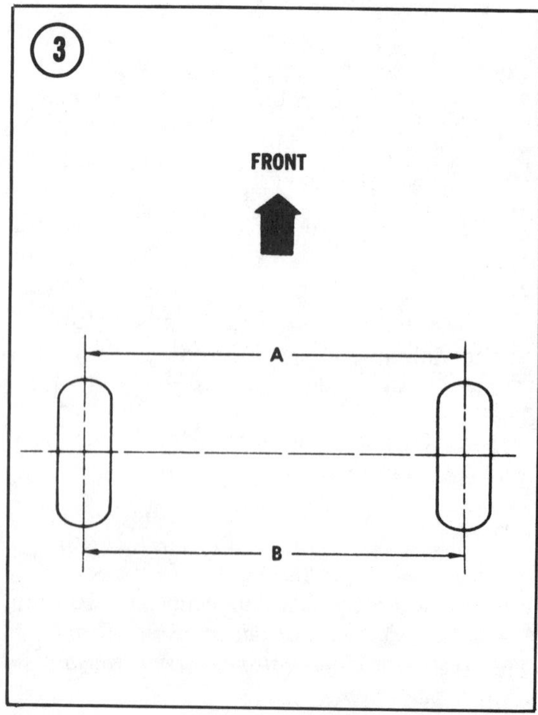

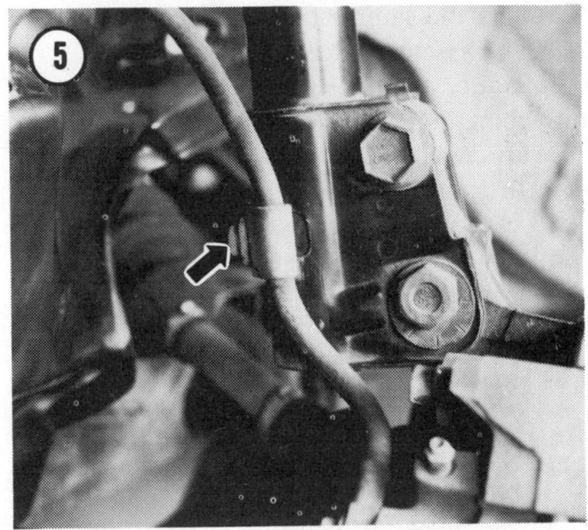

3. Check the front strut mounting bolts for tightness and tighten them as required, referring to **Table 1**.
4. Check the front wheel bearings for tightness and tighten them as required, using procedures discussed later in this chapter.
5. With the front of the car raised, try to move the control arm back and forth. If movement is felt, tighten the pivot bolt to 48 ft.-lb. (65 N•m) and check for movement. Movement indicates a worn control arm pivot bushing.
6. Check the stabilizer bar for damage and inspect its mounting bushings for wear and deterioration. Tighten the mounting bolts.
7. Remove any excessive weight load.
8. Check rack-and-pinion mechanism and tie rods for looseness.
9. Check wheel balance.
10. Check *rear* suspension for looseness.

Camber

Camber is the inclination of the wheel from vertical. See **Figure 2**. With positive camber, the top of the tire leans outward. With negative camber, the top of the tire leans inward. Camber alignment and adjustment must be performed by a front end specialist.

Toe-in

Since the front wheels tend to point outward when the car is moving forward, they are adjusted to point slightly inward at rest. This means distance A (**Figure 3**) should be slightly less than distance B.

Toe-in is changed by adjusting the tie rods. To adjust toe:

1. Loosen the nut at the steering knuckle end of the tie rod (**Figure 4**).
2. Loosen the rubber boot at the other end of the tie rod.
3. Rotate the rod as needed to adjust toe. See **Table 2**.
4. Tighten the cover and locknuts on the tie rod.

FRONT STRUTS

NOTE

*If Step 2 in **Front Suspension Inspection** indicates weak springs or unserviceable shock absorbers, have them serviced by a General Motors dealer; a special compressor is required to dismantle and assemble the strut.*

Replacement

1. Raise the front end of the car and place it on jackstands. Remove the front wheels.

NOTE

Once vehicle is secured on jackstands, remove jack and reposition under hub and rotor assembly on side of strut being removed. This will allow repositioning of the lower control arm during service.

2. Remove clip attaching the brake hose to the strut. Do not disconnect the brake line. See **Figure 5**.

10

3. Mark the camber cam adjuster bolt and the strut for assembly. See **Figure 6**.
4. Remove the upper strut-to-knuckle attaching bolt and the cam adjuster bolt from the lower end of strut (**Figure 7**).
5. Unscrew the nuts which attach the upper end of the strut (**Figure 8**) to the vehicle body and remove the strut assembly from the car.

CAUTION
Do not allow the strut to contact the drive axle boot during removal.

Installation

1. Install the strut to the upper body. Install the 3 upper strut-to-body attaching nuts finger-tight (**Figure 8**).
2. Raise the lower control arm with a jack and install the lower strut-to-knuckle bolt and the camber cam bolt (**Figure 7**).
3. Align the camber cam adjustment marks made during disassembly (**Figure 6**).

CAUTION
The camber cam bolt is used to move the wheel and upper knuckle assembly in or out as required to provide proper camber adjustment. If the adjustment marks are not aligned exactly, camber adjustment will be off.

4. Tighten the strut-to-knuckle attaching bolt and the camber cam bolt to 140 ft.-lb. (190 N•m). Tighten the upper strut-to-body nuts to 18 ft.-lb. (24 N•m).
5. Install the brake line clip at the strut (**Figure 5**).
6. Install wheel and lower vehicle.

NOTE
If the strut assembly was replaced with a new unit, it will be necessary to have the front end aligned by a General Motors dealer or qualified front end specialist.

FRONT HUB AND WHEEL BEARINGS

Adjustment

Front wheel bearings are sealed and non-adjustable. Service consists of inspection and replacement of the hub and bearing assembly only.

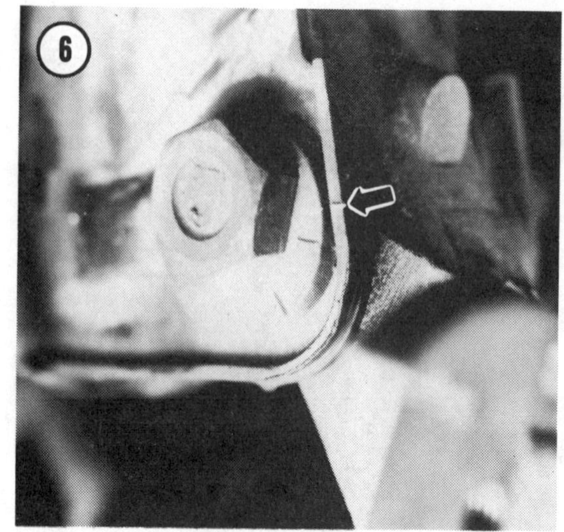

Inspection

To check looseness of the front wheel bearing, perform the following procedure.

1. Remove the brake caliper from the wheel as described in Chapter Twelve. Support caliper as shown in **Figure 9** with wire or other holding device. Do not allow caliper to hang from the brake line.
2. Mount a dial indicator as shown in **Figure 10**.
3. Grasp disc and attempt to move disc with push-pull movement. If disc movement exceeds 0.005 in. (0.127 mm), replace the hub and bearing assembly.

Replacement

The bearing assembly is shown in **Figure 11**.

1. Remove wheel cover and loosen the axle nut and front wheel nuts.
2. Jack up the front end of the car and place it on jackstands. Remove the front wheel.
3. Remove the axle nut loosened in Step 1 (**Figure 12**).
4. Remove the brake caliper as described in Chapter Twelve. Support caliper as shown in **Figure 9**. Do not allow caliper to hang from brake line.
5. Remove the hub and bearing securing bolts (**Figure 13**). Then remove the rotor splash

9

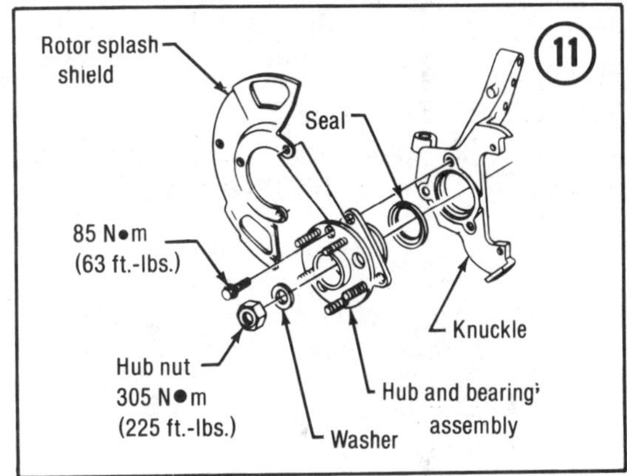

11

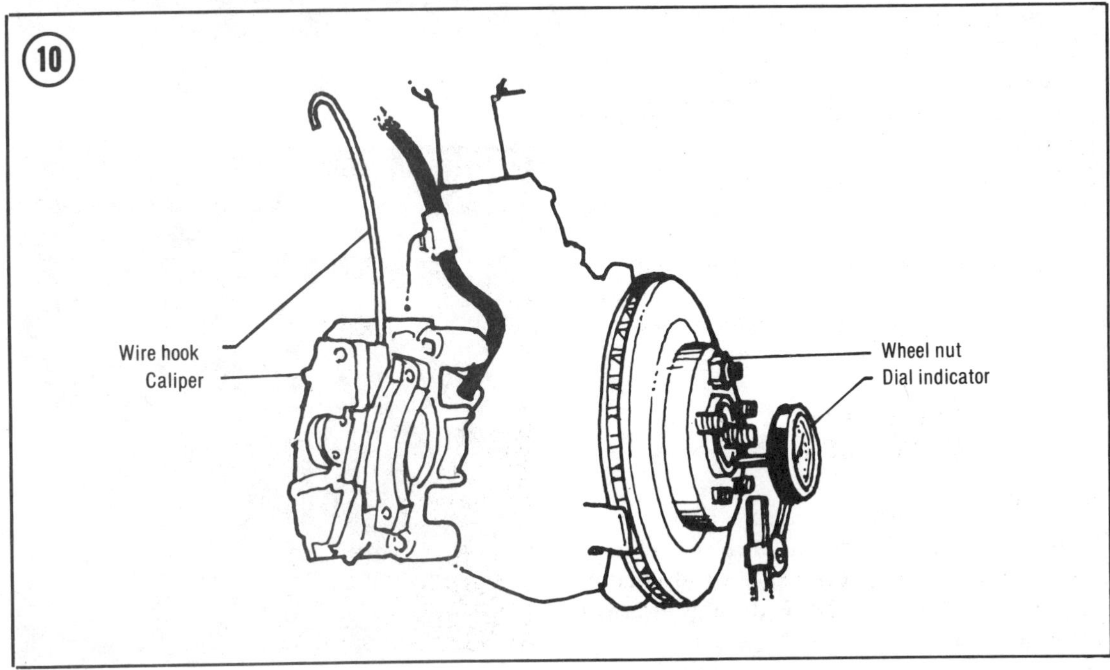

10

shield in front of the hub and bearing assembly.

NOTE

If old hub and bearing are to be reused, scribe alignment marks on hub and steering knuckle bolt holes to ensure exact reassembly alignment.

6. Attach a bearing puller to the front hub assembly (**Figure 14**) and remove the hub and bearing as an assembly.
7. Check bearing for wear, pitting, and cracks. Clean and inspect all bearing mating surfaces and steering knuckle bore (**Figure 15**) for dirt, nicks, and burrs.
8. If steering knuckle seal is damaged, or if a new front wheel bearing is being installed, install a new steering knuckle seal into the steering knuckle bore using an equivalent size drift. See **Figure 16**. Apply grease to seal and knuckle bore.
9. Push the bearing onto the driveshaft. Install a new washer and hub nut.

NOTE

Make sure to align steering knuckle and hub bolt hole alignment marks made during removal (Step 5) if old hub and bearing are being reinstalled.

10. Tighten the hub nut (**Figure 12**) until the bearing is seated (about 70 ft.-lb.). Do not apply full torque.
11. Install the rotor splash shield onto the hub and bearing assembly (**Figure 13**). Tighten attaching bolts to 63 ft.-lb. (85 N•m).
12. Install the brake caliper as described in Chapter Twelve. Make sure brake hose is not twisted.
13. Install the wheel and lower the car.
14. Tighten the hub nut to 225 ft.-lb. (305 N•m). Tighten the wheel nuts to 103 ft.-lb. (140 N•m).

BALL-JOINT REPLACEMENT

Ball-joints are used on each lower arm (**Figure 17**) and are secured by 3 rivets (**Figure 18**). To determine the condition of ball-joints, each have built-in wear indicators along the grease nipple. See **Figure 19**. When

12

13

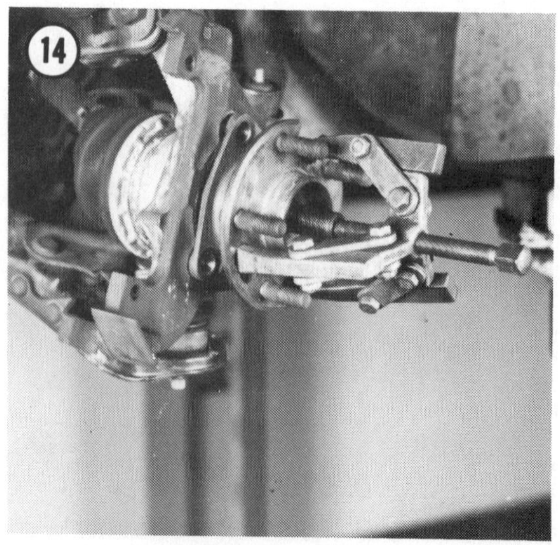

14

15

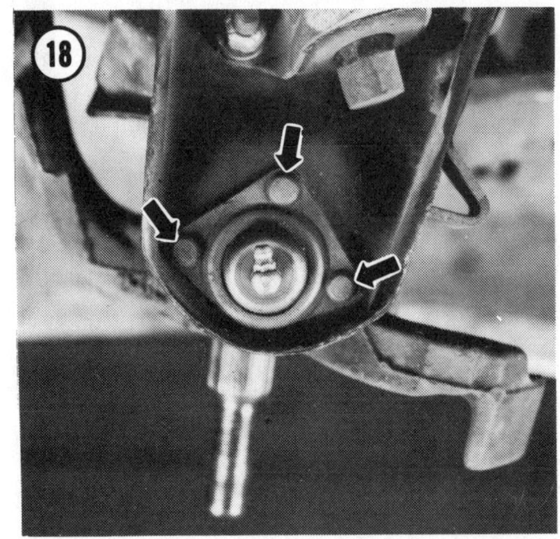
18

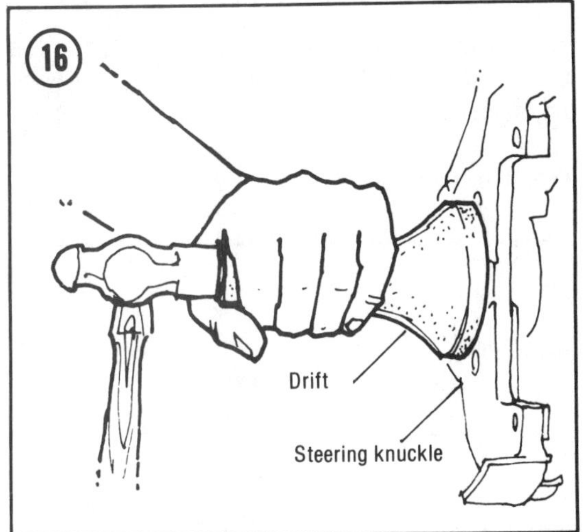
16
Drift
Steering knuckle

17

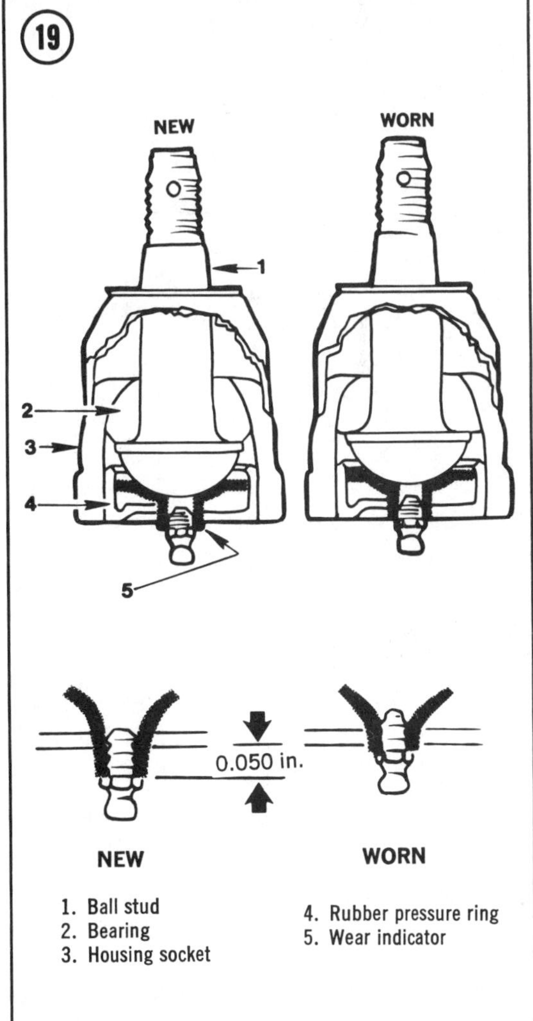
19
NEW
WORN
1
2
3
4
5
0.050 in.
NEW
WORN
1. Ball stud
2. Bearing
3. Housing socket
4. Rubber pressure ring
5. Wear indicator

nipple extends below the ball-joint seat, the joint is okay. When the indicator draws into the seat, the joint must be replaced.

1. Jack up the front end of the car and place it on jackstands. Remove the front wheels.
2. Use a 1/8 in. drill bit to drill a 1/4 in. deep hole in each of the 3 ball-joint rivets (Step 1, **Figure 20**).
3. Use a 1/2 in. drill bit and drill off each rivet head. Drill only enough to remove the rivet head (Step 2, **Figure 20**).
4. Remove each rivet with a drift punch and hammer (Step 3, **Figure 20**).

WARNING
Wear safety glasses when removing rivets to prevent possible eye injury.

5. Loosen the ball-joint pinch bolt in the steering knuckle (**Figure 21**) and remove the ball-joint.
6. Install a new ball-joint assembly. Secure with replacement bolts. Tighten bolts to 8 ft.-lb. (4 N•m). See **Figure 20**, Step 4.
7. Referring to **Figure 21**, install the ball-joint pinch bolt in the steering bolt knuckle. Bolt should slide in slot easily. If not, check stud alignment. Tighten to 45 ft.-lb. (60 N•m).
8. Install the wheel and lower the car.

CONTROL ARM

Refer to **Figure 22** for these procedures.

Removal

1. Loosen the front wheel nuts, jack up the front end of the car and place it on jackstands (under the frame). Remove the front wheels.
2. Remove the stabilizer bar as described in this chapter.
3. With the vehicle secured with jackstands, place the floor jack underneath the lower control arm.
4. Referring to **Figure 21**, remove the ball-joint pinch bolt in the steering knuckle. Position the jack to hold the lower control arm.
5. Remove the control arm pivot bolts (**Figure 22**) and the control arm.

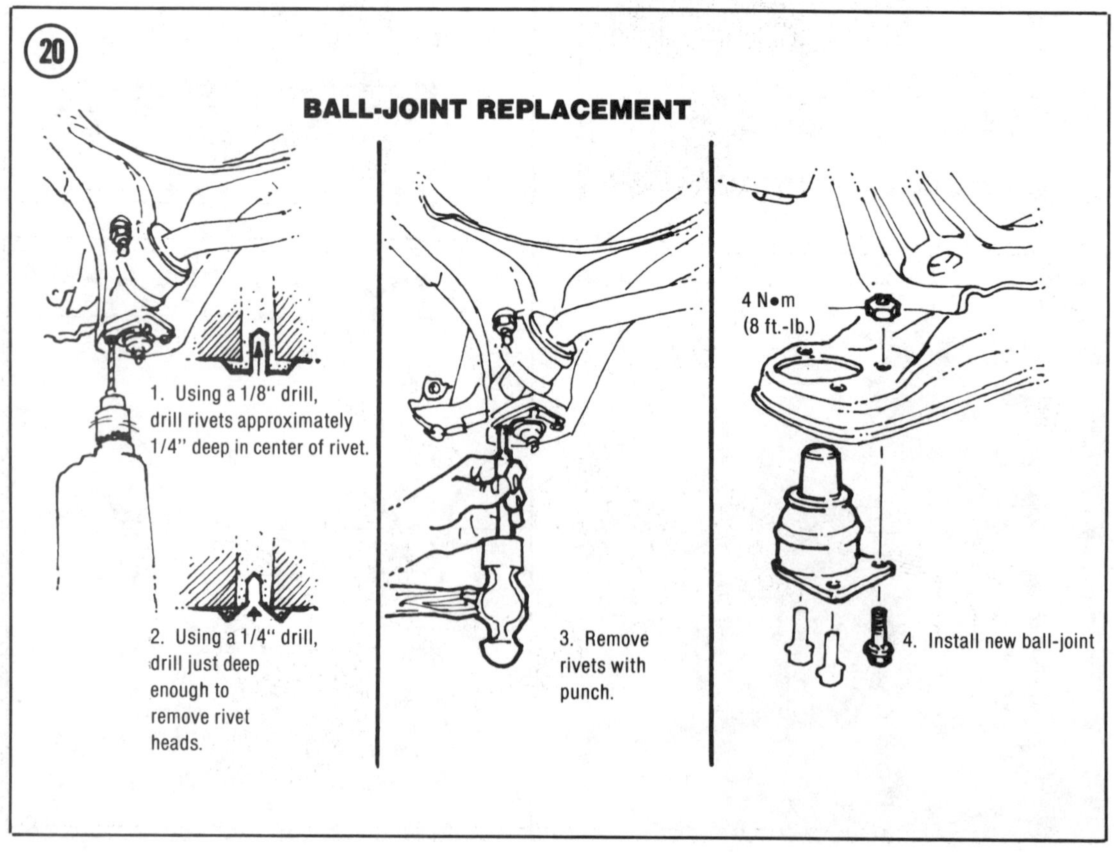
20
BALL-JOINT REPLACEMENT
1. Using a 1/8" drill, drill rivets approximately 1/4" deep in center of rivet.
2. Using a 1/4" drill, drill just deep enough to remove rivet heads.
3. Remove rivets with punch.
4 N•m (8 ft.-lb.)
4. Install new ball-joint

Installation

1. Install control arm with new pivot bolts.

NOTE

*Install pivot bolts with bolt head facing toward rear of car. See **Figure 22**.*

2. Install the pivot nuts.
3. Hold the control arm in place and tighten the nuts to 48 ft.-lb. (65 N•m).
4. Refer to **Figure 21** and install the ball-joint pinch bolt in the steering bolt knuckle. Bolt should slide in slot easily. If not, check stud alignment. Tighten to 45 ft.-lb. (60 N•m).
5. Install the stabalizer bar as described in this chapter.
6. Install the wheel and lower the car.

STEERING KNUCKLE

Refer to **Figure 23** for this procedure.

Removal

1. Loosen the front wheel nuts, jack up the front end of the car and place it on jackstands. Remove the front wheels.

NOTE

Support the control arm with a jackstand.

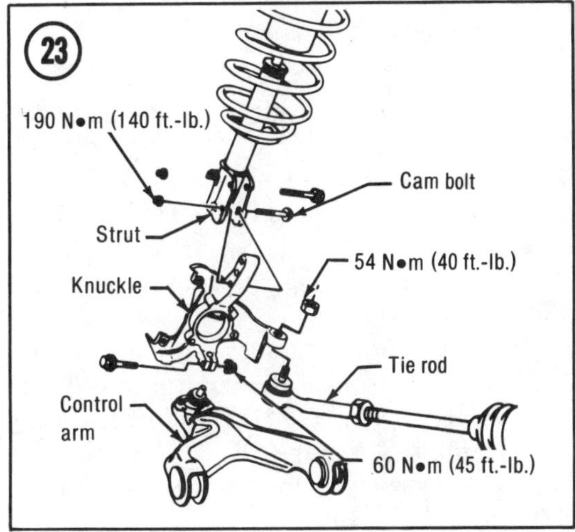

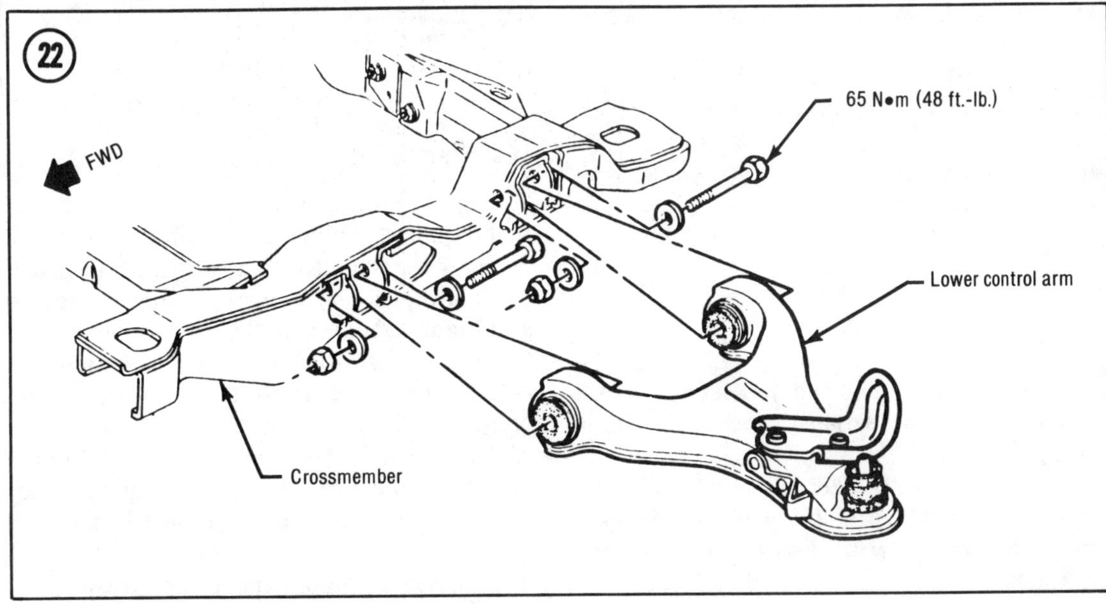

10

2. Remove the front hub and bearing assembly as described in this chapter.
3. Refer to **Figure 6** and mark the alignment position of the camber cam bolt.
4. Remove the upper strut-to-knuckle bolt and the camber cam bolt (**Figure 7**). Position strut clear of knuckle.
5. Remove tie rod nut at side of knuckle (**Figure 4**). Remove the tie rod end from the steering knuckle with GM tool part No. J-6627 or equivalent. See **Figure 24**.
6. Remove the ball-joint pinch bolt in the steering knuckle (**Figure 21**). Remove the steering knuckle and, at the same time lower the drive axle carefully to prevent damage to the axle boot.

Installation

1. Place steering knuckle in position. Install ball-joint pinch bolt to steering knuckle finger-tight (**Figure 21**).
2. Install knuckle-to-strut attaching bolts finger-tight.
3. Install front bearing and hub as described in this chapter.
4. Place a floor jack underneath the control arm and raise to load the control arm. Align the camber cam bolt as marked during disassembly (**Figure 6**). Tighten the knuckle-to-strut and the camber cam bolt to 140 ft.-lb. (190 N•m).
5. Install the tie rod end to the steering knuckle using a clamp tool and a 1 1/8 in. socket. See **Figure 25**.
6. Tighten the ball-joint pinch bolt in the steering knuckle to 45 ft.-lb. (60 N•m). Make sure pivot bolt can rotate in slot before applying torque.
7. Install wheel.
8. Remove jackstands and lower vehicle.

STABILIZER BAR

Removal

1. Raise the car on a hoist or jackstands.
2. Disconnect the exhaust pipe at the front pipe connection.
3. Remove the stabilizer bar plate from the crossmember (**Figure 26**) and the bracket from the control arm (**Figure 27**). Remove the stabilizer bar.

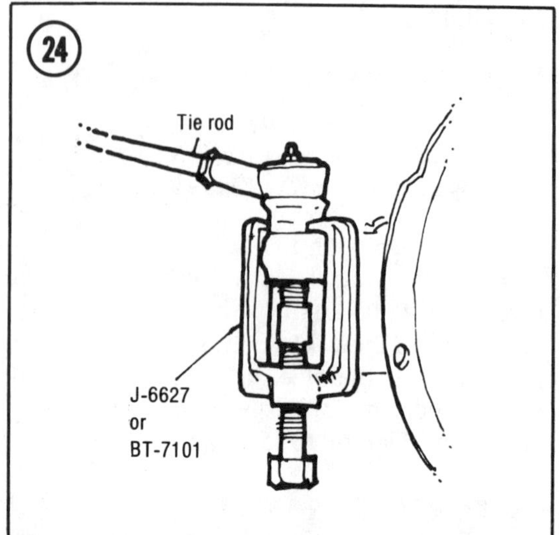

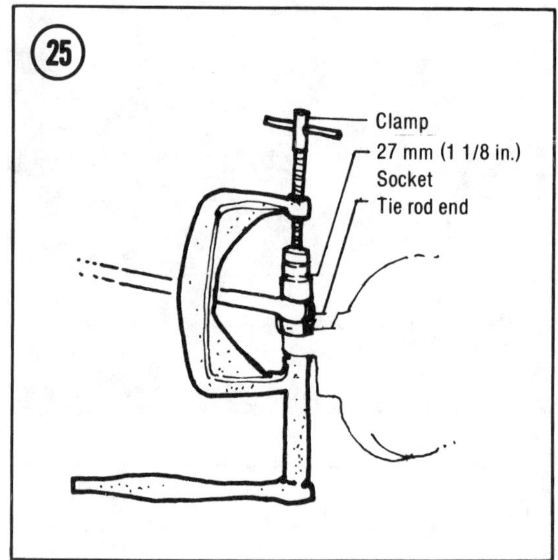

Installation

1. Install bushing on ends of stabilizer bar, making sure bushings are centered correctly.
2. Hold the stabilizer bar in place and install the body plates and brackets. See **Figure 26** and **Figure 27**. Tighten the crossmember plate bolts to 40 ft.-lb. (55 N•m). Tighten the control arm bracket bolts to 35 ft.-lb. (45 N•m).
3. Reconnect the exhaust pipe. Tighten attaching bolts to 15 ft.-lb. (20 N.-m). Replace the exhaust pipe connection seal if damaged or worn.
4. Remove jackstands and lower the car.

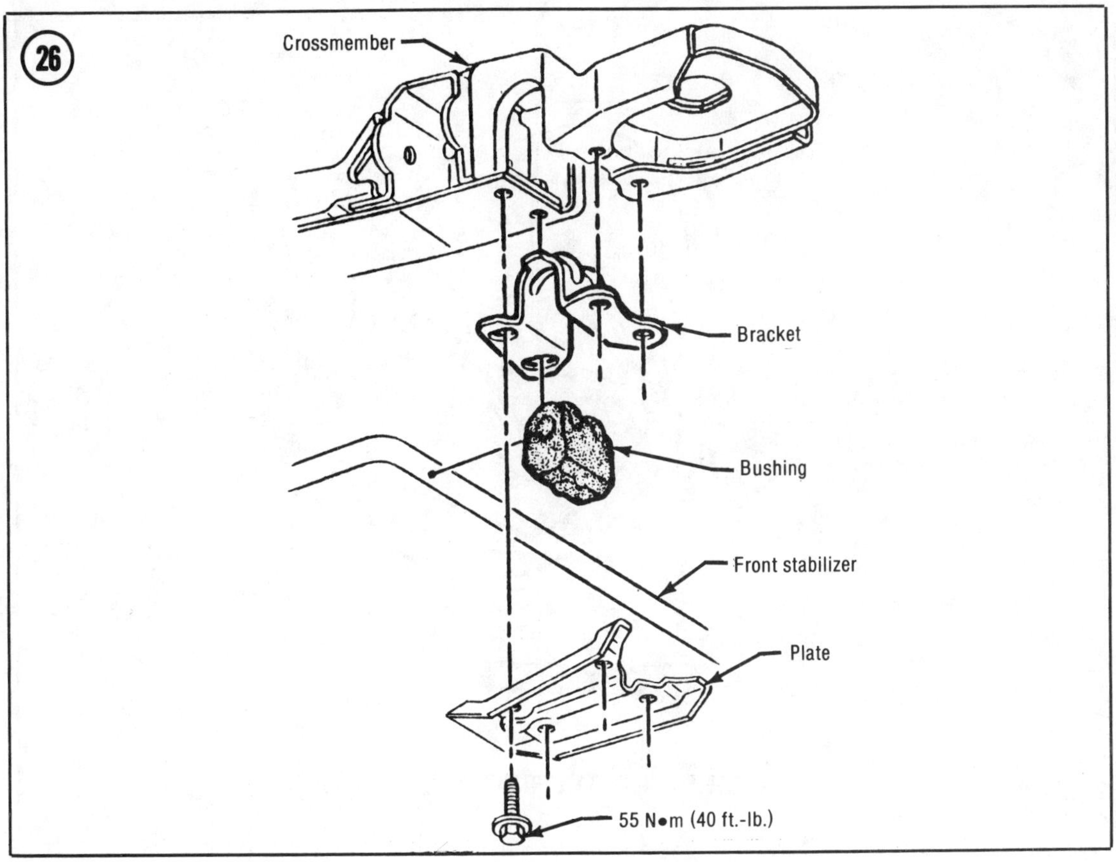

26
Crossmember
Bracket
Bushing
Front stabilizer
Plate
55 N•m (40 ft.-lb.)

27
Lower control arm
Do not remove studs from control arm.
Bushing
Crossmember
End of stabilizer should be equal distance from bushing on both sides.
45 N•m (35 ft.-lb.)

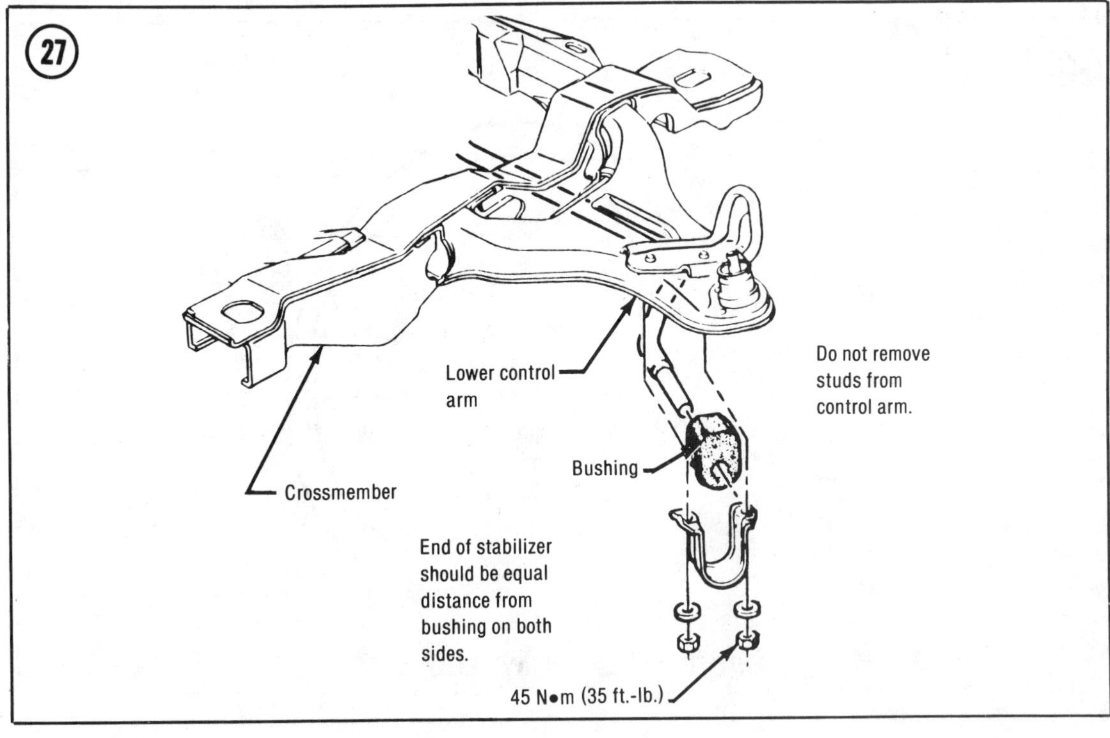

28

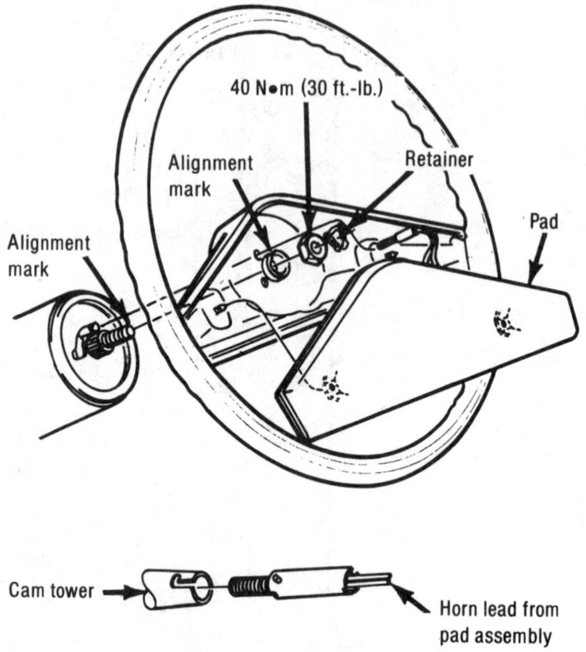

40 N•m (30 ft.-lb.)
Alignment mark
Retainer
Pad
Alignment mark
Cam tower
Horn lead from pad assembly

STANDARD STEERING WHEEL

29

40 N•m (30 ft.-lb.)
Alignment mark
Insulator
Eyelet
Spring
Cap
Retainer
Alignment mark

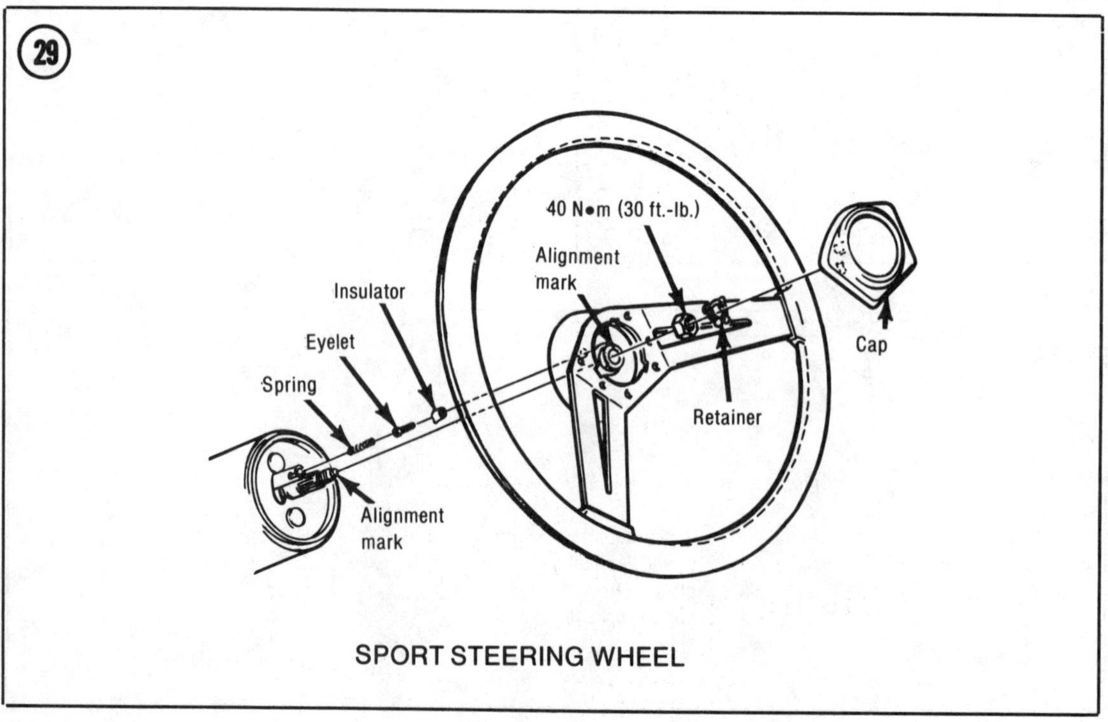

SPORT STEERING WHEEL

STEERING WHEEL

Refer to **Figure 28** (standard wheel) or **Figure 29** (sport wheel) for this procedure.

Removal

1. Disconnect battery ground cable.
2A. On standard wheel, remove 2 pad screws at underside of steering wheel and remove the pad.
2B. On sport wheel, pull off center cap.
3. Remove retainer and wheel nut.

NOTE

*Refer to **Figure 28** or **Figure 29** and note position of steering wheel alignment marks.*

4. Thread steering wheel puller anchor screws into threaded holes in steering wheel. Turn tool to center bolt clockwise against the steering shaft and remove the steering wheel. See **Figure 30**.

Installation

1. Match alignment mark on steering shaft and steering wheel, then install the steering wheel.
2. Install steering wheel nut and torque to 30 ft.-lb. (40 N•m).
3. Install nut retainer.
4. Install center pad (**Figure 28**) or cap (**Figure 29**).

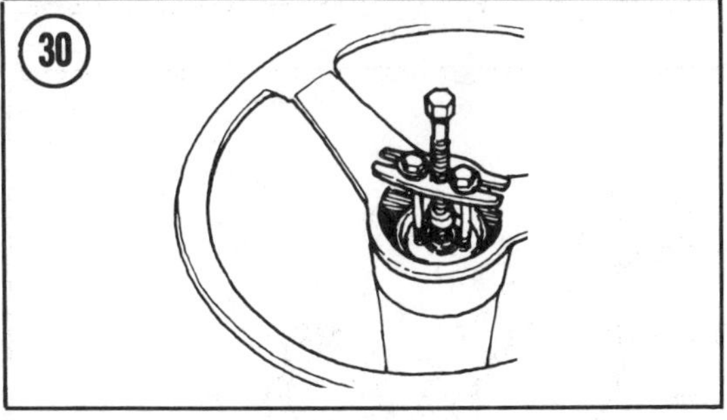

STEERING COLUMN

Refer to **Figure 31** for this procedure. See also **Figure 32** (standard column) or **Figure 33** (key release standard column) for disassembly view drawings.

Removal

1. Disconnect the battery ground cable.
2. Remove the steering wheel as described under *Steering Wheel Removal.*
3. Move the driver's seat all the way back.
4. Remove the steering column trim cover.
5. *Air-conditioned vehicles only*: Remove the sound absorber beneath the steering column.
6. Disconnect the bracket attaching the shift cable to the steering column.
7. Remove the bolt attaching the steering column to the intermediate shaft.
8. Disconnect all wiring harness connectors. See **Figure 34**.

NOTE

Check at this point to make sure all electrical wiring and control cables are detached from the steering column. Disconnect any wiring or control connections as required.

9. Remove bolts attaching the steering column support bracket to the bottom of the instrument panel. Remove the support bracket.
10. Pull the column rearward and remove the assembly from the vehicle.

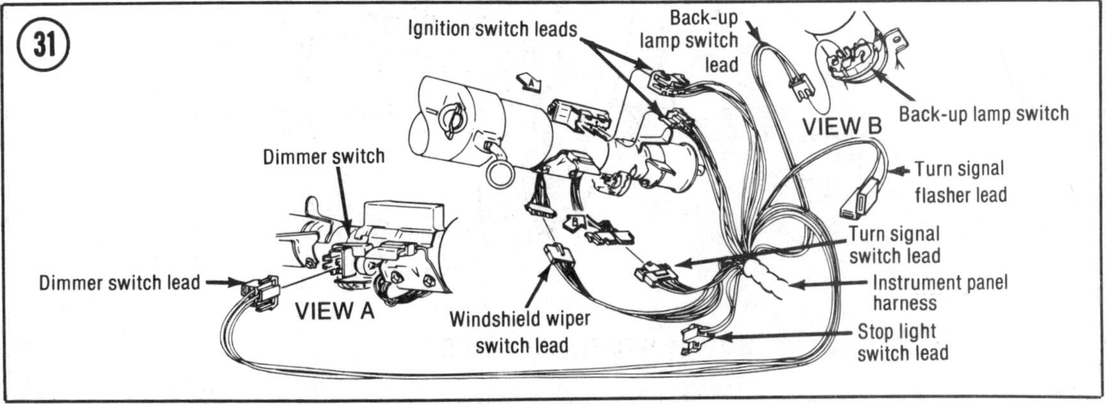

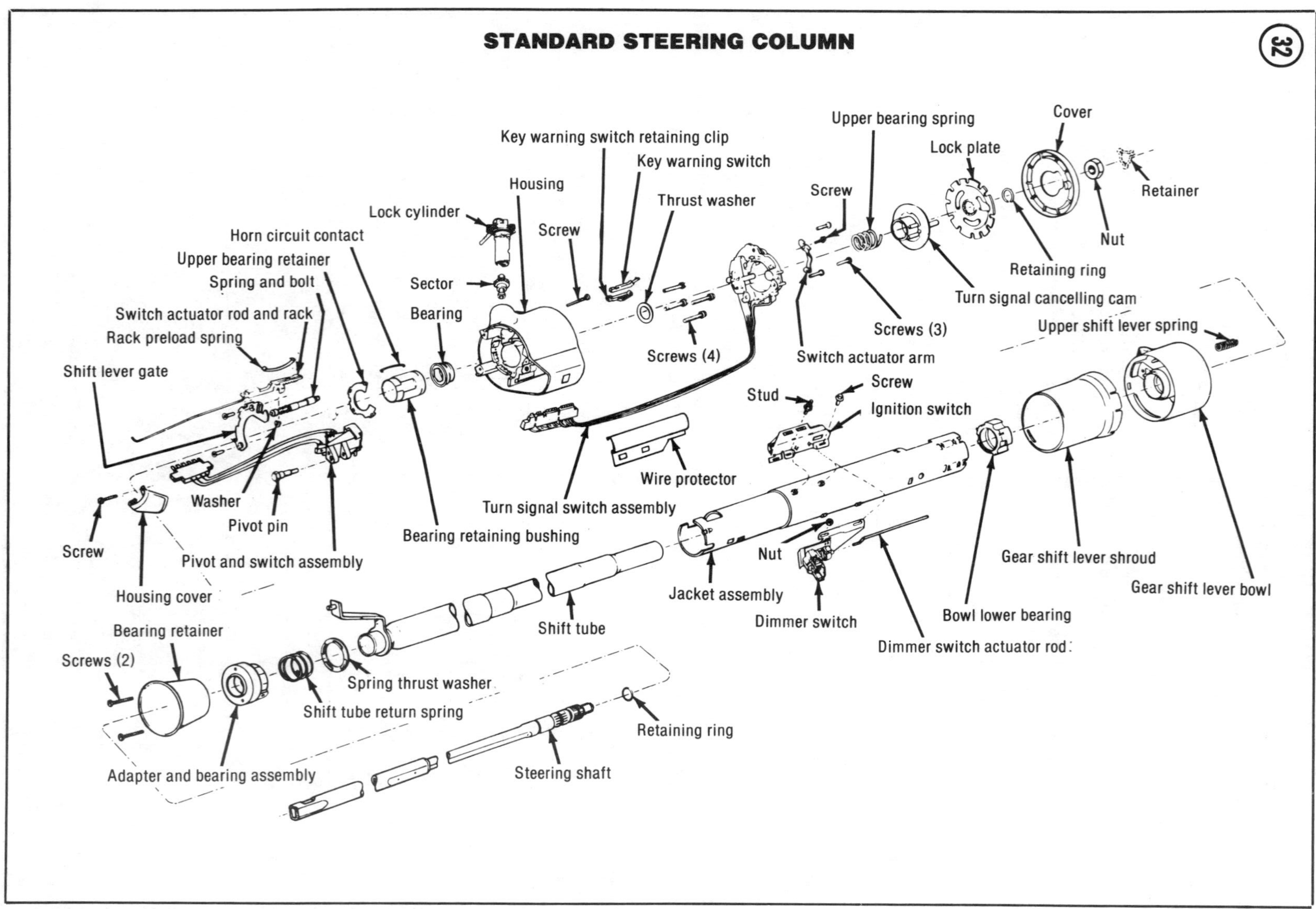
STANDARD STEERING COLUMN
32
Upper bearing spring
Cover
Key warning switch retaining clip
Key warning switch
Lock plate
Housing
Thrust washer
Screw
Retainer
Lock cylinder
Screw
Nut
Horn circuit contact
Upper bearing retainer
Retaining ring
Spring and bolt
Sector
Turn signal cancelling cam
Switch actuator rod and rack
Bearing
Screws (3)
Upper shift lever spring
Rack preload spring
Screws (4)
Switch actuator arm
Shift lever gate
Screw
Stud
Ignition switch
Wire protector
Washer
Turn signal switch assembly
Pivot pin
Bearing retaining bushing
Screw
Nut
Gear shift lever shroud
Pivot and switch assembly
Gear shift lever bowl
Housing cover
Jacket assembly
Shift tube
Dimmer switch
Bowl lower bearing
Bearing retainer
Dimmer switch actuator rod
Screws (2)
Spring thrust washer
Shift tube return spring
Retaining ring
Adapter and bearing assembly
Steering shaft

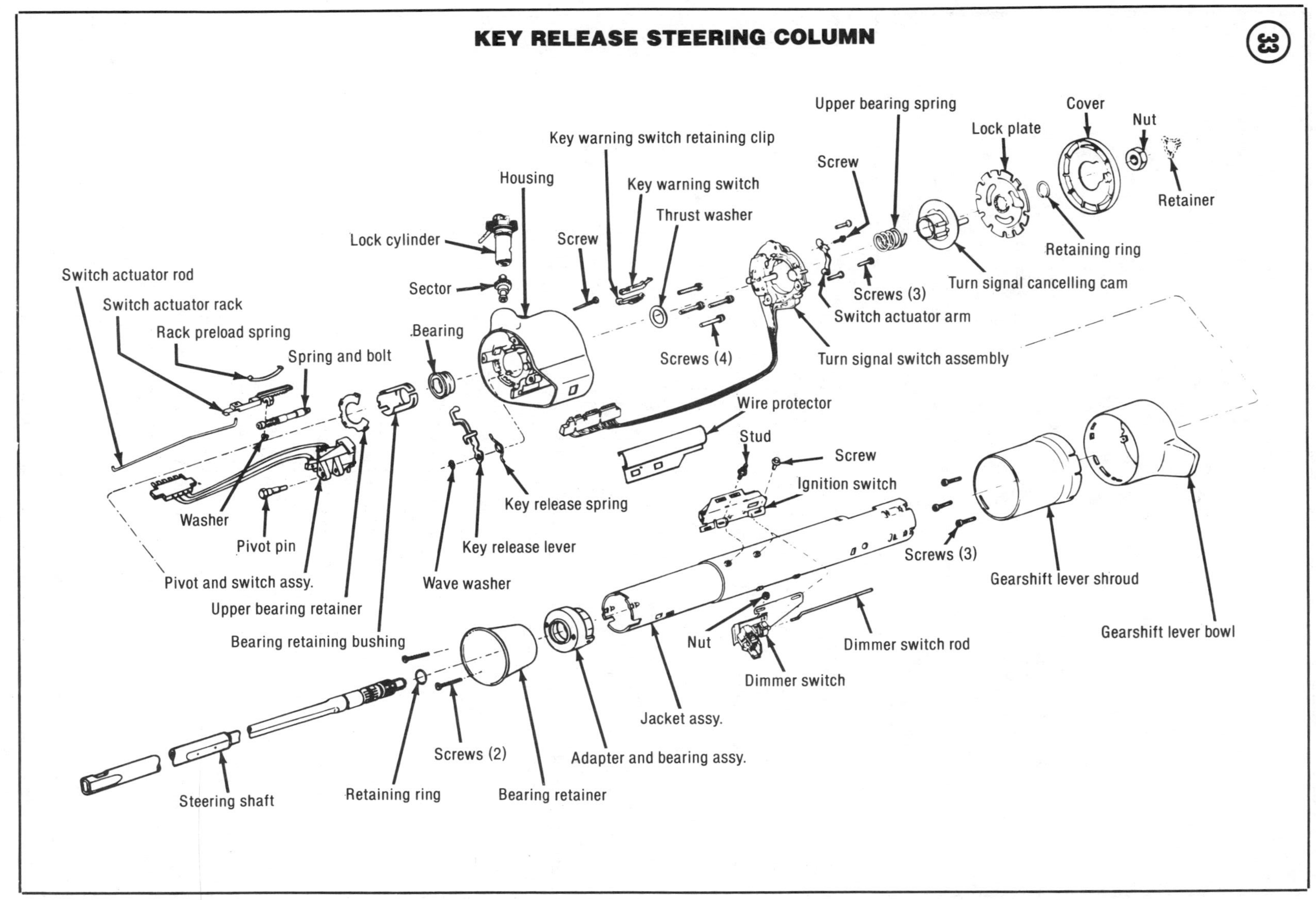
KEY RELEASE STEERING COLUMN
33
Upper bearing spring
Cover
Nut
Lock plate
Key warning switch retaining clip
Screw
Housing
Key warning switch
Retainer
Thrust washer
Retaining ring
Lock cylinder
Screw
Switch actuator rod
Turn signal cancelling cam
Sector
Screws (3)
Switch actuator rack
Switch actuator arm
Rack preload spring
Bearing
Spring and bolt
Screws (4)
Turn signal switch assembly
Wire protector
Stud
Screw
Ignition switch
Key release spring
Washer
Pivot pin
Key release lever
Screws (3)
Gearshift lever shroud
Pivot and switch assy.
Wave washer
Upper bearing retainer
Gearshift lever bowl
Bearing retaining bushing
Nut
Dimmer switch rod
Dimmer switch
Jacket assy.
Screws (2)
Adapter and bearing assy.
Steering shaft
Retaining ring
Bearing retainer

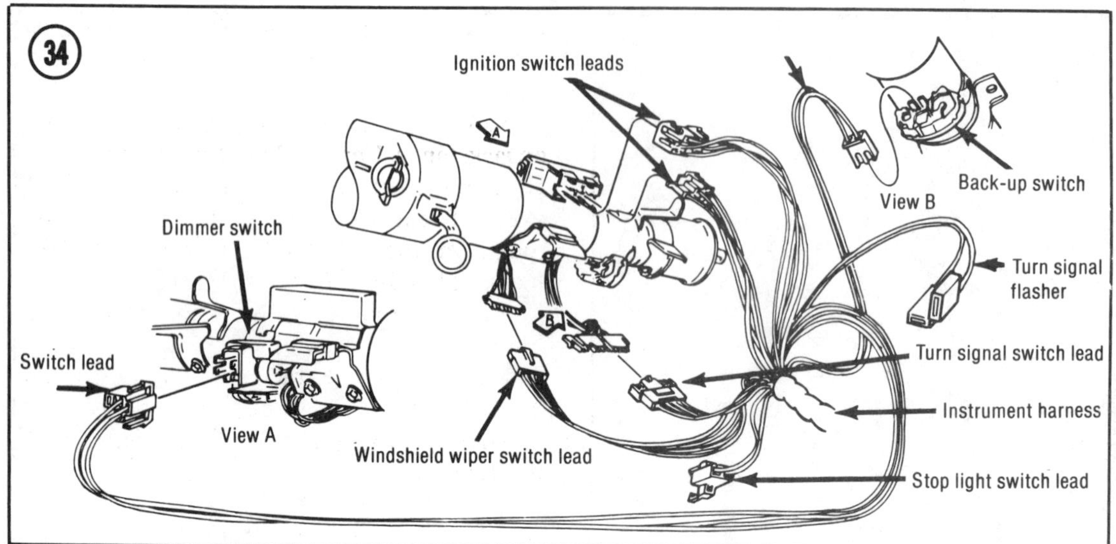

CAUTION
Handle the steering column carefully when removed from car. Do not drop or lean on the column as damage to the column could result and weaken the column assembly.

Installation

1. Attach the steering column to the intermediate shaft. Tighten attaching bolt to 45 ft.-lb. (63 N•m).
2. Install steering column at bottom of instrument panel. Tighten steering column support bracket attaching bolts evenly to 20 ft.-lb. (28 N•m).
3. Connect all wiring connectors. See **Figure 34**.
4. Install the shift cable bracket to the side of the steering column.
5. *Air-conditioned vehicles only*: Install the sound absorber.
6. Install the steering column trim cover to the underside of the steering column.
7. Install steering wheel as described in this chapter under *Steering Wheel Installaton.*
8. Connect negative battery terminal.
9. Road test vehicle and check performance. Operate all switches to make sure each is connected properly.

NOTE
Wet windshield before testing windshield wiper switch to prevent scratching of windshield.

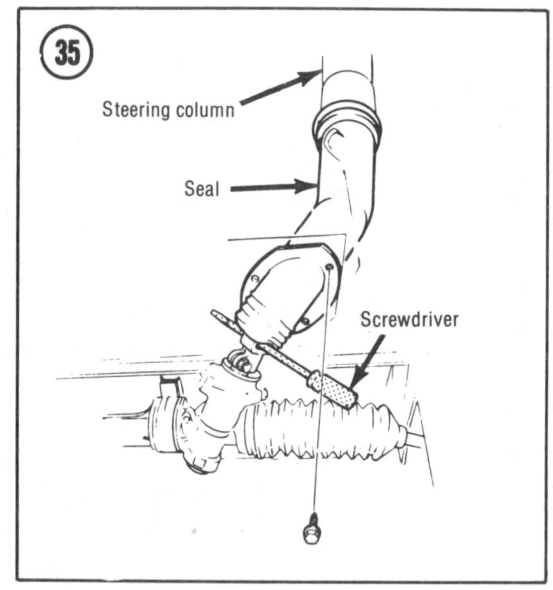

INTERMEDIATE SHAFT

Replacement

1. Disconnect the battery ground cable.
2. Remove the steering column as described in this chapter under *Steering Column Removal.*
3. Loosen bolts attaching shaft seal to steering column and remove seal. See **Figure 35**.
4. Loosen clamp bolt and remove intermediate shaft from the pinion shaft. See **Figure 36**.

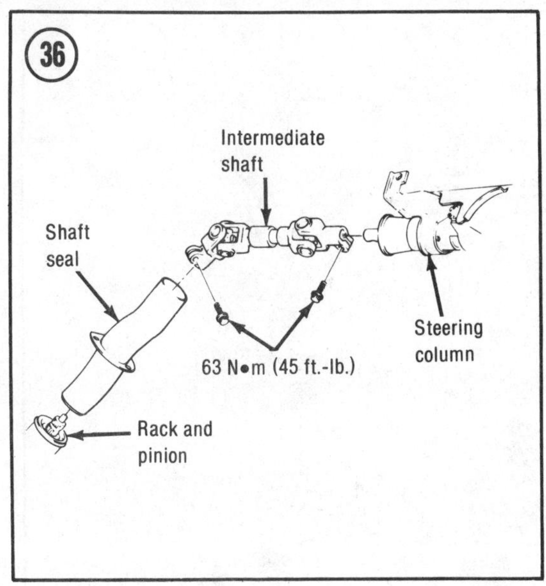

5. Reverse Steps 1-4 to install the intermediate shaft. Tighten shaft bolts to 45 ft.-lb. (63 N•m).

RACK-AND-PINION ASSEMBLY

NOTE
General Motors has indicated that 1980-1981 vehicles equipped with power steering may experience a temporary reduction of power steering assist after a cold start. While this condition disappears after engine warm-up, a seal replacement in the power steering gear assembly will eliminate it. Return your vehicle to a dealer for inspection and correction, if not already done.

Refer to **Figure 37** (manual steering) or **Figure 38** (power steering) for this procedure.

Removal (Manual and Power Steering)

1. Disconnect the battery ground cable.
2. Disconnect the rack-and-pinion shaft from the intermediate shaft. Insert a screwdriver in end of steering column shaft to prevent falling of steering shaft seal.
3. *Power steering only*: Disconnect the pressure and return lines from the steering gear valve housing (**Figure 38**). Plug the lines and ports in the valve housing to prevent entry of dirt.
4. Jack up the front end of the car and place it on jackstands. Remove both front wheels.
5. Remove the tie rod end nut (**Figure 39**) from left and right sides. Disconnect the tie rods from the wheel spindle arms using GM tool part No. J-6627 or equivalent (**Figure 24**).
6. Remove the rear cradle attaching bolts. Then support cradle with a jack.
7. Remove the 4 rack-and-pinion bracket bolts (**Figure 40**). Lower and remove the rack-and-pinion assembly from underneath the vehicle.

Installation (Manual and Power Steering)

1. Install rack-and-pinion assembly with brackets, supports and 4 nuts (**Figure 40**). Tighten nuts to 24 ft.-lb. (32 N•m).
2. Install intermediate shaft onto rack-and-pinion assembly and tighten pinch bolt to 45 ft.-lb. (63 N•m).
3. Connect tie rods to the steering knuckles using a clamping tool with a 1 1/8 in. socket. See **Figure 25**.
4. Install tie rod nuts and torque to 40 ft.-lb. (54 N•m).
5. *Power steering only*: Connect the pressure and return lines to the steering gear valve housing.
6. Lower vehicle. Have front end specialist adjust toe-in.

Disassembly (Manual Steering)

Removable components are the outer tie rod, boot seal, inner tie rod, rack bearing, pinion shaft seal and shaft assembly, roller bearing assembly, rack bushing and valve housing mounting grommets.

Refer to **Figure 41** for this procedure.

NOTE
Steps 1-7 describe replacement of outer tie rod.

(37) **MANUAL RACK-AND-PINION STEERING ASSEMBLY**

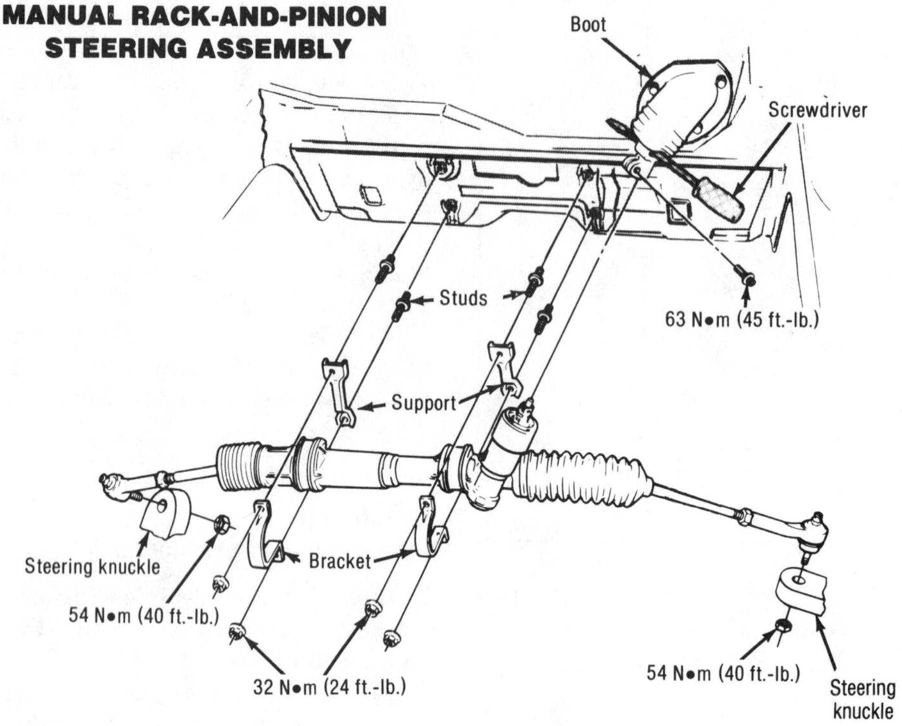

(38) **POWER STEERING RACK-AND-PINION ASSEMBLY**

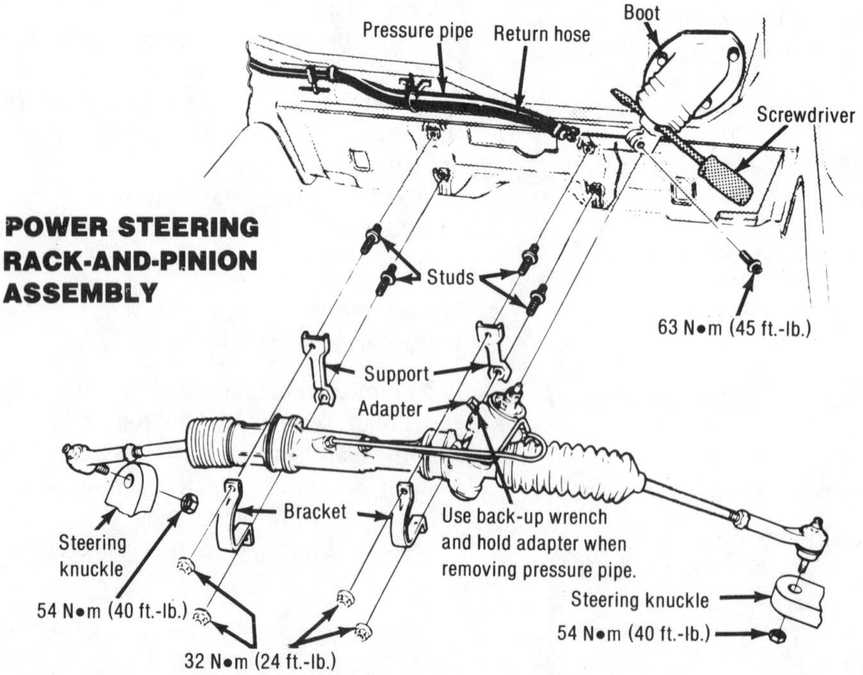

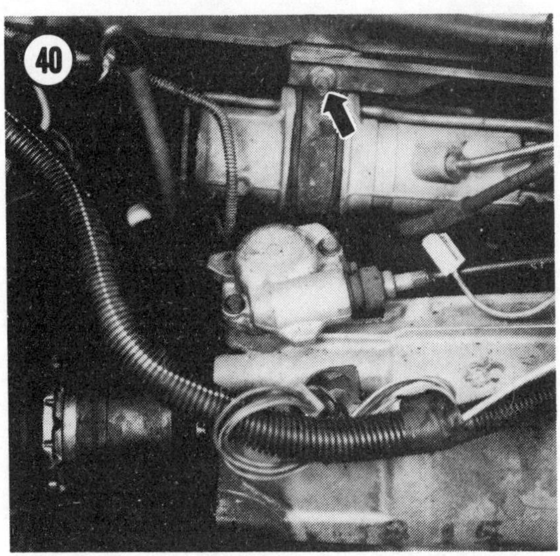

41

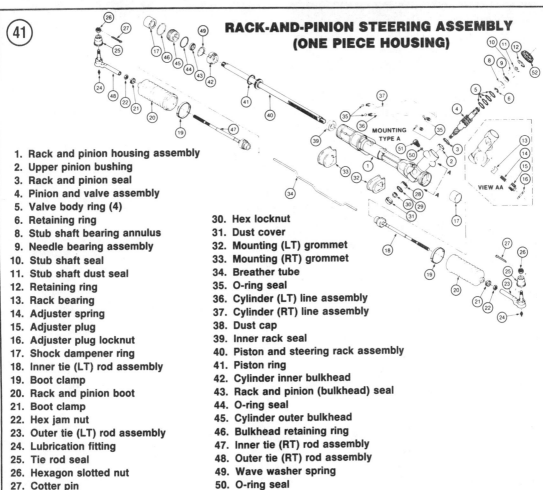

RACK-AND-PINION STEERING ASSEMBLY (ONE PIECE HOUSING)

1. Rack and pinion housing assembly
2. Upper pinion bushing
3. Rack and pinion seal
4. Pinion and valve assembly
5. Valve body ring (4)
6. Retaining ring
8. Stub shaft bearing annulus
9. Needle bearing assembly
10. Stub shaft seal
11. Stub shaft dust seal
12. Retaining ring
13. Rack bearing
14. Adjuster spring
15. Adjuster plug
16. Adjuster plug locknut
17. Shock dampener ring
18. Inner tie (LT) rod assembly
19. Boot clamp
20. Rack and pinion boot
21. Boot clamp
22. Hex jam nut
23. Outer tie (LT) rod assembly
24. Lubrication fitting
25. Tie rod seal
26. Hexagon slotted nut
27. Cotter pin
28. Ball bearing assembly
29. Retaining ring
30. Hex locknut
31. Dust cover
32. Mounting (LT) grommet
33. Mounting (RT) grommet
34. Breather tube
35. O-ring seal
36. Cylinder (LT) line assembly
37. Cylinder (RT) line assembly
38. Dust cap
39. Inner rack seal
40. Piston and steering rack assembly
41. Piston ring
42. Cylinder inner bulkhead
43. Rack and pinion (bulkhead) seal
44. O-ring seal
45. Cylinder outer bulkhead
46. Bulkhead retaining ring
47. Inner tie (RT) rod assembly
48. Outer tie (RT) rod assembly
49. Wave washer spring
50. O-ring seal
51. O-ring adapter
53. Seal adapter

1. Loosen jam nut from inner tie rod (**Figure 39**).
2. Remove the tie rod end nut. Detach tie rods from steering knuckles using GM tool (or equivalent) shown in **Figure 24**.
3. Unscrew the outer tie rod from the inner tie rod.

NOTE
Count number of turns required to separate the outer tie rod from the inner tie rod. This number will be used when assembling inner and outer tie rods.

4. Assemble new outer tie rod to inner tie rod by screwing on approximately the same number of turns as needed to remove it. This will give approximate toe angle.
5. Install tie rod to the steering knuckle using a clamping tool and a 1 1/8 in. socket. See **Figure 25**. Install nut and tighten to 40 ft.-lb. (54 N•m).
6. Tighten inner tie rod jam nut to 50 ft.-lb. (70 N•m).
7. Lower vehicle from hoist and have a General Motors dealer or competent front end specialist adjust the toe angle to specifications in **Table 2**.

NOTE
*Step 8 describes replacement of the boot seal. See **Figure 42**.*

8. To replace the boot seal, perform Steps 1-3 above. Then cut inner boot clamp with pliers, loosen and remove outer clamp and remove boot. Install new boot. Perform Steps 5-7 above to complete installation.

NOTE
The following procedures describe disassembly of the rack-and-pinion assembly. Disassemby must be performed with the rack-and-pinion unit removed from the car.

9. Hold rack-and-pinion in a vise with soft jaws near the center of the housing.
10. Remove the outer tie rod and boot seal as described above.
11. Hold rack in vise with soft jaws and remove both inner tie rod assemblies (**Figure 43**).

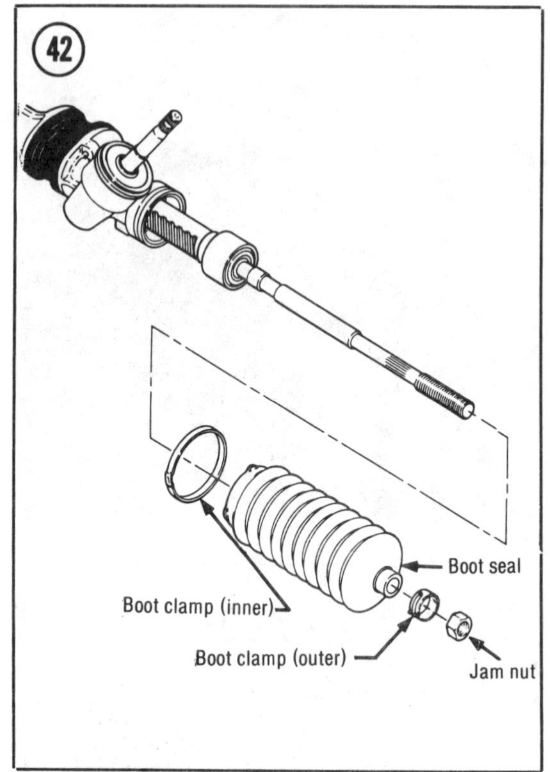

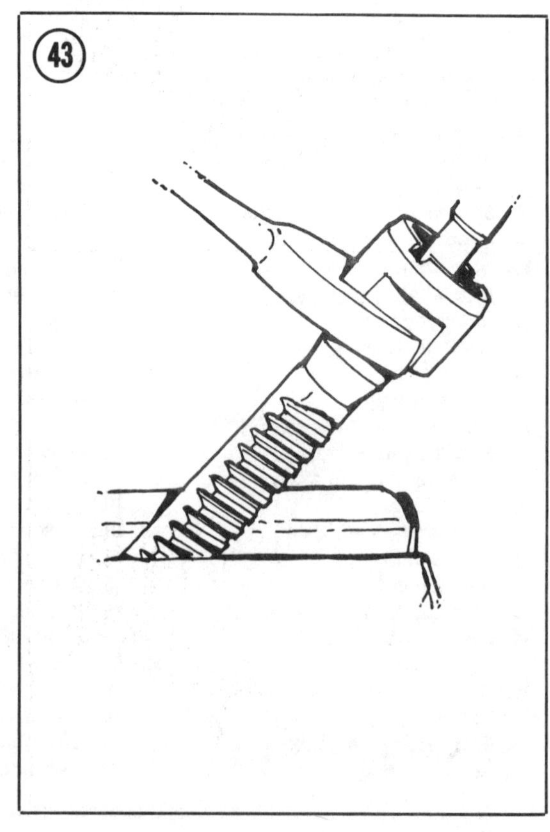

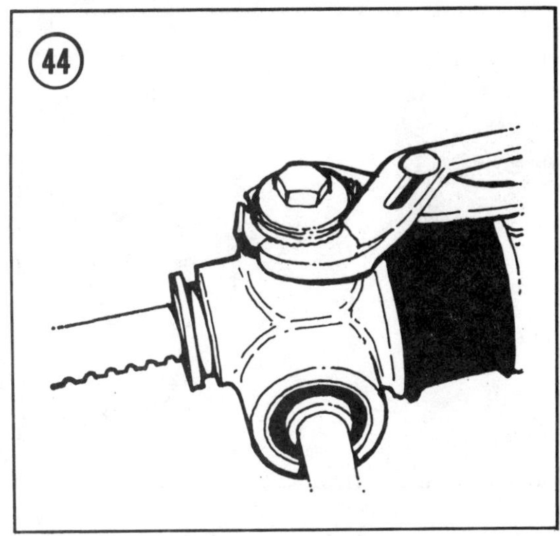

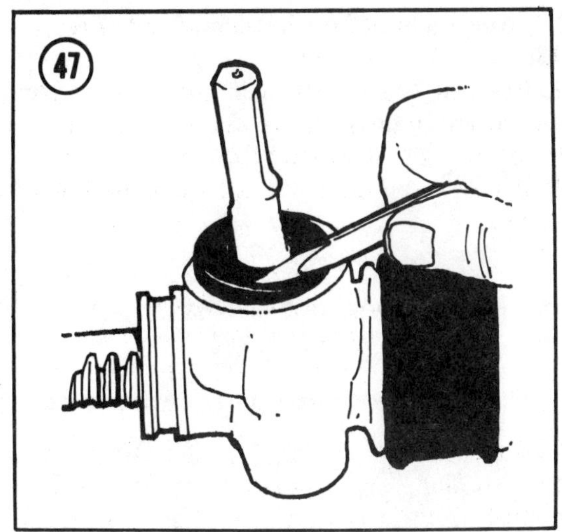

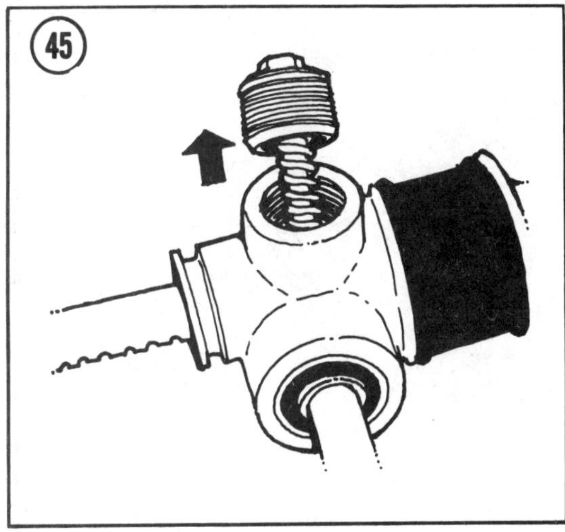

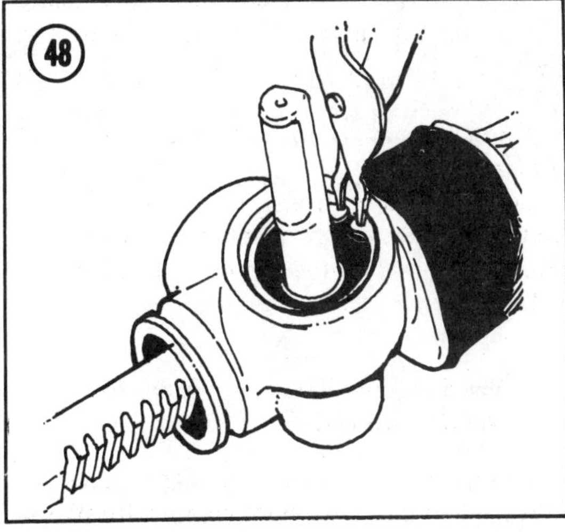

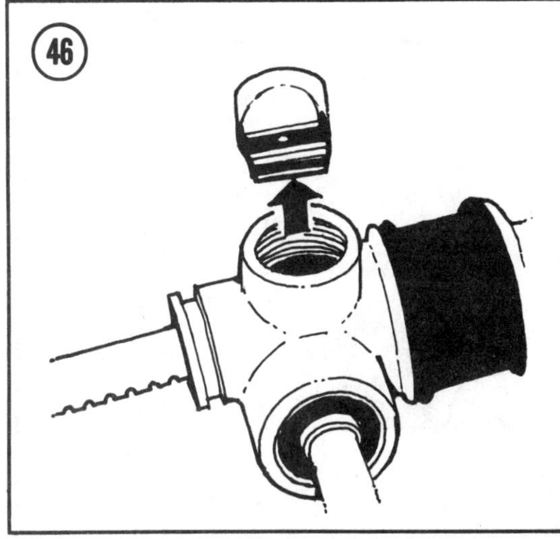

12. Remove locknut (**Figure 44**), adjuster plug and spring (**Figure 45**).

13. Remove rack bearing from housing (**Figure 46**).

14. Clean surface of seal. Pierce seal at one of the round spots on seal surface. Pry seal out (**Figure 47**).

15. Remove retaining ring (**Figure 48**) from bore with snap ring pliers.

16. Hold end of shaft in soft jaw vise. Tap housing to separate pinion assembly from housing (**Figure 49**).

CAUTION

Do not allow rack to slide from housing; it could be damaged.

17. Remove rack from housing (**Figure 50**).
18. Further disassembly is not necessary unless parts are damaged or worn. See *Inspection* procedure.

Inspection

NOTE
To replace some of the following parts, an arbor press is required. If press is not available, refer procedure to General Motors dealer or machine shop.

1. Clean all parts except inner tie rod assemblies in solvent. Blow dry.
2. Check mounting grommets. If damaged, replace them both. To do this, cut the old grommets off. Lubricate inside of new grommets with chassis grease and slide them on.
3. Check rack bushing for wear. If worn, remove retaining ring (25, **Figure 41**) and remove bushing with suitable inside bearing puller (**Figure 51**). Press new bushing in until it bottoms and install the retaining ring.

NOTE
*Bearing pullers of the type used in **Figure 51** can normally be rented from tool rental agencies.*

4. Check pinion and bearing assembly. If worn or damaged, drive bearing out with a drift. See **Figure 52**. Drive new bearing in until it bottoms and install *new* pinion.
5. Check roller bearing for wear (2, **Figure 41**). If worn, remove the roller bearing

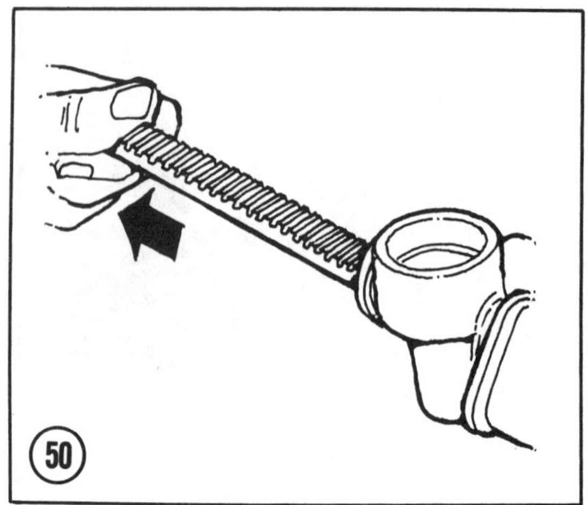

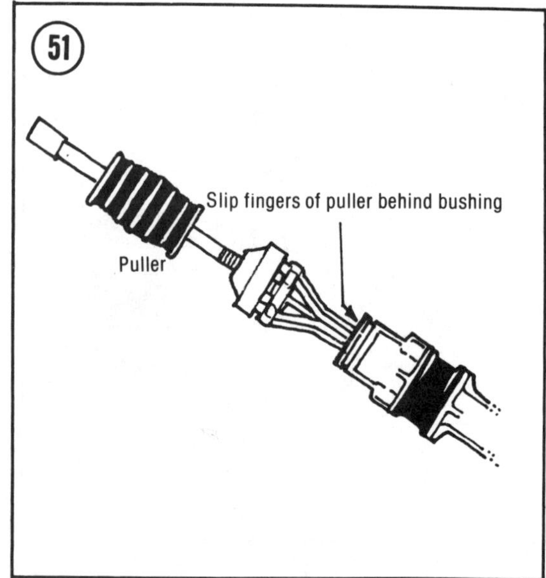

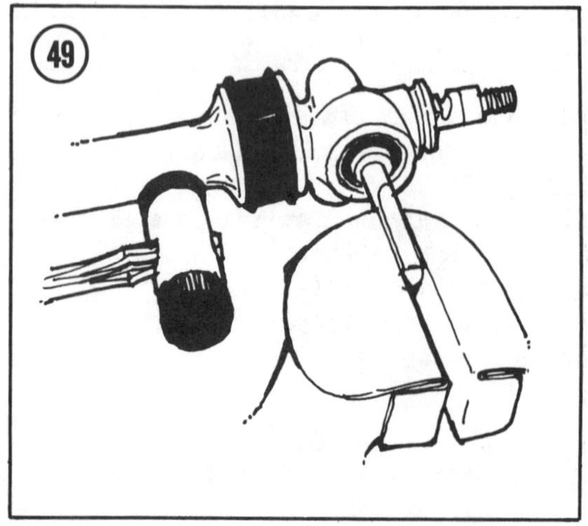

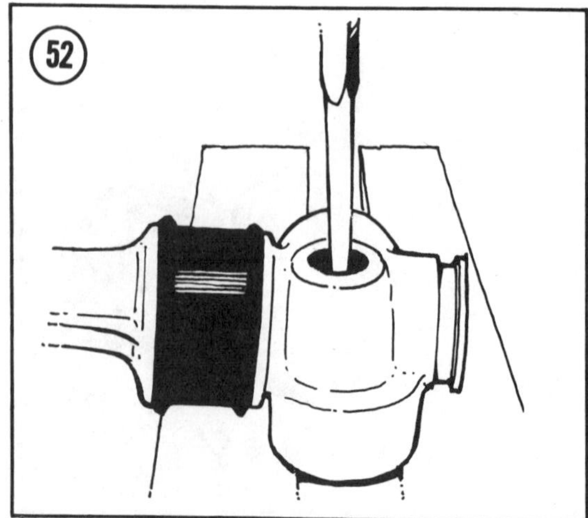

assembly by pressing out with a drift. Press in a new roller bearing until it bottoms in housing.

Assembly

1. Install rack into housing with teeth facing pinion. The flat on the teeth should be parallel with the pinion shaft.
2. Measure and set 2.50 in. (63.5 mm) from lip of housing to end of rack. See **Figure 53**.
3. Insert pinion with flat at 75° from vertical. See **Figure 54** (*start position*). Tap on pinion shaft with soft hammer until pinion seats. Measure and reset rack as described in Step 2; it will move when pinion is installed. Pinion flat should be vertical. See **Figure 54** (*finish position*). If the pinion flat is at +/-30° from vertical, remove the rack-and-pinion and begin at Step 1 of assembly.

CAUTION

If the rack isn't centered properly after performing Steps 1-3, steering wheel travel will be limited.

4. Install pinion ring with snap ring pliers. Beveled edge of retaining ring must be up.
5. Liberally coat top of pinion ring bearing with anhydrous calcium grease (**Figure 55**). Install pinion and seal flush with housing (**Figure 56**). Seal can be seated by tapping evenly all round with a hammer.

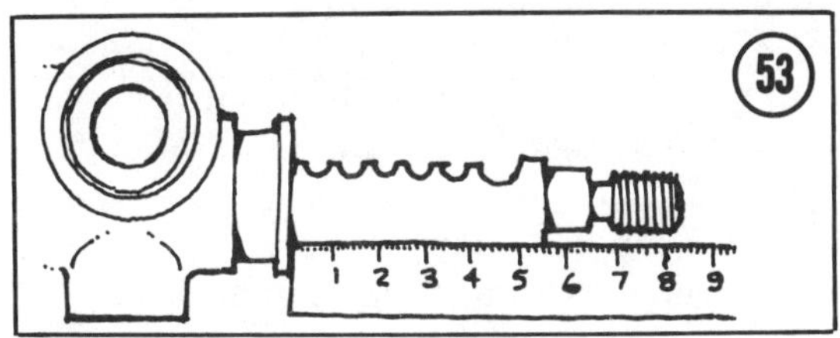

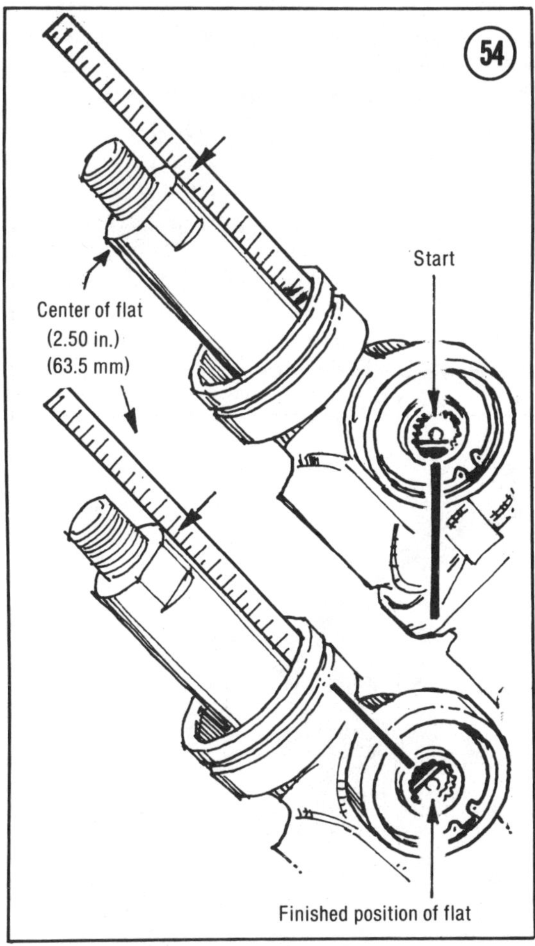

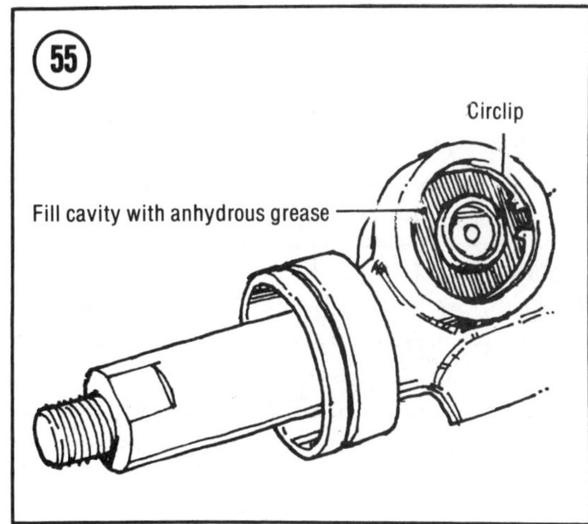

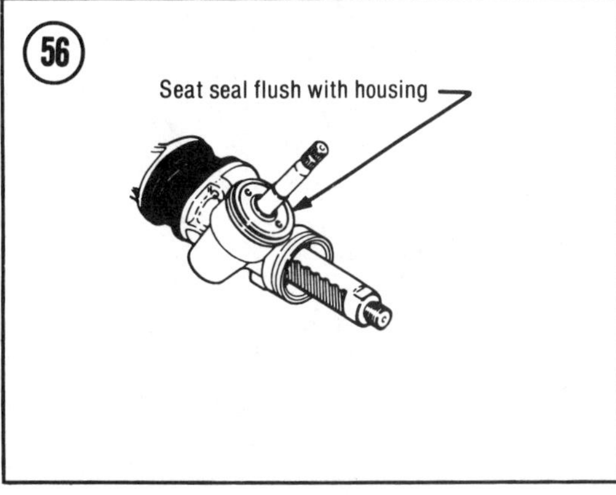

10

6. Coat rack bearing with lithium gease and install it.

7. Coat both ends of preload spring and adjuster plug threads with lithium grease.

8. Install adjuster plug and spring into housing. Screw adjuster plug in until it bottoms, then unscrew 45° to 60°. Torque required to turn pinion should be 8-10 in.-lb. (0.9-1.1 N•m). Turn adjuster plug in or out to adjust as required. Tighten locknut to 50 ft.-lb. (70 N•m). See **Figure 57**.

9. Lube both ends of rack with lithium grease. Fill rack teeth with lithium grease. Move back and forth several times by turning pinion shaft, adding grease to rack teeth each time.

10. Install inner tie rod assemblies to rack. Turn inner rod assemblies until they bottom out.

CAUTION
Hold rack with vise or wrench to avoid internal gear damage.

11. Stake both tie rod housings to rack flats. See **Figure 58**.

NOTE
After staking both tie rod housings to the rack flats, measure clearance between housing stake and rack with a feeler gauge. This measurement must not exceed 0.009 in. (0.25 mm).

12. Slide one of the large clamps on the housing. Place boot lip into position over undercut. Slide clamp over boot at undercut and tighten with side cutter pliers.
13. Slip end of boot into rod undercut. Do not assemble clamp over boot until toe adjustment is made.
14. Thread jam nut onto tie rods.
15. Install tie rods ends (**Figure 59**). Do not tighten jam nuts until toe adjustment is made.

Repair (Power Steering)

Disassembly and repair of power steering units requires special tools and experience and should not be attempted by the amateur mechanic. Refer repair of power steering units to your dealer or a competent specialist.

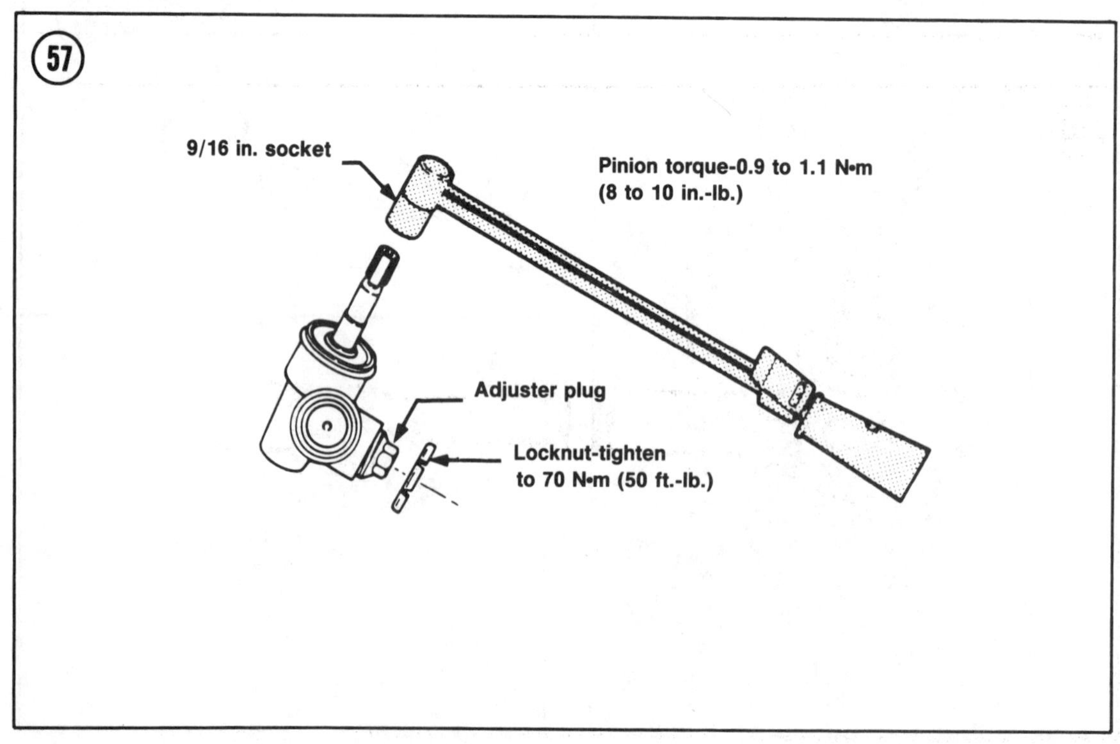

58

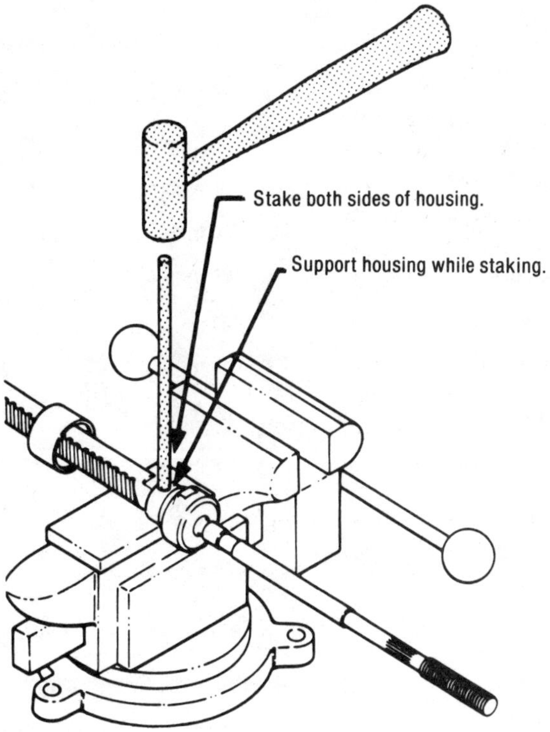

Stake both sides of housing.

Support housing while staking.

59

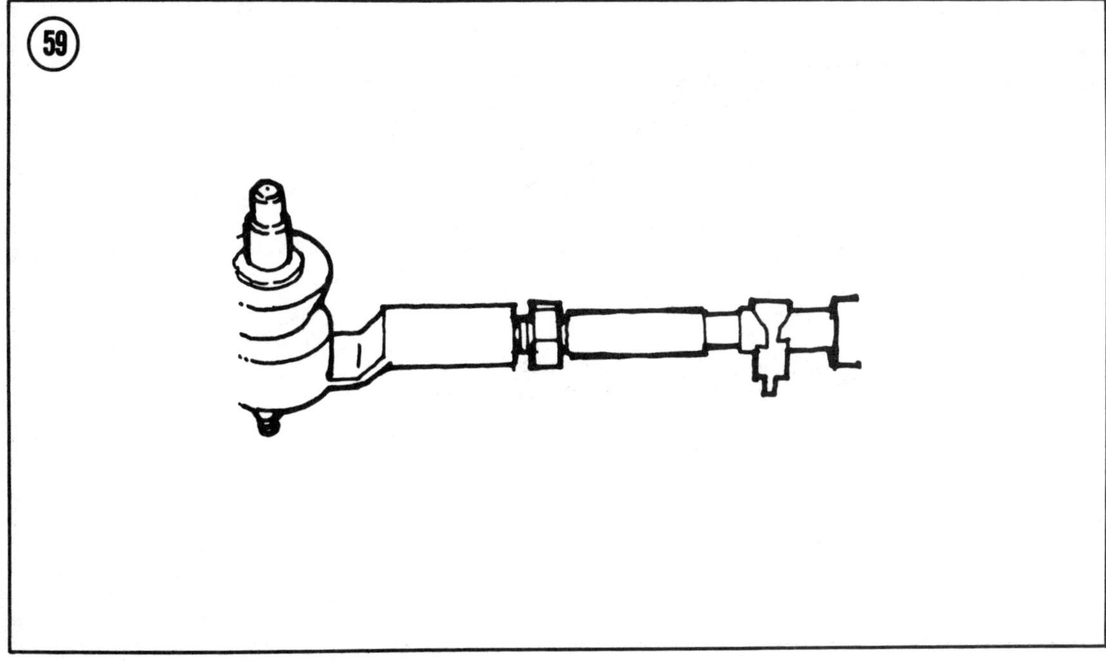

Table 1 TIGHTENING TORQUES, FRONT SUSPENSION

Item	Torque	
Outer tie rod jam nut	50 ft.-lb.	(70 N•m)
Inner tie rod housing to rack	70 ft.-lb.	(95 N•m)
Adjuster plug locknut (manual steering)	50 ft.-lb.	(70 N•m)
Pinion preload (manual steering)	8-10 in.-lb.	(0.9-1.1 N•m)
Steering wheel to shaft nut	30 ft.-lb.	(40 N•m)
Steering column to intermediate shaft	45 ft.-lb.	(63 N•m)
Steering cover to housing screws	100 in.-lb.	(11 N•m)
Stabilizer bar to plate	40 ft.-lb.	(55 N•m)
Stabilizer bar to bracket	35 ft.-lb.	(45 N•m)
Lower control arm pivot bolts	48 ft.-lb.	(65 N•m)
Upper strut to body bolts	18 ft.-lb.	(24 N•m)
Lower strut to knuckle bolts	140 ft.-lb.	(190 N•m)
Ball joint stud bolt	45 ft.-lb.	(63 N•m)
Hub to knuckle bolt	63 ft.-lb.	(85 N•m)
Hub nut	225 ft.-lb.	(305 N•m)
Tie rod to knuckle	40 ft.-lb.	(54 N•m)

Table 2 WHEEL ALIGNMENT SPECIFICATIONS

	Service Setting	Service limit
Camber (left and right side to be within 1/2°)	+1.0°	0° to 1°
Toe-in	2.5 mm	0.0-2.5 mm

NOTE: If you own a 1981 or later model, first check the Supplement at the back of the book for any new service information.

CHAPTER ELEVEN

REAR AXLE AND SUSPENSION

The solid axle attaches to the body through 2 lower control arms, a track bar and shock absorbers. See **Figure 1**.

The control arms maintain the fore and aft relationship between the chassis and the rear axle assembly. The track bar attached to the right side of the axle housing and to the left side of the underbody controls the side-to-side movement of the rear axle assembly. A stabilizer bar is welded to the inside of the axle housing.

Springing is by 2 variable rate coil springs positioned between a seat in the underbody and a seat welded to the rear axle housing. The shock absorbers provide dampening.

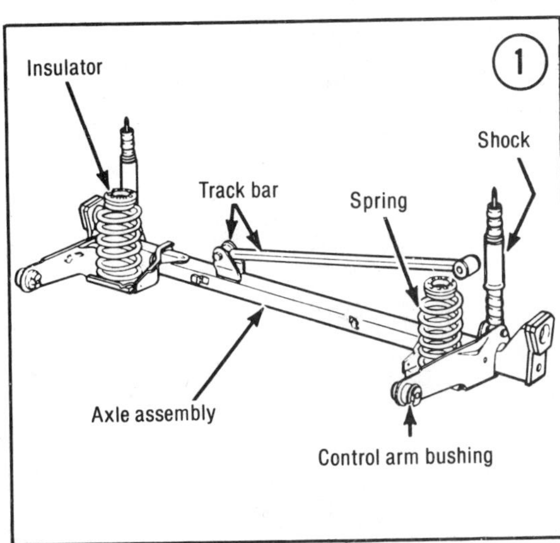

This chapter provides repair and replacement procedures considered practical for the home mechanic. Torque specifications are included in **Table 1** at the end of this chapter.

CAUTION

*All fasteners used in the rear suspension must be replaced with parts of the same type. **Do not** use a replacement part of lesser quality or substitute design, as it may affect the performance of vital components and systems or result in major repair expenses. Torque values (**Table 1**, end of chapter) must be used during installation to assure proper retention of these parts.*

REAR SHOCK ABSORBERS

Refer to **Figure 2** for this procedure.

Replacement

1. Open trunk lid and open the inside trim cover. **Figure 3** is typical. On some models, the trim cover is not used.
2. Remove the upper shock mount with a wrench.
3. Raise vehicle rear end and support on jackstands.

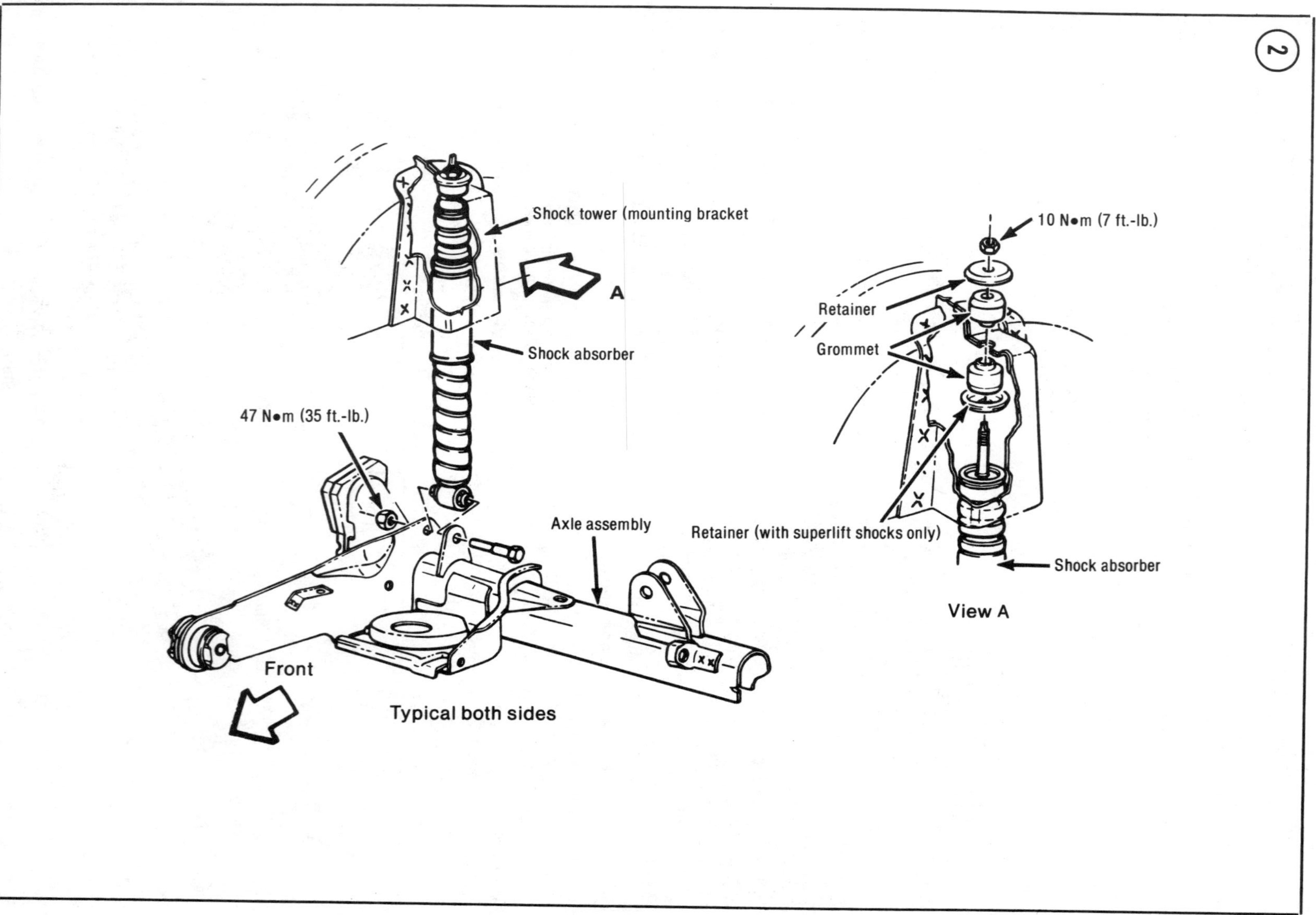
2
Shock tower (mounting bracket
A
Shock absorber
47 N•m (35 ft.-lb.)
Axle assembly
Front
Typical both sides
10 N•m (7 ft.-lb.)
Retainer
Grommet
Retainer (with superlift shocks only)
Shock absorber
View A

4. Remove nut securing lower end of shock absorber.
5. From underneath vehicle, pull old shock absorber free.
6. Install lower end of new shock absorber. Install lower nut finger-tight.
7. Extend upper stem through mounting hole and install nut finger-tight. Install grommets and washers as shown in **Figure 2**.
8. Torque lower nut to 35 ft.-lb. (47 N•m).

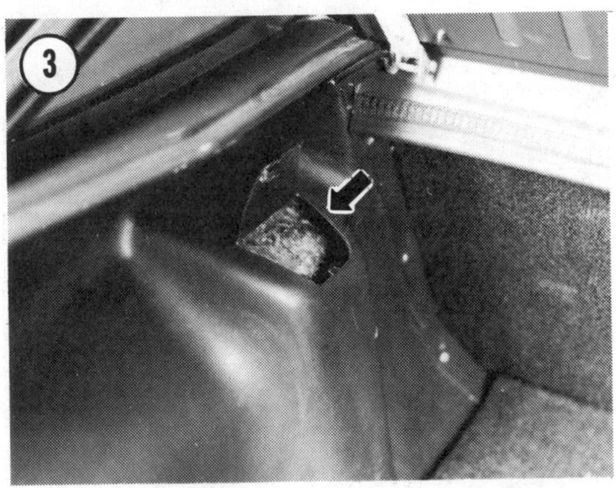

9. Lower vehicle and torque upper nut to 7 ft.-lb. (10 N•m).
10. Close inside trim cover.

REAR SPRING

Refer to **Figure 4** for the following procedures.

Removal

1. Raise vehicle rear end and secure with jackstands.

WARNING
Do not raise car using a twin-post type hoist. The swing arc tendency of the rear axle when rear axle assembly bolts are removed may cause car to slip from hoist.

2. Remove bolt attaching the right and left rear brake line brackets to the control arm. Allow brake line to hang freely. See **Figure 5** and **Figure 6**.

NOTE
Do not disconnect brake line or brakes will have to be bled.

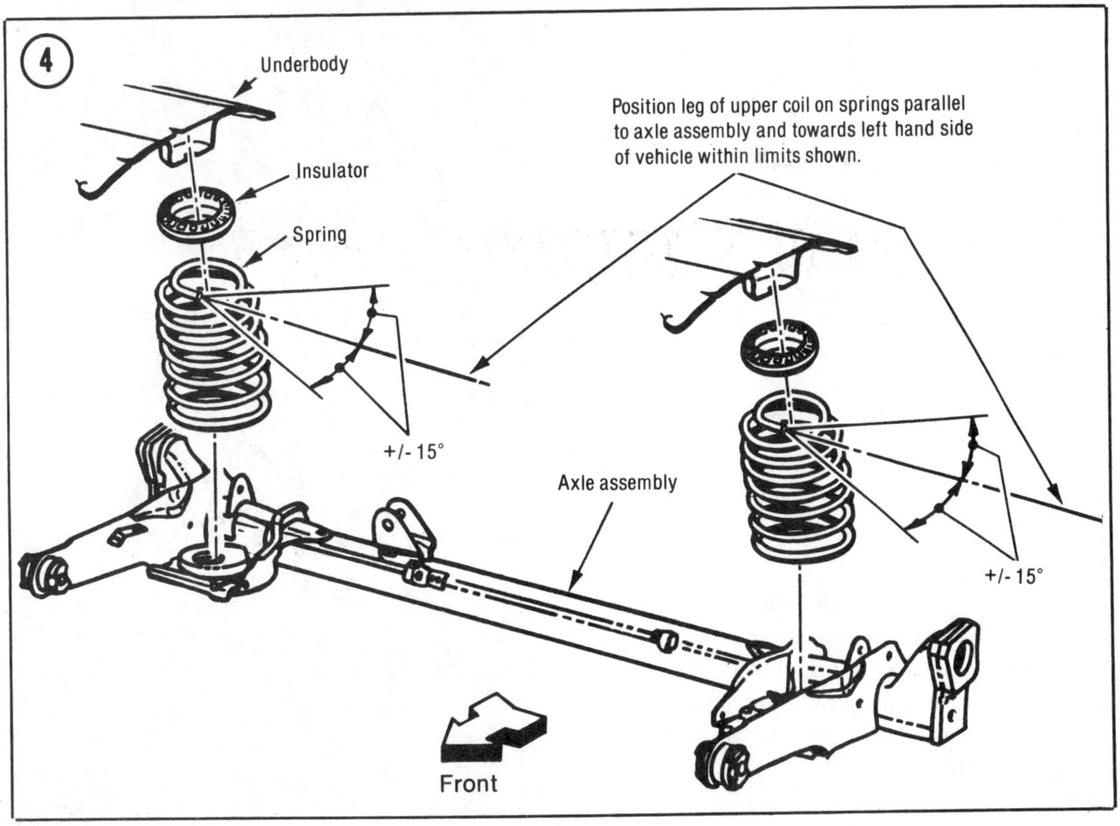

3. Remove bolt attaching track bar to rear axle. See **Figure 7**. Lift track bar from axle bracket and set aside.
4. Remove both lower shock absorber attaching nuts (**Figure 2**).
5. Lower axle with floor jack as required to allow removal of springs and spring insulators from their mounting pads.

NOTE
Each time jack is repositioned, also reposition jackstands underneath vehicle, as required, before performing any service work.

CAUTION
When lowering axle, do not stretch brake hose.

Installation

1. Install insulators on top of springs. See **Figure 4**. Install spring between upper and lower seats.

NOTE
Make sure upper spring coil is parallel to axle assembly and faces outboard to specifications shown in ***Figure 4****.*

2. Raise axle. Reconnect shock absorbers. Torque lower nut to 35 ft.-lb. (47 N•m).
3. Reconnect track bar to axle. Torque nut to 33 ft.-lb. (45 N•m).
4. Install brake line brackets to control arm. Torque screws to 8 ft.-lb. (11 N•m). See **Figure 5** and **Figure 6**.
5. Remove jackstands and lower vehicle.

TRACK BAR

Replacement

The track bar and its mounting brackets are shown in **Figure 8**.

1. Securely block the front wheels so the car will not roll in either direction. Jack up the rear end of the car and place it on jackstands.
2. Remove bolts attaching track bar to rear axle and upper body. Remove track bar.
3. Install track bar to upper body attachment bracket. Install bolt and nut finger-tight. Make sure nut faces rearward.

5

6

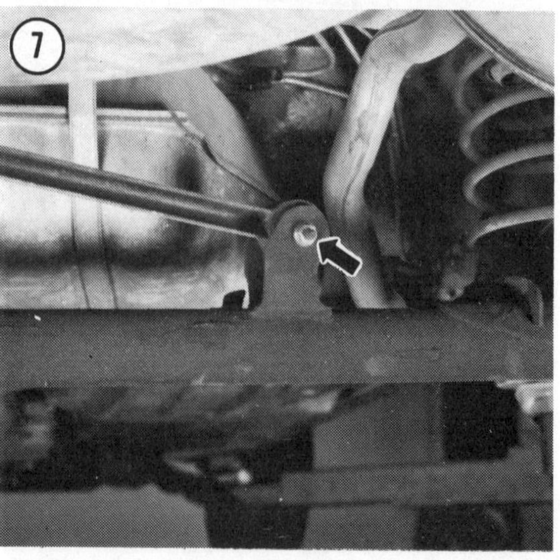
7

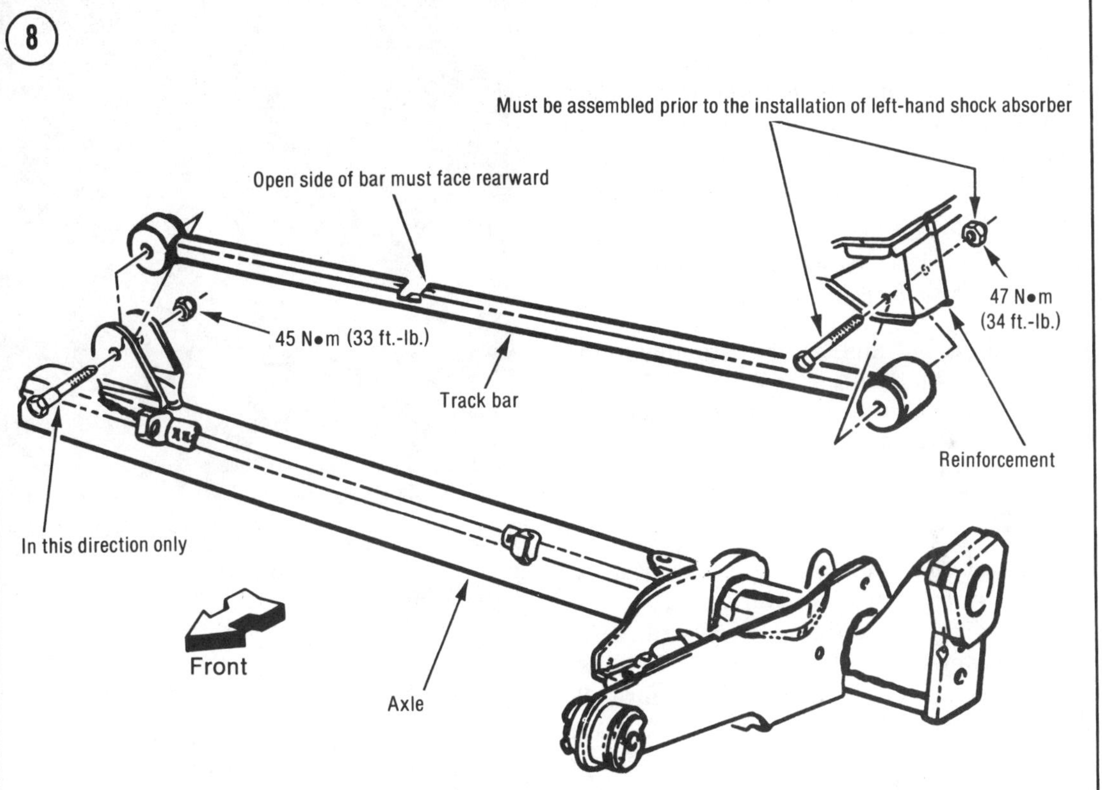

8

Must be assembled prior to the installation of left-hand shock absorber

Open side of bar must face rearward

47 N•m (34 ft.-lb.)

45 N•m (33 ft.-lb.)

Track bar

Reinforcement

In this direction only

Front

Axle

NOTE

Make sure to install open side of track bar facing towards rear of car. See ***Figure 9****.*

4. Install track bar to axle attachment bracket. Install bolt and nut finger-tight. Make sure nut faces rearward.
5. Torque lower nut to 33 ft.-lb. (45 N•m). Torque upper nut to 34 ft.-lb. (47 N•m).
6. Lower vehicle.

REAR WHEEL HUB AND BEARING

Removal

1. Securely block both front wheels so the car will not roll in either direction. Jack up the rear end of the car and place it on jackstands.

2. Remove the rear wheel and brake drum as described in Chapter Twelve.
3. Remove the hub and bearing assembly-to-rear axle attaching bolts (**Figure 10**). Then remove the hub and bearing assembly from end of axle.

CAUTION
Handle hub and bearing assembly carefully during removal and installation to prevent damage to bearing.

4. Install the hub and bearing assembly to the rear axle. Tighten bolts to 35 ft.-lb. (55 N•m).
5. Install brake drum and wheel as described in Chapter Twelve. Tighten wheel lug nuts to 103 ft.-lb. (140 N•m).

Inspection

To check looseness of rear wheel bearing, perform the following procedure.
1. Remove brake drum as described in Chapter Twelve.
2. Mount dial indicator as shown in **Figure 11**.
3. Grasp bearing flange and attempt to move flange with push-pull movement. If flange movement exceeds 0.005 in. (0.127 mm), replace the hub and bearing assembly.

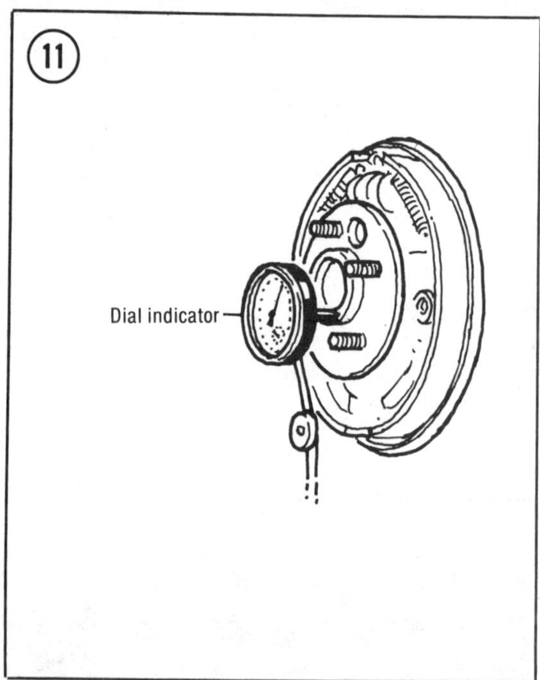

REAR AXLE ASSEMBLY

Removal

1. Securely block both front wheels so the car will not roll in either direction. Raise car with a jack and support with jackstands. Remove the rear wheels.

WARNING
Do not raise car using a twin-post type hoist. The swing arc tendency of the rear axle when the rear axle assembly bolts are removed may cause car to slip from hoist.

2. Remove the rear brake drum as described in Chapter Twelve.
3. From underneath the vehicle, remove the parking brake cable guide hook. See **Figure 12**.
4. Refer to **Figure 5** and **Figure 6** and remove both rear brake line brackets from the car chassis.
5. Disconnect the lower end of both shock absorbers (**Figure 2**).
6. Disconnect the lower end of the track bar attached to the axle (**Figure 7**).
7. Lower rear axle and remove rear springs and insulators as described in this chapter.

CAUTION
When lowering axle, do not stretch brake hose.

8. Remove rear brake lines from axle attachments.

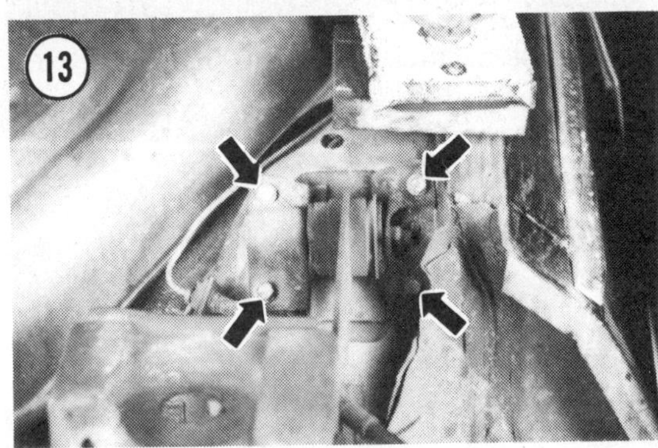

NOTE
Tape over ends of brake lines to prevent entry of dirt (if disconnected).

9. Detach brake cable from rear axle mounting brackets.
10. Remove rear wheel hub and bearing assembly as described in this chapter.
11. Move brake backing plate out of way.
12. Have 2 assistants steady the rear axle. Then remove 4 control arm bracket- to-underbody attaching bolts and lower rear axle to ground. See **Figure 13**.

Installation

1. Inspect rear axle and control arm welded joints. Replace all fasteners before reassembly.
2. Place control arm bracket onto control arms and position at a 45° angle. See **Figure 14**. Tighten nuts to 34 ft.-lb. (47 N•m).
3. With the help of 2 assistants, place the axle assembly onto a jack and raise into position. Attach control arm-to-underbody attaching bolts (**Figure 13**) and tighten to 20 ft.-lb. (27 N•m).

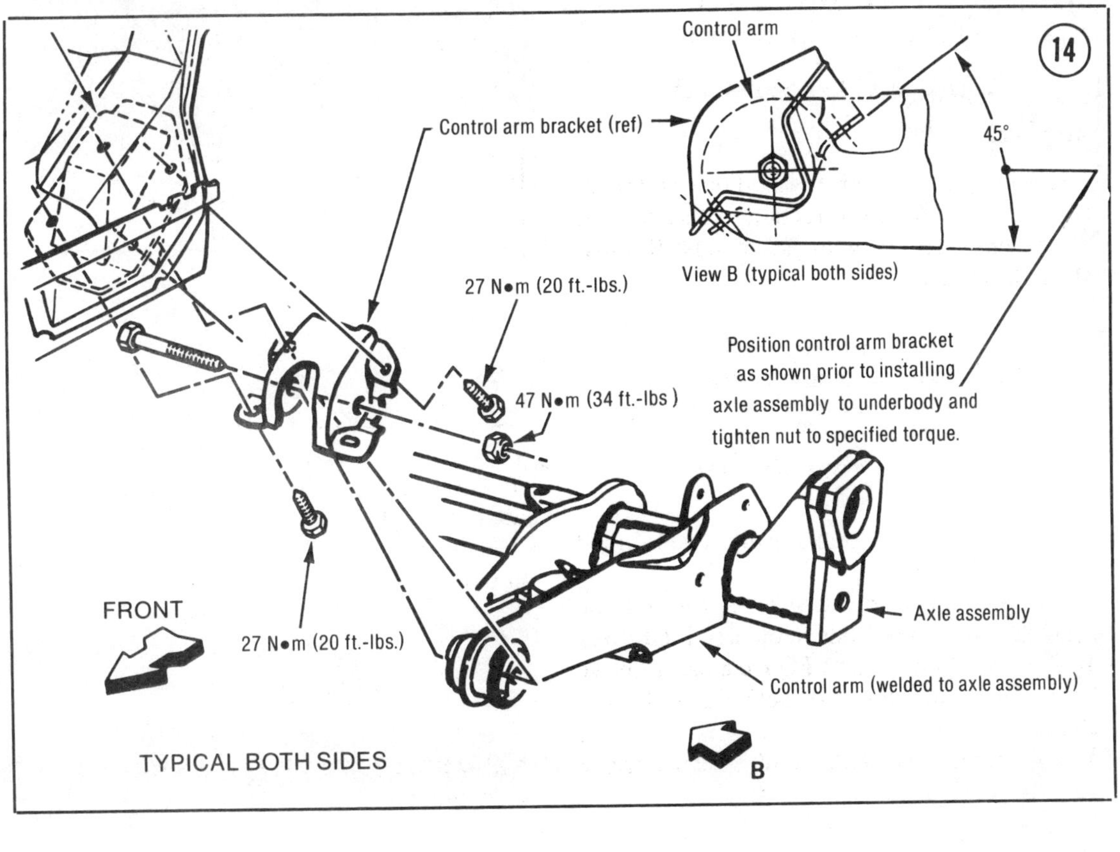

4. Install brake backing plate.

5. Install hub and bearing assembly as described in this chapter. Tighten bolts to 35 ft.-lb. (55 N•m).

6. Attach brake line connections to frame.

7. Attach brake cable to axle assembly.

8. Install insulators on top of springs. Raise axle and install springs between upper and lower mounts. Make sure springs are installed in direction described under *Rear Spring, Installation.* See **Figure 4**.

9. Reconnect shock absorbers. Torque lower nut to 34 ft.-lb. (47 N•m). See **Figure 2**.

10. Install track bar to rear axle as described in this chapter. Tighten nut to 33 ft.-lb. (45 N•m). See **Figure 7**.

11. Install brake line brackets to control arm brackets. See **Figure 6**. Tighten attaching screws to 8 ft.-lb. (11 N•m).

12. Connect parking brake cable to guide hook (**Figure 12**). Adjust parking brake as described in Chapter Twelve.

13. Install brake drums as described in Chapter Twelve.

14. Install wheel and torque lug nuts to 103 ft.-lb. (140 N•m).

15. Remove jackstands and lower car.

16. If brake line was disconnected, bleed brake system as described in Chapter Twelve.

Table 1 TIGHTENING TORQUES, REAR SUSPENSION

Item	Torque	
Brake line bracket	8 ft.-lb.	(11 N•m)
Control arm to control arm bracket	34 ft.-lb.	(47 N•m)
Control arm to underbody	20 ft.-lb.	(27 N•m)
Hub and bearing assembly	74 ft.-lb.	(100 N•m)
Shock absorber upper nut	7 ft.-lb.	(10 N•m)
Shock absorber lower nut	34 ft.-lb.	(47 N•m)
Track bar to axle	33 ft.-lb.	(45 N•m)
Track bar to underbody	34 ft.-lb.	(47 N•m)

NOTE: If you own a 1981 or later model, first check the Supplement at the back of the book for any new service information.

CHAPTER TWELVE

BRAKES

The brake system has 2 independent circuits. Each independent brake circuit operates one front brake and one rear brake, diagonally opposite. In the event of complete failure of one circuit, the other circuit still provides 50% of the total brake effectiveness.

NOTE
General Motors has indicated that brake corrosion and proportioning valve problems exist with 1980 models that can cause premature rear brake lock-up. Return your vehicle to a dealer for inspection and correction, if not already done.

The cable operated mechanical parking brake acts on the rear wheels when the parking brake pedal is depressed. The rear brake shoes expand to provide emergency or parking brakes.

This chapter describes repair procedures for most parts of the brake system. Service to the vacuum booster is limited to removal and replacement; major work on this unit should be referred to a General Motors dealer. If you are inexperienced in working on brake hydraulic components, it's recommended that you limit your service to removal and replacement. Entrust the rebuilding of the master and wheel cylinders to your General Motors dealer, or replace defective units with new ones.

Table 1 provides braking specifications. **Table 2** provides torque specifications. They are found at the end of the chapter.

TESTING BRAKES

After performing service procedures to the braking system as described in this chapter, the brakes should be tested on a dry, clean, smooth, level roadway (preferably with little traffic flow). Brake performance cannot be determined when the roadway is wet or greasy or covered with loose dirt that does not allow the tires to grip equally.

The brakes should be tested at different vehicle speeds and with light and heavy pedal pressure. However, when applying the brakes, do not lock the wheels and cause the wheels to slide. Locking and sliding the wheels should not be used as a determining factor when testing brakes. A braking action where heavy pressure is applied but the wheels do not lock will stop the vehicle in less distance than when the wheels are locked.

When testing your vehicle's brakes, consider also the following conditions that will affect brake performance.

a. *Tires:* Tires which are worn or improperly inflated will cause unequal braking. Make sure that your tire's tread pattern is

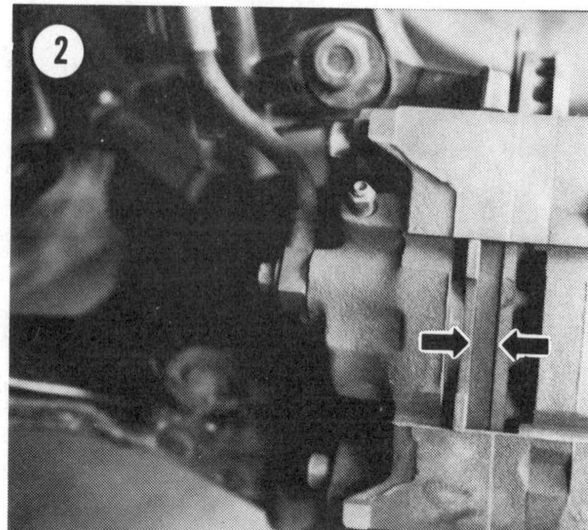

equal between the right and left sides and that the correct tire pressure is used. See Chapter Three.

b. *Alignment*: Incorrect front end alignment will cause the brakes to pull to one side. When experiencing brake pull, have the vehicle's front end alignment checked by a suspension specialist before continuing brake tests.

c. *Vehicle weight loading*: When carrying excessive weights in the car, the most heavily loaded wheels will require more braking than the others and cause unequal braking. When it is necessary to carry heavy objects, try to distribute the weight equally between the vehicle's left and right sides. Remove the weight as soon as possible. Fuel economy as well as braking efficiency is affected.

BRAKE INSPECTION

Disc Brake Pads

Inspect the brake pads every 7,500 miles for wear.

1. Raise vehicle front end and secure with jackstands.
2. Check both ends of the outboard pad by observing at each end in the caliper. See **Figure 1**. At this point on the outboard pad, the highest rate of pad wear occurs. The inner pad can be inspected by looking down through the inspection hole in the top of the caliper. See **Figure 2**.

NOTE

*The outside front disc brake pads use a built-in wear indicator (**Figure 3**) that will rub against the brake disc when the pads require replacement.*

3. Replace all 4 shoes if the lining of any pad is worn to within 0.030 in. (0.76 mm) of the rivet head at either end of the pad.

Drum Brake Shoes

Every 7,500 miles, inspect the brake shoe lining wear. To do this, remove the brake drums as described in this chapter. Measure thickness of linings. See **Figure 4**. If any one is less than 1/32 in. above rivet heads, replace all 4 shoes.

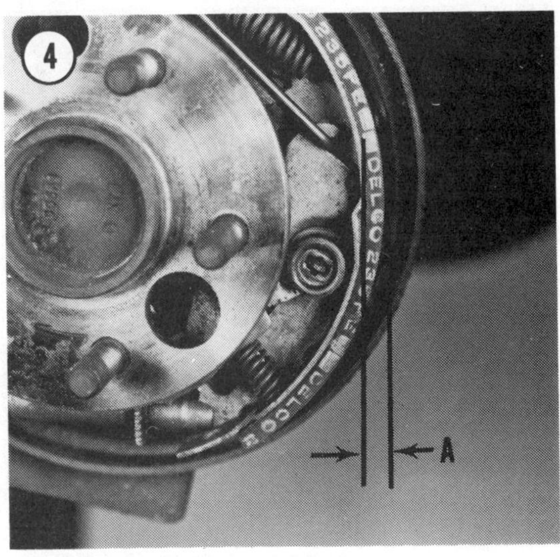

A. 1/16 in.

CAUTION

Make sure to replace all 4 brake pads or shoes even if only one is out of specification.

ADJUSTMENT

Front Disc Brakes

The front disc brakes are adjusted automatically. Therefore, no adjustment procedure is necessary or provided.

Rear Drum Brakes

Periodic adjustment is not required. The rear brakes self-adjust anytime the car is driven in reverse with the brakes applied. However, a manual brake adjustment procedure is provided for when the the brakes have been repaired. In such case, use the following procedure.

1. Jack up the rear end of the car and place it on jackstands. Release the parking brake from inside the driver's compartment.
2. Using a punch, knock out the stamped area at the brake drum (**Figure 5**).

CAUTION

When the hole is punched or drilled out, the drum must be removed and the metal fragment taken out of the brake assembly.

NOTE

On vehicles where no stamped area is in the brake drum, a hole must be drilled into the backing plate. All backing plates have 2 rounded flat areas in the lower half of the plate where the parking brake cable is installed. Drill a 1/2 in. hole into the round flat area on the backing plate opposite the parking brake cable. This will allow access to the brake adjusting wheel.

3. Insert General Motors tool part No. J-6166 or a thin-bladed screwdriver through the brake drum and turn the brake adjusting screw until the rear wheel can just be turned by hand.
4. Repeat this procedure on the opposite wheel. The drag should be equal at both wheels.
5. Back off the adjusting wheel at each rear wheel 30 notches. Turn each wheel. If the wheels still drag slightly, back off adjusting screw an additional 1 or 2 notches.

NOTE

*After backing off adjusting screw 32 notches, the brakes should be free of any drag. However, if drag is still felt, parking brake is applied or parking brake adjustment is incorrect. If parking brake is cause of drag, release parking brake and adjust parking brake as discussed under **Parking Brake**. Then repeat Steps 1-5.*

6. If hole was drilled or punched in the brake drum, obtain a hole cover from a General Motors dealer (part No. 4874119) and install in the brake drum (**Figure 5**).
7. Check parking brake adjustment.

Parking Brake

The parking brake must be adjusted whenever the rear brake cables are disconnected or when the parking brake pedal operates with less than 9 notch clicks or more than 16 notch clicks from fully released.

1. Depress the parking brake pedal exactly 2 notch clicks.
2. Jack up the rear end of the car and place it on jackstands.
3. Tighten equalizer adjusting nut from beneath vehicle until the left rear wheel can just be turned rearward but is locked when turned forward. See **Figure 6**. Turning of wheel should be done by hand.
4. Fully release the parking brake lever and rotate rear wheels; there should be no drag.
5. Lower vehicle.

Brake Pedal Height

With the brakes cold and the engine not running, measure the distance from the top of the brake pedal pad to the floorboard while firmly depressing the brake pedal as shown in **Figure 7**. Pedal height should be 3 1/2 in. (89 mm) for manual brakes and 2 3/4 in. (70 mm) for power brakes. If height specification is incorrect, perform brake inspection and adjustment procedures as described in this chapter.

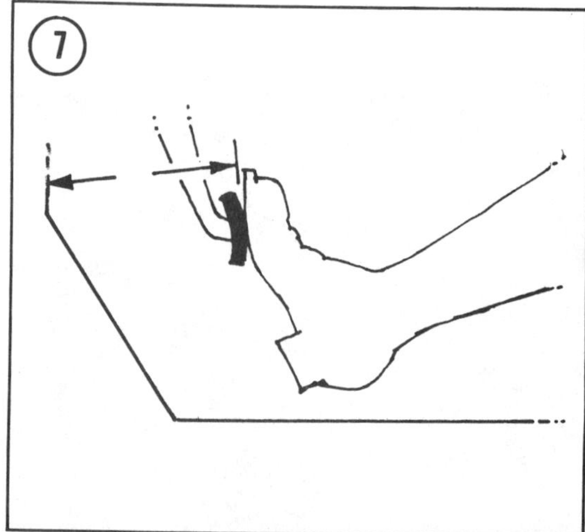

NOTE
When depressing brake pedal, an approximate force of 50 lb. must be exerted on manual brakes and 100 lb. on power brakes.

BRAKE PAD REPLACEMENT

The calipers must be removed to replace the brake pads. Follow the *Caliper Removal* and *Installation* procedures in this chapter.

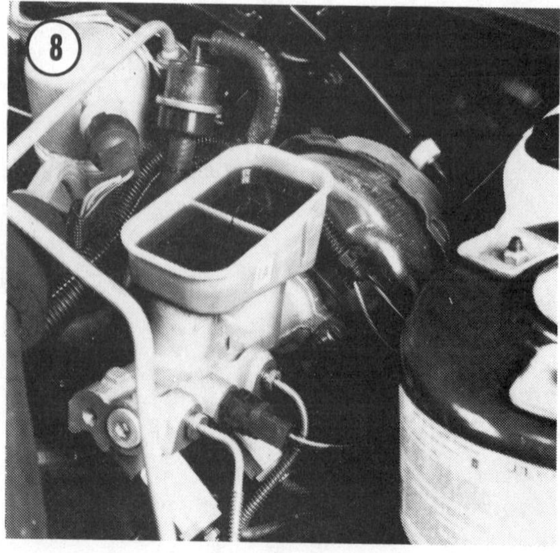

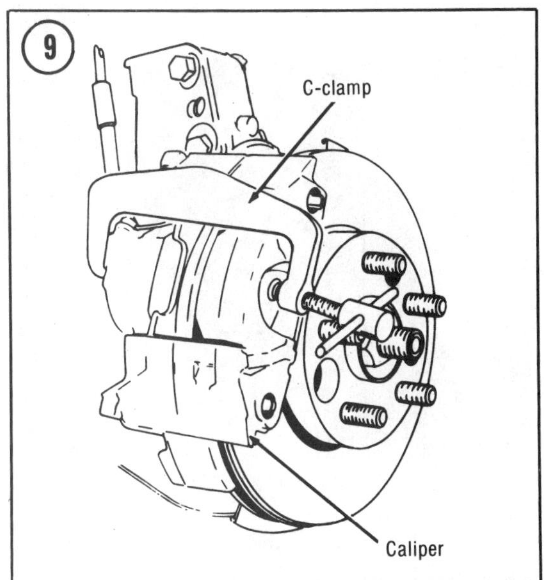

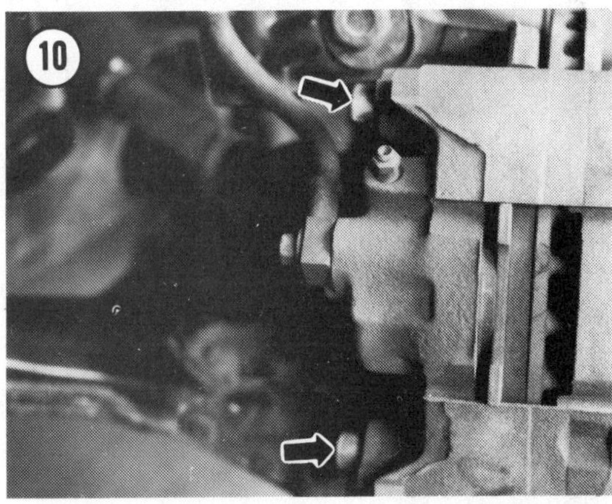

CALIPER

Removal

1. Check brake fluid level in the reservoir. If the reservoir is more than 2/3 full, siphon fluid out to bring the level to 1/3 full. See **Figure 8**.

WARNING
Discard the brake fluid removed; never reuse brake fluid.

2. Raise vehicle front end and place on jackstands. Remove front wheels.

NOTE
The next step is necessary only if brake pads will be removed.

3. Install a C-clamp on the caliper with the fixed end on the caliper housing and the adjustable end on the metal back of the outboard shoe (**Figure 9**). Tighten the C-clamp to bottom the piston in the caliper bore. Remove the C-clamp.
4. Remove the 2 bolts that secure the caliper mounting bracket to the steering knuckle. See **Figure 10**.
5. Remove the caliper from the disc. Hang caliper from front suspension using a chain or wire hook (**Figure 11**). Do not stretch or kink brake hose.
6. If caliper was removed simply to replace brake pads, the brake hose need not be disconnected. Otherwise, disconnect it from the caliper.
7. Pull the inboard pad outward until the shoe retainer spring clears the piston. Remove the outboard pad by prying on the pad retention lugs as shown in **Figure 12**. Pull shoe out of caliper.

CAUTION
Disc pads must not be interchanged between calipers. Mark disc pads if they are to be reused.

8. Repeat for opposite caliper.

External Inspection

1. Wipe the inside of the caliper clean. Clean the exterior of the dust boot and check for cuts, cracks or other damage.

CAUTION

Do not use compressed air to clean the caliper. This could unseat the dust boot.

2. Check the inside of the caliper for evidence of fluid leakage. If present, overhaul the caliper.
3. Check condition of brake pads. Make sure springs are not broken. See **Figure 13** (outboard pad) and **Figure 14** (inboard pad).

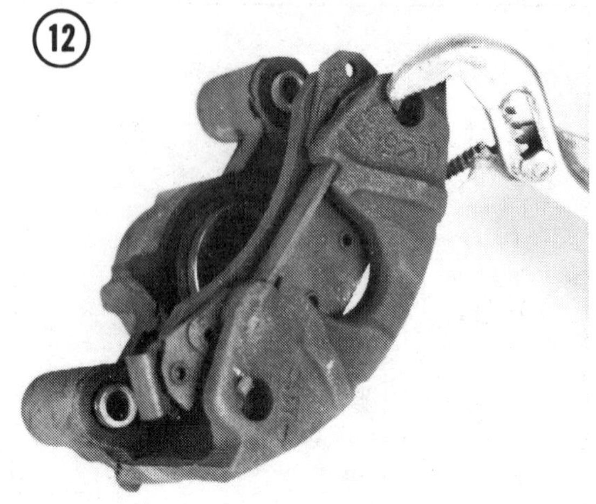

Disassembly

Refer to **Figure 15** for this procedure.

1. Clean the caliper exterior with clean brake fluid or denatured alcohol and place on a clean work surface.
2. Drain brake fluid from caliper.
3. Remove the retainer bolts, sleeves and bushings.
4. Pad the caliper with clean shop towels and remove the piston by directing compressed air into the caliper inlet hole (**Figure 16**).

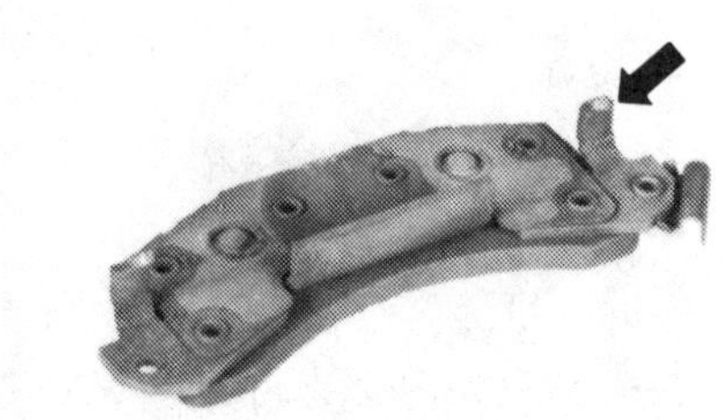

CAUTION

Use just enough air pressure to ease the piston out of the bore. If the piston is blown out, even with padding, it may be damaged.

5. Pry the boot out of the caliper with a screwdriver. See **Figure 17**. Be careful not to damage the caliper bore.
6. Remove the piston seal from its groove in the caliper bore with a piece of wood or plastic.

CAUTION

Do not use a metal tool of any type as it may damage the bore.

7. Remove bleeder valve from caliper (**Figure 18**).

Internal Inspection

CAUTION

Always use clean brake fluid or denatured alcohol to clean any caliper parts except pad linings. Never use other solvents as they cause rubber parts to deteriorate.

1. Clean all parts, except those in the repair kit, in clean brake fluid. Use dry, filtered compressed air to dry parts. Blow out all passages in the caliper and bleeder valve.

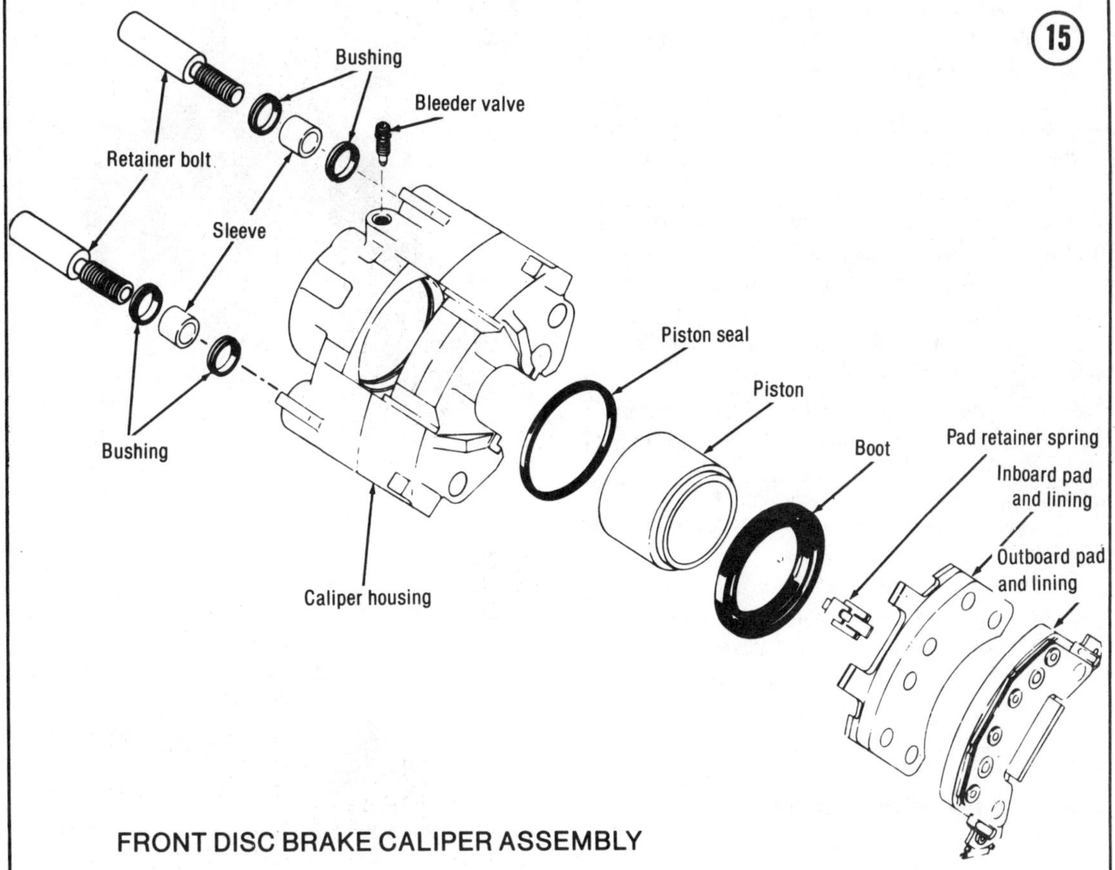

15

Bushing
Bleeder valve
Retainer bolt
Sleeve
Piston seal
Piston
Boot
Pad retainer spring
Inboard pad and lining
Outboard pad and lining
Bushing
Caliper housing

FRONT DISC BRAKE CALIPER ASSEMBLY

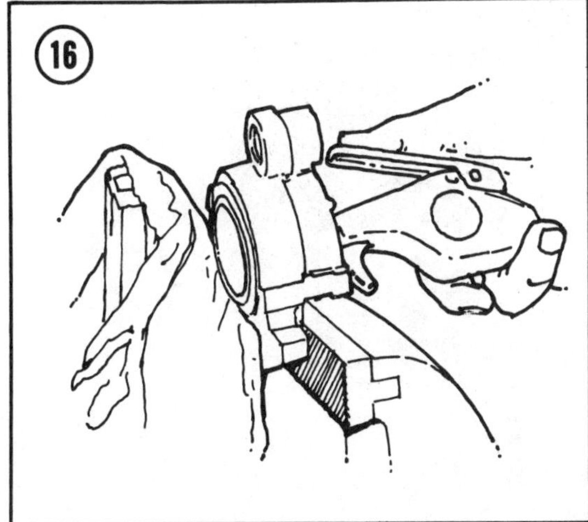

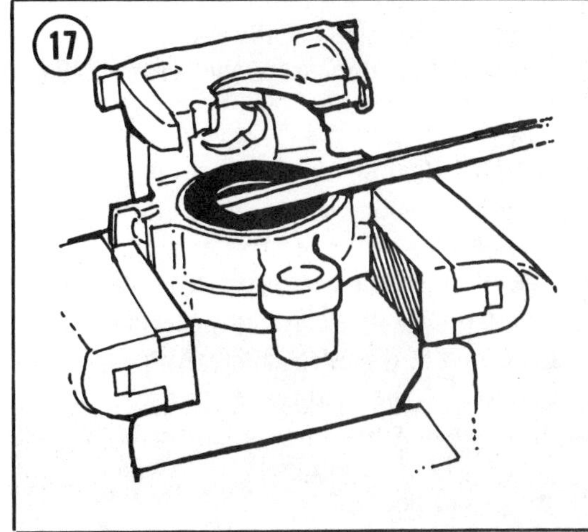

CAUTION
Lubricated shop air deposits a film of mineral oil on metal parts. This may damage rubber parts.

2. Check the retainer bolts for corrosion, breaks in the plating or other damage. Do not clean the bolts; replace them.
3. Carefully examine the piston outside diameter (**Figure 19**) for scoring, nicks, corrosion and worn or damaged chrome plating. If any surface defects are detected, replace the piston. It cannot be resurfaced by any means.
4. Check the caliper bore in the same manner as the piston. The caliper bore is not plated and stains or minor corrosion can be polished with crocus cloth.

CAUTION
Do not use emery cloth or any other abrasive. Thoroughly clean the caliper after using crocus cloth. If the bore cannot be cleaned in this manner, replace the caliper.

Assembly

Refer to **Figure 15** for this procedure.

CAUTION
Always use a complete repair kit when reassembling caliper.

1. Lubricate the caliper bore and the new piston seal with clean brake fluid. Install seal in bore groove.
2. Lubricate the piston with clean brake fluid. Install a new boot over the piston so that the fold faces the open end of the piston.
3. Insert the piston into the caliper bore. Then force the piston down to the bottom of the bore.
4. Position the dust boot outer diameter in the caliper housing and seat with GM tool part No. J-29077 (or an equivalent size drift). **Figure 20** shows the boot properly installed.
5. Install the bleeder valve (**Figure 18**).
6. Lubricate new sleeves and bushings, inside and out, and the unthreaded portion of the retainer bolts with Delco Silicone Lube part No. 3549912 (or equivalent). Install small bushings and sleeves into retainer bolt holes.

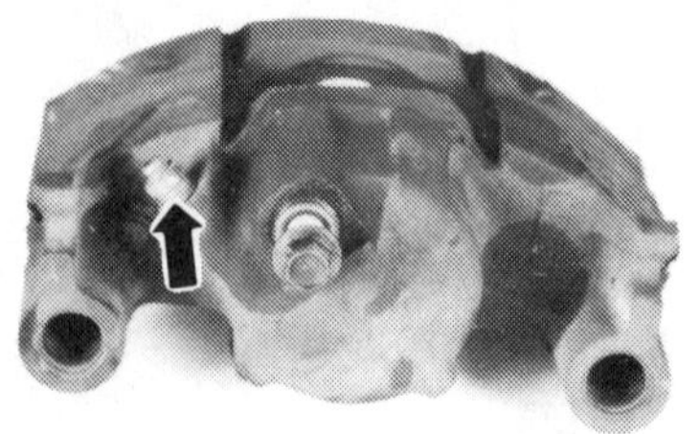

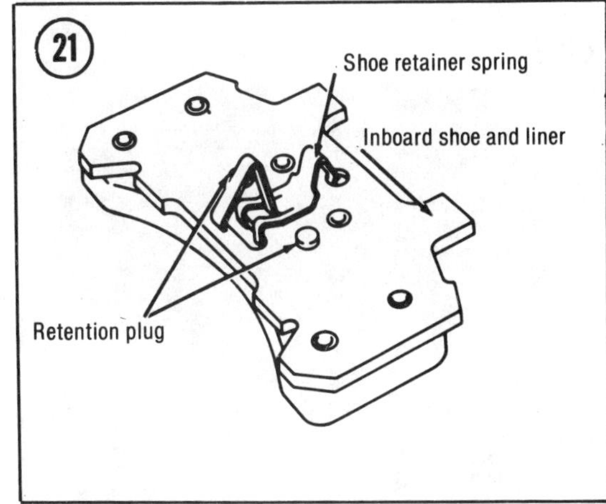

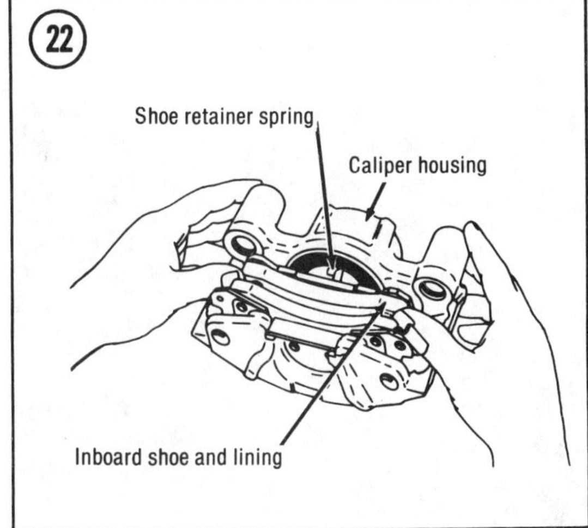

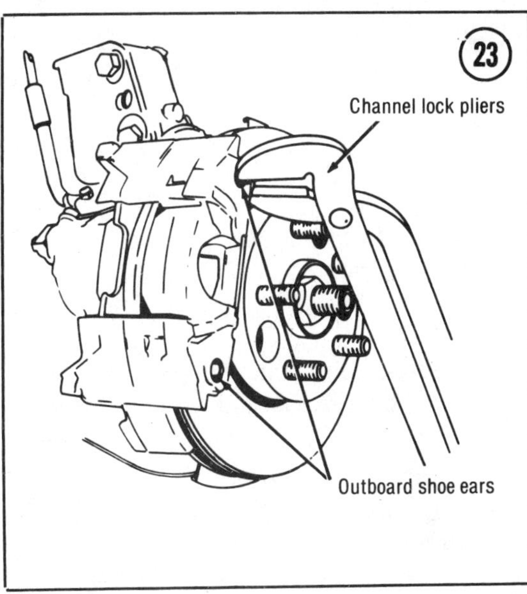

Installation

CAUTION

If original pads are to be reinstalled, they must be installed in original positions. If you didn't mark them when removing the caliper, all 4 must be replaced.

1. Install retaining spring in inboard pad. See **Figure 21**. Install single-leg end first.
2. Install inboard brake pad in caliper. Press pad in so that retainer spring seats inside the piston. See **Figure 22**. Install outboard brake pad in caliper. Secure the retaining spring to caliper as shown in **Figure 23**.
3. Install caliper over brake disc. Line up the mounting holes and install mounting bolts (**Figure 10**). Torque to 21-35 ft.-lb. (28-47 N•m).

NOTE

If brake inlet fitting was removed during removal, bleed brakes as discussed in this chapter.

4. Install wheels and lower vehicle.
5. Top up master cylinder with fresh brake fluid to within 3/4 in. of top of reservoir (**Figure 8**).
6. Pump brake pedal several times until pedal feels firm. Make sure fluid level in master cylinder is still correct; top up if necessary.

WARNING

Do not move vehicle until pedal feels firm. Bleed brakes if necessary.

BRAKE DISC

Inspection

Check brake disc surface for deep scratches, excessive runout and uneven thickness. Small marks on the disc are not important, but deep radial scratches reduce braking effectiveness and increase pad wear.

Depending upon condition, the brake discs can be resurfaced or reconditioned. If disc is badly worn or damaged, it must be replaced.

If scoring is light (less than 0.015 in. or 0.38 mm, or disc is covered with rust, resurface with a flat sanding disc. When done properly, the brake disc surface will have a nondirectional pattern.

CAUTION

When resurfacing or reconditioning a brake disc, both sides must receive equal treatment.

Minimum disc thickness of 0.964 in. (24.27 mm) is stamped on disc face. After reconditioning, the disc must measure at least 0.964 in. (24.27 mm). Discard any disc which is less than minimum thickness, regardless of condition.

1. To check runout, mark circumference of disc every 30° with chalk. Mount a dial indicator so that it contacts disc face about 1 in. (25 mm) from the edge. See **Figure 24**. Rotate the wheel and note dial indicator reading at each 30° mark. Maximum runout at any point must not exceed 0.0005 in. (0.013 mm).
2. Check the thickness of the disc with a micrometer. Make about 12 measurements around the disc, 1 in. from the outer edge. Measurements should not vary more than 0.0005 in. (0.013 mm).

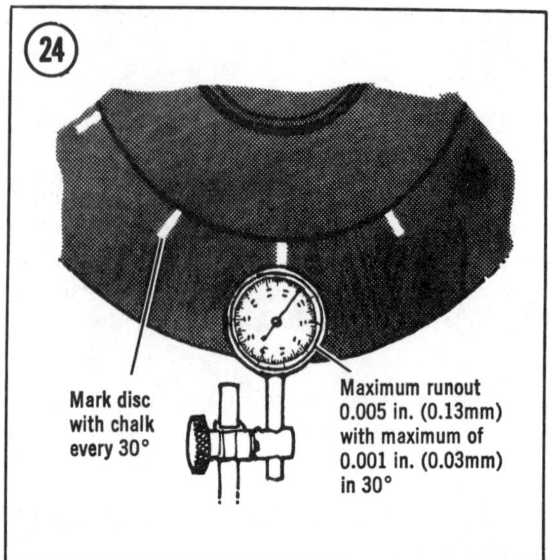

Removal/Installation

1. Raise front of vehicle on jackstands.
2. Remove wheel and hub nut.
3. Remove brake caliper as described under *Caliper Removal.*
4. Pull the disc off the hub assembly and remove.
5. Reverse these steps to install.

REAR DRUM BRAKES

Brake Drum Removal/ Installation

1. Raise vehicle rear end and secure with jackstands.
2. Remove the rear wheels.
3. Remove PAL nut and pull off brake drum. See **Figure 25**.
4. Inspect as described under *Inspection.*
5. Install brake drum and wheel. Torque wheel nuts to 103 ft.-lb. (140 N•m).

6. Adjust foot brake by applying the brake several times while driving the car in reverse. Adjust parking brake as described under *Adjustments, Parking Brake.*
7. Lower vehicle.

Inspection

1. Blow brake dust and dirt from the brake drum. Remove grease and oil with cleaning solvent blow and dry.

WARNING

Brake dust is harmful to inhale. It is highly recommended that you cover your mouth and nose when using compressed air to clean the brake assembly and to immediately leave the area until the dust settles.

2. Clean the drum braking surface with alcohol.
3. Inspect brake drums for scoring, cracking, taper, out-of-roundness, evidence of heat, etc. Drums which are scored or worn should be turned by a dealer. Cracked drums cannot be turned; replace them.

NOTE
If brake drums are turned by a dealer or garage, brake shoes must be replaced with oversized shoes.

4. Remove glaze on serviceable drums with fine emery cloth.

Brake Shoe Replacement

Figure 26 shows a rear brake assembly and should be referred to as necessary for disassembly and assembly procedures. It is a good idea to complete all work on one side of the car at a time, leaving the other brake assembled for reference.

1. Remove the brake drums as described under *Brake Drum Removal/Installation.*
2. Remove the brake return springs (**Figure 27**).
3. Remove the hold-down springs with pliers, then remove the lever pivot. Slide out the hold-down pins from the rear of the brake backing plate. See **Figure 28**.

NOTE
The hold-down springs are different lengths. The long spring is used on the front and the short one is used on the rear.

4. Lift up the actuator lever and remove the actuating link. Then remove the actuator lever, actuator pivot and return spring. See **Figure 29**.
5. Spread brake shoes apart. Remove parking brake strut and spring.
6. Disconnect the parking brake cable from the parking brake lever.
7. Disconnect both brake shoes by removing the adjusting screw. Remove the adjusting screw and spring. See **Figure 30**.

CAUTION
Mark shoe positions if they are to be reused.

8. Remove the retaining clip from the secondary brake shoe and remove the parking brake lever (**Figure 31**).
9. Clean and inspect the brake drum as described under *Brake Drum Inspection.* Replace or recondition drums as required.
10. Carefully pull lower edges of wheel cylinder boots away from cylinders. Excessive interior fluid indicates piston cups are leaking. Rebuild or replace wheel cylinder as required. See *Wheel Cylinder, Overhaul* in this chapter.

NOTE
A slight amount of fluid is normal; it lubricates the piston.

11. Check tightness of all backing plate mounting bolts. Clean all rust and dirt from shoe contact faces on backing plate with fine emery cloth.

CAUTION
If original shoes are being reinstalled, they must be installed in original positions as marked when removed.

CAUTION
Your hands must be clean while handling brake shoes. Do not permit oil or grease to come in contact with linings.

12. Lubricate parking brake cable with Delco Brake Lube part No. 3540032 (or equivalent).
13. Lubricate fulcrum end of parking brake lever with Brake Lube. Connect lever to secondary shoe and secure with new retaining clip (**Figure 31**). Make sure lever moves freely.
14. Lightly lubricate backing plate shoe contact surfaces with Brake Lube.
15. Connect the brake shoes together at bottom with the adjusting screw and spring (**Figure 30**).

NOTE
Make sure the coils of the spring do not contact the star wheel on the adjusting screw.

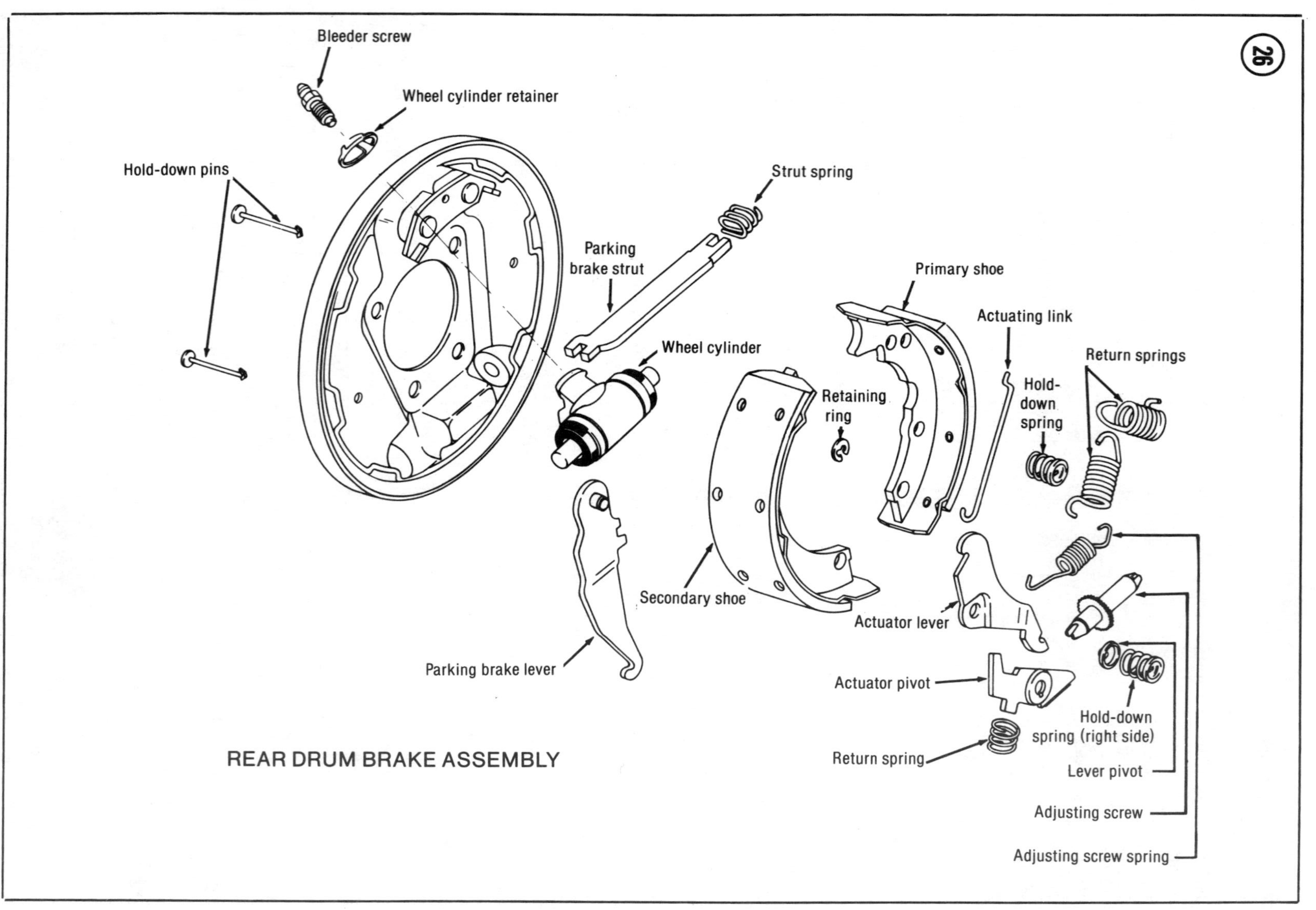
26
Bleeder screw
Wheel cylinder retainer
Hold-down pins
Strut spring
Parking brake strut
Primary shoe
Actuating link
Wheel cylinder
Return springs
Retaining ring
Hold-down spring
Secondary shoe
Actuator lever
Parking brake lever
Actuator pivot
Hold-down spring (right side)
Return spring
Lever pivot
Adjusting screw
Adjusting screw spring
REAR DRUM BRAKE ASSEMBLY

27

28

Hold-down pins
Return springs
Hold-down springs
Lever pivot

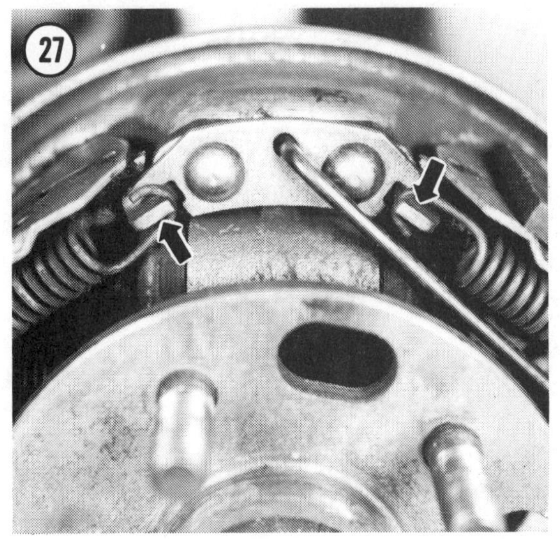

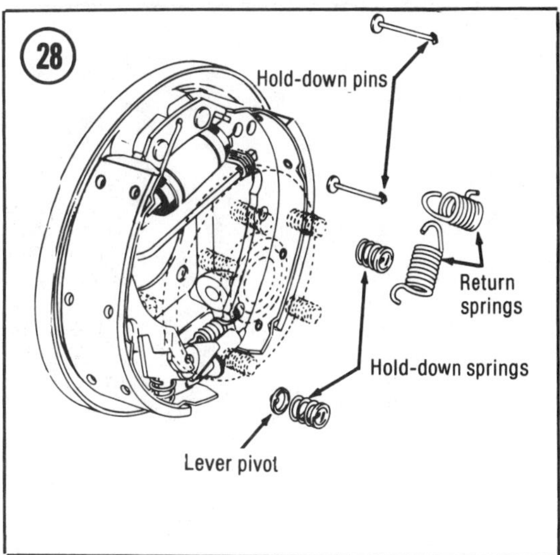

29

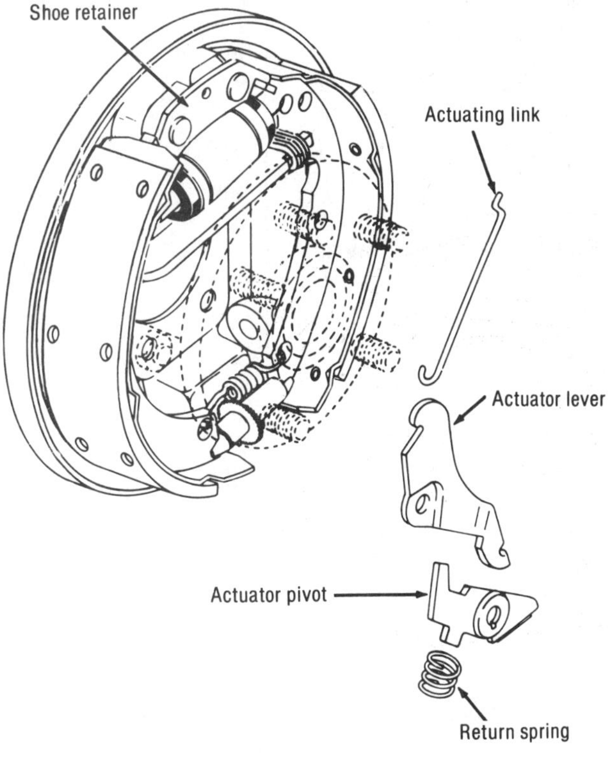

Shoe retainer
Actuating link
Actuator lever
Actuator pivot
Return spring

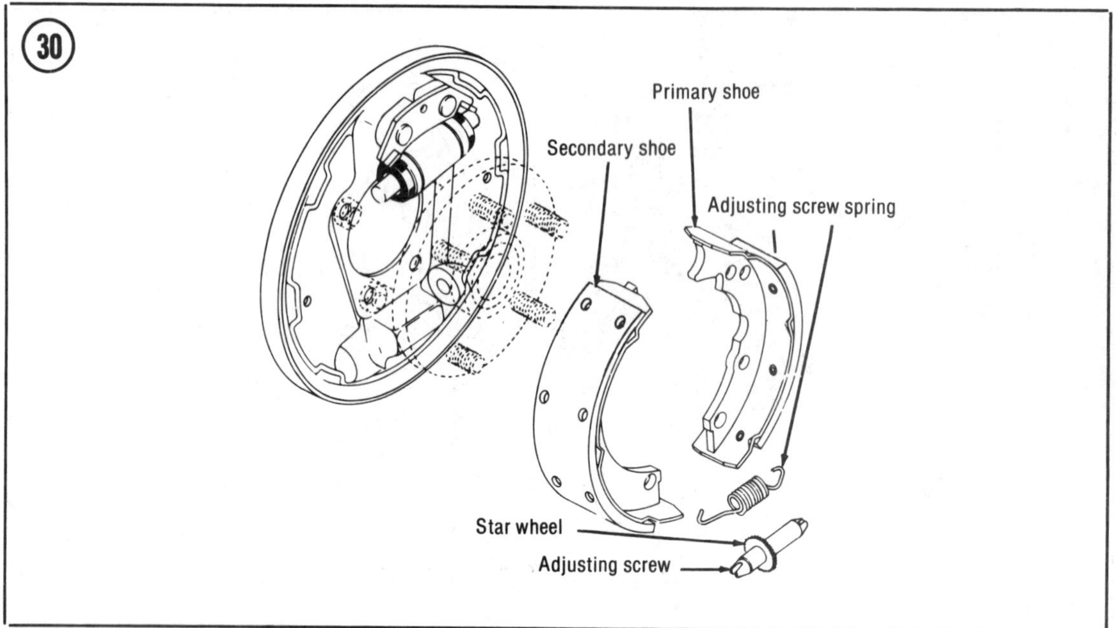

CAUTION

Left- and right-hand springs are not interchangeable.

16. Install parking brake cable to parking brake lever. Then spread the brake shoes apart and temporarily engage shoes to the wheel cylinder at top of backing plate.

17. Spread the brake shoes apart and install the parking brake strut and spring. See **Figure 32**. Make sure that end of strut without the spring engages the parking brake lever and that the end with the spring engages the primary shoe.

18. Install the actuator pivot, actuator lever and return spring. Install the actuating link in the shoe retainer. Lift up the actuator and hook the link into the lever. See **Figure 29**.

19. Install the hold-down pins from rear of backing plate. Install the lever pivot and hold-down springs from front of backing plate. See **Figure 28**.

NOTE

Make sure to install the long hold-down spring on the front shoe. The short spring goes to the rear shoe.

20. Install the shoe return springs with pliers.

21. Install the brake drums as described under *Brake Drum Removal/Installation*.

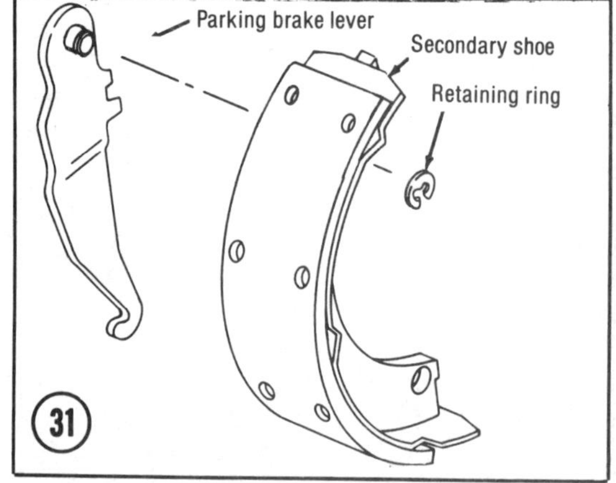

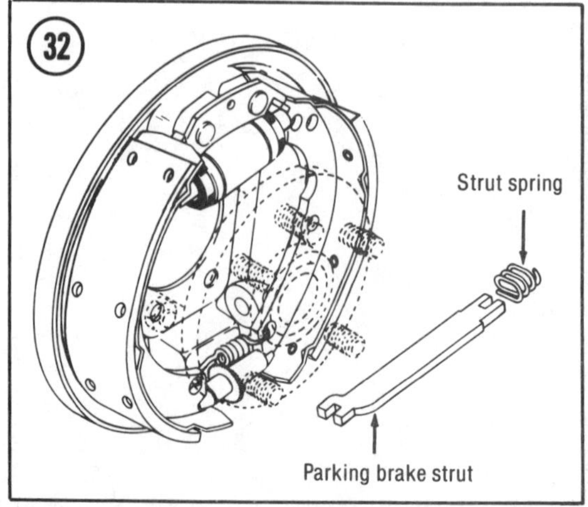

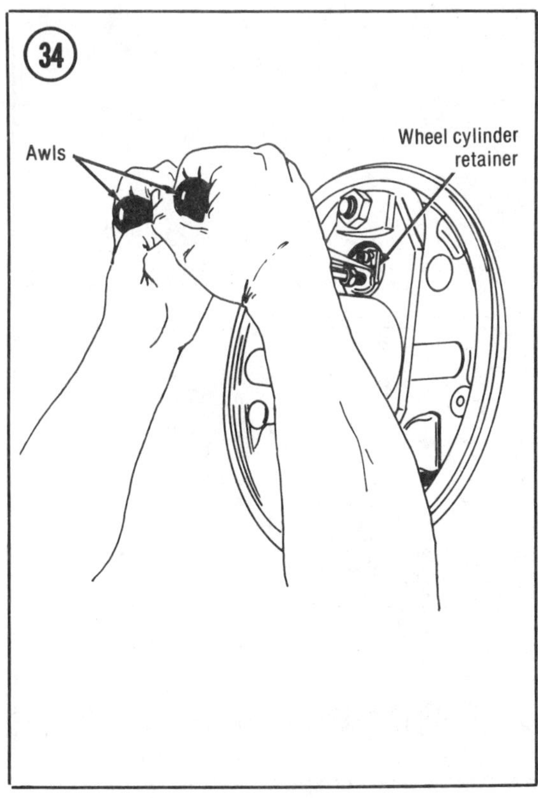

22. Adjust brakes as described under *Adjustment, Rear Drum Brakes.*
23. Install the wheels and wheel nuts. Lower the car and tighten the wheel nuts to 103 ft.-lb. (140 N•m).

WHEEL CYLINDER

Removal/Installation

Refer to **Figure 33** for this procedure.

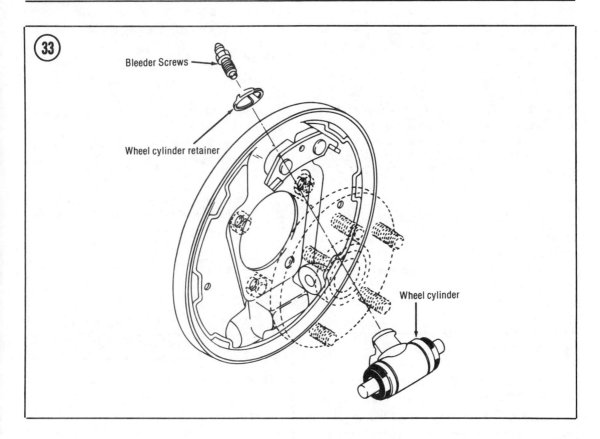

1. Raise the vehicle rear end and place on jackstands.
2. Remove wheel. Back off brake adjustment, if necessary, and remove drum.
3. Remove the brake shoes as described under *Brake Shoe Replacement.*
4. Clean all dirt and foreign material from brake line connection at the wheel cylinder. Disconnect brake line from the cylinder at rear of backing plate.
5. Insert 2 awls or pins into access slots between the wheel cylinder pilot and retainer tabs (**Figure 34**). Then bend both retainer tabs away simultaneously and remove the wheel cylinder.

6. To install, position wheel cylinder between cylinder and axle flange and hold in place with a wooden block.
7. Install new wheel retainer clip over wheel cylinder abutment on rear of backing place and secure by pressing into place using a 1 1/8 in., 12 point socket as shown in **Figure 35**.
8. Reverse Steps 1-3 to complete installation. Bleed brake system as described under *Bleeding Hydraulic System.*

Overhaul

Refer to **Figure 36** for this procedure.

1. Remove the rubber boots from each end of the wheel cylinder.
2. Take out the pistons, pistons cups and spring expander.
3. Remove the bleeder screw from the cylinder.
4. Thoroughly clean all parts with brake fluid, then blow dry with compressed air.
5. Examine the cylinder bore for scoring, pitting or heavy corrosion. Very light scratches may be removed with crocus cloth. Flush out with alcohol and blow dry. Replace wheel cylinders which show more extensive damage.
6. Make sure the bleeder screw hole is unobstructed.
7. Lubricate all parts with clean brake fluid.
8. Install new pistons, cups and spring expander provided in repair kit. Do not reuse old parts.
9. Install new rubber boots.
10. Install bleeder screw.

MASTER CYLINDER

Removal/Installation

1. *Manual brakes only*: Disconnect master cylinder pushrod from brake pedal.
2. Disconnect electrical leads at master cylinder (**Figure 37**).
3. Place rags under master cylinder to protect painted surfaces.

CAUTION

If any brake fluid spills onto the paint, immediately wipe the area, then wash with soapy water.

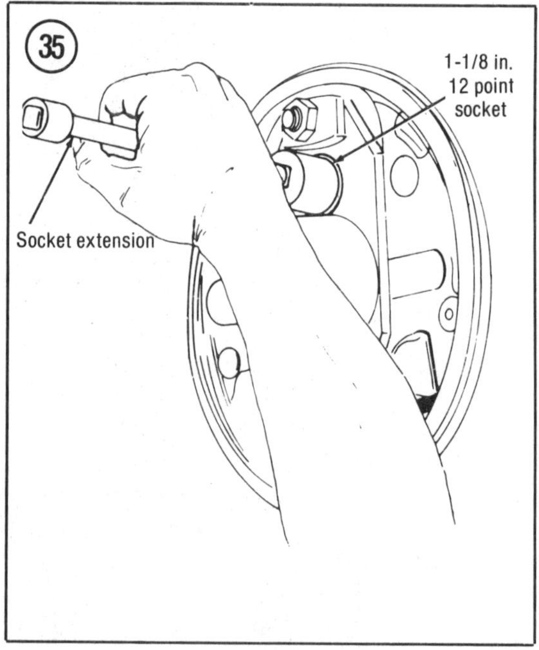

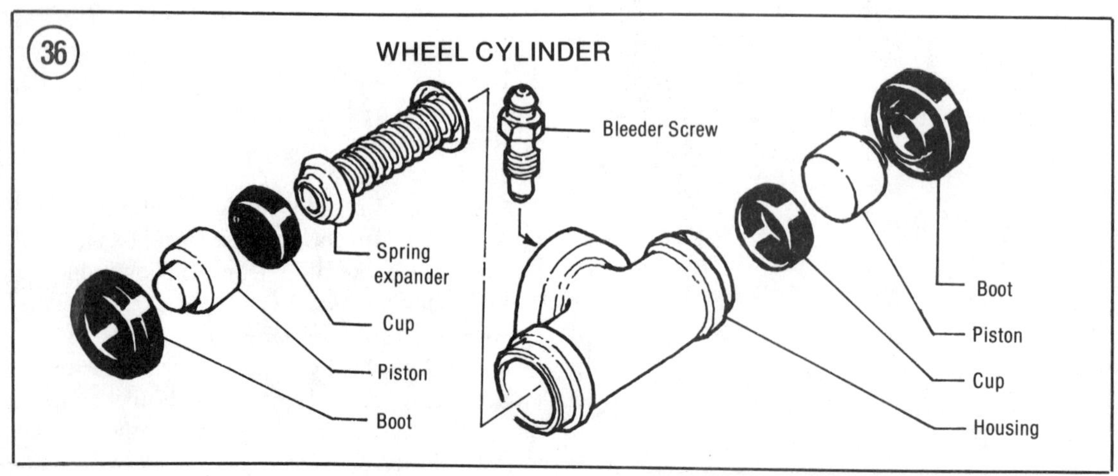

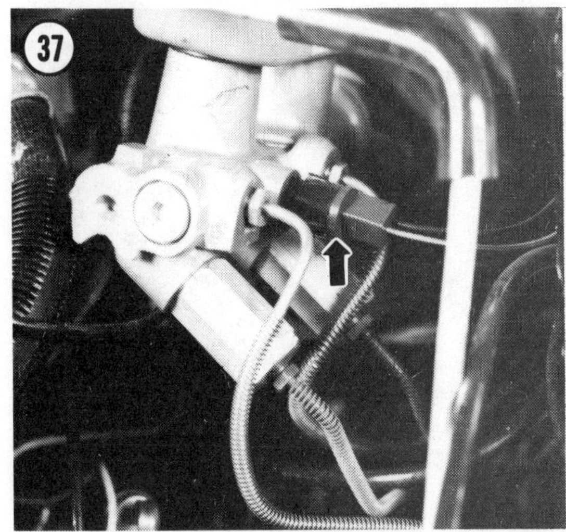

4. Clean all dirt and foreign material from the master cylinder brake lines. Disconnect brake lines from master cylinder. Cover ends of lines to prevent entry of dirt. See **Figure 38**.
5. Remove nuts securing master cylinder to firewall (**Figure 39**) or power booster (**Figure 40**).
6. Installation is the reverse of these steps. Tighten master cylinder attaching nuts to 22-30 ft.-lb. (30-45 N•m). Fill reservoir and bleed brakes as described under *Bleeding Hydraulic System.*

Disassembly

Refer to **Figure 41** while performing the following procedure.

1. Clean the outside of the master cylinder before taking it apart.
2. Remove reservoir cover. Drain fluid out.
3. Place master cylinder in a vise with soft jaws.
4. Depress primary piston and remove lock ring.
5. Refer to **Figure 42** and remove proportioning valves from outside of master cylinder body. Then remove failure warning switch and O-rings.
6. Remove the primary piston and secondary piston by directing compressed air into one of the outlets at the end of the master cylinder and plugging the other 3 outlets. See **Figure 43**.

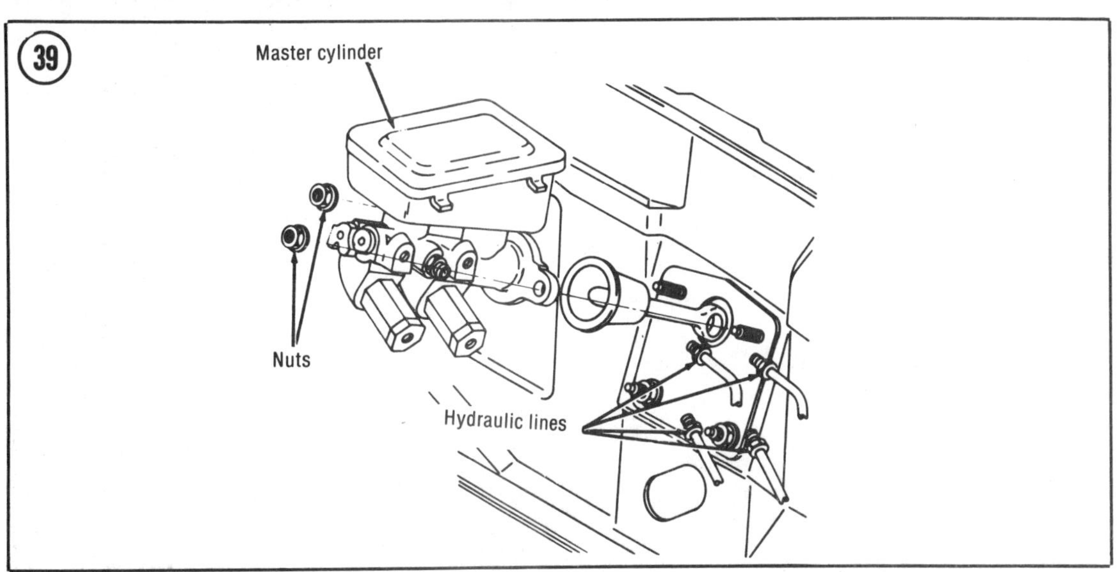

12

NOTE
Do not disassemble the primary piston. Replace it completely as provided in repair kit.

7. Remove the Allen head plug at the rear of the master cylinder. Then pull out the switch piston assembly as shown in **Figure 44**.

Inspection

1. Clean all parts in clean brake fluid or denatured alcohol which does not contain benzene. Do not use gasoline, kerosene or trichloroethylene. If in doubt about a solvent, do not use it; use brake fluid.
2. Replace the pistons for wear, chipping or other visible defects. Replace as needed.

NOTE
When using a master cylinder repair kit, install all parts supplied with kit.

3. Make sure all passages and openings are unobstructed. Blow the cylinder bore out with dry, filtered compressed air.
4. Check the cylinder bores for scores, pitting, corrosion or wear. If any damage is noticed, the master cylinder will have to be replaced.

CAUTION
Do not attempt to hone or clean up cylinder walls as the cylinder body is made of aluminum.

Assembly

Refer to **Figure 41** for this procedure.

1. Install seals on secondary piston as shown in **Figure 45**.
2. Install seal retainer on secondary piston.
3. Lubricate master cylinder bore and secondary piston seals with clean brake fluid.
4. Install secondary piston spring on piston. Install complete assembly in cylinder bore.
5. Lubricate primary piston assembly with clean brake fluid and install in the cylinder bore. Hold pressure on assembly and install snap ring.

NOTE
Perform Steps 6 and 7 if failure warning switch and switch piston assembly were removed during disassembly. If not, proceed to Step 8.

6. Install new O-rings on proportioners and failure warning switch and lubricate with clean brake fluid. Install as shown in **Figure 42**. Tighten proportioning valves to 18-30 ft.-lb. (24-41 N•m). Tighten failure warning switch to 15-59 in.-lb. (1.7-5.6 N•m).
7. Install new O-rings and retainers on switch piston and lubricate with clean brake fluid. Install switch piston assembly to rear of master cylinder. Install new O-ring on rear plug and tighten to 40-140 in.-lb. (4.5-16 N•m).
8. Fill the master cylinder reservoir with clean brake fluid and bench bleed the master cylinder as described in next procedure.

Bench Bleeding

1. Install plugs in 4 outlet ports.

NOTE
Plastic plugs that come with a replacement cylinder can be used. Otherwise, purchase suitable sized brass plugs from an auto parts supplier.

2. Hold master cylinder in a vise with the front end tilted down slightly.

CAUTION
Do not tighten vise too tightly.

3. Fill reservoir with clean brake fluid.
4. Press in on primary piston assembly. Watch for air bubbles in reservoir fluid.

41

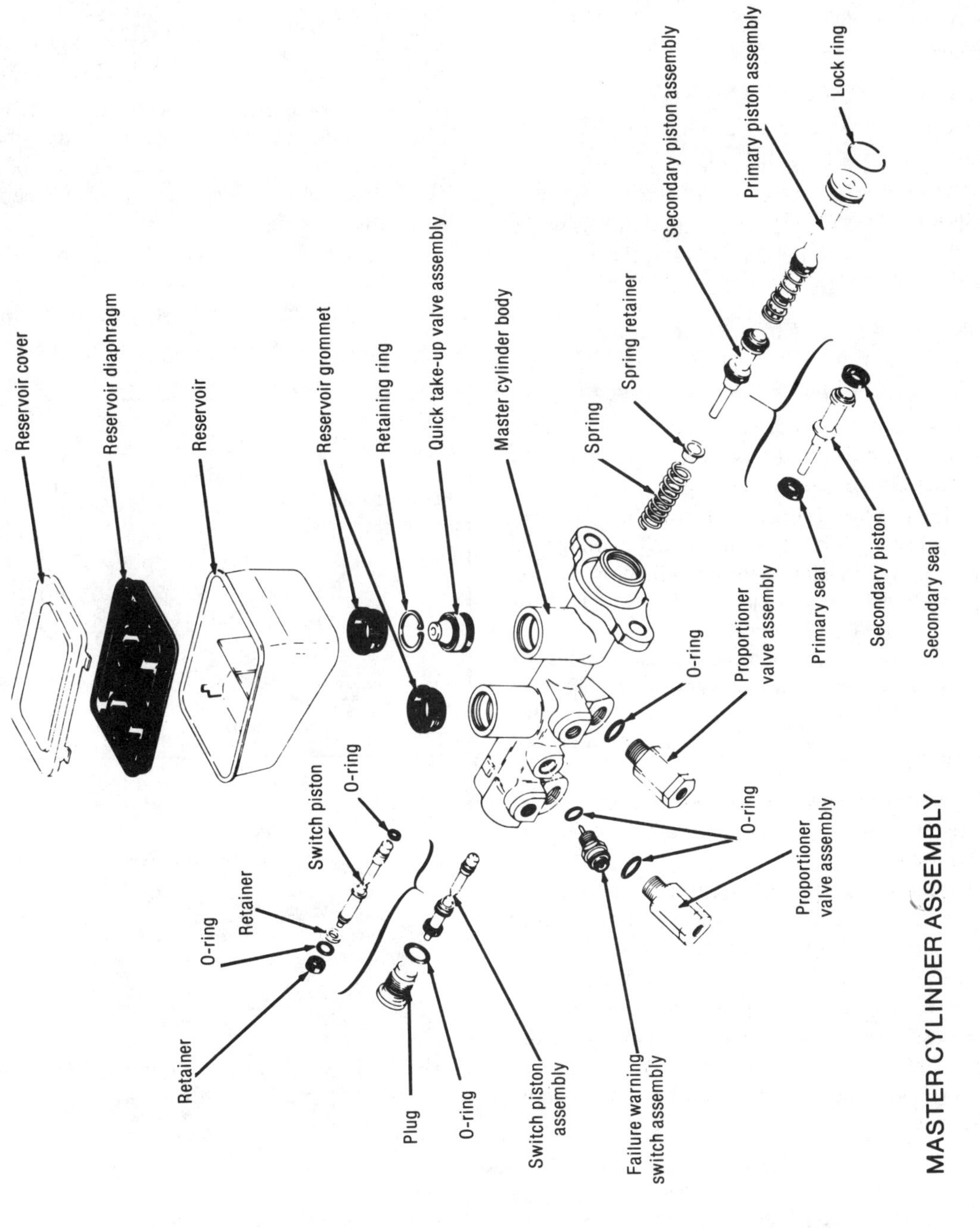

Reservoir cover
Reservoir diaphragm
Reservoir
Reservoir grommet
Retaining ring
Quick take-up valve assembly
Master cylinder body
Spring
Spring retainer
Secondary piston assembly
Primary piston assembly
Lock ring
O-ring
Proportioner valve assembly
Primary seal
Secondary piston
Secondary seal
Switch piston
O-ring
Retainer
O-ring
Retainer
Plug
O-ring
Switch piston assembly
Failure warning switch assembly
O-ring
Proportioner valve assembly

MASTER CYLINDER ASSEMBLY

5. Release pressure on primary piston. Watch for air bubbles in reservoir fluid.
6. Repeat Step 5 until no bubbles appear.
7. Reposition master cylinder in vise so that the front end is tilted slightly up.
8. Repeat Steps 4 through 6.
9. Install reservoir diaphragm and cover.
10. Install master cylinder as described under *Master Cylinder, Removal/Installation.*

POWER BOOSTER

Service to the power booster is limited to removal and installation. While the unit is rebuildable, special tools and experience are required and it is recommended that this work be referred to a General Motors dealer.

Removal/Installation

Refer to **Figure 46** for this procedure.

1. Remove the master cylinder as described under *Master Cylinder, Removal/Installation.*

CAUTION
Make sure you have placed rags underneath master cylinder/power booster assembly to prevent spillage on vehicle paint.

2. Disconnect the vacuum booster pushrod from the brake pedal inside the car.
3. Remove nuts attaching power booster to firewall and remove the power booster.
4. Reverse the removal steps to install the power booster. Tighten power booster-to-cowl attaching nuts to 22-33 ft.-lb. (30-45 N•m). Install master cylinder on booster and tighten attaching nuts to 22-33 ft.-lb. (30-45 N•m). When installation is complete, fill and bleed the brake system as described in this chapter. Road test the car to ensure that the brakes are operating correctly.

BLEEDING THE BRAKE SYSTEM

The brake system must be bled to remove air from it after any portion of the system has been disconnected (e.g., replacement of a brake hose, caliper, etc.) or when the pedal feels spongy or soft.

Fluid that is expelled during bleeding should be discarded; it may contain foreign matter and if it has been in service for a while it will have absorbed atmospheric water which

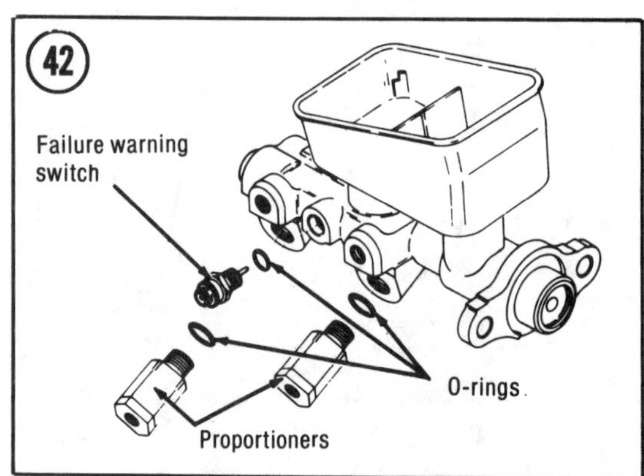

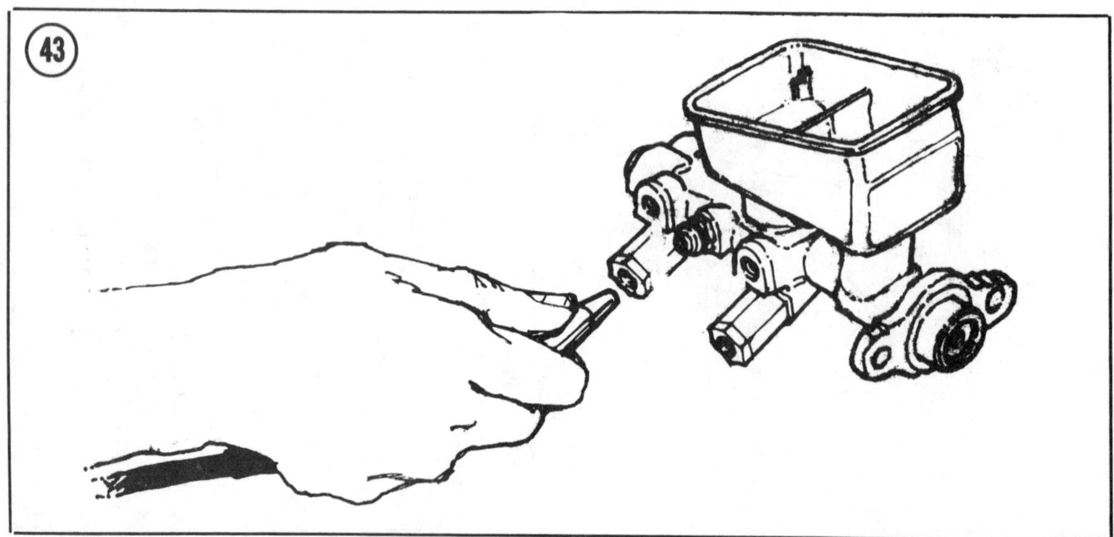

44

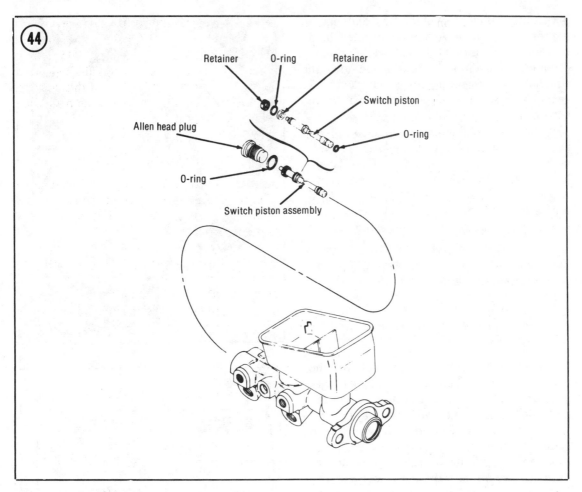

Retainer
O-ring
Retainer
Switch piston
O-ring
Allen head plug
O-ring
Switch piston assembly

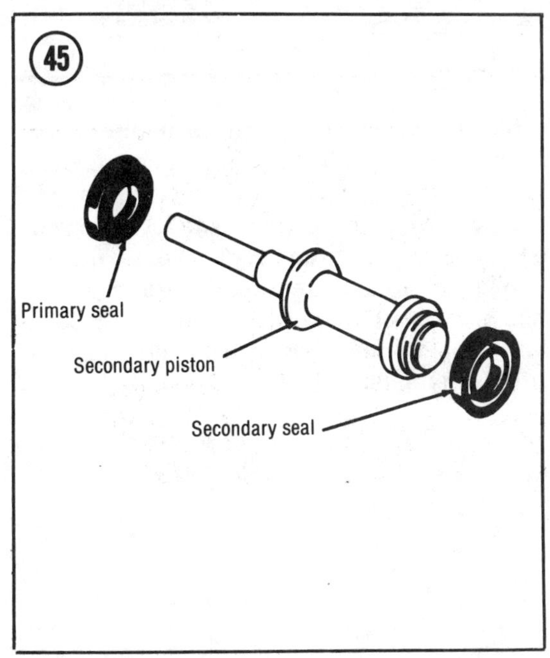

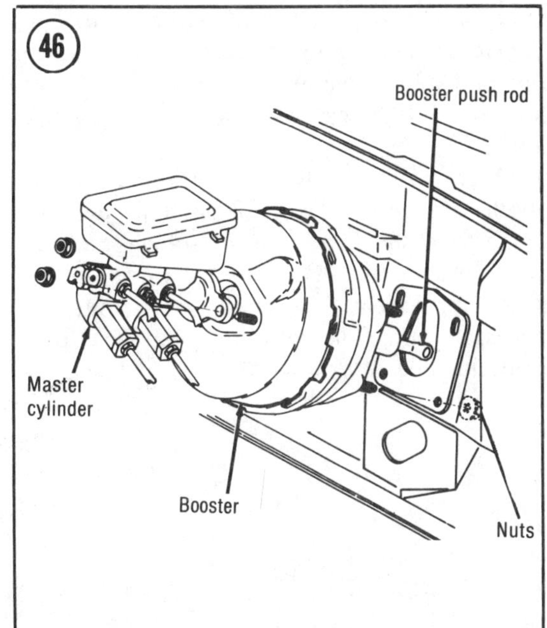

lowers the boiling point of the fluid and makes it prone to vapor lock during repeated hard braking applications (such as mountain driving). In addition, it is a good idea to completely replace the brake fluid every 2 years because of the water it will have absorbed.

Whenever handling brake fluid, do not get any on the brake shoes, brake discs, calipers or body paint. Brake shoes or brake pads will be permanently damaged, requiring replacement. Body paint can be damaged also unless you wipe the area with a clean cloth and wash it immediately with a soapy solution.

NOTE
The brake system can be bled using a pressure type bleeder or by using an assistant. Because it is unlikely that a hobbyist mechanic will have a pressure tank bleeder, the second, less expensive method is described.

1. Check the brake fluid level in the reservoirs and top them up to the upper mark if necessary. Leave the caps off and cover the reservoirs with clean shop rags to prevent fluid from being ejected and getting on painted surfaces.
2. Connect a plastic or rubber tube to the bleeder valve on the right rear wheel. Suspend the other end of the tube in a jar or bottle filled with a few inches of brake fluid. See **Figure 47**. During the remaining steps, keep this end submerged at all times and never let the level in the reservoir drop below 1/2 full level.
3. Open bleeder valve on right rear wheel about one turn. Have an assistant depress brake pedal slowly to floor. As soon as pedal is all the way down, close bleeder valve and let pedal up. Repeat this step as many times as necessary until fluid with no air bubbles flows from the tube.

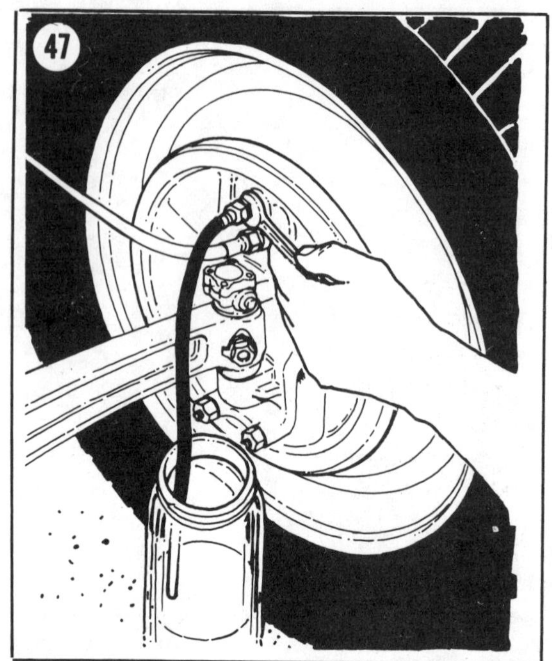

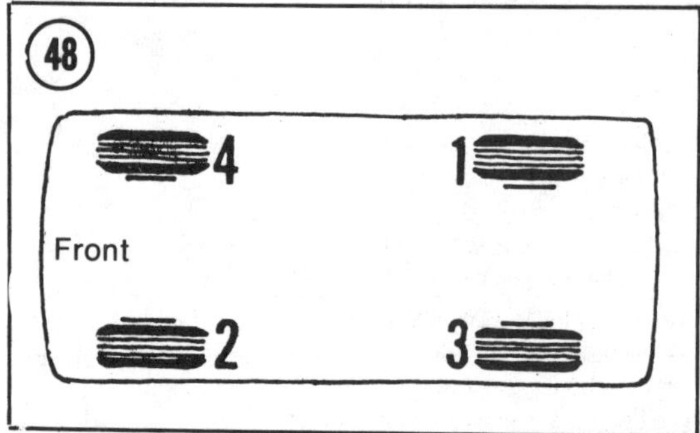

4. Bleed the remaining valves in the same manner as described in the steps above. Follow the sequence shown in **Figure 48**. Keep checking the master cylinder reservoir to be sure it doesn't run out of brake fluid.
5. When all wheels are bled, discard the brake fluid in the jar or bottle; never reuse such fluid. Top up the master cylinder reservoir with clean fluid.

Table 1 BRAKE SPECIFICATIONS

Master cylinder		
Piston diameter	0.874 in.	(22.2 mm)
Wheel cylinder		
Diameter	0.689 in.	(17.5 mm)
Discs		
Diameter	11.00 in.	(279.4 mm)
Thickness		
Minimum	0.965 in.	(24.47 mm)
Maximum	1.040 in.	(26.42 mm)
Maximum end play	0.005 in.	(0.127 mm)
Parallelism	0.0005 in.	(0.0127 mm)
Maximum out-of-round	0.005 in.	(0.127 mm)
Drums		
Diameter	7.874 x 1.575 in.	(200 mm x 40 mm)
Power head		
Diameter	7.874 in.	(200 mm)

Table 2 TIGHTENING TORQUES, BRAKES

Item	Torque	
Caliper bleeder screws	110 in.-lb.	(13 N•m)
Wheel cylinder bleeder screws	50 in.-lb.	(6 N•m)
Brake hose to caliper screw	33 ft.-lb.	(45 N•m)
Brake pipe to rear wheel cylinder	150 in.-lb.	(17 N•m)
Caliper mounting bolt	28 ft.-lb.	(38 N•m)
Master cylinder attaching nuts	25 ft.-lb.	(30 N•m)
Booster attaching nuts	25 ft.-lb.	(30 N•m)
Wheel cylinder installation bolts	150 in.-lb.	(17 N•m)
Brake pipes to master cylinder nuts	150 in.-lb.	(17 N•m)
Failure warning switch	30 ft.-lb.	(35 N•m)
Proportioner valves	25 ft.-lb.	(30 N•m)
Brake pedal to dash	18 ft.-lb.	(25 N•m)
Brake pedal swing bolt nut	49 ft.-lb.	(65 N•m)
Parking brake attaching bolts	7 ft.-lb.	(9 N•m)

SUPPLEMENT

1981 AND LATER SERVICE INFORMATION

This supplement contains service and maintenance information for 1981 and later GM X-car (Buick Skylark, Chevrolet Citation/Citation II, Oldsmobile Omega and Pontiac Phoenix) models. The information supplements the procedures in the main body (Chapters One through Twelve) of the book, referred to in the supplement as the "basic book."

The chapter headings and titles in this supplement correspond to those in the basic book. If a chapter is not included in the supplement, there are no changes affecting 1981 and later models.

If your vehicle is covered by this supplement, carefully read the supplement and then read the appropriate chapters in the basic book before beginning any work.

CHAPTER THREE

LUBRICATION, MAINTENANCE AND TUNE-UP

SCHEDULED MAINTENANCE

Table 1 summarizes all scheduled maintenance required for 1981-on models.

Fuel Filter Replacement (Fuel Injected Engines)

WARNING
Before opening any fuel system connection on a fuel injected engine, relieve the system pressure as described in the Chapter Six section of this supplement.

Fuel injected engines use a disposable inline filter canister bracket-mounted on the driver's side of the engine block. No factory specifications are provided for filter replacement, but it is a good idea to install a new filter at every tune-up. To replace the filter:

1. Relieve fuel system pressure. Loosen the fuel inlet and outlet fittings at the filter canister. Remove the inlet and outlet lines. Cap the lines to prevent fuel leakage.
2. Loosen the bracket clamp screw. Pull the filter from the bracket.
3. Installation is the reverse of removal. Be sure the arrow on the filter canister faces in the direction of fuel flow.

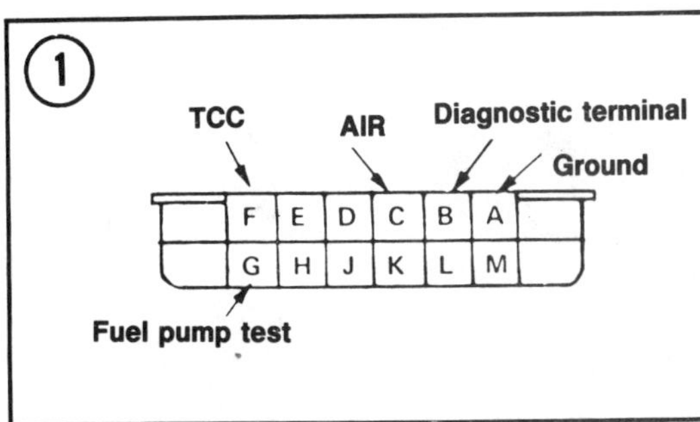

CYLINDER HEAD BOLT TORQUE

On 1981 and later 4-cylinder engines, coat cylinder head bolts with thread sealer and torque to 85 ft.-lb. (115 N•m).

SPARK PLUGS

The 1981 and later V6 engine uses R43TS spark plugs with a 0.045 in. (1.15 mm) gap.

IGNITION TIMING

Ignition timing of the fuel injected 2.5L engine is the same as for carburetted models, except that electronic spark timing is bypassed by grounding the B and A terminals in the 12-terminal ALCL diagnostic connector instead of disconnecting the 4-terminal EST connector at the distributor. The ALCL diagnostic connector will be found just to the right of the fuse box. A jumper wire installed between the 2 terminals (**Figure 1**) will let the engine operate in the bypass timing mode without being influenced by the electronic control module.

CARBURETOR ADJUSTMENTS

An idle speed control (ISC) assembly is used with 1981 and later carburetors to maintain the correct idle speed. The ISC is controlled by the electronic control module (ECM) in the Computer Command Control (CCC) system. Since idle speed is electronically controlled, no attempt at idle speed adjustment should be made.

Table 1 SCHEDULED MAINTENANCE (1981-ON)

Interval	Service
Every 7,500 miles (12 months)	• Change engine oil[1] • Check fluid levels • Lubricate chassis • Inspect steering and suspension • Inspect axle boots and seals • Check brake lines • Check manual transaxle fluid level • Check exhaust system • Adjust clutch pedal free travel
First 7,500 miles, then every 15,000 miles	• Check and rotate tires • Check disc brakes
First 7,500 miles, then every 30,000 miles	• Check carburetor choke and hoses • Check carburetor or throttle body mounting torque • Check idle speed (engines without ISC or IAC)
Every 15,000 miles	• Check and adjust drive belts • Change engine oil filter[1] • Check cooling system[2] • Check rear drum brakes • Check parking brake adjustment • Check throttle linkage • Inspect fuel tank, cap and lines • Check crankcase vent system • Change fuel filter[3]
Every 30,000 miles	• Replace spark plugs [1] • Check and adjust ignition timing • Check ignition wiring • Drain and refill cooling system • Check manual steering gear seals • Inspect air cleaner operation • Replace air cleaner filter • Replace crankcase vent filter • Replace PCV valve • Check EGR system operation
Every 100,000 miles	• Change automatic transaxle fluid and filter[1]

1. SEVERE SERVICE OPERATION: If the vehicle is operated under any of the following conditions, change engine oil @ 3,000 mile or 3 month intervals and oil filter @ alternate oil changes. Clean and regap spark plugs every 6,000 miles. Change automatic transaxle fluid and filter every 15,000 miles.
   a. Extended idle or low-speed operation (short trips, stop-and-go driving)
   b. Trailer towing
   c. Operation @ temperatures below 10° F for 60 days or more with most trips under 10 miles
   d. Very dusty or muddy conditions
2. Check coolant protection and condition once a year.
3. Carburetted engines only.

CHAPTER FOUR

ENGINE (4-CYLINDER)

ENGINE SPECIFICATIONS

Some specifications and tightening torques for the 4-cylinder engine differ for the 1981 and later models. See **Table 2** and **Table 3**.

FUEL INJECTION PRECAUTIONS

Before opening any fuel system connection on a fuel injected engine, relieve the system pressure as described in the Chapter Six section of this supplement.

ROCKER ASSEMBLY AND PUSHRODS

The 1985 4-cylinder engine uses hydraulic roller lifters (**Figure 2**) to reduce valve train friction. The lifters are held in place and prevented from rotating by lifter guides and guide retainers. See **Figure 3**. Pushrods used with this engine have been shortened from 9.754 in. to 8.3996 in. and camshaft profile is slightly modified to accommodate the lifter change. The camshaft, pushrods and lifters are not suitable for use as a replacement in earlier engines.

Service procedures remain unchanged with the additional step of removing the retainers and guides when lifters are removed. All lifters should be replaced whenever a new camshaft is installed.

ENGINE MOUNTS

The lower right-hand engine mount on 1985 models is a hydraulic design for better engine dampening (**Figure 4**). A single low torque axis transmission mount replaces the 2 mounts used on earlier models. See **Figure 5**.

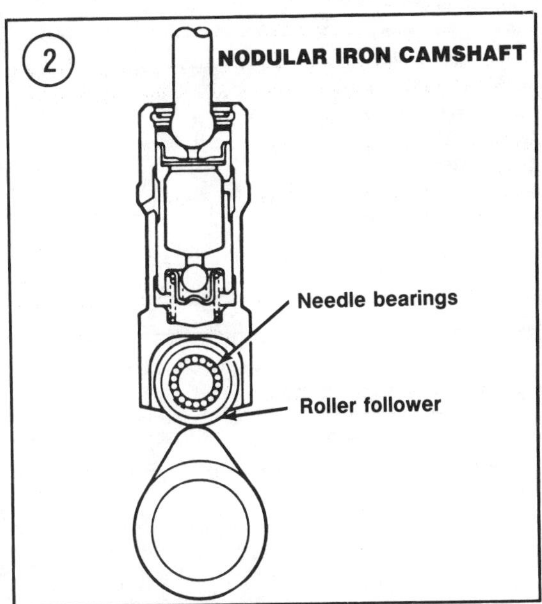

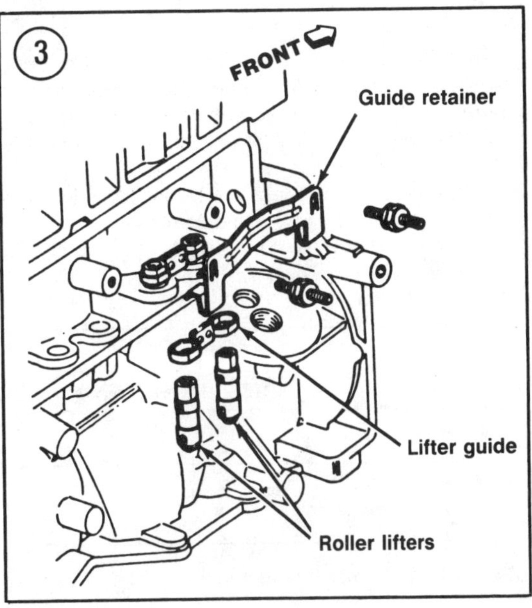

13

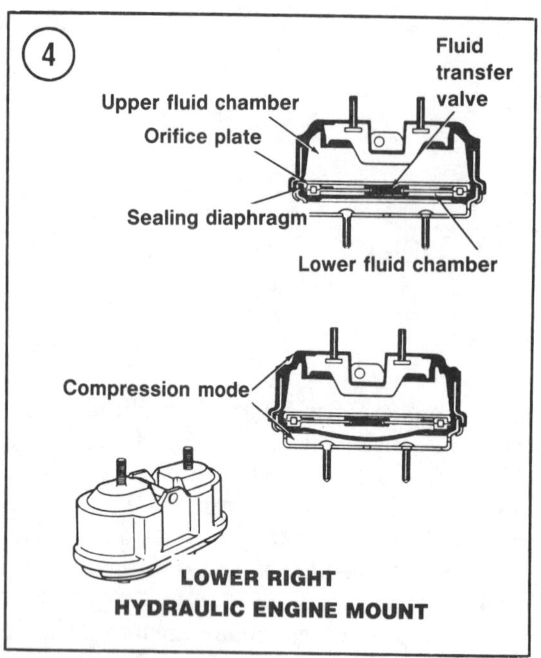

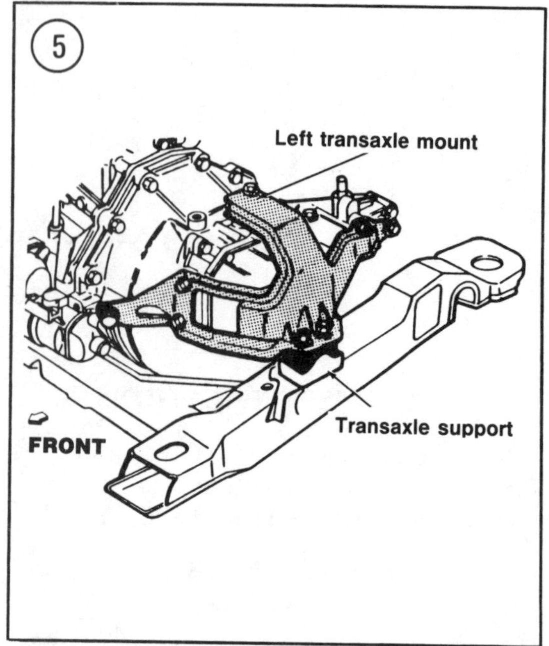

Table 2 4-CYLINDER ENGINE SPECIFICATIONS (1981-ON)

Cylinder bore	
Out-of-round	0.0014 in. (0.0356 mm)
Piston	
Clearance in bore	
Top	0.0025-0.0033 in. (0.0635-0.0838 mm)
Bottom	0.0017-0.0041 in. (0.0430-0.1041 mm)
Piston compression ring	
Ring width	
Top	0.0620-0.0625 in. (1.575-1.583 mm)
2nd	0.0775-0.0780 in. (1.9685-1.9812 mm)
Gap	
Top	0.010-0.022 in. (0.381-0.635 mm)
2nd	0.010-0.027 in. (0.2286-0.4826 mm)
Camshaft	
Lobe lift, intake and exhaust	0.398 in. (10.3124 mm)

Table 3 TIGHTENING TORQUES (1981-ON 4-CYLINDER)

Fastener	ft.-lb.	N•m
Cylinder head bolt*	85	115
Throttle body assembly	15	20

* Coat threads with thread sealer.

CHAPTER FIVE

ENGINE (V6)

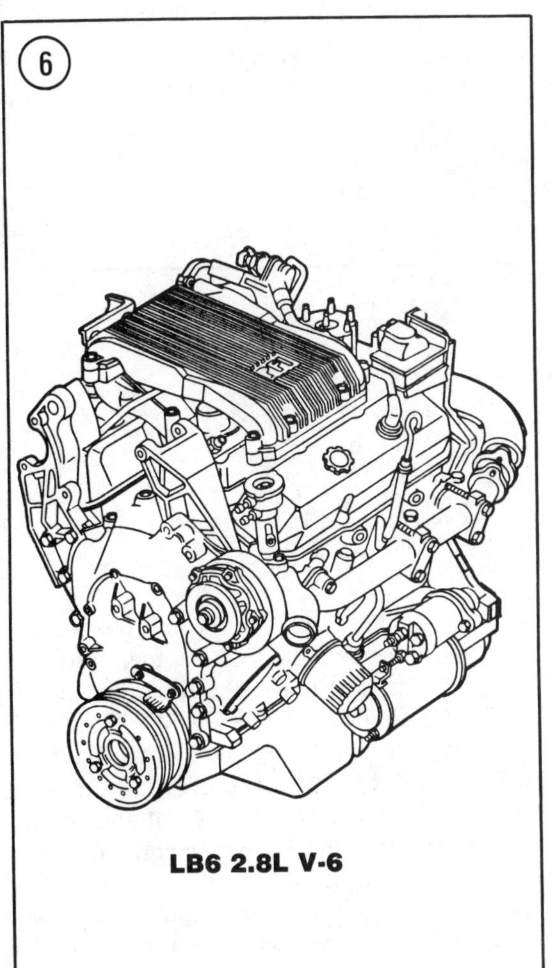

LB6 2.8L V-6

H.O. ENGINE

A high output (H.O.) version of the V6 is optional in some 1981-1984 models. The H.O. V6 differs primarily in camshaft profile, valve timing and an 8.9:1 compression ratio.

The H.O. V6 is replaced in 1985 models by the PFI V6 (**Figure 6**). This engine uses a port fuel injection (PFI) system instead of a carburetor.

Service procedures specified in Chapter Five of the basic book remain unchanged for the H.O. V6. New procedures required to service the PFI V6 are provided in this supplement.

Plenum Removal/Installation

Refer to **Figure 7** for this procedure.

1. Disconnect the negative battery cable.
2. Disconnect all vacuum lines at the plenum.
3. Remove the 2 bolts holding the EGR tube to the plenum.
4. Remove the 2 throttle body bolts.
5. Remove the throttle cable bracket.
6. Remove the 10 bolts holding the plenum to the intake manifold. Remove the plenum and gaskets. Discard the gaskets.
7. Installation is the reverse of removal. Use new plenum gaskets. Tighten the plenum bolts to 18 ft.-lb. (25 N•m).

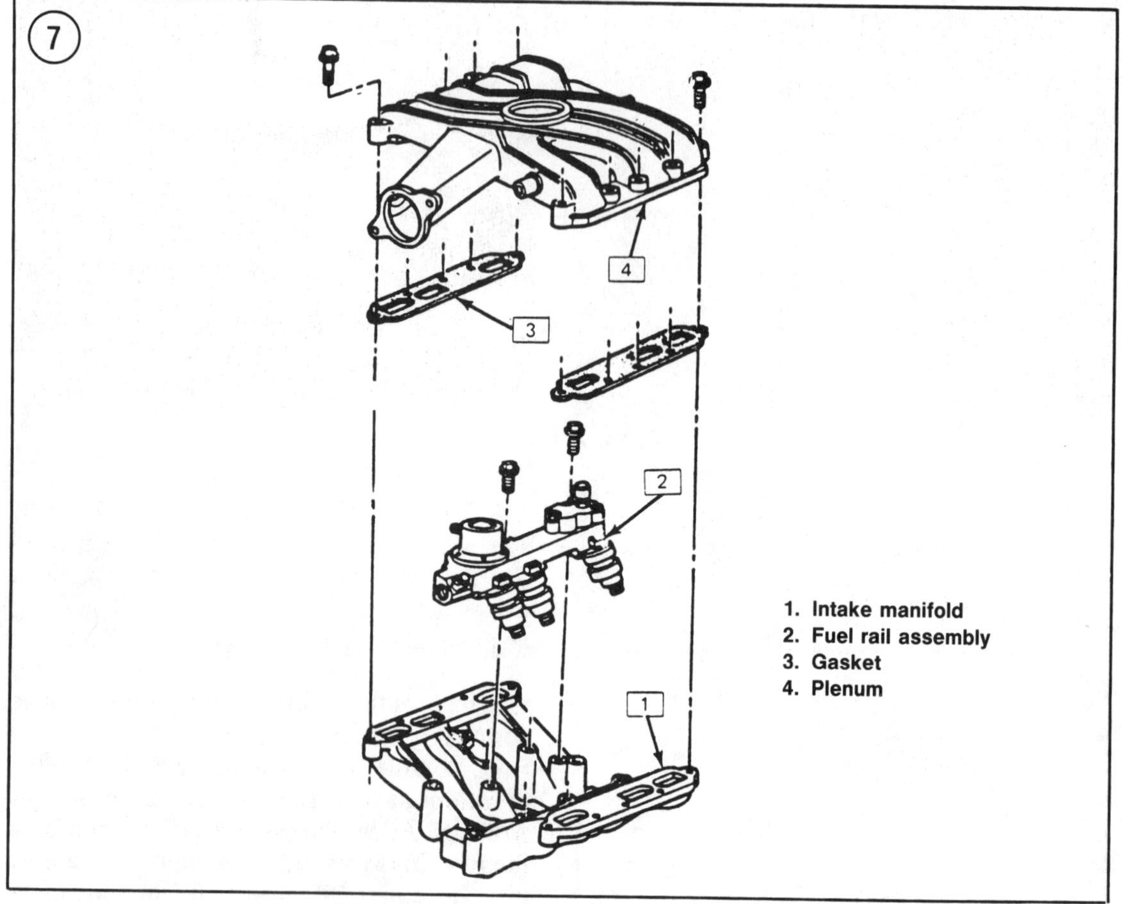

CHAPTER SIX

FUEL AND EXHAUST SYSTEM

CARBURETORS

All 1981 4-cylinder and 1981-1984 V6 engines use the Rochester E2SE carburetor. Service procedures are essentially unchanged. Specifications are provided in **Tables 4-6**.

ELECTRONIC FUEL INJECTION

All 1982-on 4-cylinder engines are equipped with a Rochester Model 300 throttle body fuel injection (TBI) assembly (**Figure 8**). The assembly contains an electrically operated injector that meters fuel into the intake air stream under the direction of the electronic control module (ECM). The ECM receives electrical signals from various sensors, refers to its stored program memory and calculates the precise amount and timing of fuel required by the engine. Fuel delivery time of the injector is modified by the ECM to accommodate special engine conditions such as cranking, cold starts, altitude, acceleration or deceleration.

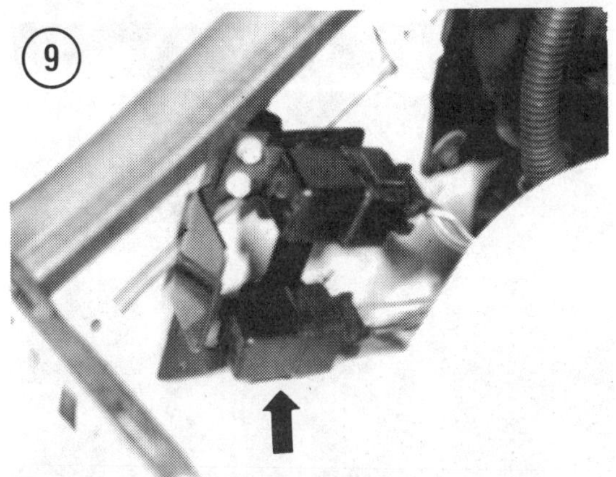

The basic throttle body assembly consists of 2 major aluminum castings:

a. A throttle body containing a valve to control air flow.

b. A fuel body assembly containing an integral fuel pressure regulator and solenoid-operated fuel injector.

System Operation

Filtered fuel is supplied to the TBI assembly by an electric fuel pump mounted in the fuel tank. When the ignition switch is turned ON, a fuel pump relay (**Figure 9**) activates the in-tank pump for 1.5-2 seconds to prime the injector. If the ECM does not receive a reference signal from the distributor, it shuts down the fuel pump.

Fuel flow is controlled by varying the duration of injection according to signals from the ECM. Excess fuel passes through a pressure regulator in the fuel body assembly and is then returned to the fuel tank. A throttle position sensor or TPS (**Figure 10**) informs the ECM of throttle valve position. An idle air control of IAC assembly (**Figure 11**) maintains a pre-programmed idle speed according to directions from the ECM.

Since the system is electronically controlled, no attempt should be made to adjust the idle speed or fuel mixture. Owner service should be limited to replacement only. If the system is not working properly, take the car to a General Motors dealer for diagnosis and adjustment.

System Pressure Relief

Before opening any fuel connection of fuel injected engines, fuel pressure must be relieved to reduce the risk of fire and personal injury.

1. Place the transaxle in NEUTRAL (manual) or PARK (automatic).
2. Set the parking brake and block the drive wheels.

3. Remove the fuel pump fuse from the fuse block.
4. Crank the engine. The engine will start and run until the fuel remaining in the lines is used up. When the engine stops, crank the engine again for 3 seconds. This will dissipate any remaining fuel pressure and permit safe disconnection of the fuel lines.
5. When fuel system service has been completed and all lines reconnected, install the fuel pump fuse in the fuse block.
6. Turn the ignition switch to ON, but do not start the engine. Inspect system connections for leaks and repair if necessary before starting the engine.

Throttle Body Removal/Installation

1. Relieve system pressure as described in this section of the supplement.
2. Remove the air cleaner as described in Chapter Six of the basic book.
3. Disconnect the electrical connectors at the idle air control assembly and throttle position sensor.
4. Carefully disconnect the injector harness (**Figure 12**) to prevent damage to the electrical connector pins.
5. Disconnect the throttle linkage (A, **Figure 13**) and return spring (B, **Figure 13**). Disconnect the cruise control linkage, if so equipped.
6. Label and disconnect all vacuum lines at the throttle body. See **Figure 14** for identification and routing.
7. Disconnect the fuel supply and return lines at the throttle body. Plug lines to prevent leakage.
8. Remove 3 bolts holding throttle body unit to engine. Remove TBI assembly and gasket from manifold.
9. Installation is the reverse of removal. Use a new gasket and tighten the throttle body attaching bolts to 120-168 in.-lb. (14-19 N•m). Tighten fuel lines to 19 ft.-lb. (26 N•m).

Throttle Body Disassembly

Refer to **Figure 15** for this procedure.
1. Remove the air cleaner stud from the throttle body assembly. Remove the 5 screws and lockwashers holding the fuel meter cover

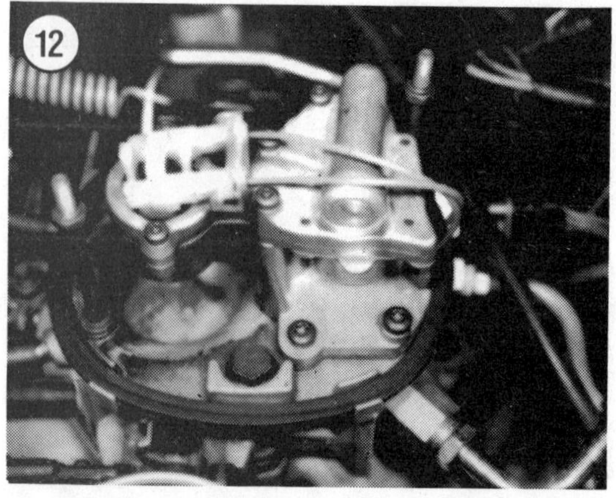

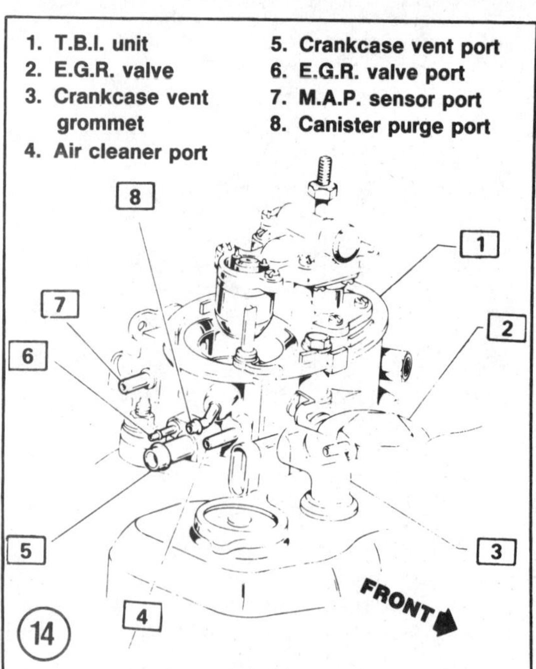

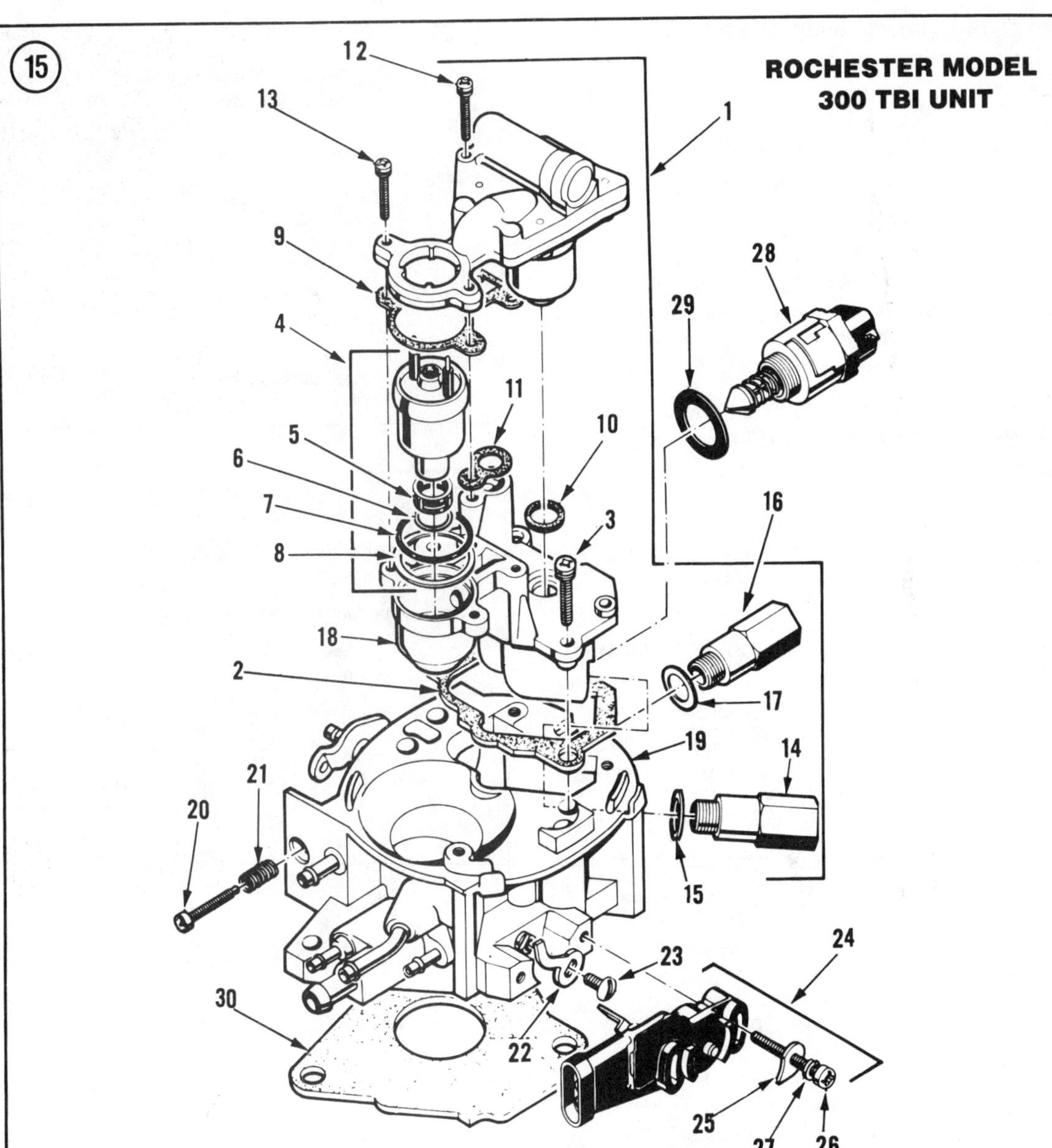

1. Fuel meter assembly
2. Fuel meter body gasket
3. Attaching screw and washer assembly (3)
4. Fuel injector kit
5. Fuel injector nozzle filter
6. Small O-ring seal
7. Large O-ring seal
8. Fuel injector backup washer
9. Fuel meter cover gasket
10. Regulator press dust seal
11. Fuel meter outlet gasket
12. Long screw and washer assembly (3)
13. Short screw and washer assembly (2)
14. Fuel inlet nut
15. Fuel inlet nut gasket
16. Fuel outlet nut
17. Fuel outlet nut gasket
18. Fuel meter body assembly
19. Throttle body assembly
20. Idle stop screw
21. Idle stop screw spring
22. TPS lever
23. TPS lever attaching screw
24. Throttle position kit sensor
25. TPS retainer (2)
26. TPS attaching screw (2)
27. TPS screw washer (2)
28. Idle air control valve
29. Control valve to T.B. gasket
30. Flange mounting gasket

to the fuel meter body (**Figure 16**). Remove the fuel meter cover and pressure regulator assembly.

WARNING

*Do not remove the screws holding the pressure regulator to the fuel meter cover (**Figure** 17). The regulator contains a large spring under heavy tension and accidental release could cause serious personal injury. The fuel meter cover and pressure regulator are serviced as a single assembly.*

2. Remove the fuel meter cover gaskets.
3. Remove the dust seal (**Figure 16**) from the fuel meter body.

CAUTION

Use care in Step 4 to avoid damaging the electrical connecting pins on the top of the injector.

4. With fuel meter gasket on fuel meter body, lift injector from body with a screwdriver as shown in **Figure 18**.
5. Rotate the injector fuel filter with a back-and-forth motion and remove from the injector base. See **Figure 19**.

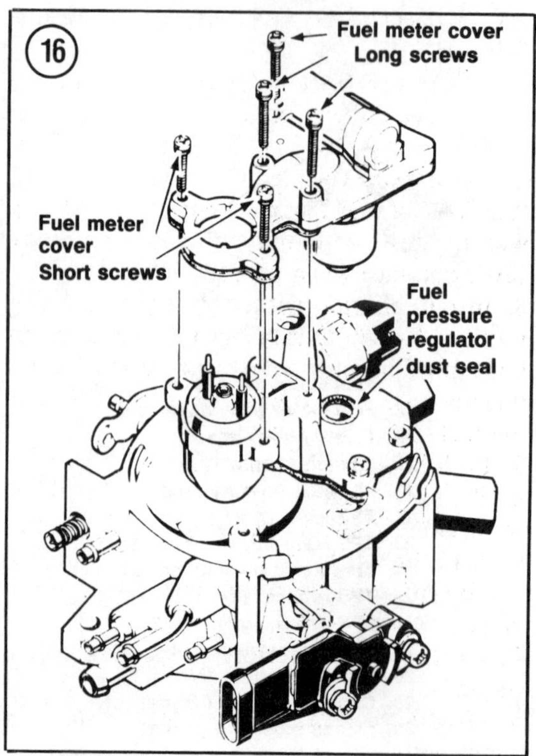

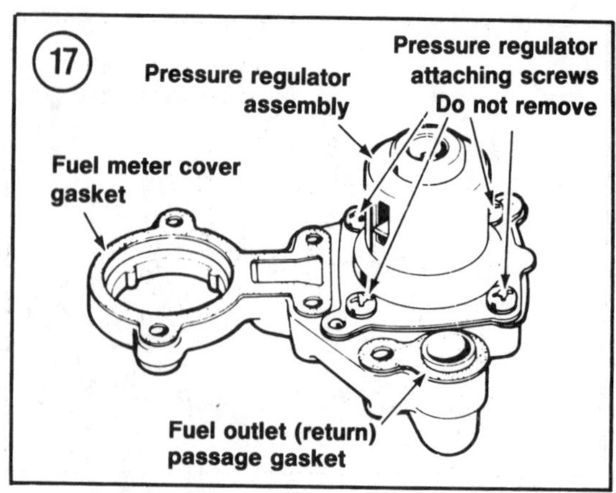

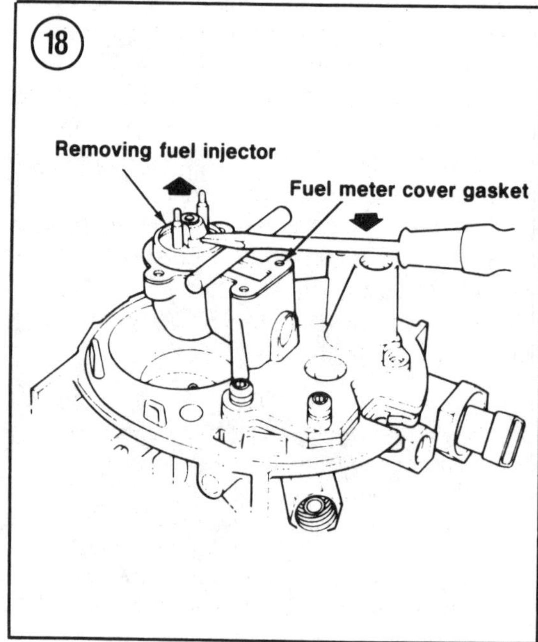

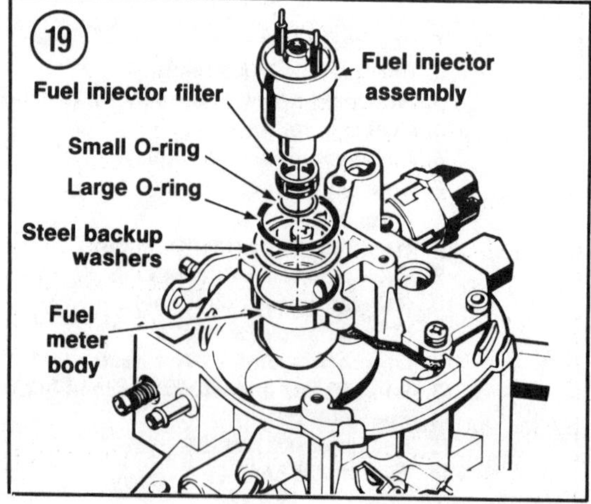

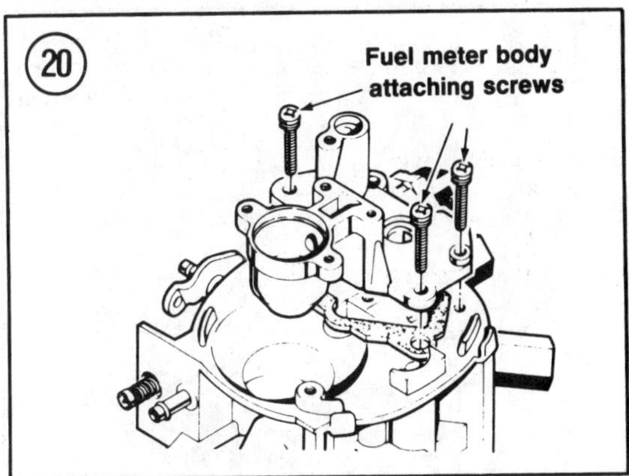

6. Remove the large O-ring and steel backup washer from the top of the injector cavity in the fuel meter body (**Figure 19**).
7. Remove the small O-ring at the bottom of the injector cavity.
8. Remove the fuel inlet/outlet nuts and gaskets from the fuel meter body.
9. Remove 3 screws with lockwashers and separated fuel meter body from throttle body assembly (**Figure 20**).
10. Remove the fuel meter body insulator gasket.

NOTE
Do not remove the throttle position sensor or idle air control assembly from the throttle body. The TPS is factory-adjusted and spot-welded to the throttle body to maintain its critical setting. It is possible to clean the throttle body without removing these components.

Cleaning and Inspection

NOTE
Do not immerse the throttle position sensor, idle air control assembly, fuel meter cover, fuel injector, fuel filter or and rubber components in carburetor cleaner.

1. Clean all metal parts thoroughly and blow dry with compressed air. Check all fuel passages to make sure they are free of burrs and dirt.
2. Check casting mating surfaces for proper gasket sealing.
3. Inspect injector O-rings for cuts, distortion or other damage.
4. Clean or replace injector fuel filter as necessary.

Throttle Body Assembly

Refer to **Figure 15** for this procedure.
1. Install a new fuel meter body gasket on the throttle body.
2. Install fuel meter body to throttle body. Apply a small quantity of thread locking compound to fuel meter body screws. Install screws with lockwashers and tighten to 35 in.-lb. (4 N•m).

NOTE
Thread locking compound is included in overhaul kits. If necessary, Thread-lock Adhesive X-10 or equivalent may be used in its place.

3. Install fuel inlet/outlet nuts with new gaskets. Tighten nuts to 260 in.-lb. (29 N•m).
4. Install fuel filter to nozzle end of injector with a twisting motion. Large end of cone-shaped filter must face upward so the filter will cover the rib of the injector base.
5. Lubricate a new small O-ring with lithium grease or equivalent. Install O-ring on nozzle end of injector and press up against injector fuel filter.
6. Install steel washer in recess of injector cavity in fuel meter body.
7. Lubricate a new large O-ring with lithium grease or equivalent. Install O-ring above steel washer and seat in cavity recess. O-ring will be flush with top of fuel meter body casting surface when properly located.
8. Install injector with a twisting, pushing motion. Nozzle O-ring must be centered in bottom of injector cavity and raised lug on injector base aligned with the cast-in notch in the fuel meter body cavity.
9. Push injector down as shown in **Figure 21** until fully seated in cavity. Electrical connector pin should be parallel with throttle shaft in throttle body.
10. Install a new dust seal in the fuel meter body recess.
11. Install a new gasket on the fuel meter cover.
12. Install fuel meter cover gasket to fuel meter body.

13. Install fuel meter cover to fuel meter body. Apply a thread locking compound to cover attaching screws. Install screws with lockwashers as shown in **Figure 16** and tighten to 28 in.-lb. (3 N•m).

PORT FUEL INJECTION

The PFI V6 uses a fuel rail containing 6 fuel injectors located under the plenum (**Figure 22**). Each injector is installed in a cylinder intake port. All 6 injectors pulse once during each engine revolution. This provides 2 injections of fuel mixed with incoming air to provide the air-fuel charge for each combustion cycle. **Figure 23** shows the major components of the PFI system.

System Operation

The PFI system operation is essentially the same as the TBI system used on the 4-cylinder engine. Since the system is electronically controlled, no attempt should be made to adjust the idle speed or fuel mixture. Owner service should be limited to replacement only. If the system is not working properly, take the car to a General Motors dealer for diagnosis and adjustment.

System Pressure Relief

The PFI fuel rail contains a pressure bleed orifice that bleeds off system pressure whenever the ignition is turned OFF. However, it is a good idea to bleed off any residual system pressure before opening any fuel connection to reduce the risk of fire and personal injury. Use the same procedure specified under *Electronic Fuel Injection* in this supplement.

Fuel Rail Removal/Installation

Refer to **Figure 7** for this procedure.

1. Remove the plenum as described in the Chapter Five section of this supplement.
2. Disconnect the cold start valve at the fuel rail. See **Figure 22**.
3. Remove the fuel line retaining bolt at the cylinder head and disconnect the fuel lines at the fuel rail. Use one wrench to hold the fuel rail fitting and a second wrench to loosen the fuel line nut. Plug the lines to prevent leakage.

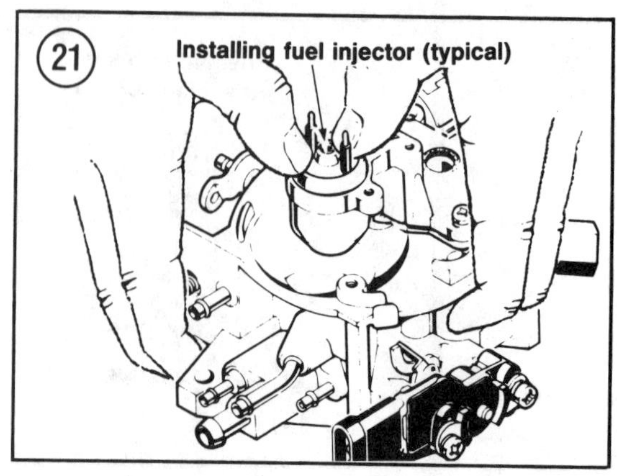
21 Installing fuel injector (typical)

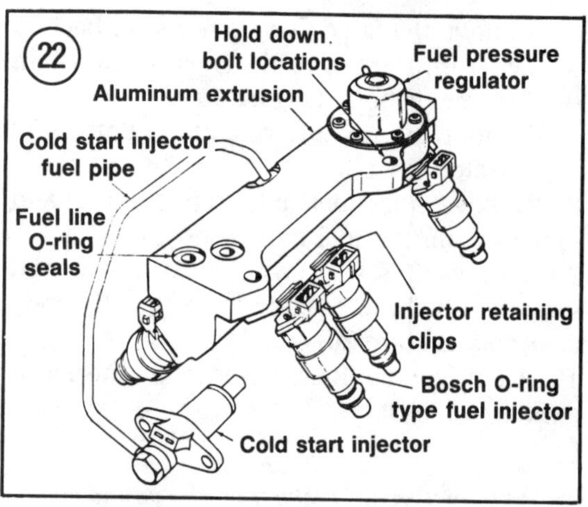

22

4. Disconnect the vacuum line at the fuel rail pressure regulator.
5. Remove the 2 fuel rail retaining bolts.
6. Carefully disconnect the electrical connectors at the injectors.
7. Remove the fuel rail and injectors.
8. Remove and discard all O-ring seals.
9. Installation is the reverse of removal. Install and lubricate new O-ring seals with clean engine oil. Tighten fuel rail bolts to 15 ft.-lb. (21 N•m).

Fuel Filter

The PFI V6 engine uses a disposable filter canister installed in the fuel line. See the Chapter Three section of this supplement for replacement procedure.

Fuel Pump

The PFI system uses an electric fuel pump attached to the fuel sending unit located in

(23)

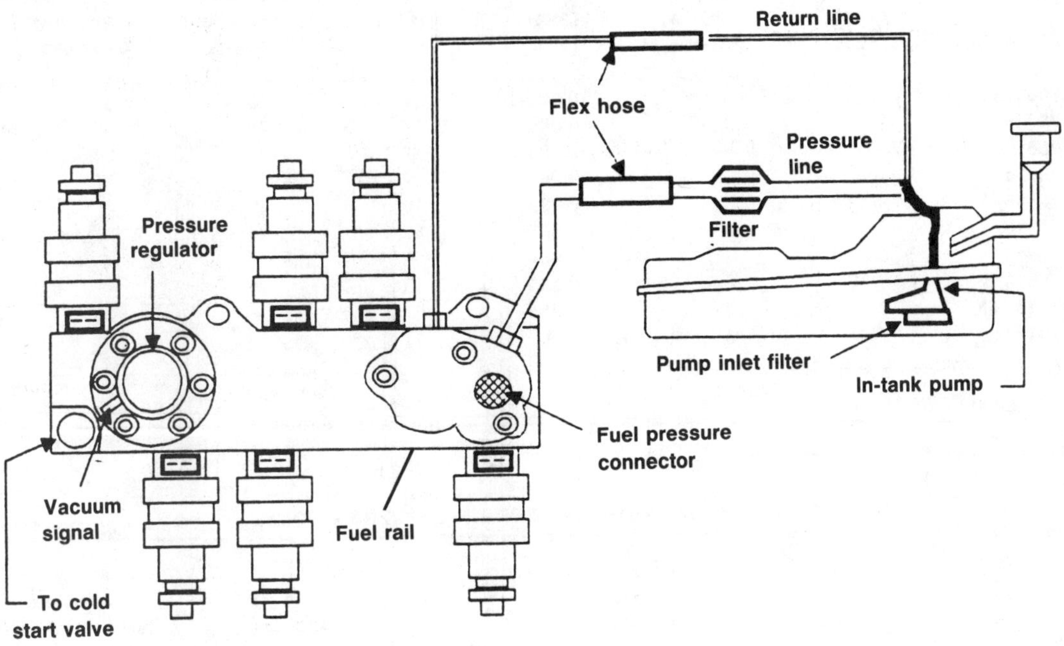

Return line
Flex hose
Pressure line
Filter
Pressure regulator
Pump inlet filter
In-tank pump
Fuel pressure connector
Vacuum signal
Fuel rail
To cold start valve

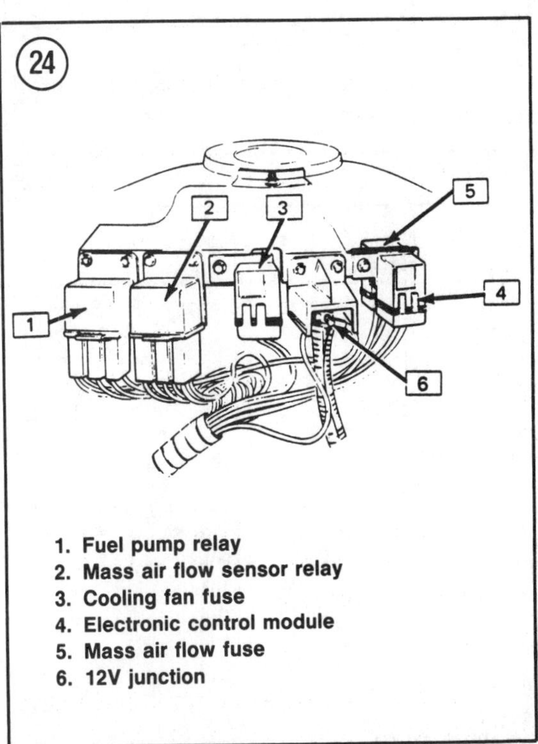

1. Fuel pump relay
2. Mass air flow sensor relay
3. Cooling fan fuse
4. Electronic control module
5. Mass air flow fuse
6. 12V junction

the fuel tank. To replace the pump, remove the fuel tank as described in Chapter Six of the basic book. Rotate the cam lock ring on the sending unit counterclockwise and lift assembly from the tank, then separate the lock ring from the sending unit. Installation is the reverse of removal.

Fuel Pump Relay

The PFI fuel pump relay is bracket-mounted to the shock tower relay assembly along with the fuel pump/ECM fuse. See **Figure 24**.

EARLY FUEL EVAPORATION SYSTEM (EFE)

Control of the EFE system by the ECM is replaced by a thermal electric switch (TES) on 1984 and later Chevrolet Citation II models.

Table 4 CARBURETOR SPECIFICATIONS (1981)

Carburetor No.	Float level (in.)	Fast idle screw (turns out)	Choke coil lever (in.)	Fast idle cam*	Primary vacuum break*	Secondary vacuum break*
17081650	1/4	3	0.085	17	25	34
17081651	1/4	3	0.085	17	29	35
17081652	1/4	3	0.085	17	25	34
17081653	1/4	3	0.085	17	29	35
17081670	5/32	3	0.085	18	19	-
17081671	5/32	3	0.085	33.5	21	-
17081672	5/32	3	0.085	18	19	-
17081673	5/32	3	0.085	33.5	21	-
17081740	1/4	3	0.085	17	25	34
17081742	1/4	3	0.085	17	25	34

* Angle in degrees.

Table 5 CARBURETOR SPECIFICATIONS (1982)

Carburetor No.	Float level (in.)	Air valve spring (turns out)	Fast idle cam*	Primary vacuum break*	Secondary vacuum break*
17082196	5/16	-	18	21	19
17082316	1/4	1	17	26	34
17082317	1/4	1	17	29	35
17082320	1/4	1	25	30	35
17082321	1/4	1	25	29	35
17082640	1/4	1	17	26	34
17082641	1/4	1	17	29	35
17082642	1/4	1	25	30	35

* Angle in degrees.

Table 6 CARBURETOR SPECIFICATIONS (1983)

Carburetor No.	Float level (in.)	Air valve spring (turns out)	Fast idle cam*	Primary vacuum break*	Secondary vacuum break*
17083356	13/32	1	22	25	35
17083357	13/32	1	22	25	35
17083358	13/32	1	22	25	35
17083359	13/32	1	22	25	35
17083368	1/8	1	22	25	35
17083370	1/8	1	22	25	35
17083450	1/8	1	28	27	35
17083451	1/8	1	28	27	35
17083452	1/8	1	28	27	35
17083453	1/8	1	28	27	35

(continued)

Table 6 CARBURETOR SPECIFICATIONS (1983) (continued)

Carburetor No.	Float level (in.)	Air valve spring (turns out)	Fast idle cam*	Primary vacuum break*	Secondary vacuum break*
17083454	1/8	1	22	25	35
17083455	1/8	1	28	27	35
17083456	1/8	1	28	27	35
17083630	1/4	1	28	27	35
17083631	1/4	1	28	27	35
17083632	1/4	1	28	27	35
17083633	1/4	1	22	25	35
17083634	1/4	1	28	27	35
17083635	1/4	1	28	27	35
17083636	1/4	1	28	27	35
17083650	1/8	1/2	28	27	35

* Angle in degrees.

CHAPTER SEVEN

COOLING, HEATING AND AIR CONDITIONING

A new thermostat housing design (**Figure 25**) is used on 1982 and later 4-cylinder engines. A handle riveted to the body of the thermostat assists in removal from the housing (**Figure 26**) and elminates the need to drain the coolant.

25

Removal/Installation

1. Remove the thermostat housing cap.
2. Grasp the thermostat handle and remove from the housing.
3. Install the thermostat in housing and push down until fully seated.
4. Install thermostat housing cap.

RADIATOR

A lightweight aluminum radiator with plastic tanks is used on some models. The plastic tanks are fitted to the brazed aluminum crossflow core with cinched header tabs and sealed with a high-temperature rubber gasket.

Service and maintenance of this radiator is essentially the same as with the copper core design, but care must be exercised in hose removal and installation and hose clamp tightening to avoid damage to the tank fittings. Excessive pressure applied to a tank fitting can crack or break it.

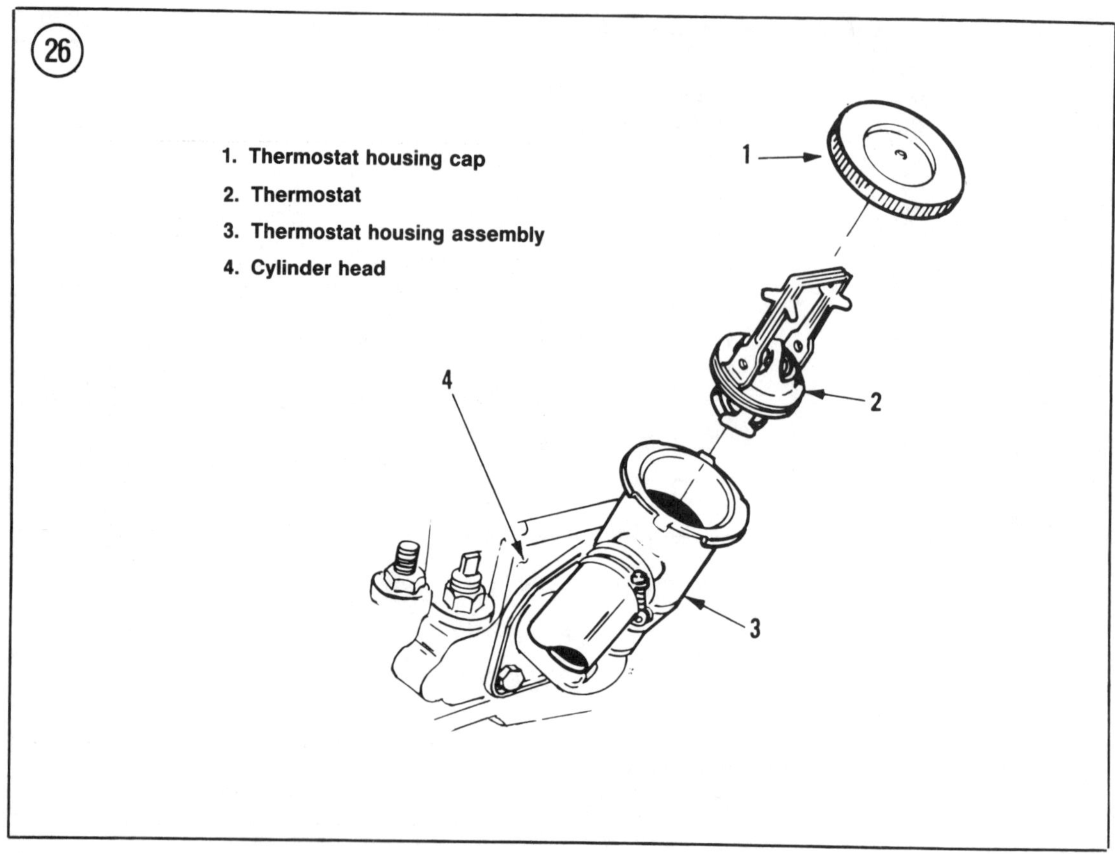

CHAPTER EIGHT

ELECTRICAL SYSTEM

HIGH ENERGY IGNITION SYSTEM

A revised version of the HEI distributor is used on 1981 and later models. This distributor uses a 7-terminal module instead of the 4-terminal module previously used. The new module provides electronic spark timing (EST) with all engines. All spark timing changes are made electronically at the direction of the electronic control module (ECM). The HEI-EST distributor contains no vacuum or centrifugal advance mechanisms. A reference pulse sent to the ECM from the distributor indicates engine rpm and crankshaft position. The ECM compares the reference pulse to its pre-programmed memory, determines the proper spark advance for the operating condition and sends a pulse to the distributor module.

A backup spark advance system is pre-programmed into the 1982 and later module used with fuel-injected 4-cylinder engines in case of EST failure.

FUSES/CIRCUIT BREAKERS

A revised fuse block is used with 1982-on models. **Figure 27** shows the fuse block design, fuse location and circuits protected. The fuel pump and crank fuses are used with fuel-injected models only.

(27)

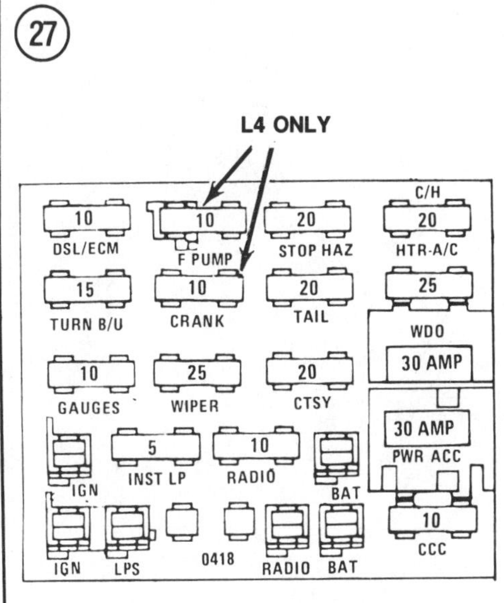

FRONT VIEW OF FUSE BLOCK

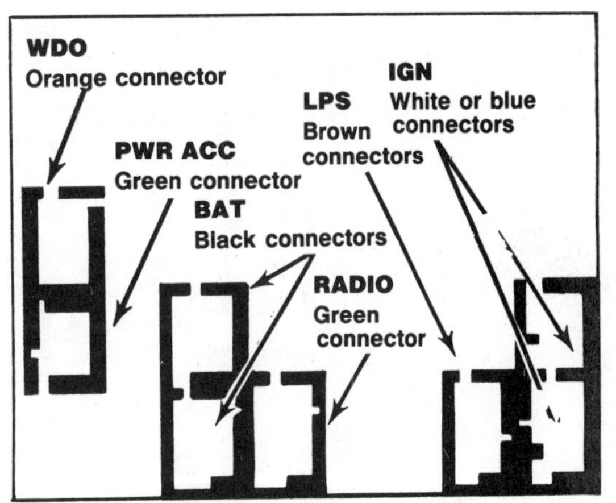

REAR VIEW OF FUSE BLOCK
CAVITY AND CONNECTOR LOCATIONS

Fuse color/ size (amps)	Fuse box circuits protected	Location
Clear (30)	Power windows	WDO
Clear (30)	Defogger, power door locks, power seats	PWR ACC
White (25)	Air conditioning, heater, trunk release	HTR-A/C
White (25)	Wiper/washer	WIPER
Yellow (20)	Brake warning system, choke heater, coolant fan	C-H
Yellow (20)	Audio alarm system, clock, cigar lighter, horns, interior lights, power antenna	CTSY
Yellow (20)	Stop/hazard lights	STOP HAZ
Yellow (20)	Turn/hazard/front park/front marker/stop lights/tail/rear marker/license lights	TAIL
Light blue (15)	Air conditioning (V6), backup and turn lights	TURN B/U
Red (10)	Electronic fuel injection (4-cylinder only)	CRANK
Red (10)	Computer Command Control	DSL/ECM
Red (10)	Computer Command Control	CCC
Red (10)	Instrument panel warning indicators, instrument panel gauges	GAGES
Red (10)	Electronic fuel injection (4-cylinder only)	F PUMP
Red (10)	Cruise control, radio	RADIO
Tan (5)	Audio alarm system, instrument panel and console lights	INST LP

CHAPTER NINE

TRANSAXLE SYSTEM

Park-Lock System

All 1984-on vehicles equipped with an automatic transaxle and floor shift have a Park-Lock system. This prevents accidentally shifting the transaxle into NEUTRAL while the key is out of the ignition switch.

A flexible cable is connected between the shift lever and a locking pin on the steering column ignition switch. When the transaxle is placed in REVERSE, NEUTRAL or DRIVE with the ignition switch in the RUN position, the cable moves the locking pin into engagement with a sliding contact in the ignition switch, preventing it from moving to the LOCK position.

Moving the gear selector to PARK allows the pin to disengage from the ignition switch contact and move to the LOCK position where it engages a cam on the flexible cable to prevent the shifter from being moved to another position until the ignition key is turned to the RUN position. **Figure 28** shows the system operation.

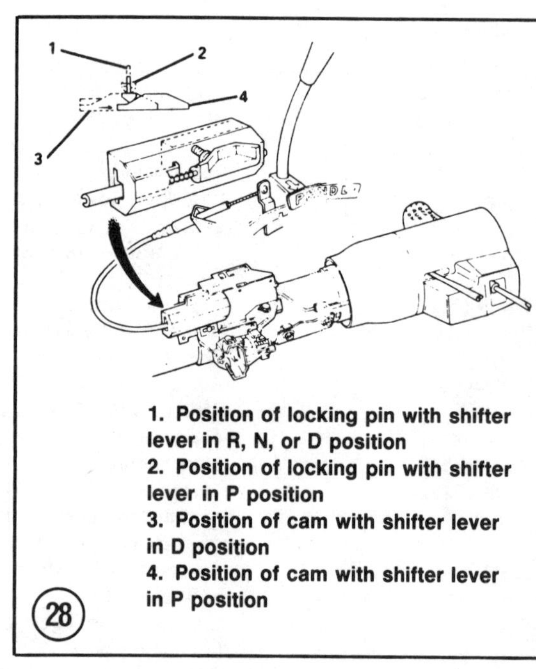

(28)

1. Position of locking pin with shifter lever in R, N, or D position
2. Position of locking pin with shifter lever in P position
3. Position of cam with shifter lever in D position
4. Position of cam with shifter lever in P position

To test system operation, insert the key in the ignition switch. With the transaxle in PARK and the ignition switch in the LOCK position, it should not be possible to move the selector lever. With the ignition switch in the RUN position and the transaxle in NEUTRAL, it should not be possible to turn the ignition key to the LOCK position.

To adjust the cable, remove the console and push the lock button on the park-lock cable connector at the shifter base to the up position. Push the cable connector forward to take up any slack and snap the lock button in the down position.

CHAPTER TEN

FRONT SUSPENSION AND STEERING

WHEEL ALIGNMENT

Alignment specifications differ for 1982-on models. **Table 7** provides the correct alignment specifications.

Table 7 WHEEL ALIGNMENT SPECIFICATIONS (1982-ON)

Camber (left and right side to be within 1/2°)	0 ±1/2°
Toe-in	
1982	0 ±2.5 mm
1983-on	0 ±0.5 mm

CHAPTER ELEVEN

REAR AXLE AND SUSPENSION

REAR AXLE AND SUSPENSION

Some rear suspension component tightening torques differ for 1981 and later models. Changes are provided in **Table 8**.

CHAPTER TWELVE

BRAKES

Some brake specifications and tightening torques differ for 1981 and later models. Changes are provided in **Table 9** and **Table 10**.

BRAKE PEDAL TRAVEL

A pedal travel measurement is used instead of pedal height on 1981 and later models to determine the need for brake inspection and adjustment.

1. With the brakes cold and the engine not running, have an assistant pump the brake pedal several times to exhaust any residual booster pressure, and then measure the distance between the top of the brake pedal and the floorboard.
2. Have the assistant depress the brake pedal with approximately 100 lb. force and hold it down while you measure the distance between the top of the pedal and the floorboard.
3. Subtract the measurement in Step 2 from the measurement in step 1 to determine the amount of pedal travel.
4. The maximum pedal travel should be 4 1/2 in. with non-power brakes or 2 1/4 in. with power brakes. If greater, inspect brakes and service as necessary.

Table 9 BRAKE TIGHTENING TORQUES (1981-ON)

Fastener	in.-lb.	ft.-lb.	N•m
Master cylinder attaching nuts			
1982-1983		29	40
1984-on		28	38
Booster attaching nuts			
1982-1983		22	30
1984-on		28	38
Failure warning switch	15-50		1.7-5.6
Brake pedal swing nut bolt		22	30

Table 10 BRAKE TIGHTENING TORQUES (1981-ON)

Fastener	ft.-lb.	N•m
Master cylinder attaching nuts*	29	40
Booster attaching nuts*	22	30
Failure warning switch*	26	35
Brake pedal swing bolt nut	22	30

* New specification is for 1982 and later models only.

INDEX

D

E

F

V

W